COLLECTED STUDIES SERIES

Public Science and Public Policy in Victorian England

Professor Roy MacLeod

Roy MacLeod

———

Public Science and Public Policy in Victorian England

———

VARIORUM
1996

This edition copyright © 1996 by Roy MacLeod.

Published by VARIORUM
Ashgate Publishing Limited
Gower House, Croft Road,
Aldershot, Hampshire GU11 3HR
Great Britain

Ashgate Publishing Company
Old Post Road,
Brookfield, Vermont 05036–9704
USA

ISBN 0–86078–535–1

British Library CIP Data
MacLeod, Roy
Public Science and Public Policy in Victorian England.
(Variorum Collected Studies Series: 509)
I. Title II. Series
354.4100855

US Library of Congress CIP Data
MacLeod, Roy M.
Public Science and Public Policy in Victorian England / Roy MacLeod.
    p. cm. — (Variorum Collected Studies Series: CS509)
1. Science—England—History—19th Century. 2. Science and state—
England—History—19th Century. 3. Science—Social aspects—England—
History—19th Century. 4. England—History—19th Century.
I. Title. II. Series: Collected Studies: CS509
Q127.G4M25   1995   95–37590
507'.942'09034–dc20   CIP

The paper used in this publication meets the minimum requirements of the
American National Standard for Information Sciences - Permanence
of Paper for Printed Library Materials, ANSI Z39.48-1984. ∞ ™

Printed by Galliard (Printers) Ltd
Great Yarmouth, Norfolk, Great Britain

COLLECTED STUDIES SERIES CS509

CONTENTS

vi

This volume contains xvi + 325 pages

INTRODUCTION

Knowledge is power, as Francis Bacon famously recalled, and since the scientific revolution of the 17th century, governments have become accustomed to wielding knowledge to the ends of statecraft.[1] Through the 18th century, that relationship bred formal structures of learned academies and other institutions devoted to the practical applications of knowledge, in both peace and in war. It is only with the mid- and late-19th century, however, that this development began to acquire its modern language and dress, as science became associated with a rationale that endorses and dignifies, by its appeals to Nature, the instruments of the nation-state. In looking at this rationale, and its underlying discourse, we can trace the paths by which the agencies of science became part of the legitimating, regulatory apparatus of modern government, the consequences of which remain prominent today.[2]

These essays were conceived in a desire – a 'research programme' would be too strong – to describe the interlocking tendencies that characterised this period in the history of science, and in the history of Britain. Selective in focus, and resisting large generalisations, they attempted to show that well before the mythic 'boffins' of the Second World War, in England, as elsewhere in Europe, the Americas, and Australasia, the practitioners of science had, by the early 20th century, created a 'scientific estate' that drew and gave strength from its associations with the instruments of government. Elsewhere, I have drawn attention to implications arising from this experience for later developments in science and government, in this century, and across the world.[3] The

---

[1] See Charles Webster, *The Great Instauration: Science, Medicine and Reform, 1626–1660* (London: Duckworth, 1975).

[2] For a wider conspectus, see the introduction and essays in Roy MacLeod (ed.), *Government and Expertise: Specialists, Administrators and Professionals, 1860–1919* (Cambridge: Cambridge University Press, 1988); also, Roy MacLeod, 'Education – Scientific and Technical', in Gillian Sutherland (ed.), *Government and Society in Nineteenth-Century Britain: Commentaries on Education: British Parliamentary Papers* (Dublin: Irish Academy Press, 1977), 196–225.

[3] See, e.g. Roy MacLeod, 'Knowledge and Power in the Pacific', in *Towards the Pacific Century: The Challenge of Change* (Honolulu: Proceedings of the XVIIth Pacific Science Congress, 1991), 87–92; with Kay MacLeod, 'The Social Relations of Science and Technology, 1914–1939', in Carlo Cipolla (ed.), *The Fontana Economic History of Europe: Vol. 5: The Twentieth Century*, Part I (London: Collins/Fontana, 1976), 301–335; and 'Changing Perspectives in the Social History of Science', in Ina Spiegel-Rösing and Derek de Solla Price (eds), *Science, Technology and Society: A Cross-Disciplinary Perspective* (London: Sage, 1977), 149–195.

emphasis in these selected essays is, however, deliberately Victorian – and, further, specifically civil, not military; domestic, not imperial; concerned more with applications of the laboratory, rather than the field sciences; and with the institutions of the few, their space defined by the 'metropolis', rather than of the many, in the countryside or provincial city. In certain respects, they are also concerned with the exploits of a handful of men (few women, alas, either grace or inform their pages) who espoused newly fashionable 'professional' ambitions, mediated by state intervention, in contrast to those who clustered for defence within the ancient citadels of 'classical' learning.

These essays are organised in three sections, and draw upon three separate but converging traditions. The first examines certain neglected aspects of the regulatory state, taking as their point of departure the administrative 'revolution in government' of the mid-19th century, and the explosive growth of central bureaucracy which seemed, at the time, to dispose of Augustan localism, mock the rhetoric of *laissez-faire*, sidestep or at least out-manoeuvre Parliament, and so frame the interests of English voluntarism and philanthropy that they were seen as elements mobilised in the purposive direction of social reform.[4] Onto this stage enters the man of science – a 'statesman in disguise', in the phrase Kitson Clark made memorable – to negotiate between the faceless men in Whitehall and the unseen populace in the country at large.[5] The result, to judge by its exemplars, is a more secure world, underlined by science, and underwritten by the rule of law. Its legacy is the book of regulation and its enforcement. State power, once extended, is never withdrawn, and the scientist–inspector becomes the Victorian equivalent of the 18th-century 'inspector–general'.[6]

In retrospect, my program was driven by a generally positive view of the state's acceptance of responsibilities in realms of policy where private enterprise had failed; the essays reveal the economic assumptions of the period in which

---

[4] The historiography of this discussion is legendary. For background, see L.J. Hume, 'Jeremy Bentham and the Nineteenth Century Revolution in Government', *Historical Journal*, 10 (1957); David Roberts, 'Jeremy Bentham and the Victorian Administrative State', *Victorian Studies*, 2 (1958–59), 210; Oliver MacDonagh, 'The Nineteenth-Century Revolution in Government: A Reappraisal', *Historical Journal*, I (1958), 52–67; and *A Pattern of Government Growth, 1800–1860* (London: MacGibbon and Kee, 1961); Jennifer Hart 'Nineteenth-Century Social Reform: A Tory Interpretation of History', *Past and Present*, no. 31 (1965), 39–61; and the summary analysis in Valerie Cromwell, 'Interpretations of Nineteenth-Century Administration: An Analysis', *Victorian Studies*, 9 (1966), 245–55. A further gloss is given in MacLeod, *op. cit.* note 2.

[5] Roy MacLeod, 'Statesmen Undisguised: Reflections on the State of British Administrative Historiography', *American Historical Review*, 78 (5) (December, 1973), 1386–1405. For some of the contradictions of expertise, see my *Treasury Control and Social Administration: Establishment Growth and the Local Government Board, 1871–1905* (LSE Papers in Social Administration, No. 23, 1968).

[6] See Oliver MacDonagh's marvellous, and surprisingly neglected, book of that title: *The Inspector General: Sir Jeremiah Fitzpatrick and Social Reform, 1783–1802* (London: Croom Helm, 1981).

they were written, and a certain acceptance of the inevitability of technical progress, in which efficiency and modernism, as hallmarks of science, were seen as equally desirable motives for administrative intervention. It was a frame of mind common among many scholars in Britain who shared, in Martin Wiener's phrase, the 'Fabian consensus' of the late Fifties and Sixties – a frame of mind in which state intervention, the administrative state or the 'social service' state, in fact – was deemed, in principle, an outcome beneficial to the many, if also profitable to the few.[7] Both 'Whig' and 'Tory' historians, however divided in the narratives and rationales of these developments, could together claim credit for the consensus they inspired.

Traversing regions beyond the better known landmarks of the 'age of reform', my essays attempted to create a distinctive place among them for the applications of science – particular cases, to be sure, to illustrate the general tendency by which the uses of science began to inform public policy in domains affected by the factors of industrialisation and economic activity characteristic of the middle stages of the Industrial Revolution. These cases illustrate some of the ways in which scientific ideas and practitioners, shaping and being shaped by law-making opinion, became commonplace features of Britain's constitutional terrain. Navigating policy through sometimes reluctant parliaments, to be implemented by newly-created bureaucracies – whose instructions typically fell well beneath the level of active party political notice – the state came to make larger claims for the moral legitimacy of central government. It seemed just as the inhabitants of Bacon's 'Solomon's House' would have wished, that the applications of science would inevitably lead to the 'effecting of all things possible, for the relief of man's estate'. Thomas Sprat, writing the first history of the Royal Society, fervently wished for a time when the 'contrary imaginations' that bedeviled political life would dissolve when confronted by the incontestable facts of nature. 'Inspectors', pledged to objective knowledge, would be the embodiment of Bacon's 'merchants of light'. Objective knowledge, impartially deployed, would be a solvent for controversy, and an antidote to discord.

Of course, the limits of objectivity are all too poignant, and soon became so in practice, not least in matters where 'expert testimony' and the credibility of witnesses were at stake. In the end, it was not enough to trace the inspiration and creation of new administrative forms without examining their inherent contradictions. While, therefore, this 'reformist' frame of mind was influential, and led to much important new work, it had its day. It was not incorrect, but it was incomplete. Its context was too specific, and its implications, insufficiently addressed. Historians, for example, now correctly question what is said to be so 'revolutionary' about this particular period in British administrative

---

[7] The point is well made (although not applied to science) in Martin J. Wiener, 'The Unloved State: Twentieth-Century Politics in the Writing of Nineteenth-Century History', *Journal of British Studies*, 33 (1994), 283–308.

history. It would be foolish to deny the need to span centuries – to trace what one historian has called the 'Great Arch' since the 16th century – if we are to canvass fully the history of the 'administrative revolution'.[8] Within this broad framework, moreover, the events of the 1830s and afterwards did not occur *ab initio*, but were shaped by recent memories and events. Notable among these must surely be the institutions of what John Brewer has called the 'fiscal-military state' of the late 18th century, with its undoctrinaire but demonstrably 'objective' rejection of unacceptably expensive and wasteful forms of government.[9] This was a period, and a range of activities – many associated with European war on land and sea – in which science and technology were also deeply implicated. From this perspective, subsequent discussions of *laissez-faire* and administrative centralism prove not so much opposing philosophies but alternative, even parallel strategies, invoking the same gods of modernisation, pragmatism, and professionalism, employing the same methods of inquiry and report, and calling with a common voice for efficient government, managed by a numerate, centralised bureaucracy – answerable to Parliament, if rarely heard in public.[10]

In attempting to throw light upon the changes at work in creating the administrative state, the following essays made a certain contribution to scholarship in the social history of science and public policy. However, they failed to illuminate the 'dark side' of liberalism which these developments also implied. A perspective within which science appeared as an ubiquitous panacea, masked the fact that science-based legislation and the appointment of inspectors whose regimes were, above all, intended to encourage and not dampen economic growth, could, when generalised, also threaten private freedoms and personal liberties.[11] No doubt, in discussing this revolution from within, these essays gave insufficient attention to its ideology, and its ideologues, while neglecting its potential victims.[12] Even idealistic motives, when enshrined in legislation, could fail of their high purpose, and it remains dangerous to confuse the passage of an apparently wise Act – and even the appointment of a central inspectorate! – with its effective implementation for the public good. Interests

---

[8] Philip Corrigan and Derek Sayer, *The Great Arch: English State Formation as Cultural Revolution* (Oxford: Basil Blackwell, 1985).

[9] John Brewer, *The Sinews of Power: War, Money and the English state, 1688–1783* (New York: Knopf, 1988).

[10] See Philip Harling and Peter Mandler, 'From "Fiscal-Military" State to *Laissez-faire* State, 1760–1850', *Journal of British Studies*, 32 (1) (1993), 44–70.

[11] See Mary Langan and Bill Schwarz (eds), *Crises in the British State, 1880–1903* (London: Hutchinson, 1985).

[12] For a critical perspective on the far from objective role of 'expertise' in social control, see the essays in A.P. Donajgrodzki (ed.), *Social Control in Nineteenth-Century Britain* (London: Croom Helm, 1977), especially Richard Johnson, 'Educating the Educators: 'Experts and the State, 1833–39', 77–108.

novel, in that it set precedents for negotiating with an elite that refused deference to any authority but truth, and which therefore set itself upon a moral high ground above partisan politics; it was familiar, in that these interests began to use the tactics that all other interest groups used, and sometimes with greater effect. Science had become an ideology *sans doctrine*. Contemporary fears of Darwinism and materialism held no place in these discussions. The government of Britain need not accept all that science promised, or proposed, to welcome its participation in the art of governing.

Yet, given this acceptance, it is striking how quickly the public was excluded from the negotiating table.[20] Where science afforded answers, governments did not need to take the public into its confidence. New technologies had earlier rendered child labour unnecessary, and slavery unaffordable, and would educate working men and women when industry needed literate workers. By the turn of the century, science-based technologies would strengthen Britain's strategic posture, by linking the empire via steamship and rail, cable and wireless. In the wake of the Anglo-Boer War, science held out hope of a cure for administrative inertia; in 1914–18, it became a source of pain, but also a path to victory; in the 1920s, it offered a future of plenty, if only to acknowledge, in the 1930s, its inability to prevent depression. The next thirty years during and after the Second World War breathed new life into the Victorian social contract between science and the public, but today, nearly a century after 'public science' seemed so full of certitude, public policy towards science, and towards the use of science, has come to evoke misgivings and distrust. Historians living in, or writing about, what David Cannadine has called 'this sceptical isle'[21] must now deal with this legacy of distrust. It is perhaps a consequence of postmodernism. It is perhaps also a result of preferring a script that has for so long played only to the actors, rather than to the audience. If these essays offer a moral – and historians rightly resist such a possibility – it would be that public science must, in the last analysis, contribute not solely to the power of the state, but to the empowerment of its people – or, in Bacon's inimitable words, to the benefit and use of life.[22]

Sydney　　　　　　　　　　　　　　　　　　　　　　　　ROY MacLEOD
December 1995

---

[20] Roy MacLeod and Kay MacLeod, 'The Social Relations of Science and Technology, 1914–1939', in Carlo Cipolla (ed.), *The Fontana Economic History of Europe*: Vol. 5: *The Twentieth Century*, Part I (London: Collins/Fontana, 1976), 301–335.

[21] David Cannadine, 'This Sceptical Isle', *The Times Higher [Educational Supplement]*, 24 (November 1995), 17–18.

[22] For Bacon's exordium, see Jerome Ravetz, *Scientific Knowledge and its Social Problems* (Oxford: Oxford University Press, 1971), 436.

these essays are cited more for their insights into hegemony than for their interpretations of political motives; but as a line of enquiry, they made their way into Gramscian accounts of the historical sociology of science,[17] and were consistent with the impressive body of work on the 'theory of interests' that was later made popular, and relevant to contemporary science, by scholars in the sociology of scientific knowledge.[18]

If Part I deals with the invocation of the state in the interests of science, and Part II with self-regulation in the interests of science, then Part III views the fine structure of science–government relations through a spectrum of case studies, spanning the width of government from the green baize of the Treasury to the herbaceous borders of Kew, from quondam pressure groups dedicated to the advancement of research, to quasi-permanent advisory committees created by the Royal Society. In each case, institutions of science emerge as identifiable interests, awakening and animating the universities, and positioning themselves *vis-à-vis* Westminster and Whitehall to influence the Admiralty, the War Office, and the home departments. Influence, rather than power, became their hallmark, as from Gladstone's first government onwards, they established such *bona fides* among the civil service and select committees as to make the bastions of the scientific 'estate' impregnable. Indeed, as one beleaguered Treasury official was heard to lament, who is to deny scientists what they ask, when only they understand what they need. The end of their mission, and the means, came to be called 'public science', usefully defined (although not by me) as a 'body of rhetoric, argument and polemic, produced by scientists' [to] 'justify their activities to the political powers and other social institutions upon whose good will, patronage and cooperation they depend'. It was a theme frequently heard from the 1880s.[19]

By the end of the century, 'public science' had acquired shape and substance in Britain, with counterpart ideologies in Western Europe and North America, driven by sentiments that linked the rhetoric of scientific method with the running of efficient empires and nation-states. Calling upon my essays and others, Frank Turner has shown how the rhetoric spun far ahead of the reality, as the advocates of science, rather more than scientists themselves, issued bold promissory notes to a public that was prepared to be persuaded. A social contract emerged between science, public servants, and elected representatives, producing a basis for public policy that was both novel and familiar. It was

---

[17] Morris Berman, 'Hegemony and the Amateur Tradition in British Science', *Journal of Social History*, 8 (2) (1974), 30–50.

[18] See Barry Barnes, *Interests and the Growth of Knowledge* (London: Routledge, 1977); Steve Woolgar, 'Interests and Explanation in the Social Study of Science', *Social Studies of Science*, 11 (3) (1973), 365–94; Brian Wynne, 'Representing Policy Constructions and Interests in SSK (Responses & Replies)', *Social Studies of Science*, 22 (3) (1992), 575–80.

[19] Frank Turner, 'Public Science in Britain, 1880–1919', *Isis*, 71 (1908), 602.

The abiding question – 'in whose interest?' – that dominates Part I, features again in the lines and subtext of Part II. These essays examine different aspects of the 'self-regulating state' of Victorian science. Self-interest in science did not, of course, equate with self-sufficiency, and it is in the study of prizes, patronage and reward mechanisms, that we see the 'estate' of science define and assert its private interests as of public importance. These essays are, to a degree, heir to a post-war tradition in the 'externalist' history of science, which took as its premise a presentist, possibly anachronistic account of 'professionalisation' as the route used by scientists in accessing power and influence in Europe and the United States.[14] In fact, these early essays departed from a largely American-inspired programme – which seemed to have served its purpose, and was saying little that was new – in order to develop an argument that seemed more relevant to understanding the role of scientists in social history. They engaged with the premise that whilst British men of science – whether amateur or professional – wilfully employed the state, and usefully framed its institutions, so they also managed to keep the state at arms' length.

In this light, the so-called 'reforms' of the Royal Society during the 1830s and 1840s, described by some historians as heralding the advent of 'modern times',[15] can be better interpreted instead as highly sophisticated, Peelite attempts to postpone, or avoid altogether, the threat of even greater reform, and to delay indefinitely such changes in the delicate relationship that might come about if governments chose, after all, to interfere in the affairs of science, as they were soon to do in the universities. The councils of science became negotiating chambers, in which concessions were made to utility and efficiency, and where expert advice was traded for certain freedoms from direct government intervention – except where such was desirable (as, notably, during the Great War) for the image and work of the institutions themselves.[16] Today,

---

[14] Everett Mendelsohn, 'The Emergence of Science as a Profession in Nineteenth Century Europe', in K. Hill (ed.), *The Management of Scientists* (Boston: Beacon Press, 1964), 3–48.

[15] Cf. the misleading impression given in Marie Boas Hall, *All Scientists Now: The Royal Society in the Nineteenth Century* (Cambridge: Cambridge University Press, 1984), as reviewed in *Historical Records of Australian Science*, 6 (2) (December 1985), 427–428; and the useful corrective afforded by Andrew J. Harrison, 'Scientific Naturalists and the Government of the Royal Society, 1850–1900' (Unpublished Ph.D. dissertation, Open University, 1988).

[16] Roy MacLeod and E.K. Andrews, 'The Origins of the DSIR: Reflections on Ideas and Men 1915–16', *Public Administration*, 48 (1) (1970), 23–48 and 'Scientists, Government and Organized Research in Great Britain, 1914–16', *Minerva*, VIII (1970), 454–7; with E.K. Andrews, 'Scientific Advice on the War at Sea, 1915–17: The Board of Invention and Research', *Journal of Contemporary History*, 6 (2) (1971), 3–40; with E.K. MacLeod, 'War and Economic Development: Government and the Optical Industry in Britain, 1914–18', in Jay M. Winter (ed.), *War and Economic Development: Essays in Honour of David Joslin* (Cambridge: Cambridge University Press, 1975), 165–204; Roy MacLeod, 'The Chemists Go to War: The Mobilisation of Civilian Chemists and the British War Effort, 1914–1918', *Annals of Science*, 50 (1993), 455–481.

associated with science are no less political, even if they traverse or ignore conventional party lines. 'Progress' in whatever ideological form it appears, bears the seeds of its own contradictions; and it is certain that Victorian science gave those contradictions their particular shape, content, and double-edge.

Despite the continuing importance of science and scientific expertise in domestic public policy – even despite the environmental movement, and its close scrutiny of the nuclear inspectorate – few social or administrative historians have followed me into these once uncharted waters.[13] Perhaps the time has come, as we near the end of the century, for a new look at these features, but from the point of view of the twentieth-century state. Twenty years after these essays were written, we inhabit a world disillusioned with state intervention and its Thatcherite alternatives. Looking back upon the essays of Part I, and on others written since, it seems clear that certain fields of scientific knowledge, when applied to regulation, may appear to have had unproblematic outcomes, but that others have demonstrably complex narratives that historians have yet to explore. But we know enough to say that environmental, factory, mines, and transport legislation do not always work in the direction intended by reformers; and where government controls of trade and traffic are involved, there emerge forms of social control that are not merely incidental to, but essential products of, the way a regulatory system functions.

That Francis Bacon was a lawyer, as well as an architect of scientific enterprise, should remind us that merely wishing to encourage the 'relief of man's estate' begs the question of which men (and women) are to be relieved, and who owns the estate. In the mid-1860s and since, the test of the 'best practicable means', as applied to alkali legislation and all its succeeding instruments, became a saleable doctrine, but also a confession of compromise, in a world in which the manufacturer, rather than the scientist, is left with the last word. The history of legislation should not neglect that of litigation. It may be argued that the sciences were applied in areas of public policy over which their practitioners had no control. One does not have to view the state as inherently sinister, in the language of Foucault, to see that science was assimilated to confer legitimacy upon actions of government, and of political groups, that, in other contexts, might more simply be described as self-interested.

---

[13] Among the exceptions are Christopher Hamlin, who has contributed extensively to our understanding of 'scientific expertise' and its limitations. See, e.g., his "Scientific Method and Expert Witnessing: Victorian Perspectives on a Modern Problem', *Social Studies of Science*, 16 (3) (1986), 485–513, and *A Science of Impurity: Water Analysis in Nineteenth-Century Britain* (Berkeley: University of California Press, 1990). Fine scholarship on many contemporary aspects of this subject, especially in Europe and North America, is associated with the work of Dorothy Nelkin and her collaborators. See, for example, Dorothy Nelkin (ed.), *Controversy: Politics of Technical Decisions* (London: Sage, 1979), and Dorothy Nelkin and M. Pollock, 'The Politics of Participation and the Nuclear Debate in Sweden, the Netherlands and Austria', *Public Policy*, 25 (3) (1977), 333–357.

ACKNOWLEDGEMENTS

For this opportunity to anthologise and reflect upon the context and significance of some of my earlier writings, I am grateful to John Smedley and Ruth Peters at Variorum. For their instruction over many years, I owe much to Professor Everett Mendelsohn of Harvard, and to Professor Oliver MacDonagh, Dr Peter Mathias, the late Dr G.S.R. Kitson Clark, and the late Dr Royston Lambert, all of Cambridge. Much of this work was written over a span of nearly twenty years, between a Fulbright Fellowship at St Catharine's College, Cambridge, and subsequent appointments at Churchill College, Cambridge and the University of Sussex. At Sussex, I benefitted greatly from the support of the (then) Department of Education and Science and the Social Science Research Council, whose assistance it is always a pleasure to acknowledge; and from the continuing friendship and encouragement of Professor Christopher Freeman, who could unfailingly see the statue in the marble. Above all, during those years and since, I have come to owe much to Dr Kay Andrews, for such help and counsel that few historians can ever expect to find, and even fewer receive.

For permission to republish these essays, I am grateful to the publishers and editors of: (I) the University of Indiana Press, for 'The Alkali Acts Administration, 1863–84: The Emergence of the Civil Scientist', *Victorian Studies*, IX (2) (December 1965), 85–112; (II) the University of Chicago Press, for 'Government and Resource Conservation: The Salmon Acts Administration, 1860–86', *Journal of British Studies*, VII (2) (May 1968), 114–150; (III) the University of Chicago Press, for 'Science and Government in Victorian England: Lighthouse Illumination and the Board of Trade, 1866–86', *Isis*, 60 Part 1, (201) (Spring 1969), 680–705; (IV) Hutchinson Publishing Group, for 'Whigs and Savants: Reflections on the Reform Movement in the Royal Society, 1830–48', in Ian Inkster and J.B. Morell (eds), *Metropolis and Province: Science in British Culture, 1780–1850* (Philadelphia: University of Pennsylvania Press, 1983), 55–90; (V) *Technology and Society*, for 'Science and the Civil List, 1824–1914', *Technology and Society*, 6 (1970), 47–55; (VI) the Council of the Royal Society, for 'Of Medals and Men: A Reward System in Victorian Science, 1826–1914', *Notes and Records of the Royal Society*, 26 (June 1971), 81–105; (VII) Noordhoff International Publishing, for 'Science and the Treasury: Principles, Personalities and Policies, 1870–85', in G.L'E. Turner (ed.), *The Patronage of Science in the Nineteenth Century* (Leiden: Noordhoff International Publishing, 1976),

115–172; **(VIII)** Cambridge University Press, for 'The Royal Society and the Government Grant: Notes on the Administration of Scientific Research, 1849–1914', *Historical Journal*, 14 (2) (1971), 323–358; and **(IX)** *Minerva*, for 'The Support of Victorian Science: The Endowment of Research Movement in Great Britain, 1868–1900', *Minerva*, 4 (2) (April 1971), 197–230.

I

THE ALKALI ACTS ADMINISTRATION, 1863–84: THE EMERGENCE OF THE CIVIL SCIENTIST

NE OF THE PRESSING TASKS awaiting the social historian is that of studying the growth of science and its applications to industry under the stimulating and regulatory auspices of the State.* This task is given added importance by the growing need, widely felt among constitutional and administrative historians, to re-analyse the traditional view of the nineteenth century "Revolution in Government" embodied in A. V. Dicey's classic *Law and Opinion*,[1] and by the need to refine our sometimes myopic conceptions of the morphogenesis of the modern State. Fortunately, it is in the applications of science to the purposes of the State, as these purposes become recognized by the public and codified by Parliament, that we find the most penetrating examples of technical regulation and control, coordination of national interest and public welfare, and incipient tendencies towards the systematic use of administrative and scientific expertise that has become so characteristic of contemporary society.

In view of this need, and these prospects, several considerations arise. First, one may inquire into the preconditions for the growth of science and the place of the expert scientist in government. Was there necessarily an ideological, Benthamite basis for the appointment of the expert? If not, what "philosophy" governed such a choice? Second, granting the gradually recognized necessity for the expert's existence, what was the scope of his action? What was his background, his fitness

* I am indebted to Professor O. O. G. M. MacDonagh, the University of Adelaide, to Dr. G. S. R. Kitson Clark, Trinity College, Cambridge, to Mr. Frank Greenaway, the Science Museum, South Kensington, and to Dr. J. S. Carter, late Chief Inspector under the Alkali Acts, for their thoughtful comments on certain issues raised in this paper.
1 A. V. Dicey, *Law and Public Opinion in England During the Nineteenth Century* (London, 1905).

I

for the job of creating new administrative machinery, of considering multiple interests and devising new scientific techniques? Third, what can be said of his role in relation to his profession, his area of public service, and his administrative superiors? To what extent was he a "public servant" — did his primary loyalty lie with his profession, the public, or Parliamentary decree? Fourth, what was the recognition accorded him and his office, by his superiors, by the Treasury, and how well did he perform his allotted task?

A second set of questions may also arise. Given the necessity to utilize the results of scientific discovery, how far and how fast could the expert's responsibility expand? What was the process by which this expansion occurred? To what extent was it a reaction to imposed circumstances, to what extent unconscious autogenous response to indefinite needs, and to what extent the unfolding of a conscious plan?

The answers to these questions may ultimately revise many notions about the background of legislative and administrative change that altered the whole complexion of Victorian life. In this regard, I would suggest that the Alkali Acts administration provides a particularly suggestive and hitherto neglected frame of reference. For here was the first administratively successful and systematically applied scientific governmental policy directed towards the positive regulation of the nation's chemical industry. Here was the first instance in Victorian contractualist society of the expenditure of public funds for the scientific protection of private property;[2] and here was one of the earliest examples of central administrative scientific control, designed from its inception to suppress an acknowledged public hazard. Finally, we see here one of the first occasions in which an expert scientific adviser, utilizing the skills of a new scientific profession, is made a Civil Servant accountable not only to Government but also to manufacturing industry and public opinion.

A study of the Victorian Alkali Acts administration reveals six definite phases of development: (1) 1863-68, experimentation in methods and administration; (2) 1869-74, realization of existing inadequacies, and more exacting regulation; (3) 1875-81, renewed demands for re-appraisal; (4) 1882-84, gradual expansion, limited planning of future needs; (5) 1885-92, elaboration of methods and means to meet those needs; and (6) 1892-1906, consolidation. In this paper, we shall be concerned only with the first four of these phases, covering the period 1863-84. These years represent the most significant features of the alkali

---

[2] *Report of the Royal Commission on Noxious Vapours* (henceforth *RNV*), *Parliamentary Papers* (henceforth *PP*), 1878 (C. 2159), xliv, 27.

issue, and coincide with the tenure of the first — and most famous — Chief Inspector, Dr. Robert Angus Smith.

I. THE ACT OF CREATION: 1862-68

By the middle of the nineteenth century, much of the once verdant countryside surrounding Widnes, St. Helens, the Mersey, and the Tyne had undergone melancholy transition to the drab lifeless grey of industrial wasteland. Dense clouds of smoke stifled young plants, and crops refused to grow. "The sturdy hawthorne," bewailed one observer, "makes an attempt to look gay every spring; but its leaves . . . dry up like tea leaves and soon drop off. The farmer may sow if he pleases, but he will only reap a crop of straw. Cattle will not fatten . . . and sheep throw their lambs. Cows, too . . . cast their calves; and the human animals suffer from smarting eyes, disagreeable sensations in the throat, and irritating cough, and difficulty of breathing."[3] The major cause of this suffering was, by all accounts, muriatic (hydrochloric) acid. Since 1823, when James Muspratt had built the first English factory for the production of soda by the Leblanc process, the alkali trade had acquired unquestioned permanence, and had signalled the beginning of heavy chemical industry in Britain.[4] From its rapidly multiplying salt pans and roasters, the contribution of the industrial revolution to Victorian civilization, came tons of vital sodium carbonate for the manufacture of glass, soap, and textiles. Consuming, in 1862, 1,834,000 tons of raw materials, and employing nineteen thousand men earning £871,000, with working capital of £2,000,000,[5] the industry was producing finished goods worth £2,500,000, was contributing to hosts of ancillary trades, and was a vital feeder for all chemical manufactures of any magnitude.[6] But from the forest of chimneys belched forth tons of cor-

[3] *Chemical News*, VI (1862), 202.

[4] Archibald and Nan Clow, *The Chemical Revolution: A Contribution to Social Technology* (London, 1952), p. 21.

[5] "Statistics of the Alkali Trade of the United Kingdom," *Chemical News*, VI (1862), 208.

[6] For general reference to the historical development of the alkali industry in Britain, see especially Stephen Miall, *History of the British Chemical Industry* (London, 1931); J. R. Partington, *A History of Chemistry*, IV (London, 1964); J. R. Partington, *The Alkali Industry* (London, 2nd ed., 1925); E. W. D. Tennant, "The Early History of the St. Rollox Chemical Works," *Chemistry and Industry*, LXVI (1947), 667; Charles Poole, *Old Widnes and its Neighbourhood* (Widnes, 1906); T. C. Barker and J. R. Harris, *A Merseyside Town in the Industrial Revolution: St. Helens, 1750-1900* (Liverpool, 1954); D. W. F. Hardie, *A History of the Chemical Industry in Widnes* ([London], 1950); and W. A. Campbell et al., *The Old Tyneside Chemical Trade* (Newcastle, 1961).

Also of considerable interest are J. M. Cohen, *The Life of Ludwig Mond* (London, 1956); Edmund K. Muspratt, *My Life and Work* (London, 1917); and J. Fenwick Allen, *Some Founders of the Chemical Industry: Men to Be Remembered* (Manchester, 1906).

rosive hydrogen chloride gas,[7] which when exposed to the moisture of the atmosphere descended in destructive clouds of acid. Later measurements suggested that at least 13,000 tons of commercial acid were being distributed over the north country at the whim of the prevailing winds. Some early attempts had been made by the manufacturers themselves to control this escape. Higher chimneys were built, in the hope that the gas would fall only after being mixed with so much air that all deleterious effects would diminish. Unfortunately, laws of gaseous diffusion were relatively unknown; the acid gas did not act as a gas, but as a mist. Muspratt's own chimney at Newton, near Liverpool, was over four hundred feet high; but its action, far from dispersing the acid, actually spread it over a wider area. Local complaints revealed the failure of the chimneys to solve the problem. Among the more articulate of the offended public were many of the landed gentry who lived to windward of the factories, in Durham, Derby, Lancashire, Cheshire, and Northumberland. In 1862, a deputation came to Lord Derby, who moved for an inquiry by the House of Lords. A Select Committee of fourteen was formed, under the chairmanship of Derby himself, so constituted as to include representatives of the landowning interest.[8]

Evidence was received from the most eminent scientists, including Lyon Playfair, John Percy, A. W. Hoffman, and Edward Frankland, and from forty-four other witnesses representing farm, local authority, or manufacturing interests. The evidence suggested that there did exist a means for condensing muriatic acid, a means which had not been widely employed because manufacturers recognized no incentive for doing so. Nothing had been done to encourage the use of such apparatus, because of the inadequacy of the nuisance laws. Nuisances, as such, were dealt with under several local or metropolitan acts, but were universally subject only to the Nuisance Removal Act, which was

---

[7] The waste product of the first stage of the Leblanc process in which common salt was treated with sulphuric acid to give "saltcake" (sodium sulfate) and hydrogen chloride. The saltcake was then furnaced with limestone and coal to give the so-called "black ash." This, on lixiviation with water, gave sodium carbonate solution, and residue "alkali waste," consisting mainly of calcium sulfide, calcium carbonate, and half-burned coal. In chemical terms:
$$H_2SO_4 + 2NaCl \rightarrow Na_2SO_4 + 2HCl\uparrow$$
$$Na_2SO_4 + CaO \rightarrow Na_2CO_3 + \underline{CaS}, \text{ ppt.}$$

[8] Of the fourteen, two were scientists (Lords Belper and Talbot); at least two were remnants of Derby's previous administration (Lords Chelmsford and Richmond); four were, in addition to Derby, estate holders in Northumberland and Cheshire (Lords Grey, Ravensworth, Stanley of Alderley, and Egerton); one was Comptroller to the Treasury (Lord Monteagle of Brandon); three others (Lords Wrottesley, Wodehouse, and De la Ware) and the Earl of Shaftesbury were also added. The Committee moved in extremely businesslike fashion: on 9 May the motion was heard; on 12 May Committee was named; on 16 May witnesses were called; on 18 July a report was agreed; and on 1 August their report was issued. The Committee was equally divided politically. There were 7 Liberals, 6 Conservatives, and 1 Liberal-Conservative. See *Chemical News*, VI (1862), 202.

directed towards scavenging and sanitation, and which actually pertained only to "city, town, or populous districts."[9] The only redress for alkali damage was action for damages at common law. This was unsatisfactory, because, "Partly in consequence of the expense such actions occasion, partly from the fact that while several works are in immediate juxtaposition, the difficulty of tracing the damage to anyone, or of apportioning it among several, is so great as to be all but insuperable; and, that even when verdicts have been obtained, and compensation, however inadequate, awarded, a discontinuance of the nuisance has not in most cases been the result" (p. 5).

The Committee were anxious to extend the provisions of the Smoke Prevention Acts, if this would suffice. However, when the alkali manufacturers submitted a statement insisting that exigencies of the trade required special legislation limited to the alkali industry, the Committee agreed to permit a special case, and further, in view of the noticeable want of unanimity among the scientists present, agreed not to prescribe the specific process by which the nuisance should be prevented. They did insist, however, that redress be made easier, and that qualified inspectors be appointed, with complete freedom of access and complete independence from local control (p. 10).

For the most part, the manufacturers admitted the wrong and approved the remedy. In March 1863 Lord Stanley of Alderley brought in a private bill proposing that all "alkali" works[10] be subjected to a fixed standard of ninety-five per cent condensation; setting penalties of fifty and a hundred pounds for first and subsequent offences, and authorizing the Board of Trade to appoint an inspector with sole powers of prosecution and appeal. The manufacturers pressed for moderation, insisting that the problem had only recently become scientifically susceptible of solution.[11] It was made clear by the industry that the State was considered an interloper and had yet to be tried and proved adequate to the task of equitable administration. In the face of this opposition, the complete freedom to take action for damages and the dictatorial powers of the Inspector recommended by the Select Committee were dropped from the Government Bill, and provision was made for damages to be recoverable by civil actions brought by the Inspector in the

---

[9] *Report of the Select Committee appointed to study Noxious Vapours, PP*, 1862 (486) xiv, 7.

[10] All works for the manufacture of sulphate of soda or sulphate of potash where HCl was evolved.

[11] If the industry "in its earlier stages had been subject to a system of inspection, and constant interference had taken place with its chemical experiments, combinations and processes, it would have been so paralysed that it never would have arrived at its present position" (Hansard, *Parliamentary Debates,* 3rd Ser., CLXXI [1863], 1163).

county courts. With the manufacturers' concurrence the Alkali Act was passed in July 1863 for a five-year pilot run (*The Times,* 27 Mar. 1863).

From the Appointed Day, 1 January 1864, to about 1868, the Alkali Acts administration was transformed from hypothetical design to working reality. What kind of central control was devised, just ten years after the removal of Edwin Chadwick from the centralized General Board of Health, and six years after its actual demise?[12] What precedents were studied, what men were chosen? Fortunately, other examples of working inspectors, particularly at the Home Office, were available; unfortunately, the Treasury saw no need to follow those precedents financially. Taking advice from the Home Office, T. H. Farrer of the Board of Trade requested positions for an Inspector and four Sub-Inspectors at salaries of £1000 and £500 — salaries comparable to those of Factory and Mines Inspectors.[13] The Treasury, however, reduced the Inspector to £700 and his Sub-Inspectors to £350, and urged the reduction of the whole staff by half.[14] Immediately, the Board of Trade argued that even Railway Inspectors received £1000, and that to offer the alkali inspectors less would prevent good scientists from applying, and forfeit the cordial cooperation of the alkali manufacturers. The Board also insisted they would need at least four Sub-Inspectors to enable "frequent and continuous" observation of the alkali works, of which there were estimated to be between eighty and a hundred, and that salaries sufficient only for part-time officials were hopelessly inadequate for men who, "having regard to the novel and delicate nature of the duties which they will have to perform . . . should possess an exclusively official character and be protected from all suspicion of local or personal influence."[15]

The Treasury compromised by sanctioning one Inspector and four Sub-Inspectors, at £700 and £400 respectively. Robert Angus Smith, F.R.S., was called from Manchester to be Inspector; with him came Alfred Fletcher, Brereton Todd, and Charles Blatherwick from London; and John T. Hobson from Manchester. Fletcher had formerly directed the industrial activities of the firm, Wilson and Fletcher; the other Sub-

---

[12] See S. E. Finer, *The Life and Times of Edwin Chadwick* (London, 1952).

[13] Public Record Office file, MH 16/1, 2 Sept. 1863, Office of the Committee of the Privy Council for Trade, to the Secretary of the Treasury. The Treasury refused, however, to sanction Factory Inspector status, because Factory Inspectors "having regard to the number and importance of the factories in the U.K. and the responsibility devolving on the inspectors involving moral as well as physical considerations . . . would constitute the highest class of inspectors." Alkali inspectors, presumably having only scientific matters to concern them, were ipso facto inferior.

[14] MH 16/1, 11 Sept. 1863, George Hamilton, Treasury, to James Booth, Committee of the Privy Council for Trade.

[15] MH 16/1, 16 Jan. 1864, J. Emerson Tennent to Secretary of the Treasury.

SECTION OF SODA FURNACE

from Charles Tomlinson, *Illustrations of Useful Arts and Manufacture* (London, 1858).

Inspectors were presumably scientifically trained, but the *Chemical News* admitted their names were "entirely unknown to us."[16] Smith was known, however, as perhaps the most celebrated sanitary chemist in the country, a student in Liebig's laboratory at Giessen, a co-worker of A. W. Hoffman and Lyon Playfair, and something of a protegé of Chadwick. At the time of his appointment he was a consulting chemist in Manchester and had just completed a report to the Royal Mines Commission on the air of mines and towns. His previous contributions to the chemical literature had established his reputation in the field of air analysis;[17] and although the original appointment records have been destroyed, he would seem to have been an obvious choice.

No departmental files exist which show the course Smith was expected to pursue. From later letters to the Board, however, it appears certain that he was not asked to give all his time, and that he fully expected to continue his own remunerative professional work. In 1880 he wrote, "I was at first appointed to attend only to muriatic acid escaping from alkali works but I found that the whole literature of escaping gases

[16] IX (1863), 72, 120. No mention of the inspectors is available at the Institute of Chemistry, nor at the Royal Institution, nor are obituary press references obtainable of those who did not ultimately become Chief Inspectors. Likewise, there is no information in official files to suggest how, or by whom, or for what reason, these particular appointments were made. In view of the procedures adopted in other instances (e.g. the Medical Department of the Privy Council), it is not improbable that the Sub-Inspectors were nominated by Smith. It is also uncertain, though clearly of considerable importance, whether the Sub-Inspectors were experimental chemists, working technologists, or (as was the case with Dr. Blatherwick) recruits from parachemical professions.

[17] *Chemical News*, XLIX (1884), 222. See also *DNB*.

at works required to be made, that no one knew what my duties could be and that I had to teach myself as well as others."[18] Plans for inspection began immediately. Smith's four assistants were assigned to four regional headquarters.[19] Smith himself continued in Manchester.

During the five months between the passage of the Act and the Appointed Day, most of the alkali makers had begun to approach near-perfect condensation. Condensing towers in which the evolving gases were passed over irrigated coke, and condensed liquid hydrochloric acid collected at the base, were put into operation even before inspections commenced. In fact, Smith conceded almost at once that "Even before I had the honour of being appointed inspector I had become familiar with the possibility of complete condensation so that all fear of pressing on an improvement to an impracticable issue was removed from the mind."[20] The main difficulty was that of devising precise means of measurement. Experiments with various kinds of aspirators were begun. By May 1865 Smith reported widespread introduction of his successful technique and general success in reducing the average escape of hydrochloric acid to 1.28 per cent — easily within the legal requirement of five per cent. Almost overnight, the evolution of acid was reduced from 13,000 tons to forty-three tons per annum; each of the sixty-four works actually registered under the Act was condensing at least the required amount, while twenty-six were condensing one hundred per cent.[21] Optimism pervaded the industry, and enthusiasm for inspection increased with the appearance of Smith's suggestions of new and profitable ways to transform the formerly wasted hydrochloric acid into hypochlorite and commercial bleach for the textile industry. The first flush of success brought cheers from Lord Derby[22] and growing demands for technical advice from the manufacturers.

A process of horizontal development became evident almost immediately. The possibility that a works might unintentionally slip below the standard led to the need for self-acting or fan apparatus to provide a continual check; the installation of these devices required

---

[18] MH 16/1, 8 Dec. 1880, Smith to Secretary of the Local Government Board, from Manchester.

[19] Fletcher in Liverpool for the Western Division (No. 1: Lancashire, Cheshire, and Flintshire); Hobson in Manchester for the Middle Division (No. 2: East Lancashire, Birmingham, Yorkshire, and London); Todd in Newcastle for the Eastern Division (No. 3: both banks of the Tyne, Middlesborough, and Seaham); and Blatherwick in Glasgow for No. 4 Division (all Scotland and Ireland). MH 16/1, minute, 11 Sept. 1863, Treasury letter to James Booth, Committee of Privy Council for Trade; RNV, 1878, p. 2.

[20] First Report of the Inspector appointed under the Alkali Act, 1864 (henceforth RAI), PP, 1865 (3640), xx, 7.

[21] Chemical News, XI (1865), 252.

[22] Hansard, 3rd Ser., CLXXIX (1865), 631-636.

new chimney designs, which in turn stimulated further innovations in works design. Soon Smith and his men found themselves peripatetic consultants to industry. Between March 1864 and January 1865 over a thousand visits were made to the sixty-four plants and to neighbouring non-alkali factories where gas evolution was equally troublesome. Witnessing the first autogenous, impulsive expansion of his statutory function, Smith cautioned the alkali makers in his annual report. It is, he wrote, sometimes advisable to consult as to the best mode of making improvements,

but it has been necessary to be very careful not to give such advice as might appear to be an interference; we have no power to decide on the mode of producing the desired result. At the same time, it so frequently happens that the necessary improvement is self-evident to those who are experienced, that any hesitation to advise would be unfair and indeed simple pedantry. This is more especially seen when the manufacturer himself has not at all thought on the subject, and is obliged either to seek advice or to remain inactive. (*First RAI*, p. 57)

Almost unintentionally, the Inspector was becoming the manufacturers' best ally; almost unconsciously, the State was providing a service to industry which would ultimately reverse the relative economic importance of hydrochloric acid waste and alkali product.

Those early developments, however, were scarcely sufficient for the immediate purpose, and all too soon the restraints upon Smith were more obvious than his powers. Although he often referred to the presence of other noxious acid gases, he could report on none but hydrochloric acid. Also, as the trade grew, it became clear that the five per cent emission allowance neither encouraged any reduction nor allowed for the effects of more works.[23] Even when condenser schemes were set, and air aspirators designed to replace cumbersome water aspirators, the goal of control was manifestly incomplete. "The appointment, I saw," Smith later wrote, "would be useless unless I imposed on myself higher duties. It was necessary to examine kindred questions."[24] All noxious fumes were a public concern, and "the inspectors cannot be indifferent."[25]

II. REVISION AND REAPPRAISAL: 1868-78

By 1868, the scheduled end of the alkali administration, it was becoming clear that Smith's impatience was justified. The Act of 1863

[23] *Second RAI*, 1865, PP, 1866 (3701), xvii, 8.
[24] MH 16/1, 8 Dec. 1880, Smith to Secretary.
[25] *Third RAI*, 1866, PP, 1867 (3792), xvi, 44, 47.

had not been a final solution. The naive expectation that roses would grow where hawthornes had fallen was unfulfilled; the early optimism faded, and it was realised, particularly by Smith, that the value of his work suffered from its implicit limitations. Moreover, laymen had not proved appreciative and the public nose was no accurate judge either of damage or of its precise cause. In many cases, Smith found, complainants referred simply to "bad smells," "sometimes making, concerning the most simple things, a most woeful tale, which sounds like the words of men in a panic when observation has lost its power" (*Third RAI*, p. 51).

Using his annual reports as broadsheet demands for greater scope and powers, Smith lamented his inability to work effectively without a wider definition of nuisance. "Is it not enough," he asked (p. 52), "that life is in some cases rendered unpleasant, or that irremovable property becomes a cause of annoyance instead of a source of happiness?" Over the five-year experimental period, the average escape of hydrochloric acid had declined from 1.28 per cent, to .89 per cent, to .73 per cent, to .62 per cent, but "still we stand still." Smith urged his superiors not to allow the Act to lapse.

They did not. In July 1868 a Bill was introduced into the Lords to continue the 1863 Act indefinitely. Smith interpreted its passage as a new mandate and immediately began to consider methods for dealing with the wider problems of atmospheric pollution. From 1869 he began to devote more of his time, and almost all of his reports, to systematic scientific studies of the atmosphere, accumulating quantitative data with which to "express in distinct language the character of a climate, and certainly of the influence of cities on the atmosphere."[26] He also gave increased attention to methods of refining the percentage emission test. Finally he requested from the Board of Trade a salary increase, in order to permit his giving full time to Government work. The Board categorically refused, without reference to the Treasury. However important the alkali work had become, the lack of any record of cooperation between the Board of Trade and the Inspectorate strongly suggests that though industry had by now recognised the State, the State had very little understanding of or appreciation for the scientific requirements of industry.[27]

In 1872, new hope kindled fresh enthusiasm. By the Public Health Act of that year Smith and his Inspectorate were transferred to the

---

[26] *Fifth RAI*, 1868, PP, 1869 (4167), xiv, 5, 34.
[27] P.R.O. file, BT 13/2, 9 Nov. 1868, Smith to Assistant Secretary, Board of Trade; Minute, 29 Dec. 1868, Sir Louis Mallet.

newly created Local Government Board, and placed under the supervision of the severely bureaucratic John Lambert, Permanent Secretary, and former Secretary of the Poor Law Board. Smith had frequently considered the public health aspects of atmospheric pollution, and though his alkali work related specifically to the protection of property, he was eager to bring his studies in line with the advancing front of sanitary effort. In his report for 1869, he had suggested the need for a "chemical climatology"; the following year he had repeated that these proposals formed an inevitable projection of his statutory responsibility.[28] The far-sighted recommendations of the Royal Sanitary Commission and the organisation of health activity which it proposed seemed particularly auspicious for the success of Smith's plans. Undoubtedly Smith would have sought applications for his research had he been in closer contact with his famous colleague John Simon at the Medical Department.

As the years passed, however, the water-tight compartmentalization of the Local Government Board, as well as the physical distance which separated Smith from Whitehall, permitted him no access to the Medical Department. Simon himself, preoccupied with his bitter conflict with Lambert, appears not to have demonstrably encouraged this important branch of public health.[29]

Despite his expanding studies in meteorology and theoretical climatology, Smith was not diverted from the pressing necessity to extend alkali legislation to other acid gases and coal smoke, and to enforce collective responsibility among alkali manufacturers, thereby equitably apportioning damage claims (*Seventh RAI*, p. 73). He realized that continuing escapes of hydrochloric acid from alkali works could be dealt with by persuasion and advice only if the precise destructive equivalents of the acid could be measured to everyone's satisfaction, so

---

[28] "It has appeared to me necessary to examine the atmosphere in order to see what amount of muriatic acid it contained in places where that is manufactured. From that I was led to examine it also in other places in order to make a full series of comparisons; and next I was naturally conducted to a comparison of the amount of muriatic acid and chlorides in relation to other substances. This part of the work may now be said to be accomplished, and the results I hope will be of use in all sanitary inquiries in future whenever the chemical method is adopted. That it will be adopted more frequently now is my belief. It is safer to examine the condition of the air by a few chemical experiments than by waiting to see how many deaths take place in a thousand of the population. That it is possible at present to substitute the chemical and microscopical entirely for the medical is not my belief, but the time has come when these must begin to assume their position, and when they have found their due place in education I do not doubt that they will rapidly take up a large portion of the time of sanitary inquirers" (*Seventh RAI*, 1871, PP, 1871 [C. 354], xiv, 4).

[29] See R. J. Lambert, *Sir John Simon and English Social Administration* (London, 1963), chs. 21-33. John Simon's classic *English Sanitary Institutions* (London, 1890) makes no mention of the alkali inspectorate or of Smith, and has but one passing reference to atmospheric pollution.

letting "weight and measure . . . take the place of opinion."[30] Moreover, the results of a private enquiry done at Smith's request in 1871 confirmed that the gradual replacement of the Leblanc process by the Solvay ammonia-soda process[31] had much diminished the proportionate injury done by hydrochloric acid, and had converted the problem to one of dealing with sulphurous and nitric acids emitted by alkali and other works. Accordingly, in 1872 Smith proposed amendment of the laws to include new powers to "enter and examine" non-alkali works which produced hydrochloric acid, in order to apply a more precise volumetric test for hydrochloric acid and to place sulphur and nitric acid works under "interrogative and tentative" inspection.

Smith's new masters, however, took no immediate notice; Smith's patience was sorely tried. In his report for 1872, he commented: "Chemical works generally are greatly on the increase, and the power to repress escapes of gases does not increase with them. . . . The Alkali Act, which was excellent for a time and has done some good, is becoming less valuable daily. When alkali works accumulate in one place they make even 1% of escape a great evil. . . . However, I am merely repeating myself."[32] And a year later he insisted, "The present method of judging by percentages is a great obstruction, because no action can be brought unless the gas going away can be measured into parts of the total evolved. Now all the random and many of the most dangerous escapes are beyond measurement, we may as well attempt to measure the speed of the wind when it has passed us."[33] Finally, his demands were heeded: in 1874, a Bill embodying many of them was entered by George Sclater-Booth (afterwards Lord Basing), President of the Local Government Board. Supported by manufacturers and landowners alike, the short Alkali Act (1863) Amendment Act of 1874 set a volumetric standard of hydrochloric acid gas escape (.2 grain of hydrochloric acid per cubic

[30] *Eighth RAI*, 1872, *PP*, 1873 (C. 582), xvi, 10-11.
[31] This involved the conversion of chlorine into calcium chloride ($CaCl_2$) in the second step of a more remunerative and largely regenerating process:

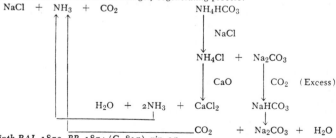

$$NaCl + NH_3 + CO_2 \qquad\qquad NH_4HCO_3$$
$$NaCl$$
$$NH_4Cl + Na_2CO_3$$
$$CaO \qquad\qquad CO_2 \ (\text{Excess})$$
$$H_2O + 2NH_3 + CaCl_2 \qquad NaHCO_3$$
$$CO_2 + Na_2CO_3 + H_2O$$

[32] *Ninth RAI*, 1873, *PP*, 1874 (C. 815), xix, 35.
[33] *Tenth RAI*, 1874, *PP*, 1875 (C. 1071), xxv, 395.

foot), extended inspection to wet copper works where salt was used and hydrochloric acid evolved, and employed the novel expedient of requiring all alkali makers to use the "best practicable means" to prevent the escape of all other noxious gases.[34] This Act intensified the restrictions of 1863, and also prepared for later additional legislation, in Smith's words, by "enforcing the acquisition of ascertained improvements."[35]

The Chief Inspector rejoiced: "The Alkali Act of 1863, after 11 years of solitary struggle with noxious gases, receives assistance from the Act of 1874, and now begins in a small degree a more vigilant, and it is to be hoped a more useful life."[36] In his next report, Smith looked forward not only to the adequate enforcement of the new volume standard, but by hard work and close cooperation between the inspectors and the manufacturers (*Tenth RAI*, p. 395), to the gradual reduction of the allowable maximum by yearly stages of .01 grain per cubic foot (*Eleventh RAI*, p. 3). By 1876, the simplicity of the test had received general approval; and most firms in addition were appointing their own resident chemists to make daily examinations.[37] The *Chemical News* eulogized the Chief Inspector: "If the Act is successful the result is mainly due to his zeal, tact, and intelligence. His method has been to lead, not to drive, the interests affected. He does not seek to lay down at once a hard and fast line, but as a truly practical man he aims at and effects gradual improvement. We can wish nothing better for the cause of sanitary reform than that all inspectors who have to deal with 'standards' may sit at his feet" (XXXI [1875], 7).

Smith's success in obtaining this Act owed much to the cooperation of the Secretary, John Lambert, and to the latter's influence over Sclater-Booth. It must be said, however, that at first neither Sclater-Booth nor Lambert had much interest in the Inspectorate, or any great appreciation of its goals. On 17 September 1874, faced with the increased work of the new Act, the Sub-Inspectors approached the President on the subject of salary. For eleven years their existence had gone unnoticed by the Whitehall departments. No reply to their request was

---

[34] Scheduled to include sulphuric acid, sulphurous acid except that arising from coal, nitric acid, sulphuretted hydrogen, and chlorine. See Alkali Act, 26 & 27 Vict., c. 124. Cf. Hansard, 3rd Ser., CCXX (1874), 336-389, 863-868.

[35] *RNV, Mins. Evid.*, Q. 188. It is interesting to note that the Passenger Acts and other widely differing examples of regulatory legislation (e.g. the Canal Boats Acts and the Salmon Acts) came to embody similar elastic mechanisms of control. I hope presently to deal elsewhere with this and other features of legislative innovation, discretionary powers, and central coordinative control.

[36] *Eleventh RAI*, 1875, PP, 1876 (C. 1339), xvi, 3.

[37] *RNV, Mins. Evid.*, Q. 14.

made. The following February, Fletcher again appealed, this time to Lambert:

An instalment of salary for January just received reminds me that the amount is exactly the same as it was in January 1864, although since then the work has constantly increased until now it is fully double of what it was then. . . . I make no complaint of this, however, but I do complain that my work does not provide me with means of living. I could not maintain and educate my family if I had no private income. . . . Kindly put the matter forward if possible. . . . Forgive my pressure — it is but transmitted.[38]

Smith supported the letter, insisting,

The Inspectors would willingly be judged by their work, which has been to carry out the Alkali Act. No succeeding work can be better carried out. If the Act failed to do all that was expected it is not the inspectors who are to blame. . . . It must not be supposed that we have been pressed both, but until lately have been disregarded. . . . My enquiries led to the last Act, and every deputation before asked my advice and after the Act took my published opinion . . .
When beginning a new Act which I may add is to a great extent carried out by extra-exertion, it is not pleasant to find those who must do the details activated by a deep feeling of being utterly neglected, or so they would say more than neglected. They are men perfectly capable of seeing clearly the importance of the position which their long experience has given and as they may be held as advisors to a large and important body, their loss to that body, to the public and to the Board would be great.[39]

Lambert, however, chose to reserve the issue — thus, to Sclater-Booth: "I believe you have quite decided not to consider the question of an increase in the salaries of the Alkali Inspectors until you have had some experience of the operation of the new Act." Sclater-Booth demurely agreed, and the Inspectors' raise was refused.[40] Lambert defended his action to Smith on the grounds that certain private individuals in Runcorn and Widnes[41] had seen little vegetative regeneration as a result of the Act, and attributed this to the lax efforts of the Inspectors. Smith denied the implied accusation, protesting that he, and not the public, had first called attention to the imperfections of the Act, which admittedly still allowed several tons of acid to escape every week. On the matter of alleged laxity under the 1874 Act, Smith angrily replied,

I suppose . . . it may not have occurred to anyone that an Act of a progressive character like that of 1874 cannot be brought to perfection on an appointed day. A Factory Act which said that children should not work alone 6 hours per day, might

---

[38] MH 16/1, 1 Feb. 1875, Fletcher, in Liverpool, to Lambert, marked "Private."

[39] MH 16/1, 24 Feb. 1875, Smith to Lambert.

[40] MH 16/1, 3 Feb. 1875, minutes, Lambert to President, and President to Lambert.

[41] MH 16/1, 26 June-29 July 1875, correspondence, Robert Holland, for Sir Richard Brooke, to Smith. The Brooke estate was particularly devastated. Brooke appealed to Wilbraham Egerton, M.P., who then brought the matter before Sclater-Booth in the Commons.

be made complete in its efficiency at once. On the first of March, we had power to begin, and we began. I have already shown that I went as far as I considered prudent, for violence may delay the next important step. But already furnaces have been stopt, improvements at great expense have been made, and new inventions are growing or being tried in order to make improvements permanent.[42]

Smith had to educate his masters. Gradually, his honest efforts won Lambert's confidence. On 9 November 1875, Smith submitted to the Board a thorough defence of the Inspectorate's work since the Act of 1874, and included special reports from each Sub-Inspector. He stressed again the difficulty of causing manufacturers and landowners to reason together. Moreover, he gave evidence to show that the major source of nuisance and complaint was no longer hydrochloric acid, but sulphur-etted hydrogen arising from the sulphide waste heaps of the alkali works. Since these deposits were not within the province of the Act,[43] the Inspectors could legally do nothing to mitigate their effects.

By mid-November, Lambert had begun to appreciate the many factors hindering efficient inspection. He dictated to Sclater-Booth:

These reports certainly show a considerable improvement and that the operation of the late Act has been very beneficial. Probably you will consider whether it will be desirable that a Bill should be prepared, for the purpose of bringing other chemical works under inspection. You will see . . . that Dr. Smith is desirous of having a conference as to the mode of dealing with sulphuretted hydrogen.
Shall these reports be acknowledged with an expression of satisfaction, and the hope that the sub-inspectors will not relax in their efforts to give full effect to the late Act? At the same time Dr. Smith may be informed that you have made application to the Treasury to increase the salary of the sub-inspectors by £100 p.a. from the 25th of March next.[44]

For the next ten years, Smith's relations with his Permanent Secretary were extremely cordial. Lambert seemed content to render unto the scientists the things that were scientific. Partly owing to the fact that Smith did not attempt to force his broader climatological schemes upon the secretariat, and partly because of his distance from Whitehall, there was no occasion for a personal and professional clash comparable to the duel between Lambert and Simon. When Smith wanted experimental apparatus, Lambert helpfully referred technical descriptions to the Treasury. Smaller sums for immediate needs were granted promptly, within the limits of the Board's vote. Lambert's solicitude was such, in fact, that when Smith wrote from Paris in 1877 proposing the useful-ness of atmospheric research, Lambert was on the point of allocating to

---

[42] MH 16/1, 24 July 1875, Smith to Lambert.
[43] *Intermediate Report of the Chief Inspector, 1863 and 1874, of his proceedings since the passing of the latter Act, PP,* 1876 (165), xvi, 1.
[44] MH 16/1, 16 Nov. 1875, Lambert to President.

I

Smith a portion of the tiny grant for Auxiliary Scientific Investigations annually allotted to the Medical Department.[45]

Despite the theoretical basis of Smith's good work, criticisms of noxious escapes continued and increased.[46] In October 1875, Victoria herself complained that the royal estate at Osborne was being rendered uninhabitable by the ammonia vapours emitted from a neighbouring cement works. Since these works were not under the Act, and since the owner was not desirous of improving his furnaces, despite a personal visit from Smith, nothing could be done.[47] Finally, demands of redress on the part of such groups as the Lancashire and Cheshire Association for Controlling the Escape of Noxious Vapours and Fluids resulted in a petition to the Lords, asking for a comprehensive review of the law. In February 1876, the Duke of Cumberland asked for a Royal Commission, which was promised in July by Richard Cross, the Home Secretary.[48] Lords Aberdare, Percy, and Middleton — all outspoken contributors to earlier debates on the Alkali Acts — led the Commission, with Aberdare as Chairman. Wilbraham Egerton (M.P. for Cheshire) followed his father, who had sat on the Committee of 1862. James Stephenson (M.P. for South Shields) came as the representative of the Alkali Manufacturers Association; and Professors Alexander Williamson and Henry Roscoe were added. The Commission was to "inquire into the working and management of works and manufactories from which sulphurous acid, sulphuretted hydrogen, and ammoniacal and other vapours and gases are given off, to ascertain the effect produced thereby on animals and vegetable life, and to report on the means to be adopted for the prevention of injury thereto" (RNV, p. 1).

In their investigation, the Commissioners visited the major centres of manufacture and exhaustively questioned 197 witnesses, including Smith, his four Sub-Inspectors, John Lambert, and John Simon. In the fourteen years since 1862, the annual value of the alkali trade had trebled, its manpower and production nearly doubled, and capital expenditure increased five-fold. But this very expansion had made it impossible to estimate advantages accruing from the Acts. Therefore, while praising the Inspectors, the Commissioners added: "All the Act could

---

[45] MH 16/1, 22 May 1877, Smith to Lambert, and Lambert to Smith.

[46] *Chemical News*, XXXVIII (1878), 181-182.

[47] MH 16/1, 16 Oct. 1875, Sir Thomas Biddulph for the Queen, to Sclater-Booth; 5 Nov. 1875 — 4 Apr. 1878, correspondence with the alkali firm of Francis and Newport.

[48] It is interesting and significant that the issue was brought to a head by Cross. That the legendary sanitary zeal of Disraeli's Government was embodied in the Home Secretary and not in the Local Government Board corroborates the assertions made by Dr. Lambert in his description of administrative conservatism in the early years of the Local Government Board. See Lambert, p. 547.

SODA MANUFACTURE

from Charles Tomlinson, *Illustrations of Useful Arts and Manufacture* (London, 1858), p. 117.

be expected to effect was the prevention of much injury which would otherwise have arisen. And this result has by general consent been obtained; although it may be a question whether the law has been so administered as to extract the utmost advantage derivable from it, and whether its stricter enforcement, and a more vigorous and systematic inspection would not have secured still greater benefits" (*RNV*, p. 3).

Testimony was heard on the effect of acid vapour on health and vegetation. Damage to property remained manifest, but the effect of fumes upon the welfare of humans was a point of contention.[49]

Of legal proceedings of inspectors under the Act, the Commissioners were cautiously critical. To date, only four prosecutions had been undertaken, as a direct result of Smith's policy of persuasion:

In the opinion of many of the witnesses, this policy, at first expedient, has been unnecessarily prolonged; and we believe that, although allowance should have been made for the shortcomings of manufacturers honestly striving to render due obedience to the law, more frequent instances of severity exercised towards those known to have been animated by a different spirit, would have been advantageous to the public, and desirable in the interests of the manufacturers themselves.[50]

On organisation of inspection, the Commissioners found a surprising difference of opinion. Manufacturers, almost universally in favour of the "best practical means" test that permitted them latitude for experiment while definite standards were still impracticable, wished continued central inspection. Local inspection, they felt, would be inefficient and would show wide variance in administrative rigour; local officers could not possess the requisite scientific and chemical knowledge and their actions would inevitably be partial, vexatious, and unconducive to general industrial improvement (*RNV*, p. 28). Furthermore, the manufacturers had been encouraged by past inspections in the belief that a central inspector would not press them with undue

---

[49] *The Times* (2 Sept. 1878), likened the comparison of affected and non-affected property to the lands of Goshen and the domains of Pharoah's servants. One doctor present, Benjamin Ward Richardson, the nominal medical head of the "Chadwickian school" of sanitarians, asserted that he was "unable to discover any evidence which showed to him proof of special deterioration of health" in Widnes or St. Helens. John Simon, however, asserted that "the expression 'injurious to health,' in many of these discussions had been used in a sense to impose upon the person who is charged with the duty of protecting health, an obligation to prove that typhoid fever, or small pox, or dysentery, or ringworm, or something of that kind, some definite disease that we name in our catalogue of diseases, is produced by those vapours. I do not think we are bound when it is a question of sanitary injury, to show injury of that kind. To be free from bodily discomfort is a condition of health. If a man gets up with a headache, pro tanto he is not in good health, if a man gets up unable to eat his breakfast, pro tanto he is not in good health. When a man is living in an atmosphere which leaves him constantly below par . . . all that is an injury to health, though not a production of what at present could be called a definite disease." See *RNV*, pp. 7, 26; *Mins. Evid.*, Q. 2852-53, 13194.

[50] *RNV*, p. 16; *Mins. Evid.*, Q. 32.

severity. "These trades," they argued, "cannot be carried on with absolute innocuousness. Occasional forbearance will be as necessary a quality in an inspector as vigilance and firmness, and more likely to be found in a Government officer than in a local officer" (*RNV*, p. 31).

All the representatives of the Local Government Board, however, including both John Simon and John Lambert, protested against the continuation of central inspection, and were adamantly opposed to any further exceptional legislation of this kind. Both Simon and Lambert said that local inspection was more effective, and that any further legislation should be of a general character, enlarging the power of local authorities, rather than extending the powers and duties of the central government.[51] The Commissioners observed, however, that everyone was compelled by acknowledged fact to admit that there was, at that time, "no sufficient reason" for believing that existing local authorities could be entrusted to discharge duties required by the Alkali Act. In the end, Lambert finally conceded that "the circumstances were unusual"; and Simon's scheme, though he never admitted it, depended upon an organised local health administration which had not yet appeared. It was obvious that a system of local inspection had the advantage of being in harmony with recent legislation and the extension of local responsibility and power, but it was clear that many local authorities did little to enforce laws which would adversely affect the interests of their most important constituents.[52]

In the end, the Commission endorsed the continuance of centralised control, and advocated greater numbers of inspectors, with increased powers to report defective works. Powers of individual redress were to be refined, and specific tests applied to determine contributory nuisance responsibility. The Final Report accepted the Inspector's desire to broaden and intensify special legislation, to fix standards for sulphur and nitrogen acid gases at one grain per cubic foot and .5 grain per cubic foot respectively; to prohibit deposit or drainage of

---

[51] Simon read to the Commission a memorandum he had written in 1872 (presumably at the time he was advocating the appointment of local health officers), in which he said, "The central government should act not as inspector of nuisances, but as inspector of nuisance authorities, and that any deviation from this principle must, on the one hand, embarrass central government with duties which it cannot properly discharge, and on the other hand, hinder local authorities from acquiring a proper sense of their duties to the public." See *RNV*, p. 29; *Mins. Evid.*, Q. 13176-81. In some respects, this view differs from those advanced by Simon while at the Local Government Board (1871-76). The fact that only two years after his abrupt resignation he was advancing opinions similar to those of his arch-enemy, Lambert, may suggest a change in attitude not betrayed in his *English Sanitary Institutions*. It is interesting to speculate upon the course public health development itself would have taken, if these self-same arguments had been applied to its own enforcement.

[52] *RNV*, p. 29. See also *The Times*, 2 Sept. 1878.

I

all alkali sulphide waste; and to place sulphuric acid works under inspection. It also extended inspection to chemical manure works, ammonia works, tar distilleries, gas liquor works, and coke ovens, with elastic instructions to adopt the "best practicable means" of suppressing noxious vapours. Finally, it recommended that all noxious works not yet under the Alkali Acts be placed under the nominal supervision of the Local Government Board, which would have power to fix standards of escape by Provisional Order as soon as such standards became industrially feasible.[53]

III. THE LEGISLATIVE RESULTS: 1879-84

One immediate effect of the Royal Commission's report was to dampen the cordial relationship between Lambert and Smith. The Local Government Board's administration of the Acts had not been very warmly praised and the fact that the Commissioners accepted Smith's recommendations over those given by Lambert was not taken well by the Permanent Secretary. With the Final Report published, Smith again wished to acquaint himself with Continental procedures before recommending specific legislation. Lambert rejected Smith's travel request with unaccustomed curtness: "The previous permission must be considered as exhausted" (MH 16/1, 27 Nov. 1878). Clearly surprised, Smith replied in the most formal letter he ever wrote to the Board, explaining in detail the obvious necessity of comparative study for "giving to others that confidence which is felt in those who have seen much." He added cheerfully, "without doubt you know the reasons well and I suppose that it was only necessary to have them in an official form." Smith estimated his expenses to be £86 and asked for £74 (4-12 Oct. 1878); Lambert (without explanation) downgraded his grant to £60.

The Final Report also ended Lambert's acquiescence in Smith's policy of enforcement by persuasion. To the Secretary stricter penalties appeared the only solution. Lambert therefore instructed Smith to begin prosecutions whenever possible. Smith reluctantly agreed and reported that the manager of Messrs. Snape and Co., Widnes, had accidentally allowed an escape of hydrochloric acid in excess of the .2 grain per cubic foot standard. Lambert wrote to the President: "You know how often it has been alleged that the Inspector omits to take proceedings, and you will be able to say whether or not Messrs. Snape should be allowed to

[53] Works not under the Act included arsenic, cement, cobalt, dry copper, wet copper, galvanising, glass, lead, salt, spelter, tin, coal tar dye, and nickel works, and potteries where glazing was done. See *RNV, Mins. Evid.*, Q. 13176-81. See also *The Times*, 31 Aug. 1870.

escape on the present occasion." Mr. Craig, the administrative clerk overseeing Alkali Acts affairs, protested that too little information was available. Sclater-Booth nevertheless obliged Lambert: "let proceedings be taken."

The Board received a heartrending plea from Snape and Company, apologizing profusely and asking that proceedings be abandoned. Lambert, with imperial coldness, minuted to Smith for reply: "The Board regret the necessity of proceeding in these cases but so much blame has been incurred by the supposed indisposition of the Board to enforce the provisions of the Act that they do not feel justified in dispensing with these actions" (22 Oct. 1878). Golding and Davis, another firm caught in the dragnet, appealed not formally to the Board, but informally to Smith. The Inspector, weighing loyalties, sent a firm reply to the manufacturer, and a minuted file of papers to Lambert, adding,

I forward the papers because, among other reasons, they show the spirit of the alkali makers and their relation to inspection. To be found fault with causes a most serious commotion. If trials were frequent this delicacy of feeling would disappear.
(14 Nov. 1878)
I do not think it well to trouble the Board with feelings, but this enclosure is only a specimen of much that I was obliged to hear and perhaps there is no harm in showing the Board for once somewhat of the inner workings of the inspection.
(16 Nov. 1878)

But Lambert remained adamant and Smith was unwillingly obliged to prosecute.[54]

Resigned to this arbitrary prosecution, both Snape and Golding and Davis paid the maximum fine of £50 without waiting for the case to be tried. Proceedings were dropped.

To an extent, this "get-tough" policy strained Smith's carefully nurtured inspector-manufacturer relationship. But it also brought Lambert wholeheartedly behind Smith's long-advocated demands for increased coverage. Indeed, the hitherto rather amateur administration of the Acts received all the calculating drive of Lambert's genius, and on 7 April 1879 a strong Bill was introduced to effect all the recommendations of the Royal Commission. In addition, it proposed to extend the jurisdiction of the nuisance clauses of the Public Health Act, 1875, and to require licence duties from all manufacturers; this application of Lambert's "secretarial commonsense" would give the local authorities a greater share in initiating the prosecution of transgressing firms, and

---

[54] "Having been so much blamed for clemency I have no desire to compensate by an act of cruelty, but as I have been blamed for taking so much responsibility upon myself, I feel inclined in this case to relieve myself if possible of some" (MH 16/1, Smith to Secretary, 14 Nov. 1878).

would enable the administration to be practically self-supporting.

Although Sclater-Booth announced confidently that the manufacturers would support the Government Bill,[55] it was blocked by threatened opposition at the second reading.[56] Lambert consequently rejected a proposed pay-raise for the Inspectors,[57] and stubbornly pressed forward an identical Bill the following session. In June 1880, Smith was approached by the alkali makers, who urged restraint. Under Lambert's hand the Board was proceeding too fast.[58] Smith wrote to Lambert that the manufacturers had begun to win the sympathy of local courts and that any regulation would not be successful which deprived them of their confidential role of participant-observers.

No time was found in the session to advance the Bill of 1880, and at the end of the year J. G. Dodson (later Lord Monk-Bretton) became President of the Board. Unsuccessful in railroading the legislation through, and apparently having less influence over Dodson than he had held over Sclater-Booth, Lambert agreed to submit the matter to Smith.[59] Smith thereupon composed a new Bill, reiterating most of the recommendations of the Royal Commission and the two preceding Bills, but easing the judicial strictures on the alkali makers and removing them from the threatened control of the local authorities.[60] Further, his Bill of 1881 sought to alter the whole emphasis of alkali legislation by regulating the acid gases themselves, rather than the processes which emitted them. By this means, standards could be applied to the offending acids regardless of how they were produced, and the need for continual temporary legislation attacking specific works would be obviated.

This Civil-Science alliance, conceded by Lambert as an act of necessity, won the immediate support of local government groups, and both Herbert Phillips, Chairman of the Association for Prevention of Noxious Vapours (Manchester and East Cheshire) and J. L. Clarke-Smith, Assistant Secretary of the National Association for the Promotion

---

[55] A deputation of manufacturers introduced by Derby in Nov. 1878, had urged Sclater-Booth to take "a substantial step in advance from previous legislation." One Widnes manufacturer complained that Derby had "painted the Devil even blacker than he really is," and that to "enhance the cost of [alkali] production by hasty or ill-judged legislation would enhance the cost of half the industrial products of the country" (*The Times*, 6 Dec. 1878).

[56] Hansard, 3rd Ser., CCXLVIII, 1406; *The Times*, 27 Feb. 1880.

[57] MH 16/1, 20 Jan. 1880, Fletcher to Sclater-Booth, minutes by Lambert.

[58] The manufacturers went to the Society of Arts to listen to F. E. Muspratt and protest against the Bill (*The Times*, 27 Feb. 1880).

[59] MH 16/1, 15 Nov. 1880, Lambert, minutes to Craig; 20 Nov. 1880, Craig to Lambert. The alkali manufacturers testified strongly in favour of Smith's method of inspection and expressed a willingness to have stricter regulations on his lines. See *The Times*, 14 Dec. 1880.

[60] Cf. Sclater-Booth's replying to deputation, *The Times*, 13 Feb. 1880.

of Social Science, sent petitions in support of the "elastic clause" for the inspection of all noxious processes (MH 16/1, 5 Mar. 1881).

Unfortunately, the Bill as submitted by Dodson to the Lords on 7 February omitted the inclusive acid provisions. It is uncertain why, although it is known that a deputation from the alkali manufacturers, introduced by John Stephenson, M.P., met with Dodson, Lambert, and the Legal Officer, Danby Fry, on 11 December 1880 (*The Times*, 14 Dec. 1880). Uninformed of this decision, Smith was disappointed at seeing the printed text of the Bill. After again suggesting the inclusive acid clause, he added, "I trust this will receive your assent. I should be glad to know the movements that I may be able to render you aid."[61] When the Bill reached Commons on 18 March, Smith was notified and told to formulate a solution agreeable to the alkali makers. This he did; and the Bill, overcoming the obstructionist tactics of cement makers, Irish members, and a generally ignorant House, passed into law at the session's end.

The Alkali, etc., Works Regulation Act, 1881, was a good compromise effecting many of the recommendations of the Royal Commission. Cement works had been omitted, and Smith's inclusive clause was missing, but the vital "et cetera" in the title laid the foundation for the future expansion of the inspector's responsibility. The Act provided for increased control in three ways: first, by extending fixed standards to sulphuric acid and nitric acid; second, by placing more than a dozen new kinds of works under the "best practicable means" test pending the formulation of fixed standards; and third, by giving the Local Government Board power to expand inspectorial control over cement and salt works by provisional order, as soon as suitable means of regulation could be devised. Lambert's interest in economy was served by the introduction of registration fees for all works emitting the scheduled acids, and by the encouragement of local authorities to provide part of the salary of local inspectors in their areas.[62]

Of equal significance, this Act, prepared by Smith's own hand, promoted Smith to the status of Chief Inspector, and authorized five additional Sub-Inspectors and assistants — effectively doubling his staff. Salary increases were allowed to the faithful Fletcher, Blatherwick, and

---

[61] On 11 Mar. 1881, he wrote to Lambert, "I fear that the Alkali works Registration Bill has not been much altered in the House of Lords. I fear I have written on it so often as to tire you" (MH 16/1, 11 Mar. 1881).

[62] This financial caution was certainly one key to success in the presence of an obdurate Treasury. In early 1880, Sclater-Booth had declared, "one of the reasons why the Alkali Acts had been somewhat restricted had been the difficulty of asking Parliament to provide a larger establishment of inspectors. . . . it was most important that the public should pay for the remedy they desired to have applied" (*The Times*, 3 Feb. 1880).

Todd; Smith himself was advanced from £800 to £1000; and expenditures for the Inspectorate generally were increased by one-half.[63] The number of works that were brought under the Act swelled the total from about 240 to just under a thousand.[64] Local authorities were asked to submit statistical returns of all noxious works in their areas, and from the information on registration applications, inspection duties were re-allocated and extended.

The combination of Lambert's acute administrative prescience and Smith's way with the manufacturers suggested a reasonably promising future. To Smith, who since 1876 had also been the Inspector under the Rivers Pollution Prevention Acts, it now seemed time to "consolidate the Departments of air and water so far as the chemistry is concerned" and to report them together (MH 16/1, 8 Dec. 1880). Fresh hope was felt for the suppression of sulphide waste heaps,[65] the acid-filled streams, and the innumerable environmental hazards which reduced the health and efficiency of the nation.

Indeed, the next three years saw the Inspectorate pass from adolescence to maturity. Two major events completed this transition. First, clause nineteen of the Act of 1881, permitting local authorities to appoint resident chemical inspectors, was adopted by the Associated Sanitary Authorities of the Liverpool-Merseyside area who selected a chemist and, over the objection of the Alkali Manufacturers' Association, stationed him in Liverpool. A compromise agreement among all interests resulted in this unique creation of a specialist regional officer, appointed by the local authority, responsible to the central authority, and paid jointly from Parliamentary and local funds — surely a far-sighted experiment in the history of central-local government relations.

Second, the Provisional Order Clause of the Act of 1881, which was directed towards cement and salt manufacturers, was projected for immediate application. As soon as the Act was passed, Smith instructed his inspectors to give special attention to cement works, deduced principles on which new furnaces might be made, and — just as he had done before with nitric acid and sulphur acids — proposed legislation for the accomplishment of successive stages of purity (MH 16/2, 12 Apr. 1883). Similarly, action was taken to discover the "best practicable means" for

---

[63] *Civil Service Estimates*, PP, 1882 (26), xlii, 120. Total expenditures for 1882-83 were estimated at £4914, plus returns from registration certificates, which were expected to amount to £4300.

[64] *Chemical News*, L (1883), 306.

[65] After 1887 the Chance process for recovery of sulphur from alkali waste resulted in a new source of sulphuric acid, and consequently profit from a former nuisance. See Alexander Findlay, *A Hundred Years of Chemistry* (London, 1948), p. 261.

salt works, as the first of several steps towards fixed standard regulation.

The Provisional Order embodying these principles passed without debate in 1884. In remarkably similar pattern, Smith's successor, Alfred Fletcher, would extend, ascertain, and adopt methods to assure the "best practicable means" for additional processes in the elaborating measure of 1892, and also prepare the way for the consolidating measure of 1906, which is the basis of vapour regulation today. But by 1884 the building was done, and Smith's weakening health slowed his eager pursuit of new experiments. Professional honours came to him, the LL.D. of Glasgow as early as 1861 and the LL.D. of Edinburgh in 1882; but problems of dealing with his growing staff and office became more burdensome. On the eve of preparing the Order of 1884, he wrote to Hugh Owen, Jr., the new Permanent Secretary:

Dr. Blakie, my assistant, young, ardent and effective in work and of apparently very fine physique has been seized with illness, presumably aggravated if not caused by exposure when doing work for the district of the Inspectors who required aid. One of them had said that Inspection was slavery.

I have it also pressed upon me that the requests for grants for labs. have not been attended to and trouble and expense is put upon the Inspectors. So we have all some troubles, but we do not intend to be beaten if possible. I am hoping not to rest much till after the session as no one else can take the reins in hand. After that time I hope to have some actual leisure which I really never have had.

(MH 16/2, 20 Feb. 1883)

He never lived to achieve this wish. Two days before the Provisional Order was taken into Commons, Smith died.

It is significant that the highest tributes to his work came from the members of the industry he was appointed to regulate, but stayed to serve.[66] Testimony to his work lay in the sustained good relations between the manufacturers and the State. His scientific work won its own reward; the Establishment, however, hardly noticed his passing. No remark occurs in the Inspectorate files, no mention in the official reports. It is ironic that his good work did not merit the notice that Simon enjoyed, when the latter resigned from the Medical Department eight

---

[66] At the height of protest in 1879, the *Chemical News* wrote: "His thorough knowledge of industrial chemistry, his suggestive and fruitful mind, his tact, courtesy and patience, his clear oversight of the whole field of operations, and of the rival interests to be dealt with, cannot be too highly esteemed. . . . His method of leading instead of driving the chemical manufacturers, and of substituting, whenever possible, remonstrance and advice for summonses and fines, is perhaps slow, but it is sure. We know well that a part of the British public value remedial agencies and reforms of every kind simply in proportion to the disturbance they create. . . . Dr. Smith remarks that, 'Some of the public would have preferred to see the inspectors frequently in court with cases of complaint, but I know well that information must grow and habit must grow, and that to torment men into doing what required much time to learn, was to return to the old system of teaching by the cane instead of through the intellect' " (XL, 304).

years before; Smith's passive nature aroused nothing of the scandal that attended his contemporary's tumultuous career.

In the last analysis, one can easily question the "good" that Smith actually achieved. The obstacles to the complete suppression of noxious gases were insuperable.[67] The conditions in chemical works of the time, and the nature of the Leblanc industry itself, while it lasted, put a total solution of the problem beyond reach.[68] As Smith himself once admitted, the Acts must be considered in terms of "diminishing the extent of devastation," rather than in terms of "manifest improvement" of property. Sources of fumes, like coal smoke, could never be adequately controlled. These, like the sulphide waste heaps, were the price of manufacture, and could be redeemed only by the passage of time. Even Smith evinced a vague sense of futility in his later reports, when he looked at the wastelands, lamented the gaps in his knowledge of the atmosphere and means of applying new techniques, and wrote: "I see this, and I labour in the contracted field of chemical works, repressing some evil, doing some good I think but not so much as I wish, for I see that it is invention that is required, and not inspection merely. Invention is slow, and if ideas are quick the trials are not so. Nature with which we struggle is so complex" (*RNV, Mins. Evid.,* Q. 115). It is to the everlasting credit of the manufacturers and the inspectors that an attempt was made to deal with nature realistically, and to strike a successful compromise between the needs of industry and the well-being of society.

It remains to suggest what tentative conclusions may be derived from this development, and what issues it proposes for further study.

First, we may deduce in Smith something about the character of the mid-Victorian Civil Scientist, and about his relationships with the public, his colleagues, and his superiors. High qualifications and universally recognized professional standing, together with broad conceptions of duty and limited conceptions of self, were testimony to his ability; his successful dealings with laymen and administrators revealed what could be done within the constraints of departmental control. Smith's almost forgotten role at the Local Government Board shows all

---

[67] *The Times* (17 Feb. 1881) sadly acknowledged an even greater futility: "In the ignorance of the sufferers consists their helplessness. They sicken and indeed they die, but they cannot prove it and cannot even describe the causation. . . . Only when people begin to know more of the air they are breathing, they will be able to protect themselves."

[68] D. W. F. Hardie, *A History of the Chemical Industry in Widnes* (London, 1950), p. 86.

too clearly that his most lasting praise was the respect of his scientific and technical peers; his only rewards were a substantial salary, and the knowledge that certain elements of society did benefit from his work.[69]

Second, we may perceive that the forces operating to expand the Inspector's role were not the result of party politics, a national mandate, or even a widely recognized conception of State responsibility for preserving mutually beneficial relations between industry and society. The concept of national responsibility grew largely from the Inspector's own work: that this work expanded in the way it did was due to an admixture of personal imagination, difficult goals, and the internal momentum of administration.

Third, we may discern the now-familiar legislative and administrative sequence of growth, which so often attended the creation of Victorian public policy, and which has been well elucidated.[70] A condition of "intolerability" was followed by inquiry, report, and tentative legislation. Discovery that the legislative requirements were inadequate led to further inquiry, further legislation, horizontal expansion, and vertical intensification. A unique characteristic of the alkali Inspectorate, however, was its peculiar dependence upon the need for a precise scientific method of control. Further research should reveal the use of scientific controls in other areas of Victorian social policy; indeed, this specific case is but one of an increasingly identifiable number of instances where the growth of departmental responsibility was accompanied by, and predicated upon, conscious scientific determinants.

Last, the alkali administration suggests certain tendencies towards the application of central control in other aspects of Victorian life. In this particular instance, centralization was introduced in a period, and into a sector of society allegedly dogmatic on the issue of laissez-faire. This development as such, however, owed little or nothing to the ideological discussions of the Benthamites.[71] That this particular kind of growth could occur, and imply notions suspiciously similar to

---

69 It is unfortunate that the state of the historical record does not, at present, permit of further generalization about the work of the Sub-Inspectors in the field. Additional research in various Local Authority correspondence files may reveal more about the important connections between local inspection and adequate control, and the relevance of these inspections to the development of central-local government relations.

70 See O. O. G. M. MacDonagh, "The Nineteenth-Century Revolution in Government: A Reappraisal," *The Historical Journal*, I (1958), 52-67; *A Pattern of Government Growth* (London, 1961).

71 Although Smith knew and admired Chadwick, his regard was based on an appreciation of the latter's practical accomplishments in stimulating sanitary science (see *Transactions of the Sanitary Institute of Great Britain*, V [1883-84], 266-294). There is no evidence, in Smith's writings or elsewhere, that he approved of the ramifications of Benthamism, or even consciously applied them in his work. Fresh research may, however, cast additional light on this important issue.

I

Benthamism, implies only that the values of centralization were well appreciated outside a particular Benthamite sphere of influence. Central control was so readily and implicitly accepted, in fact, that not until fifteen years after the Alkali Acts had begun was any serious discussion heard about its propriety in a free society. Central control was, rather, a calculated expedient, a straightforward device to secure agreed ends, permitted by the agreement of a majority concerned with its operation. Its rationale was explicitly stated by the Royal Commission on Noxious Vapours: "when the law is impotent, it is within the legitimate province of the State to apply other means for reducing these evils to a minimum, and with that object to enforce the adoption of processes as effectual to the best in use, or at least by a system of inspection to render such enforcement possible hereafter" (RNV, p. 28). What ensued was, as we have seen, the reaction of individual men to the logic of this responsibility.

Central control in alkali administration was achieved with relative ease. Why was this so? A number of explanations may be adduced. First, one may agree with MacDonagh that the farther an issue tended to be from the heat of public debate, the more successfully it could be handled by the State. Certainly, one reason why the alkali inspectorate enjoyed a relatively unperturbed existence, while the hotly debated General Board of Health crashed and fell, was that it lay just within this "safety zone" of public ignorance and national apathy. Moreover, the efforts made by the inspectors to simplify redress and to encourage collective responsibility eventually won the near-unanimous cooperation of manufacturers and landowners alike. Third, the uniform administration of agreed scientific standards, with the kind of helpful solicitude shown by the inspectors themselves made cooperation a virtue and success almost unavoidable. In this light, one is inclined to see in the Alkali Acts administration one of the most fruitful instances of Victorian social policy. It became clear to every interested observer that statute law and administrative practice could grow no faster than relevant scientific knowledge. By fashioning instruments of policy and persuasion, and by encouraging the advancement of the science upon which statutory duty depended, the emerging Civil Scientist not only secured the application of new knowledge to industry and the public welfare, but empirically fashioned the substance of national policy, and suggested a new range of national attitudes in the making of modern Britain.

II

Government and Resource Conservation: the Salmon Acts Administration, 1860-1886[1]

No area of Victorian administrative history is more richly documented or less adequately explored than that concerning the development of public policy by professional or scientific "specialists" within the civil departments of Government. Traditionally, texts on the evolution of the modern state have concentrated upon the role of political philosophy, economic motivation, and parliamentary expedience in determining the direction and timing of government involvement in the private sector. In recent years, however, there has been a growing interest in the anatomy and function of institutional change within the so-called "Nineteenth-Century Revolution in Government."[2] Now a number of attempts are being made to describe the manner in which science, technology, and "special professional knowledge" were used administratively by the state to conserve and protect the wealth of the nation.[3]

The Salmon Acts administration reveals this phenomenon of development particularly well. These acts embodied what one contemporary observer called the first permanent attempt by Parliament to protect and regulate private property in the public interest.[4]

---

1. I am grateful to the Governors of Imperial College of Science and Technology, South Kensington, for permission to use and quote the Huxley Papers. I am also indebted to Professor O. O. G. M. MacDonagh for his comments on an earlier draft of this paper. R. M. M.

2. See O. O. G. M. MacDonagh, "The Nineteenth-Century Revolution in Government: A Reappraisal," *Historical Journal*, I (1958), 52-67; O. O. G. M. MacDonagh, *A Pattern of Government Growth* (London, 1961); Asa Briggs, "The Welfare State in Historical Perspective," *Archives Européenes de Sociologie*, II (1961), 221-58; J. Hart, "Nineteenth-Century Social Reform: a Tory Interpretation of History," *Past and Present*, No. 31 (1965), 39-61; V. Cromwell, "Interpretations of Nineteenth-Century Administration: An Analysis," *Victorian Studies*, IX (1966), 245-55.

3. For general surveys see G. Kitson Clark, *The Making of Victorian England* (London, 1962); W. L. Burn, *The Age of Equipoise* (London, 1964). For special studies see R. J. Lambert, *Sir John Simon, 1816-1904, and English Social Administration* (London, 1963); H. Parris, *Government and the Railways in Nineteenth-Century Britain* (London, 1965); R. MacLeod, "The Alkali Acts Administration, 1863-84: The Emergence of the Civil Scientist," *Victorian Studies*, IX (1965), 85-112.

4. The Salmon Acts were, with the later Alkali Acts, "the first and . . . only Acts which sanction the expenditure of public money on inspection in cases where the object of such inspection is . . . mainly the protection of private property." *Report of the Royal Commission on Noxious Vapours*, 1878 (C. 2159), XLIV, 27. This generalization is valid only for England and Wales. The establishment of the Irish Linen Control Board, about 1750, seems to have been the first such legislation in the British Isles as a whole.

Their administration involved the first permanent staff appointed to supervise the fisheries of England and Wales and laid the foundations for British nature conservancy policy. Government intervention in the salmon fisheries followed different lines of development in Scotland, Ireland, England, and Wales during the course of the century. The following pages, however, will be confined to salmon administration in England and Wales during the period 1860-86, in what was essentially the "heroic age" of policy-making by the salmon inspectors at the Home Office and the Board of Trade.

I.   Salmon and the State, 1861-1866

During the eighteenth century the salmon of Great Britain, the most prized freshwater fish, had actually been the poor man's staple food. By 1828, however, there was mounting evidence that the national salmon catch was dwindling.[5] Because, by the middle of the century, the growth of population had begun to outstrip the nation's meat-producing capacity, and methods for preserving and importing food from abroad had not yet been developed,[6] the reduced supply of salmon caused growing concern. After the *Times* reported in 1861 that, despite new means of distributing fish throughout the kingdom by railway, the salmon which had sold fifty years earlier at 1½d a pound was now thought cheap at 2 shillings,[7] natural historians and others who feared the consequences of scarce food and vaulting prices[8] demanded remedial government action.

Legal efforts to protect salmon rivers from pilfering and overfishing were not unknown. As early as Magna Carta salmon had enjoyed some form of legal protection against poaching and "fixed engines,"[9] and this protection had increased with the passage of

5.   See An Angler [Sir Walter Scott], "Salmonia or Days of Fly-Fishing," *Quarterly Review*, XXXVII (1828), 534.

6.   Only cereals were imported, since fresh meat could not yet be satisfactorily frozen and shipped. See J. T. Mitchell and J. Raymond, *The History of the Frozen Meat Trade* (London, 1912). In 1866 the Royal Society of Arts, in response to the problem, appointed a special Food Committee to investigate "the production, importation and preservation of food." Sir Henry Wood, *A History of the Royal Society of Arts* (London, 1913), p. 459.

7.   *Times*, 28 Mar. 1861.

8.   "A prime salmon is quite as valuable on the average as a Southdown sheep, and has been known at certain seasons to bring as much as ten shillings per pound weight in a London fish shop." "The Salmon Question," *Quarterly Review*, CXIII (1863), 389.

9.   The term "fixed engines" referred to fixed nets and other fishing devices frequently employed in nonnavigable rivers. Technically, fixed engines included "stake nets, bag nets, putts, putchers, and all fixed instruments for catching or for facilitating the catching of fish." See *Parliamentary Papers*, 1862 (243), IV, 241.

years. Moreover, diminishing economic returns from the fisheries had been of constant concern to many gentlemen anglers and netmen, who had repeatedly approached Parliament for redress.[10] Lord Derby once said he knew hardly a session of Parliament without its salmon bill.[11] But these early efforts were unsuccessful, chiefly for two reasons. First, there were considerable hostility and misunderstanding among the five conflicting interests along the salmon rivers. These interests included the upper proprietors, usually sportsmen, anglers, and rod fishermen, who were most interested in protecting the spawning salmon; the lower proprietors, whose nets gathered the largest share of river salmon, but who were less interested in replenishing salmon stocks; the tidal fishermen, who enjoyed a common-law right to the tidal and estuary waters, and who were commercially inclined to catch salmon before they entered fresh water; the mill owners, whose dams blocked the streams, and who were uninterested in salmon; and the riverside factory owners, to whom rivers had become convenient sewers for industrial wastes.[12] This confusion of interests resulted in a proliferation of nets, river obstructions, and effluents, which blocked the salmon's ascent, polluted the riverways, and destroyed the fry.[13] "The salmon," wrote the *Times,*

> endeavor to come to our doors and we drive them away . . .
> they are trapped in all kinds of nets, at all times of the year;
> killed when they are uneatable, or before they are half
> grown; poisoned by the washing of mines and gas works;
> and persecuted to such a degree that it is a marvel that the
> breed is not extinct.[14]

The second difficulty facing Parliament was the absence of satisfactory means for reconciling the needs of salmon and the interests of the mill owners. Little was known about the process

---

10. *Times,* 5 Sep. 1854. See Henry Marshall, *A Few Suggestions for Restoring and Preserving the Salmon Fisheries of Great Britain* (London, 1885), p. 2.
    11. *Times,* 17 May 1861.
    12. A. Russel, *The Salmon* (Edinburgh, 1864); "Mr. Russel on the Salmon," *North British Review,* XLII (1865), 168.
    13. "The Salmon Question," *Quarterly Review,* CXIII, 389.
    14. *Times,* 28 Mar. 1861. With the recurrence of unproductive fishing seasons, counsels of fear spread among the fishing communities, especially, and at first, in Scotland. One zealous Scottish pastor advanced a spirited proposal for "radical reform" of the fisheries, demanding either the drastic use of fixed engines to catch all fish swimming in a given river, or else governmental action "to buy up all the fisheries in the Kingdom, and to work them in strict accordance with rules based on the principles of natural science and the results of practical observation." *Edinburgh Review,* XCIII (Apr. 1851). On other "nationalization" proposals see Dugald S. Williamson, *Thoughts on the Present Scarcity of Salmon* (Stranraer, 1852), p. v. See also "The Decline of the Salmon Fisheries," *Scotch Reformers' Gazette,* 1853-54.

mendations. Few members commented upon the bill, but Joseph Henley, M.P. (Conservative), successfully protested against the inclusion of trout and other fish,[24] and Colonel Pennant, also a Conservative, rejected a clause introducing fishery boards on the grounds that these would interfere with private property rights.[25] Henley also objected strenuously "to the payment out of public funds of an unlimited number of inspectors, who would be always putting their noses into everybody's face and their hands into everybody's pocket."[26]

Among the Liberals, Hussey Vivian, M.P., the famous South Wales manufacturer who relied on the rivers as outlets for his factory wastes, protested in committee against "damaging the great commercial interests of the country for the sake of preserving a few fish."[27] The *Field* joined in the attack against centralization, objected to yet another example of an "indiscriminate mania for legislation," and asked that the salmon fisheries be kept out of Parliament, "for bad as they are, worse may come of it."[28] But most Liberals, including W. E. Forster, and most river proprietors supported the bill. Lord Stanley of Alderley argued that if salmon never again sold for a penny a pound, at least it would become "more plentiful and cheaper than it was at present."[29]

The original bill had fifty-seven clauses; the act as passed had only thirty-six and by Conservative opposition was shorn of many important features.[30] No fishery boards were to be established, and no extensive powers were to be given to bailiffs. The act did sweep away fixed engines and forbade future construction of mill dams and weirs without passes, but mill owners were merely em-

---

24. Which, it was feared, might impose on magistrates the necessity of "a very intimate knowledge of natural history." *3 Hansard* 163: 1374.

25. This, he felt, would interfere with the rights of persons having property in rivers. *Ibid*. 163: 1375.

26. *Ibid*. "The next thing," he foresaw, "would be to appoint inspectors for the preservation of foxes, pheasants or any other game." *Ibid*. 164: 938.

27. *Ibid*. 164: 770.

28. *Field*, XV (1860), 413. "With private enterprise and intelligence we would have been content until such knowledge, had been diffused at this point as to make trickery impossible . . . We foresee another fishery board . . . with a fishery police of inspectors and bailiffs, with salaries, places and patronage for a troup of corrupt place hunters whose chief recommendation will be that they know as much about the habits of salmon as they do of the icthyosphere."

29. *3 Hansard* 164: 1343.

30. In Oct. 1860 the *Field* urged Scottish and English proprietors to stop "hurrying and thirsting for commissions and boards," and advised that "if we are to be taken in hand by a Board whose officers are to be appointed under ministerial patronage . . . then we say, let us alone." The journal wished to see only a clarifying and consolidating measure. Once fixed engines were declared illegal, the *Field* thought county police would be sufficient to guard against contravention. *Field*, XVI (1860), 438; XVII (1861), 101.

powered, not compelled, to attach such passes to existing mill dams.[31] Although the act did authorize central inspectors, it technically gave them power only to approve the placement and form of fish gratings, and no power whatever to institute proceedings for violation of the law. For the purposes of local administration, the new law simply renewed the old power of justices to appoint conservators "for the preservation of salmon, and enforcing for that purpose the provisions of this Act," and gave them neither specific duties to perform nor powers to exercise. The *Field* self-righteously approved: "It will be found that the jurisdiction of educated, resolute and clear headed country gentlemen will be found as fully effective as . . . the cumbrous machinery of Government Boards and bailiffs."[32]

The Salmon Act of 1861 (24 & 25 Vict., c. 109) began its life with the fishing season of 1861-62. The *Times* thought the terms of the act a certain remedy: "It is not much that is asked of us. The supply is offered on very reasonable terms. The ground requires no preparation; the crop is self-sown; we have only to abstain from rooting it up in the ear, or trampling it underfoot."[33] In fact, landowners did begin to assemble and discuss the implications of the new law. Within two months several meetings were held along the major rivers. At Darlington Town Hall, for example, a motion introduced by Henry Pease, M.P.,[34] resulted in the distribution of handbills to fishermen and proprietors along the banks of the Tees, and in an application to Quarter Sessions at Durham and Northampton for the appointment of boards of conservators.[35] At Cockermouth the Honorable Percy Wyndham, M.P., presided over a meeting of frontage owners on the Derwent and was joined in resolutions supporting the act by Lord Naas, M.P., John Steel, M.P., and Wilfred Lawson, M.P.[36]

The first inspectors appointed by the Home Office under the

---

31. See James Patterson (Special Commissioner for English Fisheries), *The Objection to Compulsory Fishways in Our Salmon Rivers Considered and Answered* (London, 1870).

32. *Field*, XVIII (1861), 79.

33. *Times*, 28 Mar. 1861.

34. Progressive Liberal M.P. for South Durham, manufacturer, and coal owner, who believed in "strict economy in our national resources." Dod's *Parliamentary Guide*, 1861, p. 265.

35. In the event that Quarter Sessions refused to pay the salaries of these officers, a subscription fund was set up to which the gentry lent their names and support. *Times*, 9 Oct. 1861.

36. *Ibid.*, 25 Oct. 1861. The group reflected the widespread bipartisan spirit of conservancy, Naas was a Tory, and Steel and Lawson were Liberals. Wyndham was a Tory but was on record as not against "cautious progress." Dod's *Parliamentary Guide*, 1861, p. 313.

new act were two Irishmen: William Ffennell, self-educated natural historian and fisheries expert, originator of the precedent-setting "Ffennell's Act" of 1848 for the preservation of salmon in Ireland, and previously a member of the Royal Commission on Salmon Fisheries;[37] and Frederick Eden, a fishery commissioner for Ireland and expert on the local administration of Irish fishery districts. Both inspectors were to continue simultaneously as fishery commissioners in Scotland, and Eden continued as chairman of the Irish Special Commission. In November 1861 Clive instructed the two appointees to "visit and inspect the different rivers of England and Wales," to communicate with proprietors of fisheries and consider any improvements suggested by them, to determine which fixed engines must be permitted to continue on grounds of "immemorial usage," to examine and approve fish passes, weirs, and nets, and to present annual reports every March.[38]

Certain immediate obstacles impeded effective policy. The absence of any useful fishery statistics and the dearth of meteorological records about weather or water conditions influencing fish harvests made the enforcement of regulations seem arbitrary and unjust. The inspectors were impressed with the fact that government regulation would cease to be politically acceptable if it were scientifically ineffective. Nevertheless, in their first report, after three months' work, Eden and Ffennell were optimistic: the Severn fisheries reported the best season for years, and Sir George Grey was assured that individuals who had first opposed the act were combining to give it effect.[39]

The act also had immediate consequences among private fishery organizations. In York the lord mayor presided over "an influential meeting of gentry," where resolutions were passed to "restore the salmon to Yorkshire." In Exeter Sir Stafford Northcote presided over a meeting attended by the Earl of Devon (Lord Courtenay),

37. William Joshua Ffennell (1799-1867), "fishery reformer"; former chairman of Suir Preservation Society and fishery inspector under the Irish Board of Works at the time of the 1848 famine. D.N.B. "With much energy and sturdiness of opinion, Mr. Ffennell preserved the bonhomie peculiar to Irishmen, which can arrange a difficulty pleasantly, and his part was one in which difficulties between conflicting interests, requiring great tact . . . were a constant occurrence." Field, XXIX (1867), 207; XVIII (1861), 422. Similar testimony to his twenty-two years of fishery service is given in Land and Water, III (1867), 173.
38. Returns Relating to the Inspector of Salmon Fisheries, 1872 (368), LIII, 2. The substance of these instructions, specified in the principal act at a time when inspectors often had to discover by personal experience both the object of their work and the means of doing it, suggests the impact of a straightforward Irish transplant to England.
39. 1st Annual Report of the Inspectors of Salmon Fisheries (England and Wales), 1862 (4301), XIX, 3-4; Times, 20 Nov. 1862; Field, XX (1862), 175.

Colonel Acland, and the mayor of Exeter, where it was agreed to press for obedience to the new law.[40] Voluntary bodies, such as the United Association for the Protection of the Fisheries of the Severn, and the Fisheries Preservation Association, prosecuted alleged offenders at Quarter Sessions. Just before Christmas the *Times* noted optimistically that "the new Act is doing its work quietly, but very effectively, and requires but very few additional provisions to make it the most perfect measure that could have been devised for the regeneration of our almost extinct English salmon fisheries."[41]

To the inspectors, however, it was soon clear that several amendments were necessary. Although the act prohibited the sale of salmon in close seasons, there was nothing to prevent fishermen from catching salmon and exporting them for sale to France. This practice increased until a short amending act, the Salmon Act of 1863 (26 Vict., c. 10), prohibited export during close seasons. Other flaws emerged. For instance, the act neglected to account for differences in the climatic conditions of Ireland and England. Section 26 required that sluices on mill dams be closed when the water was not needed for milling in order that the water could be sent through the fish passes. This worked well in some Irish rivers, which received heavier rainfall and had water going over the dams continuously, but in some parts of England and Wales there was less rain and thus less water available for the fish.[42] Moreover, a licensing system was needed to pay for the policing of rivers, and some arrangement was needed for sharing the expense of salmon cultivation. There was as yet no means to compensate mill owners whose property was dismantled under the act.[43] Finally, some lower river fishermen, suffering more from the act than their upper river neighbors, had begun to devise new netting devices to escape its stipulations.

To meet these difficulties, the inspectors began to formulate practical suggestions for greater control. Their early reports to the Home Secretary reflected the same counsel of hope and confidence in the inevitability of near-perfection reminiscent of the alkali inspectors, the gas inspectors of the Board of Trade, and the Privy

---

40. *Times*, 1 Dec. 1862. In one case a £5 fine was levied upon a workman for selling a salmon allegedly found dead in a river during close time.

41. *Ibid.*, 23 Dec. 1862.

42. See Francis Day, *British and Irish Salmonidae* (London, 1887), p. 121; J. Willis Bund, *Salmon Problems* (London, 1885), pp. 10 *et seq.*

43. *2nd Ann. Rep.*, 1863 (84), XXVIII, 56. See Lambert, *Sir John Simon.*

Council medical inspectors under John Simon.[44] Like these, their counterparts, the salmon inspectors saw that the act's deficiencies were "becoming generally known, and the remedies proposed for some of those deficiencies showed a great concurrence of opinion."[45] Accordingly, the salmon inspectors looked for reform in those who committed the error. A list of local violations was compiled, including the continued use of fixed engines, neglect of fence times and closed seasons, wanton destruction of unseasonable fish and fry, and continued pollution by mines and manufacturing. In 1863 the inspectors urged the appointment of a tribunal for deciding the legality of all fixed engines and amendments to make enforcement easier, compensation adequate, and rewards uniform.[46] Next, they informed the Home Secretary that equal responsibility for river care should be legally enforced.[47] Voluntary associations and local gentry were unable and unwilling to meet the whole costs of river management. Ffennell and Eden argued that "every man who benefits by protection should be made to contribute towards the expenses of such protection,"[48] but to implement this principle, three specific legal provisions were needed: the representation of all interests on local executive bodies, some means of apportioning administrative expense, and the provision of local bylaws where "regulations of general utility were exceptionally injurious." The inspectors found models for the first principle in the Scottish and Irish fishery boards, and proposed to adopt in England a hybrid of the Scottish system of assessing water rates and the Irish system of selling fishing licenses.[49]

The inspectors' proposals were embodied in a government bill

---

44. *2nd Ann. Rep.*, XXVIII, 56. They added, "No Fishery Act of modern times has been received with so little opposition, and has so quickly gained over the greater proportion of opponents." Compare the similar attitudes of the alkali manufacturers towards the Alkali Act of 1863.

45. See *Report, Select Committee on the Salmon Fisheries*, 1868-69 (361), VII, 525.

46. *2nd Ann. Rep.*, XXVIII, 57.

47. Some justices at Quarter Sessions had strenuously supported the act and had appointed conservators, but the latter had no specific powers and could only by voluntary means collect subscriptions, employ watchers (or "water bailiffs"), and direct prosecutions. *4th Ann. Rep.*, 1865 (193), XXIX, 8.

48. *2nd Ann. Rep.*, XXVIII, 66.

49. The fisheries tribunal was another Irish precedent. Parliament had forbidden fixed engines in Ireland by the Act of 1842, but the act was limited in effect by difficulties of enforcement. An amending act was passed in 1848, following agitation by river proprietors on behalf of draught-net fishermen, many of whom had been thrown out of work by the 1842 act. An act in 1850 clarified the applicability of the principal act to fixed engines but failed to resolve the issue. Finally, in 1863, a Special Commission was formed to study the problem of fixed engines and their relevance to fishery fluctuations between relative conditions of renovation and decay. Frederick Eden served on this Commission. See *4th Ann. Rep.*, XXIX, 13.

introduced by T. G. Baring (later Lord Northbrook) late in 1864 and again in 1865. In his 1868 report Eden argued that "there are no persons so anxious for an Amending Act as those who have done the most to carry out the present one,"[50] and the *Field* initially agreed: "A Bill drawn up in such a spirit of moderation and fairness . . . cannot but command our support and appreciation."[51] But Cavendish Bentinck, M.P. (Conservative), protested against a proposed clause which empowered conservators to appoint bailiffs with authority to cross private property — a proceeding he held "contrary to the first principles of English law";[52] and Lord Malmesbury prophesied the destruction of private rights by reforming zealots "carried away by a salmomania."[53] Indeed, when the *Field* perceived that the Government proposed to strengthen the powers of conservators, it belligerently withdrew its support:

> There never was a government in modern days which did so much to advance centralisation and the placing of power over property and persons in its own hands as the present one. On all sides the spread of this deadly influence is felt and the more it spreads the more influence it has and the capability of spreading its influence grows.[54]

With some difficulty the Government overcame these objections.

The Salmon Act of 1865 incorporated much of what had been excluded from the 1861 act. It appointed locally elective boards of conservators over "fishery districts," which comprised complete river areas and watersheds throughout England and Wales. It empowered these conservators to impose and administer license duties on fishing instruments and to employ bailiffs empowered to inspect all weirs, dams, and fixed engines.[55] Such authorized local officials would no longer be open to "the imputation of meddling invidiously with their neighbors."[56] It also set up a Special Commission of three specialists on the Irish-Scottish model to determine

---

50. *Ibid.*, XXIX, 21.
51. *Field*, XXI (1864), 336.
52. *3 Hansard* 180: 363. A similar point of controversy about the legality of appointing inspectors to enter private property had already been settled in connection with the Factory Acts. The issue of property inspection along inland waterways arose again in the inspection of canalboats.
53. *Ibid.* 180: 857. Lord Stanley of Alderley carried the bill through the Lords, much as he had against opposition to the Alkali Act of 1863.
54. *Field*, XXV (1865), 22.
55. Soon many voluntary associations disbanded and re-formed as ginger groups within boards of conservators. See *Times*, 27 July and 26 Aug. 1865. The proposed imposition of a "rate-in-aid" to supplement license fees predictably elicited protest from the *Field*, which thought the motion unworthy of an English country gentleman. *Field*, XXIV (1864), 456.
56. *5th Ann. Rep.*, 1866 (280), XX, 15.

the legality of fixed engines[57] and compelled fish gaps, fish passes, or fish ladders on all mill dams. It did not give power to make bylaws, but Ffennell welcomed it as a further instalment towards "rendering the law a reality."[58]

Contemplating his success, Ffennell speculated on the implications of what the inspectors had done. The value of the salmon harvest had almost doubled from £18,000 in 1863 to £30,000 in 1865. Moreover, it was now evident to all that

> the grand mistake or error on the part of the Riparian Proprietors in England was, that they submitted so long to every species of abuse to their rights and interest, in many instances having become almost sceptical of their existence. This hopeless state of things has gone by, for it has been made manifest that the Salmon Fisheries of England can be restored to an extent well worthy of the care and attention that are now being rendered to them.[59]

This was written eight months before overwork and ill health forced Ffennell to retire, and only ten months before his death. By intervention into the domain of private rights, the state, through its inspectors, had paradoxically strengthened and defended those rights. By encroaching upon individual liberty to fish or to impede fishing, it had suggested means for improving fish yields and for financing the construction of new apparatus. By taking into account the interests of many contesting groups, it had constructed a broad legislative base for the betterment of them all. Most important in the long run, by force of practical instruction and education, the inspectors had created local reservoirs of further law-making opinion. And this in the first five years.

II. Reanalysis and Reform: the Second Phase, 1867-1873

Despite its auspicious beginnings, by June 1866 central supervision of salmon affairs had begun to falter. Frederick Eden,

---

57. Ffennell noted with satisfaction that "the legislature has provided a means by which these matters may be determined and set at rest forever without further delay, and at the same time relieving the fishery interests from the consequences of protracted and expensive litigation." *Ibid.*, XX, 5. The first three commissioners (Eden, Admiral Wallace Houston, and James Patterson) were appointed in Feb. 1866. In June and Sep. 1866 the first two were replaced, respectively, by Captain T. A. B. Spratt, R.N., and Major Henry Scott. See *Returns of the Dates of Appointments of the Special Commissioners for English Fisheries*, 1868-69 (302), L, 1; *Times*, 12 Sep. 1867. Both Eden and Houston had seen service in Ireland, and Patterson, a barrister, had published a digest of the Salmon Act of 1861.

58. *5th Ann. Rep.*, XX, 4.

59. *Ibid.*

Council medical inspectors under John Simon.[44] Like these, their counterparts, the salmon inspectors saw that the act's deficiencies were "becoming generally known, and the remedies proposed for some of those deficiencies showed a great concurrence of opinion."[45] Accordingly, the salmon inspectors looked for reform in those who committed the error. A list of local violations was compiled, including the continued use of fixed engines, neglect of fence times and closed seasons, wanton destruction of unseasonable fish and fry, and continued pollution by mines and manufacturing. In 1863 the inspectors urged the appointment of a tribunal for deciding the legality of all fixed engines and amendments to make enforcement easier, compensation adequate, and rewards uniform.[46] Next, they informed the Home Secretary that equal responsibility for river care should be legally enforced.[47] Voluntary associations and local gentry were unable and unwilling to meet the whole costs of river management. Ffennell and Eden argued that "every man who benefits by protection should be made to contribute towards the expenses of such protection,"[48] but to implement this principle, three specific legal provisions were needed: the representation of all interests on local executive bodies, some means of apportioning administrative expense, and the provision of local bylaws where "regulations of general utility were exceptionally injurious." The inspectors found models for the first principle in the Scottish and Irish fishery boards, and proposed to adopt in England a hybrid of the Scottish system of assessing water rates and the Irish system of selling fishing licenses.[49]

The inspectors' proposals were embodied in a government bill

---

44. *2nd Ann. Rep.*, XXVIII, 56. They added, "No Fishery Act of modern times has been received with so little opposition, and has so quickly gained over the greater proportion of opponents." Compare the similar attitudes of the alkali manufacturers towards the Alkali Act of 1863.

45. See *Report, Select Committee on the Salmon Fisheries*, 1868-69 (361), VII, 525.

46. *2nd Ann. Rep.*, XXVIII, 57.

47. Some justices at Quarter Sessions had strenuously supported the act and had appointed conservators, but the latter had no specific powers and could only by voluntary means collect subscriptions, employ watchers (or "water bailiffs"), and direct prosecutions. *4th Ann. Rep.*, 1865 (193), XXIX, 8.

48. *2nd Ann. Rep.*, XXVIII, 66.

49. The fisheries tribunal was another Irish precedent. Parliament had forbidden fixed engines in Ireland by the Act of 1842, but the act was limited in effect by difficulties of enforcement. An amending act was passed in 1848, following agitation by river proprietors on behalf of draught-net fishermen, many of whom had been thrown out of work by the 1842 act. An act in 1850 clarified the applicability of the principal act to fixed engines but failed to resolve the issue. Finally, in 1863, a Special Commission was formed to study the problem of fixed engines and their relevance to fishery fluctuations between relative conditions of renovation and decay. Frederick Eden served on this Commission. See *4th Ann. Rep.*, XXIX, 13.

Colonel Acland, and the mayor of Exeter, where it was agreed to press for obedience to the new law.[40] Voluntary bodies, such as the United Association for the Protection of the Fisheries of the Severn, and the Fisheries Preservation Association, prosecuted alleged offenders at Quarter Sessions. Just before Christmas the *Times* noted optimistically that "the new Act is doing its work quietly, but very effectively, and requires but very few additional provisions to make it the most perfect measure that could have been devised for the regeneration of our almost extinct English salmon fisheries."[41]

To the inspectors, however, it was soon clear that several amendments were necessary. Although the act prohibited the sale of salmon in close seasons, there was nothing to prevent fishermen from catching salmon and exporting them for sale to France. This practice increased until a short amending act, the Salmon Act of 1863 (26 Vict., c. 10), prohibited export during close seasons. Other flaws emerged. For instance, the act neglected to account for differences in the climatic conditions of Ireland and England. Section 26 required that sluices on mill dams be closed when the water was not needed for milling in order that the water could be sent through the fish passes. This worked well in some Irish rivers, which received heavier rainfall and had water going over the dams continuously, but in some parts of England and Wales there was less rain and thus less water available for the fish.[42] Moreover, a licensing system was needed to pay for the policing of rivers, and some arrangement was needed for sharing the expense of salmon cultivation. There was as yet no means to compensate mill owners whose property was dismantled under the act.[43] Finally, some lower river fishermen, suffering more from the act than their upper river neighbors, had begun to devise new netting devices to escape its stipulations.

To meet these difficulties, the inspectors began to formulate practical suggestions for greater control. Their early reports to the Home Secretary reflected the same counsel of hope and confidence in the inevitability of near-perfection reminiscent of the alkali inspectors, the gas inspectors of the Board of Trade, and the Privy

---

40. *Times*, 1 Dec. 1862. In one case a £5 fine was levied upon a workman for selling a salmon allegedly found dead in a river during close time.

41. *Ibid.*, 23 Dec. 1862.

42. See Francis Day, *British and Irish Salmonidae* (London, 1887), p. 121; J. Willis Bund, *Salmon Problems* (London, 1885), pp. 10 *et seq.*

43. *2nd Ann. Rep.*, 1863 (84), XXVIII, 56. See Lambert, *Sir John Simon.*

severely ill since June 1865, had asked to retire.[60] William Ffennell, nearing sixty-seven, was in extremely poor health following the effects of cold weather and had only a few months to live. His reports declined in quality,[61] and arrears in the office mounted. Fishery work fell upon the sole office clerk, Thomas Baker,[62] who, distrustful of "experts,"[63] almost ruined the inspectors' close relationship with the fishery interests by his blend of "secretarial common sense" and formal proclamations.[64] The necessity for two fresh inspectors became painfully clear.

A replacement for Eden was found in Francis Trevelyan Buckland, the eldest son of William Buckland (Dean of Christ Church, Oxford).[65] At the age of forty-one Buckland enjoyed a reputation as a popular writer and amateur natural historian. He was also known as a man "who held the ordinary usages of society in supreme contempt when they appeared to interfere with his zeal of experiment and research."[66] In 1865 Buckland had established at South Kensington a collection of fishery displays and had begun "the first successful attempt to divert the attention of the nation towards pisciculture."[67] More recently as editor of *Land and Water*,

60. One reviewer cynically observed, "It seems to be quite an established part of our system now, whenever we do get a good man, to use him up as speedily as possible." *Field*, XXVIII (1866), 414; *Land and Water*, III (1867), 173.

61. *Field*, XXVII (1866), 415.

62. PRO, Thomas Baker to Ernest Percival, Home Office, 14 Oct. 1868, HO 45/9342/1797.

63. See Thomas Baker, *The Insidious "Red Tape" System of Government in England* (London, 1870), p. 207, where he cited the Privy Council's medical officer (John Simon) as a "capital illustration of how completely the great majority of Members of Parliament are in the hands of experts."

64. Thomas Baker, a barrister by training, and former clerk to Southwood Smith at the General Board of Health, wrote several legal manuals and compendia: *The Laws Relating to Burials in England and Wales* (London, 1855; six eds. by 1898); *The Laws Relating to Public Health* (London, 1865); and *The Laws Relating to Salmon Fisheries* (London, 1866). He was also an antivaccinationist and a confirmed believer in anticontagionist Chadwickian sanitary policy.

65. F. T. Buckland (1826-80), B.A. (Christ Church, Oxford); medical student, 1848-51; Assistant Surgeon, Life Guards, 1854; on staff of the *Field*, 1856-65; editor of *Land and Water*, 1866; author of many articles on natural history and fish culture, including: *Curiosities of Natural History* (London, 1857-72); *Log Book of a Fisherman Zoologist* (London, 1875); *Natural History of British Fishes* (London, 1881). See also C. Bompas, *Life of Frank Buckland* (London, 1885); a memoir by Spencer Walpole, "Mr. Frank Buckland," *Macmillan's Magazine*, XLIII (1881), 303-09; *Times*, 7 Feb. 1867.

66. *D.N.B.* As the *Field* commented in 1880, "he never aimed at becoming a profound writer on science; his knowledge of species may not have received recognition among the scientific men of his day, but he had the great merit, as a pioneer of popular writing, of making natural history attractive for the multitude." Cited in R. N. Rose, *The Field, 1853-1953* (London, 1953), p. 70.

67. His home in Albany Street, filled with wide varieties of improbable animals, was one of the zoological showpieces of London. His practical knowledge and familiarity with the current state of the fisheries made him a valuable authority on the subject of fish economy, and his genial humanity made him a popular figure. *Nature*, XXXIII (1885), 385-86.

the sportsman's journal he initiated with Ffennell in 1866, he had vigorously applauded the 1865 act and had called for greater attention to the salmon issue.[68]

On February 18, 1867, Buckland began his first official duties.[69] In March he was joined by Spencer (later Sir Spencer) Walpole, the future historian and youngest son of the Home Secretary, who was then a third-class clerk at the War Office. Walpole, twenty-eight, had been his father's secretary at the Home Office from 1858-60, and there is little doubt that he was advanced to Ffennell's vacant £700 post on his father's recommendation.[70]

The new appointments were not unanimously acclaimed. There was criticism on grounds of both policy and personality. Ffennell and Eden had served simultaneously as fishery inspectors for England and commissioners for Scotland, and Eden had also been chairman of the Special Commission for England established in 1866. This integrated British system came to an end when Buckland and Walpole were appointed inspectors for England and Wales alone. Moreover, correspondents of the *Field* questioned Buckland's research skill and cited a woolly address he had previously given to the Thames Angling Society. Many others were unimpressed by the knowledge that Buckland had "lectured before learned societies, told many humorous stories and anecdotes, and found that salmon do not jump at weirs to amuse bipeds."[71] Even *Land and Water* criticized Buckland's penchant for unusual experiments and his tendency to speculate in supposedly factual reports.[72] For his part, Walpole came under attack because of his relationship with the Home Secretary. One Colonel Whyte, a prolific correspondent on fishery matters, lamented that "in an age when the smallest appointments are submitted to competitive examination, . . . so great an interest as the fisheries of England should be committed to the care of a man without due qualification."[73] In a similar vein other critics questioned whether the War Office was an appropriate school in which to learn the best ways of developing salmon fisheries and sadly predicted that "we have not much chance of a con-

68. *Land and Water*, I (1866), 25, 53, 467.

69. Spencer Walpole, the Home Secretary, offered Buckland the post of salmon inspector on Feb. 6, 1867, in a letter delivered during a dinner at the Piscatorial Society. Buckland accepted the post immediately; on Feb. 12 he visited the Fishery Office for the first time. Bompas, *Buckland*, pp. 182-83.

70. *D.N.B.* (2nd Supplement, 1912).

71. *Field*, XXVII (1867), 245; XXIX (1869), 366.

72. *Land and Water*, V (1868), 237.

73. *Ibid.*, V (1868), 227.

tinuance of that improvement in our salmon fisheries which has been so well begun by better men."[74]

The Cassandras were soon disappointed. Delicate in health, quiet and even-tempered in manner, Walpole was the perfect counterpoise to the ebullient Buckland, and they formed a smoothly efficient team. Although beginning without experience of fishery law,[75] they demonstrated startling initiative. Walpole's first move was to dispense with Baker, the office clerk whose legalistic responses to fishermen's requests had alienated the fishermen.[76] In March 1867 the inspectors began their rounds, and in April 1868 their first report was acclaimed by the *Field* as a "great improvement in style and manner" over previous salmon records.[77] In his section of the document, Buckland emphasized the need for the practical study of salmon reproduction and migratory habits, the precise measurement of pollution, and the means of improving fish passes and ladders. He preached to fishermen that "nature has ordained certain laws which regulate the habits of this most nutritious and valuable of migratory fish."[78] The objective was to make the laws of men more nearly coincide with the laws of nature. "We must not forget," wrote Buckland, "that the ultimate verdict of whether a salmon ladder be good or bad be left to the decision of the salmon themselves; all we can do is to find out what they want and accommodate them."[79]

74. *Ibid.*, V (1868), 247.
75. Walpole later recalled that "the old traditions of the office were snapped at the period of Mr. Buckland's appointment, and the new inspectors, without the experience of an experienced colleague, had to map out their own policy." M. Holland, "Sir Spencer Walpole," in Spencer Walpole, *Essays Political and Biographical*, ed. Francis Holland (London, 1908), p. 298. *Land and Water*, IX (1879), 10, soon altered its editorial policy in favour of the inspectors, although the *Field* continued to be cynically hostile.
76. This seemingly straightforward discharge was not completed without a long legal battle between Baker, who charged that he was being ousted through the nepotistic collusion of the Home Secretary and the younger Walpole. A suit for libel was begun by Baker, and correspondence between solicitors, which threatened to involve the Home Secretary himself, continued until compensation was agreed upon by Lord Stanley, acting as referee. Walpole wrote to his uncle, Ernest Percival, his father's private secretary: "This will show you that I have reason in saying with Cromwell — 'the Lord deliver us from a lawyer.' " PRO, Walpole to Percival, 6 Oct. 1868, HO 45/9324/17,970. Thomas Baker recorded his struggles in *A Battling Life, Chiefly in the Civil Service* (London, 1885), pp. 128-31.
77. *Field*, XXXI (1868), 257.
78. *6th Ann. Rep.*, 1867 (44), XVIII, 4.
79. *Ibid.* One year later, after a complete survey of England and Wales, he reasserted: "There can be no doubt that a continuous and diligent inquiry, carried out in a scientific spirit, will demonstrate to us what are the requirements necessary to bring rivers to the highest state of civilisation and development of which they

Buckland next initiated statistical enquiries into the salmon sales at Billingsgate and other major markets, and into such factors as the numbers of licenses, fishermen, and prosecutions recorded during each fishing season. He also encouraged comparative studies of conservators' efforts to deal with the infringement of close seasons. On the vexed question of pollution, Buckland consulted Professor Edward Frankland of the Royal College of Chemistry and thus opened a new avenue of investigation into the study of river conditions. To provide a national focus for fishery information, Buckland received permission from the Committee of Council on Education to move his Museum of Economic Fish Culture into the Science and Art Department buildings in South Kensington. There salmon habits were studied and experiments in new prototypes of fish ladders begun.

In his own section of their joint second report, Walpole stressed that many principles of 1861 and 1865 were still unfulfilled in practice. The number of boxes of salmon sent to Billingsgate failed to indicate a sustained increase in salmon harvests. Although the value of the salmon had increased by an estimated 60 per cent, a much greater improvement was considered possible.[80] The rods accused the nets, the nets accused the rods, and both nets and rods complained of increased pollution and river traffic. Clearly the Government's policy of conservation by consent was not always effective.[81]

The weaknesses of the Acts of 1861 and 1865 were now clear — they had condensed and simplified salmon legislation, but they had also interfered with some of the earlier safeguards for dams and weirs and had failed to give fishery boards vital powers of supervision over their districts. Walpole accordingly proposed penalties for manufacturers who discharged into any "salmon river or tributary any solid or liquid matter as may be proved to make that portion of the river uninhabitable."[82] Further, Walpole urged that *all* fishing in any given watershed area be incorporated under the

---

are capable. . . . Human knowledge of the nature of salmon fisheries and the great variety of circumstances in which they exist throughout the kingdom is by no means yet complete. To perfect it, a constant study of the questions of engineering and of the law must be pursued." *7th Ann. Rep.*, 1867-68 (160), XIX, Preface.

80. During the period 1867-70 the number of men employed in salmon fishing fluctuated between 4,600-5,980; prosecutions for offences between 260-413; and convictions under the Salmon Acts between 197-328. Fluctuations in salmon activity derived largely from unpredictable differences in the amount of rainfall during successive fishing seasons. See *10th Ann. Rep.*, 1871 (C. 320), XXV, 55-57.

81. *7th Ann. Rep.*, XIX, 87.

82. *Ibid.*, XIX, 81-82; *Times*, 7 Apr. 1868. This provision was not made applicable to all rivers until 1948.

appropriate fishery board and that all fishing instruments be under license.[83]

In 1869, following a deputation to the Home Office by J. P. Dodds,[84] Earl Percy, and eleven M.P.s, the inspectors' requests were embodied in a new bill, introduced by Dodds with the concurrence of the Government and referred for consideration to a Select Committee. Under the chairmanship of Dodds, the committee met throughout 1869. The 1869 bill, considered by the *Field* a feeble gesture,[85] failed for lack of time and was referred to Dodds's Select Committee in 1870.[86]

The problems which had confronted the Royal Commission in 1861 were still relevant in 1870. Even now there was no fish pass acceptable for all rivers, and the inspectors were criticized for enforcing regulations opposed to the received wisdom of the conservators.[87] After twenty-one sittings, the Committee of 1870 essentially confirmed the Royal Commission's recommendations of 1861. It also recommended that the salmon industry be placed under the supervision of a "recognised central authority, subject and responsible to one of the departments of government." To this authority would be entrusted powers to enforce improvements; to "constitute, alter, unite, divide and dissolve, fishery districts"; and to co-

---

83. *10th Ann. Rep.*, XXV, 43. To critics who questioned his authority to range so far over policy issues, Walpole answered, "I conceive it my duty not only to give detailed account of my inspections, but also look forward to suggestions for regulation and improvement." "It may seem presumptuous of me to suggest that greater powers should be given to the Inspectors of Fisheries than the present law has delegated to them, but the fact is that our present want of power is so palpable that it is absolutely necessary that additional powers should be accorded to us . . . If our inspection is to be real, it is clear that persuasion ought not, as it is now, to be our *dernier ressort.*" *7th Ann. Rep.*, XIX, 87; *Times*, 10 May 1869.

84. Chairman of the Tees Board of Conservators and M.P. for Stockton. See J. P. Dodds, *The Salmon of the Tyne and Dams* (London, 1856); *Times*, 5 Mar. 1869; *Biograph and Review*, IV (1880), 453-56.

85. *Field*, XXXIII (1869), 414.

86. Evidence was heard from thirty-three witnesses: three inspectors; one special commissioner; three chairmen, six members, and two secretaries of boards of conservators; five engineers; one chief constable; two fishery lessees; six fishermen; two mill owners; and two others. See *10th Ann. Rep.*, XXV, 4.

87. *Field*, XXXIV (1869), 235, angrily demanded, "the country is paying these two gentlemen some £1200 or £1400 for their services and what have they done for it? . . . they have pottered about over the kingdom at vast extra expense; they have published reports which have certainly not been worth the cost of printing. How long the British taxpayer will stand this sort of thing remains to be seen." When Walpole attempted to mollify opposition from the mill owners at the Select Committee, the *Field* denounced him for attempting "more mischief to the cause of the salmon fisheries than any other witness out of thousands who have been . . . examined." *Ibid.*, XXXV (2 Apr. 1870).

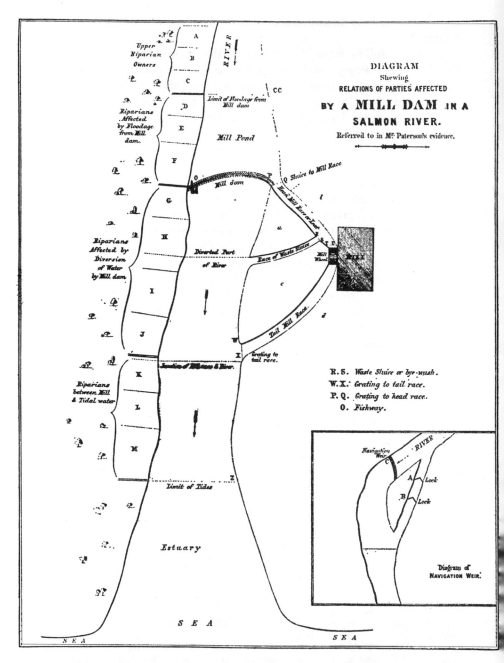

Vested interests along a typical salmon river. From *Report of the Select Committee on Salmon Fisheries*, 1868-69 (361), VII, 525.

ordinate the activities of local boards and the tribunal of special commissioners.[88] Until such time as a national "department of fisheries" could be established to amalgamate salmon affairs with other fishery business and to identify the salmon industry more closely with the commercial interests of the country, the committee advised that the salmon inspectorate be transferred from the Home Office to the Board of Trade. The committee thus proposed a nationally organized, regionally based plan to strengthen existing administrative provision "without such extensive changes in the existing fishery laws as might excite reasonable apprehension of the owners of mill property and retard legislation . . . (and) without any counter-balancing prejudice to other interests."[89]

Buckland's next annual report was a point-by-point analysis of the feasibility of the committee's recommendations. The previous year had seen an abundant harvest, but adverse weather conditions were putting salmon preservation methods to a severe test.[90] Fortunately, new knowledge about the habits of salmon permitted more informed regulation of nets and close times, and even the chronic problems of fish-pass technology were gradually giving way to experiments in Buckland's South Kensington museum. Like Walpole, Buckland took every opportunity to stress the broader implications of salmon policy for other natural resources. "Salmon fisheries do not form the only sort of agriculture that require development by means of scientific attention and regulation in this country." For thousands of acres of water not suited for salmon, yet suitable for other fish, "proper scientific cultivation could produce . . . large quantities of food for the poorer classes if their natural resources received a little regulation."[91] The study of "applied fish economy" generated new proposals which led directly to the question of government support of research and the regulation of other national reserves.

Both inspectors favoured centralized control on grounds of utility, but given the desirability of greater supervisory powers, neither Walpole nor Buckland was in favour of transferring their

88. *Report, Select Committee on Salmon Fisheries*, 1870 (368), VI, §§6-8. The committee foreshadowed future organizational developments in fishery administration by suggesting that "jurisdiction in fishery matters should be transferred to the Board of Trade until, at least, the fisheries of the country are thought to be sufficiently developed to justify the establishment of a separate fishery department" (§6).
89. *Ibid.*, VI, §16.
90. *10th Ann. Rep.*, XXV, 7.
91. *Ibid.* A factor which he felt would have the desirable side effect of keeping the "industrious mechanic" at the fishing stream rather than in the public house.

work from the comparative freedom of the Home Office to the departmental jurisdiction of the Board of Trade. Buckland anxiously asserted:

> There can be no doubt that the authority of the Home Office produces great moral effect in carrying out the various provisions of the Act, and I should be sorry if a system which works now so well in practice were changed for another which experience might prove were not so efficacious.[92]

The inspectors felt that the beneficial character of individually applied personal recommendations could be maintained only in their flexible, semiautonomous position under the Home Secretary.[93]

While the best form of central organization could not be settled swiftly, Walpole insisted that amending legislation was necessary immediately.[94] An abortive bill of 1871 was followed in 1873 by a

---

92. *Ibid.*, XXV, 8.

93. Buckland described at length his policy towards the mill owners — the longstanding enemies of the salmon: "I have sometimes been called to task for not 'fighting' the salmon cause sufficiently against say, weir or mill owners. The element of 'fighting' is not, in the present days of enlightenment, at all called for. An injudicious zeal in the cause entrusted to an individual by the public, may often damage that cause more than promote it. As I have said in former reports, salmon do not form the sole food of the people; bread comes before salmon. . . .

"I have found weir owners, as a class, most willing to advise fishery interests, . . . providing these interests do not interfere with their legal rights of water and their trade.

"In cases of this kind, where Parliament, I may almost say, appears to hesitate — or at all events is reluctant — to interfere seriously, I feel convinced that 'persuasion is bettter than force', and that private interviews and subsequent conversations will often succeed in obtaining for the salmon what no act of Parliament in the absence of the local executive could obtain.

"What the Public requires of me, as a Government officer, is to use my best endeavours to increase the supply of salmon. Long experience has shown how best to do this in individual cases. Those not actually engaged in the work can know nothing of the details required. Though my writings sometimes seem opposed to the salmon cause, yet I can assert, that what I say and do in this important matter is founded upon anxious thought and views of all sides of the question. Facts are the great things to be desired, and these can only be obtained by accurate observation out of doors, and by the dissecting knife and the microscope indoors. The science — for it ought to be elevated to a science — of salmon culture is yet in its infancy. I make it my daily business to endeavor to deduce from the facts that come before me the general laws of nature which are higher than the laws of man." *Ibid.*, XXV, 18.

94. *9th Ann. Rep.*, 1870 (C. 79), XIV, 29. The bill introduced in 1871 by J. P. Dodds, purporting to follow the committee's recommendations, varied from them in some essential particulars and was attacked by mill owners and both upper and lower water interests. The bill antagonized the conservators by its provision for representative elections and alienated the mill owners by proposing to extend the powers of the special commissioners. A deputation to the Home Office was led by John Whitwell (M.P. for Kendal, Westmorland), Nathaniel Buckley (M.P. for Staleybridge, Lancaster), the Duke of Beaufort, and Lord St. Vincent. The bill was also discussed at the Society of Arts, where these objections were aired. *Land and Water*, XI (1871), 227; XII (1871). *Field*, XXXVII (1871), 238, 360; XXXIX (1872), 212.

bipartisan private bill introduced by Lewis Dillwyn, M.P. (Liberal), William Lowther, M.P. (Conservative), Ralph Assheton, M.P. (Conservative), and Alexander Brown, M.P. (Liberal).[95] The Dillwyn bill, designed to effect the Select Committee's recommendations to give greater powers of enforcement to the inspectors and the Home Office, alarmed the *Field*, which, speaking for the rod fishermen and upper proprietors, called it "unnecessary, . . . dishonest . . . and radically a bad Bill."[96] Conservative M.P.s representing riparian property owners claimed that the local bailiffs provided under the bill "were frequently old poachers . . . appointed on the principle, . . . set a thief to catch a thief";[97] yet, in the course of the second reading, H. A. Bruce, Home Secretary, wearily supposed that "if any question was ripe for legislation, . . . the subject of salmon fishing might be so, for no single session, since he was in Parliament had passed without the introduction of some Bill related to it."[98] The measure passed at the session's end.

The Act of 1873 (36 & 37 Vict., c. 71), following thus the Acts of 1861, 1863, 1865, and 1870, completed the groundwork of legislation. The *Field* criticized the new measure for not abolishing weirs altogether and for apparently pandering to the lower proprietors and estuary netsmen. "Until we have a free run from the mouths of rivers to the really unpoisoned sweet upper streams with a reasonable restraint upon the wholesale capture at present claimed and exercised by the nets, it is impossible that anything like efficient reform can be carried out."[99] But *Land and Water* applauded this attempt to recognize the conservators' demands for bylaws and equitable representation,[100] and Walpole and Buckland welcomed the act as a useful instrument.[101] In fact, local

---

95. Dodds, owing to his chairmanship of the Tees Board, which supervised rather unusual river conditions, was reluctant to allow too many uniform compulsory powers to the Board of Conservators. The conservators in general, however, favoured having such powers. See *Report, Royal Commission on Salmon Fisheries*, 1902 (Cd. 1188), XIII, *Mins. Evid.*, Q. 22,645.

96. *Field*, XXXIX (1872), 264.

97. 3 *Hansard* 214: 1375.

98. H. A. Bruce added, "It was the business of the government representing the people to see that proper measures were taken in respect of salmon fishing with a view to the supply of food, and also to encourage the employment of the people." *Ibid.* 214: 1379.

99. *Field*, XLI (1873), 291, 368. The editor admitted that salmon fishing was "surrounded by and connected with other rights and issues," and supposed that nearly everyone who was involved in the bill found himself overpowered by these conflicting interests. *Ibid.*, XLI (1873), 344.

100. *Land and Water*, XI (1871), 2.

101. "The Legislator," Buckland wrote in 1874, "under proper advice has wisely fitted the law to the benefit of the salmon, for the simple reason that salmon refuse to take cognisance of the edicts of the law." *13th Ann. Rep.*, 1874 (C. 971), XII, 9. In view of these changes, Home Secretary Bruce felt the work of the

power to regulate local policy stimulated greater local interest and, while in theory casting more paper work upon the Home Office and ostensibly making for greater central supervision, actually gave freer rein to local interests.[102] Surveying the results of inspection, Buckland concluded that "this new Act is a wise measure cast in accordance with natural facts and with due consideration for all rights and interests . . . I venture . . . to hope that we are now, in 1874, entering upon a new age of increased prosperity for the salmon fisheries of England and Wales."[103]

III.   Expansion and Consolidation, 1874-1880

From 1874 onwards, with the basic work behind them, the salmon inspectors looked beyond salmon problems and conjectured about the reclassification of all freshwater fisheries.[104]

Thus an inquiry into the destruction of freshwater fry in Norfolk and Suffolk led Buckland to suggest close times for those fish, and for all other freshwater fish in England and Wales.[105] Indeed, not content with problems of freshwater fish, Buckland and Walpole extended their inquiries into coast and sea fisheries as well. In 1873 at the suggestion of Ralph Lingen at the Treasury, the Home Office permitted Walpole to take over the oyster inspections hitherto conducted by H. Cholmondeley Pennell at the Board of Trade, on grounds that "the causes which interfere with the development of our Salmon Fisheries are to some extent similar to those which are interfering with other interests."[106] In 1875 Buck-

special commissioners was done. The commissioners were disbanded by the Salmon Fisheries Act, 1873 (36-37 Vict., c. 13). See 3 *Hansard* 215: 89.

102. Walpole reflected, "The elaborate regulations which the Act made for the due framing of by-laws ensure in every case their adequate consideration. The law might possibly be more vexatious if it were less complicated." *13th Ann. Rep.*, XII, 91.

103. *Ibid.*, XII, 75.

104. "It is quite certain that the Acts passed, since 1861, relative to salmon have greatly increased the supply of that fish. Why not, therefore, extend protection to other fish besides salmon?" As an afterthought he added, "having given my serious considerations to the cultivation of fish under every possible condition . . . I may, perhaps, be pardoned for introducing the subject in this place, as this Report is the only official means for bringing the facts related to the fisheries before Mr. Cross and the members of the Legislature, many of whom are practically interested in the subject." *16th Ann. Rep.*, 1877 (C. 1751), XXIV, 22.

105. "I am gradually collecting facts, which, when put together, will I trust, be deemed sufficiently weighty to induce the legislature to preserve the fry of fish which are bred in our freshwater lakes, rivers, ponds, etc., as well as upon our own foreshores, and thus develop what ought to be a valuable natural industry, now so cruelly neglected and allowed to run to waste." *15th Ann. Rep.*, 1876 (C. 1466), XVI, 27.

106. PRO, Walpole to Henry Winterbotham, Home Office, 10 May 1873, BT 13/36. Cf. *Report on the Fisheries of the English Lake Districts*, 1878 (C.

land and Walpole began studies on the conditions of the Norfolk crab, lobster, and oyster fisheries. In 1877 they inquired into the crab and lobster fisheries of the whole United Kingdom and the following year unobtrusively added a study of the herring fisheries of Scotland.

Their enthusiasm eventually led them, in 1877, to a study of the destruction of fish generally, a question which, in the opinion of T. H. Farrer,[107] Permanent Secretary of the Board of Trade, had supposedly been dealt with by a committee from his department ten years before.[108] Farrer warned the ambitious inspectors that "for the past few years there had been a disposition on the part of the Home Office to undertake matters connected with the Sea Fisheries, without communication with the Board of Trade."[109] But the logic of expansion was ineluctable. In 1877 Buckland called the attention of the Home Secretary "to the desirability of passing legislation for other fish." Buckland's overtures were embodied in the Freshwater Fisheries Act of 1878, introduced by A. J. Mundella and carried with the unanimous endorsement of a Select Committee. This act empowered conservators to set up fishery boards for trout and char rivers containing no salmon and extended the salmon close season regulations to all freshwater fish. Two years later Walpole's suggestions for consolidation of the law[110] were finally embodied in the Salmon and Freshwater Fisheries Consolidation Act, 1880.

2004), XXI, ix. "The science of fish culture has indeed now advanced so much that it is difficult, if not impossible, to consider one kind of fish without at the same time becoming aware that the interests of the other fish may be in the same way affected; thus for example, the fry of sea fish and shrimp are of great value as food for the salmon; or to take another instance out of many, the supply of mussels to the public market is most valuable . . . In a Salmon Report, it would be out of place to go further into this important matter; suffice to say that, considering the present high price of food, and the gradual increase of population no attempt should be neglected to cause every acre of water to produce fish food in some form or other." *16th Ann. Rep.*, XXIV, 5.

107. Sir Thomas Henry Farrer (1814-99), educated Eton and Balliol; called to the bar in 1844; joined Board of Trade, 1848, when Sir Stafford Northcote, a friend from Eton days, was Assistant Secretary; became Assistant Secretary of the Marine Department, 1854; Permanent Secretary of the Board, 1865-86; dogmatic free trader and noninterventionist; established brilliant administrative reputation at the Board of Trade, and wrote frequently on fiscal and monetary policy. See T. H. Farrer, *The State in Its Relation to Trade* (London, 1883).

108. PRO, "Jurisdiction Respecting Sea Fisheries," Board of Trade, Departmental Memorandum, T. H. Farrer, 16 Dec. 1879, p. 4.

109. *Ibid.*, p. 3. See *Report of Inspectors of Fisheries for England and Wales and Commissioners for Sea Fisheries, on Sea Fisheries of England and Wales*, 1879 (C. 2449), XVII, v.

110. "Any official," he wrote, "would incur grave responsibilities who neglected to impress the importance of such consolidation on the Government." *19th Ann. Rep.*, 1880 (C. 2587), XIV, 77.

In December 1880 Buckland, aged fifty-four, died from over-exposure to wet and cold during an inspection tour. News of his death was received with mixed feelings. Especially of late the *Field* had criticized his speculative and sometimes verbose literary style, which frequently failed to present a clear quantitative appraisal of fishery conservation work. "Mr. Buckland, . . . who is an optimist of the most advanced school, admits to nothing and holds that everything is all right and we have nothing to fear." Indeed, Buckland's zealous pursuit of interesting artifacts tended to damage his reputation as a professional inspector. Some found his reports increasingly diffuse, inconclusive, and illogical and criticized "the bewildering Jack-o-Lantern facility with which he turns to something else — Norfolk Broads, crabs, lobsters, or some other subject not at all germane to the salmon fisheries."[111] By contrast, Walpole's reports, which ended in 1887 when he became, at Gladstone's request, lieutenant governor of the Isle of Man,[112] were considered all that was "practical, sensible and logical."[113]

With Buckland's death and Walpole's departure, "the amateur naturalist" era in fishery regulation came to a close. Walpole remembered his colleague as "the constant advocate of . . . fish culture," whose efforts were indispensable to "the development of an industry which was the object of his life."[114] And to date their accomplishments were impressive. "By some of the most stringent legislation which was probably ever sanctioned,"[115] as Walpole later wrote, the state had won the upper and lower proprietors to the need for state control; it had empowered conservators to inflict temporary penalties for permanent profits; and it had wielded new knowledge about fish and fisheries techniques to place first salmon fisheries, then freshwater fisheries as a whole, on a sound economic and technical basis. In 1880 the salmon industry was estimated as

---

111. *Field*, XLIX (1877), 346.
112. *Ibid.*, LVII (1882), 301. During his inspectorship Walpole frequently contributed articles on finance and trade to the *Pall Mall Gazette* and wrote, in 1874, a life of his grandfather, Spencer Perceval. In 1878, after he received a legacy of £10,000 from Lord Egmont, Walpole produced the first two volumes of his *History of England from 1815*, all of which was written by "flickering light of railway oil lamps." See Walpole, *Essays Political and Biographical*, pp. xiii-xiv.
113. A reviewer noted that "Mr. Buckland's report is seventy five pages of the total report, or more than half of the whole, . . . Mr. Walpole continues to say all that is required of him in twenty pages." *Field*, XLVII (1876), 510.
114. "He lost no opportunity," Walpole added, "of familiarising the public with the subject; he was in constant communication with the leading fish culturists both in this country and abroad. It is in part to his exertions that Australia owes the introduction of trout in its waters. In this country his name among fishermen has become a household word." *20th Ann. Rep.*, 1881 (C. 2901), XXIII, 3.
115. *15th Ann. Rep.*, XVI, 61.

worth £100,000 p.a.[116] Buckland's conception of the nation's rivers as "water farms" had begun to bear fruit. Many areas for improvement remained, but the inspectors had established a tradition of systematic observation and good public relations.[117] In fact, the ultimate fate of nature conservancy policy, especially at a time when centralization was so actively opposed, depended to a large extent on the inspectors' success in keeping the general public continuously aware of the need for preservation and in energetically pursuing fishery policy in the lobbies of Government. This fact acquired added force from the events of the following two decades.

IV.   Salmon, Science, and Government, 1881-1886

The Act of 1873 stipulated that all new local bylaws were to have the approval of the Home Secretary. The provision necessarily implied greater official dependence on the advice of the salmon inspectors and was one of several factors motivating Sir William Harcourt's approach, within weeks of Buckland's death, to Thomas Henry Huxley, professor in the Royal School of Mines and eminent scientific publicist, educator, and natural historian:

> I have often regretted that the Civil Service of the Crown in its numerous branches offers so few places for the occupation of men of science, and I have always desired if it lay within my power to do something towards this deficit.
>
> The death of my friend F. Buckland and the vacancy thereby caused the place of Inspector of Fisheries seems to give me such an opportunity. It is not a *grand* place nor as good in its emoluments as I could desire, for it is worth only £700 p.a. But it is a pleasant occupation — does not require much labour or time — and would leave its holder ample leisure for other pursuits. Salmon have the good taste to addict themselves to healthy and picturesque localities and what little work there is to do might seem as a nirvana to hard worked brains and sedentary philosophers.
>
> Could I tempt you to accept such a holiday task. I should not make the suggestion if I thought it would interfere with your higher labours, in which the world has a deep concern . . . You would find in Mr. Walpole an experienced assistant and a gentle colleague who would take the drudgery off your hands and do whatever is necessary when you are otherwise engaged.[118]

---

116. This was in contrast to the evaluation of £18,000 in 1863, and £30,000 in 1868. See Walpole's report, *16th Ann. Rep.*, XXIV, 53.

117. *Field*, XLIX (1877), 346.

118. Imperial Col. of Sc. and Tech., Sir William Harcourt to T. H. Huxley, 23 Dec. 1880, Huxley Papers, XVIII, fol. 5. These papers provide an invaluable

This letter conveyed at least three impressions about the attitude of the Home Office toward the salmon inspectorate: first, that it was a part-time activity, of no onerous kind; second, that it counted as one of the few places in the "Scientific Civil Service"; and third, that the inspectorate had become a routine appointment within the administrative machine. The Home Secretary was adamant that a man of science, and not "one of these sportsmen who beset me," should have the post.[119]

Huxley at first declined and accepted ultimately only after Harcourt and Gladstone arranged to let him continue his other employments.[120] From one point of view, this "tempting piece of scientific pluralism"[121] would give him many opportunties to visit the fishmongers and salters halls and to lobby the livery companies in support of technical education. Moreover, the relation between the fisheries and the Government had always been of interest to him.[122] As he wrote to Col. John Donnelly (permanent secretary of the Science and Art Department, who supervised the Royal School of Mines), he "could get great things done in the matter of fish culture and fish diseases at South Kensington, if poor dear X's [Buckland's] rattle trappery could be turned to proper account, without in any way interfering with the work of the School."[123] Moreover, this appointment seemingly offered an opportunity to make a contribution to a definite sphere of policy: "of the few innocent pleasures left to men past middle life — the jamming of common-sense down the throats of fools is perhaps the keenest."[124]

insight into Huxley's association with the Home Office and the fishery interests, as well as into his many other activities. A complete index to the holdings at Imperial College exists in W. R. Dawson, *The Huxley Papers* (London, 1946).

119. Imperial Col. of Sc. and Tech., Harcourt to Huxley, 25 Dec. 1880, Huxley Papers, XVIII, fol. 11. In the Commons Harcourt was asked to appoint a "thoroughly practical man"; he replied that the new appointment had been postponed so "that the whole matter could be considered and the department made more useful." *Field*, LVII (1882), 301.

120. He therefore received £600 for his post at the Royal School of Mines, Jermyn Street, £200 for his lectureship in biology at the Normal School of Science, and £700 for his inspectorship. Imperial Col. of Sc. and Tech., Huxley, 11 May 1885, Huxley Papers, XXX, fol. 136; Harcourt to Huxley, 27 Jan. 1881, *ibid.*, XVIII, fol. 18.

121. C. Bibby, *T. H. Huxley: Scientist, Humanist and Educator* (London, 1959), p. 128. Bibby's otherwise excellent book makes no other reference to Huxley's contributions in the field of fisheries.

122. Huxley had given evidence before the Scottish Select Committee on Salmon in 1860, the Royal Commission on Trawling for Herring in 1862, and the Royal Commission on the Sea Fisheries in 1864-65.

123. Huxley to Col. John Donnelly, 27 Dec. 1880, in Leonard Huxley, *Life and Letters of Thomas Henry Huxley* (London, 1903), II, 290.

124. Huxley to Farrer, 18 Jan. 1881, in *ibid.*, II, 291. On his first inspection Huxley reportedly ordered a man to sit down and later wrote to his wife, "We

The *Field*, however, did not welcome his appointment and saw it as the untimely triumph of one who "professed to be scientific" over those practical individuals who were actually needed for the job.[125] This recurring theme of antiscientific prejudice was magnified by the fear that the professional man of science would not descend to frequent inspections and visits with fishermen. The experience of the next three years seemed, in fact, to bear out these forebodings.

In February 1881 Huxley wrote to his son that "there is more occupation than I expected, but no serious labour."[126] In part the serious labour was assumed by Walpole, who tried assiduously to maintain good relations with fishery interests.[127] But in early 1882 Walpole left the Home Office. Despite pressure from the fishery interests, no replacement was found until January 1883, when Charles Edward (later Sir Charles) Fryer was appointed assistant inspector.[128] Thus for a year the post was Huxley's alone, and angry conservators demanded a return to the amateur "practicality" of Buckland. During the three years Huxley remained at the Home Office, his reports betrayed his impatience with trivial objections, his chronic ill health, and a lifetime of overwork.[129] Moreover, as the conservators repeatedly stressed, his work emphasized his scientific rather than his inspectoral role, and he confined himself to studying the influence of meteorological conditions on fishing and the presence of salmon disease.[130] The more routine work — "sitting all

---

have begun very well, we have sat upon a duke." *Ibid.*, II, 299. His enthusiasm was caricatured by *Punch*, Mar. 1881.

125. *Field*, LVI (1881), 346.

126. L. Huxley, *Life and Letters of T. H. Huxley*, II, 292.

127. Walpole and Huxley also became good friends. See Imperial Col. of Sc. and Tech., Walpole to Huxley, 17 Feb. 1881, Huxley Papers, XXVIII, fol. 122; dinner invitations, 18 Mar. 1882, etc., *ibid.*, fol. 124. Leonard Huxley even asked Walpole to assist in writing the *Life and Letters* of his father. See *ibid.*, II, 292-98. Walpole recalled marvellous conversations with Huxley "founded on knowledge, enlarged by memory, and brightened by humour." *Ibid.*, II, 295. And Huxley once wrote, in a letter to his wife from Wales, "Walpole is a capital companion — knows a great many things and talks well about them, so we get over the ground pleasantly." *Ibid.*, II, 299.

128. *Field*, LXI (1883), 76.

129. Imperial Col. of Sc. and Tech., Walpole to Huxley and Mrs. Huxley, 18 Mar. 1882 - 19 Dec. 1886, Huxley Papers, XXVIII, fols. 125, 127, 128, 130, 132, 134.

130. The last of these efforts was probably the most important. In Dec. 1881 Huxley left for Wales to study the epidemic of salmon disease which had appeared in Conway. Rejecting fears that the epidemic was caused by chemical pollution, Huxley reported that the cause was biological. "We must look for the origin of the disease to the *Saprolegniae* which infest dead organic bodies in our fresh waters. Neither pollution, drought or overstocking will produce the disease, if the *Saprolegniae* is absent. The most these conditions can do is to favour the

day in a crowded court," as he wrote to his wife, "hearing a disputed case of fishing rights, or examining witnesses who stuck firmly to views about fish which had long been exploded by careful observation"[131] — did not appeal to him at all. There were many and competing claims on his time.[132] Salmon inspection was a distraction, and not always a welcome one.

Fishery work did proceed, if not with any great encouragement from Huxley and the Government. In 1883, following the efforts of Sir Edward Birkbeck, an International Fisheries Exhibition was held in Edinburgh.[133] The Exhibition was well attended and endowed by the United States and by every major European country except Great Britain, a fact not overlooked by critics of the Government's neglect of research. The speakers unanimously agreed that government support for research was vital: "without further knowledge any legislation or attempts to improve our fisheries by better modes of fishing, or by protection or culture, must be dangerous, and indeed, unreasonable."[134] In October of the same year the British Association endorsed a proposal to establish a "British Marine Zoological Laboratory," on the model of the six government-sponsored laboratories existing in France and the analogous stations built by Austria in Trieste and by Italy in Naples. This proposal ultimately resulted in the Marine Biological Association, founded in 1884 under the leadership of Edwin Ray Lankester and the Prince of Wales, dedicated to cultivating the pure and applied sciences underlying fishery cultivation.[135]

---

development or the diffusion of these *materiens morbi* where the *Saprolegniae* already exist." Imperial Col. of Sc. and Tech., Huxley Papers, LVII; T. H. Huxley, "A Contribution to the Pathology of the Epidemic Known as the 'Salmon Disease,' " *Proc. Roy. Soc.*, XXXIII (1882), 381-89.

131. L. Huxley, *Life and Letters of T. H. Huxley*, II, 303-04. In 1881, for example, Huxley was offered the Linacre Professorship at Oxford but declined on grounds of overwork. In the same year he delivered a paper to the International Medical Congress on the "Connection of Biological Science with Medicine" and read a paper on the "Rise and Progress of Paleontology" to the B.A.A.S. at York. In 1881-82 he sat on the Royal Commission on the Medical Acts and filled the intervals between his scientific lectures and speaking engagements with scientific articles.

132. Cf. T. H. Huxley, "Oysters and the Oyster Question," *Proc. Roy. Inst.*, X (1884), 336-58.

133. Sir Edward Birkbeck, Bt. (1833-1907), M.P. for North Norfolk, 1879-95, and East Norfolk, 1885-92; chairman, Royal National Lifeboat Association.

134. George Romanes, F.R.S., to *Times*, 30 Oct. 1883.

135. The Marine Biological Association opened a laboratory at Plymouth in June 1888 and a hatchery at Ormesby. The Plymouth laboratory was built at a cost of £12,000. Its income derived from the Fishmongers Company (£400 p.a.), from private subscriptions, and from a Treasury grant of £5000 outright, plus £500 p.a. for three years, rising to £1000 p.a. from 1892, which was won through the influence of its royal patron. In 1892 the income of the M.B.A. amounted to

But this prospect of a new research endeavor found the ill and ageing Huxley unmoved. In any event he had no especial wish to taint science with politics. Following the 1883 Exhibition he complained bitterly to Sir Michael Foster, the Cambridge physiologist: "Will you tell me what all this has to do with my business in life, and why the last fragments of a misspent life that are left to me are to be frittered away in all this drivel?"[136]

By the autumn of 1883 Huxley, now president of the Royal Society, confessed to his friend Colonel Donnelly that he wanted to retire, and would, were there not "the blessed Home Office to consider. There might be Civil War between the net men and the rod men in six weeks, all over the country, without my mild influence."[137] But he found himself unable to sacrifice his other interests indefinitely. At fifty-nine, as his depression deepened, Huxley lost all patience with salmon, fishery boards, and the Home Office:

> The mere thought of having to occupy myself with the squabbles of these idiots of country squireens and poachers makes me sick — and is, I believe, the chief cause of the morbid state of my mucous membranes. All this week I shall be occupied in hearing one Jackass contradict another Jackass about questions which are of no importance.[138]

In late 1884 Huxley left for Italy to recover his health. For months the Home Office extended his leave of absence. In the spring of 1885 he wrote Walpole that inspection had ceased to interest him and that salmon work was too time-consuming:

> The Office would be quite perfect, if they did not want an annual report. I can't go in for a disquisition on river basins after the manner of Buckland, and you have exhausted the other topics. I polished off the Salmon Disease pretty fully last year, so what the deuce am I to write about.[139]

Given the state of knowledge and the impracticability of improving legislation, Walpole had no convincing answer. In May 1885, just after his sixtieth birthday, Huxley resigned his professorship, his

---

£2200. By contrast, the marine laboratory under Anton Dohrn in Naples cost £20,000 to build and £7000 p.a. to operate. At the same time the U.S. Fishery Commission had a budget of £70,000, and even the Scottish Fishery Board received upwards of £21,000 for fishery research. See PRO, Marine Biological Association to Chancellor of the Exchequer, 2 Nov. 1906, T 1/1069A/19726/1906.

136. L. Huxley, *Life and Letters of T. H. Huxley*, II, 333.
137. *Ibid.*, II, 370.
138. *Ibid.*
139. *Ibid.*, II, 298.

inspectorship, and his presidency of the Royal Society.[140] Salmon inspection came again to an abrupt halt.

When Huxley left the Home Office, Home Secretary Harcourt himself lost interest in salmon affairs. In the choice of a successor for Huxley, the fishery boards this time prevailed, and Arthur Davies Berrington, former chairman of the Usk Board,[141] was appointed in October 1885, expressly with the intention of renewing the personal relationship between the inspectorate and the fishermen which Huxley's scientific and academic preoccupation had pushed aside.[142] In the *25th Annual Report* Berrington attempted to carry on the practical informative work begun by Buckland and Walpole and thereafter neglected by Huxley.[143] But his efforts were overtaken by events. In 1887 Berrington and salmon inspection were submerged into the administrative offices of the Board of Trade. Because all policy had now to pass through a hierarchy of officials, the personal contact with the fishery interests which Berrington had sought was irretrievably lost. The move was resented by the conservators. John Willis Bund, for example, complained that in the golden days of independence under the Home Office, "the Inspector's promises were carried out." Now, he found "a great deal more trouble in carrying out the work of the fisheries, a great deal more correspondence, and a great deal more interference and we do not get half such good results."[144] In every case, however, such com-

---

140. In May he received an honorary D.C.L. from Oxford and a Civil List pension; in 1892 he was made a Privy Councillor, reportedly "the first Man of Science . . . ever . . . admitted, on grounds of science, to that Charmed Circle." Imperial Col. of Sc. and Tech., Walpole to Huxley, 23 Aug. 1892, Huxley Papers, XXVIII, fol. 146.

141. Arthur D. Berrington was formerly a private secretary at the General Board of Health, 1854-55, and the Metropolitan Board of Works. He retired from the Usk Board in 1884 after helping for eighteen years to make the Usk "the first salmon river in England." *Field*, LXVII (1886), 320. *Second Report, Royal Commission on Civil Establishments*, 1888 (C. 5545), XXVII, *Mins. Evid.*, Q. 18,514; *Report, Royal Commission on Salmon Fisheries*, 1902 (Cd. 1188), XIII, *Mins. Evid.*, Q. 22,564-22,569.

142. "An Inspector sitting merely in London cannot possibly give a useful opinion on the delicate points which come before him. His attendances in different parts of England and Wales should be frequent, and he can do more good work on the river bank than at the Home Office. In this way he will be brought into a closer personal contact with the Conservators, and it may be hoped that a feeling of mutual confidence will spring up which must greatly facilitate the smooth working of the fishery laws." *25th Ann. Rep.*, 1886 (C. 4713), XV, 15.

143. The change was gratefully received by the practical-minded fishery boards, one of which commended Berrington as "a gentleman with all the qualities and knowledge essential for the satisfactory execution of the duties attached to the office as they were carried on by Messrs. Walpole and Buckland." PRO, John Ridley, Tyne Conservators, to A. J. Mundella, 27 July 1886, BT 13/36 (E. 7481).

144. *Second Report, Royal Commission on Civil Establishments*, 1888 (C. 5545), XXVII, *Mins. Evid.*, Q. 18,552. J. W. Bund was a chairman of the Severn Fishery Board and a frequent author on fishery affairs. See Bund, *Salmon Problems*.

plaints were met by the defiant resistance of civil servants at the Board of Trade, who, willing to err only on the side of caution, were determined to create the formal procedure necessary for the safe conduct of a large public department. Scarcely three decades after salmon policy had begun, Berrington and salmon inspection were defeated, like John Simon's medical inspectors at the Local Government Board, by the accumulating wisdom of "secretarial common sense."

V

By the end of the century salmon work had ceased to expand. Although by 1902 a total of 18,306 papers had been registered in the new Harbour and Fisheries Department,[145] only 2,750 of these related to fishery questions, and only 1,900 pertained to the Salmon and Sea Fisheries Acts. Despite reports of bad fishing seasons, Berrington's requests for more accurate statistics and new consolidating legislation went unheeded.[146] Buckland's Museum of Economic Fish Culture fell into neglect and disuse.[147] Reviewers of Berrington's *29th Annual Report* found "nothing in particular to be proud of" in the way of salmon policy, and as the administrative dilemma predicted by Berrington achieved alarming reality, the Fishery Department languished.[148]

After 1886 the Government sought few additional statutory powers. At the turn of the century the Board of Trade's authority

---

145. The Harbour Department was merged with the Fisheries Department in 1898.

146. *Field*, LXXV (1890), 841.

147. *Ibid.*, LXXVI (1890), 622. In 1889 a Treasury Committee quoted Huxley in support of transferring the museum and the Buckland Professorship in Fish Culture to the Marine Biological Laboratory at Plymouth or to the Natural History Museum. See *Report of the Committee Appointed by the Treasury to Enquire into the Science Collections at South Kensington*, 1889 (C. 5831), XXXIV, 7. Again, in 1898, a Select Committee recommended that the museum be closed, on grounds that it was obsolete and that its alcohol preservatives were dangerous to the public. A memorial was circulated by Walpole and Bund, and Walpole led a deputation to the Board of Trade to complain that "successive governments have come and gone, betraying no interest whatever in the Museum." *Field*, XCV (1900), 168. "With a very moderate expenditure," Walpole mused, "and with intelligent supervision it might have been made, by this time, a complete and comprehensive collection, illustrating the science and practical aspect of the fisheries of this country." *Ibid.*, XCV (1900), 185. By 1901, however, the museum had not been closed.

148. "The fishery department . . . is rapidly gaining a reputation for dilatoriness as the L.G.B. unconcernedly possessed for many years past. Nor does it seem, as in the case of the L.G.B., that the recent delay in dealing with various pressing questions has been owing to the pressure of business, for many of the points . . . could be settled by a competent inspector without a moment's hesitation." *Ibid.*, XCIX (1902), 347.

was quite limited. It could construct a fish pass over a dam and recover costs in default; it could approve of the form and dimensions of fish passes and gratings; it could supervise bylaws and license duties; it could grant certificates for the formation and alteration of fishery districts and set the number of conservators and could occasionally grant provisional orders for the purchase of land for fish passes. But the once visible evidence of a rational policy for the fisheries, as demonstrated by the early inspectors, had gone. Far from having their statutory authority increased over the years, even the consultative role of the later inspectors was severely reduced. While Walpole and Buckland had once toured the whole country all year around, the inspector now rarely moved outside of Whitehall. The boards of conservators gradually assumed the task of dealing with sea fisheries committees,[149] applying the principles of salmon legislation to other freshwater fish, and restraining river pollution. The central department became less and less informed about local variations in fishery supervision except through the formal conservators reports or through scandal inquiries. Moreover, because the Treasury suppressed applications for additional staff, chronic Whitehall conditions of overwork claimed the full time of the existing clerks. Thus Charles Fryer, assistant inspector, lamented, "I do not know what a Sunday is, and I seldom know what a holiday is. I get no regular weekly or annual 'close time'."[150]

The situation had not improved by 1903, when, following the recommendation of the Royal Commission, fishery work was consolidated and transferred to the Board of Agriculture.[151] The Salmon and Freshwater Fisheries Acts, as administered by the

---

149. These were created by the Sea Fisheries Regulation Act, 1888, which provided for the formation of districts including contiguous estuaries and inland waters. Sea fisheries committees clashed with salmon conservators over modes of fishing permissible at different times of the year and over the jurisdiction of different authorities over pollution and sewage. *Ibid.*, LXXII (1888), 165.

150. *Report, Royal Commission on Salmon Fisheries*, 1902 (Cd. 1188), XIII, *Mins. Evid.*, Q. 22,818.

151. The Board of Agriculture, thus transformed into the Board of Agriculture and Fisheries, became the Ministry of Agriculture and Fisheries in 1919, and the Ministry of Agriculture, Fisheries and Food in 1955. The Salmon and Freshwater Fisheries Act, 1923, consolidated earlier legislation and is still in force. The River Boards Act, 1948, placed each river system under a single local authority, which became responsible for the unified control of salmon, trout, and freshwater fish, canal drainage, and the prevention of river pollution. The cost of the river boards is now met out of county rates, supplemented by license fees. Each board is limited to forty members and has one member appointed jointly by the Ministry of Agriculture, Fisheries and Food and the Ministry of Housing and Local Government. Since local authorities appoint about 60 per cent of each board's membership, the representation of the fishing interests per se has been considerably reduced. See *Report of the Committee on Salmon and Freshwater Fisheries*, 1960-61 (Cmnd. 1350), XV, §§14-22.

fishery boards, covered over three thousand net fisheries and over two thousand licensed net fishermen in twenty-three rivers, which together provided catchment areas for 25,600 square miles of the 58,000 square miles in England and Wales. Since only about 10,000 square miles were used for salmon cultivation, there was a clear possibility of doubling or trebling the yield. But even in those areas which were under constant cultivation, certain rivers refused to show improved results. Certain contradictions were at first difficult to explain. For example, it was known that the Severn suffered chiefly from weirs, the Tyne from Newcastle's pollution, and the Usk from the trade of Newport. But the fact that the busy Usk produced more salmon than the quiet Wye remained a mystery until it was shown that the Wye had been depleted by inept management.

Moreover, the inspectors laboured under a severe lack of information. When once asked why salmon legislation had not proved more effective, H. A. Bruce (then Lord Aberdare) replied that the "numerous and multiform" causes of decline were in most respects traceable to the "altered condition of the times we live in."[152] Indeed, in 1876, after several lengthy attempts to understand why salmon yields varied so greatly from year to year and from river to river, Buckland himself concluded that it was unreasonable to expect a constantly improving harvest. "The habits of the salmon are in reality little understood, and their mysterious habits are . . . so affected by floods, droughts and every possible change of the weather, that the control of men in capturing them from year to year must of necessity depend upon natural causes."[153]

Thirdly, it was notorious that relatively little of the massive effort against pollution had achieved success.[154] The inspectors were helpless to act on the question of pollution as long as the Government referred all pollution questions to public health authorities,[155] who were interested only in the chemical purification of water for human consumption. The Government's consistent refusal

152. Cited in F. Eden, "The Salmon Fisheries," *Fortnightly Review*, XXX (1881), 629-30; see also Archibald Young, "Scotch Salmon Fishery Legislation: Its Defects and Their Remedies," *Trans. National Association for the Promotion of Social Science* (1880), pp. 254-55.

153. *15th Ann. Rep.*, XVI, 4; *Times*, 3 May 1876.

154. Henry Ffennell, "A Resuscitated Industry," *ibid.*, 30 Dec. 1892; *ibid.*, 29 Dec. 1894.

155. In 1876 Buckland had observed that "the best method of obtaining the future purification of our rivers will be to discover methods by which waste materials now thrown away, may be converted into saleable and commercial value." *16th Ann. Rep.*, XXIV, 33. "The legislature had determined not to deal with the question of river pollution on fishery grounds, and I have neither the desire nor the right to dispute their decision." *17th Ann. Rep.*, 1878 (C. 2096), XXI, 53.

to allow the biologists a greater influence in the subject thwarted
Walpole's best intentions. In the end he threw up his hands altogether in a literary gesture of despair:

> So far as my own duties are concerned, I must simply state
> that as salmon are dependent on clear water, and as the
> river systems of this country are certainly not, as a whole, be-
> coming clearer, I do not imagine that it is possible, under
> present circumstances, for the local Conservators to develop
> the production of rivers entrusted to their management to a
> much greater degree than they have already succeeded in
> doing.[156]

Finally, the three fundamental principles of 1861 — the preservation of salmon during a fixed close time, the free ascent of salmon,
and the prevention of pollution — were still widely disregarded.
In the fifty-one fishing districts, 593 bailiffs were employed, but
only 440 were employed permanently. Large river areas were un-
inspected, and poaching in some rivers was a flourishing pastime.
The free ascent of salmon continued to be blocked, after over thirty
years of legislation, by the owners of dams who refused to build
fish passes and by the inefficient fish passes installed by some local
boards. The fishery interests felt that the Government had not
invested enough men and money in the fisheries, while the inspector felt that attempts at innovation were suppressed by the
voice of departmental authority.

It was clear that what had begun boldly had lapsed into a
pathetic history of indifferent half measures. The over-all outcome
for the British salmon fisheries had been a short burst of improvement, followed within a decade by a sluggish rate of growth. By
and large, the issues graphically defined in the 1860s still lacked
the general public enthusiasm necessary for transforming limited
fishery acts into a broad policy for national resource conservation.

---

156. *Ibid.* As late at 1919, in reviewing wartime attempts to cultivate fish
as food, the Secretary to the Board of Agriculture and Fisheries wrote: "Our salmon
rivers are a sadly neglected national asset, and it is a somewhat melancholy duty
for the Board, which has no effective powers for preserving or developing their
resources, to publish an annual report which must in effect be a report of annual
decline. As long as there is no effectual check on industrial or sewage pollution,
and as long as this evil is aggravated by continuous abstraction of water and the
presence of artificial obstructions, the progressive decline of our salmon and freshwater fisheries is inevitable. A few of our salmon rivers are still reasonably pure
and comparatively prolific. A Board armed with effective powers could conserve
and develop these, and might rescue others before their ruin has been completed.
But if these ends are to be secured, the Administration must be in a position to
regulate not merely fishing operations but the fisheries themselves, and must be
provided with the means of checking or controlling the causes which threaten the
rivers with extinction." *Report of the Proceedings under the Salmon and Freshwater Fisheries Acts for the Years 1915, 1916, 1917, and 1918,* 1920 (Cmd. 497),
XXII, Preface.

VI

The administration of the Salmon Acts illustrates several characteristics of the growth of government and the formulation of public policy in the late nineteenth century. The tension between upper and lower proprietors, net and rod fishermen, and the mill and factory owners reveals the extent to which the character of law and opinion was influenced by social groups which had a common objective but quite dissimilar views on the manner in which to achieve it.[157] Likewise, the process by which inspectors resolved diverging opinions into productive channels demonstrates the manner in which specialist expertise could be applied to legal affairs. Finally, the process by which factions once hostile to state intervention were won to its support exhibits the role of law and its agents in the formation of law-making opinion.

Because the inspectors were influenced by the attitudes and opinions of their time, they provide a classic description of the way in which Victorian "experts" could use Benthamite imperatives and legislative controls without being tutelary Benthamites, and without advocating state intervention as an end in itself. The inspectors were knowing agents of change, but they did not necessarily applaud its implications and consequences. Ffennell and Eden were more strongly in favour of the tighter government controls familiar in Ireland, but even they gave no evidence of approving state control as a long-term policy. Buckland shunned political discussion wherever possible, preferring to keep natural science out of politics, and Huxley, though aware of the need for government scientific policy, was by no means a doctrinaire supporter of government-sponsored science.

Similarly Walpole had no clear preference for government involvement. In the words of his *D.N.B.* biographer, he was ideologically sympathetic to the "Manchester School" traditions; "he was a believer in *laissez-faire*, he was equally distrustful of toryism and socialism."[158] As he wrote to Huxley, soon after the transfer of the fishery work to the Board of Trade:

> When I read of the prodigious development of a Fisheries Department, and the excessive activity of a paternal Government to appoint Secretaries, Inspectors and Lord knows what, I am inclined to think that the cheapest thing for the

---

157. Cf. John Goldthorpe's illuminating analysis, "The Development of Social Policy in England, 1800-1914," *Trans. Fifth World Congress of Sociology* (Washington, 1964).
158. *D.N.B.* (2nd supplement, 1912).

country, and *entre nous*, the best thing for the fisheries would have been for the Government to have given us £5000 a year for life, on condition that we should do nothing for it.[159]

In his *History of England*, published just four years before his death, Walpole viewed with alarm the "increasing determination to arm the State with authority to prevent abuse"; his words suggest strongly mixed feelings about the "growing disinclination in the complex conditions of modern society to rely on the doctrines of laissez-faire."[160]

If one seeks, therefore, a general philosophy underlying their actions, one finds not legalistic Benthamism but an ethical utilitarianism strongly identified with an idea of progress. In the transition of their function from that of protecting fishing interests to providing useful services for landowners and fishermen, the inspectors were cautious and empirical. This approach is illustrated by their reaction against the extension of "secretarial common sense" and "legal mentality" into delicate areas of central-local relations and questions of scientific research. They heuristically identified private interest with the public good and sought to apply government stimulus to a value system based on self-improvement. If they had a philosophy of intervention, it was an operational one: a set of practical alternatives and proposals to smooth local differences and to create institutions of the size and kind necessary to make desirable legislation practicable.

Their methodology was utilitarian, but their equipment was incomplete. Their efforts to supplement voluntary endeavour, to reconcile dissenting interests, and to curtail the dissipation of resources exemplified a very modern approach to the role of government in domestic affairs. Yet to implement the three cardinal principles of the 1861 act required more knowledge of natural

---

159. Imperial Col. of Sc. and Tech., Walpole to Huxley, 19 Dec. 1886, Huxley Papers, XXVIII, fol. 134. Two decades later Walpole, en route to the secretaryship of the Post Office, confided again to Huxley: "The Fishery People [i.e. the Fishery Department] have gone far beyond the ideas of two such old fashioned folk as you and I, and seem to be bent on interfering with fishermen everywhere and in everything. I sometimes wish that they would meditate on your advice that fishermen should be free to fish how they like, when they like and where they like. However, I reflect that it is no longer any affair of mine; and that it never answers for anyone who has left an office to interfere in the management of his successor; so I fell back (like you will) upon Silence." Imperial Col. of Sc. and Tech., Walpole to Huxley, 22 June 1893, *ibid.*, fol. 147.

160. Spencer Walpole, *The History of Twenty-five Years* (London, 1903), III, 331. It is interesting to observe that no mention of the revolutionary regulatory precedents of salmon legislation appears in Walpole's earlier *History of England* (London, 1890), VI.

history and fishery technology than the Victorian scientific community possessed. All fishery legislation proceeded on the assumption that an adequate fish technology was within practical reach and this in turn required an investment in sound fundamental research. But the endowment of environmental research implied a financial and constitutional commitment which Victorian Governments were not prepared to accept. The result was a series of legislative and administrative compromises which exhausted the amateur inspectors, frustrated their scientific successors, annoyed the fishery interests, and cast unfamiliar problems upon ill-equipped secretariats. Although fishery bills continued to make their time-honoured appearance on the parliamentary timetable, successful nature conservancy demanded coherent policies which were not destined to come during the nineteenth-century "revolution in government."

III

Science and Government in Victorian England: Lighthouse Illumination and the Board of Trade, 1866-1886

The use of light to guide the mariner as he approaches land, or passes through intricate channels, has, with the advance of society and its ever increasing interests, caused such a necessity for means more and more perfect as to tax the utmost powers both of the philosopher and the practical man in the development of the principles concerned, and their practical application.[1]

INTRODUCTION

THE GROWTH of government participation in the conduct of British science has long interested historians of science and technology who recognize the significance of social factors in the application of scientific ideas. Within recent years, however, the subject has also become attractive to students of social, economic, and administrative history. In part this new interest has arisen from current preoccupations with the expanding demands made by science on the country's budget and with the necessity to design appropriate policies for the administration of fundamental and applied research. Just as the postwar years of welfare-state-making found historians looking for the historical roots of the social services, so we have now begun to probe beneath "current history" for lessons and experience bequeathed by the past.[2]

* This investigation was assisted by a grant for research in science policy from the Department of Education and Science. For the use of records and archive material I am indebted to the kindness of the Elder Brethren of Trinity House. The Tyndall diaries have been quoted by kind permission of the Librarian of the Royal Institution.

[1] Michael Faraday, Lecture at the Royal Institution, 6 March 1860.

[2] For general surveys see E. Mendelsohn, "The Emergence of Science as a Profession in Nineteenth Century Europe," in K. Hill, *The Management of Scientists* (Boston : Beacon Press, 1964) pp. 41–43; Sir E. Ashby, *Technology and the Academics* (London : Macmillan, 1958); and D. S. L. Cardwell, *The Organisation of Science in England;*

Reprinted from Isis, Vol. 60, Part 1, No. 201
© 1969 by the History of Science Society Inc.

6

Perhaps one of the chief ways in which the general historian can assist this endeavor lies in the discovery and analysis of events which illustrate how policies involving science, technology, and economics have become part of the experience of government. We know, for example, that by the middle of the nineteenth century, Parliament had already taken significant steps toward the regulation of public health, transportation, welfare, and safety. And as greater powers were sanctioned, so government found it necessary to have "systematic means" of regulation at its disposal.[3] Increasingly this involved the use of scientific and technical knowledge and the employment of "experts" possessing such knowledge.

This quiet, piecemeal introduction of science into central policy began to raise questions about research methods which were wholly unfamiliar to professional civil servants educated in "Greats" or the practice of law. By the early 1870's Gladstone's financial reforms together with codified principles of competitive entrance gave civil servants a corporate identity and a more precise conception of duty. But the Rule of Law, particularly when reflected in financial retrenchment, came increasingly into conflict with the spirit of constantly improving administration which the new "experts" were intended to provide. These conflicts were rarely clear contests between right and wrong or mere bouts between progressives and conservatives; invariably they involved questions of choice where different scientific judgments had first to be weighed against each other and then tested against political and economic goals. This paper seeks to illustrate the nature and implications of this process of choice for both public administration and the scientific community.

On 18 March 1881 John Tyndall, aged fifty-three, resigned from his post as scientific adviser to Trinity House and the Board of Trade. This unexpected move by a well-known and respected scientist suddenly deprived the government's maritime department of its foremost authority on the applied physics of light and sound. The issue flickered briefly in the press and then was publicly forgotten.[4] But the official correspondence leading up to Tyndall's resignation, comprising over four hundred letters and memoranda over twenty years, left a lasting impression on the Board of Trade, on Tyndall, and on his scientific colleagues. History has surmised that Tyndall was defeated, and probably on reasonable grounds, yet no successor was appointed to his post for nearly fifteen years. On

a *Retrospect* (London: Heinemann, 1957). For a reassessment of one area of government policy toward science see R. MacLeod, *Specialist Policy in Government Growth, 1860–1900* (unpublished Ph.D. thesis, University of Cambridge, 1967).

[3] *Cf.* R. MacLeod, "The Alkali Acts Administration, 1868–1886, The Emergence of the Civil Scientist," *Victorian Studies*, 1965, 9 : 85–112 ; R. MacLeod, "Government and Resource Conservation," *Journal of British Studies*, 1968, 5 : 114–150.

[4] Little mention of this conflict appears in the authorized biography of Tyndall by A. S.

Eve and C. H. Creasey, *The Life and Work of John Tyndall* (London : Macmillan, 1945), and none in the many biographies of Joseph Chamberlain, then president of the Board of Trade. Tyndall's views, however, are set out in three consecutive articles: "A Story of the Lighthouses," *Nineteenth Century*, 1883, 24 : 61–80; "A Story of the Lighthouses," *Fortnightly Review*, 1888, 44 : 805–828 ; and "A Story of the Lighthouses," *Fortnight. Rev.*, 1889, 45 : 198–219. These polemical works must of course be carefully assessed in the light of official records, departmental correspondence, and Parliamentary Papers.

closer scrutiny, however, several points at issue become clear, and the conflict, ostensibly remote from our age, reveals its place in the history of science and public affairs.

LIGHTHOUSES AND THE STATE

Near the end of the 1850's a number of circumstances focused public attention upon the lighthouse service of the United Kingdom. At the beginning of the decade over 42% of the world's maritime commerce was British. By 1880 Britain was to command 55% of all sea-going trade, representing a fixed capital outlay of more than £110,000,000.[5] During the same period, however, 800 to 1,200 lives and nearly 1,200 ships were annually being lost in wrecks at sea. In the years 1852–1860, 10,336 ships, or one in every 210 British ships and one in every 232 foreign vessels, were destroyed in collisions or smashed against the rocky shores of the British Isles.[6] And if in the same period the National Lifeboat Institution assisted in saving 11,500 lives, another 7,200 were lost—"not solely by the visitation of God," said *The Times*, "but in a great degree through the obstinacy and perversity of man."[7]

Men knew the sacrifice was preventable. Admiralty enquiries had shown consistent correlations between shipwrecks and reports of old and unseaworthy ships, unqualified masters and inexpert crews, negligent loading, imperfect charts, and defective equipment.[8] In response, successive governments had seized legislative instruments to assist supervision and control. In 1836 a Select Committee recommended a Mercantile Marine Board to supervise and inspect ships, a Code of Maritime Laws, nautical schools, courts of inquiry, and altruistic provisions to encourage better habits among crews. In 1845 a second committee recommended further amendments in the laws of pilotage, signals by sound rockets and mortar apparatus, lifebelts and buoys, and codes for protection of wrecked property. All these recommendations were adopted in a series of Merchant Shipping Acts, but their effect in reducing loss of life and property was disappointing.[9] Despite the increasing powers of the government, often acquired

[5] Admiralty records listed 3,397,000 tons under sail and 168,000 tons under steam in 1850. T. H. Farrer, *The State in its Relation to Trade* (rev. ed., London: Macmillan, 1902), p. 157. Recent analyses suggest that in 1850 there were 25,984 ships under the British flag or British ownership, representing 3,565,000 tons, and that the number increased to 28,971 ships and 5,779,000 tons in 1866. After 1866 there were more steam ships but fewer ships altogether. B. R. Mitchell, *Abstract of British Historical Statistics* (Cambridge : Cambridge Univ. Press, 1962), p. 218.

[6] See the *Admiralty Register of Wrecks and Casualties to Vessels which occurred in the Sea on the Shores of the United Kingdom during the year 1854–55*, 1855.(75).xxxiv.3; and subsequent annual *Registers* through the

Returns of Wrecks, Casualties and Collisions reported on or near the Coast of the United Kingdom in each year, 1861–70, 1871.(139). lxi, 13. [The citation for Parliamentary Papers notes the following: the year (or session), the session number (in parentheses) or the command number (in square brackets), the volume number (in lower case roman numerals), and the page number (in arabic numerals)].

[7] *The Times*, 26 Sept. 1861.

[8] Beginning in 1852 shipping casualties were recorded every year by the Admiralty. The Board of Trade began compiling wreck statistics in 1855. See W. Muston, *Wreck Inquiries* (London : Stevens & Sons, 1885).

[9] Between 1840 and 1843, 611 ships and 766 lives were lost on the average annually. W. S. Lindsay, *History of Merchant Ship-*

8

over bitter opposition from free traders and ship owners, losses continued to increase.[10]

Because the loss of property was less sensational than the loss of life, shipwrecks attracted rather more humanitarian compassion than commercial concern. Under these circumstances the government's attention was directed to the improvement and control of safety devices. Among the more traditional and significant of all preventive means were naturally the nation's lighthouses—"the true guardians," as David Stevenson wrote, "of this country's naval greatness."[11]

In 1857 the Crimean War ended. But the peace left vivid memories of Scutari, of Britons "overtaxed from want of calculation and underfed from want of foresight."[12] As the threat of war had helped catalyze reform in the British civil service, so the coming of peace freed public energies to press for the enforcement of reforms which war had delayed. The same outraged public sensibility which helped the crusade of Florence Nightingale and which now moved through Parliament fresh legislation to reform the army, to reclaim inebriates, to suppress industrial wastes, and even to appoint, for a time, a centralized General Board of Health, also denied the inevitability of lost life at sea. The ghastly spectre of watery death made an appeal to action which a naval nation could not neglect.

In 1859 a confluence of events brought this growing awareness of avoidable tragedy to kindling point. In September of that year the *Royal Charter,* an Australian trader and passenger trip within twenty-four hours of its destination, was smashed against the rugged Anglesey coast and the *Pomona* sank off Blackwater Bank, near the coast of Ireland. Altogether 870 passengers and crew were killed in these two shipwrecks alone.[13] Rarely had any sea disasters occasioned sorrow and suffering to so many.[14] The cost of lives that year was five times greater than that of the previous year and three times that of the year following.[15] The value of material losses in 1859 alone soared over £1,500,000.[16]

In November Sir David Brewster, the contentiously brilliant optical physicist,[17] presented the issue to the public in the *North British Review:*

---

ping and Ancient Commerce, Vol. III (London : Sampson, Low, Marston, Low & Searle, 1876), p. 463.

[10] The increase did not, however, exceed 1% of total shipping (*ibid.,* p. 509).

[11] *Good Words,* 1864, 5 : 105.

[12] *Annual Summaries of The Times,* Vol. I, for the year 1855, p. 76.

[13] The *Royal Charter* wreck, which cost over 400 lives, was described by Charles Dickens in *The Uncommercial Traveller* (London : Chapman & Hall, 1861), pp. 7–20. Dickens had previously developed the theme of shipwrecks with Wilkie Collins in *The Wreck of the Golden Mary,* which originally appeared in the Christmas 1856 number of *Household Words.*

[14] See *Wrecked in Sight of Home, or the loss of the "Royal Charter"* (London : Blackie & Son, 1896), p. 13 ; *The Times,* 26 Sept.

1861; Robert Fitzroy, "Notice of the *Royal Charter* Storm," *Proceedings of the Royal Society,* 1859, 10 : 561–567.

[15] See Lindsay, *History of Merchant Shipping,* Vol III, p. 506.

[16] See *Returns of the Number of Wrecks, Casualties and Collisions reported to the Board of Trade as having occurred on or near the coasts of the United Kingdom in the last ten years,* 1871.(139).1xi.669.

[17] Sir David Brewster (1781–1868), F.R.S. 1815, educated (Edinburgh University) for the ministry but later turned to science and scientific journalism; editor of *Edinburgh Magazine* (afterward *Edinburgh Philosophical Journal* and *Edinburgh Journal of Science*); received Rumford and Royal Medals for discoveries concerning the polarization of light; first director of the Royal Scottish Society of Arts, 1821; knighted in 1831; Vice

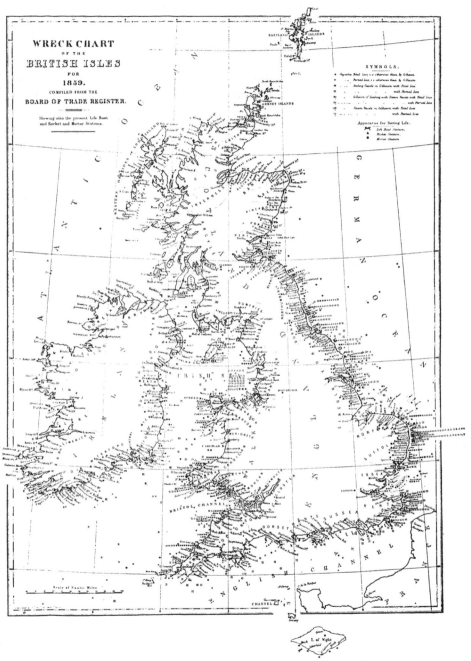

Wrecks in 1859

10

The time is not distant when it [the lighthouse question] must be investigated in all its bearings by the legislature. The establishment of new lights on various parts of our coasts, the universal introduction of the system, and the invention of better distinguishing lights than those we possess, are topics of ever-increasing importance which must sooner or later force themselves on the attention of Parliament.[18]

In the wake of the *Royal Charter* and Brewster's article a Royal Commission was appointed to inquire into the number, quality and position, sufficiency, expense, and management of British lighthouses.[19]

The Commission, under the chairmanship of Admiral Baillie Hamilton, consisted of two naval officers and two representatives of the shipping interests. The Commission visited all British and French lighthouses and circulated a set of questions to men of science who had special knowledge of optics. From the outset it had been under pressure to recommend the appointment of men of science, as well as engineers and naval officers, to every lighthouse board. "Public opinion would hardly tolerate continued neglect," Brewster assured the Commission. "It would be better surely to double the lighthouse dues, than to leave our glimmering and misleading lights, superintended by unpaid and irresponsible commissioners and ignorant engineers" beneath "the state of science in England."[20] Brewster's prophetic remarks were forced home by the losses of 1860, when extraordinarily bad weather caused 250 wrecks in a single two-week period.

Unlike the earlier inquiries into lighthouse administration in 1836 and 1845 the Commission also appointed a scientific member, Dr. John H. Gladstone, F.R.S.[21] The addition of a man of science was cheered by Brewster as marking a happy departure from Establishment amateurism; but, as events soon revealed, Gladstone's presence was not as useful as might have been expected. Scientific questions of lighthouse efficiency became entangled with nonscientific issues of lighthouse policy. This was particularly the case in the use of different lighthouse illuminants.

For some years lighthouse authorities had realized that new methods of creating light by gas and electricity were being used on city streets and awaited only appropriate modifications to make them available for the prevention of shipwrecks. From time to time, the authorities considered the installation of different improved illuminants, but it had proved extremely difficult to assess the contribution such improvements made to shipping safety. It was easy enough to assert in principle that brighter lights would save more ships, but causal relationships

Chancellor, Edinburgh University, 1860; President, Royal Society of Edinburgh, 1864. He was actively concerned in securing government support for scientific activity; helped to found the British Association in 1831; and defended Charles Babbage's *Reflexions on the Decline of Science in England and on Some of its Causes* (London: B. Fellows, 1830). See *Quarterly Review*, 1830, 43: 305–342.

[18] [Sir David Brewster] "Life Boats—Lightning Conductors—Lighthouses," *North British Review*, 1859, 31: 495.

[19] *Report of the Royal Commission appointed to inquire into the Conditions and Management of Lights, Buoys and Beacons,* 1861.[2793].xxv.1.

[20] [Sir David Brewster], "British Lighthouses," *N. Brit. Rev.*, 1860, 32: 517.

[21] John Hall Gladstone (1827–1902); Professor of Chemistry, Royal Institution, 1874–1877; President, Physical Society 1874–1876; President, Chemical Society, 1877–1879. *Cf.* J. H. Gladstone, "The History of Lighthouse Illumination," *Macmillan's Magazine,* 1862, 5: 378–385.

in individual cases were difficult to establish. Under the circumstances even the best lighthouse authorities were unsure how to evaluate competing claims for illuminants and how to decide whether power, intensity, or ease of manipulation was more important. In the end the question was usually decided on grounds of expense. To choose otherwise would require intensive research and development work, from authorities which the Commissioners found apathetic and ill-equipped.

In 1861 the Commission recommended the use of double lights and brilliant lights for bad weather and the introduction of methods for distinguishing between lighthouses. The Commission also cited approvingly their evidence that the "science of lighthouse illumination is in a transition state, and capable of further development."[22] Dr. Gladstone assured the Commission that many potentially profitable studies were awaiting only the appointment of men to undertake them.[23]

ADMINISTRATIVE RESISTANCE TO INNOVATION

Much of the Commission's criticism focused on Trinity House, the ancient authority for ensuring uniformity in administration since the reign of Henry VIII.[24] The semi-official powers of Trinity House extended over a wide spectrum of maritime affairs. From Elizabethan times it had levied light dues upon all ships using British ports—by this means maintaining lightships, buoys, and light-houses. By 1830 it had acquired supervisory jurisdiction over the lighthouses which were not privately chartered or operated by local authorities. A similar function was performed in Ireland after 1783 by the Ballast Board for the Port of Dublin (later the Commissioners of Irish Lights) and in Scotland after 1786 by the Commissioners of Northern Lights.

Over the years these three bodies amassed great wealth and influence. By 1844, for example, the twenty Elder Brethren of Trinity House included three cabinet ministers and five ex-ministers,[25] and their meetings had become chiefly social events for retired naval officers and eminent public officials. To some extent the same was true of the other bodies. The Ballast Board of Dublin was composed not of naval men at all, but of merchants, bankers, magistrates, and railway directors. Until the middle of the century the Scottish Board was composed entirely of law officers. Neither had an engineer or a man of science on its staff.[26]

---

[22] The last coal fire, at St. Bees, had been extinguished as recently as 1822; even oil had been in use only since 1730, and now the Commissioners found inventions being tested "which promise to transcend far the powers of even the four-wick mechanical lamp in producing light." *Report of the Royal Commission,* 1861, p. vi.

[23] *Ibid.,* p. xxx.

[24] In the 16th century Trinity House was a vital administrative component of the English Navy and acted as agent for ships' stores, for appointing pilots, regulating land buoys and beacons, and exercising judicial powers

in Admiralty cases. These activities were financed by the collections of beaconage and buoyage dues. The sole right of erecting beacons and sea marks in England was conferred upon Trinity House by Queen Elizabeth I. C. R. B. Barrett, *The Trinity House of Dept-ford Strond* (London : Lawrence & Bullen, 1893), pp. 1–26.

[25] The twenty included the Master and the Deputy Master (the acting chairman). A brief history is given in *Trinity House Today* (n.d.), Vol. 25, pamphlet 1 (Trinity House Library).

[26] ". . . the government of lighthouses in

12

As early as 1834 this situation had been compared unfavorably with the distinctive centralized and scientific administrative system of France and other continental powers.[27] Indeed, such invidious comparisons had prompted the Board of Trade to appoint Michael Faraday as its occasional consultant on lighthouse management in 1836.[28] But Faraday devoted comparatively little time to this particular work, and his presence made little impact upon Establishment policy.

In 1854, in reply to repeated public criticism of the extravagant spending of Trinity House and the Irish and Scottish Boards on luxurious cruises and sumptuous dinners, Parliament entrusted their financial supervision to the Board of Trade. Parliamentary committees in 1845 and 1854 had also recommended the establishment of a unified central authority on the American or French model, either by granting fresh powers to the Admiralty or by elevating the Elder Brethren of Trinity House to official status. But the repeated opposition of the rival Scottish and Irish Boards defeated every attempt at centralization. As a compromise with tradition, therefore, each Board was permitted to operate semi-autonomously. In deference to its seniority, Trinity House was given power to approve requests for improvements by the Scottish and Irish Boards. Formal authority to hear appeals and to sanction expenditure was vested in the Board of Trade, but the three-tiered decision structure made swift action exceedingly difficult.[29] Moreover, the Board of Trade had only restrictive powers of the purse; it had no authority to initiate expenditure or to make proposals for new works. All such activities were the responsibility of the individual lighthouse Boards. Not surprisingly, the burden of efficiently administering this manifestly inefficient system bore heavily on the clerks of the Board of Trade.

By the late 1850's the Board of Trade also faced difficulties of its own. Over the preceding two decades it had tried to assimilate a considerable corpus of fresh statute law into a long-established department. But because the president of the Board was without cabinet rank, and because the post was commonly used

the U.K., their management and construction, are all confided to bodies of gentlemen of various employment, none of which necessarily afford them an opportunity of acquiring a knowledge of those branches of science which bear upon lighthouse illumination." *Report of the Royal Commission*, 1861, p. xxix. Spain, Denmark, Sweden, and Austria had centralized Ministries of Marines which were responsible for lighthouses. In the U.S., marine functions were vested in the Treasury until 1852 when in response to public criticism a lighthouse board was established and endowed with a staff of scientific and technical specialists. See Major George Elliott, *Report of a Tour of Inspection of European Lighthouses* (Washington : GPO, 1875).

[27] As Brewster observed, "It is difficult to understand how a Board comprised of lawyers with a small percentage of municipal

functionaries . . . could discharge those scientific duties which in France were entrusted to Admirals, engineers and men eminent in science." "Lifeboats—Lightning Conductors —Lighthouses," *N. Brit. Rev.*, 1859, *31* : 514.

[28] Public Record Office file MT 10/128. Faraday to Emerson Tennant, Board of Trade, 1 Feb. 1856. Faraday's salary was fixed at £800 per annum. See L. Pearce Williams, *Michael Faraday* (New York : Basic Books ; London : Chapman & Hall, 1965), p. 489.

[29] As one critic observed, "the whole management of the lighthouse service appears to be impeded by the opposing action of three separate governing bodies ; and it does not clearly appear what advantage is gained to counter-balance the delay which results. . . ." *Report of the Royal Commission*, 1861, p. xxv.

"as a convenient depository for politicians of high rank called statesmen by courtesy,"[30] the Board's administration was largely in the hands of its senior civil servants, particularly those who supervised harbor and marine affairs. This staff was led by the well-known civil servant Thomas Henry (later Lord) Farrer, a "high priest of financial orthodoxy"[31] and a man remembered as "signally able, dogmatic . . . and seldom weakened by deficiency in self-estimate."[32] Farrer's strong belief in economy as the first condition of efficiency and in defensive spending on well-tried programs dominated the Board's policies until 1886.

The philosophy personified in Farrer was the third and most critical obstacle to change cited by the Commission of 1861. The lighthouse service was, after all, an expensive enterprise.[33] Since the revelations of the 1830's and 1840's successive governments had been sensitive about its cost; indeed, this was why the lighthouse authority accounts had been transferred to the Mercantile Marine Fund in 1854. But to the Commissioners the methods of the Board of Trade in administering this fund seemed overcautious. Despite evidence that frequent inspections encouraged more efficient lighting, the Board of Trade sanctioned very little money for inspection costs in England, and less for Ireland. The various Local Authority lighthouses had virtually no inspections at all. Under such circumstances the Commission concluded: "The Board of Trade has steadily kept economy rather than progress in view, but the saving they have thus effected has been represented as sometimes a false economy, and it has unquestionably led to much unsatisfactory correspondence, and in some instances to prejudicial delay."[34] To remedy this chronic malaise the Commissioners proposed that the lighthouse system be consolidated under a single central authority, receiving a

[30] Ibid., p. 409. J. L. Garvin, The Life of Joseph Chamberlain, Vol. I (London : Macmillan, 1932), p. 409.

[31] Ibid., p. 435.

[32] Ibid., p. 410. Sir Thomas Henry Farrer, First Baron Farrer (1814–1899); educated Eton and Balliol; barrister, Lincoln's Inn, 1844; Assistant Secretary, Marine Department, Board of Trade, 1850; Assistant Secretary to the Board, 1854; Permanent Secretary, 1865–1886; baronetcy, 1883; member of L.C.C., 1889–1898; author of various economic treatises, including The State in its Relation to Trade (1883, rev. ed., 1902); bitterly opposed to such "financial heresies" as local subsidies from Imperial funds, the reduction of the sinking fund, and increased expenditure on the army and navy. Farrer married Charles Darwin's niece, and Darwin's son Horace married Farrer's daughter. In his long career "he exercised considerable influence on the development and character of English commercial legislation." "Though dogmatic in his view . . . especially distrustful of the extension of state interference, and a free trader of unyielding temper, he yet maintained cordial relations with successive ministers, and as head of a department he was popular and successful because of the confidence with which he treated his subordinates." Dictionary of National Biography, Supplement, Vol. II (London, 1901), pp. 201–202.

[33] In 1861 the maintenance expenses of lighthouse authorities were as follows: Trinity House, £159,353; Commissioners of Irish Lights, £46,824; Commissioners of Northern Lights, £33,561; a total of £239,738. By 1883 annual maintenance expenditures had risen to Trinity House, £197,672; Irish Lights, £73,780; Northern Lights, £47,645. With expenditure on improvements the annual appropriation administered through the Mercantile Marine Fund in 1883 was approximately £352,600. Accounts of the Mercantile Marine Fund, 1862.(219).xxx.540; 1883.(272).1xii.3. These expenses were chiefly concerned with the maintenance of buildings and salaries. New scientific experiments would have been relatively quite inexpensive (under £2,000 per year). For the cost of alternative systems see n. 130 below.

[34] Report of the Royal Commission, 1861, p. xxxiv.

public vote from the Consolidated Fund, having a staff of scientific members to inspect all lights, and being required to report annually to the Royal Society and Parliament.

The Commission's recommendations in 1881 were at first heatedly discussed and then quickly forgotten. *The Times* admitted that administrative defects existed, particularly in the case of the Local Authorities, but insisted that the deficiencies were overstated; after all, the existing machinery was effective enough to win the praise of other nations:

> We have our own way of doing things and our way is not remarkable for simplicity or system. We are all for "self government" and all against "centralisation". We have a national antipathy to "Boards" and we are in the habit of looking to results rather than to means. . . . Complex and ill-organised as our system may appear, the results cannot be termed discreditable.[35]

Scientific Men and Engineers

The Commission of 1861 recognized that British lighthouses were among the most impressive structures of their kind in the world. They and their engineers had become household symbols of virtuous self-help and man's triumph over nature. Over the years great dynasties developed from the early lighthouse engineers. In Scotland Robert Stevenson, who built Bell Rock lighthouse in 1807–1812, began four generations of lighthouse engineers,[36] and in England Nicholas Douglass, who built the Bishop Rock lighthouse in the Scilly Isles in 1707, was followed in the profession by his sons and grandsons. Both his grandsons, William and James, became famous in their own right: it was James who rebuilt Eddystone a third time and who became in 1862 the Chief Engineer to Trinity House.[37]

Until long after Faraday's appointment to the Board of Trade, lighthouse operation was traditionally considered a question of engineering, and little technical advice was sought from theoretical men of science. This was natural when only candles were used for illumination and when optical devices were no more sophisticated than reflecting mirrors. With the introduction of oil, gas, and electric lamps and complex lens systems, however, the increased need for scientific knowledge brought men of science into closer contact with the Establishment

[35] *The Times*, 4 April 1861.

[36] His three sons won fame building the Skerrymore lighthouse and applying optics to lighthouses (Allan), establishing coastal beacons (David), and conducting experiments in illumination and condensing systems (Thomas). His grandsons included Robert Louis Stevenson. See David Stevenson, *Life of Robert Stevenson* (Edinburgh : Adam & Charles Black, 1878). See also David Stevenson, *Lighthouses* (Edinburgh : Adam & Charles Black, 1864); Thomas Stevenson, *Lighthouse Illumination* (2nd ed., Edinburgh : Adam & Charles Black, 1871), and "On an Improved Optical Arrangement for Azimuthal Condensing Apparatus for Lighthouses," *Nature*, 1875, *12* : 333–335.

[37] Sir James Douglass (1826–1898), educated as apprentice to ship-building engineers ; assisted as engineer in lighthouse construction, 1854-1870 ; appointed Chief Engineer to Trinity House, 1862 ; knighted 1882, M.I.C.E., 1861, F.R.S., 1887. *DNB*, Suppl., Vol. II, p. 150. Douglass was once self-consciously described as compensating for a lack of scientific training with an "unerring instinct." William Leisching, *The Story of Britain's Coastwise Lighting and Pilotage* (privately printed, n.d.), Pamphlet 1, Box 27, Trinity House Library. See also Thomas Williams, *Life of Sir James Nicholas Douglass, F.R.S.* (London : Longmans, Green, 1900), pp. 10–44.

engineers. From the second quarter of the century the lighthouse service witnessed an increasing number of confrontations between the advocates of "science" and the advocates of "common sense."

Between 1815 and 1860 the engineers enjoyed several institutional advantages over their new rivals. They were already in positions of high civil authority, they had a professional ethos, and they enjoyed social prestige based on impressive records of achievement. Practical men who had braved the brute force of nature to fashion pillars of stone and mortar had a strong emotional case against speculative men of ideas who merely designed appropriate lighting devices. Wherever an engineer found himself in conflict with a man of ideas on a subject involving as much technological application as abstract science, the engineer—particularly the Scottish engineer—had an obvious claim on public sympathy.

The civil and mechanical engineering profession in Britain had begun on a tide of progressive enthusiasm. By the middle of the century, however, certain sections of the profession had become more rigid, narrow, and unprogressive in their attitudes toward innovation.[38] This was reflected in the long struggle of the Scottish Board engineers against the introduction of Brewster's dioptric system, which delayed its use in Britain for over twenty years after it had become commonplace on the Continent.

The lighthouse engineers were, on the whole, content with the Board of Trade, which had demonstrated similar diffidence toward the encouragement of new scientific ideas. Whenever the revelations of the Wreck Abstracts or the reports of parliamentary inquiries aroused the concern of influential M.P.'s or shipowners, the Board assisted technical research on new safety techniques; but when the pressure of events subsided, the Board was inclined to reconsider its financial accountability and to withdraw its research support. This discontinuous policy of sudden overspending and rapid retrenchment was not conducive to the smooth development of illumination experiments. Instead, it revealed a profound misunderstanding of the unpredictable nature of scientific research.

This was demonstrated in 1860 when Trinity House sought Board of Trade sanction for a series of experiments with electric lights, to be performed by Michael Faraday. The Board of Trade, still under the scrutiny of the Royal Commission, agreed. The earliest of these experiments showed, however, that an electric light, although eight times as powerful as a first-order dioptric oil light (that is, one with a single ring of burners), was vastly more expensive to install and operate, and Trinity House asked to stop the tests. The Board of Trade felt obliged to keep the experiments going, partly for political reasons and partly because so much had already been invested in them. While Captain Bar-

---

[38] For further discussion on this point see S. G. Checkland, *The Rise of Industrial Society in England, 1815–1885* (London : Longman's, 1964), pp. 78–100. Prof. Checkland, in common with Prof. Bernal, argues that "with electricity, science for the first time held the initiative in social change." See J. D. Bernal, *Science and Industry in the Nineteenth Century* (London : Routledge & Kegan Paul, 1953), Ch. 5. It can be argued, however, that gas illumination played an earlier and, at the time, equally significant role in the encouragement of scientific innovation by social need.

III

tholomew Sulivan[39] (Nautical Adviser to the Marine and Harbour Departments) admitted that "the result of the experiments hitherto is not decisive enough to justify an extension of the system at present,"[40] he and Farrer both urged that experimental research be continued. In the end a scientific committee was appointed to investigate French electric apparatus and to make experiments "under the immediate charge of scientific men."[41] But when these good intentions found no immediate reward, and when political pressure eased, the Board's enthusiasm gave way to cynicism and gloom. Sometime afterward, when approached for more tests, Capain Bedford[42] approved them with great reluctance:

> I suppose this must be sanctioned . . . I hope with all these progressive appliances wrecks may be reduced in numbers and navigation facilities increased . . . though we are not much encouraged by the past to think that this will be the case. The more facilities, the greater heedlessness, increased collisions, and sunken wrecks seem to be the order of the day.[43]

By 1869 a long series of such disappointments had prejudiced the Board against any uncertain, speculative, or new departures in the field of illumination.

THE CASE OF JOHN WIGHAM

In 1866, after thirty years of service as a consultant inspector, Faraday asked the Board of Trade to appoint in his place John Tyndall, his student, colleague, and friend, who had already assumed most of Faraday's duties at the Royal Institution.[44] Farrer agreed to Tyndall's appointment without hesitation. Memories of Faraday's services, for which he had asked so little payment, were fresh in mind.[45] But Tyndall's optimistic tenure had scarcely begun before a dispute over salary between the Irish and Scottish Boards threatened to mar his cordial ties with Trinity House and the Board of Trade.[46] The trifling dispute was settled

[39] Sir Bartholomew J. Sulivan (1810–1890), entered Royal Navy in 1830 ; served aboard H.M.S. *Beagle,* 1831–1836 ; surveyed Falkland Islands, 1838–1839 ; naval command 1841–1854 ; Naval Officer of Marine Department, Dec. 1856–April 1865. Retired Rear Admiral, 1865, Vice Admiral, 1869, Admiral, 1877 ; C.B., 1855 ; K.C.B., 1869. F. Boase, *Modern English Biography,* Vol. III, col. 821. Sulivan as a young Lieutenant had served on the *Beagle* under Fitzroy and knew Darwin well. See Henry N. Sulivan, *Life and Letters of the late Admiral Sir Bartholomew James Sulivan, K.C.B., 1810–90* (London: John Murray, 1896).

[40] MT 10/34 [4478]. Minute, Sulivan and Farrer, 9 April 1863 ; MT 10/65 [2890]. Secretary, Trinity House, to Secretary, Marine Department, Minute, Farrer, 18 Jan. 1865. The experiments failed to produce a reliable light, chiefly because of untrained lighthouse keepers and inefficient steam engines.

[41] "In the present case [Dungeness] had

not two men neglected their duties at once, the accident would not have happened. And we may hope for much improvement and simplification of apparatus. You ought not to be discouraged in the experiment on electric light." MT 10/55 [6515], Farrer to Bedford, 5 March 1866.

[42] George A. Bedford (1809–1879), entered Royal Navy, 1823, promoted Captain, 1854, retired Vice Admiral, 1876 ; F.R.C.S., 1859. See Boase, *Modern English Biography,* Vol. I, p. 218.

[43] MT 10/145 [1181]. Minute, Capt. Bedford, 21 March 1868.

[44] MT 10/128 [8879]. Secretary, Trinity House, to T. H. Farrer, 8 Dec. 1868.

[45] As soon as he found himself unable to fulfil his duties Faraday asked to return his £350/year salary and was reluctant to accept even a small pension from the government. MT 10/128 [721]. Minute, Farrer, 7 March 1867.

[46] Farrer and Capt. Arrow (Deputy Master of Trinity House) wished to continue paying

by a convenient compromise,[47] but it soon proved to be an inauspicious omen.

Tyndall discovered that following the inquiries of the 1830's and 1840's the lighthouse authorities had permitted research in three sectors—wireless telegraphy, fog signals, and illuminants. Of these three subjects the infant telegraphic system was the most novel and speculative. The question of fog signalling, whether by rockets or sirens, provided an opportunity for the application of much basic research currently being done on the transmission of sound which Tyndall himself had helped inaugurate.[48] The issue of illuminants, however, involved fundamental problems about the propagation and behavior of light which were not fully understood. The possibilities of using gas as an economic substitute for mineral oil and of one day substituting electricity for both oil and gas raised questions which could be answered only by further observation and experiment. Such research was already underway, in the private workshops of individual men.

In 1863 John Wigham, an amateur inventor from Dublin,[49] developed a series of gas burners of gradually ascending power which were said to be many times

Faraday a salary of £300 as long as he lived and to offer an additional £400 to Tyndall, wherever "scientific help is constantly needed, especially with the electric light and other experiments" (MT 10/128 [721]. Minute T. H. Farrer, 7 March 1867). The £700 was to be paid half by Trinity House and half by the Board of Trade. Although Capt. Bedford thought the sum quite high, he agreed that "Science should be well paid" (*ibid.*, Minute, Bedford).

The Irish Board, having no long-standing tradition of engineers, was anxious to receive the attentions of a talented scientist (MT 10/128 [2526], Secretary, Irish Lights, to Farrer, 20 July 1867). But the Scottish Board, already equipped with an engineering adviser, had no wish to pay an additional sum for the scientific advice of the Trinity House adviser and resented the Trinity House monopoly of authority (MT 10/128 [1937]. Minute, Bedford, May 1867).

47 The Scottish and Irish Boards were given independent access to Tyndall's services (MT 10/128 [2138]. Farrer to Bedford, 20 June 1867). Tyndall's salary of £400 was ultimately divided as follows : £200 from Trinity House; £200 from the Board of Trade, including £100 from the vote for lighthouses abroad and £100 from the Mercantile Marine Fund. The latter sum represented £50 from the Scottish Board and £50 from the Irish Board. MT 10/128 [118]. Minute, Hamilton, 6 Jan. 1872. See *Correspondence showing the Mode in which the Remuneration to the Scientific Adviser to the Board of Trade and the Trinity House is charged,* 1872.xxxvi.119.

48 *Cf.* J. Tyndall, *Lectures on Light* (delivered in the United States, 1871–1872) (London : Longmans, Green, 1873), and "On Atmosphere in Relation to Fog Signalling," *Contemporary Review,* 1874, 25 : 148–168. In 1872 Sir Frederick Arrow and Capt. Webb visited and inspected the fog signals of the U.S. and Canada, and in 1873 Tyndall advised a special committee of the Board of Trade in an elaborate series of experiments on fog warning devices at South Foreland. Between 1873 and 1884 Trinity House conducted experiments on the comparative value of sirens and whistles actuated by steam and by compressed air from caloric engines. Other experiments were conducted by Trinity House officials in the 1890's, culminating in the studies of sound distribution by Lord Rayleigh's committee in 1901. See Capt. Thomas Golding, *The Trinity House from Within* (London : Smith & Ebbs, 1929), p. 52.

49 John Richardson Wigham (1829–1906). Born in Edinburgh of a Quaker manufacturing family, moved to Dublin at age 14 ; apprenticed to brother-in-law's firm, Edmundson and Co., ultimately succeeding to ownership of firm devoted to providing small gas works for lighting private homes ; became engineer to Commercial Gas Co. of Ireland (designed gas works at Kingstown); and became prominent commercial figure in Dublin. Member of Dublin Society and Royal Irish Academy ; Associate Member, Institution of Civil Engineers, and Fellow of the Institution of Mechanical Engineers. *DNB*, 2nd Suppl., Vol. III, pp. 662–663.

more powerful than oil lamps.[50] Although Wigham enjoyed no official connection with the lighthouse authorities, his apparatus was adopted in 1865 by the Commissioners for Irish Lights, who received Board of Trade sanction for a gas light on Howth Bailey, a promontory in Dublin Bay. When John Tyndall first inspected Howth Bailey lighthouse in 1869, at the invitation of the Board of Trade, he found the beam twelve times as strong as any in England. The light penetrated haze and was powerful enough to give an unmistakable glow during dense fog.[51] After photometric measurements Sir William Thomson eagerly seconded Tyndall's praise.

The use of gas had much to recommend it. Gas burners could be easily lighted and required less constant care; there were no oil lamp glasses to be broken; the flame could be modulated to suit the weather; and when fitted with an automatic flashing apparatus the flame could be varied rapidly in such a way as to send identifying flashes of light in any succession and for any duration. The lighthouse could even be made to spell its own name.[52]

These advantages notwithstanding, there was from the outset a sharp division of opinion about the illuminant's practical usefulness. Although the gas burner produced a brilliant pillar of light, much of the light from the high flame was "ex-focal," hence was diffused into the sky. The opponents of gas said that this light was wasted and that the lower flame of an oil light of the same brightness was preferable, but Wigham insisted that an ex-focal glare could make the lighthouse known in fog when a powerfully condensed beam of light with a small angle of divergence could not. Tyndall concluded, in his report to the Board of Trade in 1869, that gas might "be beaten in point of cheapness by mineral oil, but in point of handiness, distinctiveness, and power of variability to meet the changes of the weather, it will maintain its superiority over all oils."[53] Deeply impressed "on grounds of policy as well as of humanity," Tyndall advised the Board of Trade that "while withholding all countenance from extravagant or fanciful experiments, it would be wise to encourage the gradual, economical and consequent healthy expansion of the system of gas illumination in Ireland."[54] Tyndall purposely restricted his recommendation to Ireland, partly because he thought the method would prove itself to the Scottish and English Boards and partly because he feared arousing personal jealousies. His fears were soon realized.

Six months after Tyndall's report on Howth Bailey, David and Thomas Stevenson, Engineers to the Scottish Lights, reported to the Board of Trade that their experiments had shown gas to be much more expensive than oil for the same

[50] Brewster had prophesied the application of gas to lighthouses in a paper to the Royal Society of Edinburgh in 1827, within a decade of the first use of gas to illuminate towns. Since Wigham's gas devices were the first designed for lighthouses, there seems to have been a "time lag" of 36 years in putting this general knowledge to a new specific purpose.

[51] *Papers relative to a Proposal to Substitute Gas for Oil as an Illuminating Power in Lighthouses*, 1868–1869.[4210].p.1v.

[52] J. Tyndall, "A Story of the Lighthouses," *Fortnight. Rev.*, 1888, *44* : 808.

[53] E. Price Edwards, *Our Seamarks : A Plain Account of the Lighthouses, Lightships, Beacons, Buoys and Fog-signals Maintained on our Coasts for the Guidance of Mariners* (London : Longmans, Green, 1884), p. 50.

[54] Tyndall, *Fortnight. Rev.*, 1888, *44* : 808.

power of light and to give candle-power measurements lower than oil at the same distance. The Stevensons used the standard 4-wick Trinity House oil burner, which had been designed and patented by the Trinity Engineer, James Douglass. The London Gas Referees were asked to investigate these strangely conflicting reports, in which, as Tyndall later quipped, "a quantity of a gas capable of giving a light . . . of 1900 candles was outshone by an oil lamp giving the light of about 270 candles."[55]

The Referees told the Board of Trade that neither Tyndall nor the Stevensons had done their experiments very systematically. The Scots had used particularly inefficient burners, overestimated the need for retort fuel, and miscalculated the amount of gas per ton of coal.[56] The Referees recommended that the Board, to begin afresh, first establish what illuminating power it desired and then work out the cost and feasibility of a light on that basis. This recommendation, however, was administratively impracticable. In the absence of a single agency empowered to take any initiative, all lighthouse authorities argued that the placement, maintenance, cost, and design of their own lighthouse were in danger of being neglected merely for the sake of a more powerful illuminant.

In 1872 Trinity House, deciding to test the Wigham apparatus for itself, investigated the gas light which they installed in the Haisbro' lighthouse on the Norfolk coast. Captain Nisbet, one of the Elder Brethren, called the new light "perfectly beautiful," but it was less easy to prove to mariners its practical superiority at close range. Because gas gave so much ex-focal light, differing relative photometric values for oil and gas stations were recorded when observations were made at different distances. The London Gas Referees accordingly recommended that both lights be tested from different distances, in different weather, over a period of six months.[57]

Without consulting Tyndall, Trinity House appointed an internal committee to act on this recommendation. In March 1873 the committee decided that the 4-wick Trinity House oil burner was 35% more powerful than Wigham's 28-jet gas burner and for practical purposes was as strong as the 48-jet burner.[58]

Not unnaturally, Wigham objected that the Trinity House experiments had been unfairly contrived. He found evidence that the Haisbro' lighthouse keeper had been officially instructed to turn the jet burners only one quarter "on." The Trinity House denied the allegation,[59] but it was difficult to assert that all was well with an experiment which showed a 4-wick burner, yielding 328 candle power, to be equal to a 28-jet burner that gave 832 candle power, and a 68-jet light which gave 1,253 candles to be identical to an oil lamp giving 328 candles.

[55] Further Papers relative to a Proposal to Substitute Gas for Oil as an Illuminating Power in Lighthouses, 1871.[C.282].1xi.15.
[56] Ibid., p. 18.
[57] MT 10/220 [2108]. Reports of J. S. Pierce and R. A. Patterson, 28 June 1872, in Further Papers relative to a Proposal to Substitute Gas for Oil as an Illuminating Power in Lighthouses (hereafter abbreviated

Further Papers), 1875.[C.1151].36.
[58] MT 10/220 [1791]. Secretary, Trinity House, to Assistant Secretary, Harbour Department, Board of Trade, 25 March 1873. Further Papers, 1875.[C.1151].27.
[59] Further Papers, 1875.[C.1151].31–34, Wigham to Robin Allen, Secretary, Trinity House, 29 April 1873; Allen to Wigham, 16 May 1873.

20

Under pressure from Wigham, Trinity House at last requested Tyndall to prepare an official experimental report on the manufacture and cost of the gas at Haisbro'. To avoid "expenditure of time, money and good temper in subsequent controversy," the Elder Brethren agreed to let Wigham's own assistants operate the gas apparatus. In March 1874 Tyndall and his assistant, Mr. Valentin, accompanied by a Committee of Elder Brethren, went aboard the *Galatea* to test officially the effects of the two Haisbro' lighthouses.[60] Arrangements were made to use Douglass' oil lamp in one and Wigham's gas lamp in the other. The lights were viewed along a line equidistant from both lighthouses at points four miles and eight miles from the shore. The consensus was that the 28-jet burner was essentially equal to the 4-wick lamp and that while the second- and third-order 48- and 108-jet burners were vastly more powerful than the ordinary oil lamp, the 108-jet lamp could not be used because of the intense heat it generated against the lens. This left the 48-jet burner as the champion of gas, against which, Tyndall later remarked, "the Trinity 4-wick lamp shrank finally into a mere speck."[61]

But the test was not over. Stimulated by Wigham's competition, Douglass proceeded to contrive a 6-wick oil burner, which he placed in the experimental lighthouse. It was found that this 6-wick lamp gave a light virtually identical in power to Wigham's 48-jet lamp. Upon their return to London, Tyndall reported this new fact to the Board of Trade. He insisted, however, that gas, by virtue of its flexibility for "flashing" and its dispersive glow, was still unmistakably superior.[62] Some officials of the Board of Trade agreed;[63] Trinity House did not. Indeed, the report Trinity House received from Douglass suggested that the 48-jet gas flame burned so high that 31% of its light was wasted. Douglass admitted that he confined his photometric measurements to focal light, which gave the Wigham burner a much higher cost-to-power ratio, but he insisted that the vaunted flexibility of gas did not justify a complete revolution in lighthouse equipment. Where flexibility was required, intermittent oil lamps which would involve no major modifications of the existing system could be used.[64]

Tyndall thought these judgments unfounded. He told Trinity House that even if the gas light "missed" the focal range of the lens system, only 4% was actually "lost." Further, he insisted that Douglass' vague platonic references to oil as a more "superior lighthouse illuminant" were incontrovertibly quashed by considerations of power and ease of manipulation. As Tyndall observed, Douglass'

60 William Valentin was the principal demonstrator in chemistry at the Royal College of Chemistry, South Kensington. The Trinity House committee consisted of Capt. Webb, Capt. Nisbet, and Adm. Collinson. *Further Papers,* 1875.[C.1151].37. Tyndall to Allen, 16 Oct. 1874.

61 Tyndall, *Fortnight. Rev.,* 1888, *44* : 810.

62 "A fixed light a long way off and a ship's light close at hand may be absolutely indistinguishable; and under such circumstances the coast light virtually ceases to be a guide to the mariner . . . . This defect will increase in gravity as our coast lights become more numerous and our ships more improved." *Further Papers,* 1875.[C.1151].38–39 ; Tyndall to Allen, 16 Oct. 1874.

63 Capt. Bedford confirmed Tyndall's views and predicted that even the "prejudice which the Elder Brethren have hitherto felt will . . . have to yield to the results of these repeated trials." MT 10/220 [7863]. Minute, Capt. Bedford, 23 Dec. 1874.

64 *Further Papers,* 1875. [C.1151]. Douglass to Trinity House, 11 Dec. 1874.

assertions begged the whole question; it was unhelpful to be told that were the gas flame reduced so as to render the two lights photometrically equal, the better shape of the new Trinity lamp flame would make it 31% superior. Not wishing to awaken argument, however, Tyndall finally confined himself to repeating his modest recommendation for a mere "partial intercalation" of gas with oil and electricity at Trinity House stations.[65]

This fresh evidence of Tyndall's optimism puzzled Trinity House, who visibly thought him needlessly stubborn. In 1875, after six years of struggle, Tyndall offered to resign. Sir Frederick Arrow, Deputy Master, persuaded him to stay in the hope that some compromise agreement could be reached, and eventually the Elder Brethren promised that Haisbro' would be given gas lamps permanently. But relations between Tyndall and Trinity House continued to deteriorate. At a distance, technological innovation seemed sacrificed to arbitrary principles of expedience and economy.

DESPAIR AND DEFIANCE: THE BOARD OF TRADE
VERSUS "IRISH INVENTION"

In 1878 the Commissioners for Irish Lights had built upon the promontory of Galley Head, which guarded forty-two miles of dangerous Irish coastline between Cape Clear and the Old Head of Kinsale, a "group flashing" quadriform gas light, on the model supplied by Wigham.[66] It was, Tyndall later remarked, "the offspring of individual genius, untrammelled by routine, coming first hand into contact with a question which required for its expansion both energy and originality."[67] A single 68-jet burner gave a power of 1,253 candles, but this burner gave 5,012 candles, or about fifteen times as much power. Shortly after its completion the Elder Brethren visited the lighthouse with their engineer. Tyndall was not invited. Not surprisingly, Douglass' report was hostile. On the basis of detailed calculations which excited Tyndall's cynical admiration[68] Douglass persuaded the Elder Brethren that oil was still preferable.

In May 1879 Tyndall was asked by the anxious Irish Commissioners to discover what truth lay in Douglass' assertions. Tyndall accordingly set out on the *Princess Alexandra* to Galley Head, where, with William Douglass, brother of James and recently appointed Engineer to the Irish Board, he tested the lights and found them quite as good as before.[69] William Douglass went on record at the time as agreeing completely. Some time later, however, Tyndall was surprised to see a statement appended by William Douglass to the Galley Head report in which he denied having made any such statement and further alleged that Tyndall had confused his comments about the distinctiveness of the light with his comments about its power. Tyndall was unable to explain Douglass' equivocation. But other

[65] *Further Papers*, 1875.[C.1151]. Tyndall to Allan, 21 Jan. 1875.

[66] Tyndall, *Fortnight. Rev.*, 1888, *44* : 822.

[67] *Ibid.*, p. 816.

[68] "I do not know a more skilful advocate than Sir James Douglass. The dexterity with which he manages, by the introduction of outlying points, to 'o'er inform' the reader, and damage his opponent's case, has often excited my admiration" (*ibid.*, p. 817).

[69] J. Tyndall, *Letters to Papers of London and Dublin* (Dublin: R. D. Webb & Sons, 1883), Vol. I, pp. 2–5 (Trinity House Library).

research and his lectures at the Royal Institution demanded his attention. After writing a remonstrance to Farrer he let the matter rest.[70]

Meanwhile the Board of Trade grew apprehensive about these expensive and seemingly unending tests. Establishment clerks Charles Cecil Trevor[71] and R. G. C. Hamilton[72] were startled to learn that one Trinity House experiment alone had cost over £850, which had to be met from the Mercantile Marine Fund. Trevor cautiously warned Trinity House that "we might . . . generally point out that if so large an expenditure is necessary in placing a gas light establishment in working order, the Board of Trade will have great hesitation in sanctioning its extension."[73] Trevor had other worries as well. For over a year the Board of Trade and Wigham had been arguing over the question of royalties for the multiform burner device. The long correspondence ended with a grant of £2,500 to Wigham, which the Board wearily welcomed as a "satisfactory termination to a disagreeable dispute."[74] The experience of this bitter contest did not, however, dispose the Board to take a more favorable view of Wigham or the claim of the Irish Lights which he seemed to represent. Captain Bedford actually looked forward to ending his experiments altogether.[75]

As the years went by, the Board's patience with Tyndall also began to wane. Thomas Farrer and Tyndall had formerly been close friends for many years. It was Farrer who had initially drawn Tyndall's attention to the introduction of gas into Irish lighthouses.[76] In 1875 it was Farrer who had agreed that his Board "ought to encourage the experiments and observations Tyndall wishes to be made" and who had cordially sanctioned the Irish Commissioners' expenses.[77] For his part Tyndall had repaid the compliment of cooperation many times over.[78] But this peace did not last. When Tyndall abdicated his lighthouse work

---

[70] *Ibid.*, p. 6.

[71] Charles (afterward Sir Charles) Cecil Trevor (1830–1921), C.B., 1882, K.C.B., 1896; Rugby; St. Catherine's, Cambridge; Barrister, Lincoln's Inn, 1855; Assistant Secretary, Board of Trade, 1867–1895; Conservator of River Thames, 1895–1906. Delegate to North Sea Fishery Conference 1881–1882, to Submarine Cables Conference, 1882–1883 and 1886, to North Sea Liquor Traffic Conference, 1886, and to Channel Fisheries Negotiations, 1886.

[72] Robert G. C. (afterward Sir Robert) Hamilton (1836–1895); University and King's College, Aberdeen, 1854; clerk in commissariat in Crimea, 1855; Education Finance Department, 1861; accountant, 1869; Assistant Secretary, Board of Trade, 1872–1878; afterward Accountant General of the Navy, Permanent Secretary to the Admiralty, Under-Secretary for Ireland, and Governor of Tasmania; K.C.B., 1844. *DNB*, Suppl. Vol. II, p. 382.

[73] MT 10/220 [3288]. Trevor, Minute, 23 April 1875.

[74] MT 10/220 [3288]. Hamilton, Minute, 17 Aug. 1876.

[75] "I think we may congratulate the Board in having escaped a very serious expense in these fog experiments, with Wigham ; after all, suppose it were more successful? What then? Are we to put up flash lights for fog signals? I really think we have paid dearly enough for Wigham's experiments already." Hamilton concurred, adding that "experiments in Ireland are a mistake. The Commons neither check expenditure nor assist in coming to just conclusions regarding them." MT 10/211 [8495]. Minutes, Bedford and Hamilton, 2 Dec. 1875.

[76] Tyndall, *Nineteenth Cent.*, 1888, 24 : 64–65.

[77] MT 10/211 [6704]. Farrer to Jennings, 24 Sept., 1875. For example, when Tyndall learned that the Irish Lights Engineer requested £700 for experiments with Wigham's burner, he advised Farrer that the sum "in relation to the object in hand is so astoundingly large that I cannot ask the Board to grant it." The sum was reduced, and the Board acknowledged its thanks.

[78] MT 10/211 [8225]. Tyndall to Farrer, 17 Nov., 1875.

From "Lighthouses," Leisure Hour, 1862, 11:665.

24

for the sake of his lectures Farrer himself went to Galley Head. Although he made no new experiments, he returned to London convinced that the multiform gas light was not greatly superior to a single tier of oil burners and would prove vastly more expensive.[79] Farrer achieved what he thought was a consensus but by implication cast doubt on the integrity of Tyndall's testimony.

In October 1879, four months after the Galley Head experiments, Wigham asked the Irish Commissioners to install a light on Copeland Island, near Belfast. The ensuing discussions exposed the cul-de-sac into which the Board of Trade had maneuvered itself. William Douglass advised the Commissioners that the 6-wick Trinity burner was superior to Wigham's burner. When the matter went through channels to Trinity House the secretary, acting perhaps more by custom than deliberate delay, approved the Engineer's recommendation. The Harbour Department, given Douglass' comparative estimates and the Trinity House reports on the expense of Wigham's experiments, refused to sanction the expense of a gas light at Copeland. No sooner had they done so, however, than they sanctioned a sum for oil improvements at Copeland which greatly exceeded Wigham's estimate for the introduction of gas.

This impolitic maneuver aroused an immediate furor. Lord Meath, Lord Monck, Sir John Barrington (the Lord Mayor of Dublin), and other leading Irishmen protested strongly to the Board. On 18 May 1880 the Board relented.[80] It proceeded, however, to ruin the effect of its concession by insisting that the gas light be supervised by William Douglass—the Irish Engineer, to be sure, but also brother to James. The Board's preoccupation with paper formality had unwittingly placed it in a position where it was discriminating against a private individual, and worse, an Irish inventor. Tyndall's pronounced sympathies toward the Irish on the home rule question were well known; this latest evidence of ostensible discrimination against Ireland and the Irish roused his temper to flashpoint.

In 1880 Joseph Chamberlain became president of the Board of Trade. The arrival of a well-known and aggressive Liberal reformer gave Wigham fresh hope, and at Wigham's instance Tyndall went to explain the position to the new president.

Tyndall's defense of Wigham was not unique. He had before defied authority and defended those whom he thought unfairly treated or compromised.[81] But in Wigham's case Tyndall saw himself pitted against a particularly obnoxious form of bureaucracy: "Mr. Wigham was a comparative stranger to me," Tyndall later reminisced, "but I saw his personal merit and his value to the State. I could by no means stand by and see him wrongfully borne down by mere authority."[82]

[79] Tyndall, *Fortnight. Rev.*, 1888, *45* : 199.

[80] *Ibid.*, p. 823; *The Times*, 10 Jan. 1885.

[81] See, e.g., his defense of Julius Mayer in the priority dispute concerning the discovery of the law of energy conservation, and his differences with James David Forbes on glacial action, *DNB*, Vol. XLVII, p. 35.

[82] Tyndall, *Fortnight. Rev.*, 1888, *44* : 813. "In what I did myself I may have offended against the canons of red tape ; if so, it was not for the first time. When red tape means order, I stand by it, but when it means obstruction and oppression, my deference to it ends" (Tyndall, *Letters to Papers of London and Dublin*, Vol. II, p. 8).

Tyndall gave Chamberlain a copy of Wigham's protest against the appointment of William Douglass at Copeland Island and appealed for the president's personal intervention.[83] Chamberlain agreed to let Wigham control the Copeland lighthouse. The light was moved to the superior position of Mew Island, County Down, where the new gas light was soon acclaimed by masters and shipping companies using the Channel routes.[84] Shortly afterward the Board also conceded to the introduction of gas at Tory Island. But the issue had already ceased to be a philosophically neutral question of scientific fact, susceptible to convincing proof by quantitative methods; it had become a question of application, involving preferences and requiring choices to be made on grounds of economy, convenience, and expedience. As such it had become caught between forceful opposing personalities who viewed each other with increasing acrimony and distrust.

Thus, Tyndall accused Trinity House of conspiring against an innocent man and condemned the Board of Trade for relying upon Farrer's impressionable visit to Galley Head in assessing Wigham's photometric evidence. "Trained in administration," Tyndall argued, "and worthy of all respect as an administrator, I fear that at Galley Head, Sir Thomas Farrer entered a field which his previous culture had not entitled him to occupy."[85] For his part, Farrer grew resentful of Wigham,[86] distrustful of Tyndall, and skeptical of the Irish Board.

THE POLITICS OF CRITICAL EXPERIMENTS

In early 1882 Chamberlain set out to end this chronic feud. He instructed Farrer to begin a series of experiments which would "bring to a final and conclusive issue" the comparative merits of gas and oil.[87] Tyndall asked the Elder Brethren to compare the highest quality of oil illumination actually maintained by the Trinity House Engineer in England with the highest quality of gas illumi-

---

[83] Tyndall added (*Letters to Papers of London and Dublin,* Vol. II, p. 7):

Speaking as an observer who stands apart from all private interest of professional jealousy in regard to this question, and mindful solely of the well-being of our seafaring men, I need say that, should the opponents of the gas system have their way, the most powerful beacon flames ever placed in a dioptric apparatus for the benefit of the mariner will be withheld from our coasts, while a most salutary and effective stimulus to other inventors will cease to act as it has obviously hitherto done.

This letter is not included in the collected correspondence published in the several Returns to the House of Commons. Farrer felt that Tyndall's appeal was in poor taste (*ibid.,* p. 8).

[84] Tyndall, *Fortnight. Rev.,* 1888, 44 : 825.

[85] *Ibid.,* 1889, 45 : 200.

[86] "[The Board] feel bound to add that, in their opinion, you have from the beginning injured your own case, even with those who were most anxious to support what was good in your invention, by irregular communications and suggestions concerning the activities of others, which, insofar as concerns the Engineers of Trinity House and Commissioners of Irish Lights, should never have been made." Farrer to Wigham (*c.* 1880), quoted in Tyndall, *Fortnight Rev.,* 1888, p. 82.

[87] *Correspondence on the Subject of a Proposed Investigation into the Respective Merits of Gas, Oil and Electricity as Lighthouse Illuminants* (hereafter abbreviated *Correspondence*), 1883.(168).3. J. Tyndall to Assistant Secretary, Board of Trade, 25 Jan. 1882. This Parliamentary Paper includes transcripts of 112 letters, written over the 20 months between 3 Oct. 1881 to 11 May 1883, or an average of two letters a week.

nation experimentally achieved by Wigham in Ireland. Tyndall also asked that the two systems be compared by reference to their value in their own countries of origin, without prejudicing any possible application of the method of one country to the lighthouses of the other. He wished

> to make it appear, by a strict comparison of what [Wigham] had done with what his rival had done, how criminal it would be to quench a genius so fertile, and so greatly needed, merely because his works outshone those of a competitor who enjoyed the joy and sympathy of the Trinity House and the Board of Trade.[88]

Arrangements for the experiment were made at Howth Bailey in September 1882. Douglass was to use the Howth Bailey lighthouse itself, where he installed his new 8-wick lamp. Wigham himself was given a shed adjacent to the lighthouse for the 48-jet gas burner. The scene, as later described by Tyndall, was hardly chivalrous: "On the one side, stood the magnificent corporation, and their well-paid Engineer, with his workshops and assistants; on the other, stood a man absolutely unaided, save through the scant protection that my position enabled me to afford him."[89] Upon the recommendation of Douglass[90] electric-light machinery was also included in the experimental apparatus, despite Tyndall's objection that the electric light would divide and divert attention from the most important comparison at hand.[91]

Tyndall's own role in the inquiry was initially uncertain. On 8 March 1882, in what he claimed to be his first "strong expression of feeling" against the government, Tyndall had privately indicted Trinity House for its indifference to innovation:

> It was long my hope that [Sir James Douglass] and Mr. Wigham might be brought to work together for the public good. This hope, I regret to say, has not been fulfilled. The attitude of Mr. Douglass towards the gas system, and towards the optical devices of its inventor, has weakened their usefulness and retarded their development. It would be wholly unreasonable to suppose that had the system been encouraged it would not have reached a higher point of power and perfection than that at which it now stands. But while every encouragement has been given —in my opinion, most wisely—to the development of the oil system, it has been

---

88 *Ibid.*, p. 203.
89 *Ibid.*, p. 204.
90 Trinity House, replying to Tyndall's attack on Douglass' report, urged the Board of Trade to broaden the base of comparison. Robin Allen argued :

> For stations where the greatest power of the oil light is deemed inadequate, the problem appears to be whether it is well to pause contented with what seems to the Elder Brethren a rude and imperfect middle course, or proceed to the use of the most powerful illuminant known, which is also perfect on those points in which the gas is most difficult, . . .

91 Tyndall predicted that the brilliant electric light would be used in the future on important land falls but that its greater cost and doubtful performance in fog would restrict its use to only a few locations (*Fortnight. Rev.*, 1889, 45 : 203, 205):

> Until the superiority of the electric light in fog is placed upon a far surer basis than that on which it now rests, I would say, let the important land falls of Ireland, at all events, be illuminated by a light indigenous to the soil, and to which all the later improvements of the flame-beacons of England are directly traceable (*ibid.*, p. 211).

withheld—in my opinion most unwisely—from the development of its rival. Those who are aware of the strength of my antagonism to any scheme tending to separate Ireland from England will be able to give due weight to the declaration which I here make, that if the test of the gas invention and its optical adjuncts could be regarded as a fair sample of the general treatment of Ireland by England, it would be the bounden duty of every Irishman to become a Home Ruler.[92]

Under the pressure of competing demands on his time, Tyndall had asked to be spared further correspondence for five weeks. Shortly afterward, having heard nothing more from the Board of Trade, he left England for his annual holiday in the Alps.

While Tyndall was still abroad, Farrer instructed Trinity House to begin the projected series of experiments on oil, gas, and electricity in haze and fog. In early August Farrer informally secured the help of Augustus Vernon Harcourt, F.R.S., formerly a Gas Referee for the Board and at that time Lee's Reader in Chemistry at Oxford, as chairman of the examining committee. It was decided to begin experimental work in October, when Tyndall returned. However, Farrer also suggested that the three official engineers (Sir James Douglass for Trinity House, his brother for Ireland, and Thomas Stevenson for the Scottish Lights) should serve on the committee with Harcourt and Tyndall.

No news of this arrangement was sent to Tyndall until late September, when the Irish Board informed him of Farrer's plans. Tyndall immediately remonstrated with Chamberlain against appointing to such a committee three engineers all well-known opponents of gas—two of whom were brothers and one the patentee of the oil lamp. Tyndall also pointed out that Douglass was being allowed to use his most advanced oil lamp while Wigham was being denied the use of the triform apparatus which he himself had invented. Tyndall demanded that Douglass and Wigham be placed "on the same level" in the committee.

The Elder Brethren replied that it was undesirable to let the Trinity House Engineer be appointed to a committee on a level with a mere Dublin "trader" who had taken out a patent for his invention.[93] In any event J. Inglis, Secretary of Trinity House, denied that there was any rivalry between them and insisted that Douglass' advice was necessary for a decision based on "practical nautical efficiency." But what Inglis neglected to reveal was that James Douglass' patent had recently appeared in a prospectus advertising shares in "The Improved Gas and

[92] *Correspondence,* 1883.(168) Tyndall to J. Inglis, Secretary, Trinity House, 8 March 1882; Tyndall, *Fortnight. Rev.,* 1889, *45* : 212.

[93] Trinity House reasoning was as follows :

Mr. Wigham, the patentee of the composite gas burner, is a manufacturer, constructing and vending to the lighthouse authorities, not only the burner itself, but the whole gas-making apparatus connected with it, he has incurred the expense of a patent, and will reap substantial profit at the hands of the shipowners in the event of success after these trials. Sir James Douglass, is not a manufacturer nor a trader in oil ; he has himself incurred the expense of a patent without any contribution by the Corporation, and has granted the free use of it to all the Lighthouse Boards, so that he makes no profit whatever by success, and the only benefittee is the shipowner (*Correspondence,* 1883. (168).24, Inglis to the Board of Trade, 28 Oct. 1882).

Oil Burners Co. Ltd.''[94] Although he had made no charge to the lighthouse authorities for his patents, Douglass had used public funds to promote a private company which could buy his invention and transfer it to other countries.[95] Such were the circumstances in which Wigham's rival was made his judge.

The Board of Trade to all intents and purposes tried to make the Illuminants Committee fair and representative. Assistant Secretary Henry Calcraft, learning of Tyndall's objection, told Trinity House that Douglass' pecuniary interest in the burner logically seemed to "disqualify him from acting on a committee which has a quasi-judicial character, though it does not prevent him from giving his most valuable aid and advice to the Committee."[96] Under pressure from the Board, Inglis, while still insisting that his engineer should not "accept a position derogatory to his standing," agreed to let him be *amicus curiae* and to appoint Captain Edward Nisbet as the voting member for Trinity House. Two months later Farrer's proposed committee of ten was completed and included James Douglass and his brother as well as Thomas Stevenson, a second Scottish representative, and Dr. John Hopkinson[97] to represent the "interests" of electricity. The list was sent to Tyndall as a *fait accompli* one month later. With Nisbet as chairman, the committee constituted a small but axiomatic majority against Tyndall and Wigham.

Smarting from the veiled insult of being refused the chairmanship and believing the committee flagrantly unfair,[98] Tyndall refused to serve in any capacity. Farrer, bewildered by this rejection of what seemed an equitable compromise, asked him to stay. But Tyndall bitterly replied:

> . . . what am I to do—holding, as I firmly hold, the action of late years by the Board of Trade, towards the great improvements in lighthouse illumination which

[94] Chamberlain was questioned in the Commons four times during 1885 about Douglass' dealings. Although the story remains shrouded in mystery, it seems that Douglass received £500 for his patent plus £25,000 worth of stock in the company. Possibly under pressure from Trinity House, the company wound up its dealings in the U.K. in Oct. 1884. Douglas thereafter formed another company, which concentrated its activities outside the U.K. Hansard, *Parliamentary Debates*, Third Series, 29.c.1119–1120 (the first number is the volume; the second, the column); 295.c. 92–93; 296.c.825; 297.c.1634; 298.c.705.

[95] Tyndall apparently did not know this until some years later, when at last he publicly questioned the "patriotic disinterestedness" claimed by Trinity House. The story was even suppressed in the correspondence between Vernon Harcourt and the Board of Trade, published by Parliament in the early months of 1883. (See *Correspondence*, 1883. (168).31; Harcourt to Board of Trade, 18 Nov. 1882, with notable elisions.) It now appeared, however, that the Board of Trade

had permitted Douglass to use public funds and laboratory facilities in perfecting apparatus which was subsequently patented and sold on the open market.

[96] *Ibid.*, p. 25. Calcraft to Inglis, 4 Nov. 1882.

[97] John Hopkinson (1849–1898), electrical engineer; educated Owen's College, Manchester, and Trinity College, Cambridge; D.Sc., London, 1871; manager and engineer in lighthouse and optical department of Messrs. Chance Ltd., Birmingham, 1872–1878; F.R.S. 1878; patented 3-wire system of distributing electricity, 1882 ; designed practical dynamo, 1886; professor of electrical engineering, King's College, London, 1890; consulting engineer to contractors of City and South London Railway; member of Council of Institution of Civil Engineers; M.I.E.E.; occupied "a dual position in the world of theory and in that of practice." See B. Hopkinson, ed., *Original Papers by the late John Hopkinson, D.Sc., F.R.S.* (Cambridge: Cambridge Univ. Press, 1901), p. lxi.

[98] *The Times*, 8 Nov. 1884.

we owe to Ireland to be adverse to the public interest, and opposed to the evidence at once strong, clear and unimpeachable.[99]

Tyndall then proposed an alternative committee of nine, including four representatives of each "side" and Harcourt, and he insisted that the concurrence of the Irish Board—the only board, he said, "of which I am in any sincere sense the scientific adviser"—should be obtained. But Chamberlain officially rebuked Tyndall for exceeding his authority and expressed regret that "so much personal feeling should be introduced to prejudice what ought to be a purely scientific and practical inquiry into facts and results."[100] Tyndall insisted that his reports were "not news or opinions, but demonstrations,"[101] and that this contest had become "a struggle of single handed talent against official power."[102] Nevertheless, under pressure from the Board of Trade the Irish Lights, "like Aesop's reed," withdrew their objection to Farrer's committee and Tyndall was left fighting alone. On 28 March 1883 he informed the president that "these wranglings must now cease. I might have ended them earlier had not the lives of our sailors, and those in their charge, been in a measure implicated in the discussion."[103] With that, Tyndall resigned.

THE DENOUEMENT

Tyndall's action awakened some interest among Irish M.P.'s and the popular press. Edward Gibson (afterward Baron Ashbourne)[104] and Colonel King-Harman asked for a public explanation and for some effort to "prevent the services of this eminent man being lost to the country."[105] The *Daily Express* attacked Chamberlain for his nonchalant acquiescence in a one-sided committee which was, by ministering to the self-interest of the Board of Trade and Trinity House, attempting "to make a fair trial impossible, and to secure a foregone conclusion."[106] The *Irish Times* interpreted the published correspondence and Tyndall's resignation as

[99] *Correspondence*, 1883.(168).39. Tyndall to Farrer, 9 Feb. 1883.

[100] *Ibid.*, pp. 43–44, Chamberlain to Tyndall, 20 Feb. 1883.

[101] A month later he wrote, "Both sides were before me, and if I pronounced in favor of one, this, I submit, is the normal process of judgment. You would not have me play the part of John Bunyan's Mr. Facing-both-ways?" . . . "The unbiased evidence of science had been given, and it was the disregard of that evidence, resulting in manifest danger to a most valuable invention, that first introduced into the discussion the warmth needed in opposing a moral wrong." *Correspondence*, 1883.(168).52. Tyndall to Chamberlain, 28 March 1883.

[102] *Ibid.*, p. 47. Tyndall to Chamberlain, 26 Feb. 1883.

[103] Tyndall, *Fortnight. Rev.*, 1889, 45 : 218. With emotion he added :
. . . my resignation of the post of scienti-

fic Adviser to the Trinity House shall also be dispatched today. It is not without a wrench that I sever myself from the Elder Brethren, with whom I have worked long in friendship and from whom I have ever received the utmost personal kindness and consideration. While differing from them, I respect them, for they have acted, I doubt not, according to their lights, as I have according to mine.

[104] Hansard, 279.c.28; *Tyndall Papers*, Diary entry, 8 May 1883; *The Times*, 11 May 1883. Edward Gibson (1837–1913), Trinity College, Dublin; Conservative M.P. for Dublin University, 1875; Irish Attorney General, 1877–1880; Baron, 1885. Lord Chancellor of Ireland, 1886–1892, 1895–1905. *DNB* (1950), p. 169.

[105] Hansard, 279.c.520. Tyndall remained associated with the Board of Trade in his capacity as a Gas Referee until 1887.

[106] *Daily Express*, 6 and 12 June 1883.

symptomatic of the government's "systematic injustice" toward Irish inventors.[107] Even the *St. James Gazette* expressed sympathy with Tyndall.[108]

Chamberlain did not attempt to explain Tyndall's resignation,[109] but Lord Sudeley neatly turned Tyndall's half-reference to home rule into a possible political motive, and the Duke of Argyll with lethal kindness conjectured that Tyndall's error arose from a misplaced patriotic support of a fellow Irishman.[110] The imputation was absurd. Wigham was a Scot who merely worked in Ireland, and Tyndall had not lived in Ireland for years. But the public received the impression that Tyndall's action had been prejudiced, rash, and unnecessary.[111] *The Times* endorsed the Establishment line,[112] and Tyndall, whose impartiality had led him to espouse Wigham, stood convicted of partiality on Wigham's behalf.[113]

Following his resignation the Illuminants Committee enjoyed an ephemeral burst of life. Sir James Douglass was placed on the committee as a voting member, while Wigham was not. With John Hopkinson's appointment, the balance of members was weighted overwhelmingly against the Irish Board,[114] which after much vacillation announced their withdrawal "from all participation in the contemplated experiments." Nevertheless, this "rump" committee met through May and June and into July. At Douglass' instance they decided to conduct tests with a

107 *The Irish Times*, 9 June 1883.

108 "The lives of sailors are at stake in this manner, and as Mr. Chamberlain is never tired of making political capital by charging unprincipled shipowners with drowning their seamen in 'the reckless pursuit of unholy gain,' he ought to have no hesitation in taking care that while he casts out the mote from the shipowner's eye he doesn't neglect the beam in his own" (*St. James Gazette*, 15 June 1883). Chamberlain had associated himself with Samuel Plimsoll's agitation and had supported Plimsoll's abortive bill of 1874. See n. 160 below.

109 Hansard, 279.c.520. Chamberlain replied only that the committee had not been imposed; that the three boards had simply been asked to send representatives; and that he had had no success in overcoming Tyndall's objections. Tyndall did not abdicate his position altogether. Following Chamberlain's remarks in Commons, he wrote : "It was not so cocky and off-hand as his first answer to Mr. Gibson, but he managed with some adroitness to put things out of true relations and to come perilously near untruth. I suppose he has found such tactics successful, but I fear that in the present instance he will find himself disabused" (*Tyndall Papers*, diary entry, 12 May 1883).

110 Hansard, 280.c.1103–1112. Argyll's *coup de grace* summarily dismissed the question as merely a "case of an Irish invention *versus* an English invention."

111 Having exercised a few platitudes, Lord Sudeley described Tyndall as a "gentleman" of "high character, straightforwardness and independence. But it was no discredit to him to say that he had the character that, when once he had formed an opinion, it was almost impossible to get him to alter it. The President of the Board of Trade had felt he was bound, as a Trustee, to look upon the matter from a practical point of view" (Hansard, 280.c.1108).

112 "We cannot doubt that the general feeling of the public will be one of regret at the loss of Professor Tyndall's services, tempered by a concurrence with the opinion expressed by the Duke of Argyll, to the effect that the Professor has made a mistake" (*The Times*, 22 June 1883).

113 Hansard, 280.c.1108.

114 *Correspondence*, 1883.(168).57. The committee began with Nisbet, Douglass, J. A. Crichton, T. Stevenson, Robert Ball, William Douglass, A. V. Harcourt, and J. Hopkinson. See Allen Stoneham, Board of Trade to Nisbet, Trinity House, 4 April 1883. Chamberlain at first denied that Hopkinson had been associated with Trinity House (Hansard, 279c.1744) but later admitted that Hopkinson was the scientific adviser to Messrs. Chance of Birmingham, the glass manufacturers who enjoyed a virtual monopoly on lighthouse work undertaken by Trinity House.

biform light (which was the highest power oil lamp at Eddystone) but to exclude the quadriform light (such as that which existed at Galley Head), despite the fact that the latter was eight times more powerful than the former.[115] This policy did not long escape criticism: indeed, Douglass' bias eventually annoyed even Thomas Stevenson.[116] In May 1883 Dr. (later Sir Robert) Ball, the Irish astronomer, resigned in disgust,[117] and by mid-July the rest of the committee had dissolved.[118] Under the circumstances it was widely agreed that no decision the committee could make would have been regarded as final or conclusive. To a question in Parliament Chamberlain replied that he had "no longer any hope of bringing [the three lighthouse authorities] into unanimous agreement."[119] The three authorities were requested to submit all future proposals for illuminants testing individually, "and the Board of Trade will endeavour to meet their individual wishes, subject of course to general consideration of expense and efficiency."[120]

Beginning in late July Tyndall released the whole story to the press.[121] What had begun as scientific difference of opinion and had developed into a departmental and parliamentary incident now exploded into a question of public morality. Because Tyndall's letters implied that the superiority of gas had been established and that the lighthouse authorities were categorically to blame for not adopting it, their publication had the effect of making his "martyrdom" complete.

Tyndall assured his readers that the Elder Brethren were well intentioned but that they had followed too closely the devices and desires of their own engineers and had closed their minds to external innovation:

> I warned them loyally and repeatedly as to the inevitable result of that course; but they deemed me a partisan, and finding at the Board of Trade a President whose views for the moment chimed in with their own, they united with him in proceedings which ended in the wreck of a relation of seventeen years' standing.[122]

Tyndall found Chamberlain guilty of relying on biased officials, of financial hypocrisy, and of "grinding despotism" in refusing to give Wigham's claims a fair test.[123]

---

[115] Chamberlain hesitated but essentially admitted this in the Commons (Hansard, 281.c.44–45). Harcourt argued, perhaps rightly, that testing with single or double devices should have sufficed because the effects of multiplication would be proportionately equal. See *Further Correspondence on the Subject of the Composition of the Lighthouse Illuminants Committee* (hereafter abbreviated *Further Correspondence*), 1883.(263).11. Harcourt to Farrer, 23 June 1883.

[116] *Tyndall Papers*, diary entry, 8 June 1883.

[117] *Further Correspondence*, 1883.(263).6. Ball to Board of Trade, 30 May 1883; Tyndall, *Fortnight. Rev.* 1889, p. 219.

[118] *Tyndall Papers*, diary entry, telegram from Wigham, 12 July 1883.

[119] Hansard, 281.c.1892.

[120] *Further Correspondence*, 1883.(263).14, Farrer to Trinity House, 10 July 1883.

[121] Tyndall, *Letters to Papers of London and Dublin*, Vol. I, pp. 1–5.

[122] *Ibid.*, Vol. II, p. 10.

[123] His "offending," said Tyndall, lay only in

> . . . my effort to protect from extinction an able and a meritorious man, who had the misfortune to raise a rival at the Trinity House, and to ruffle the dignity of the gentlemen of the Board of Trade. Struggling single-handed, relying solely on his own industry and talents and with no public funds to fall back upon at pleasure, Mr. John Wigham . . . during the brief period of his permitted activity, had made advances in the act of lighthouse illumination which placed him far ahead of all competitors. This man I did my best to

Chamberlain replied publicly to Tyndall's attack, claiming that Tyndall's behavior had departed "so widely from the judicial impartiality which is the ordinary characteristic of men of science,"[124] and had compounded his error of judgment by "unworthy and ungenerous insinuations against the personal integrity of those who had the misfortune to differ from him on a matter which ought to be capable of scientific determination."[125]

The issue had become so controversial that over a year elapsed before the Trinity House again approached the Board of Trade for sanction to conduct further experiments.[126] The Board of Trade witnessed the irony of a committee composed solely of Elder Brethren, with no scientific adviser, who chose to move the experiments to the South Foreland where land was purchased, rooms were built, and fresh equipment was provided at a cost of £4,000, ten times the cost of Tyndall's proposed trials at Howth Bailey the year before.[127] The work went forward; representatives from the Commissioners of Irish Lights and the Commissioners of Northern Lights were invited, as were representatives of the shipping interests of the United States, France, and eight other countries. But any hopes that this calculated maneuver would produce objective results were soon disappointed. In December, without having made tests with the improved quadriform gas light, Trinity House declared its experiments at an end.

In its report, issued the following year, the committee concluded that gas was too expensive for the power achieved; that "for the ordinary necessities of lighthouse illumination, mineral oil is the suitable and economical illuminant and that for salient headlands, important land falls and places where a very powerful light is required, electricity offers the greatest advantage."[128] The report against

protect from the effects of personal jealousy and bureaucratic irritation . . . . It was my earnest desire to utilise Mr. Wigham's genius for the public good. It was the object of officials whom he had offended to extinguish him. They did what they could to weary him, worry him, and take the heart of enterprise out of him ; and they certainly succeeded in checking the development of his system . . . . Had it not been for an opposition which, considering the interests at stake, seemed to me at times criminal, that system would assuredly be far more advanced than it now is. (*The Times*, 25 Nov. 1884.) These comments were collected and published privately by Wigham in pamphlet form, to Tyndall's considerable annoyance, in 1885 (*Tyndall Papers*, diary entry, 8 Feb. 1885).

[124] Chamberlain continued :
A review of all the circumstances connected with the Committee . . . will show that the arrogance of which the Professor complains consists in my inability to adopt . . . his opinion on a question involving a large expenditure of public money as to

which he was at issue with the most experienced practical authorities, and in my endeavour to protect from unworthy and ungenerous insinuations the characters of scientific men as honourable as himself and equally entitled to respectful consideration. (*The Times*, 10 Nov. 1884.)

[125] *The Times*, 17 Nov. 1884.

[126] *Nature*, 1884, *30* : 362–363; Hansard, 284.c.883.

[127] The final cost of the South Foreland experiments actually exceeded £8,800 (*Further Correspondence*, 1887.(i).lxxiii.89).

[128] *Report to the Trinity House of Deptford Strond on the Investigations made by the Committee of its members into the Relative Merits of Electricity, Gas and Oil as Lighthouse Illuminants*, Pt. I, 1884–1885. [c.4551].lxx.69. *Fairplay*, 4 Feb. 1887, p. 18. *Nature* remained objective and aloof from the debate : "the general result of a very large number of observations appears to have been that there is but little to choose between oil and gas as far as their illuminating powers are concerned, and that electricity is greatly superior to both" (1886, *33* : 281).

gas did not arouse much surprise. Wigham found it "unequalled as a record of partisan proceedings by a public department,"[129] and the *Daily Express*, not without glee, denounced the report as yet another chapter in the "history of jobbery and scheming" of the Trinity House.[130] But *The Times* assured its readers that "the minds of the average landsmen will have no difficulty in accepting the general conclusion of the Committee."[131] *The Irish Times* refused to accept the report as final:

> . . . the question arises, will the mercantile community be satisfied to adopt the advice of the Trinity House, and substitute for a light which they pronounce to be unquestionably superior, anything inferior to it, for the sake of a paltry saving in cost. . . . We venture to think that the unanimous voice of the community will be against them in this conclusion.[132]

But this was too easy an assumption. Trinity House and the Board of Trade had become convinced of the impracticability of gas on the unassailable grounds of cost. The Galley Head, although built without any of the difficult structural problems plaguing the Eddystone or Wolf Rock lights, had cost more than £20,000, and the annual maintenance cost of its gas burners was said to exceed any in the world.[133] Even if gas lights generally gave a more powerful light, gas lights in diform or triform lamps were 2¼ times as expensive to use as oil at first-order power.[134] Trinity House was inclined to prefer an adequate light at nominal cost, rather than a vastly more powerful light at twice the price. The Board of Trade felt that if research and development could eventually make gas more economical, oil could be made proportionately more so. Thus, development costs on improvements of the 6-wick oil dioptric could be more easily justified to a parsimonious Treasury.

In fact, once the authorities had settled on what constituted the "better" illu-

---

[129] J. Wigham, "Irish Lighthouses and the Board of Trade," *Fairplay*, 21 Jan. 1887.

[130] *Daily Express*, 1 Sept. 1885.

[131] *Glasgow Herald*, 8 Sept. 1885 :

They opposed the introduction on the Irish coast again and again . . . . They became bound, of course, as the new plan of gas illumination was extended from one lighthouse to another, to take special cognisance of the matter. That they did in the most grudging spirit. When the lighthouse at Galley Head had made its famous mark among the sea signals of the world, they paid it a visit, but . . . reported against it by the hand of their engineer. It was this increasing animosity to gas as a lighthouse illuminant that formed the main cause of the rupture with Professor Tyndall.

[132] *The Irish Times*, 29 Aug. 1885; cf. *The Freemason's Journal*, 31 Aug. 1885.

[133] The Trinity House committee judged

that the annual maintenance costs at comparable orders of intensity were £20,000 for gas, £17,000 for electricity, and £11,000 for oil. *The Times*, 28 Aug. 1885. In 1884 only 11 of the 149 lighthouses in Britain were equipped with gas burners; of these, 9 were in Ireland and 2 in England.

[134] Cdr. Joshua Cole, R.N., writing in *The Times*, 1 Jan. 1885. Later after the initial heat of controversy had cooled, Tyndall admitted the truth of this :

As compared with oil, it is clear that gas is equally effective as an illuminant for lighthouses on the mainland ; but it has not yet been demonstrated that it is cheaper ; consequently its extension is not rapid. There may be a great future for gas as a lighthouse illuminant, especially if the process of manufacture be simplified and the price of gas was reduced, or an effective means of transporting and storing large quantities of gas discovered. Oil will then have to look to its laurels.

minant, they could easily justify their choice to sanction or decline. The politicians and secretariat of the Board of Trade did not choose to endorse and buy a larger gas development scheme, because they were not sufficiently impressed with the importance of investing in greater power and potential effectiveness. As Sir William Thomson (later Lord Kelvin) observed, "when the British [government] resolves that the object is of importance . . . the most obstructive of anti-reformers and the most apathetic of boards will be thoroughly converted."[135] Had Tyndall succeeded in impressing the administration, no cost within reason would have been refused. The professor and the inventor lost their case on grounds more personal and political than scientific.

If Tyndall's political naïveté wrought his undoing, he had secured a victory of principle, which in the hands of his successor became an accepted instrument of policy. Sixteen years after his resignation Lord Rayleigh, brother-in-law of A. J. Balfour, nephew of the Prime Minister, overcame Trinity House policy and introduced a 190-gas-jet burner at Howth Bailey. In reply to his critics Rayleigh quietly conjectured that ". . . the existence of an independent Irish establishment may perhaps be taken to imply that the Trinity House should not, in all matters insist upon their own views. After all," he surmised, "there may sometimes be an advantage in having doubtful experiments tried by those who believe in them."[136]

Retrospect

As old age approached, Tyndall grew disillusioned with his fellow scientific advisers[137] and with the Liberal Party, whose position toward Ireland and Egypt embittered him.[138] Tyndall's hostility toward Chamberlain slowly cooled,[139] and his resignation from the government in 1886 "obliterated all bitterness on [Tyndall's] part" against him.[140] Possibly Chamberlain's defiant stand on behalf of the Merchant Shipping Bill in 1884 and his support of regulations against the undermanning, overloading, and overinsuring of ships redeemed him even further in Tyndall's eyes.[141] Against Farrer, Tyndall also held no lasting

---

[135] William Thomson, "Lighthouses of the Future," *Good Words*, 1873, *14* : 224.

[136] *Scientific Adviser's Reports* (Trinity House), p. 16, entry, 9 March 1899.

[137] He was, for instance, grieved to learn in 1889 that his old friend and fellow Gas Referee, Vernon Harcourt, had taken out a patent for a pentane standard while still a government official responsible for judging that standard. "I *cannot* understand it," wrote Tyndall, "his case seems as bad as that of Douglass." Eve and Creasey, *Life and Work of John Tyndall*, p. 257 ; diary entry, 15 March 1889.

[138] In a letter to *The Times*, 24 Nov. 1885, Tyndall announced that he was almost prepared to vote Conservative : "It was not in sympathy with the hide-bound Toryism of the past that I would act thus, but as a protest against the more dangerous and

tyrannical Toryism which threatens our future." See *Tyndall Diaries*, entry, 6 Feb. 1885.

[139] Garvin, *Life of Joseph Chamberlain*, Vol. I, p. 384.

[140] *Tyndall Papers*, MSS notebooks, "Religious and Political," Tyndall to Wigham, 27 June 1886.

[141] See S. H. Jeyes, *Mr. Chamberlain: His Life and Public Career* (London : Sands & Co., 1903), pp. 164–168 ; Garvin, *Life of Joseph Chamberlain*, pp. 414–422. *Punch* assisted his image by picturing him as a cherub, sitting aloft amidships "to keep watch over the life of poor Jack." See A. MacKintosh, *Joseph Chamberlain : An Honest Biography* (London : Hodder & Stoughton, 1903), p. 80 ; David Masters, *The Plimsoll Mark* (London : Cassell, 1955).

grudge: "In his case a bureaucratic spirit has swamped the feelings of an English gentleman."[142] In 1885 Tyndall returned to Surrey while his brother-in-law, Lord Claud Hamilton, repeatedly but unsuccessfully urged the Board of Trade to invite him back to Whitehall.[143] In 1887, afflicted by ill-health, Tyndall resigned his post at the Royal Institution. In 1892, following the disastrous wreck of the German ship *Eider*, he bitterly attacked the Elder Brethren for maintaining a light at St. Catherine's Point which was unable to penetrate thick fog.[144] But this was his last effective protest. The following year, at the age of seventy-three, he died in his sick-bed.[145]

For some years Wigham, whose prospects were renewed by the publicity of Tyndall's resignation, continued correspondence with the Board of Trade. Assisted by T. W. Russell, an Irish M.P. who annually submitted the Board of Trade to scrutiny, Wigham tried to have the experiments renewed. He was frequently supported by petitions from shipowners' associations, whose interest he had finally stirred.[146] But the last significant, official, and devastating word on the subject was left to Baron de Worms, who informed Dr. Cameron, M.P., in May 1891 that the Board of Trade was "not prepared to suggest to the General Lighthouse Authorities to incur further expense in investigating the inventions of Mr. Wigham or of other inventors. It is the duty of the Board of Trade to control expenditure rather than initiate it."[147]

In the meantime Sir James Douglass went from strength to strength, becoming President of the Mechanical Section of the British Association in 1886 and F.R.S. in 1887. He retired in 1892 and died in the same year. Thomas Williams, Douglass' official biographer, whose final appraisal is remarkable for its subtle assumptions, admitted that Douglass' actions were not always above criticism. "There were those who . . . thought him, sometimes, to be wanting in breadth of perception; to be biased in favour of his own views; prone to see things only in one light. And, to a certain extent, such persons judged correctly."[148] This judgment history has confirmed.

During the years 1885–1900 provision for coastal lighting was greatly extended.

---

[142] *Tyndall Papers*, diary entry, 2 Jan. 1885.
[143] Hansard, 299.c.1617 ; 303.c.478.
[144] See *The Times*, 4 Feb. 1892 ; Tyndall, "On Coast Protection," *New Review*, 1892, 6 : 430–440 ; *The Freemasons' Journal*, 6 April 1892 ; *Daily Express*, 6 April 1892 ; *Chambers Journal* 3 Sept. 1892 ; and press clippings in the *Tyndall Papers*.
[145] He died tragically after an accidental overdose of chloral was given him by his devoted wife Louisa. The incident is related in the journal which Louisa compiled after his death and gave to the Royal Institution.
[146] *Further Correspondence*, 1887.(i).lxxiii. 60,64,84 *et passim*. Petitions were sent from Liverpool, Belfast, and Bristol.
[147] Hansard, 353.c.482.
[148] Williams curiously adds :

He did not want to find, and would not discuss, a better way now that it was too late to walk in it. So some people said he *was* "narrow". In this restricted sense, he *was* narrow ; but therein lay one of the chief secrets of his strength". . . . In *arriving at* an opinion as to the best course to adopt, in given circumstances he was careful and patient in the extreme, collecting with unwearied diligence all necessary data to enable him to judge aright ; but having *completed* that process, he was far too wise a man to fritter away his energy, and destroy his usefulness, by considering when the time had come for action, whether, after all, there might not be some better way of attaining his purpose. (*Life of Sir James Nicholas Douglass, F.R.S.*, pp. 193–194).

Although no direct causal relationship could be proved between the use of light-houses and the avoidance of wrecks,[149] the continuing loss of life and property encouraged improvements in lighthouse facilities. One Admiralty report listed 1,095 lights in 1897, which reflected an increase of 200 coast lights in England and Wales over the preceding ten years.[150] Where there had been only fifty harbor, coast, and pier lights at the beginning of the century, there were over 900 in 1897.[151] Optical techniques were gradually refined,[152] and management became more efficient. Many problems remained, such as the difficulty of dis-tinguishing lights[153] and the need for lights capable of penetrating fog. But after Tyndall's death and Douglass' retirement the illuminants question lost its emotive appeal. Indeed, it became clear that the personal clash of the 1870's and 1880's had created false impressions about the relative values of different illuminants. In part this was because no strictly numerical valuation could be placed on the competing claims. The question of a "better light" had been confused with the question of a more intense light, a brighter light, or one which would give a greater amount of light with less intensity. Even the question of usefulness and ease of manipulation had been distorted. As E. Price Edwards, formerly private secretary to the Deputy Master and close associate of Tyndall, wrote at the time: "Oil can be conveniently transported and safely stored; and the certainty and simplicity of its action are great recommendations. The lamps are easily manipu-lated by the keepers, and if paraffin be used it is the cheapest kind of illuminant available."[154] Even Tyndall acknowledged the usefulness of oil,[155] admitting that any illuminant's suitability depended on the object and location of the lighthouse. Gas could be more easily adapted to the requirements of fixed, in-termittent, revolving, and group-flashing lights, but since coal gas required a generating station, it could not be used for rock lighthouses at all.

With the invention of the incandescent mantle (itself a result of competition with the new electrical industry), inefficient wicks were no longer used. Incan-descent oil was cheap, more easily combustible, and self-contained. At the same time coal-gas illuminants could be used in particularly inaccessible places where

[149] Statistics for the period are prolific, but the extent to which lighthouses alone were a factor in preventing loss of life and property is difficult to judge. For example, the Wreck Abstracts for 1882–1883 revealed 3,076 deaths among 12,533 sailing crew, and 765 deaths among 4,263 steamer crew, all on the coasts of Britain. But no deaths were cited as due to the "want of lights or buoys on coasts at home" (Class V—"others"). *First Report, Royal Commission on Loss of Life at Sea,* 1884–1885. [C.5577].xxxv.719–720. It is at least arguable, however, that much of the loss due to overloaded ships, negligent ship-owners, and ignorant crews could have been alleviated by better coastal lighting.

[150] See J. Kenward, "Lighthouse Progress, 1887–1897," *Nature,* 1898, *56* : 283.

[151] F. M. Holmes, *Celebrated Mechanics and their Achievements* (London : S. W. Partridge, 1896), p. 50.

[152] "Recent Improvements in Lighthouse Illumination," *Nature,* 1895, *53* : 56–58.

[153] William Thomson, "On Lighthouse Characteristics," *Lectures on Naval Archi-tecture and Engineering, Glasgow Naval and Marine Engineering, 1880–1881* (London/Glasgow : William Collins, 1881).

[154] Edwards, *Our Seamarks,* p. 46.

[155] In 1889, six years after his resignation, he wrote : "Electricity and oil are, it appears, to keep the field for the future. For all ordi-nary purposes the latter is considered suffi-cient, while, on the more important landfalls, it is proposed to mount the former ; gas, as I foresaw, is completely ignored." (*Fortnight. Rev.,* 1889, p. 205).

the cost of building expensive gas-generating plants was offset by the need for fewer men to control the light. Yet, because so little interest was demonstrated in gas lighting, no stimulus was given to the improvement of gas installations or to methods for making them more economically competitive, despite the fact that the competition had vastly benefited the oil system.[156] Other petroleum products, like compressed oil gas, came to be used in lighted buoys and smaller beacons and occasionally in lightships. Acetylene, although expensive and dangerous, was also introduced from time to time. Electricity, as Tyndall and Thomson feared, was not useful in areas of heavy fog and involved high construction and maintenance costs.[157] It is ironical that had Douglass and Trinity House been content to let their oil apparatus be tested against gas over a long period, it would have proved itself superior on its merits, at least until electricity could be provided to lighthouses on a cheaper and more efficient basis.

CONCLUSIONS

The illumination controversy spectacularly illustrates the dilemma of administrators confronted by alternative technical systems and obliged to weigh scientific advice against political and economic expediency. In this context it is ingenuous to ask whether Tyndall's vested interest in "scientific truth" was more worthy than Douglass' concern for technical uniformity or Farrer's preoccupation with economy. As this study suggests, the Establishment case against gas had a certain validity. Gas and oil each had certain virtues, but the use of either depended upon the particular requirements of local circumstances. The prestigious academic adviser was not necessarily *wholly* right *all* the time.

The merits of both sides, however, were obscured by personal rivalries and resentment, based in large part on a fundamental misunderstanding of the nature and the need for long-term research and the propriety of considering new and exciting policy options. In this sense Tyndall emerges from the conflict not so much as the apologist of a particular technique, but rather as the advocate of a policy for fundamental research applied to broader, more far-reaching public needs. He realized that this policy would be subject to change as—in this case —the technology of oil and electric illumination improved. But this improvement would happen more readily if government supported and encouraged the efforts of individual scientists and technologists. Indeed, so long as creative work in applied science was done outside the Establishment by men gifted with that "energy and intellectual capacity" which Lord William Armstrong called "the real source of national superiority,"[158] it followed that such men should receive not only financial aid for their inventions, but also assistance through the stages

---

[156] In 1885, Cdr. F. E. Chadwick, U.S.N., reported from South Foreland to Washington that "the competition of the Wigham system had undoubtedly resulted in bringing about a much greater effectiveness in oil, and also at the same time in producing another gas light, which would seem is . . . largely superior in effectiveness and economy to that of Mr. Wigham. Mineral oil also now shows an effectiveness which far surpasses anything thought possible with this illuminant a few years since. . . ." *Further Correspondence,* 1887.(1).lxxii.57.

[157] Chance Brothers, *A Few Notes on Modern Lighthouse Practice* (Birmingham, 1900).

[158] Quoted in Tyndall, *Fortnight. Rev.,* 1888, pp. 627–628.

of development and production. Without efforts by the state to sustain a vital and creative environment for innovation,[159] the country's potential reserve of systematic technologists would be wasted, and their potential contribution to national scientific and economic growth would remain unrealized.

Such a policy for innovation obviously required a greater appreciation of scientific research among those responsible for making decisions. It also required efficient apparatus for obtaining and weighing the best available expert advice. Finally, and most important, it required harmony of action which only statesmanlike conduct could ensure. Tyndall's experience showed that expert advisers must recognize the limitations of their advice in the arena where administrative and political forces interplay.[160] By insisting so vigorously on Wigham's behalf, Tyndall succeeded only in polarizing rival interests, ruling out easy reconciliations, and making compromise impossible. In this case Tyndall's temperamental devotion to science and to an individual he thought ignobly wronged led him to underestimate the responsibilities of Thomas Farrer. Ironically, Tyndall's resignation was much of his own making. As contemporary experience repeatedly showed,[161] academic experts in the service of Victorian government ran the risk of Ibsenesque struggles with administrative expedience. The necessary combination of sophisticated political judgment with scientific integrity was not generally available or widely appreciated. The academic expert still inclined toward the tragic hero rather than the statesman of science.

[159] This need is at last receiving active official attention in Britain. See *Second Report on Science Policy,* Cmnd. 3420 (London : HMSO, 1967); A. Wedgwood Benn, "The Government's Policy for Technology," *New Technology,* Jan. 1968, pp. 1–3.

[160] For a recent assessment of the experts' limitations, see Sir Solly Zuckerman, present Chief Scientific Adviser to H. M. Government, "Scientists in the Arena," Third Annual Lecture of the Science of Science Foundation, April 1967.

[161] Compare the experience of Sir John Simon and the government's Medical Officer: R. J. Lambert, *Sir John Simon, 1816–1904, and English Social Administration* (London: MacGibbon & Kee, 1963); and R. MacLeod "The Frustration of State Medicine, 1880–1899," *Medical History,* 1967, *11* : 15–40.

IV

Whigs and savants: reflections on the reform movement in the Royal Society, 1830–48

Introduction: the distorting mirror

Between 1846 and 1848, responding to overt pressure from within and the subtle threat of pressure from without, the Royal Society (henceforth RS) approved the most important alterations of its statutes ever considered in the 186 years of its history. These "reforms" were to have a dramatic effect on the self-image of the Society; they were also to have a profound effect on the public persona of the Society in its dealings with Parliament, with government and with men of science and other learned societies in London, the provinces and abroad.

For over thirty years, historians have seen this "age of reform" in the RS as an important part of the "professionalization" of science. Today, reading Lyons's semi-official account, the internal history of the RS since 1848 is presented as merely a chapter of consolidation, the natural consequence of enlightened policies set in motion by early Victorian "professionals".[1] This form of corporate self-description is not uncommon among institutions. Yet the historian's task is to expose the circumstances which such an account may unconsciously conceal.

In a rich comparative discussion of the "state of science" in nineteenth-century Europe, Merz drew attention long ago to allegations of "decline in science" in Britain between 1780 and 1815, and explored the prevalence of the amateur tradition in this country.[2] Historians have since continued to debate the merits of the declinist position, and its relevance to subsequent events in the organization of British science.[3] However, in 1951, Foote attempted to place these events in context, to understand the "great reforming energy" which accomplished this transformation, set against the background of reform provoked by the declinist attack, and the argument wielded by a small group of "scientific reformers".[4] He gave particular prominence to Charles Babbage, and to his *Reflections* (1830), which criticized the RS, as John Playfair and Charles Lyell had earlier criticized the universities for failing to recognize and reward the cultivators of English science.[5] Foote asserted that these events coincided with a time of 'reform in practically every phase of English life'. He also argued that the declinist attack had direct consequences for British science in two ways: by challenging antiquated forms, it helped to strengthen the Society; and by prompting the foundation of the British Association for the Advancement of Science (henceforth BAAS), it opened the way to improved relations between science and the state, and gave new impulse to the efficient transformation of scientific ideas into action.[6] In 1961 Williams located the climax of the declinist campaign in the contested presidential election of 1830, when J. F. W. Herschel was defeated by the Duke of Sussex.[7] Subsequently Mendelsohn argued that these events were important principally because in their wake emerged the BAAS, representing "professional" science.[8] None of these accounts considered the effect of these events on the *subsequent* history of the RS. None was concerned with the political context of the reform movement outside the small band of "noisy ones" involved in the contest. Nevertheless, the connotation of 1830, as a step towards professionalization has become received wisdom.[9]

Recent scholarship has shown the professionalization model to be at best oversimple, and at worst untenable.[10] Indeed, the professionalization model has impoverished our understanding of the social order of science, ignoring actors' intentions, individual interests, regional motives, and political expectations.[11] In fact the motives, prejudices, and confusion surrounding the key events of 1830–48 convey far more than the emergence of a new professional class dedicated to the "disinterested search for truth". Discovering these factors has meant exploring what Cannon has called 'history in depth'.[12] Rediscovering the RS, and its world of metropolitan science, entails abandoning anachronistic distinctions between traditional and modern, and between amateurs and professionals.[13]

The deepest difficulty in interpreting the history of institutions in this period lies in untangling the complex relationship between events in the RS and parallel events in British political life. During these decades new mercantile, trading and professional interests gained influence in the management of metropolitan science. Their influence, giving way to pressure, eventually, for internal self-management by these new interests, began in the 1820s and culminated in 1848, the year which, for the RS, as for Europe, was the year of revolution. The events of 1830–48 also reveal the gradual and unexpected process by which traditional loyalties to Crown and Church were replaced by new contractual allegiances, or "hegemonies", based upon service to knowledge and utility to the State.[14] During this period the RS discovered, in Bagehot's phrase, the 'efficient secret' of the British constitution: a 'disguised republic', combining the dignity of monarchy and the 'representative power' of cabinet government.[15] Between 1830 and 1848, the RS experienced a version of the political and economic turbulence raging throughout Europe. Augustus de Morgan acknowledged that the 'Great epidemic which produced the French Revolution . . . showed its effect on the scientific world.'[16] The leadership of the RS, with strong ties to Crown and Parliament, was unable to ignore public charges of Toryism and favouritism, especially when such charges were supported by the interests of "reform" and "improvement" and wielded by a self-styled "philosophical party".[17]

The end of the Napoleonic Wars saw many traditional British institutions strengthened by the experience of those two decades. In common with restored Europe, British society in 1815 rested upon a pyramid of monarchical rule, assured of privileges ostensibly conferred by right and birth. In the institutions of English science, as in political institutions, the period between 1815–48 saw two great forces pitted against each other – men who owed allegiance to the traditional ruling classes, and men who looked to the new agencies of manufacturing and commercial power, and who made their bids for institutional power in the name of liberalism and specialized knowledge. However, these opposing interests were not always distinguishable. Few philosophers exemplified either extreme; most fell in between, and the RS was merely one alembic within which their interests were compounded.

Following the end of the war in 1815, Britain fell into severe recession. "Cheap government" became a watchword, drawing credit from the belief that the impoverishment of the country owed much to the incompetence of Tory governments, in power since 1800, and to the extravagance of the monarchy. Couched in class and party terms, this belief gained wide currency among middle-class liberals and working-class radicals. Economic and social distress contributed to political disquiet and social disorder. Civil peace could be had only at the price of electoral and administrative reform. Enfranchising the people would herald the end of sinecures and placemen, and the free air of representative government would cleanse the warrens of despotic institutions. The wars of 1793–1815, so the argument ran, had not been fought and won only to allow the British aristocracy to suppress liberalism and democracy at home.[18]

These circumstances affected British science beteen 1815 and 1850 in two significant ways. First, until Peel's government of 1841, there was little disposition to increase government spending (except through military or naval arrangements) on the pursuit of natural knowledge. Second, the institutions of science with aristocratic or royal connections were politically suspect; if they were staffed by court favourites, they were ripe for attack. Voluntary initiative and institutional self-help thus became not only corollaries of austerity; they were political common sense. Not until the spirit of reform reached the institutions of science would they be seen as fit recipients of public trust.

These economic and political factors, coupled with traditional intellectual rivalries with France, helped to shape the debate concerning the position of British science and the reform of the RS between 1830 and 1848. In these years, to borrow the felicitous phrase of Burn, Britain presents a 'distorting mirror', from which we receive conflicting images.[19] To resolve them, it is convenient to divide the reform period of the RS into three arbitrary phases: (1) from 1820 to about 1831, a period of apprehension; (2) from about 1830 to about 1836–8, a period of accommodation and reconciliation between the RS and different metropolitan and provincial interests; and (3) from 1836 to about 1849, a period of adjustment, in which the RS, succumbing to pressures for constitutional reform, acquired a new Benthamite image of philosophical integrity, public utility, open competition, and efficient administration. The first phase corresponds approximately with the discontented reign of George IV, from the riots surrounding the Six Acts to Catholic Emancipation, with the succession of Tory governments from Liverpool to Wellington; from the overtures of the declinists through Humphry Davy's tenure as PRS; from the death of Sir Joseph Banks to the election of the Duke of Sussex. The second phase coincides with the reign of William IV, the passing of the Reform Act, the short life of Grey's Whig Government, and subsequent party divisions between Peel and Melbourne; with the creation of the BAAS, the passing of reform legislation affecting both factories and poor relief, and the Duke of Sussex's tenure as PRS. The third phase begins with Peel's first administration, with early Victorian campaigns for administrative reform, and with constitutional reform in the RS. This phase coincides approximately with the Chartist agitation, with the elimination of protectionism, the repeal of the Corn Laws, and the succession of Melbourne's weak liberalism by the unsteady coalition of Lord John Russell. It ends with the arrival in Cambridge of Prince Albert as Chancellor, and the creation of the Natural Sciences Tripos, with electoral reform in the RS, the beginnings of the Great Exhibition, and the death of Peel. Throughout the period, the 'distorting mirror' reveals the RS following in both method and metaphor an uneven parallel in its transition from what Bagehot described as monarchical to parliamentary government, at the same time reflecting the new dispositions of political power in British society.[20]

I

Years of apprehension

In the history of the scientists' revolt, the turning point is by all accounts the contested presidential election of the Duke of Sussex in November 1830. That contest was the culmination of earlier attacks on the RS. During Sir Joseph Banks's courtly regime, the RS was assailed from several different sides.[21] The provincial towns, through their Literary and Philosophical Societies were creating important new traditions, effectively uniting mercantile, literary and philosophical interests.[22] Philosophical interests in London had advanced their own activities by creating new learned societies, which Banks opposed.[23] From 1820, the result was an undeclared "Thirty Years' War" in which the Astronomical and the Geological Societies, who shared the RS's premises in Somerset House, became its prominent rivals. Gradually, they helped to establish by 1850, in Gramsci's phrase, the counter-claims of the new 'organic' hegemony against the 'traditional' hegemony of Banks.

These claims were also being asserted by reforming interests within the Royal Institution (RI) and the medical profession. It would be surprising to find the RS unaffected by the RI's experience; both were caught simultaneously, as were the medical corporations, in cross-currents of public debate. Between 1800 and 1840, the RI played a central role in confirming a new social image of science and a model for its support.[24] The RI gave experience to men who later proved influential in the RS. Roget, an ambitious

60

and versatile physician, and Brande, a favourite of Banks and a supreme civil administrator of science, were both recruited by Davy from the RI as Secretaries to the RS.

In preparing the ground for reform within the RS, the RI may also have provided a politically neutral ground for reformers and conservatives, a listening post for reverberations from public criticism, and an accessible and uncontentious practical body whose existence spared the RS from the necessity of giving popular practical interests special prominence.[25] Similar considerations arose in medicine. Medical men had always been prominent in the RS, but in the period 1800–48 their number (between 20 and 30 per cent of the Fellowship) and influence attracted particular notice.[26] By 1815 the Fellowship of the RS had become a mark of social status for medical men, particularly those of humble birth who aspired to the highest reaches of professional practice and social acceptance. Medical men on many sides of the reform movement, from Roget to Charles Bell, found the Fellowship an important social acquisition. To critics of the RS the persistence of "non-scientific" medical men was a perennial grievance. The three mystical initials FRS were ridiculed in translation as Fees Raised Since.[27] With the RI, the other learned societies and the medical corporations, the RS formed an interlocking directorate of metropolitan science. All reflected certain representative features of patronage and social place, and all represented a formidable interpenetration of scientific, cultural and careerist interests. In this sense, the reform movement in British science was embedded in the expectations of several different groups, all seeking to maintain status, influence and power.

In 1820 these expectations were still far from realization. The coincidence of the deaths of Banks and George III in 1820 released a fleet of political discontents upon an uncertain sea. Thus, Babbage wrote to Whewell:

... all sorts of plans, speculations and schemes are afloat, and all sorts of people, proper and improper are penetrated with the desire of wielding the sceptre of science. Whether this elective throne shall be filled by a philosopher or a peer, a priest or a prince, is a problem. . . .[28]

In 1820 the RS underwent its first presidential election for over forty years. Sir Humphry Davy was elected. He was acceptable both to philosophers and peers, and was devoted to preserving the delicate equilibrium of the society. Though Davy mended bridges with the sister societies previously ostracized by Banks, he altered little the role of President, preferring Banks's model of a benevolent monarchy of letters of which he was the titular head. His monarchy saw few sustained attempts at reform. Instead, the crown rested upon two "estates": rich men and men of rank who encouraged science by purse and patronage; and men of science who were thus patronized. Successful government depended upon the harmonious co-operation of both, secured by good administration. Davy's administration was conducted largely through the efforts of Brande, as Senior Secretary, and Davies Gilbert, as Treasurer. In 1824 Brande was joined by Herschel, who served until 1827. That year, however, Herschel and Gilbert collided, and their collision affected the RS's future for the next two decades.

In 1827, aged 35, Herschel was one of the most celebrated philosophers of his day. Elected to the RS in 1813, he became a founder member and officer of the Royal Astronomical Society in 1820. Since Cambridge, with Babbage, Peacock and Whewell, he remained a central figure in a cultural network whose influence pervaded English science and letters.[29] Politically and philosophically, his sentiments were liberal, though not Whiggish, and certainly neither radical nor utilitarian. His life had been unmarked by religious or civil turbulence; he was too young to remember Robespierre. Gilbert, aged 60, in 1827, had little in common with his younger colleague.[30] He bore memories of the anti-Jacobin mob burning Priestley's house in Birmingham. From 1806 to 1832, he was Tory MP for Bodmin, and an admirer of the conservatism of Fox and Burke. In 1810 he had warned in Parliament that the tumultuous storm of democracy would lead to a gulf of despotism. In the 1820s he spoke for public order in the face of Peterloo, and against Catholic emancipation in the face of his party.

In 1827 events at Westminster and in the RS followed a parallel course. Electoral and administrative reform were the dispositive issues. In February 1827, Liverpool's health destroyed, Canning formed a government held together only on mild reforming lines. Gilbert saw himself caught between the horns of corruption and revolution. The same dilemma confronted the RS. Gilbert's fears of political reform outside the RS were fanned by fears of 'mob rule' within, of 'disorder leading ultimately to dictatorship'.[31] It followed that, like Parliament, the institutions of science wanted only an alteration or two. Like a monarch, the President could, by tradition, hold the chair until death or abdication. Councils were coteries of friends, selected by the President; financial accounts

62

were closed except to him and the Treasurer. Papers were read infrequently, and only by the President's permission, and publication was slow. Fellowship elections were casual affairs, conducted at ordinary meetings and often on the nomination of the President. The new Royal Medals, awarded from 1826, were virtually in the gift of the officers.[32]

In March 1827, opposition to the RS's courtliness came to a head when Gilbert received a demand from a small group of Fellows to publish a statement of property belonging to the Society. Subsequently, a committee of Fellows, including Herschel, Babbage and Sir James South, was asked to report on Fellowship elections and the appointment of officers. Its report recommended a ceiling of 400 Fellows; elections restricted to four new Fellows each year, to reduce purely social interests; and a more powerful Council, empowered to select its successors and to oversee finance.

On Davy's retirement in the summer of 1827, Gilbert was invited to be President. Neither he nor Davy saw the selection of a President as different from the nomination of a candidate to a pocket borough. But Gilbert's response was tempered by recent events. With Davy's support, Gilbert called upon Sir Robert Peel to be President. The danger Gilbert saw was of outrageous republicanism. 'The Great Contest that I allude to,' he told Peel, 'is the Conflict of Aristocratic and Democratic Power. I wish the Royal Society rescued from the latter.'[33] Peel declined the invitation. In his stead, Gilbert was elected President in November 1827. In December 1827 he squashed the Fellowship Committee's report without further discussion. The result was only to drive discontent underground. In 1827 Herschel resigned as Secretary, resolved to fight against the injustices he had seen.[34]

In the presidential election of Sussex in 1830, three issues linked philosophy and politics. First, in 1829 three leading statesmen of the *ancien régime* of English science, Wollaston, Young and Davy, had just died. Into this vacuum rushed speculation about the "new men" who might succeed them. Second, simmering discontent with the financial and electoral administration of the Society came to the boil. Third, the Society's proximity to medical politics threatened to convert it 'into an engine for party purpose and self-interest'.[35] It was even rumoured that Henry Warburton had been offered the Presidency in return for his support of a successful Anatomy Bill.

Gilbert feared that the power of the old order in science was passing, as part of the process which was transferring political power in the State from the aristocracy to the middle classes. Both as an MP and PRS, he tried to soften the impact of this process. As his Secretary, he chose Roget, a close associate of leading utilitarians. But his efforts at accommodation were to no avail. Gilbert and Roget suffered steady rebuke from Herschel, Babbage, South, and correspondents in *The Times*.[36] The public was treated to the spectacle of South, President of the Astronomical Society, accusing Gilbert, PRS, of perfidy and incompetence. With the publication of Babbage's *Reflections* in May 1830, all hopes of peace were lost. Moreover, the RS could not free itself from the web of intrigue among the medical corporations. In April one FRS used *The Lancet* to describe the abuse of the Society by those whose fashionable practices rendered it 'a medical advertising office, a very puff shop for the chaff of medical scribblers'.[37] To such medical men, the absence of reform in the RS was doing irreparable harm to the reform of English medicine.

Faced by a constitutional crisis, Gilbert looked for a safe successor. His purpose was to secure for the Society the continuance of aristocratic interest, liberalized in practice, serenely removed from the disquiets of civil war. By August 1830 he had approached the Duke of Sussex, whose well-known hospitality at Kensington Palace assured continued yet liberal royal patronage and a plausible safeguard against radicalism in medical and scientific affairs.[38] In the event, his strategy sadly underestimated the participatory sentiments of a substantial number of London Fellows.

In early November 1830, a Requisition signed by thirty-two Fellows was sent to Gilbert demanding the publication of all correspondence concerning his own plans and the negotiations with Sussex.[39] This procedure was unprecedented; all Gilbert's fears of the *vox populi* were apparently being realized. Alarmed by this combination, Gilbert explained to a meeting the circumstances of his invitation to Sussex. When he had finished, the meeting passed two resolutions. The first asked that in future officers should be selected for 'acquaintance with the conditions and interests of Science'. The second, moved by Herschel and seconded by Faraday, asked that the Fellowship should choose its future officers, albeit from a list drawn up by the President and Council. The meeting ended with a vote asking Sussex to retire.

The resolutions of this unprecedented meeting were by nature purificatory; neither implied a revolutionary break with the statutes, but both broke sharply with custom, at a time when customary forms were under great pressure. The country itself had just emerged from a bitter general election in July and August. Throughout the country, middle-class radicals were pressing for reform, uniting with such working-class interests as the Radical Reform Association and the British Association for the Promotion of Cooperative Knowledge. The autumn saw reports of rick-burning and Swing's signature in the South, and a flurry of unstamped papers, demanding concessions to working-class interests.[40] Gilbert personally associated the Fellows' request with the firing of hayricks on his Sussex estate that autumn. Demands for reform did not require the July Revolution to spark off calls for a new Government, but November saw the arrival of Grey's administration – the first Whig Government in decades, with leaders in political, medical and educational reform (including Brougham, the new Lord Chancellor) holding high office.

The same month, Wellington issued his famous refusal to countenance any measure of reform. Party lines at Westminster seemed mirrored in the battle lines at Somerset House. But the Requisitionists signalled neither revolution nor a victory for reform. The picture is more complicated, reflecting only the complex nature of political alignments. The Council (including many of the rebels) was itself divided on the subject of patronage. Faraday, no radical in politics, disappeared from the discussion. Most of the Fellowship remained aloof. By whom should Gilbert have been bound? Under these circumstances, the announcement of Herschel's candidature against Sussex forced a choice. Gilbert was prepared to accept constitutional alteration, while at the same time he rejected the concept of an exclusively "philosopher's Parliament". Such a change would destroy the social basis upon which the Society depended.

At the next meeting of the Council on 18 November, Gilbert procedurally disallowed the resolutions passed at the unconstitutional meeting of 11 November, and announced his intention of resigning. This effectively mobilized opposition. Spurred by Babbage, a declaration of support for Herschel was circulated. This important document reveals that of the eighty signatories at least thirty-three were not "scientists". Forty-five were not authors in *Philosophical Transactions*, although twelve of these – Lyell for one – were certainly considered "scientific". Some of the eighty represented reforming parliamentary interests (both among Tories and Whigs)[41] and several represented legal reform or utilitarian sympathies.[42] Three (Brodie, Green and Warburton) had been active in reform in the Royal College of Surgeons since the 1820s, while, of the physicians, four (Chambers, Holland, Prout and Elliotson) were prominent members of the medical establishment. Significantly, the Declarationists included experienced Fellows, who saw the constitutional integrity of the Society as the central issue. Of the sixteen past or present Councillors who signed, seven were actually on Gilbert's Council at this time. There was no distinct separation of opposing party interests. Barlow, Ellis and Sedgwick, for example, supported Herschel, but were not in Herschel's prospective cabinet.[43] In fact, Barlow and Ellis, although they ostensibly supported Herschel, actually remained on Sussex's Council after 1830! Their concern was that shared by many metropolitan improving interests. Under the circumstances, it is not surprising that the list contained few titled gentlemen, or clergymen, or for that matter, Fellows resident outside London.

The Herschel Declaration demonstrated the diversity of opinion within the Society; compromise was required, but capitulation would have been disastrous. In any case, Gilbert (and Sussex) had the support of over 400 Fellows, including substantial representatives of the Church, the Army, the Navy, and much of the legal and medical establishment, who did not sign. To alienate these elements would have, in Gilbert's eyes, reduced the influence of the Society in the affairs of the nation.

Meanwhile, in a small book entitled *Science without a head*, Augustus Granville imparted a cool perspective to the contest.[44] His survey of the 651 current Fellows argued that only one in five could be regarded as an active philosopher: most were merely *savants en credit*. His sharpest arrows were reserved for his medical confreres (fifty-five physicians and eleven surgeons) whose motives for earning the FRS had little to do with useful inquiry. Superficially, Granville confirmed the justice of Babbage's attack. But there were two important differences. Granville's book was also a treatise on political sovereignty. He rejected the suggestion that science was in decline and made no claim for science as a profession. Instead he argued for the replacement of inefficient privilege by efficient patronage, regulated by a new constitution. Second, Granville believed the reform of leadership lay not in the choice of an enlightened politician or even a good astronomer: the first committed the Society to definite political alignments; the second had merit, but other qualifications were essential in a President. In effect, Granville's book parried the "noisy men" with a spirited defence of the constitution (and *ipso facto*, Gilbert) and concluded by supporting the election of Sussex. It is difficult to gauge Granville's influence on the majority of Fellows. Some in the liberal camp attempted to dissuade Sussex.[45] For reasons which remain obscure, Sussex declined to withdraw. Perhaps like Gilbert, he feared the prospect of victory by a reforming movement, led by petty sectional interests, to which Herschel had been drawn.

The famous poll on St Andrew's Day, 1830, was 119 to 111, narrowly in favour of Sussex. His narrow victory would have been wider had more of the 600 Fellows voted. The outcome was to Gilbert's manifest relief. At the same time, historians have interpreted it as a loss for the reforming party. As Williams put it, 'the cause of reform had been soundly beaten, and the reformers retired in disgust'.[46] Even *The Times* lamented that 'the first scientific establishment in the Empire has obtained a Prince and missed a Philosopher for its President'. But the question was not a simple gloss on the principle of peers versus the people. The outcome challenged the Society to find a political model which would successfully govern English science in a period of rapidly shifting allegiances. Gilbert rejoiced: 'I have retreated over a Gold Bridge with Purple Banners.'[47] But he knew that the work of adjustment had just begun.

II

Years of adjustment, 1830–8

For the next eight years, Sussex, aided by Gilbert, tried to create a *rapprochement* between the RS and the political life of the country. This was made easier by the fact that, like the institutions of State, the Society continued largely unaltered in its ways. Fellowship elections continued in what Granville called 'a desultory fashion' at every ordinary weekly meeting where a quorum of twenty-one was present.[48] Herschel left the country to begin his observatory at the Cape of Good Hope; Babbage, Murchison and Sedgwick turned to the new BAAS. In 1832 Babbage took an unsuccessful excursion into national politics. His electioneering play, 'Politics and poetry, or the decline of science', eloquently conveyed his belief, with Gilbert, that the two were really one.[49]

The 1830s witnessed an expansion in local scientific activity, led by the BAAS. As in the country's political life of the last decade, the place of London in the "strategy of agitation" had changed; the provinces, and provincial scientific societies supplied much of the energy behind this new activity.[50] Under Sussex, the RS quickly accommodated itself to the BAAS's existence, while in fact accepting little internal change. Moreover, Sussex began to cultivate the Fellowship. His combination of political wisdom and intellectual taste was vital; for the years 1830–8 were a period of great contention within the Society.

It was no less a period of contention in the country, with four general elections occurring in the space of ten years. Both in Parliament and the RS, Sussex supported the 'most that could be pushed, and the least that would satisfy the country . . . '.[51] At his first meeting in December 1830, he announced his intention to hold soirées on Monday in the season, to encourage 'a familiar and useful intercourse of wealth and talent of men of rank and men of genius and other grandees of society'. In the uneasy calm following the Reform Bill, nothing could be 'better calculated', said the *Gentleman's Magazine*, to promote harmony and good feeling between the 'three Estates of the Kingdom'.[52] To share power, more Vice-Presidents (an average of six per year instead of two) were created, and were selected from old friends and adversaries alike. Opposition was accommodated in the Council. Of the eighty declared supporters of Herschel, eleven became Council members within two years, and a further eight, within the next decade.

In the meantime, the major work of administrative reform was shelved. This was, ironically, made easier by the fact that during the years 1832–5, the country, and much of the Fellowship, were preoccupied with parliamentary reform (1832), factory and poor law legislation (1833–4) and with ecclesiastical, educational and medical issues.[53] Within the medical world, the cholera outbreak of 1831 forced attention to the inadequacy of official medical arrangements.[54] In their protest against the Royal Colleges, Thomas Wakley and Charles Hastings pursued a model similar to that of the British Association, in forming the Provincial and Medical Surgical Association at Worcester in July 1832.[55]

Between 1834 and 1835, following Gilbert's retirement, Sussex's Council contained several of these reformist surgeons, while other figures, including Peel, improved the public image of the Society and of English science.[56] Peel's brief term as Prime Minister

68

between 1834 and 1835 saw a baronetcy for John Barrow in 1835, and civil list pensions for Georgy Airy (who became Astronomer Royal), Mrs Somerville and Faraday. In 1836 the pensions earlier awarded to Brewster, Dalton and Ivory were increased.[57] However, Peel's labours were interrupted by Melbourne's Whig Government, which, for six years between 1835 and 1841, generally did little to encourage science.[58] But Sussex, working through the Reform Club and the Lords, mediated between Melbourne and Warburton's parliamentary radicals, and managed to keep the Government's sympathy. It was ostensibly at his request that Herschel, his former opponent, was given a baronetcy in the Queen's Coronation Honours in 1838.[59]

The years between 1830 and 1837 also saw a new alliance between the cultivators of science and wider commercial, economic and political interests. In 1831 James Douglas, the political economist, claimed that philosophers required

the union of the patronage of the government with the interest taken in its prosperity by the nation at large. This interest could only be universally diffused by a general and voluntary society.[60]

What had begun as a protest against the inadequacy of royal patronage had grown into a debate about the sources of patronage generally. The remedy, Burke once said, lay in association. In fact, this role soon became the special task of the BAAS.[61] The radical image of the BAAS at first had proved startling, especially when associated with the provinces.[62] Recalling the decade 1830–40, Babbage saw that science 'like other kinds of enterprise...has resorted to association for the furtherance of its object and for the support of its expenses to the contributions of its associates'.[63] The BAAS served the RS's interests in three ways. First, it offered a convenient public forum for the promotion of science without at the same time compromising the RS. This took two forms. Some public concession was desirable politically. As Lyell wrote to Darwin in 1838:

... in this country, no importance is attached to any body of men who do not make occasional demonstrations of their strength in public meetings ... nothing is to be got in the way of homage or influence, or even a fair share of power, without agitation.[64]

The BAAS gave philosophers (including FRSs) a chance to turn public orators at no direct cost and at considerable indirect gain to the Society. Moreover, the Fellows of the RS could work, if necessary, through the BAAS in seeking government support for tidal observations (1834), an Antarctic expedition and magnetic observatories (1839). The presence of claims launched by *two* organizations, one avowedly committed to self-help, ensured a better hearing.

Second, the BAAS offered a timely concession to men who desired the status of philosophers without implying the social sanctions that the letters FRS had hitherto bestowed. As Babbage wrote in 1832,

It is highly probable that in the next generation the race of scientific men in England will spring from a class of persons altogether different from that which has hitherto supplied them.[65]

The BAAS's existence relieved the RS from direct responsibility for the democratic consequences such a development might imply.

Finally, the BAAS, widely reviewed in the major weeklies of London, deflected gossip away from the metropolis itself, while providing the RS with a social laboratory in which to test national feeling. Borrowing parliamentary language, the BAAS helped the RS restore itself as an upper house of science, aided now by a substantial Commons. What Tyndall called 'the great travelling congress' could work together with the 'old stationary palladium of British science'.[66]

In the late 1830s, it was perfectly plausible for a visiting savant to write that 'England is not the land of science – es existirt dorten nur ein Weitgetriebener Dilettantismus'.[67] It was plausible, but not quite accurate: many undercurrents were disturbing the superficial calm of the English scientific establishments. Far from disappearing, complaints about the "state of science" revived. Bulwer Lytton's influential *England and the English* (1833), which contained a chapter strongly suggestive of Babbage's influence, revived the twin questions of patronage and recognition. 'Science is not higher on the continent than with us,' the argument went, 'but being more honoured, it is generally more cultivated.'[68] While Britain led in manufacturing and practical science, the 'circle of speculative science' was narrow and confined. According to Lytton, this deficiency could only be made good by endowing science at the ancient English universities, and by bestowing public honours on its devotees. As Granville argued in his second book, *The Royal*

70

Society in the Nineteenth Century (1836), the required remedy was fundamentally political. The existing system of patronage was inimical to the philosophical interests of a wider franchise. Remedy required that patronage by rank be displaced by the patronage of fellow philosophers.

In 1838 Sussex resigned. In his last presidential address, he had welcomed Herschel, whose return could well have opened an old wound. Peel, still out of office, was canvassed, but again declined, asking that 'the chair should be filled by some distinguished man who had devoted his time and faculties to some branch or other of science'.[69] Eight years before, the election for the Presidency was hotly contested. Now, tactfully avoiding interference with 'the free use of the franchise which every Fellow possesses and is expected to ... exercise',[70] Sussex welcomed the Council's nomination of the Marquess of Northampton, a man 'without more pretensions to science or philosophy than a good education and a taste for such studies would naturally justify'.[71] Northampton, aged 48, a graduate of Trinity College, Cambridge, a former Whig MP (1812–20), an FRS since 1830, and a mineralogist of note, was easily underrated. For the previous two years, he had been among the reform party in the Council, and was a favourite compromise candidate. Through him, achieving recognition for "philosophical patronage" became the dominant theme in the next phase of reform.

III

Years of accommodation, 1838–49

By 1849 the RS had completed the third and final instalment of its internal reform. A decade which culminated in revolution in Europe, witnessed in Britain the collapse of Chartism, the beginnings of reform in the civil service, in public health and the universities, and recognition of the RS as a responsible public body.[72] At Westminster, Peel's administration fought through a programme based on sound finance, efficient administration and social legislation. In analogous fashion, Lord Northampton, similarly encumbered by an unreformed civil service managed by his Senior Secretary, Roget, guided the RS towards electoral reform, and to the recognition of new "philosophical" constituencies within the Fellowship and the Council.

Returning to government in September 1841, Peel watched the

"philosophical" movement grow in influence. Though aware of the odious power which patronage confers, Peel nevertheless used his patronage to encourage the process. Peel's efforts reached beyond pensions to grants for scientific purposes, and knighthoods for scientific reformers.[73] Yet Peel's support of science and the Society could not alone restore the Society's image. In 1842, Augustus de Morgan, never an FRS, claimed that

> The RS is the focus of aristocratic science and scientific aristocracy. . . . It has justly survived not merely by the labours of those who cultivated science, but also by the financial support and promotion of those who did not. If it were suggested, however, that the RS had a public responsibility, as well as a right to service, it was not clear that it had done its duty.[74]

By the mid 1840s, despite Sussex's efforts, the RS was neither completely 'dignified' nor 'efficient'.

When Victoria ascended the throne in 1837, the monarchy was at a low ebb. Like Victoria, Northampton had the task of restoring lustre to the sceptre of English science. Steps were taken to sustain the *entente* with the BAAS and to improve diplomatic relations with those learned societies which had become what one observer called 'antechambers to the Royal'.[75] In his first address, Northampton announced the launching of Ross's expedition to the Antarctic, pressed on the Government by the BAAS, and the programme of colonial magnetical observations organized by Sabine. Continuing Sussex's tradition of soirées, he similarly pursued Sussex's Whiggish interests in encouraging "scientific utility" and in improving the *Philosophical Transactions*.

For fifteen years, thanks to the conciliatory posture of Sussex and Northampton, the Society's Council Minutes were silent on the subject of constitutional reform. Like Sussex, Northampton avoided being carried away by extremists of either group.[76] As he wrote to Granville 'You see, my dear doctor, that we are accepting little by little your suggestions; all the rest will come by and by.'[77] In fact, by 1847, Northampton realized that he was virtually controlled 'by what is called *his* Council'. Increasingly, the Council, and not Northampton, was held responsible for the Society's actions – to contain radical sentiment, to curtail professional self-advertisement, and to eliminate favouritism. As the reformers of 1830 had shown, these reforms depended upon modifications in the practice of Fellowship elections, in the selection of the Council, and in the tenure of the President. To check the indiscriminate admission of new Fellows, Northampton re-established proposal forms on which grounds for nomination were required.[78] The issue of presidential tenure came next. In 1848, after a decade in which, by general consent, he gave more general satisfaction to the Society than any President since Banks, Northampton recognized that no future President could ever again reign so long, lest he become 'too absolute – nay jobbing – or at all events, if he lives to be old, he is likely to become superannuated, and not to know it'.[79] By 1848, however, these sentiments were overtaken by more sweeping proposals which had slowly gathered impetus in the preceding three years.

In May 1846 a debate arose among some of the Fellows over the award of one of the previous year's Royal Medals, to T. S. Beck, the physiologist, for a paper on the nerves of the uterus. Contrary to custom, Beck's paper had not been previously presented to the Society or published in the *Philosophical Transactions*. As usual, the President, advised by the Council, had chosen the winners. When Beck's award was announced, Dr Robert Lee, FRCP, an obstetric physician and former Council member, claimed that his own work on the same subject had been overlooked and then, after a cursory reading, rejected by the Council. Lee was ultimately overruled; but the radical medical press, and the medical community generally, were enraged.[80] Immediately, the charges precipitated the dissolution of the Committee of Physiology; eventually, they were to prompt Northampton's retirement.[81] Coupled with a threat of legal proceedings they ultimately forced Roget's resignation. The issues of principle involved were seized upon by William (later Sir William) Grove, who was to play a central part in the main events of the next three years. Grove, then aged 34, an Oxford graduate and patent lawyer, was elected FRS in 1840, and was on the Council from 1845. In 1846 he published his best known work on the *Correlation of Physical Forces*. To the reformers, his combination of legal and philosophical talents proved decisive. Shortly after the Beck affair, Grove took steps to mobilize a charter committee of the Council to consider alterations in the Society's constitution. The political symbolism of the Chartists was not lost on him or his contemporaries.[82] Before the summer recess of 1846, with little public display but with great determination, the charter committee recommended 'organic changes of the most comprehensive kind'.[83] The committee recommended a triennial term for the President, more efficient organization of the subject committees, and most important, the restriction of new Fellows to fifteen each year, chosen by ballot. Irritant sand had produced a reformist's gem.

Since 1830, the Fellowship had broadly accepted the argument that its President should be a man of position, preferably with access to the Crown, Parliament, and departments of State. But the internal government of the Society was a different matter, requiring a new form of ministerial responsibility. Great significance, therefore, attached to the committee's recommendations, which implicitly redefined the Council, in parliamentary language, as a cabinet, and the President, by implication, as no more than its prime minister, and to that policy which would open the gate of Fellowship to men of lesser means but greater philosophical ability.

Throughout the autumn and winter of 1846–7, these issues became prominent in those sections of the medical press which spoke for the corporate conscience of medical reform. *The Lancet* aimed an attack upon Roget, whose twenty years in office had, in its view, blocked the representation of new interests. These charges, of great importance to medical FRSs, came to a head at a Special General Meeting of the Society, held on 11 February 1847, specifically to consider the proprieties of the Beck affair. At a time when the Royal College of Surgeons was contemplating the election of Fellows by examination, the recognition afforded by Royal Medals was vital to medical standing.[84]

Meanwhile, in early 1847, appeared an anonymous publication, signed 'FRS', entitled *Thoughts on the Degradation of Science in England*. The author, later alleged to be Charles Babbage, revived the rumours of decline in British science, and attacked the Society's administration, which, in his view, had since turned this decline into calculated degradation. The tract was far more political in its overtones than Babbage's book of 1830, but despite its rebarbative prose, it aroused far less debate. In fact, the Council had already begun to respond, although its response was muted: nothing was done to remedy the failure of the sectional committees, whose comparison with those of the BAAS invited scorn; and for legal reasons which are not fully revealed in the Council's Minutes, the recommended changes in the charter and statutes were dropped, save for those concerning Fellowship elections. In the event, following legal advice from the Law Officers of the crown, this single proposal was approved by the Council on the Society's behalf, on 10 February 1847. The equivalent of electoral reform had

74

been achieved, at last, and apparently without revolution. Were it not for the medical presence, it might have been silent as well.

None the less, the result of this simple change was far-reaching. Given the age structure of the Society, the elective limitation to fifteen Fellows immediately reduced the size of the Fellowship. Where there were 764 Ordinary Fellows in 1847, there were only 630 in 1860, of whom 330 were said to have 'higher scientific qualifications'.[85] The RS was the only major learned society in England to shrink in size in this period; and within two decades, there was a formidable queue of eligible men, including a large number of disappointed physicians.[86] To satisfy sceptics, important features remained unaltered. The statutes permitted, for example, any number of the Fellowship to be elected in certain privileged classes based on rank; and the Society remained highly medical, about 20–25 per cent of all Fellows elected between 1848–1900. The Society's finances suffered, but not catastrophically. Moreover, the reputation of the Society vaulted. The list of fifteen names each year, as Granville said, enabled anyone to 'judge of the real worth of our present standing in the opinion of the scientific world'.[87]

Reflecting the Liberal Government of Lord Russell which had replaced Peel in 1846, the Council which had introduced these changes bore the timely complexion of a coalition cabinet.[88] Its political sympathies were conciliatory, if not quite reformist; and favourable to the mixture of political sympathies which combined in what might be called the "philosophical" party. Thus the events of the following few months must be understood not as an assault against the Society but as an attempt by a coalition cabinet to consolidate its policies.

With the election procedures altered, the philosophical integrity of the Society could be strengthened. To air demands for these further reforms, a ginger group, representing a broad base of philosophical interests, was well advanced by February 1847, when J. P. Gassiot and Grove proposed the creation of a new society within the Society. In April 1847 twenty-seven Fellows met at a London hotel to form the Philosophical Club. It was to meet monthly on Thursdays at 5.30 p.m., just before the meeting of the RS, its purpose being to 'promote the scientific interests of the RS [*sic*] and to facilitate intercourse between fellows cultivating different branches of natural science'. To honour the year of its foundation, membership was limited to forty-seven Fellows, who were required to have contributed a scientific paper to one of the metropolitan learned societies (a rule inspired by the BAAS).[89]

The Club bore a close relation to the coalition cabinet of the RS. Superficially it appeared a creature of that cabinet, representing key metropolitan and professional interests.[90] Grove was appointed Treasurer, and Edward Forbes, Thomas Graham, Leonard Horner and John Royle formed a Committee of Management. There was to be no President, merely a chairman to guide discussion. But a substantial number had experience of government.[91] Despite the presence of a strong medical interest, the Club's direction was deliberately philosophical rather than professional: those elected were mainly men who already earned their living by means other than the cultivation of science. Almost immediately they began to influence public opinion, not by fostering political cabals, but by strengthening the position of the RS among the learned societies of London.

With the creation of this philosophical vanguard, the RS had the 'elements of a great organisation . . . '. 'Let [its Fellows]', urged an FRS in *The Athenaeum*, 'by some means seek a reunion with the cultivators of the natural sciences which they have lost.'[92] The two issues to which the Club gave immediate prominence were the unification of the different scientific societies in one locality, preferably in one building; and the normalization of relations with the other societies. The first object it pursued for over two years, leading eventually to the acquisition of Burlington House in 1852; the second, it proposed for a time to achieve by inviting the Linnean, the Geological, the Astronomical and the Chemical Societies to send their best papers to the *Philosophical Transactions*. Both aims indicated the Society's new will to leadership.

Within the Society, the fuse lit by the Beck affair was kept alight. Gradually, the RS had moved towards open government through the publication of accounts, rotation of committees, restriction of members, election by merit, and had nearly limited the tenure of its officers. But these policies were informal, and could still be overturned by an unsympathetic President or Secretary. At a heated Council meeting on 9 February 1848, Sir Henry De la Beche advanced, and then, on reflection, withdrew a proposal to restrict the office of President to two years, which would have reduced the President to the status of merely a superior member of Council.[93] But what would be the future principle of government in the Society – monarchical or parliamentary, aristocratic or philosophical; in Bagehot's phrase, 'dignified' or 'efficient'?

Early in the revolutionary year of 1848, Northampton indicated his wish to resign. His succession unavoidably again brought into focus the constitutional role of the officers. In March 1848 *Punch* supplied an advertisement for a new President:

Wanted, a Nobleman who will undertake to dispense once a month, upon rather a liberal scale, tea, lemonade, and biscuits, for a large assembly. The company is select, and he will be allowed to mix with some of the greatest men in England. Sealed tenders, stating most liberal terms, to be sent in to the Royal Society, marked 'President'. No scientific or literary men need apply.[94]

As if to anticipate criticism, Northampton proposed the Earl of Rosse, the astronomer. Herschel, again proposed, was weary of the fray, and willing to defer to Rosse. There were few other possibilities. Edward Sabine, an "artful dodger" perhaps, but certainly an astute politician, again (unsuccessfully) suggested Peel. Babbage had protested against an aristocrat, but the election went the President's way. Rosse, who believed in continuing an element of Tory paternalism in the Society's government, offered the best compromise, though his residence in Ireland for most of the year hardly promised a major social force in London.[95]

As the election drew near, others urged the replacement of Roget to remedy the 'negligent manner in which the business of the Society has been conducted for years past'.[96] In May, *The Athenaeum* speculated that both Roget and Northampton might soon retire, providing an opportunity to complete the Society's reform.[97] In fact, in what amounted to a general election, the Council was captured by the progressive movement in the Society, including Airy, Horner, Gassiot, Lyell, John Phillips, Grove and Wheatstone. The Philosophical Club had revealed its new-found strength. Altogether, thirteen members of the Council belonged to the Club. But the Secretaryship was not to be decided by reforming interests alone. The time had come when, following the electoral reform of 1847, new constituency boundaries had to be defined. Increasingly, they would be defined in favour of the philosophical specialities. The medical fraternity, for example, claimed Roget's post as their own by right. As W. B. Carpenter wrote to Grove: 'If battle is not between the Reforming and Conservative parties, but between the physicists and the naturalists, we must support our own sciences.'[98] And Walter White, the RS's Assistant Secretary, asked perceptively, would 'science or faction conquer'?[99]

Following a heavily contested election, Thomas Bell (dental surgeon and Professor of zoology, King's College, London) became the new Junior Secretary; and in January 1849, the Council, under Bell, began the work of detailed administrative reforms long deferred under Roget. Seven new sectional committees were created, each consisting of between twelve and twenty specialists to consider papers, and to make recommendations for the Copley and Rumford Medals, and for the use of the Donation Fund. Hereafter, administrative decisions would never be far from philosophical interests. Would science or faction conquer? Ironically, in the future they were indistinguishable.

The election on St Andrew's Day, 1848, was a significant turning point in the Society's history – not because it heralded the advent of a scientific liberalism based on reform, but because it replaced conservative principles based on patronage with principles based on disciplinary prerogative. Hereafter, the Society would be both 'dignified' and 'efficient'. There exists no better index of its improved public reputation than the good opinion of men of all parties, and particularly, of Russell's Liberal Government, which had watched closely the events of 1848. In October 1849, Russell offered the Society an unprecedented parliamentary grant 'for the promotion of science and the encouragement of scientific men'.[100] This bespoke not only the confidence of a Liberal Government; it was tacit recognition that the Society had set itself in order.

Conclusion

By 1850 the Society had repaired its public and philosophical image.[101] After twenty years, science was no longer without a head. The Reverend Abraham Hume remarked that this was a 'pleasing set off to the well known observations, both correct and important' respecting the decline of science in England.[102]

From the reform decades of 1830–48, several considerations arise. This essay has suggested first, that the events of 1830 were not, as Williams has written, 'a victory of the amateurs'; it was, instead, like the Reform Bill of 1832, a victory for moderation.[103] Equally, the "triumph" of 1848 was not so much a victory for Whiggism, as a victory for coalition, conservatism and compromise – ultimately for a Peelite strategy of assimilation and accommodation. In this context, the language of politics becomes more than a matter of metaphor. Parliamentary representation, electoral reform, a self-

78

determining extended franchise – these were the issues which dominated England and which were reflected in all her major institutions. The institutions of science were not excepted. As *The Times* perceptively observed:

The Royal Society, like all other institutions, must take account of the fact that democratic principles now govern the world in all fully civilised communities – the chief scientific society must in all matters itself be scientific.[104]

In Bagehot's terms, the government of the Royal Society moved from absolute to constitutional monarchy. Within another generation, the transformation was complete; the President would become, not a peer, but a prime minister, *primus inter pares*, presiding over a cabinet rather than a *curia regia* of Council members. Within two decades it was agreed to keep presidential tenure to the same limits which, by custom, each British government observed. And no longer could cabinet officers be appointed without regard to the constituency interests representative of specialized disciplines.

It should now be clear that the application of a simplified model of professionalization has honoured the events of 1830–47 more in the breach than in the observance. It is far from clear that the 'uprising of scientists at the RS in 1830 was in part a proclamation that science could now stand on its own, that it had the prestige of a profession'.[105] Such an assessment depends too much upon the accounts of Babbage and Brewster; it also distracts the reader from the historical context within which the uprising occurred. That context was as much political as professional, as much concerned with the parochial concerns of a traditional elite, fearful of abrupt change, as with the intellectual interests of an organic elite seeking recognition.[106] This becomes all the more clear when the fearful events of 1830 are reinterpreted in the light of those of 1848.

This essay has applied a general political model in place of a professionalization one, partly because contemporaries generally saw events in these terms, and also because these events were distinctly part of political developments which were affecting virtually every quarter of English life. Some trappings of professional behaviour, including the tendency to foster group solidarity, to promote exclusiveness in an elite united regardless of differences in general education, social rank or economic standing, are clearly present. But the agonies of professionalization (*pace* Babbage) – at least in relation to occupations, qualifications and contractual obligations – were not a central factor in English science then, nor indeed, for another four generations. Savants had become more democratically "men of science", but they were still "philosophers", not yet given to the pursuit of what J. A. Thomson later called 'Brodwissenschaft'.[107]

Nevertheless, the institutions of English science did create a route to professional enterprise. This was nowhere clearer than in medicine and in those technical occupations and institutions associated with commerce and the useful arts, where the social recognition afforded philosophers often ensured both profit and status. Many of these professions, however, were similarly dominated by autocratic metropolitan institutions.[108] In these professions, demands for reform were bound to win attention. In the nature of events these demands arose, first, from men who were in sympathy with liberal sentiments and who were determined, for a mixture of reasons, to couple the power of knowledge with commercial manufacturing and trading interests. For this reason, the history of the RS offers a prismatic perspective on those issues of power, status and patronage central to metropolitan culture.

This essay has stressed the particular relation between contemporary reform movements in science and in medicine. Between 1830 and 1850 the London scientific establishment, like the medical establishment, accepted that it must justify its social status by elevation of its philosophical character – in Huxley's words – by raising 'the level of its scientific reputation'. The scientific establishment sustained the new role by asserting the utility of "pure science", and by restricting entry to its elite. In *The Athenaeum*'s phrase, the 'survivors are of the opinion that the smaller the number the greater the honour'.[109] As a result, the RS won increased prestige and government patronage. The medical establishment achieved similar ends by creating a respectable professional image, linked with government sanction, and ultimately justified on grounds of improving standards of science. In medicine, as in science, the major institutions deflected competition and criticism, partly by departmentalizing knowledge in disciplines, and partly by encouraging the universities to defend these departments, and so offer themselves as both social and intellectual selectors for the metropolitan elite.

This essay has also focused on the twin issues of hegemony and patronage. Perkin has described the Victorian era as witnessing the replacement of 'old vertical connections of dependency and patronage' by the 'horizontal solidarities of class'.[110] As we have seen, this process, if it can be said to have ever occurred in science, had scarcely begun by 1850. Vertical connections of class, were, in fact, replaced by vertical connections of family and interest,[111] reinforced not merely by the authority of expertise, but also by restriction of access. The achievement of the RS by 1848 was, in Huxley's words, 'not to create an academy of immortals, but to save the Fellowship of the Society from becoming a strain and an imposition'.[112] In this process, there was an apparent shift from reward by patronage to recognition by merit; from recognition of rank to the reward of ability. But the real significance of this shift should not be exaggerated. While increasing competition and creating a rewards system, the RS did not affect, or seek to affect, the economic base of the would-be philosopher. The "amateur" tradition, preserved by the *corps d'élite* in the RS, naturally persisted as long as that elite remained intact. That elite would eventually be modified in complexion, not principally in economic terms, but in normative expectations. In the process, the RS may be seen to have merely exchanged one form of cultural capital, based on social ascription by class, family and friendship, for another, based on the material and social prerogatives of an educated elite. To complete the transformation, new forms of patronage, operated by representative peers were required. For, as Weld observed in 1848, 'It is the want of patronage that drives science from the halls of our universities; for she has no such rewards to confer on her students as those attached to the bar or to the Church.'[113] Within two decades, the major institutions of science, as other British institutions, had, by accommodating themselves to the threat of rising class interests, successfully set anchors to windward, and had retained for the metropolis, joined in holy trinity with Oxford and Cambridge, primacy both in intellectual and political authority.

It remains to ask why the RS, like the Royal Colleges of Physicians and Surgeons, failed to act until well after 1900, in the interests of the general practitioner or the rank and file of science. By confining its resources to prizes, by confining its elections to virtual prize fellowships, the RS inevitably became part of the competitive struggle for survival in nineteenth-century intellectual life. Yet, in practice, the actual encouragement of specific areas of science was left to others – the learned societies, the BAAS, field clubs, eventually the universities, university colleges and schools. In the debates which filled the pages of *Nature* and supplied the motives of the scientific movement some twenty years later, the RS stayed at a safe distance from "bread and butter" matters. Even a new generation of "Young Turks" in the 1870s and club rule from the famous 'Xs', did not quickly alter the picture. In both cases, it can be argued that neither the medical nor the scientific establishment could have won greater social advantage by advocating greater participation. But in both cases, radical alternatives, seeking a broader base for professional development, were rejected as socially, and therefore, professionally, undesirable. It surprised no one that parliamentary democracy was limited to the confines of a small, closely examined and socially reproduced elite – in Coleridgian terms, a clerisy of science.

Paradoxically, owing largely to the character of its reform between 1830 and 1850, many of the most important developments in late Victorian applied science and science education took place largely outside the compass of the RS. Its successive Councils preferred a policy of *dégagement*, justified by the need for a suitable division of labour, but also by the need to distinguish between industry and insight, between enthusiasm and excellence.[114] As a result, in pursuing its philosophical independence, the RS almost inadvertently underwrote a policy of professional science, increasingly detached from the wider and more popular scientific, technological and educational interests of the country. Science was perhaps not without a head, but it was, as Huxley and others later claimed, without a nervous system. It is ironic that the absence in England of a national system of scientific "organization", lamented for the next fifty years from Matthew Arnold to Arthur Balfour, could scarcely have been more thoughtfully arranged.

Acknowledgements

This paper is a much shortened version of a longer essay which examines more closely the institutional history of the Royal Society and scientific London in the first half of the nineteenth century. For their help and comments the author wishes to thank the editors, Dr Kay Andrews, and Mr N. H. Robinson. For permission to use their manuscripts the author is grateful to Trinity College, Cambridge, the Royal Society of London, and the Royal Institution. Since this paper was submitted, several relevant works have appeared which I have been unable to take into account. These include David Miller, 'The Royal Society of London, 1800–1835: a study in the cultural

82

politics of scientific organisation', unpublished Ph.D thesis, University of Pennsylvania, 1981, and Jack Morrell and Arnold Thackray, *Gentlemen of Science: Early Years of the British Association for the Advancement of Science*, Oxford, 1981.

Notes and references

1 H. Lyons, *The Royal Society, 1660–1940: A History of its Administration, under its Charters*, Cambridge, 1944; D. Stimson, *Scientists and Amateurs: A History of the Royal Society*, New York, 1948.

2 J. T. Merz, *A History of European Thought in the Nineteenth-Century*, 4 vols., Edinburgh and London, 1904, **1**, pp. 230–48.

3 N. Reingold, 'Babbage and Moll on the state of science in Great Britain', *British Journal for the History of Science*, 1968, **4**, 58–64.

4 G. Foote, 'The place of science in the British Reform Movement, 1830–1850', *Isis*, 1951, **42**, 192–208.

5 C. Babbage, *Reflections on the Decline of Science in England*, London, 1830; M. Moseley, *Irascible Genius: The Life of Charles Babbage, Inventor*, London, 1964. For criticisms of the universities: C. Lyell, 'State of the universities', *Quarterly Review*, 1827, **36**, 216–68; and M. Sanderson, *The Universities in the Nineteenth-Century*, London, 1975, pp. 26–72.

6 G. Foote, op. cit. (4), p. 208; also, Foote, 'Science in early nineteenth-century England', *Osiris*, 1954, **11**, 438–54. cf. R. MacLeod, 'Introduction. On the advancement of science', in R. MacLeod and P. Collins, *The Parliament of Science*, London, 1981, pp. 17–42.

7 L. P. Williams, 'The Royal Society and the founding of the British Association for the Advancement of Science', *Notes and Records of the Royal Society*, 1961, **16**, 221–33.

8 E. Mendelsohn, 'The emergence of science as a profession in nineteenth-century Europe', in K. Hill (ed.), *The management of scientists*, Boston, 1964, pp. 3–48. A tendency to ascribe professional attributes to science without a close reading of recent history was commonplace by the 1870s: T. H. S. Escott, *England: Its People, Polity and Pursuits*, London, 1879, p. 452; and H. Spencer, *The Principles of Sociology*, London, 1893.

9 cf. D. Knight, *The Nature of Science*, London, 1976, pp. 92 *et seq.*; and S. F. Cannon's corrective *Science in Culture*, New York, 1978, pp. 137–65.

10 The best review of professionalization is devoted to American

science but applies to Britain: N. Reingold, 'Definitions and speculations: the professionalisation of science in America in the nineteenth-
century', in A. Oleson and S. Brown (eds.), *The Pursuit of
Knowledge in the Early American Republic*, Baltimore, Md, 1976,
pp. 33–69. For the difficulty of assigning professional labels to
different disciplines in Britain, see R. Porter, 'Gentlemen and
geology: the emergence of a scientific career, 1660–1920', *The
Historical Journal*, 1978, **21**, 809–36.

11   I. Inkster, 'Science and society in the metropolis: a preliminary
examination of the social and institutional context of the Askesian
Society of London, 1796–1807', *Annals of Science*, 1977, **34**, 1–32; A.
D. Orange, *Philosophers and Provincials: The Yorkshire Philosophical Society from 1822 to 1844*, York, 1973.

12   W. F. Cannon, 'History in depth: the early Victorian period', *History
of Science*, 1964, **3**, 20–38.

13   J. B. Morrell, 'Individualism and the structure of British science in
1830', *Historical Studies in the Physical Sciences*, 1971, **3**, 183–204.

14   The concept of hegemony, taken from Gramsci's theory of cultural
supremacy, embraces the distinction between the social roles of
"traditional" intellectuals (scholars) and "organic" intellectuals
(including technical and bureaucratic experts): G. Williams, 'The
concept of "Egemonia" in the thought of Antonio Gramsci: some
notes on interpretation', *Journal of the History of Ideas*, 1960, **21**,
586–99; M. Berman, 'Hegemony and the amateur tradition in British
science', *Journal of Social History*, 1975, **8**, 30–50.

15   W. Bagehot, *The English Constitution*, London, 1867, pp. 252–67.

16   S. de Morgan, *Memoir of Augustus de Morgan*, London, 1882, p. 42.

17   "Philosopher" and "philosophical" are used throughout in their
contextual sense to describe those holding a "philosophical" (as
distinguished from a received) view of nature, or a member of a
"philosophical circle".

18   A. Briggs, *The Age of Improvement, 1783–1867*, London, 1959, pp.
184–235; J. Droz, *Europe between Revolutions, 1815–48*, London,
1967.

19   W. L. Burn, *The Age of Equipoise: A Study of the Mid-Victorian
Generation*, London, 1964, pp. 15–54.

20   Bagehot, op. cit. (15).

21   J. Barrow, *Sketches of the Royal Society and the Royal Society Club*,
London, 1849, pp. 16–52, describes Banks's court.

22   C. Lyell, 'Scientific institutions', *Quarterly Review*, 1826, **34**, 153–79;
R. Schofield, *The Lunar Society of Birmingham: A Social History of*

84

Provincial Science and Industry in Eighteenth-Century England, Oxford, 1963; A. Thackray, 'Natural knowledge in cultural context: the Manchester model', *American Historical Review*, 1974, **79**, 672–709; S. Shapin, 'The Pottery Philosophical Society, 1819–35: an examination of the cultural uses of provincial science', *Science Studies*, 1972, **2**, 311–36.

23 Following the secession from the RS of the Linnean Society in 1788, the disrobing of the "old lady" continued with the creation of the Geological Society (1807), the Astronomical (1820), the Zoological (1828), and the Geographical (1830) Societies.

24 M. Berman, *Social Change and Scientific Organisation: The Royal Institution, 1799–1844*, London, 1978. The interpenetration of the RI and the RS can be deduced from biographical notes included as appendices in Berman's thesis of the same title (Ph.D thesis, Johns Hopkins University, 1971), but not reproduced in his book.

25 The Society of Arts from the 1770s had cultivated good relations with the RS: D. Hudson and E. W. Luckhurst, *The Royal Society of Arts, 1754–1954*, London, 1954.

26 Slightly more physicians (thirty-three in all) were elected to the RS in the decade 1810–19 than in the four previous or subsequent decades: *Record of the Royal Society*, London, 1940; W. Munk, *Roll of the Royal College of Physicians of London*, London, 1861.

27 A. C. C. Swinton, *Autobiographical and Other Writings*, London, 1930, p. 62; *Natural Science*, 1894, **4**, 2–3; A. T. Basset (ed.), *A Victorian Vintage*, London, 1930, p. 124; A. B. Granville, *Autobiography*, London, 1874, **i**, p. 66.

28 Babbage to Whewell, 15 May 1820, Whewell Papers, Trinity College, Cambridge.

29 J. F. W. Herschel, *A Preliminary Discourse on the Study of Natural Philosophy*, London, 1830; S. F. Cannon, op. cit. (9), 29–71.

30 Gilbert (1767–1839) became an FRS in 1791 and soon entered politics. During Fox's administration he attracted praise for his knowledge of public finance and government administration, and for his assistance with inquiries into weights and measures, copyright and mining. During Liverpool's administration, he nurtured good relations between the RS and the Admiralty; through his intercession, more scientific places were created on the Board of Longitude and Babbage received the first grant given for his calculating engine.

31 A. C. Todd, *Beyond the Blaze: A Biography of Davies Gilbert*, Truro, 1967; and 'The life of Davies Gilbert, 1767–1839', unpublished Ph.D thesis, University of London, 1958, p. 654.

32 R. MacLeod, 'Of medals and men: a reward system in Victorian science, 1826–1914' *Notes and Records of the Royal Society*, 1971, **26**, 81–105.

33 Todd, op. cit. (31, 'Life'), p. 698; Todd, op. cit. (31, Biography), pp. 205, 237 (quotation).

34 Herschel to Babbage, 15 December 1829, Herschel Papers, RS, 2, 242.

35 *The Lancet* (1829), 20 June 1829, **1**, 383–4.

36 e.g. "Argus" (?Babbage), *The Times*, 30 June 1830.

37 *The Lancet*, (1829–30), 3 April 1830, **1**, 16.

38 Following the recent death of George IV, the Duke of Sussex was brother to the new King, William IV. Educated at Göttingen, his liberal and cosmopolitan credentials were impeccable. From 1811 as Grand Master of the Freemasons and from 1816 as President of the Royal Society of Arts, he had drawn a closer circle between the Crown and progressive policy.

39 W. Fitton, *A Statement of Circumstances Connected with the Late Election for the Presidency of the Royal Society*, London, 1831.

40 P. Hollis, *The Pauper Press: A Study in Working Class Radicalism*, Oxford, 1970, pp. vii, 30.

41 e.g. G. P. Scrope, Liberal MP for Stroud, 1833–68; and R. Vyvyan, Tory MP successively for Cornwall, Okehampton, Bristol and Helston, 1825–57.

42 Including E. R. Daniell, barrister and Governor of the RI, 1816–31; H. Hallam, historian and barrister; and R. H. Solly, one of the original promoters of the RI.

43 Fitton, op. cit. (39), p. 29. A close examination of the proposed Councils reveals remarkable similarities. Both Sussex and Herschel, for example, would have dropped Sir John Franklin, Sir Everard Home, Sir Thomas Lawrence and Adam Sedgwick; Herschel and Sussex would have both retained Roget as Secretary. They were also agreed to keep George Rennie, John Pond, Henry Kater, Faraday, and Gilbert himself. Both parties would have *added* William Cavendish and John Lubbock. In fact, the area of disagreement centred upon only twelve places. Clearly few new men were involved on either side. Herschel's cabinet was highly philosophical but hardly professional. The Duke's was decidedly representative of the *patronat*. Clearly there would have been differences in spirit but scarcely a revolution in values.

44 A. B. Granville, *Science Without a Head; or, the Royal Society Dissected*, London, 1830.

45 W. Tooke wrote to Sussex asking him to withdraw: Williams, op. cit. (7), p. 230.

46 ibid, p. 230.

47 *The Times*, 1 December 1830, and Gilbert quoted in Todd, op. cit. (31, *Biography*), p. 265.

48 A. B. Granville, *The Royal Society in the Nineteenth Century*, London, 1836, p. 218.

49 Moseley, op. cit. (5), pp. 122–5.

50 Briggs, op. cit. (18), p. 207. P. D. Lowe, 'Locals and cosmopolitans: a model for the social organisation of provincial science in the nineteenth-century', unpublished MPhil. thesis, University of Sussex, 1978, pp. 16 and *passim*. The creation of new provincial societies, a movement beginning in the 1810s and 1820s, reached its first climax in the 1830s.

51 N. Gash, *Politics in the age of Peel*, 2nd edn., London, 1977, p. 10.

52 *Gentleman's Magazine*, 3 May 1834, **1** (n.s.) 540.

53 G. B. A. M. Finlayson, *England in the Eighteen-Thirties*, London, 1969, pp. 31–6.

54 M. J. Durey, 'British Society and the cholera', Ph.D thesis, University of York, 1975, pp. 1–11.

55 E. M. Little, *History of the British Medical Association, 1832–1932*, London, 1932, pp. 117 *et seq.*, and C. Brook, *Battling Surgeon*, Glasgow, 1945.

56 Kater remained a Councillor, but resigned as Treasurer. His successor in 1830, Lubbock, endowed the Society's financial affairs with all the respectability of a successful banker. Barrow provided a useful naval link; Murray, a link with the Tories; Vigors, a link with the liberal landed Whigs; John Rennie, with the engineers; Lord Melville, with the Admiralty and the House of Lords; and Peel, whose parliamentary influence guaranteed a steadying hand, with the forces of moderate reform.

57 Return of Civil List Pensions, 1840, p. 302. His object, Peel explained, to Mrs Somerville, was 'a public one, to encourage others, and to prove that great scientific attainments are recognised among public claims': M. Somerville, *Personal Recollections from Early Life to Old Age, of Mary Somerville*, London, 1874, p. 177.

58 Melbourne awarded no Civil List pensions to men of science during 1837–40. For the insult accorded Faraday by Melbourne: L. P. Williams, *Michael Faraday*, London, 1965, p. 353; and E. P. Hood, *The Peerage of Poverty*, London, 1859, pp. 213–15.

59 Barrow, op. cit. (21), p. 124.

60 J. Douglas, *The Prospects of Britain*, Edinburgh, 1831, p. 59.

61 Between 1833 and 1849, the BAAS assisted over fifty men and 300 projects with sums amounting to £15,000: R. MacLeod, 'The Royal Society and the Government grants: notes on the administration of scientific research, 1849–1914', *The Historical Journal*, 1971, **14**, 323–58.

62 For the political principle of association, in opposition to the autocracy of science: T. Robinson, *Presidential Address to the British Association at Birmingham*, 1849, pp. xxx–xxxi; J. M. Baernreither, *English Associations of Working Men*, London, 1891; F. H. Giddings, *The Principles of Sociology: An Analysis of the Phenomena of Association and of Social Organisation*, London, 1899; E. C. Black, *The Associations: British Extra-Parliamentary Political Organisation*, Cambridge, Mass., 1963; R. MacLeod, op. cit. (6), pp. 20, 38.

63 "FRS", *Thoughts on the Degradation of Science in England*, London, 1847, p. 49.

64 K. M. Lyell, *Life, Letters and Journals of Sir Charles Lyell*, London, 1881, **ii**, p. 45.

65 C. Babbage, *On the Economy of Machinery and Manufactures*, London, 1832, p. 313.

66 Tyndall to Spottiswoode, 21 January 1878, Tyndall MS (RI), II, fo. 1273.

67 Leibig to Berzelius, 26 November 1837, quoted in T. E. Thorpe, *Essays in Historical Chemistry*, London, 1923, p. 588.

68 E. B. Lytton, *England and the English*, London, 1833, p. 17.

69 Granville, op. cit. (27), **2**, p. 224; Peel to Granville, 31 October 1838.

70 Barrow, op. cit. (21), p. 124.

71 Spencer Joshua Alwyne Compton, second Marquis Northampton (1790–1851), was a 'well-educated nobleman, a traveller . . . versed in the laws and institutions of his country . . . fit for any situation that an English gentleman could be qualified to hold': Barrow, op. cit. (21), p. 128.

72 A. Whitridge, *Men in Crisis: The Revolutions of 1848*, New York, 1949; J. Sigmann, *1848: The Romantic and Democratic Revolutions in Europe*, London, 1973.

73 Briggs, op. cit. (18), p. 331; R. Owen, *Life of Richard Owen*, London, 1894, **i**, pp. 230, 236. Murchison was knighted in 1846; Richard Owen was offered, and declined, a similar honour. Peel's scientific weekends at Drayton Manor in the early 1840s were attended by Playfair, Wheatstone, Owen, Brodie and George Stephenson among others: Parker, *Sir Robert Peel*, London, 1899, **ii**,

88

304–7; **iii**, pp. 162, 225, 433–5, 447. In the 1840s De la Beche, Playfair, Owen, Horner and others repeatedly gave evidence to select committees on questions ranging from smoke and noxious vapours to factory and health legislation: W. M. Fraser, *A History of English Public Health, 1834–1939*, London, 1950, p. 19. Peel also used William Buckland as his informal scientific adviser. Babbage, alas, was disappointed.

74 A. de Morgan, 'Science and rank', *Dublin Review*, 1842, **13**, 275–6.

75 *Sharpe's London Magazine*, 1845, **280**, p. 581.

76 Lyons, op. cit. (1), pp. 257–8.

77 Granville, op. cit. (27), **2**, p. 222.

78 Barrow, op. cit. (21), pp. 127, 132.

79 Northampton to Herschel, 26 May 1845, Herschel Papers, RS, HS 5. 266.

80 The correspondence was published, with editorial comment supporting Lee against the Society in *The Lancet*, 1846, **1**, 526–9, 583–5.

81 *The Lancet*, 1846, **2**, 408.

82 The committee was chaired by Northampton and included the Vice Presidents (Rennie, Lubbock, Wrottesley and Hooker), the two Secretaries (Roget and Christie) and the Foreign Secretary (Sabine) as well as Grove himself.

83 *The Lancet*, 1846, **2**, 408; Lyons, op. cit. (1), p. 260.

84 Z. Cope, *The Royal College of Surgeons of England: A History*, London, 1959, pp. 64–7.

85 D. Martin, 'The Royal Society today', *Discovery*, 1960, pp. 292–3.

86 L. Levi, 'On the progress of learned societies, illustrative of the advancement of science in the United Kingdom during the last thirty years', *Report of the British Association for the Advancement of Science*, 1868, 169–97; *Daily News*, 27 April 1871. In that year there were fifty candidates, of whom nineteen were physicians, five chemists, four geologists and one a mathematician.

87 Granville, op. cit. (27), **i**, p. 66.

88 The Council of 1846–7 still included Brande, of Davy's day, and George Rennie, Roget and Paris, of Gilbert's Councils; but it also included a coalition of philosophers, e.g. Samuel Christie, Samuel Cooper, Edward Sabine, Henry De la Beche, Edward Forbes, William Hopkins, George Porter, Baden Powell, Sir John Richardson, W. H. Sykes and W. H. Smyth. Four men (Cooper, Forbes, Porter and Richardson) were on the Council for the first time.

89 J. P. Gassiot to Herschel, 5 March 1847 and 1 April 1847, Herschel Papers, RS, HS 8. 55–6; T. G. Bonney, *Annals of the Philosophical*

Club of the Royal Society, London, 1919; T. E. Allibone, *The Royal Society and its Dining Clubs*, Oxford, 1976, pp. 199–205.

90 The "forty-seven" included five surgeons and two physicians; another six were then professors at King's College, London; four others were professors at UCL; and four were governors of the RI. Among ten geologists or palaeontologists, three (Horner, Lyell and De la Beche) were, or would become, Presidents of the Geological Society. Remarkably, none of the officers of the RAS or the Linnean was represented. The Club insisted upon an accommodating policy towards the learned societies. Forbes urged Grove to avoid setting dates of meetings to clash with other societies: it was 'very important that they should gradually learn to look on the Philosophers as a sort of higher council or guardian angel for them all': Forbes to Grove (n.d., probably 1849), Grove Papers, RI.

91 In 1845–6 the twenty-one officers of the RS included eight members of the new Club; in 1846–7 there were fourteen, including the Treasurer (Rennie), the Junior Secretary (Christie) and the Foreign Secretary (Sabine). Of the forty-seven, only seventeen had been Fellows in 1830, and not all were administrative reformers; only five had signed the Fellows' Requisition, and only nine signed Herschel's Declaration that year. Of the forty-seven, thirty had served on the RS Council between 1831 and 1846. By their second meeting on 6 May, thirteen additional Fellows had accepted, and by June their numbers were complete.

92 *The Athenaeum*, 27 May 1848, p. 509.

93 W. White, *The Journal of Walter White*, London, 1899, p. 82.

94 *Punch*, 18 March 1848.

95 Northampton to Rosse, 21 March 1848, Herschel Papers, RS, HS 5. 274. According to Lyell, Faraday declined to stand, but was prepared to support either Robert Brown or Richard Owen as 'good men of European reputation': Sabine to Grove, 1 February 1848, Grove Papers, RI; "FRS", op. cit. (63), p. 59; Rosse to Sabine, 6 November 1854, RS, Mc. 5. 181; Rosse to Sabine, from Birr Castle, Parsonstown, 23 March 1848, Sabine Papers, RS, SA 1112. On Sabine, see N. Reingold, *Dictionary of Scientific Biography*, **12**, 49–53.

96 Sabine to Grove, 28 November 1848, Grove Papers, RI.

97 *The Athenaeum*, 27 May 1848, p. 509.

98 Carpenter to Grove, 22 November 1848, Grove Papers, RI.

99 White, op. cit. (93), p. 86.

100 Minutes of the Government Grant Committee, 11 November 1849, cited in MacLeod, op. cit. (61). The model for the parliamentary

90

grant was the voluntary research fund begun over a decade before by the BAAS: Minutes of Government Grant Committee, 7 March 1850. The vocabulary of voluntarism had been assimilated into the grammar of government.

101 The appointment of assistant secretaries of the calibre of Charles Weld (1843–61), and Walter White (1861–85), the publication of accounts, and the expectation of regular attendance from the two Secretaries and the Foreign Secretary in return for substantial salaries, all sustained an image of greater diligence: A. Strange, 'The government of the Royal Society', *Nature*, 1870, **3**, 1–2; White, op. cit. (93), p. 209.

102 A. Hume, *The Learned Societies and Printing Clubs of the United Kingdom*, London, 1853, pp. 41–2.

103 D. C. Moore, 'Concession and cure: the sociological premises of the first Reform Act', *Historical Journal*, 1966, **9**, 39–59; and his *Politics of Deference*, London, 1975.

104 *The Times*, 29 November 1848.

105 Cannon, op. cit. (9), p. 145.

106 Berman, op. cit. (24). For alternatives worth pursuing, Cannon, ibid., pp. 150–63.

107 J. A. Thomson, *Progress of Science in the Century*, London, 1908, p. 46.

108 cf. R. N. Shaw and T. G. Jackson (eds.), *Architecture: A Profession or an Art?*, London, 1892; P. Smith, *History of Education for the English Bar*, London, 1860; F. C. Thompson, *Chartered Surveyors: The Growth of a Profession*, London, 1968; B. Heeney, *A Different Kind of Gentleman: Parish Clergy as Professional Men in Early and Mid-Victorian England*, Hamden, Conn., 1977.

109 *The Athenaeum*, 23 December 1865, p. 891.

110 H. Perkin, *Origins of Modern English Society, 1780–1880*, London, 1969, p. x.

111 As late as 1874, Galton found that 120 of 180 FRSs then alive belonged to only thirteen different families: *English Men of Science*, London, 1879, p. 40; and his *Index to Kinsmen of FRSs*, London, 1904.

112 T. H. Huxley, *Proceedings of the Royal Society*, 1885, **39**, 281.

113 C. R. Weld, *A History of the Royal Society*, London, 1848, **ii**, p. 467.

114 RS Council Minutes, 30 November 1875, Report of Election Statutes Committee.

V

Science and the Civil List
1824 – 1914

*Introduction**

It is generally recognised that the rate and direction of research in natural science is partly dependent on the influence of external social, political and economic considerations. Particularly since the late 1930's, much attention has been paid by historians of science to the question of how and to what extent economic environmental incentives have influenced individual scientists.[1] While it is difficult to prove a general case, it is clear that in the specific circumstances, economic factors may impel particular fields of research or innovation in certain directions. Much of what is known as 'science policy', as so far as this is concerned with studying the effects of the allocations on the direction of research, or the eventual application of research, accepts this basic premise.[2]

Given this broad premise, however, it is surprising that few historians have looked into the more intimate, relationships between an individual's economic circumstance and his scientific performance. While it has never been seriously argued that scientific work occurs in a social vacuum, it is still unconventional — and widely considered not quite 'proper' — to enquire into the personal economic reasons that have motivated or restricted men of science in choosing science as a career, or in following particular lines of research. By many

---

*   This investigation is part of a larger study of the endowment of research and was supported by a grant in science policy from the Department of Education and Science. I am indebted to the Governers of the Imperial College for permission to quote the Huxley Papers, and to the Librarian of theRoyal Institution for the use of the Tyndall Papers, and to the Cambridge University Library for the use of the Stokes Papers.

1   *Cf.* J. D. Bernal, The Social Function of Science (London: Routledge, 1939); R.K. Merton, 'Science, Technology and Society in Seventeenth Century England', *Osiris*, 4, (1938), Pt.11, pp. 360-632.

2   *Cf.* Harvey Brooks, *The Government of Science* (Cambridge, Mass.: MIT Press, 1968); C. Freeman and A. Young, The Research and Development Effort in Western Europe, North America and the Soviet Union (Paris: OECD, 1965).

historians of science, these factors are thought trivial and uninteresting and in any case not significant enough to affect the inexorable development of scientific ideas. To the limited academic study of scientific ideas as such, this form of historical enquiry may be philosophically uninformative; given the cumulative character of science, new ideas will arise, and who or what brings them to light are arguably questions of social, but not intellectual importance.

The limitations of this view, however, are obvious. In so far as the historian's duty is to understand the process of scientific change, and in so far as that process is the reality of life within science in a given historical moment, the impact of social and economic circumstance is not irrelevant to the steps men take, and the recognition they receive. Instead of advancing one's field of vision the historian is driven to ask broader questions, some of which take sociological and administrative form. Within the rational structure of conceptual science, social devices for endowing, encouraging and rewarding science have a strong bearing on the highly internal subjective quality of life as it is lived on the frontiers of research. The historical study of such devices and the assumptions on which they operate are important to the study of scientific activity as a social process.

This form of enquiry is particularly important to the history of science in 19th century Britain. The 'scientific revolution' of the 17th century was, at least in England, in the hands of the relatively affluent class of men, working within a particularly religious and rationalistic context, whose economic position endowed them with sufficient leisure to pursue their scientific interests. By the mid 19th century, the class structure of British science had gradually changed. Two broad social groups — professional and artisan families — provided increasing numbers of young British scientists. By and large neither group automatically possessed the leisure or the independent wealth to do research. Especially for such men 'prospects' had a good deal to do with the choice of science as a 'calling' and not infrequently deflected young men towards careers in law or medicine.

Increasingly, good men needed outside help to do research. Slowly, this need was recognised by government and led ultimately to the concept of full cost research support. One early step towards a complete system of endowment in England took the form of Crown pensions, awarded on the recommendation of the Prime Minister, from the royal 'Civil List'. The political and economic importance of the Civil List attracted public attention. The question of royal maintenance naturally aroused party interest, and from time to time brought to light the assumptions underlying the British form of constitutional monarchy. But the historical significance of the Civil List, and particularly the pension awarded from the Civil List to deserving subjects, is usually overlooked. The pension list has long had an importance which surpasses its economic value. In recent times Crown pensions have also carried a measure of national recognition which is both political and social in character. From the standpoint of science, the Civil List pensions have an important historical lesson.

I. Origins of the Civil List Pensions

The concept of the 'Civil List' was an offspring of the Glorious Revolution of 1688. The term itself was originally devised to distinguish between military expenditure and the upkeep of the Royal Household and civil administration under the Crown. Before William III, there was no distinction between the expenses of the government (the 'civil service') and the household expenses of the monarch. The hereditary taxes and revenues levied by the Crown were expected to meet all costs of living as well as charges of administration, enforcement of justice and representation of England abroad. The Crown's resources of revenue included rents from the royals estates, war booty, capital ships and confiscated property. To this system, as witnessed the experience of Charles II and James II, the Crown's considerable independence from Parliament was chiefly due. One of the first acts of the Crown was, therefore, to debit portions of this for civil expenditure. The Civil List, based on royal incomes from hereditary rents and certain national revenues, was the result.

In effect, the Civil List was the price paid by the people for the constitutional monarchy. On the accession of each monarch, a committee of the House of Commons considered the amount to be settled on the Crown. Until the 18th century, the Civil List remained technically Royal Wealth; if annual revenues exceeded annual expenses, the surplus went to the Crown. On the accession of George III, however, Parliament under Pitt removed the hereditary revenues from the King's pleasure, giving him in return a fixed estate of £800,000 (later increased to £900,000) to sustain the civil service and otherwise support the honour and dignity of the Crown.

Despite these attempts at control, the management of the Civil List remained a constant source of irritation between parliament and the King. Sometimes by bad management, but sometimes despite careful preparation, the Crown habitually overspent its income, and had continually to appeal for extra funds. Moreover, it could endow pensions which, so long as they totalled no more than the sum allowed by parliament, were unaccountable to any higher authority. No regulations governed their patronage, and their awards were often thinly disguised marks of favour. The amount allegedly spent to support political favour in the Commons alone was staggering. One estimate in the reign of Queen Anne suggested that 76 MPs divided £150,000 p.a. among them. Between 1769 and 1780, successive parliamentary committees tried unsuccessfully to repair this grievance. At last, in 1782, an Act originally framed by Edmund Burke in 1780 was passed (22 Geo. III, c.82) which expressly limited the patronage of Members, and in effect, further restricted the ascendancy of the Crown over the Commons. The pension list was made subject to more strict control and the total amount to be distributed in pensions was limited to £170,000. Secret pensions were forbidden, and no pension could exceed £600, or be given for any other reason except for the relief of distress or the reward of merit .[3]

---

3   Henry Dunckley, 'The Civil List and Grants to the Royal *Family'*, *Contemporary Review*, 56 (August 1889), p. 296. The Civil List is treated at length in Anson, *The*

Despite this Act, 'merit' was loosely defined and large abuses continued. In 1793, the pensions list amounted to over £80,000 for Ireland and £90,000 for England. At the turn of the century the Civil List became an easy target for reformers among Radicals and Whigs. Lord Brougham once proclaimed, '... If there be justice in Parliament ...' the List 'must ere long be rescued from its present perversion and cease to afford the materials of corrupt influence'.[4]

Gradually, amendments and reforms were made in the allowed classes of expenditure, and in 1816 an 'auditor of the Civil List' was appointed. On the accession of William IV in 1830, the Civil List was reduced to £510,000 and relieved of all charges relating to Civil Government other than those connected with the Royal dignity and the support of the Royal Household. (I Will. IV. c.25) Within the five classes of the Civil List (Privy purse, retinue allowances, household expenses, royal bounty and pensions) pensions were limited to £1,200 a year and to a ceiling of £75,000. These reforms eventually curtailed flagrant abuses, but pensions were still largely confined to rewards for military, diplomatic or political service, and as such, remained a valuable source of patronage.[5] Rarely, if ever, were they considered as a means of awakening or rewarding broader national cultural interests. In the event, the possibility that the Civil List could be put to such uses gained greater support. The arguments appealed to no one more forcefully than to Sir Robert Peel.

II. Peel's Policy for Science

In 1831, Peel, then Home Secretary in Wellington's ministry, argued that pensions ought to be given only to persons 'who either have rendered a service to the public, or who are nearly related to those who have, and to enable those who have rank and title and no means of maintaining them to live at least in dignity'.[6] The reform of government administration and spending, including the pension awards for public services outside military and political affairs, formed a fundamental part of Peel's domestic policy, while his scientific spirit had become a national byword. This spirit had commended itself to George IV who, in 1825, had approved Peel's plans to 'reward and encourage men distinguished by their literary talents and scientific attainments' by creating Royal Medals for men of science and literature distinguished by original research. The spirit also prevailed upon William IV, who granted baronetcies in 1835 to Robert Southey,

---

Law and Custom of the Constitution, vol. 11, p. 163. For recent comments on the pension as applied to literature, see Paul F. Matthiesen and Arthur C. Young, 'Gassing, Gosse and The Civil List',*Victorian Periodicals Newsletter,* No. 32, Fall, 1967, pp. 11-16.

4 Lord Brougham, 'The Civil List—and Retrenchment', *Edinburgh Review,* 32 (1820), pp. 487-488.

5 See Sir Herbert Maxwell, *Life and Times of the Rt. Hon. William Henry Smith, M.P.* (Edinburgh: Blackwood, 1893), vol. 11, p. 211.

6 Charles Parker, *Sir Robert Peel* (London, 1899), vol. I, p. 99.

the poet, and Isaac Barrow, the natural philosopher.[7] In 1831 Sir James South received a pension of £300 and several other scientists were knighted, and in 1832 James Ivory received a pension of £100.

Peel's policy was unquestionably elitist. He had been in the van of economic reform, but was strongly opposed to any attempt to give parliament complete control over national rewards. In February 1834, only months before Peel succeeded Melbourne as Prime Minister, Lord Althorpe, Chancellor of the Exchequer, moved a resolution in the Commons to limit the Civil List pensions to 'certain public claims, especially art and science'. The Crown, on the advice of the Prime Minister could hence forth grant pensions up to a total of £1,200 per year,

> to such persons as have just claims on the royal beneficence, or who, by their personal services to the Crown by the performance of duties to the public, or by their useful discoveries in science and attainments in literature and art, have merited and gracious consideration of the sovereign and the gratitude of their country.[8]

The first scientific candidate to be brought within the new scheme during Peel's first ministry (December 1834 April 1835), were Sir George Airy, who was granted a pension of £300 a year,[9] and Mrs. Mary Somerville, Peel explained,

> ... As my object is a public one, to encourage others to follow the bright example which you have set, and to prove that great scientific attainments are recognised among public claims ... if that provision will enable you to pursue your labours with less of anxiety, either as to the present or the future, I shall only be fulfilling a public obligation ...[10]

Herschel's greetings were among her most enthusiastic. 'Although the Royal notice is not quite so well swift as lightning in the selection of its objects', he smiled, 'it agrees with it in this, that it is attracted by the loftiest'. Such events 'seem to mark the progress of the age we live in and give Peel credit for this tact in perceiving this mode of making a favourable impression on the public mind'.[11]

In 1835 Faraday received £300, and the following year pensions went to Dalton, Brewster and Ivory. No one could seriously question the validity of the claims, but they were still associated with political favour. To keep his freedom

---

7   Ibid. vol II, p. 304. William IV to Peel, 21 January 1835.
8   Hansard, *Parliamentary Debates*, Third Series, 21.c.4961 (18 February 1834).
9   Parker, op. cit. p. 307. Peel to Airy, 17 February 1835. Following Airy's death, his pension was settled on his wife.
10   Martha Somerville, *Personal Recollections, from Early Life to Old Age, of Mary Somerville* (London: John Murray, 1874), p. 177. Following her husband's financial reverses, Lord John Russell later added £100 to Mrs. Somerville's grant.
11   Ibid.

of manoeuvre, Peel remained unalterably opposed to increased parliamentary control. On the accession of Victoria in November 1837, the Chancellor proposed a Select Committee, following the precedent of 1830, to assess the size and conduct of the Civil List.

On 8 December the Chancellor proposed a second committee to look into pensions of all kinds, and met a brilliant speech from Peel in opposition. Publicly, Peel argued that it would do little good to reduce the 300-odd pensions currently on the list, and useless to ransack old memories. But privately he may well have considered the patronage that would await a future Prime Minister, anxious to advance science and literature without prying Radical opposition. But the Radicals did not easily give way. Handley accused Peel of justifying the pensions merely by their antiquity.[12] After a division (295-233) gave the government a majority of 62, the Select Committee was approved.

From 23 November to 5 December the Civil List Committee held eight meetings. Peel, as a member, proposed two amendments which would have delayed reductions in the pension fund below the ceiling of £75,000 set at the accession of William IV, and rejected attempts for annual Parliamentary scrutiny. But on both amendments he was over-ruled. In its Report, the committee recommended that the figure of £1,200 p.a. be grafted onto the Civil List Act, and that annual returns be laid before Parliament.[13]

The Civil List Bill passed through its third reading, over bitter opposition. The Bill proposed to accept the Select Committee's recommendations, and to endorse the 1834 Resolution of the House. George Grote, M.P. (City of London), violently objected that the provision begged important questions about the way in which the sum of £1,200 was fixed, and whether it really contributed to 'the comfort and dignity' of the Sovereign. Did it 'encourage pursuits and habits of a scientific or literary tendency, which, though beneficial to the public generally were not profitable for the individual person ... ? It cannot be so', he argued, 'The prize is one which is both too small and too much out of reach to produce any such effect upon anyone'.[14] Moreover, there were potential disadvantages to the scheme: 'You pay a compliment to one man of science or to one public man, but you create a feeling of dissatisfaction and wounded pride in the bosoms of a dozen others'.[15] Finally, mixing awards for merit with awards for charity without defining which were which was exceedingly bad form: '... the scientific world have a right to know when any particular man of science is singled out for a pension charged on a public fund, whether the grant implies scientific superiority or whether it is intended for mere relief or assistance'.[16] In the absence of such announcements, the system would seem exceptional, irregular and arbitrary.

---

[12] Hansard, Parliamentary Debates. Third Series, 39. c. 894.
[13] Report of the Select Committee on the Civil List, 1837-38 (22), xxiii, p. 6.
[14] Hansard, 39.c.1288-1289.
[15] Hansard, 39.c.1290.
[16] Hansard, 39.c.1291.

Peel also rose to oppose the motion. In his view, however, the sum of £1,200, far from being too large, was far too small. Moreover, annual scrutiny by Parliament would be inefficient and counter productive. Besides, members were losing sight of the original motives for granting pensions. 'Was it not said', Peel reminded the House, 'that despotic nations rewarded science and selected eminent scientific and literary men, anxious to pay them a just compliment, whilst they also afforded them a substantial reward?'[17] The measure was intended to distribute awards formerly given only for military or political service, 'when a literary man of eminence was selected for royal favour, then the whole class was elevated and complimented in the act'.[18] The House was, in restricting the pension fund, going back on its resolution of 1834.

On a division, Peel lost his point, and was defeated with the Radicals, 125-23. In the Lords, Brougham denounced the practice of appropriating money at a single date for an entire reign, but his objections were also overruled. The Civil List Act, 1837, became law. (1 Vict. c.2.) The wording of the Act made no reference to destitution; it was clearly contemplated as a distinctive mark of national gratitude for eminent personal services.[19]

In the meantime, the Pensions Committee, which Peel had strongly opposed, had begun its meetings. The twenty-one members of the committee, including the Chancellor, Lord Russell, Grote, Howe and Handley, but noticeably not Peel, decided to survey, by letter, all current pensioners. It was necessary to do this because no warrants of awards had ever been kept. The results were impressive. Under 'Rewards for Literary and Scientific Services', there were only sixty-four names, and charges amounting (in 1834) to only £9,204 out of a total pension expenditure of £140,000. After six months, in July 1838, the committee reported, recommending that the reasons for each award should henceforward be published; that the amount granted and age of the recipient would be reviewed from time to time; that pensions would not be granted to Peers, merely because they were in reduced circumstances, and that all awards to pensioners entering public services would be summarily stopped.[20] The annual sum of £1,200, implying a total annual outlay of £20,000 was felt to have obvious economic advantages over a fixed grant of £75,000. The committee applauded the creation of more systematic pension schemes, which had begun to substitute a 'strictly-defined and regulated system of reward for a system which depended on the arbitrary selection of the Crown, or the recommendation of the existing Government, exposed to the bias of party or political considerations'. As such, this development was well in line with the 'progressive advancement of sound constitutional principles ...'[21]

---

[17]   Hansard, 39.c.1307.
[18]   Hansard, 39.c.1308.
[19]   See Sir Arnold Talbot Wilson, 'Civil List Pensions', *Nineteenth Century and After*, vol.121, (March 1937), pp. 273–283.
[20]   *Second Report of the Select Committee on Pensions, 1837-38* (621), xxiii, p. 15.
[21]   Ibid., pp. 12, 15.

Returning to office, in September 1841, Peel sought to extend provision for science within the limits set out by the Civil List Act. His efforts met with the enthusiastic thanks of the scientific community. 'There are few ways', wrote John Herschel, in January 1842, 'in which the Royal Bounty can be more availably bestowed for the interests of science than by relieving men of a very high order of attainment, and who have distinguished themselves for original research, during those years while their powers are still unimpaired and available for discovery, from the necessity of looking either to public or private instruction as their chief means of support'.

> The higher and far the most important pursuits of science — those which are directed to the improvement of its theories — are in a very remarkable degree unremunerative, and the man who gives his genius fair play must lay aside all hope of fortune.[22]

Advised by Airy, Dean Buckland, and other close scientific friends, Peel made awards of £100 to such eminent men as John Curtis, the entomologist, J. D. Forbes of Edinburgh, Professor Richard Owen, and Sir William Hamilton. In 1843, Lady Bell, widow of Sir Charles Bell, the anatomist, received a pension of £200, and Robert Brown — little known in England, but on Buckland's testimony, recognised in Germany as 'the first botanist now living'— received a grant as well.[23] Pensions to active scientists were virtually 'fellowships', and Peel framed his letters of award with this concept in mind. Each 'pensioner' was assured that his acceptance would be 'compatible with entire personal and political independence'.[24] For some, the money was critical. Forbes, for example, received £200 and warmly thanked Peel for the means of pursuing, with greater freedom of 'of mind and steadiness of purpose than I could otherwise have done, the scientific occupations which you have been pleased to mention ...[25] Richard Owen, whose expensively illustrated *British Fossil Reptiles* made great demands on his purse, rejoiced that the pension 'happily enabled him to meet these without difficulty or anxiety'. [26] This warm response stirred Peel to even greater efforts on the scientists' behalf. In 1844, a committee under Richard Owen memorialised the government for £1,000 to arrange and display the rich collection of sub-tropical fauna housed in the British Museum and the India Office. The Prime Minister was quick to help the memorialists reach their goal.[27] In 1845, Peel moved a step further, and

---

22 Parker, op. cit., vol. III, p. 444, Herschel to Peel, 2 January 1842.
23 Parker, op. cit., vol. III, pp. 445-447, Buckland to Peel, 19 August 1843.
24 Peel Papers (British Museum), Add.Mss. 40, 574, L 71. Peel to J. D. Forbes, 15 September 1845.
25 Peel Papers, Add. Mss. 40,574, L 73. Forbes to Peel, 19 September 1854.
26 Richard Owen, *Life of Richard Owen* (London: John Murray, 1894), vol. 1, p. 207.
27 Ibid., p. 236.

Roderick Murchison was given a knighthood for his services as director of the Geological Survey, while Owen was offered, but declined, a similar honour.[28]

Peel's noble purpose was succeeded by political indifference. In 1835, acting on Peel's memorandum, Lord Melbourne, his Tory successor, invited Faraday to call at his office. There, after describing the practice of giving literary and scientific pensions as 'a piece of gross humbug', Melbourne offered Faraday £300. In reply, Faraday excused himself and coolly sent the Prime Minister his compliments:

> After the pithy manner in which your Lordship was pleased to express your sentiments on the subject ... it only remains for me to relieve you, as far as I am concerned from all further uneasiness. I will not accept any favour at your hands nor at the hands of any Cabinet of which you are a member.[29]

After some time, Melbourne apologised, and Faraday accepted a pension from the King's hands. But this earlier humiliation was by no means forgotten.

Peel's flexible concept of an award for merit was gradually reshaped into a narrower plan for meeting financial need. This was illustrated forcibly in 1854, when Lord Wrottesley, chairman of the newly formed Parliamentary Committee of the British Association, requested Lord Aberdeen, then Prime Minister, to reconsider the claims of men of science. This was the third appeal; Wrottesley had made a similar request of the elder Lord Derby in April 1852, during Derby's first ministry (February - December 1852). Then, the Government had refused a recommended pension of £200 for John Phillips, Professor of Geology at Oxford and Trinity College, Dublin, and founder member of the British Association. Wrottesley and Sir Robert Inglis protested that only 13% of the sum annually available for pensions had fallen 'to the lot of science'.[30] Indeed, the percentage remained at about this level for the rest of the century (See Table 1).

28 Ibid. Owen accepted a knighthood in 1884.
29 See L. Pearce Williams, *Michael Faraday* (London: Chapman & Hall, 1965). The story is variously recounted. See Edwin Paxton Hood, *The Peerage of Poverty* , First Series, Third Edition (London: Judd & Glass, 1859), pp. 213-215.
30 Aberdeen Papers (BM), Add. Mss. 43, 252. f. 223. Wrottesley to Aberdeen, 19 March 1854.

TABLE 1

Civil List Pensions received by Men of Science (or their Relatives)*
1772-1924

	Men of Science (or relatives)	Others	Men of Science as percentage of totals
1772-1829	nil	987	nil
1830-1839	9	100	10.0
1840-1849	13	100	13.0
1850-1859	8	55	12.7
1860-1869	18	107	14.4
1870-1879	11	104	8.0
1880-1889	13	93	12.3
1890-1899	15	168	12.2
1900-1909	21	92	18.0
1910-1914	11	66	14.0
Totals	**119**	**1,812**	**6.6%**

*Explorers are not included in this category.

A second application made by Lord Rosse, President of the Royal Society, in October 1853, also failed. As Aberdeen explained, the Government was 'compelled to require that poverty should be the attendant of merit; and that the pension should be as much the relief of pecuniary distress as the acknowledgment of intellectual attainments'. Rosse referred the matter back to the Parliamentary Committee, and deplored Aberdeen's attempt to associate the pension fund with a means test. If this went on, Wrottesley agreed, it would

> render absolutely nugatory, so far as Science and its Cultivators are concerned, all the benevolent intentions which Parliament and the country must be supposed to have entertained in their favour when the provision in question was created.[31]

Pensions might be an inappropriate method of rewarding wealthy men of science, but Wrottesley believed that few awards would go to science at all if poverty were made a prerequisite. In retrospect, his position seems strikingly

---

[31] Ibid.

elitist, and rather uninformed. Nonetheless, he could argue, with some conviction that, if poverty were the test,

> the honoured names of Airy, of Owen, of Hamilton and Adams would never have appeared on the pension list; and that small encouragement to abstract science which has hitherto been dispensed by the British Government would virtually have been withdrawn.[32]

Aberdeen refused to sanction Peel's interpretation — not, however, because he was against science, but because he was in favour of rewarding public service in general. Against Phillips he saw competing and more forceful claims upon the royal bounty. 'The general belief', he said, 'that these Civil List pensions were intended by Parliament exclusively for Science and Literature, is altogether incorrect; and it is right that this should be clearly understood.[33] There was only £1,200 per year to be divided among people who had 'just claims on Royal beneficence'. The entire sum could easily be spent without reference to science or literature at all. Aberdeen regretted he could not be more 'extensively beneficial', but observed that several deserving men would not appear on the list. In the end, Phillips received no pension.

The fact that Peel's vision of a reward for merit alone was not to be realised applied with particular force to men in Applied Science. Awards for inventors were categorically ruled out, no matter how meritorious or important. For example, in December 1861, Sir William Fairbairn, recently knighted for his service to engineering and for his presidency of the British Association, asked Palmerston, then Prime Minister, to award a pension to Richard Roberts, a well-known inventor of textile machinery. Palmerston felt certain Roberts would 'scarcely fall within the limits of the rules by which the grant of civil list pensions are governed'. Furthermore,

> ... the whole amount disposable is very small, and it is scarcely ever possible to give to any person more than a hundred pounds a year; and one should think that if the invention of Mr. Roberts has been greatly advantageous to the manufacturers of cotton, those who have grown rich by the use of his invention might, among them, well be able to give him a better annuity than the Civil List could afford.[34]

These characteristically mid-Victorian appeals to 'fair trade and no favour' led scientists to expect nothing at the Government's hands. Charles Babbage, supporting a circular on behalf of George Boole's widow, angrily denounced the pension's 'continuing political bias'. Babbage had been pleased with the Civil List Act of 1837. As he told George Stokes, Secretary of the Royal Society, 'It was professed to be for the reward of *eminence* in Science and

---

32   Ibid.
33   Aberdeen Papers, Add Mss. 43, 252, f. 283. Aberdeen to Wrottesley, 29 March 1854.
34   William Pole, *The Life of Sir William Fairbairn* (London: Longmans & Green, 1877), p. 391.

Literature and as such it won public approbation. It was not then supposed that it would be made first a pauper list and then a mere means of purchasing political power'. But the awards had become debased. Now, any successful application he said, 'must appear to be the wish of parties who have political power'. His instinct was to fight back by marshalling political influence: 'If the Royal Society, the London University and King's College would sign [Boole's petition] as corporate bodies', he wrote Stokes, 'it would no doubt be successful'.[35]

Political economy and political power were, in turn, subject to the whims of public popularity. A striking case was that of James Prescott Joule, discoverer of the mechanical equivalent of heat. In January 1872, Henry Roscoe and Balfour Stewart, both of Owens College, Manchester, tried to raise a fund for their colleague. 'We feel', they wrote Stokes, 'that the pre-eminent scientific merits of our friend Dr. Joule have

> partly through his own retiring disposition, not been sufficiently appreciated by the prominent men in this district and it seems to us that a proper recognition of his great service ought, if possible, to take place during his lifetime'.[36]

In May 1878, an official appeal was made but it soon foundered. While Faraday, Brown and Owen had apparently received pensions irrespective of financial need, Joule's circumstances were judged 'not sufficiently low' to justify an award. Huxley and Hooker protested that because the grant was confined to cases of 'indigent merit' and because so many clams were pressed upon the government, the annual £1,200 was being dribbled away in sums of £25.[37] But the rub was that Joule was felt to have less public support: 'While Joule was unknown, everyone knew of Faraday'. In the end, Joule received £300 from the Civil List (and another £200 from the Royal Society's Government Grant Fund), but the moral was clear. A candidate need not only be indigent, impressive, worthy and politically acceptable; he need be popular as well. The influence of this upon the social conscience of scientists was inescapably adverse.

During the last quarter of the century, scientists seeking pensions won little systematic response from Government. From time to time Victoria took some interest in the pensions, but her motives were activated more by pity for the poor than by appreciation of merit.[38] The Civil List was occasionally criticised in the press. It remained a target for anti-monarchical sentiment, as in parliamentary debates in 1971 and 1873. Cases of abuse still arose as when £500 was granted to two daughters of a distinguished nobleman who had for many years drawn a salary of £8,000 and who had held a pension himself after retirement. At the

35   Stokes Papers (Cambridge University), Babbage to Stokes, 24 January 1865.

36   Stokes Papers, Roscoe and Stewart to Stokes, 30 January 1872.

37   This was not strictly true. The smallest pensions awarded were of £50 and these were given only four times, all after Joule's time.

38   Tyndall Papers (Royal Institution), vol. III, f. 2,745, Hooker to Tyndall, 20 May 1878.

other extreme, however, one Chancellor was attacked for bestowing awards in such a way as to reflect discourteously on the 'poverty of gentlefolk'.[39]

III. Characteristics of the Civil List Pensioners

The Civil List paid the price of its own assumptions in confusion and distress. Peel had intended the awards to be for youngish men, in the prime of their creative lives, and assumed that such men would not, by and large, have independent means. But Wrottesley wanted pensions for distinguished men, past their prime, regardless of their means, as a form of public honour. Aberdeen wanted them for the poor. There was naturally confusion between these objectives, which placed the pensions in an ambiguous middle ground. They went neither systematically to young men, nor necessarily to distinguished men. Instead, the average age of pensioners merely increased without any corresponding increase in merit. As Table 2 shows, most winners were between sixty and seventy years of age, and were quite poor.

TABLE 2

Age and Discipline of Scientific Pensioners at Time of Award*

Field	Age					
	30-39	40-49	50-59	60-69	70-79	Total
Astronomy	-	1	-	1	-	2
Mathematics	1	-	1	2	-	4
Physics	1	3	3	1	1	9
Chemistry	-	-	-	4	1	5
Natural History	3	2	-	4	3	12
Geology	-	-	1	-	-	1
Agriculture	-	-	-	-	1	1
Physiology	-	-	-	-	1	1
Medicine	-	-	-	-	-	-
Engineering	-	-	1	2	-	3
Anthropology	-	-	-	-	-	-
Totals	5	6	6	14	7	38

* This includes those pensioners (38 of 73, or 52%) for whom dates the same period of birth and death can be found. The table naturally excludes posthumous awards made to next of kin.

---

39   Maxwell, op. cit., pp. 210-12. Richard Jefferies, a popular author, was refused a pension in 1885, but granted one after Smith's intervention in 1887.

Ironically, even when a pension was given it usually failed to provide an adequate living. Most grants were below £150 p.a., and two-thirds of these were under £100 (See Table 3).

TABLE 3

Sums Awarded in Civil List Pensions to Men of Science or their
Relatives
1770-1914

	£50	£50-99	£100-149	£150-199	£200-249	£250-300	Total Awards
1770-1830	-	-	-	-	-	-	-
1830-1839	-	2	1	1	3	2	9
1840-1849	-	2	5	-	5	1	13
1850-1859	-	5	1	-	2	-	8
1860-1869	-	8	9	-	1	-	18
1870-1879	-	3	4	3	1	-	11
1880-1889	-	5	4	2	1	1	13
1890-1899	2	9	3	-	1	-	15
1900-1909	1	11	6	2	1	-	21
1910-1914	1	7	3	-	-	-	11
Totals	4	52	36	8	15	4	119

In this fact appears the quintessential paradox of the civil pensions. If they were to be neither inducements for research nor rewards for illustrious careers, neither were they adequate to support the widows and families of men no longer able to do research or earn a livelihood (See Table 4). Moreover, when one compares the decreasing number of pensions given to living scientists and in the increasing number being given to relatives, as a kind of posthumous award, it appears that the decade ending 1879 was the last in which a scientist could confidently expect to receive in his own lifetime the benefit of his pension (See Table 5).

TABLE 4

**Wealth at Death of Civil List Pensioners leaving Estates
in England and Wales*
1770-1914**

Size of Estate	1770-1869 Pensioners receiving annual sums of:				1870-1914 Pensioners receiving annual sums of:				Totals
	£50	£50-99	£100-149	£150	£50	£50-99	£100-149	£150	
£500	-	-	2	-	-	3	-	-	5
£500-999	-	1	-	-	1	1	-	-	3
£1,000-4,999	-	1	-	5	1	2	5	1	15
£5,000-9,999	-	-	1	1	1	3	3	3	10
£10,000-24,000	-	-	-	2	-	-	1	1	4
£25,999-49,999	-	-	1	-	-	-	-	1	2
£50,000	-	-	-	-	-	-	-	-	-
Totals	-	2	4	8	3	7	9	6	39

*   The sample of 68 (67%) includes those Pensioners who were Fellows of the Royal Society
or who are mentioned in the DNB.

TABLE 5

Distribution of Pensions to Living Men of Science
and their Relatives
1770-1914

	Living	Posthumous	Total Awards
1770-1820	-	-	-
1830-1839	8	1	9
1840-1849	11	2	13
1850-1859	8	-	8
1860-1869	16	2	18
1870-1879	9	2	11
1880-1889	6	7	13
1890-1899	5	10	15
1900-1909	7	14	21
1910-1914	3	8	11
Totals	73	46	119

In looking at the group of pensioners as a whole, one sees that successful candidates were chosen for many different reasons. Not all of them were nationally eminent, as measured by mention in the *Dictionary of National Biography:* In fact, the percentage of pensioners noted in the DNB decreased between 1850 and 1899 and began to increase again only with the turn of the century. On the other hand, the number of pensioners who were elected Fellows of the Royal Society after 1860 — a convenient index of scientific merit — tended to increase over the same period. Only one-third of the pensioners honoured in the 1850s were Fellows, but this lends support to the hypothesis that many needy scientists were provincial, and not from the metropolitan pool from which Fellows were usually drawn (See Table 6).

TABLE   6

Fellows of the Royal Society and DNB Entries
among Civil List Pensioners
(Living and Posthumous)*
1770-1914

	Awards to FRSs	Awards to DNB Entries	Total Awards	FRSs as Percentage of Total Awards	DNB recipients as Percentage of Total Awards
1770-1830	-	-	-	-	-
1830-1839	7	9	9	77 %	100 %
1840-1849	9	12	13	70 %	90 %
1850-1859	3	7	8	37 %	80 %
1860-1869	7	14	18	38 %	77 %
1870-1879	5	7	11	45 %	63 %
1880-1889	4	6	13	38 %	45 %
1890-1899	8	6	15	54 %	40 %
1900-1909	11	11	21	50 %	50 %
1910-1914	8	6	11	72 %	54 %
Totals	6 2	6 8	1 1 9		

* The sample of 68 (67%) includes those pensioners who were Fellows of the Royal Society or who are mentioned in the DNB.

The distribution of awards by field of science shows that about half the winning candidates were in natural history (See Table 7). Large areas of pure science were unrepresented. Mathematics and geology, two very popular fields by Victorian standards, surprisingly received no pensions at all.

TABLE   7

Fields of Science Represented by Civil List Pensioners

	1770–1829	1830–1839	1840–1849	1850–1859	1860–1869	1870–1879	1880–1889	1890–1899	1900–1909	1910–1914	Total Awards
Astronomy	-	3	1	1	1	1	-	1	3	1	12
Mathematics	-	2	1	-	2	2	-	1	2	-	10
Physics	-	3	3	1	3	1	1	4	5	3	24
Chemistry	-	1	-	-	3	-	1	2	-	1	8
Natural History	-	-	5	1	5	2	6	1	4	2	26
Geology	-	-	2	1	-	-	-	1	-	2	6
Agriculture	-	-	-	-	1	-	-	-	1	-	2
Physiology	-	-	-	-	-	1	1	-	-	-	2
Medicine	-	-	-	-	1	-	-	-	-	-	1
Engineering	-	-	-	-	-	1	1	-	-	-	2
Anthropology	-	-	-	-	-	-	-	1	-	-	1
Mining	-	-	-	-	-	-	-	-	1	1	2
'General Science'	-	-	1	3	-	1	-	-	-	-	5
'Inventors'	-	-	-	1	2	-	2	-	-	-	5
Unknown	-	-	-	-	-	2	1	4	5	1	13
Totals	-	9	13	8	18	11	13	15	21	11	119

The proportion of pensions given to scientific men varied from decade to decade. The periods 1860–1869 and 1900–1909 were particularly fruitful, although it is unclear what factors made them so. The dates do suggest possible sympathies between the changing political leadership and the scientific community. Certainly, Palmerston (1859–1865) was not a great friend of science, and few were given in his time, while Lord Russell (1865–66) and Lord Derby (1866–68) were well disposed towards their scientific friends. Disraeli (1868–1870) might have seized an opportunity to win prestige if strong representations were made, but Gladstone apparently let scientists find their own rewards. In any case, the sympathies of Lord Salisbury (1895–1902) and A. J. Balfour (1902–1905), both of strong scientific interests and accomplishments, were certainly more reliable.

Men of science were forever writing round for colleagues in distress. For example, John Judd, Professor of Geology at South Kensington trying to raise a sum for S. Highley, went first to the Geological Society, and then to the Scientific Relief Fund, but all to no avail. As John Crisp wrote, 'Highley was a hopeless case, relative to the rest of deserving men'.[40] Even scientists with official scientific positions, including professors at the Royal College of Chemistry, Dublin, or in London, had extreme difficulty in winning pension rights — the unremitting struggles for pensions, in fact, dominated a large part of their social correspondence.[41]

In 1890, following a memorial drawn up by Hooker and signed by several men of science, George Stokes, PRS, was asked to approach the Chancellor personally, on behalf of two daughters of the Rev. Miles Berkeley, FRS, a Royal Medallist. Two of Berkeley's four daughters had become missionaries in Zanzibar; the other two wished to begin a school. The Chancellor replied that the list of candidates was too long, and scientists were among the most vulnerable.[42] As J. D. Hooker remarked,

> The fault is in the system not the minister. The £1,200 is a charity and there is no other resource available. What is really wanted is an annual grant analogous to the 'good service pensions' of the army and navy which are not so much rewards of merit as recognition's as such.[43]

By the end of the century, alternative forms of rewards, recognition and recompense had become available. The Scientific Relief Fund, begun by Gassiot and adopted by the Royal Society in 1859, made small grants to indigent scientific families on the recommendation of the President of any learned society. The expenditure was at first of limited use. For nearly 30 years the Fund's capital did not exceed £7,500 and its annual income was less than £250. But in 1886 Sir William Armstrong donated £20,000 to the Fund on the condition that his gift be equally matched from some other sources, and many, including Ludwig Mond, helped greatly.[44] This, together with the Government Grant Fund, and the pension funds of the Civil Service, helped to satisfy some of the very different demands put by science on the Civil List. In 1901, on the accession of Edward VII, pensions were removed from the Civil List and entered in the Consolidated Fund instead,[45] but the total allowance remained unchanged over the years.

The 'Civil List Pensions' became an anachronism. They continued to be granted by the Crown on the recommendation of the Prime Minister, but their importance and visibility diminished. In 1936 with the accession of George VI, it was officially admitted that though the fund could be used 'partly to merit cases of hardship and partly to reward merit' it had become the practice 'to grant

---

40 Stokes Papers, Judd to Stokes, 24 May 1886; Crisp to Judd, 27 May 1886.

41 Stokes Papers, W. N. Hartley to Stokes, 5 March 1892.

42 Stokes Papers, Thisleton-Dyer to Stokes, 22 February 1890, Huxley Papers (Imperial College), vol. 3, f. 356. Hooker to Huxley, 18 January 1890.

43 Tyndall Papers, vol. III, f. 2,745. Hooker to Tyndall, 20 May 1878.

44 *Nature*, 33 (11 March 1886), p. 433.

45 *Report of the Select Committee on the Civil List*, 1901. (87).v. p. 6.

pensions only where there are both merit and hardship'.[46] The same year, recognising that 'changes in national conditions during the last hundred years justify some increase', the annual limit was raised to £2,500, or an average total annual expenditure of about £50,000. By the Civil List Act of 1952, on the accession of Queen Elizabeth, the sum was raised to £5,000.[47] In 1949, the Government decided that publicity attaching to the awards was still so great that public statement of the grant of awards could prove embarrassing to their recipients.Thereafter, lists of pensioners, though submitted to Parliament, were no longer printed for general use. Eminence, not poverty, is still considered to be the chief, and statutory criterion; but its signification is no longer clear.

Conclusion

Historically, Civil List pensions to men of science, arts and letters were a welcome mark of national esteem, but fell far short of successfully stimulating research in youth, rewarding success in old age, or caring for the pensioner's family after death. Paradoxically, the reforms in Civil List administration which did away with the corruption of centuries of political misuse, helped to reduce the financial impact of such awards. The small sums, rigidly accounted for, were another legacy of the Age of Reform which could be regarded as a mixed blessing. Peel's attempt to create a fund for amply encouraging merit had, in the hands of his successors, become a mere token, awarded to those of the elite in the humblest circumstances. Far from enriching a life of honours, they could become symbols of poverty and humiliation.

The experience of Civil List pensions confirmed the belief of scientific reformers that *ad hoc* state aid could never supply the continuous support men of science and their work needed. The life of science required for its nourishment sufficient income and security to guarantee freedom from financial want which had discouraged men from taking science as a career. The Civil List, as one of the few small tributaries of Government aid, ironically added to the torrent of criticism of Government indifference towards science and letters. As such it contributed to the growing sense of identity among men of science, for whom adequate personal means were a necessary prerequisite to the development of a vigorous tradition of original research.

---

[46] Report of the Select Committee on the Civil List, 1936-37. (114).vi.p.8, para 18.
[47] Statutes, Civil List Act, 1952, section 13 (2).

Plate 6

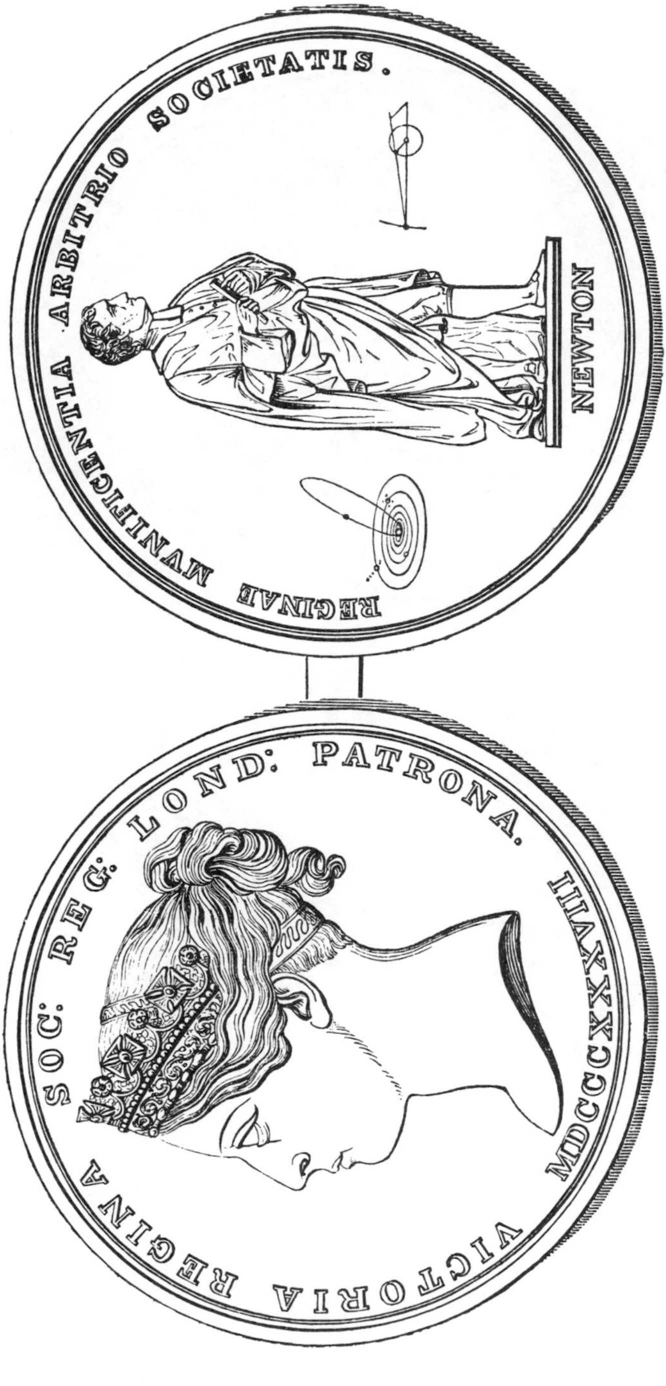

ROYAL MEDAL.

Design of the Royal Medal in 1838

Plate 5

Royal Medal awarded to James Ivory, F.R.S. in 1826

Facing page 84

Almost immediately, however, the medals became objects of intense and bitter dispute. The regulations approved by the Council in January 1826 specified that medals should be given (one gold and one silver replica) for 'the most important Discoveries or Series of Investigations completed and made known to the Royal Society, in the year preceding the day of their award' (21). But this rule was no sooner made than broken. Much to the disgust of Babbage, who had prepared a special paper on mechanical notation for the occasion, the first medals were not awarded for 'recent work' at all. Following a Council resolution of 26 November 1826, one was given to John Dalton for his work on the atomic theory twenty years before, and the other to James Ivory for his paper on refraction, published in the *Phil. Trans.* in 1823 (22).

In 1830, Babbage accused the Council of bad faith in failing to make publicly known the rules which governed the award, and prophesied an inglorious end to the original high purpose of the scheme. The medals would, he said, cease to excite 'competition among men of science' because 'no man could feel the least security that he should get them, even though his discoveries should fulfil all the conditions on which they were offered' (23). Babbage's argument was coloured by personal ambition; as he later recalled, his failure to win the Medal had been one of the three major disappointments of his young career (24). But his criticism had force. Three years later, Bulwer Lytton, quoting Helvetius, ominously reminded his countrymen that 'the degree of public virtue in a State depends exactly on the proper distribution of public awards' (25). It appeared that, within their mandate, the Council had chosen to use the royal bounty to remedy long-standing debts of gratitude among men of science, rather than to reward fresh work. There was, no doubt, justification of this policy. Among the distinguished investigators of the day, Dalton, at age 60, and Ivory, at 61, were among the least fêted (26) (though Ivory had received the Copley in 1814), and it was not unjust for them to receive the first royal awards (27). But it was also felt, as Davy explained in 1826, that the merits of a man's work could be seen only in the perspective of time.

> Discoveries are sometimes made of great interest, which require time and new labours for their confirmation; and when their importance is great, and their bearings extensive, years even may pass away before a full conviction of their truth can be obtained.

> Accordingly, in the case of Ivory and Dalton, the Council had looked to labours which have been sanctioned by time, the importance of which is generally felt, though not sufficiently acknowledged; which may be said

In 1824, Peel, then Home Secretary, and well aware of the 'Declinists' position, raised the question of state encouragement for science with Sir Humphry Davy, President of the Royal Society (9). In his presidential addresses, Davy had expressed a strong interest in rekindling the ethos of discovery lost by the Society during its aristocratic interlude under Sir Joseph Banks (10). Nonetheless, negotiations went on slowly and not until late 1825 did the time seem ripe for action. Then, 'at a period when the attention of government to science had not undergone any marked change', as Charles Babbage sourly observed, 'a most unexpected occurrence took place' (11). Peel proposed to George IV that medals be instituted for rewarding recent original contributions to science. Pensions, honours and medals had long been established forms of royal patronage on the Continent and in the literary and political life of England. Moreover, Peel noted, amid the proliferation of provincial botanical, geological and astronomical societies in the first decade of the new century, it would be politically wise 'to extend the influence of those establishments (such as the Royal Society) which have been derived from the Crown' (12). Sir Henry Lyons suggests that the King's agreement was an 'unexpected act of royal recognition of the Society's increasing activity and national utility' (13), but Peel's argument was probably more compelling. The Home Secretary recommended the creation of two gold medals, worth 20 guineas each, to be awarded 'in such manner as shall by excitement of competition among Men of Science seem best calculated to promote the objects for which the Royal Society was instituted' (14).

George IV had inherited few of the scientific and technical interests of his father (15), but he approved Peel's proposal, and increased the value of the medals to 50 guineas (16). In December 1825, following the King's agreement, the President and Council of the Royal Society drafted regulations for awards. The first medals were announced in 1826, and Babbage hailed them as the 'commencement of a new era' (17). Davy had called the Copley Medal 'the ancient olive crown of the Royal Society' (18); the 'Royal' was to be its modern coronet. Other medals, like the Rumford (created in 1800), the Davy (1877), the Darwin (1890), the Buchanan (1897), the Sylvester (1901) and the Hughes (1902) were or would be established to reward contributions in particular fields. But the Royal Medals, alone with the Copleys, were to be awarded annually 'for scientific work of exceptional merit' (19) of significance to science as a whole. Although they were not, by definition, to be limited to British subjects, it was envisaged that they be given for work done in Britain. As Babbage remarked, even those who doubted the policy of establishing medals for the encouragement of research 'saw much to admire in the tone and spirit in which they were offered' (20).

Royal Society. The Royal Medals are historically important for at least three reasons. First, they were one of the earliest instruments of royal patronage created specifically to encourage original scientific research. Because fundamental discovery has been responsive to external stimulation only within relatively narrow limits and over relatively long periods of time (4), the Medals can be useful in testing hypotheses about the potential effect of external rewards upon the social and professional structure of the scientific community.

In political and institutional terms, the Royal Medals also illustrate the manner in which a reward system can operate, the professional and personal ends it can be made to serve, and the intellectual norms it can help establish. Historians of scientific ideas have often remarked upon the circular pattern of reward and achievement which sometimes helps elevate men to 'greatness', but the relevance of the pattern itself in reinforcing a scientist's claim to recognition has only recently received systematic attention (5). In this context, the Royal Medals provide useful sociological evidence.

Finally, the history of the Medals, and the features of the scientific élite it helped define, offer an insight into the subtle process of reform taking place within the Royal Society, both during the 'Scientists' movement of the 1830s and 1840s, and through the remainder of the century.

1. ORIGINS AND EARLY YEARS

The Royal Medals have their immediate beginnings in the broad context of Sir Robert Peel's endeavours to encourage meritorious work in natural science. Virtually alone among British Prime Ministers of the first half of the nineteenth century, Peel had a profound respect for original investigation and an eager interest in the practical benefits of research. Historians are familiar with his 'scientific weekends' at Drayton Manor in the early 1840s, where his house parties were attended by Lyon Playfair, Charles Wheatstone, Richard Owen and George Stephenson. Peel's advocacy of Liebig, his enthusiasm for agricultural chemistry, his respect for the reformed Royal Society, and his collaboration with the Prince Consort in helping create the Great Exhibition of 1851 are all well known (6). Until Peel's untimely death in 1851, British men of science – and men of art – had a powerful patron (7).

Among Peel's many efforts for science, two schemes were of particular importance to individual scientists. One was the reform of the Civil List in 1835, and the regular allocation of public money through pensions to men of science and their families (8). The second, though the earlier in time, was the inauguration of the Royal Medals.

VI

OF MEDALS AND MEN: A REWARD SYSTEM
IN VICTORIAN SCIENCE
1826 – 1914

> Though discoveries in science may be the result of genius or accident, and though the most important discoveries may have been made by individuals without public assistance, the progress of such discoveries may at all times be materially accelerated by a proper application of public encouragement. (1).

INTRODUCTION

BY the 1820s the attack begun by John Playfair and Lord Brougham in the *Edinburgh* and the *Westminster* against the 'decline' of exact science in Britain had spread to criticism of the English Universities, the Royal Society and the government. In the critics' view, the 'scientific spirit' had a much firmer grip on France and Germany, whose universities and scientific academies accorded science social respect unknown in England (2). Recent scholarship, however, has shown that the concept of national scientific 'decline' or 'ascent' is extremely difficult to define. Indeed, international comparisons of scientific strength and the 'gaps' they seemingly disclose can be made only with reference to some external index, such as the award of prizes, papers published, or sums of money spent and men employed. Even current use of such indexes is open to considerable question (3).

But whatever one may think of the Declinists' claims – and it is clear that some state initiative was visibly wanting – it is not widely known what results were achieved by the rewards and honours schemes launched in the wake of the Declinist attack. Remarkably little attention has been given to those developments which, in some cases, had a profound impact on the social system of Victorian science.

This paper is a study of one of these schemes – the Royal Medals of the to have acquired their full authority only within a very short period, and which consequently, may be considered as within the literal meaning of the foundation (28).

The logic of repaying old debts and making 'safe' awards, coupled with the difficulty of evaluating recent work, perhaps also governed the Council's decision in 1827 to award Davy a Royal Medal for his Bakerian Lecture – 'considered as the last link, in the order of time, of the splendid chain of Discoveries in chemical Electricity which had been continued for so many years of his valuable life'. The Duke of Sussex himself later remarked that the only obstacle to Davy receiving the medal in its first year was the fact of Davy being President at the time (29). In the following year, a similar 'tribute of gratitude and regret', as Sussex put it, was given to Wollaston, as a last public offering to his services. 'The fame of these two illustrious men', Sussex admitted, 'is established upon too firm a basis to require or receive any additional strength or permanence from any honours which we can pay to their memories' (30).

But it remained true that the regulations had said one thing and the Council had done another. In March 1827, the Council attempted to legitimize its policy by passing a resolution limiting awards to a 'Discovery or Series of Investigations on any one principal subject or branch of knowledge which shall have been sufficiently established or otherwise completed within *five* years of the day of award (my stress) and for which a Royal Medal had not previously been bestowed' (31). But this did not help the Society escape criticism. In 1829, the circumstances surrounding awards to Charles Bell and Eilhard Mitscherlich aroused the resentment of some scientific Fellows – not because the medals were necessarily wasted, but because their award was capricious. As Sir James Smith charged in 1830, one was given to Bell 'for intricate anatomical investigations and disputed physiological deductions on the evidence of a single member of the Council – the rest making no pretentions to anatomical knowledge', and the other to Mitscherlich for work admitted by the President 'to be very little known in this country' and of which no one in the Council knew anything 'except by report' (32). As if to offset criticism, one of the medals for 1830 went to Sir David Brewster. But the Council could not escape so easily.

In 1830 Davies Gilbert was succeeded as President by the Duke of Sussex (33). The Duke, brother of the King, was unpopular with the scientific Fellows; it was clear that he would receive little sympathy from them unless rewards were distributed in the most judicious fashion. Moreover, whatever forms of patronage might thrive within reach of the Society, the medals were conspicuous evidence of the Council's good faith, and too visibly connected with science to be awarded on any but scientific grounds.

In 1830, a committee consisting of the President, Sir J. W. Lubbock, John Children, Michael Faraday, Capt. Kate, Davies Gilbert and Peter Roget was asked by the Council to 'consider of the regulations, both written and practically followed, under which the honorary rewards of the Society have been awarded; and to report to the President and Council the fittest modes, according to their judgement, of conferring these rewards in future'. A report was presented in August 1831, and an Appendix added in December 1834, both of which analysed the Society's medal and lecture policy in the closest detail (34). The Copley regulations were altered slightly, but no changes were recommended for the Royals (35).

Meanwhile, in 1831 and 1832, no Royal Medals were awarded, and the complaints of Babbage and the reformers quietly slipped from mind. The decision not to make awards may have been an act of diplomacy; certainly, the medals were a focus of controversy at a time when the Council wished to minimize contests between the reformers and themselves (36). At all events, the Duke of Sussex felt it necessary to announce apologetically at the Anniversary Meeting in 1833 that there were 'many circumstances connected with the original grant and distribution of those Medals as well as causes leading to their temporary discontinuance with which the Fellows may not generally be acquainted'.

The explanation Sussex gave was ingenious and convincing. For the first five years, he recalled, no Medals were actually available, and the first 10 winners had, in fact, been given empty boxes (37). In 1826, Sir Francis Chantry had been entrusted with selecting a design for the obverse side of the medal, and Sir Thomas Lawrence with the reverse. But each, through over-delicacy or procrastination, died before finishing the design and though the work was transferred to other hands, the death of George IV in 1830 delayed it even more. Under the circumstances, Sussex said, it was best to suspend further awards until the new King, William IV, had made known his views. Not until 3 years later, in 1833, did William give his assent to restore the Medals. Sussex heralded the decision as 'a glorious commencement of a philosophical chivalry, under whose banners the greatest among us may be proud to be enrolled' (38). But whether he had actually asked William for his assent sooner, Sussex did not say. Significantly, he did say that the Council had decided to alter the Medal regulations in such a way as seemed 'best calculated to comprehend every department of science and to prevent the jealousies which might arise from recurrence of similar subjects in immediate or too close succession' (39). Hereafter, awards would be given in triennial sequence on subjects to be decided by the Council three years ahead of each award. For the first three year cycle, which would begin in 1836, the upper limit of eligibility for a candidate's paper was left at five years before the date of award.

The King's letter was formally conveyed to the Royal Society on 23 March 1833; on 28 March the Council determined by lot that the series would be as follows:

Field	For awards in
1. Astronomy	(1836)
2. Physiology	(1836)
3. Geology and Mineralogy	(1837)
4. Physics	(1837)
5. Mathematics	(1838)
6. Chemistry	(1838)

Two committees, each of seven men, were appointed to nominate candidates for awards in astronomy and physiology, respectively, for 1833 and to set 'prize questions' in each subject for 1836 (40).

Almost from the start, however, it was clear that the new system would not work. Reporting on 18 April, the Astronomical Committee disagreed with Sussex's bland assumption that merely setting 'prize questions' would bring about distinctive discoveries. Discoveries could not be timed like examination papers, to suit the convenience of examiners. 'Some points in astronomy might indeed be indicated', the committee admitted, 'on which scientific persons might be advantageously employed' but only where 'industry and patience are the main qualities required' (41). The Physiology Committee, reporting in May, was less critical, but proposed as its prize question the discovery of 'the laws by which the Functions of the different Organs belonging to the Animal System are associated with each other' (42). Such an ambitious task must have been suggested with tongue-in-cheek.

It seems the Council took the point; perhaps science was not a matter of discovery 'to order'. By a resolution of 13 May 1833, the Council decided simply to give the two medals for 1836 to the two most important unpublished papers transmitted to the Society in astronomy and physiology. In the meantime, the 'Physiology' Medal for 1833 went to Auguste de Candolle for his *Physiologie Végétale* (published 1832), and the 'Astronomy' Medal to Sir J. F. W. Herschel for his paper on 'The Orbits of Revolving Double Stars'.

Despite the setback to its new regulations, the Council refused at first to recast its 'prize' policy. In November 1834 two new committees were appointed

– in geology and mineralogy, and physics – and given the same instructions as before (43). Again, the Physics Committee (which had four members in common with the Astronomical Committee of the previous year) announced its unwillingness to set a prize question for 1837. The 'Physics' medal for 1834 went, at the recommendation of Whewell and Peacock, to J. W. Lubbock, for his papers on the tides. The Geology Committee, while 'declining to express any opinion on the controverted positions contained in his work' awarded their medal for 1834 to Lyell for his *Principles of Geology* (44). The Committee also, with the example of Lyell's work in mind, suggested as a prize for 1837, 'Contributions towards a System of Geological Chronology, founded on an examination of Fossil Remains and their attendant Phenomena'. If no such work was forthcoming, their prize would go to the best paper in the field between 1834 and 1837.

In 1835, disillusioned by its experience with set prize questions, the Council abandoned this policy, and medals were thereafter awarded on the basis of nomination alone. But any method in which powerful men like Whewell and Peacock could choose candidates virtually unopposed was clearly open to bias, possible abuse, and sharp criticism (45). When Sir J. F. W. Herschel received a second medal in 1836 for his catalogue of nebulae, some may have wondered. When Whewell received it, in 1837, some may have been openly suspicious. But when it was announced that only one medal would be available in 1837, despite the plans of the 'geological committee' in 1834, it seemed evident that the Society was drawing upon too small a sample of active men in deciding the distribution of its awards.

The importance of this fact during the Medal's early years is suggested by the experience of 'multiple winners'. During the period 1826 to 1914 there were six multiple winners, all of whom were elected to the Royal Society before 1847. James Ivory, Michael Faraday, Thomas Graham, George Newport and Charles Wheatstone each received two, and J. F. W. Herschel received three. Of these only one (Newport) received his first medal before becoming an F.R.S. The other first awards ranged between two years after election (in Graham's case) to twenty years (Herschel). Having once won a medal the probability of receiving a second or third naturally depended on factors other than sheer accomplishment, such as the number of competing claims in any one year. Thus the 'lag' between the first and second awards could vary from only three years in the case of Wheatstone and Herschel, to 12–15 years in the case of Newport, Ivory, Graham and Faraday. It is perhaps significant that no multiple awards occurred after 1848, the first year the revised statutes of the Society were in operation. From the early 1850s onwards, the increasingly scientific standards of the Council and the growing number of productive scientists in the Society made multiple awards presumptuous and impractical.

Between 1826 and 1837 there were no formal restrictions on the nature of publication eligible for an award. With Victoria's accession in 1837, the Council, still under the Duke of Sussex, kept the triennial cycle, but narrowed the qualification by requiring that awards could be made only for papers published in the *Phil. Trans.* This was undoubtedly an attempt to 'upgrade' the awards.

But over the years, this restriction aroused hostility, owing to the sheer delay involved in getting work published. The unscientific demands made by the triennial 'prize' schedule were also annoying. But political and personal contests associated with the Medal cast both these difficulties into the shade. In 1845, Sir George Airy, the astronomer, and Thomas Snow Beck, a physiologist, received the two medals. Airy was a clear choice, but Beck was only 31 and not yet a Fellow (he was elected in 1851). Moreover, the paper on the nervous system of the uterus for which he received his award had not, contrary to the regulations of the Council, been published in the *Phil. Trans.* In November, the legality of the award was questioned by Dr Robert Lee, a rival physiologist and a Fellow since 1830. Lee's opposition to Beck's award was both professional and political. For years Lee had warred against Dr Peter Roget, also a physician, and since 1827, Secretary of the Society, and Roget, it appeared, had supported Beck's nomination.

Lee's protest was considered by the Council, but with only three dissenting votes, his objections were overruled. 'The Medal has been awarded', said the President, 'the thing is done, and it is too late to say anything more about it'. The President did, however, refer the matter back to the Physiology Committee, asking R. B. Todd and William Sharpey to draw up a paper on Beck's claims. In December, their report, which also sustained Beck's award, was approved by the Council and printed in the *Proceedings* (46).

The President claimed that the Council had acted on the recommendation of the Committee of Physiology. But on 2 April 1846, Lee attacked the President's assertion. On the contrary, Lee said, fifteen papers were submitted to that Committee, and the Committee had waited until William Lawrence, referee on all Lee's papers, had left the Committee Room before reaching a decision. This seemed to Lee clear evidence of a plot against him. Lee claimed that his own paper on the uterus had been read before the Society on 19 June, but had remained unrefereed for four months while Beck's paper, which had not been read, had nonetheless been properly refereed by Todd and Sharpey in good time. Lee demanded a competent tribunal to investigate these 'irregular, unjust and most unphilosophical proceedings . . . . ' (47), but his claim was not considered, and his angry fulminations in the *Athenaeum* were ignored (48). However, the moral force of Lee's argument added fuel to the reform movement, which hastened Roget's resignation in November, 1848, and cast a shadow over the Medal's history. Sixteen years later, Dr J. E. Gray, the zoologist, was still recalling Beck's alleged 'job' and telling Walter White, the Society's Assistant Secretary, that he wished, for the sake of good will, the Royal Society had no such medals to give (49).

Incidents such as this were not uncommon, although most were less conspicuous. In 1848, Col. Edward (later Sir Edward) Sabine, a former Secretary of the Society (1827–1833) and future President (1861–71), threatened to leave the Committee of Physics because he had been denied the Medal in 1847 for his papers on metallurgy and magnetism published in the *Phil. Trans.* the same year. 'What little things change men's dispositions', remarked Walter White. Sabine was by no means alone. Jealousies and rivalries were never far below the surface, as the experience of Sir David Brewster and Charles Babbage amply revealed – where 'self and not science' was the prime mover.

'When will philosophers be true to their calling?' White asked his diary (50). But this begged the real question. Scientists competed because competition was becoming part of their vocation, and the award made, or was thought to make, all the difference. Tremendous pressures bore heavily on some men. For example, in 1846, Richard Owen received a Royal Medal for his fossil work. In 1848, Gideon Mantell added important details and pointed to certain significant omissions in Owen's paper, but Owen fought to suppress Mantell's criticism, and felt the authority of his medal proved him 'right'. When Mantell himself got the medal in 1849, the case was closed. But for over three years, Mantell struggled to 'legitimatize' his criticisms through the recognition of his peers. 'I think he (Mantell) ought to have it', White wrote in his Journal 'but I do not like to see a philosopher so anxious for a mere medal' (51). White could have spared his moralizing; given the circumstances, virtue could be its own reward, but it carried little weight in the scientific community or the outside world. When Lyell received the Medal in 1839, he declined a party in his honour offered by his publisher, George Murray. In 1857, however, an older and wiser Lyell, remarked, 'I know better now; publicity is what a man in my position wants' (52).

The requirement of 1837 that winning papers be first published in the *Phil. Trans.* clouded the Medal's prestige for years. Gathering doubts prompted Samuel Christie, Secretary of the Society, to issue in March 1850, a circular letter to selected Fellows. In reply, Sir George Airy, the Astronomer Royal, went so far as to say that 'the Royal Medals are viewed with contempt':

The institution of the Royal Medals has, in my opinion, totally failed in so far as it has produced any effect at all, I believe the effect to have been that of lowering the character of the Society. The grand and radical fault is, the confining of the adjudication of the Medals to the authors of Papers printed in the *Trans* . . . . . The Fellows of the Society are thus invited and encouraged to withdraw themselves from competition with the world and to enter only into the petty contests of a single society. No service whatever, I believe could be contrived so distinctly tending to degrade the scientific tone of the Society's *Transactions* (53).

Airy also criticized the limited eligibility period for the Medal, and the difficulty of having to make awards in given subjects. Inevitably, from the astronomer's point of view, unfavourable comparisons could be drawn between the Royal Medals and the medal of the Royal Astronomical Society. But even within the Royal Society the Royal Medal, Airy said, was seen to be inferior to the Copley, 'simply from the circumstances that it (the Copley) is unrestricted in regard to place or manner of publication of papers and unlimited in regard to time'. Every person connected with foreign academies knew that the peculiar value of the Copley arose from the fact that 'the Prize has been offered to the competition of the world' (54).

In his reply to Christie, Humphrey Lloyd, of Trinity College, Dublin, agreed that the rule requiring publication in the *Phil. Trans.* had tended to 'lessen the honour of the award' (55). Perhaps they need not be offered openly to the whole world, but at least they should be 'disposed of for the encouragement of British Science generally' (56). Baden Powell of Oxford argued that limiting awards to contributions published in particular scientific papers might prove invidious for a man who simply deserved the medal 'for his general services to science' (57), while Sir J. F. W. Herschel agreed that the limitations in force were too narrow. Because 'the Royal Medals were . . . intended as an encouragement to British Science generally and especially its cultivation in the Royal Society', Herschel proposed that one medal should go to a Fellow, and one to someone outside the Fellowship. The triennial cycle he thought unworkable: 'Discoveries do not arise in stated order of time.' Instead medals could be given in specific subjects, or used in concert with the new Government Grant – 'the one to stimulate invention, the other to enable the inventor on the recognition of his merit as such to reduce his invention to practice' (58).

In the last reply, Robert Brown, the physiologist, recommended that the medals should be distributed equally between biology and physics (59). The Medal should also be given greater prestige; otherwise, Brown warned Christie, it might, by some form of Gresham's law, undermine the character of the Copley, 'the highest public mark of approbation of the Royal Society'.

The Council received Christie's report, and on 13 June 1850 abandoned both the principle of prior publication in the *Phil. Trans.* and the triennial system. Awards henceforward were made simply for 'the two most important contributions to the advancement of Natural Knowledge published originally in Her Majesty's dominions within a period of not more than 10 years and not less than 1 year of the date of award'. The period of 'gestation' was thus extended from three to ten years. In place of the triennial cycle, it was decided that one Medal should be given each year in 'each of the two great divisions of Natural Knowledge' (60).

The reformed regulations could not, of course, pretend to do away with party or favour. Some men of science found the whole business distasteful. As Faraday wrote to Thomas Andrews in 1843:

> I have always felt that there is something degrading in offering rewards for intellectual exertion, and that societies, or academies, or even kings and emperors, should mingle in the matter does not remove the degradation, for the feeling which is hurt is a point above their condition and belongs to the respect which a man owes himself (61).

Others, perhaps less otherworldly, felt that substantial rewards were necessary and valuable to science, but that medals were too volatile a commodity. In 1850, Babbage had remarked that the Society's actions seemed to be inspired by a certain set, and that it was possible to predict with fair accuracy who would receive medals from year to year. In Babbage's view, situations could develop in which the Council, having given a medal to someone, then found it necessary to give a second medal to someone of an opposing faction to destroy the impression of favouritism created by the first. Afterwards, the Council would probably have to give a medal to a third candidate who had deserved it all along (62). Inevitably, personal preferences would be expressed, and the most active Fellows would generally have the greatest chance of expressing them. After 1850, these Fellows (and the greater part of the Council) were genuinely men of science rather than dilettanti, but this does not mean that cliques vanished. In 1854, Edward Forbes's claim was passed over in favour of young Joseph Hooker. Unfortunately, Forbes died within a few weeks of the award (63), and all grieved at the apparent injustice. Of course, the reverse happened too, when medals were used as rewards for older men with long standing reputations, rather than for new and exciting discoveries (64).

The case of John Tyndall is instructive. In the autumn of 1853, the 'Biology

Committee' decided to recommend Darwin for 'their' Medal, but the 'Maths, Physics and Chemistry Committee' was undecided. For the 'Physics' Medal, five names were placed before the Council – Cayley, Frankland, Hoffman, Sylvester and Tyndall. The Council recommended Tyndall, and told him so; whereupon Tyndall wrote Hirst a jubilant letter, rejoicing that he had beaten Hoffman (65). In the meantime, however, sentiment in the Society rose against Tyndall. He had been elected a Fellow only the year before, and some doubted whether his work on magne-crystallic action was original and unassisted (66). When Tyndall heard of these rumours he immediately released Christie and the Council from any obligation to him. 'I should be doubly unworthy of any such distinction', he wrote, 'were I willing to accept it when coloured by a doubt'. To John Peter Gassiot, Tyndall wrote even more strongly: 'However highly I may value such a mark of distinction I should, under present circumstances, feel it to be my duty respectfully to decline it'. Gassiot accepted Tyndall's decision with becoming grace: 'I would sooner hold the position you have so promptly taken than be the recipient of twenty medals' (67). In 1864 Tyndall was belatedly awarded the Rumford Medal. But never again would the Royal (or the Copley) be offered him.

CHARACTERISTICS OF THE ÉLITE

Over the period 1826 to 1914, a total of 173 Medals were given to 166 different men. With few exceptions, two awards were given each year. In 1831 and 1832, as we have seen, none was given, and in 1837 and 1853 only one was given each year (to William Whewell and Charles Darwin, respectively).

Ninety-one, or 54% of the Medals over the entire period went to men in the physical sciences, while the earth sciences and the life sciences shared about 73, or 42%. Only two went to engineers (see Table 1). Awards were always made by the Council. The restriction of awards to papers in the *Phil. Trans.* often meant that only Fellows could be considered. After 1850, the Fellowship barrier probably acted as a useful screening mechanism for potential candidates. Whatever the virtues of the fact, 159 medallists (86%) were, or became, Fellows or Foreign Members of the Royal Society. Of the recipients who were not, only two (Oswald Heer, 1877 and Antoine Balard, 1830) were both foreigners and not foreign members. Only six British medallists never became Fellows: George Chrystal (awarded in 1911), Peter Guthrie Tait (1886), John Hewitt Jellett (1881), Thomas Anderson (1872), John Westwood (1885) and Albany Hancock (1858).

TABLE 1. DISTRIBUTION OF MEDALS BY SUBJECT‡
1826-1914

		A	B	C	D	E	F	G	Eng	Totals
					Subject					
1826–35	.	6	2	5	1	1	—	1	—	16
1836–45	.	6	4	5	—	1	—	3	—	19
1846–55	.	5	3	4	1	3	4	—	—	20
1856–65	.	5	2	3	1	3	1	3	1	19
1866–75	.	2	1	8	4	1	4	1	—	21
1876–85	.	5	2	2	2	2	4	2	1	20
1886–95	.	2	6	1	2	2	3	4	—	20
1896–1905	.	5	5	1	3	1	2	3	—	20
1906–1914	.	5	1	1	4	1	2	4	—	18
Totals	. .	41	26	30	18	15	20	21	2	173

‡ Subjects are defined in the terms used by the Royal Society's Government Grant Boards:

A Mathematics and Astronomy
B Experimental Physics
C Chemistry
D Geology and Palaeontology
E Botany
F Zoology and Comparative Anatomy
G Physiology and Medicine
Eng Engineering

TABLE 2. THE TENURE OF WINNERS IN THE ROYAL SOCIETY AT TIME OF FIRST AWARD

Number of Winners Receiving Awards Before Election		Number of Winners Receiving Awards After Election		Total
≦ 5 years before .	4	≦ 5 years after . .	29	
6–10 years before	4	6–10 years after .	35	
≧ 11 years before	3	≧ 11 years after .	84	
Totals . .	11		148	159

As Table 2 shows, most winners did not receive their Medals until long after their election to the Society. Not less than 84 of these 159 Fellows (54%) had at least eleven years standing in the Society, and a further 30% of these had been Fellows for more than fifteen years.

TABLE 3. AGE INCIDENCE OF WINNERS BY SUBJECT
1826–1914

Age			Subject							
		A	B	C	D	E	F	G	Eng	Totals
21–25	. .	–	–	–	–	–	–	–	–	–
26–30	. .	2	–	1	–	–	2	1	–	6
31–35	. .	5	3	7§	–	–§	–	1	–	18
36–40	. .	4	3§	5	1	3	1	3	–	21
41–45	. .	3§	4§	3	–	–	5‖	3	–	21
46–50	. .	6	5	3	2	2	2‖	5	–	26
51–55	. .	6	4‖	3‖	4	3	2	6	–	30
56–60	. .	3‖	–	1	4	3	2	–	–	14
61–65	. .	2§‖	1	2	3	2	3	1	–	16
66–70	. .	1	–	2	3	–	–	1	1	8
71–75	. .	1	1	–	–	–	1	–	1	4
76–80	. .	1	–	–	1	–	–	–	–	2
Totals	. .	38	24	29	18	14	20	21	2	166

Physical Sciences (A–C): 91
Earth Sciences (D): 18
Life Sciences (E–G): 55
Engineering (Eng): 2

166

§ Number includes first award of a multiple winner
‖ Number includes a Non-F.R.S. winner

Legend:
A Mathematics and Astronomy
B Experimental Physics
C Chemistry and Metallurgy
D Geology, Palaeontology, Mineralogy and Geography
E Botany
F Zoology and Comparative Anatomy
G Physiology and Medicine
Eng Engineering

Table 3 shows the pattern of age incidence by field, while Table 4 shows the median age distribution, by decade, for the entire group of winners. The youngest winner was William Bowman (Field G), (1842, aged 26); the oldest was General Sir Richard Strachey (A), (1897, aged 80). The average age of award varied only slightly between 46 and 50 in all fields except chemistry

(C), geology (D) and botany (E). The median age in chemistry was much lower than average; it was higher in botany, and highest in geology. The youngest individual winners did not, however, appear in chemistry, but in mathematics (George Boole, 1844, aged 29), and zoology (Charles Hargreaves, 1848, aged 28). The comparative youth of the *average* chemistry winner raises interesting historical questions. The number of Royal Medallists is, of course, too small to demonstrate trends, but it would be interesting to see whether the recognition pattern in different fields was changing significantly over time.

TABLE 4. MEDIAN AGE OF WINNERS IN DIFFERENT SUBJECTS BY DECADE†
1826–1914

	A	B	C	D	E	F	G	Eng	Average
1826–35 · ·	38·0	46·5*	46·8	37·0*	35·0*	–	55·0*	–	43·1
1836–45 · ·	38·6	41·3	37·2	–	33·0*	–	31·3	–	36·3
1846–55 · ·	44·8	35·0	50·2	59·0*	40·5	40·8	–	–	45·1
1856–65 · ·	53·2	40·5*	48·0	53·0*	59·0	48·0	52·3	71·0*	53·1
1866–75 · ·	62·0*	42·0*	51·0	57·3	61·0*	51·3	64·0*	–	55·5
1876–85 · ·	50·8	52·0*	45·5*	66·5*	50·0*	41·8	54·0	66·0*	53·3
1886–95 · ·	63·0*	43·8	44·0*	54·0*	51·0*	53·6	41·5	–	50·1
1896–1905 ·	50·0	54·0	55·0*	70·0	39·0*	66·0*	49·3	–	54·8
1906–1914 ·	52·8	62·0*	61·0*	57·0	55·0*	54·0*	49·5	–	55·9

† Multiple winners are given by age of first award
* Samples of two or less

Of the 129 Fellows receiving medals after the electorial reform of 1847, 113 (or 68% of all winners) were elected since that date. The age distribution of winners among post-1847 Fellows is similar to that given in Table 3, except that they appeared relatively less frequently in the 31–35 age group and rather more in the group over age 36. From the Royal Society's viewpoint, the most 'profitable' decades were 1851–1860, when 28 future Medallists were elected and 1881–1890, when 25 were elected. The least 'profitable' decade was 1861–1870, in which only 19 future Royal Medal winners were elected. Whether this generation represented a 'trough' in British scientific excellence, remains an intriguing question. It is interesting that awards to chemists show a sharp drop after 1875. These were the same critical decades in which, as Sir Eric Ashby and D. S. L. Cardwell remind us (68), German university science had reached a peak of prestige, and British failure to advance chemical research

VI

and education later cost the nation dearly in international industrial and technological competition.

Although the selection process is not described in Council records, a list
of 'Medal Claims, 1873–1909', now preserved in the Society's Library, gives
some tantalizing insights. The men chiefly responsible for most nominations
between 1873–1883, for example, were Joseph Hooker, Alexander Williamson,
George Stokes, Edward Frankland, Norman Lockyer, Warren de la Rue,
Balfour Stewart, Frederick Abel, Thomas Hirst, Henry Debus, Ray Lankester,
Thomas Huxley and Michael Foster. The 'Young Guard' (69) of science
probably exerted more than their share of influence over the Society in the
second half of the century. Of the eight scientific members of the famous
'X-Club', five received Royals (70), and one (Tyndall) narrowly missed. Four
of these eight are among the most active on the list of nominators.

Many factors, including the persistence of a man's 'proposer', the Council's
opinion of his work, and the extent of competition within his 'area' naturally
affected his chances and speed of recognition. Again, the evidence is too slight
to be conclusive, but the contests raise interesting speculations. For example,
in 1857 and 1858 John Lindley and Albany Hancock received medals for their
work in botany, and both seemed indebted for support to Hooker, son of the
Director of Kew and himself a medallist in 1854 (71). In 1875, two men were
recommended – William Crookes, by G. G. Stokes, and William Froude, by
C. W. Merrifield – for the physical science medal. In the end, Crookes won
that year, and Froude was deferred until 1876. Whether Stokes's word counted
for more than Merrifield's is an open question; the evidence is simply suggestive.

The records also suggest the level of 'competition' a man encountered. In
1883 there were five nominations for the two medals – P. M. Duncan and T. A.
Hirst, in physical science, and Carl Schorlemmer, H. N. Moseley and J. Burdon
Sanderson in biological science. The winners were Hirst and Burdon Sanderson.
In 1884 there were four candidates – George Darwin (nominated by William
Abney) and D. H. Hughes (by Stokes), in physics, and Daniel Oliver (by
Foster) and D. Ferrier (by Lauder Brunton) in biology. The winners were
Darwin and Oliver; Hughes was put off until 1885, and Ferrier was rejected
altogether. In 1885, Francis Galton and E. R. Lankester were nominated in
biology. As Galton's claims were opposed by Huxley (72), Lankester won that
year, and Galton had to wait until 1886.

By the 1880s, the queue of deserving candidates had grown embarrassingly
long. Even after vigorous screening, an average of four candidates were nominated each year, and the wait for recognition grew accordingly. Some years
saw much more competition than others; in 1905 for example there were

seven candidates; in 1903, only two (Sir David Gill and Horace Brown). Inevitably, some men waited an exceedingly long time. John Henry Poynting, for example, was unsuccessfully nominated by J. J. Thomson in 1900, but was put up again in 1904 and finally won in 1905. Gill, Brown and D. H. Scott were proposed in 1902, and all were passed over. Gill and Brown won the following year, but Scott was deferred to 1905, and again to 1906. Joseph Larmor, proposed in 1901, did not receive a medal until 1915. Ramsay Traquair, first proposed in 1904, was proposed four times again until he finally won in 1907. John Aitkin, proposed in 1905, received his only in 1917.

When awards were postponed or delayed, recognition sometimes came too late. Sir David Gill, considered for the Copley in 1903, was given the Royal Medal instead, and died before he could be reconsidered (73). Others were proposed repeatedly, with no success. One notable example was H. L. Callendar, put up with a short testimonial by John Perry in 1905. Callendar received a $3\frac{1}{2}$-page recommendation, again by Perry, the following year, but again in vain. It is ironic that Callendar served for 15 years on the Society's Government Grant Board, deciding who should receive grants in physics.

Being of lesser rank, the Royal was usually awarded before the Copley, and a few outstanding scientists could reasonably expect to receive both medals during their life-time. In other cases, the Royals were means of rewarding men of the first rank who had already won the Copley and could go no higher in the Society's scale of honours. For the majority, however, the Royals sometimes became 'Copley substitutes', and the Medals, far from encouraging young researchers, were used to reward senior men who could not, for technical reasons, be awarded a Copley, or a Copley twice.

The fact that most winners were of about ten years standing in the Society suggests that awards were given for the most part to established, recognized scientists, most of whom were nearing middle age. This was not commonly believed at the time. Huxley, recalling his own experience, told the anniversary dinner of the Royal Society in 1892 that the Royal Medal was usually given to younger men and by this means attracted youth to science:

> In his (Huxley's) younger days, if a man took to science it was thought he was going to the bad; the receipt of the medal made an entire revolution in the minds of his friends and he was a respectable person from that time (74).

Indeed, if one considers as a group those Fellows of the Society who received their medals eleven or more years after election, one finds a gradient favouring older, more established men. This is particularly noticeable for the years following the reforms of 1847, and seems to be co-variant with the increasing dominance of university professors among the winners (as among the Council of the Society and the community of science generally). As A. W. Rucker remarked in toasting the Medallist in 1891, five of the eight preceding winners had long experience of provincial colleges (75), and this professoriate reinforced the gerontocratic quality of the Council. As Thiselton Dyer sourly remarked in 1894, in speaking of the Copley:

> If a man wishes to see his name enrolled in the same list as Darwin and Pasteur, as Joule and Helmholtz and as Kelvin and Ludwig, he must be content to wait till the scientific *orbis terrarum* gives an unspoken but unqualified assent (76).

There were what seemed spasmodic attempts to 'restore the balance' by nominating younger men. Thus in 1896, although one medal went to Sir Archibald Geikie, aged 61, the other went to Charles Vernon Boys, then only 41. Despite denials by Lord Lister (then President) and Lord Rayleigh (Secretary) (77), *The Times* insisted that the opinions of older Council members had been overridden in the reward of a younger man, instead of another more 'experienced' person (78).

CONJECTURES AND CONCLUSIONS

Behind every awarded medal lay a complex history of competition, sacrifice, and, sometimes, disappointment. One can guess at 'missing' names which perhaps should have been on the list, but which are now largely forgotten. One of the chief tasks awaiting future historians is the 'discovery' of these men – the unrecognized scholars, or the 'second rank' scientists – who have played such a large unwritten role in the development of scientific ideas.

By their award, Medals codified schools of thought, and legitimized scientific paradigms. But it is less clear whether they really achieved Peel's original objective – to encourage fresh scientific discovery within British science as a whole. If Medals were, after 1855, going on balance to older and more established men of science, it is arguable that they were becoming more a means for recognizing past glory and long service to science than a means of stimulating younger scientists to greater zeal. This was reflected by the timing of many awards. Faraday, for example, first received the Royal Medal in 1835, three years after he had been awarded the more prestigous Copley. Airy received his in 1846, ten years after he had become Astronomer Royal, and in the same year that he was elected President of the Royal Society. Alfred Ewing received the medal in 1896, after he had been repeatedly honoured by the Geological Society, and had become a leading man of science (79). The Rev. John Kerr received one in 1898, virtually on his deathbed (80). William Ayrton received his in 1901, long after his most significant work in electricity, and when he was on the threshold of retirement. To men of such accomplishment, Royal Medals were merely tokens of esteem. For some men of science and their biographers, they were not even worth mentioning (81).

It is possible to ask whether the Crown and the Council could have distributed its patronage more wisely in a different way (82). Michael Foster, for example, said in recommending Daniel Oliver in 1884, that the Medal ought to be given also for self-sacrificing service to museums and education, as well as for published research (83). Unquestionably, the Medal did have a significant impact, and did alter the course of some men's lives as a standard of recognition and acceptance. Late in life, Huxley recalled the time when 'the value of the medal was inexpressible to him'; winning the Medal 'thereby determined my career' (84). Perhaps it was inevitable that the Medal, as any reward system, could become an instrument of personal influence. As Hooker once remarked to Huxley, 'I cannot see that the majority of the Council are ardent truth seekers, or care for more than to back, each, their own profession' (85). A closer study of Medal claims would no doubt throw much revealing light on the internal politics of the Society.

Brewster argued in 1835 that, had it not been for the creation of the British Association in 1830, Peel's two distinct, though small steps in the favour of science would have been lost amid the loud demands for political reform that absorbed the attention of his successors. Certainly the British Association, at least in its first quarter century, did as much as, if not more than the Royal Society or the Royal Medals for the advancement of natural knowledge in a general way throughout the country (86). At the outset, Peel's plans were originally intended to *stimulate* scientific work by traditional methods. But as we have seen, events implicitly conspired to transform his scheme from an objective stimulant to a highly subjective and personal reward. The debate of the 1820s had shown that science had an inadequate role in the universities, insufficient representation in the Royal Society, and inadequate encouragement from the Crown and the State. But the experience of the learned societies in the 1860s and 1870s revealed that the more fundamental task of government was to secure the direct encouragement of science by the provision of research grants and stipends on a national basis to promising individuals who lacked the time and the means to devote to science. Medals, both in theory and practice, no longer served the utilitarian role envisaged for them. They had to be combined with formal honours and financial stipends if they were to be successful incentives. In 1900, after decades of experience, the Council concluded that the creation of further medals would serve no useful end (87), and placed more emphasis upon the endowment of research (88). This policy was long overdue. Nearly one hundred years before, Jeremy Bentham had advised that 'the most simple and efficacious method of encouraging investigations of *pure theory* – the first step in the career of invention, consists in the appropriation of sufficient funds to the researchers requisite in each particular science' (89). Not until the government and the universities accepted responsibility for providing this direct financial encouragement could science become a practicable vocation, and its practice a truly national enterprise.

ACKNOWLEDGEMENTS

This investigation was supported in part by a research grant from the Department of Education and Science. The author gratefully acknowledges the courtesy of the Librarian and Archivist of the Royal Society. The Huxley Papers have been quoted by kind permission of the Governors of Imperial College.

NOTES

(1) J. Bentham. 'The Rationale of Reward', Ch. 2 in John Bowring, *The Works of Jeremy Bentham* (Edinburgh, 1838–1843), Vol. 2, p. 256.

(2) See especially, Charles Babbage, *Reflexions on the Decline of Science in England, and on some of its Causes*, (London, 1830), Edward W. Brayley, *The Utility of the Knowledge of Nature*, (London, 1831). The period is dealt with in some detail in George A. Foote, 'The Place of Science in the British Reform Movement, 1830–1850', *Isis*, **42**, 192–208 (1951), and most elegantly in J. T. Merz, *A History of European Thought in the Nineteenth Century*, (Edinburgh, 1896), Vol. 1, Chapter 3. For a recent and interesting contribution, see Nathan Reingold, 'Babbage and Moll on the State of Science in Great Britain: A Note on a Document', *Brit. J. Hist. Sci.*, **4**, 58–64 (1968).

(3) Cf. O.E.C.D. *Gaps in technology: comparisons between member countries*, 1968–70.

(4) See R. MacLeod. 'The Institutionalisation of Basic Research: The Government Grant to the Royal Society, 1850–1914' (in the press).

(5) See, e.g., Stephen Cole and Jonathan R. Cole, 'Scientific Output and Recognition: A Study in the Operation of the Reward System in Science,' *Amer. Social Rev.*, **32**, 377–390 (1967); Harriet Zuckerman, 'Nobel Laureates in Science: Patterns of Productivity, Collaboration and Authorship', *Amer. Social Rev.*, **32**, (1967).

(6) See Charles S. Parker, *Sir Robert Peel*, (London, 1899), Vol. I, pp. 99–100; Vol. 2, p. 304–7; Vol. 3, pp. 162, 225, 433, 444–47. Recollections of Peel's good intentions towards science are legion. Peel was considered for the Presidency of the Royal Society in 1838, and 1848. In the 1840s he assisted in the creation of the Royal College of Chemistry,

and in the preparations for the Great Exhibition of 1851. He also encouraged Prince Albert to admit men of science to the Privy Council. (*Proc. Roy. Soc.*, **7**, p. 567). It was also through Peel's influence that Sir Roderick Murchison, as director of the Geological Survey, received his knighthood. (T. Wemyss Reid, *Memoirs and Correspondence of Lyon Playfair*, (London, 1899), p. 156).

(7) See J. Mordant Crook, 'Sir Robert Peel: Patron of the Arts', *History Today*, (January 1966), 3–11.

(8) See R. MacLeod, 'Science and the Civil List, 1830–1914', *Technology & Society*, **6**, 47–55 (1970).

(9) Parker, *op. cit.*, Peel to Sir Humphrey Davy, P.R.S., 13 December 1824.

(10) Cf. Sir Humphrey Davy, *Six Discourses to the Royal Society*, (London, 1827).

(11) Babbage, *op. cit.*, p. 115.

(12) Parker, *op. cit.*, Vol. I, p. 387, Peel to George IV, 26 November 1825.

(13) Sir Henry Lyons, *The Royal Society: 1660–1940*, (Cambridge 1944), p. 247.

(14) Royal Society MSS., DM. 1.74, Peel to Sir Humphry Davy, P.R.S., 3 December, 1825.

(15) D. McKie, 'The Crown and Science: Elizabeth I to Elizabeth II,' *Discovery*, July 1960, pp. 288–290.

(16) At the same time two similar medals were given to the Society of Antiquaries. Through the efforts of the Bishop of Salisbury, ten literary fellowships of £100 p.a. were also established for 'meritorious and not wealthy members of that society'. See Sir David Brewster, 'The Decline of Science in England', *Quarterly Review*, **43**, 382 (1830).
See Sir Nicholas Harris Nicolas, *Observations on the State of Historical Literature and on the Society of Antiquaries and other Institutions for its Advancement in England*, (London, 1830), p. 200.

(17) Babbage, *op. cit.*, p. 116.

(18) See E. C. Smith, 'The Copley Medal and its Founder,' *Nature*, **174**, 1034 (4 December 1954).

(19) The grant was subsequently confirmed by William IV in 1833, by Victoria in 1837, Edward VII in 1901 and by each successive monarch since. Lyons, *op. cit.*, p. 250. Until 1939, a gold medal together with a silver replica was given to each winner. Since 1939, the gold medal has been given alone.

(20) Babbage, *op. cit.*, p. 116.

(21) Council Minutes, 26 January 1826.

(22) Council Minutes, 26 November 1826.

(23) Babbage, *op. cit.*, p. 120.

(24) The others were his failure to become a Secretary of the Royal Society, and his lack of success in getting (until 1828), the Lucasian chair at Cambridge, See Maboth Moseley, *Irascible Genius: A Life of Charles Babbage, Inventor*, (London 1964), p. 104.

(25) Edward Bulwer Lytton, *England and the English*, (London, 1833), Vol. 1, p. 163.

(26) Brewster bewailed their plight in his review of Babbage's *Reflexions*: 'Mr Dalton, the most distinguished chemist in Britain, and the man who has given to chemistry her numerical laws, has been allowed to spend the flower of his days in drudgery of teaching the elements of mathematics at Manchester and has never been honoured by a single mark of national gratitude. Mr Ivory, the first mathematician in England, after exhausting the vigour of his life as a mathematical teacher at Marlow has retired, as his humblest colleague would have done on a superannuation, and has been allowed to spend his latter years in comparative poverty and obscurity'. *Edinburgh Review*, **43**, 320 (1830).

(27) In 1833, Dalton also received a Civil List pension from the Crown, one so small that Sussex expressed official regret 'at the very narrow limits within which the munificence of the king and the generosity of the Nation should be confined'. *Proc. Roy. Soc.*, **3**, 220 (1830–1837).

(28) Charles Weld, *A History of the Royal Society*, (London, 1848), Vol. 2, p. 403.

(29) *Ibid*, p. 427.

(30) *Proc. Roy. Soc.*, **3**, p. 220.

(31) Royal Society MSS, DM. 1. 76, Peel to Davies Gilbert, 27 March, 1827, conveying Royal Assent.

(32) Sir James South, *Charges against the President and Councils of the Royal Society*, (London 1830), pp. 9–10.

(33) See L. Pearce Williams, 'The Royal Society and the Founding of the British Association for the Advancement of Science', *Notes and Records Roy. Soc. Lond.*, **16**, 221–283 (1961).

(34) James Hudson (ed.), *Report on the Adjudication of the Copley, Rumford and Royal Medals: and Appointment of the Bakerian, Croonian and Fairchild Lecturer*, 1831 and 1834. (hereafter, Medal Committee).

(35) Royal Society MSS, DM. 1. 72. Medal Committee to Council, 20 October 1831.

(36) Sir Henry Lyons has suggested the possible political importance of the medals in the heated electoral contest between the Duke of Sussex and John Herschel in 1830. Lyons, *op. cit.*, p. 250.

(37) *Report, Medal Committee*, pp. 215–6. The first medals were not available until 1833. *Proc. Roy. Soc.*, **3**, (1830–37), See Lyons, *op. cit.*, p. 247; *Record of the Royal Society of London*, (London 1940), p. 67.

(38) *Proc. Roy. Soc.*, **3**, 219 (1830–1837).

(39) *Report, Medal Committee*, (Appendix, p. 10).

(40) Council Minutes, XII, p. 40. The Astronomy Committee included Baily (V.P.), Airy, Lubbock, Peacock, Rigaud, Sheepshanks, and Whewell; the Physiology Committee included Maton (V.P.), Brodie, Brown, Clift, Sir A. Cooper, Green and Roget.

(41) Council Minutes, XII, p. 48.

(42) Council Minutes, XII, p. 51.

(43) Council Minutes, XII, p. 137. The Geology and Mineralogy Committee consisted of de la Beche, Gilbert, Greenough, Konig and Sedgewick; the Physics Committee, of Baily, Cumming, Lubbock, Peacock, Pepys, Powell, Roget and Whewell.

(44) Council Minutes, XII, p. 147.

(45) See Royal Society MSS, MC. 2. 147. Geo. Peacock to Roget, 26 November 1834 and W. Whewell to Roget, 26 November 1834, concerning the selection of Lubbock over Faraday that year. Faraday received the medal in 1855.

(46) Royal Society MSS, MC. 4. 102, 108–9. R. Lee to President and Council, 1 December and 12 December, 1845.

(47) Royal Society MSS, RR. 1. 150, R. Lee to President and Council, 2 April 1846.

(48) William White, *The Journals of Walter White*, (London 1899), p. 77.

(49) *Ibid.*, p. 191.

(50) *Ibid.*, p. 83.

(51) *Ibid.*, p. 92.

(52) *Ibid.*, p. 119.

(53) Royal Society MSS, MC. 4. 334, Airy to Christie, 18 March 1850.

(54) *Ibid.*,

(55) Royal Society MSS, MC. 4. H. Lloyd to Christie, 18 March 1850

(56) *Ibid.*

(57) Royal Society MSS, MC. 4. 338, Baden Powell to Christie, 24 March 1850.

(58) Royal Society MSS, MC. 4. 340 J. W. F. Herschel to Christie, 10 April 1850.

(59) Royal Society MSS, MC. 4. 342 Robert Brown to Christie, 11 April 1850.

(60) *The Record of the Royal Society of London*, (London, 1940), p. 117.

(61) Quoted in J. H. Gladstone, *Michael Faraday*, (London, 1873), p. 110.

(62) Babbage, *op. cit.*, p. 130.

(63) Huxley Papers, Vol. 2, f. 7, Huxley to Hooker, 6 November 1854; Vol. 3, f. 13, Hooker to Huxley, 7 November 1854.

(64) Compare the contest between Edward Frankland and Alexander Williamson over the award of the Davy Medal to John Newlands in 1887. *Huxley Papers*, Vol. 16. f. 272. Frankland to Huxley, 5 November 1887.

(65) Tyndall Papers (Royal Institution), Vol. 2, f. 279, Tyndall to Hirst, 5 November 1853.

(66) A. S. Eve and C. H. Creasey, *Life and Work of John Tyndall*, (London 1945), pp. 45–49.

(67) Council Minutes, Vol. 2. pp. 266–267, Tyndall to Christie, 24 November 1853, and Tyndall to Gassiot, 18 November 1853.

(68) Sir Eric Ashby, *Technology and the Academics*, (London 1958), p. 33 D. S. L. Cardwell, *The Organisation of Science in England: A Retrospect*, (London 1957), p. 84.

(69) See Leonard Huxley, *Life & Letters of J. D. Hooker*, (London, 1918), Vol. 1, p. 541.

(70) Including T. H. Huxley (1852), J. D. Hooker (1854), Edward Frankland (1857), George Busk (1871) and Thomas Hirst (1883). See: R. MacLeod, 'The X-Club: A Social Network of Science in Late Victorian England', *Notes and Records Roy. Soc. Lond.*, **24**, 305 (1970).

(71) Huxley Papers, Vol. 3, f. 34. Hooker to Huxley, 3 November 1857.

(72) Huxley Papers, Vol. 2, f. 276, Huxley to Hooker, 24 October, 1885.

(73) See George Forbes, *David Gill: Man and Astronomer*, (London, 1916), p. 356.

(74) See *The Times*, 1 December 1892.

(75) See *The Times*, 1 December 1891.

(76) Letter to *The Times*, 11 December 1894.

(77) Baron Rayleigh, *John William Strutt, Third Baron Rayleigh*, (London 1924), p. 173; *The Times*, 4 December 1896.

(78) *The Times*, 1 December 1896

(79) L. F. Bates, *Sir Alfred Ewing*, (London, 1946), pp. 21–25.

(80) '. . . I cannot think of anything else in my scientific relations', wrote Kerr in later years, 'that would give me an equal amount of pleasure except a new and valuable discovery', Royal Society MSS, MC. 17. 188, Kerr to Rucker, 6 November 1898.

(81) The award to Sir William Flower in 1882, is not, for example, mentioned in Charles J. Cornish, *Sir William Flower*, (London, 1904).

(82) In 1828, W. H. Wollaston gave a benefaction of £2000 to the Royal Society, asking that a fund be created to promote scientific research. A sum of £3410 was collected for the new fund – called the Donation Fund – which was the first of its kind in the history of the Society. For the first 13 years of its existence, however, the Fund was little used, despite the fact that needy men of science, especially ones outside the Society and living away from London, could doubtless have turned its assistance to great advantage.

(83) *Medal Claims*, 1873–1909 (Royal Society Library).

(84) Addresses at Anniversary Dinners, 1892, and 1894. See *The Times*, 1 December 1892 and 1 December 1894.

(85) Huxley Papers, Vol. 3, f. 34, Hooker to Huxley, 3 November 1857.

(86) Brewster hoped that the first objective of the British Association would be to appeal for such support. *Edinburgh Review*, **60**, 384 (1835).

(87) In 1900 the Council announced that: 'Every year the Council have to award several medals, including the Copley, Royal, Rumford, Davy Darwin, Buchanan, Sylvester and Hughes Medals, or some of these, and have been led by experience to the conclusion that it is neither to the advantage of the Society nor in the interests of the advancement of Natural Knowledge that this already long list of medals should in future be added to and that, therefore, no further bequests to be awarded as prizes for past achievements should be accepted by the Society'. *The Record of the Royal Society of London, op. cit.*, p. 117.

(88) Cf. R. MacLeod, 'The support of Victorian science: the endowment of science movements, 1868–1900', *Minerva*, **9** (in the press).

(89) J. Bentham, 'The Rationale of Reward', Ch. 2 in John Bowring, *The Works of Jeremy Bentham*, (Edinburgh, 1830–1843), Vol. 2, p. 256.

VII

Science and the Treasury: Principles, Personalities and Policies, 1870–85

Introduction

In the concluding essay in this volume, W. H. Brock considers ways in which Victorian men of science could, as individuals, receive patronage. He pays particular attention to the fact that State aid actually comprised a small fraction of the resources which could be said to have gone towards scientific activity. He rightly draws attention to the place of voluntary effort in science, and to the continuing tradition of amateurism throughout the country. He rightly emphasizes the advantages of private endowments to scientific research and education. No one can deny the importance of private and individual initiative, and its corollary of 'amateurism' in the development of British research until at least the First World War. Although such comparisons are notoriously difficult to quantify, one is also prepared to agree that direct State aid to fundamental research was not only proportionately less significant than private endeavour, but was also not necessarily the ideal form of patronage.[1] It was not until the end of the nineteenth century that the 'modern' university, with its familiar compromise between the direct demands of teaching and the indirect encouragement of research, came to provide the locus of fundamental research—a position which would eventually be complemented by the provision of government-aided research institutes.[2]

This being said, it remains clear that by the middle of the nineteenth century, British governments had already a considerable tradition of support for science,[3] and had undertaken considerable responsibilities in aid of scientific activity in the broadest sense, through the 'patronage' of honours, medals and prizes, through the endowment of trigonometrical, tidal, ordnance, and geological surveys and expeditions, and through the maintenance of specific government scientific posts and inquiries.[4] Indeed, the government's interest in scientific knowledge, particularly in new areas of testing and inspection, and investigation specifically related to government administrative policy, was increasing dramatically. Taking a broad definition of science, government expenditure on 'civil' scientific activities rose from £70,115 in 1859–60, to £261,184 in 1869–70 and to £346,528 in 1879–80.[5] The extent to which this constituted 'direct aid', and the question whether such aid was ideal or necessary, can be debated, but the fact of expenditure cannot.

It is important to draw a distinction between the support of what we today would call fundamental research, and what we now call scientific services, or science-related activities. This distinction is, indeed, one of the central points at issue in the campaigns of the 'scientific reformers' of the nineteenth century—an issue which was (and still is) frequently misunderstood. Science expenditure, in fact, presented a bifocal image. Researchers looking at government spending could claim that little went to research, while government officials, looking at the same expenditure, reached exactly the opposite conclusion. In a sense, both were right. At the time, this implicit misunderstanding failed to make clear important changes in the nature of research and in the real costs of doing science.

As the volume of scientific men and work increased, the costs of scientific research were growing rapidly,[6] and the case for State aid to meet these costs was argued.[7] One cannot say in retrospect that increases in the real capital and recurrent costs of doing research were so large that they could be met *only* through State investment. However, there was, by the 1860s, a significant weight of opinion that private initiative, which had traditionally shouldered the burden of both fundamental and applied science, was no longer adequate; that, as a result, British achievement was 'small when compared with that which is needed in the interests of Science'. There were repeated instances of 'unremunerative research in which the benefit conferred on

Science and the Treasury, 1870–85

the Nation by those who have been voluntarily engaged in it establishes a claim upon the State for compensation for their time and labour'.[8]

This opinion was given force by the growing size and economic expectations of the scientific community.[9] However, the cost of paying individual scientific men a living wage, although certainly important, was not the only calculation. By the 1870s, routine work in the physical sciences was becoming very expensive. There were new disciplines (notably solar physics, meteorology and electrical physics), which required apparatus and observations that could not be accommodated in existing laboratories or other institutions. The emergence of these new disciplines not only required new and elaborate instruments, but greater numbers of staff, more expensive materials, skilled assistance, new laboratories, and provision for full-time collaborative efforts over sustained periods. The Devonshire Commission recognized the latter, in particular, when it reasoned that 'the Endowment of Modern Science requires Investigation and Observations extending over areas so large and periods so long that the means and lives of nations are alone commensurate with them'.[10] This was at first mere contention, but it burst upon the public in many forms, and in no form put more succinctly than in the concluding words of the Devonshire Report:

> The progress of Scientific Research must in a great degree depend upon the aid of Governments. As a nation we ought to take our share of the current scientific work of the world. Much of this work has always been voluntarily undertaken by individuals and it is not desirable that Government should supercede such efforts; but it is bound to assume that large portion of the National Duty which individuals do not attempt to perform, or cannot satisfactorily accomplish.[11]

The position was clear enough to the editor of the *Quarterly Journal of Science*, who felt that 'All that remains now to be determined is whether as much has been done in this direction as the best interests of the nation require.'[12]

If this were to take place, the role of the State as patron required expansion and redefinition. There are many assumptions hidden in the writings of Victorian apologists for science,[13] which historians have rarely examined. Taking 'statesmen of science' at face value has contributed to an oversimplified view of the State's responsibilities towards science. On the one hand there is agreement that the State had always done much for science, that *science* did not lack patronage, though individual scientists often did,[14] and that the chief role the State could play was that of helping to 'professionalize' scientific activity through the creation of academic degrees, protective patents, awards, honours and jobs.[15] On the other hand, given the obvious merit of supporting science in both education and research, it appears self-explanatory that the State had a duty to assist.[16] The question for discussion by generations of students has thus become simply: Why was government so supine? Or, more charitably, why did the process of recognition take so long? This question is predicated upon two assumptions. First, that there *was* a single monolithic entity which could be summarily defined as the 'State' or 'government', with a uniform philosophy of administration; and, second, that if men of science did ask for help, the 'government' was in some way morally obliged to give it. It can be argued that these assumptions have misrepresented the actual situation. On the contrary, the 'government', consisting of many different departments and departmental points of view, offered remarkably different opportunities for administrative development; moreover, far from acceding uncritically to every request made by scientists, each department had a duty to examine all such applications for expenditure in the light of other priorities.

In reviewing these assumptions it becomes important to look at the mechanisms by which 'State' patronage could be given, and the reasons why it was withheld or granted. In examining this patronage, our attention is immediately focused upon the Treasury, the centrepiece of civil administration, the department which 'held the clue to most others' in Whitehall.[17] It was, as Sir William Flower, Director of the British Museum (Natural History) remarked: 'The Dread Department . . . which sat in judgement on them all, and had or withheld the means of encouragement to all.'[18] Today, the Treasury correspondence files offer a prospect of the entire business of domestic and imperial government.[19] A number of case-studies of individual departments and incidents have emerged which are beginning to com-

Science and the Treasury, 1870–85

plete the picture, but the task of documenting systematically the role of the Treasury in relation to departmental objectives and pressure group policies has yet to be attempted. The prospect of doing so has improved within the last four years, with the publication of two important studies of the Treasury as an entity, [20] and with growing interest in the relations of central departments during the nineteenth century 'revolution in government'.[21] As yet, however, there is no survey of the Treasury in its views towards science, and the remarks that follow can only be provisional, impressionistic, and exploratory.[22]

Science, Government and the Principles of State Aid

The years 1870 to 1885 represent one of the most critical and convenient periods in which to study the development of Treasury policy towards science. In this period, the Treasury, itself being transformed, transformed its manner and methods of dealing with the claims of science. Within these years, one may also see important developments in the administrative context within which the Treasury came to work, and in the approach of particular individuals to the problems of defining and achieving Treasury control over expenditure requiring expert judgement.[23] This period was a prelude to the development of Treasury policy towards science, which has become a lasting feature of British administration.

By the 1860s, the State was impinging upon science in many ways. The Devonshire Report brought much of this to public view (see Morrell, Table 1, p. 59 above). But this survey, arguably the most impressive at the time, was, in important ways, incomplete. For example, it did not take account of the 'scientific expert', who had already become a key figure in certain areas of administrative law, particularly in the enforcement of statute law by the Board of Trade fisheries and coal mines legislation, explosives legislation, conservation of fisheries, and safety of lives at sea), the Government Chemist (food and drugs legislation), or the alkali, factories, fisheries, and mines inspectorates.[24]

Moreover, the Devonshire Report merely drew attention to some of the government's many recurring responsibilities for scientific work in public departments. The Commission did not consider it 'necessary to take evidence regarding the detailed work of the public departments', but if it had, it would have included, for example, research into aspects of public health and preventive medicine (including vaccination), undertaken first by the Medical Department of the Privy Council (1858–70), and later by the Local Government Board, as well as research of relevance to agriculture, commerce, and the use and development of natural resources at home and in the Empire.[25] In addition to the responsibilities of some central departments for specific researchers, the Government also supported scientific and technical inquiry through a range of Commissions and Committees on scientific, technical, and educational matters. Among the most notable inquiries were those into cholera (1854), cattle plague (1866), pollution of rivers (1866), scientific instruction (1876), vivisection (1875), accidents in mines (1879), technical instruction (1884), and safety at sea (1885). Between 1838 and 1896, the cost of such Commissions amounted to £186,039.[26]

Finally, the State was involved in the encouragement of scientific education and research through the support of individuals and institutions. This was a more complicated sector. Motives for the support of research were mixed, but usually revolved around notions of international prestige, and a sense of scientific and cultural necessity, combining philosophical utility with material advantage, a necessity urged with greater forcefulness as the appeals of scientific interest groups increased in volume.[27]

In very general terms, and with the benefit of hindsight, government aid to scientific activity may be divided arbitrarily into several clear, yet sometimes overlapping categories:

Expenditure on 'Scientific Services' in Connexion with Administration. This included expenditure connected with agriculture, health, and the development of natural resources, as well as the supervisory work of 'scientific' inspectorates and inquiries.

The Promotion of General Inquiries Outside Departmental Sponsorship. This included grants to learned societies, including the Parliamentary Grant to the Royal Society for scientific investigation (£1,000 in 1849, rising to £4,000 in 1876);[28] and for the *Catalogue of*

Science and the Treasury, 1870–85

Scientific Papers (£8,000 for 1873); to the Royal Geographical Society (£500 annually from 1854 with occasional *ad hoc* payments for expeditions); the Royal Society of Edinburgh (£300 annually from 1834); and the *ad hoc* grant to the Scottish Meteorological Society of £1,000 for 1876. This category also includes payments made through specific societies or associations, such as the Solar Physics Committee (£500 annually from 1880); the Marine Biological Association (£2,500 each year during 1886–8, £500 each year until 1891, and £1,000 annually thereafter); and the Solar Eclipse, Transit of Venus, and *Challenger* Expeditions, for which manpower, instruments, and transport were provided.

International Prestige and Co-operation. Support for surveys, expeditions and inter-national conventions with economic and strategic advantages, including the Arctic Expedition of 1875; the Antarctic Expedition of 1900; the North Sea Fisheries Investigation; and the Washington Geodetic Conferences, 1882 and 1884.

Public Education in Arts and Sciences. The establishment and support of scientific museums, such as the Science Museum, South Kensington; the British Museum (Natural History); and the museums administered by the Science and Art Department in Scotland and Ireland; the support of Kew and other botanic gardens; the support of certain university professorships at London University and the Scottish universities between 1850 and 1890; and the Normal School of Science (1882).

These categories, for different financial years, produced the pattern of expenditure represented in Table 1. By 1875, the total of public money spent annually on scientific activity, *excluding* education, was admitted by the Devonshire Commission to exceed £321,000—a figure which included some expenditure within the Army and Navy Estimates. From the data given in Table 1, a more liberal calculation, *excluding* military research, might suggest a figure of about £347,000 on civil research alone—or probably nearer half a million pounds per annum for 'civil' and 'military' science. This figure of £347,000 represented 2.7 per cent of the gross civil estimates for 1875–6, a

Table 1

Expenditure by Government on Science and Science-Related Activities, in Selected Years, 1850–1900

Category	*Financial Years (figures in £ sterling)*						
	1850/1	1859/60	1869/70	1875/6	1879/80	1889/90	1899/1900
I. Expenditure on 'Scientific Services'	19,000	38,584	111,607	230,995	285,952	374,117	445,074
II. The Promotion of 'General Enquiries'	2,696	6,439	12,600	12,300	20,600	22,600	30,600
III. International Prestige and Cooperation	—	7,649	—	4,637	4,000	—	300
IV. Public Education in Arts and Sciences	12,632	25,092	146,931	99,872	95,337	255,654	141,813
Totals	34,328	77,764	271,138	347,804	405,889	652,371	617,787
Total as a percentage of Civil Estimates	·9%	·9%	2·8%	2·7%	2·7%	4·1%	2·6%

Source: Civil Estimates, 1850–1900

Science and the Treasury, 1870–85

proportion which naturally varied from year to year.[29]

The 1860s and 1870s witnessed several important developments in all these sectors, such as John Simon's rapid consolidation of a new concept of State medicine, complete with scientifically trained, permanently paid medical inspectors, and grants for auxiliary scientific investigations wrested from the reluctant heads of the Treasury.[30] The same period saw the consolidation of the Government Grant to the Royal Society, the creation of a new Meteorological Council, and the launching of several major scientific expeditions to observe the transits of Venus, solar eclipses and the ocean floor.[31] Meanwhile, the premise that State aid of this magnitude was justified was becoming generally accepted. In the mid-1860s, Lord Russell had railed against the inadequacy of public aid, 'while science pauses in despair before the giant of false economy, where he stands with uplifted club ready to strike back the rash intruder who would penetrate into the mysteries he conceals'.[32] By the turn of the decade, after repeated pronouncements from the British Association and the learned societies, the scientific lobby forming around *Nature*, and the active 'endowment' sentiment in educational circles, the position had changed. Arthur Helps thought it clearly established that only public aid could provide sufficient resources; if an individual wished science to advance, 'he will find that the only mode, or at least, the chief mode of action that he can adopt is through government'.[33] The *Spectator* agreed, observing that the outright support of science had become 'a national extension of the State's acknowledged duty to print money, provide standards of weights and measures, build lighthouses, conduct surveys and guard public records and monuments'.[34]

The Treasury and its Tribulations

When the claims of the 'scientific movement' of the 1860s reached the government, they found a Treasury, after half a century of internal reform, greatly improved in morale, stature and authority; at the same time, its structure presented handicaps which precluded direct, positive action.

The Treasury, in principle, dealt with spending departments. But in dealing with science it had to contrive procedures for dealing with issues that involved several different spending departments and out-side pressure groups, each with its own idiosyncracies and self-interests. As such, 'science' was not excluded from the acceptable objects of public expenditure. The Treasury could not decline to aid science merely on grounds that it might open 'a serious door'.[35] That door was open, and the Treasury's task was instead to restrain overambitious expenditure. Therefore its job, *proprement dit*, was not to define criteria according to which certain kinds of scientific work would pass and others not. However, the need to give explicit reasons for sanctioning expenditure ineluctably forced Treasury clerks to weigh policies, make choices and articulate a range of 'acceptable' proposals.

In wrestling with these proposals, one sees something of the Treasury's attempt at a social construction of its own objectives. The Treasury's formal authority could not be confused with its interpreta-tion of its authority, a fact which adds an important complexity to the study of Treasury control. There were few memoranda setting out general policy—even towards superannuation, let alone science. Indeed, with the exception of recruitment, its 'departmental' objec-tives were never made explicit and its policies were in a continuing state of development. In regard to issues of national policy, the Treasury did not take a position. In regard to science, this would have required an overall knowledge of scientific activities which few, if any, Treasury clerks could ever possess.

In the context of late-Victorian Whitehall, three factors were of paramount importance in influencing Treasury attitudes towards public expenditure. The first was the budgetary tradition within which the Treasury had come to work. This tradition, shaped steadily during the 1860s under Gladstone's watchful genius, was governed principally by three beliefs: first, the desirability (indeed, the urgent necessity) of reducing the National Debt; second, a strong Liberal preference for individual action; and third, a profound faith in the vir-tue of Free Trade.[36] These beliefs contributed overall to a spirit of rigorous national accounting, to the reification of 'thrift' as a moral virtue, and to a committed confidence that, with money left to fructify in the pockets of the people, private initiative would ultimately secure its own rewards.

Science and the Treasury, 1870–85

In retrospect, debt management, representing a tremendous uphill struggle against irrestible forces, eventually proved unsuccessful, while Free Trade survived in Treasury policy until the present century; and both concepts, implying the maintenance of a balanced, minimal budget, were ultimately forced to give ground to the expansionist impulses of a society demanding more from its government. But in each case, whether in colonial development, social welfare, public education, or science, the Treasury ideology provided a heavy counterweight.[37]

A second significant feature was the increasing authority and power wielded by the Treasury itself. The Treasury had become first among equals. In March 1863, for the first time in British financial history, all services were required to surrender their standing balances to the Exchequer. Moreover, the permanent establishment was acquiring more power previously left in political hands. In 1867, the Office of Permanent Secretary was created in the Treasury, and the prospect of a powerful permanent establishment, with all the implications of 'policy-making' by statesmen-in-disguise, became an important possibility. Finally, the Treasury was given new responsibilities, if often without well defined powers. In 1868, the creation of the Comptroller and Auditor-General's Department set out new and higher standards of financial accounting. This development underlined a third feature of the Treasury's position.

In the late 1860s and early 1870s, the Treasury was still suffering from the Civil Service Reforms of the mid-century that began to transform central government, and that refashioned the Treasury's own staff, recruitment, and work arrangements. As Stafford Northcote, Disraeli's Chancellor between 1874 and 1880, told the Playfair Commission in 1875, 'The Civil Service has been undergoing a great transformation of late years; indeed, it may be said to have been in the crucible for the last twenty'.[38] Following Gladstone's Order in Council of 1870, open competition, tempered by selection and a practice of recruiting staff who had seen service in other departments, helped raise the intellectual standard of juniors. Between 1870 and 1900, the 'unambitious and unclubbable' gave way to the Balliol Double First. Greater mobility between the Treasury and other departments gave the Treasury greater confidence and what

Roseveare has called 'a purposeful sense of community'. Moreover, some delegation of work was made possible, and procedure revised so that junior clerks had more responsible work. In many ways this operated to make the Treasury a more competent body. But the methods by which the Treasury would meet its responsibilities to keep spending departments up to the mark were left to the Treasury establishment itself. This situation was complicated by internal administrative factors that exaggerated the Treasury's defensive posture.

The 'new Treasury', in common with many government departments witnessing 'the 19th century Revolution in Government', was severely overstretched. Throughout the 1860s, new administrative instruments governing conditions of service, pensions, allowances, office hours, honours, discipline, sick leave, and superannuation, were devised throughout Whitehall, and added greatly to the Treasury's work. The tendency of new departments to spawn fresh work—and the Privy Council to spawn new departments[39] —produced a growing volume of correspondence. Unhappily, the Treasury's increasing responsibilities fell upon a reduced staff. As a direct result of Gladstonian economics, the permanent staff of the Treasury was reduced in 1870 to a mere twenty-five, and was held to that for a decade. This meant, almost invariably, an overload of work for those Divisions affected by new legislation, and resulted in the delays, frustrations and disappointments with which generations of pressure groups and spending departments became depressingly familiar.

The Treasury tried, in many ways successfully, to rise to these new challenges. In the early 1870s, it re-formed into five Divisions, each with jurisdiction over specific departments (see Table 2). This reorganization was intended to improve the flow of government business, and this it achieved. However, the departments within each Division were not functionally distinct. Indeed, the water-tight nature of the Divisions meant that decisions on 'sub-political' subjects, including science, which could potentially affect several spending departments, had a good chance of being dealt with in very different ways by each of the different divisions. Moreover, the work could fall on each of the Divisions quite unevenly. Thus, for the entire period

Science and the Treasury, 1870–85

between 1870 and 1890, the Third Division, which embraced many scientific works—under the Privy Council Office, the Office of Works, the Home Office or the Science and Art Department—had a total of only three Principal Clerks, six First Class Clerks, and five Second Class Clerks; since promotion normally took place within each Division, this total of fourteen, in fact, represented only twelve different men, four of whom seem to have taken the largest share of the work.[40] There were apparent advantages in having a small number of staff intimately associated with the work of specific departments. However, there were clear disadvantages if few in that number were experienced in the subjects they were called upon to consider. Not surprisingly, in no one's case was science a *forte*.

The disadvantages of 'narrowness' were offset in some ways by office routines. Following the procedural reforms of the 1870s, incoming papers would receive their first Minutes by the Second Class Clerks, and would be sent upwards. Questions requiring decisions on precedents would be referred to the Assistant Secretary (who answered for Divisions 1 and 2) or to the Permanent Secretary, who signed for Divisions 3 and 4. In cases requiring the attention of the Chancellor, papers would be sent up by the Permanent Secretary and eventually referred down again for action.

Throughout the period 1870 to 1900, the ideology and structure of the Treasury gave its critics an easy target. As Roseveare comments: 'The undermanned establishment, strenuously administering a negative principle, seemed well designed to impede, with the maximum of friction, and poorly equipped to collaborate in purposeful government.'[41]

This general aspect of the Treasury was potentially at its worst in regard to science. The image of harassed Treasury officials, being force-marched by 'experts', wielding only the power to say 'no' (and that unconstructively), did not leave an edifying impression. Nevertheless, the Treasury was forced by the ineluctable pressure of circumstances to consider how and under what terms to admit expenditure on science within its purview. It was obliged, particularly during the 1870s and 1880s, to acquire a broader view of the purposes for which public money could justifiably be spent. In essence, these decisions often required Treasury officials (and particularly those

Table 2

Organization of the Treasury Establishment
1870 to 1914

Permanent Secretary

Parliamentary Financial Secretary

Parliamentary Clerk

Staff

—*Assistant Secretary*

—*First (or Finance) Division*
Finance generally, Banking & Currency; the Mint, Exchequer & Audit Dept, Bank of England, National Debt Office, Public Works Loan Commissioners, Estimates, etc.

1 Principal Clerk
2 1st Class Clerks
2 2nd Class Clerks

—*Second Division*
Foreign Office, Colonial Office, War Office, Admiralty, Woods, Municipal Corporation, etc.

1 Principal Clerk
1 1st Class Clerk
1 2nd Class Clerk

Supplementary Dept ———
Accounts Branch

Registry Branch

Treasury Solicitor

Science and the Treasury, 1870–85

—Third Division
Home Secretary, India Office, Privy Council Office, Office of Works, Channel Islands, Education, Science & Art Dept, Poor Law, etc.

1 Principal Clerk
1 1st Class Clerk
1 2nd Class Clerk

—Fourth Division
Revenue Depts., Post Office, Board of Trade, Superannuation, Telegraphs, Civil List Pensions, etc.

1 Principal Clerk
1 1st Class Clerk
2 2nd Class Clerks

—Fifth Division (known as the Dept of the Auditor of the Civil List and Assistant to the Secretaries until 1881)

The Royal Household, Legal Establishments, and Courts of Law, Criminal Prosecutions, Sheriffs' Accounts, etc.

1 Auditor of the Civil List or Principal Clerk
1 1st Class Clerk
1 2nd Class Clerk

Source: Establishment files, cited in H. Roseveare, *The Treasury: the Evolution of a British Institution* (New York, 1969), p. 211.

in Division 3, dealing with departments more vulnerable than others to new legislation) to reject any generalized philosophy of *laissez-faire*, in favour of a series of pragmatic definitions, based upon an understanding of what custom and usage would tolerate. These definitions were almost invariably riddled with exceptions, and it is this 'exceptional' pattern of spending that characterized government activity in science well into the present century. The fact that it was not systematic gave rise to repeated tensions and frustrations, and to accusations of Treasury meanness. But the apparent arbitrariness of government aid could provide an important degree of freedom and elasticity in administrative procedure. Invariably, this worked to the overall advantage of those who could understand and use the system.

The Context of Treasury Control

Given the nature of the Treasury's ideology and structure; given the nature of departmental estimates within which 'science' figured; given also the interdepartmental nature of scientific activity, it is difficult to see how overall or specific Treasury criteria could be easily defined, or once defined, defended. In dealing with science, the Treasury clerks tended to apply the same reasoning they used with reference to literary or scholarly patronage. In this spirit, the Treasury always took pains to foster the impression that all increases in expenditure were prima facie undesirable, justified only in 'special and exceptional' circumstances.[42] At the same time, the relation of knowledge and power through science had a novel justification, and the use of public funds in applying science to public improvements was philosophically unexceptionable. The arguments of immediate utility had clear favour, but more complicated questions arose when the prospect of utility was more remote, or when utility could not be urged as a criterion.

Here classical political economy was not of immediate help. Jeremy Bentham, writing in 1820, had argued the case with deductionist elegance:

That which governments ought to do for the arts and sciences of immediate and remote utility, may be comprised in three

Science and the Treasury, 1870–85

things—1. To remove the discouragements under which they labour; 2. To favour their advancement; 3. To contribute to their diffusion.[43]

But Bentham also admitted that:

Though discoveries in science may be the result of genius or accident, and though the most important discoveries may have been made by individuals without public assistance, the progress of such discoveries may at all times be materially accelerated by a proper application of public encouragement.[44]

This seemed to imply an open ended commitment, which could only be defined in particular cases. If the argument from 'utility' was elusive, the argument for 'cultural value' was even more vague. The issue here was the support of science for its own sake. Whatever justifications of prestige or improvement could be found, the fact remained that this work represented a material cost. The question was whether it should by right become, at least in part, a public charge. At the end of the century, W. E. H. Lecky summarized the dilemma confronting the government:

There are forms of science and literature and research which can by no possibility be remunerative or at least remunerative in any proportion to the labour they entail or the ability they require. A nation which does not produce and does not care for these things can have only an inferior and imperfect civilization.[45]

The story of attempts to define a workable system of government aid often turned on the verdict of circumstances. It became a story in which patronage, in pursuit of thrift, found compromise in preparing the way for a system of subsidy that only men of science could operate. The situation was not made any easier by evidence of ragged disagreement between men of science themselves, who, far from acting as a united interest group (as, say, the medical profession did through the British Medical Association), reflected violent disagreement. Some men of science saw State aid as potentially mischievous;[46] others saw it more as a stimulant to be taken in moderation.[47] Some wanted aid in the form of grants for both training and research to universities, while others saw the essential question as that of direct aid to individuals.[48] 'The time . . . has not yet arrived', wrote Richard Proctor, the amateur astronomer and science journalist, 'when the nation would look with satisfaction on any wide scheme of scientific endowment.'[49] There is some evidence that the Treasury took wilful advantage of this disunity to limit spending,[50] and a failure to achieve a concerted policy among scientists often seems to have delayed government action. A notable example arose in 1877, in the debates on Supply, when Bernhard Samuelson, the noted educational reformer, asked whether the Government were going to defray the cost of the Loan Collection. This critical step, which led ultimately to the present Science Museum,[51] was delayed, according to Lord Sandon, Vice-President of the Council, by the controversy then raging as to the importance of having such a Collection at all. The government were interested, Sandon announced, but first it was necessary 'that there should be something like unanimity among men of science'.[52]

This unity seemed impossible to achieve; indeed, one is impressed by the differences encountered by what were, at least at first, the minority views of small reformist lobbies in science and science education in the 1860s and 1870s.[53] Yet, within a broad band of 'progressive' opinion, there was evidence of growing feeling that science should be free, as Playfair put it, 'from the embarrassments of poverty or the temptations of wealth'. Those who accepted this as necessary and desirable found spokesmen in George Gore, Alexander Strange, Charles Appleton,[54] and George Harris, a scientific popularizer. For Harris, science, wherever it was not specifically practical, required State patronage, both

1. to aid the originators of new inventions in science which may be of great ultimate value to the public, but which the discoverers may not be able to afford, or which it may not be worth their while to perfect; and

2. to encourage experiments in science which those practically engaged in them may not have the means, or ability, or leisure to carry out; but which it may be of the highest and most essential importance to the State to complete.[55]

Science and the Treasury, 1870–85

There was, of greater significance, a growing belief that science itself, in expanding the domain of natural knowledge, required greater attention. The character of the development could not be consciously demonstrated (and so the very fact could be summarily dismissed as a self-serving assertion of a minority interest group), but the impression gained ground with repetition. In 1871, the Treasury refused outright to continue the State aid to expeditions it had furnished in the 1850s and 1860s. Yet, it could be protested that:

> owing to the great advances in all branches of science, the arising of new problems and the perfecting of scientific instruments for observations impracticable in former times, there is much greater necessity for such expeditions now than there was in the days of Parry, Franklin or the Rosses.[56]

This programme, if indeed necessary, required a critical sense of judgement on the part of the patron. The questions before the Treasury were formidable. Were funds to be limited to capital and equipment expenditure, or were personal stipends to be involved? What were the implications of any government aid? Was there danger of excessive centralization (as opposed to fair play for all), or of jobbery and corruption, or of multiplying costly and unproductive sinecures. The Treasury had both to be, and to be seen to be, at least as innocent as Caesar's wife. Finally, assuming state aid were given, should it be given solely as departmental Votes, answerable in some way to Parliament? Or should it be given only through 'learned societies', with the attendant risk of losing all hope of routine public accountability? The learned societies, since the creation of the British Association in 1831, had spearheaded the campaign for public recognition of science, and the Parliamentary Committee of the British Association had urged government attention to matters of finance.[57] By the 1870s, the principle was well established, and Disraeli's Chancellor, Stafford Northcote (later Lord Iddesleigh) could say with transparent candour that 'they all desired to recognize the claims of scientific bodies to assistance from national funds'. The difficulty was '. . . to draw a line and say where that assistance should begin and where it should end. It was one of the most perplexing questions with which successive governments had to deal—how national aid could best be given for the promotion of scientific research.'[58]

Gladstonian Finance and the Problem of Endowment

Of senior statesmen, Gladstone had undoubtedly the largest influence upon Treasury policy. When he became Chancellor of the Exchequer in 1859, he confronted the situation left by the vast expenditures of the Crimean War, which cost £70 million and doubled income tax from 7d. to 1s. 4d. in the pound. Gladstone set out to achieve a balanced budget. When he became Prime Minister in 1868, he expressed his determination to reduce expenditure. Arguing that 'Economy is the first and great article in my financial creed', and benefitting by the economic boom conditions between 1868 and 1874, he succeeded remarkably. By 1872–3 there was an actual surplus of £6 million on an expenditure of £70.7 million. His views on public finance and political economy, drawing strength from success, were explicitly set out to a Midlothian audience in 1879:

> The Chancellor of the Exchequer should boldly uphold economy in detail, and it is the mark of a chicken-hearted Chancellor when he shrinks from upholding economy in detail, when, because it is a question of only two or three thousand pounds, he says that is no matter. He is ridiculed, no doubt, for what is called candle-ends and cheese-parings but he is not worth his salt if he is not ready to save what are meant by candle ends and cheese parings in the cause of the country.[59]

The immediate topic was defence, but Gladstone extended the principle across Government activity. He could be persuaded, for interests of expedience, and political advantage, to act so as to advance the interests of science; the *Challenger* Expedition and the creation of the Devonshire Commission can easily be interpreted in this light. But with regard to regular endowment, Gladstone was implacably opposed. 'Endowment', he told an Edinburgh audience in 1860, 'gravitates towards torpor as its natural consummation'. This attitude obviously did not endear him to the 'endowment faction', any more than did his general political views, or his views on science. Gladstone

Science and the Treasury, 1870–85

did admit in public that 'there is truth . . . in the assertion that we are backward in appreciating or pursuing abstract knowledge',[60] but his conclusions did not lead to the deliberate support of abstract enquiry. However, his attitudes towards the pursuit of science should not be confused with his attitude towards the usages of scientific knowledge in practical terms. Science, to pay its own way, had merely to exploit its advantages. As he explained to the Institution of Civil Engineers in 1872:

> A fair field and no favour is the maxim of English administration. A field so fair, so extensive and so promising that all industry may find its place, and such an absence of favour that one as well as another may hope for success. If, under these conditions the State does nothing for science, it cannot be helped, nor need it be lamented, considering how little science stands in need of the aid.[61]

Among Gladstone's opponents, wide differences emerge. Disraeli, concerned more with Destiny than thrift,[62] took little interest in science, and, apart from a critical caricature of the Royal Society in the late 1860s,[63] was disinclined to pronounce on the merits or otherwise of State support. When Disraeli was elected a Fellow of the Royal Society in 1876, the press criticized the step as 'a delicate piece of flattery', remarking that 'Mr Disraeli, among the devotees of science, is a figure too inconspicuous for serious contemplation . . . [his] genius . . . has not a touch of the true scientific spirit.'[64] Stafford Northcote had little to say in support of science, although he was perhaps more aware of its power as an aid to statecraft.[65] The two Conservative statesmen who did give science more than a passing reference were Lord Salisbury and the 15th Earl of Derby.[66] Both men spoke in favour of increasing scientific endowments before the Devonshire Commission, and both returned to the question repeatedly. In November 1872, Salisbury testified that, like the Church, 'research is unremunerative', and given 'that it is highly desirable for the community that it should be pursued, . . . the community must be content that funds should be set aside to be given, without any immediate and calculable return in work, to those by whom the research is to be pursued'.[67]

Salisbury kept the issue alight, insisting on the justice of the claims of science to a place in higher education, both before and during the Oxford Reform Bill debates.[68] Derby agreed with Salisbury during the Devonshire Commission. Moreover, he publicly exalted the dignity of scientific discovery and the lustre it conferred upon the society that gave it sponsorship. Science, Derby told an Edinburgh audience in December 1875, soon after the Devonshire Commission had completed its work, 'had this advantage over almost every other form of successful human effort; that its results are certain; that they are permanent; that whatever benefit grows out of them is worldwide'. If, as he told medical students at Liverpool in October 1881, 'The student of abstract science gratifies in the fullest measure the intellectual requirements for his nature . . . he may be sustained by a perfectly just conviction of the ultimate utility of his work.'[69] The problem was to secure provision for him. Science required leisure and it was in the national interest to secure it aid, both public and private. Derby countered Liberal economics, rebuking

> . . . a certain class of thinkers, of whom I speak with respect, but who, I think, argue for the abuse of a thing against its use. The fact remains that the most enduring and valuable work done in the line of pure science will not bring a shilling to the man who does it, and while that is so . . . there seems nothing unreasonable in saying that society shall in one way or another, make provision for those who are doing so much for society.

Derby saw the fears of jobbery exaggerated: '. . . men who work to make money, or men who care for reputation of the popular sort, do not choose such pursuits . . .'. His conclusion was direct: '. . . whatever is done, or whoever does it, I think that more liberal assistance in the prosecution of original scientific research is one of the recognized wants of our time'.[70]

Once at the Treasury, the claims of science were reviewed within a context that was partly political, and partly administrative. In particular, differences in attitude among successive chancellors, Financial Secretaries, Treasury Clerks, and Permanent Secretaries, could have an extremely important effect. While the entire canvas must be seen as shaded by the larger issues of finance and expenditure discussed

Science and the Treasury, 1870–85

above, there were important possibilities for changes in the colour and texture of Treasury negotiations.

The five Chancellors who served in the period from 1868 to 1886 represented interesting variations. Robert Lowe (Chancellor, 1868–73), who reflected his premier in many ways, had a rough passage at the Treasury.[71] Gladstone consoled him in 1871:

> No man wants so much sympathy as the Chancellor of the Exchequer, no man gets so little. Nor is there any position so lamentable for him as to be defeated in proposing some new charge on the public conceived or adopted by himself. He is like an ancient soldier wounded in the back. Whereas even defeat in resisting the raids of the House of Commons on the public purse is honourable, and always turns out well in the end.[72]

At first he took a distinctly negative view of science and its institutions. To a department in 1869, seeking funds for the Meteorological Society of Scotland, he criticized the idea of giving aid to societies, especially the Royal Society, 'as a sort of agency of government'. He said: 'I think it a very bad plan for any government to select societies as their agents, and to give them large sums of money, because the tendency is to give large salaries, and they give rise to a suspicion of jobbery.' Lowe, reflecting on his experience in education, brought his views on voluntaryism to bear on science: 'We are called upon for economy [he told his department]. Now, the first maxim of economy is that Government should not be called upon to do that which there is a reasonable probability people will do for themselves.' Lowe apparently feared the corrupting power of government aid—'For the moment [voluntary societies] finger government money, it seems as if it produces a revolution in their minds, and the whole objective seems to be perverted ... to the getting of the greatest possible amount of Government money.'[73] In June the same year, Lowe rejected a proposal to give government aid to the Faraday Memorial, to the accompaniment of criticism from the Liberal *Telegraph*, and from the Liberal benches in the Commons,[74] and increased the wrath of scientific men by abolishing Stenhouse's job as Assayer to the Mint, worth £600 per annum.

Gradually, however, Lowe became more accessible to scientists.

For their part, men of science set to work upon him and his chief, with dinners at the Royal Society and regular deputations. In 1870, he was introduced to the X-Club, and in January 1871, he was invited to visit Darwin with Sir John Lubbock[75] and T. H. Huxley, and evidently respected Darwin immensely.[76] In May 1871, Lowe as Chancellor was unanimously elected a Fellow of the Royal Society.[77] For the rest of his tenure, he seemed constant in his support of scientists for Civil List pensions,[78] and remained a cordial guest of the X-Club.[79] He was, perhaps, pleased to find some circle where his good works could be recognized at no great cost to the public; in May 1871, responding to his welcome at the De Morgan testimonial, he remarked on the great zest which a long run of unpopularity gave to a little applause.[80] Indeed, when Lowe wanted to spend, he could be generous. His biographer credits him, in the midst of the Alabama claims crisis, with helping to outfit the *Challenger* expedition, and with sanctioning both £8,000 for buying Peel's pictures for the nation, and £50,000 for purchasing antiquities for the British Museum. It was also Lowe's intervention that helped secure the first grant of £2,000 per annum for John Simon's Medical Department.[81] By 1873, perhaps encouraged by the Devonshire Commission and the claims of science, Lowe even extracted from the Treasury authority to raise the salary of Dr T. A. Hirst as Director of Studies at the new Royal Naval College from £1,000 to £1,200.[82] In the event, Lowe's successors were in turn fêted and cajoled by men of science. Ten years later, E. Ray Lankester told the British Association in Southport that 'The time will come ... when there will be more than one member of the Government who will understand and appreciate the value of scientific research.'[83] In the event, more than a generation was to elapse before Lankester's hopeful vision found a response.

The Quest for Criteria

In the lengthy process of defining what criteria should govern State aid to science, the Treasury's responses were guided by several general administrative principles common to all Treasury business. Repeatedly, however, one is impressed by the way in which these principles were overtaken or neglected or simply allowed to disappear

Science and the Treasury, 1870–85

for pragmatic reasons. One may, for convenience, collectively describe them in three contexts: (1) the overall context of Treasury control, within which an issue would be considered; (2) the social context of the issue, which could make the issue more or less politically visible, and often remove it beyond any permanent sense of Treasury control; (3) the substantive nature of the issue, where the Treasury, unguided by advice or experience, was obliged to consider the amount and method of payment suitable to a given proposal.

(1) The overall context of Treasury control was not easy to define, and much more difficult to operate. The intention of the Treasury, in the mind of Gladstone, was 'economy, pure and simple'. Yet, by 1856, Charles Trevelyan was already prepared to admit that 'We are beginning to see that there can be no real economy which is not combined with efficiency and that the highest efficiency is generally the best economy.'[84] This opened to the Treasury two alternatives, controlling spending through the central departments, or sanctioning limited grants-in-aid.

In the first case, chief responsibility passed to the ministerial head of a department. In October, 1869, before the first sweeping changes in scientific expenditure were felt, and at a time when Gladstonian budgets had produced a surplus in the Exchequer, George Hamilton minuted his considered view to James Stansfeld, Lowe's Financial Secretary from 1869 to 1871, that: 'The primary object of every Minister is and must be to place his own Department and the interests committed to him in the greatest state of efficiency—the cost I venture to state will be necessarily secondary.'[85] By the 1870s, however, this represented a counsel of perfection. Hamilton's successors realized this. In particular, Ralph Lingen's policy in the 1870s was to secure restraint, 'in criticizing and in insisting upon some measurable proof in support of the propositions for increased expenditure'.[86] Once items were included in a departmental Vote, it was the prerogative of the department to decide how this vote should be spent. The Treasury, while cautious of all prospective increases, was not in a position to criticize internal departmental expenditure. Treasury control, therefore, operated mainly through the requirement of prior approval, through insistence upon lengthy justification and the threat of delay. As Wright summarizes: 'By linking delay on the supply side with delay in approving expenditure on establishments', the Treasury could operate a vice-like policy of negation. Indeed, the chief effort of the Treasury in the late nineteenth century, was directed towards refusing to admit the necessity of departmental expansions. Support for science was to be kept temporary and limited, despite the obvious fact that scientific activity was growing in size, complexity, and cost. This, in all probability, affected the most diffident applicants the most severely, and one will never know how many applications for scientific patronage were not submitted for this reason.

However, the Treasury's position suffered from fundamental weaknesses. William Baxter, Lowe's Financial Secretary from 1871 to 1873, told the Select Committee on Expenditure in 1873, that Treasury control provided the 'means of preventing a great many proposals for increases which are never heard of again',[87] but Lowe himself was doubtful, and the Treasury entered the 1870s looking back to the 1860s as a time of rigorous control and ahead to a time of over-ambitious spending. Hamilton's highly moral position in the 1860s, embodied in the belief that 'a great deal of the good we do in this world might perhaps be measured by the evil we prevent',[88] was by the 1870s a pious hope. Moreover, scientists would not consent to having others make such Faustian distinctions between 'good' and 'evil'.

The question of government austerity could take on added importance at particularly critical times, notably during the blow to the Exchequer by the budget of 1876–7, when surpluses were wiped out, and during the economic depression of the late 1870s, when all negotiations became more difficult. Arguably, a sense of 'national austerity' may have helped to control public expenditure.[89] However, with Treasury officials, the 'relativities' in assessing cost and efficiency were never at issue. The Treasury insisted on deciding on questions of principle. Yet, on these grounds, the Treasury was increasingly vulnerable.

Treasury control was weak for several general reasons. First, it could only reiterate general rules, or force issues into open conflict. The Department of Science and Art was often involved in such

Science and the Treasury, 1870–85

struggles, although probably not as frequently as the War Office or the Admiralty, and its record of successes was achieved at the price of much ill-feeling. The general experience was that the Treasury could be forced to back down if faced with sufficient determination. This premise acquired the legitimacy of a natural law when no less an authority than Alpheus Todd pronounced that:

> The Treasury as a general rule invariably gives way when applied to by any Board or other department presided over by a Cabinet Minister, for their sanction to spend money. They may delay at first, and if a sufficiently plausible reason for the application be not given, the Secretary of the Treasury may appeal to the Chancellor of the Exchequer, and a correspondence may ensue between the Departments, but the Treasury invariably gives way in the end.[90]

The Treasury's effective power was 'to remonstrate, to exhort, and to recommend'. The ultimate sanction of refusing to authorize an overpayment was a weak weapon with which to stop a determined department.

Second, the Treasury had to deal with each case on its merits, applying, where possible, the unwritten rules of principles and precedents. In a despairing moment, reviewing the discontinuities in superannuation procedures, Lingen minuted:

> As no two circumstances are ever completely identical, 'special cases' are a necessary feature in each. I doubt most extremely whether . . . equal or impartial justice is possible . . . from the application of properly classified scales for retirement and superannuation.[91]

Treasury control suffered from the lack of a concept of a unified civil service[92] (let alone a 'scientific civil service'). Any attempt at setting out unified rules of procedure aroused immediate departmental jealousies. This was aggravated by the separation of departments into notional 'classes'. The 'first class' departments (including the Home Office, the War Office, the Foreign Office and the India Office) usually received deferential treatment, while 'second class' departments, including the Science and Art Department, the Board of

Trade, the Local Government Board and the Board of Agriculture, which accidentally, but significantly, had 'scientific interests', were less likely to be dealt with as peers. This did not necessarily stop their development, but it did affect the pace of their expansion.[93]

Third, the Treasury's methods often failed because they forced departments to take up defensive positions from which the departments could never retreat without suffering considerable loss of face. Official letters of rebuke or referral, drawn up in the pontifical Treasury style, read like divine injunctions, and provoked conflict. This situation was recognized by Gladstone in 1865, who suggested sending draft circulars before issuing formal letters on such questions as proposed reductions in estimates: 'For if any of [the departments] raised difficulties in an official correspondence, the impediment will be harder to overcome.'[94] As late as 1891, G. J. Goschen, (Chancellor from 1887 to 1892) had repeatedly to stop sharply worded memoranda on their way to the Admiralty. 'The draft is too strong', he once wrote, 'not for what the Admiralty deserve, but for what is prudent. The receipt of such a letter produces anger not penitence or shame.' The point might equally have been made about letters to the Science and Art Department, and even the occasional ill-worded reminders sent to the Royal Society. During the 1870s and 1880s, the Treasury seemed to prefer these 'long verbal bombardments'.[95] By the next decade, however, personal contact, the development of semi-official correspondence as a conciliatory device, and the representation of Treasury clerks on important interdepartmental committees,[96] altered the relationship between the Treasury and the spending departments, and permitted a degree of negotiation. This affected government matters in general no less than scientific activity in particular. But it had important consequences for science.

The rise of the scientific civil servant was the fourth limiting factor in the context of Treasury control. Possibilities for more explicit forms of government accountability for expenditure on science developed as government took men of science into its service. Wright's study suggests that the Treasury, knowing its own weaknesses, and fearing collision, was at worst 'niggardly or small minded'; and that it expressed a willingness to 'accept the judgement of the Minister and a wish for agreement and accommodation

Science and the Treasury, 1870–85

wherever possible'.[97] But the experience of civil servants does not necessarily bear this out. Men of science, once in departments, had obvious departmental interests; how could they be adjudicated? In many areas, having located the most able scientific men in the central departments, the best hope of control was to back them solidly. But whether this would contrive to produce economy in the narrow sense, was often in doubt. Ralph Lingen eventually admitted this, when he remarked in 1871, after a particularly hostile duel with John Simon, that 'I do not know who is to check the assertions of experts when the Government has once undertaken a class of duties which none but such persons understand.'[98] In the event, the Treasury tried to hold its own, declaiming for example against Simon's 'unlimited missionary action', and giving way to his plans for an enlarged inspectorate only because of its weight of accumulated evidence, plans for economy, and promise of temporariness.[99] Devising methods of dealing with the Treasury taxed the ingenuity of Simon and other 'civil scientists' (e.g. Angus Smith),[100] but generally the 'experts' won, at least as long as they remained unbowed by their own departmental 'superiors'.[101] The principle of efficiency was calculated to win over the most bitter opposition.

The second form of Treasury aid, if easier to operate, was equally difficult to control. Within the six classes of the Civil Estimates, provision was made for several 'grants-in-aid'. These grants were not strictly routine, but they furnished an important exception to the general rule that all expenditure must be accounted for in detail by the Accounting Officer, that the appropriation of the money be examined by the Chancellor and Auditor General, and that any unexpended balance disclosed thereby be surrendered to the Exchequer. Among other good works, they allowed the government to contribute to the Metropolitan Fire Brigade, to certain hospitals and exhibitions, and to certain immediate charges of a national kind. It was recognized from about the middle of the century (although not codified by the Committee of Public Accounts until 1896) that:

> ... these grants-in-aid constitute a useful and economical arrangements, when the State, though willing to render some assistance to a service, does not wish to treat it as a Government

service, and also when the expenditure towards which the aid is given is an uncertain quantity and cannot be accurately estimated.[102]

With reference to science, this category, entitled 'Scientific Works and Experiments', arose formally in the Estimates in 1843, under Class 4 ('Education'); it consisted mainly of votes for the meteorological and magnetic observations conducted in Canada, Britain, and the Cape. After 1859, grants given to the Royal Society, other learned societies, the Scottish universities and London University, were added to the list. In 1866, these votes to scientific societies (and a new grant to Edinburgh University) were grouped together in Class 4 under the designation of 'Learned Societies'. In 1873–4, these two categories were combined to become 'Learned Societies and Scientific Investigations'.[103] The sums involved were significant, averaging between £8,350 and £9,000 between 1856–7 and 1905–6.[104] These grants, however, were virtually by definition, *ad hoc* solutions to particular problems, and their piecemeal nature generated wide differences in administration.[105]

If grants-in-aid presented the Treasury with obvious dilemmas, they also provided an obvious solution. Special claims like the *Challenger* Expedition could be met more easily through the grant-in-aid mechanism.[106] Moreover, once the scientific societies received public funds, they became 'honest brokers', acting as agents of economy and efficiency. Rarely, of course, were these estimates greatly increased, and at any suggestion of increase, direct Treasury intervention could easily be asserted.

(2) A far more serious threat to Treasury control came with the danger that a Treasury decision could be overriden by political influence or public pressure, reflected in ministerial or parliamentary intervention. The Treasury had to give way to political pressure, either on the part of the Chancellor or his Cabinet colleagues. Undoubtedly, the Foreign Office, the War Office and the Admiralty were the most intransigent departments, partly because they wielded such evident power.[107] Thus, Lingen gave way on a military estimate in 1871, by effecting a calculated retreat. 'I am not convinced, but I doubt it being expedient to overrule in relation to an existing charge the

Science and the Treasury, 1870–85

strongly repeated opinion of a Secretary of State of Mr Cardwell's experience.'[108] The refusals of the Admiralty to recognize Treasury control in any form, appealing to the historical separation of the Admiralty from civil policy, became classic. In scientific matters, immediate national crises (e.g. the cattle plague, or an outbreak of cholera or smallpox) could stimulate the Treasury to pay sums for specific researches, but these examples did not really set dangerous precedents (although the prolonged efforts of medical reformers to keep public fears alive, may have kept public expenditure under way).[109] A more insidious fear was pressure from outside and above. In 1892, W. N. Hartley reminded George Stokes of the circumstances of the Royal College of Science: 'We have it on record that three years after the college was established the Treasury endeavoured to abolish it, but the House of Commons insisted on its being carried on.'[110] The permanent staff of the Treasury could be overruled, and where this happened,[111] the damage to 'professional pride' could be lasting.

This was particularly clear in the early 1870s. Increasingly, the Treasury was asked not whether the State should, or could, from its resources aid science, but whether there was certain scientific work which the State was actually bound in honour to support. This criterion, clearly not of the Treasury's making, was nevertheless thrust upon it. When scientific issues were ventilated in Parliament, in Parliamentary Questions, or Supply Debates, the press also could sense intrigue and make trouble. The early 1870s, when Gladstonian economies had their most ruthless run, were particularly hard for the Treasury. Of course, not only science was affected. Arthur Helps, Clerk to the Privy Council, referred in October 1872, to the 'infinite absurdity of the Treasury'. He wrote: 'The Treasury is always at war with almost every office; and the degree and interference we have to endure is almost intolerable.'[112] In 1872, the press took the side of J. D. Hooker, FRS, Director of Kew Gardens, against both Lowe and Gladstone's Chief Commissioner of Works, A. S. Ayrton, in a flurry that helped to precipitate a Parliamentary debate, and eventually the Cabinet reshuffle of 1873.[113] 'It is not money on Kew', *The Times* remarked, 'which burdens the country and perplexes the Chancellor of the Exchequer . . . better to spare a wound from a "Woolwich Infant" than to deprive the greatest botanical establishment in the world of the most competent men.'[114] In October the same year, at the height of the cattle plague, *The Times* blasted the Treasury for discouraging veterinary officers from applying for compensation. This was, and was seen as, a direct threat to the operation of Contagious Diseases (Animals) Act. 'It is possible that in framing the [offending] Minute', *The Times* added, 'Their Lordships may not have sufficiently reflected upon the character of its expressions, or upon the inexpediency of any appearance even of tying the hands of zealous officers at a critical and dangerous time'.[115] But this kind of Treasury ignorance was insupportable.

(3) Where the Treasury's ignorance had little public consequence, however, men of science were in a different position. The same year, *Nature* recounted the sad story of a Treasury refusal to assist observations on tidal phenomena. In May 1872, a Memorial (signed by Sir William Thomson, later Lord Kelvin) was sent to the Treasury by the British Association asking for a grant of £150. The subject, of obvious utilitarian interest, had occupied the British Association from its earliest days, and the Association had contributed £600 of its own funds towards it. However, after an appreciable delay, hopes were dashed. The Treasury replied that while 'fully sensible of the interesting nature of such investigations [they felt that] if they acceded to this request, it would be impossible to refuse to contribute towards the numerous objects which men of science may desire to treat scientifically'. The conclusions *Nature* drew were twofold: first, 'So long as individuals and bodies of individuals ... attempt to do what should properly devolve on the State, so long will a Government, destitute, like ours, of a particle of the scientific element, neglect its legitimate duties'. Second, in its censuring judgement, the Treasury 'plaintively confesses its total inability to grasp any State scientific problem, lest it should have to deal with them all.'[116] If the Treasury clerks could never completely escape this criticism, they could at least offset it by more careful use of their power.

Indeed, one has the impression that if Treasury clerks were oblivious of the disasters they caused, they were also never completely aware of their power. This was particularly significant in areas where 'policy' or the direction of political mandate (if any) was not clear. We

Science and the Treasury, 1870–85

know little of most of these men in the Treasury, yet it is clear that 'minute' references by junior clerks, struggling to make sense of novel propositions, formed the basis of policies, while the Treasury, for most of the period, was so ordered that the Permanent Secretary saw only the final correspondence. It was often these junior clerks, ill-informed as many were, who gave to the notion of 'Treasury control' a sense of leaden indifference to the needs of science.

Two examples, drawn from the Third Division (Education, Science, etc.) will suffice. When, in 1867, it was agreed to transfer the Meteorological Council from the Board of Trade to the Royal Society, there were certain objective constitutional issues. The costs of the new Meteorological Council were to be met by public funds, yet its officers were not to be public officers and were not entitled to superannuation. The prospect was that of defraying the cost of a department over which the Treasury had no control. George Ward Hunt minuted anxiously: 'I fear the arrangement will be a bonus of expense and irresponsibility.'[117] Hunt himself was in the position of trying to fathom not whether it was in the national interest to make the transfer—a matter already decided at a political level—but whether it was wise to abandon storm signals and continue other observations.

A second example is that of F. A'Court Bergne (1842–1908), who entered the Treasury as a Third Class Clerk in the First Division in 1861, and who became First Class Clerk (hence with authority to draft nearly final minutes) in 1875. In 1884 he was transferred to the Third Division, where he had direct responsibility for many scientific departments. Bergne had a difficult time at the Treasury; in 1884 he was passed over for promotion to Principal, in 1887 he was reprimanded for intemperate language in writing to the Irish Education Office, and, in 1893, he was censured for a breach of manners, following a quarrel with the Parliamentary Clerk. His brusque style was well known, and was discounted; but his negative attitude tended to sour everything he touched.[118] Unhappily, this included science. In 1878, Clements Markham, the famous geographer, applied to Sir Stafford Northcote on behalf of the naturalist, Captain Fielden, asking for some official recognition of Fielden's service to the Polar Expedition. Bergne minuted abrasively: 'I should be inclined to refuse as Fielden has already been well paid and his services were purely civil.'

Bergne was right, but his ungenerous style was hardly civil. Fielden's request was refused. Towards the Marine Biological Association (MBA), Bergne behaved in a similarly cavalier fashion:

> I do not believe that any addition to food supply will be secured by anything that is done at the Biological Laboratory. I think that when the time comes, asking the Association to show cause for a continuation of their grant, they will find this very difficult to do. The grant will be spent on scientific research and will be very difficult to withdraw from the people who will get the handling of it, but I don't believe that a single herring or sole will be caught the more for all the Association's efforts.
>
> But if we find that there is duplication of work we may cut down the expenditure on both bodies; for this reason it is necessary to know what they are doing (which we shall do in the Reports) and to be in a position to stop the Fishery Boards from trying to begin abstract studies. For this reason as the Fishery Board is pledged to practical work, I think it very necessary that the Board should nominate one of its members on the Council of the Association, for they cannot plead ignorance of what the latter body is doing.
>
> After a year or two I expect to find a consensus of opinion among practical men that neither body has done any good at all; if we then put them to proof we may get rid of the grants to both.[119]

Given this kind and quality of opinion, the senior officials of the Treasury had every reason to resist the claims of science. Indeed, for as long as they were required to *overrule* their juniors, a more generous line of argument could not develop.

The Administrative Response

It is with reference to such questions as these that the Treasury ultimately had either to turn to advisers, or to relinquish all hope of control. In effect, the Treasury did both. Quantitatively, the outcome of *particular* discussions may have been decided on financial grounds of many different kinds. But in more qualitative terms, which had

Science and the Treasury, 1870–85

reference to the whole spirit of spending, the likelihood of improved, less frustrating relationships between science and administration, became of central importance. In these situations, issues of public relations became matters of personal relations. And in these personal relationships, where substantive ignorance was probably irrelevant, the all-important requirement was personal respect. This respect took years to build, and varied greatly with the personalities involved.

In the period from 1870 to 1894, three Permanent Secretaries held the stage, Ralph (later Lord) Lingen (1870–85), Reginald (later Lord) Welby (1885–94), and Francis (later Sir Francis) Mowatt (1894–1903); a 'succession of past masters in all the *arcana* of Gladstonian finance'.[120] Under George Hamilton (1859–70), the Treasury treated science civilly, but on an *ad hoc* basis, with no particular regard for general policies. His successor, Lingen, came upon a situation where science was expanding both within government departments and in outside claims for support, and the need for some regular principles became manifest. It was not until the succession of Welby and Mowatt that improved personal relations, and the smoother conduct of business they implied, moved appreciably and regularly to a different plane.

Lingen was brought by Robert Lowe to the Treasury from the Education Department, where they had both won fame for implementing the Revised Code, the system of capitation grants, and the philosophy of 'payments by results'. Lingen's biographer recalled his complete qualifications to 'preside over the Treasury under a Government which carried almost aggressively into practice the old Liberal doctrine of economy'.[121] Admittedly, to the world 'his strength lay not so much in his capacity to make changes as in his ability to negative claims upon the public purse'.[122] Even Gladstone described him as a 'ferocious economist'.[123] At first, Lingen's opinion was, predictably, that science deserved no special treatment, and that men of science were simply lobbyists in their own cause. The question of what 'higher national interests' they might serve, and whether they were better equipped to define them than he was, did not immediately arise. It was ironic, however, that within his first few months as Permanent Secretary, the government was under pressure to subsidize the *Challenger* Expedition, to expand scientific and technical education, and to get under way the first Royal Commission ever constituted to consider specifically the position and prospects of scientific education and research. When the Devonshire Commission began its work, however, Lingen categorically rejected a proposed increase in the payment of expert witnesses: 'witnesses eminent enough to seem to call for exceptional allowance may firmly be expected to have more than usual interest in their subject and to be willing to assist the Commissioners without remuneration'.[124]

Throughout the early 1870s, Lingen remained cool towards science, especially where it seemed to trail off into the remote and unaccountable expanses of education; in particular, he distrusted the Science and Art Department. One has only to recall this Department—conceived with the blessing of the Prince Consort, delivered by the skill of Lyon Playfair, and which embraced the combined talents of the Royal School of Mines and the Royal College of Chemistry (including Huxley, Goodeve and Guthrie)—to recognize its crucial symbolic and practical significance to public approval of science.[125] The Department was of particular and continuing embarrassment to Lingen. As he minuted to W. H. Smith in 1875, 'This is a very difficult department to deal with financially. The statements in the estimates are very little guide to the grants paid to individuals for its administration.'[126] In the same communication, he expressed grave foreboding:

> I need not remind you how formidable a place education under one name or another occupies in the Civil Service Estimates ... nor how much more formidable from the same point of view is the growing civil expenditure than the military. I think it particularly needful at a time when the application of the endowments of the Kingdom may be said to be in process of change, to keep the tightest hand over this implausible part of public expenditure which is exposed to many influences besides the love of knowledge or the desire to spread it.[127]

Among these 'influences', Lingen took particular exception to that of Norman Lockyer.[128] Lockyer, while a War Office clerk, had begun the journal *Nature*, and was, by 1870, widely canvassing for 'scientific reform'. Lingen tried to stop Lockyer's appointment as Secretary of

Science and the Treasury, 1870–85

the Devonshire Commission on the grounds that he was still at the War Office, that the Commission needed a full-time Secretary, and that the Treasury was unwilling to pay Lockyer two salaries. Lingen was overruled, but his misgivings continued. 'Observe', he minuted to W. H. Smith in 1875, 'that Mr Lockyer (who purports to be a clerk in the War Office) . . . is Secretary to the Science Commission on whose report all sorts of proposals for the expansion of this Department may be expected.'[129] After the Commission had finished its work, it was proposed to transfer Lockyer from the War Office to the Department of Science and Art. Lingen again ruled against this. When the Department, in turn, refused to accept Lingen's ruling, he agreed reluctantly to give in: 'I propose to give them what they ask for under protest; they are sure to send us in another rigmarole, but I would then remain mute until we have to deal with their Estimates, 1876–77. You will see that . . . they make some important and rather short-sighted admissions.' He bitterly added: 'We are partners intended to sleep with unlimited liability.'[130]

With the Department itself, Lingen had no patience. 'It is evident', he minuted in October 1875, 'that the creation of such a place [as Lockyer's] will thereby become a personal question, instead of remaining a public one to be examined on public grounds only . . . South Kensington will never get into order as long as this kind of irregularity is tolerated.'[131] When it was suggested that a heliostat purchased for the Transit of Venus Expedition could be made over to Lockyer for his solar physics work, Lingen was much distressed, and commented that 'The service is demoralized by matters of this kind. The money's worth is a matter of indifference.'[132] This revealing admission—that there were principles above price in Treasury policy—provides a rare clue to Lingen's personal beliefs.

If the trajectory of Lockyer's career disturbed Lingen's confidence in the probity of scientists, Lingen did not altogether despair of science. His dealings with scientific societies proved more satisfactory. Indeed, while Lingen took umbrage at what seemed a chronic tendency among scientists to 'demand', he frequently expressed his gratitude for what he called 'occasional flashes of reasonableness'. Thus, in 1871, Sir George Airy, the Astronomer Royal, wrote to cancel a request for government money to publish the results of the

Solar Eclipse of that year. Airy, Lingen considered, was a 'reasonable man', and he minuted accordingly: 'The Treasury receives a good many less civil and reasonable letters from less distinguished correspondents.'[133] Still, there were limits. In 1877, Lingen was faced with the difficulty of deciding how far to aid the learned societies. The issue arose specifically in connexion with a request from the Scottish Meteorological Society, which requested support equal to that of the Royal Society in the conduct of 'English' meteorological observations. Lingen demurred. He admitted that learned societies, had from 'time to time, been admitted by successive governments, on no one settled principle, to receive aid', but he felt that 'with so large an expenditure [on science] in hand, almost the whole of which is the growth of quite recent years', the government could not be asked to 'make grants to particular societies as if there were no other way of promoting science, and if it were doing nothing else towards that object'.[134] It was decided to 'put some check on this sort of provincial raid on public money'. As a gesture of 'reasonableness', however, he was prepared to grant £1,000 for 'past services'.[135]

These, and other examples, suggest strongly that from the 1870s onwards, Treasury control of science contained a paradox. It was only with some measure of scientific understanding that Treasury control could operate. Yet, this understanding increasingly relied upon a practice of transferring greater responsibility to expert assessors outside Whitehall, and often to the very interest group which was seeking support. Eventually, this involved a recognition of institutions or individuals who could be counted upon to act as 'public spokesmen'. Increasingly, the Treasury looked to the Royal Society to become its own standing committee on science.

The Royal Society, with its long history of providing advice to governments,[136] was an obvious choice. Indeed, an Advisory Council of scientists, comprising Fellows of the Society, but responsible to a special Minister of Science, had formed one of the chief recommendations of the Devonshire Commission's *Eighth Report* in 1875. But this particular form of Advisory Council did not precisely meet the Treasury's needs. A council of scientists with first loyalties to a Minister could arm that Minister against the Treasury, and could not be relied upon for 'objective' advice. But the Royal Society, working

Science and the Treasury, 1870–85

with the Treasury, could prove a valuable partner. During the 1840s and 1850s, the Royal Society, with the British Association, had pressed for greater support of science. In so doing, they came to recognize a pattern of cooperative action. In 1853, for example, Earl Granville took the occasion of a Parliamentary Question on navigational aids to remind Lord Wrottesley that:

> It was of very great importance for the Government, and for the interests of science itself, and with a view to obtain all reasonable money grants for the country ... to show that when they did give grants for scientific purposes, they exercised economy in administering the grants.[137.]

By the 1880s, the Royal Society had largely accepted this responsibility. Within its Council men could be found who by policy and temperament could be relied upon to take a respectful attitude, 'even indeed, a conservative attitude', towards the spending of public money.

Such a man was Sir Joseph Hooker, President of the Royal Society between 1873 and 1878, who was prepared to admit that the Treasury had been very generous to science. To Lingen he wrote:

> Assuredly, you have not taken too much credit upon yourselves for subsidising science. You might have added large sums for the Greenwich Observatory and Kew, for although both these Institutions are supposed to be mainly utilitarian, they are in their scientific aspects very liberally dealt with in my opinion. Then there is the *Challenger* expedition, and the Arctic and the publication of the Royal Society catalogue. As to the Nautical Almanac, I suppose that fully half of its matter, or half the labour involved in its preparation, is in the interests of Scientific Observatories.[138]

In Hooker, as in Airy, Lingen found a staunch reluctance to see science bound by fetters of gold. This corresponded perfectly to Lingen's desire to get value for money. Occasionally, he managed to restrain scientific spending. For example, in November 1878, he successfully refused a request for more staff for the beleaguered Meteorological Council, instead advising the Council to 'extract [from the entire subject] for the more active prosecution those parts of it which in your judgement are the most likely to be of present use [and] ... to economize in other directions'.[139] But, thanks largely to the work of Airy and Hooker, and within the Vote given to the learned societies, Lingen was prepared to be flexible. As usual, specific cases provided the occasion for judgements, and naturally, where the Royal Society had a strong interest, Lingen advised George Ryder, in December 1878, 'to interfere in the least possible degree with [the Council's] appropriation of the grant, unless their annual report ... affords ground for dissatisfaction or inquiry'. The Treasury should not, Lingen felt, 'abnegate the right of control'. Yet, he added, revealingly:

> Science as such is no part of the provision of political government and nothing can be more out of place than direct discussions about it in official correspondence. My Lords select the most promising *savants* and give them their heads, so long as they show no signs of running wild, or of spending too much or of producing no result.[140]

In December 1881, Lingen elaborated his position in a letter to Hooker's successor, William Spottiswoode. As before, his views were focused on a specific case, and again the case was meteorology. Lingen offered an attempt at a consistent view:

> My Lords consider generally that scientific enquiry is not the direct business of government, but rather of Societies and bodies which, under your conditions, government may occasionally assist, e.g., by such grants as those of £4,000 and £1,000 now made to the Department of Science and Art and to the Royal Society.
>
> If any more special grant is ever in question, the object of it should be definite, of great importance, beyond any public views, and promising of success.[141]

With this, Spottiswoode agreed.

Time and again, the prospect of close collaboration with the Royal Society gave Lingen a sense of comradeship in defence of thrift. In June 1881, he assured Lord Frederick Cavendish that £20,000 for the

Science and the Treasury, 1870–85

Transit of Venus Expedition was quite in order, especially as he had himself had 'a good deal of discussion' with the President of the Royal Society. 'They gave their services *gratis*', he said, as if to press home the obvious lesson of this high moral posture, adding, 'and are beyond all question, preferable to any official body for such a duty.'[142] The request was sanctioned without difficulty. Again, in reference to the forthcoming Solar Eclipse Expedition, Lingen admitted frankly his impression that:

> The scientific tendency of the time is to multiply observations, and if the Government once interfered, the only remaining precaution is for it to be advised as well as it can be, that the way chosen is the best and that no unnecessary expense is incurred.
> ... The Royal Society has been, thus far, a tower, not only of strength, but of economy to the Government.[143]

Spottiswoode took away instructions to work within his grant of £4,000, and this the Royal Society attempted to do. Throughout the early 1880s this spirit of cooperation flourished.

Lingen tried repeatedly to add to the Society's responsibilities—its advice was not only free, in terms of public money; it worked. He was even inclined to let the Solar Physics Observatory go to the Society,[144] but this the Society resisted. In February 1882, the Royal Society did somewhat reluctantly acquiesce in a proposal to increase its government grant from £1,500 to £3,000, and to add the sum of £2,000 to the grant taken since 1876 under the Vote of the Department of Science and Art for 'scientific investigations'. This proposal was part of A. J. Mundella's plan to create a scheme of 'State Fellowships' for science. Lingen was indignant; his prejudice against the Department and in favour of the Royal Society brought a quick response. 'I think it most mischievous', he thundered, 'to make a Parliamentary Department the channel of doles.'[145] In 1876, he had condemned this as 'opening the door to a sort of expenditure doubtful both in kind and degree'.[146] In 1882 he observed:

> The Royal Society is the most eminent and the most generally representative of all the central scientific associations. If the direct prosecution of scientific enquiry is not, as I contend it is

not, the business of Government, its indirect prosecution (supposing that with all our enormous endowments it is necessary to resort to the Exchequer at all) cannot be better forwarded than by liberal grants to this Society.

A remarkable grasp of science and its needs then emerged:

Real discoverers are not of the sort that South Kensington would either attract or select. Real discovery cannot be ordered like so much clerical or other labour, although plenty of people who can be ordered are ready to take wages for it. The judicious assistance and encouragement of a body like the Royal Society ... is probably the least mischievous form of aid, although even that implies the question 'what are you doing?' and 'when may we look for results?' which I believe to be more grievous than poverty with its freedom, to the investigator who is worth anything, and who must far oftener turn back than go forward.[147]

With this, the Royal Society agreed. The issue of State Scholarships lay dormant until the early years of the First World War.[148]

By 1885, and the date of his retirement and elevation to the peerage, in the 'formal arrangements of a dying government', Lingen had become thoroughly familiar with science, and had opened fresh channels of communication with scientists and politicians. His minute on the proposed £5,000 grant in aid of the new Marine Biological Association, in 1885, reveals a new manner of working. 'I have had', he reported, 'a good many discussions on horse-back, after the manner of the ancient Persians on this question with Lord Dalhousie. Subject to budget considerations, I am rather favourably disposed ... It is very desirable that it should not be wholly dependent on Parliamentary funds, but be in a position like that of the Royal Society.'[149] Indeed, the history of the Marine Biological Association reveals a strikingly more sophisticated approach to the problems of government aid. The baronial interests of the Treasury must be served, but the Treasury could take a larger view. As Spring-Rice commented: '... a good deal is to be said in favour of not leaving such work to private enterprise. It requires organization and cooperation and is not

Science and the Treasury, 1870–85

directly productive, and necessarily requires expenditure of time and money.'[150]

If Lingen had not learned the gentle art of conciliation until late in the day, Reginald Welby and Francis Mowatt, his successors as Permanent Secretary, began from a position of strength. Welby, chiefly remembered as an epicurean, an intensely 'clubbable' Etonian of great wit and erudition, succeeded Lingen, to the rejoicing of his colleagues; he became what Sir Algernon West called 'easily the most powerful man in the British Empire'.[151] Although he inherited a strong sense of Lingenian negativism, he did not act as quickly to defend public virtue. As Dr Roseveare comments: 'His room became a kind of gigantic "in-tray" and it was a Treasury joke, upon the occasion of a celebrated murder, that if the criminal had the sense to conceal the body on Welby's desk he would have certainly escaped detection.'[152] Welby's position was in many ways different from his predecessors'. From the 1880s onwards, as he remarked, 'The wind was in the sails of the spending departments'; the old spirit of economy was weakened, and with new colonial, imperial and military commitments, financial orthodoxy was regularly receiving blows to the body. His letters convey a more generous (or perhaps more realistic) sense of public duty. It is no accident that during his nine years in office, which saw a succession of five Chancellors, the atmosphere of bitterness between Treasury and science notably subsided. Science was not necessarily better endowed, but it had no longer to seek special justification. Under the circumstances, Welby had officially an almost passive view of Treasury control; as he told the Royal Commission on Civil Establishments in 1887: 'My view of the control or check entrusted to the Treasury is that it is purely a financial check, instituted for purely financial purposes, and from the moment it interferes in any shape or kind with policy, it is departing from its proper sphere.'[153]

Welby was not always consistent in this interpretation. In particular, this general rule did not apply to examples of apparent 'immorality', notably the Department of Science and Art, or Norman Lockyer's ingenuous request for the heliostat in 1876. Yet it was Welby who, ten years later, questioned critically the work of Lockyer and Donnelly, and disputed the wisdom of continuing the Treasury's 'sop to South Kensington'.[154] On the other hand, where public virtue was found, it was rewarded. Welby, and Mowatt following him, learned from their predecessors, for example, the value of giving funds to the Royal Society, and then leaving the Society to manage them effectively. The real job was not to deny expenditure on expertise, but to delegate it and fix an upper limit.[155] Mowatt, who resigned in 1903 following differences with Chamberlain's protectionist policies, was an even more gentle man, who, while defending Liberal economies, saw probably more clearly than many of his predecessors (and successors) the necessity to give creative men freer rein.[156] With Mowatt, the growing practice of personal consultation, through committees and commissions, reached its first significant stage. When the proposed Polar Expedition came before the Treasury in 1900, Mowatt minuted:

> I am afraid that personally, I find it difficult to view the present proposal solely through Treasury spectacles, but I have tried to keep out of this Memorandum anything like advocacy. Till now, this Country had made the study and the survey of the Ocean its own. The *Challenger* expedition put us absolutely at the head of all enquiries into such matters and its results are immensely appreciated throughout the world. Whether the Government think we have done enough, and may leave the rest to other nations, is the question now to be decided.[157]

Mowatt's reaction revealed the great distance the Treasury had come. Thirty years of cumulative experience had shown the value of science, and the public responsibility of men of science. What remained was the question: To what *extent* could scientists continue to justify public spending on science as a national goal? With the coming of the new century, this question would acquire an entirely new meaning.

Conclusion

Despite the acknowledged desirability of private initiative and voluntary endeavour, growing costs of science had, by 1870, provoked demands for public patronage. The government, already contributing measurably to scientific activities, was called upon to deal with the new claims of a growing scientific community. The Treasury, un-

Science and the Treasury, 1870–85

dergoing the same fundamental internal changes that were affecting all central departments, was called upon to devise procedures to deal with science. Its approach to science was at first indistinguishable from its approach to any other set of claims for public money. It operated in a budgetary context defined by a succession of strong Chancellors and Permanent Secretaries. However, recognizing ultimately its inability to challenge claims based upon authoritative expertise, it sought means for securing expert advice. By the end of the period, machinery of increasing sophistication had been devised whereby the Treasury could rely upon men of science in helping them to take responsible decisions. This development cannot be separated from the influence of personalities. Mutual regard and an extreme sensitivity to the 'reasonableness' of demands came to characterize the relationship between the Treasury and its scientific advisers. The possibility that this might create difficulties for younger, provincial, less well-known men of science remained distinct, as succeeding generations would abundantly prove.

Dr Brock ends his discussion of patronage with the question: How did a nineteenth-century scientist earn his living? We must reverse the question and ask from the Treasury's point of view: What claims of science were sufficient to justify expenditure from the public purse? Too often, the historical discussion of the scientific movement is represented as a battle between polar opposites, of enlightened public interest versus obscurantist bureaucracy, in which scientists were pitted against legalistic authorities who knew the price of everything but the value of nothing. The literature on the organization of science in Britain is pervaded with the assmption that in the nineteenth century, no less than now, the case for supporting science was manifestly clear to anyone who took the trouble to consider it. However, the case for supporting science to the limits of the scientists' own self-defined needs was not obvious. In an industrializing democracy, government departments had enormously increased responsibilities, the immediate implications of which were not always clear. The Treasury, in particular, imbued with a sense of moral responsibility, could not accede automatically to any interest group, no matter how well placed or well motivated. The Treasury was no more able than anyone else to estimate the potential contribution of science to the national economy, a practice which has since been described as 'multiplying an un-forseeable gain by an unknowable probability'.[158]

More often than not, however, the Treasury appeared despotic when it was actually being cautious. Two questions arise. First: What made it so cautious? Second: Was this caution merited? Historically, there have often been fundamental differences between what governments want and what objectives scientists, individually or in groups, have been desirous of promoting. The Treasury, for whom science was always so 'exceptional', required to be convinced of the legitimate claim of science to public money. It is arguable that Treasury control, operating in this unsophisticated way, was perfor-ming a vital public service. That it did not necessarily work against the best interests of science itself is clear. Energetic appeals, when launched and sustained by men of science well placed in society, who could marshall effective utilitarian, cultural, or 'prestige' arguments to the support of a united case, usually succeeded.

The 'benefits' of working within such constraints, however, can be exaggerated. On balance, the Treasury's approach, whether reasoned or not, probably delayed innovation and discouraged many good men. It was clearly a rearguard action. The signs were plain, even by the late 1880s, when Norman Lockyer optimistically announced that henceforward 'science is to be aided on precisely the same ground that we aid the army and navy. It is no longer a question of merely paying for sweetness and light, or of giving a poor dog a bone.'[159] By the turn of the century, governments throughout Europe were moving to strengthen their scientific efforts, and Britain was no exception. Indeed, by 1900, when the National Physical Laboratory was es-tablished, the Treasury's participation in science had extended even into the direct encouragement of manufacturing industry.

The two major stumbling blocks to the endowment of science by the State proved to be the widespread inability of civil servants to ap-preciate the difficulty, purposes, and ultimate value of fundamental research, coupled with the inability of men of science to recognize the difficulty and necessity of accountability. It was this collective diffi-culty, more than mere obscurantism on either side, which resulted in case after case of false economies, fragmentation of effort, and in the weary, frustrating routine of scholastic controversy, which became so

Science and the Treasury, 1870–85

familiar to generations of scientists.

The late nineteenth century witnessed a transformation within the terms of patronage, and the development of 'modern' patterns of endowment. In grasping for the means to keep control over public expenditure, the Treasury was forced to admit its own limitations. Gradually, the Treasury began to move from *ad hoc* decisions towards general policy—a development which many would say is far from complete. What became vital in this development was a sense of shared responsibility between patron and client. In general terms, central government needed guidance, and machinery more efficient than traditional, cumbersome Royal Commissions and Select Committees. It required the institutionalization of advice through which 'reasonable claims' could be advanced. As successive governments came to use science as an instrument of policy, they became reconciled to the fact that scientists themselves had to decide what the main problems were, and how they should be dealt with.

By 1914, the cost to public funds of 'civil' scientific activities in Britain, excluding education, amounted to about £2 million, or about 3.6 per cent of the total civil expenditure.[160] Although this comprised only a fraction of the nation's total 'patronage' of science, it already presented important problems of allocation and control. Government activity in the 1870s and 1880s had raised questions not merely of size, but of procedure and direction in spending—issues which became profoundly important during and after the First World War. Indeed, these early controversies disclosed some of the most fundamental problems which would face all governments in their use and support of science—the problems of securing adequate accountability for public funds spent in the public interest. By the 1890s, the pressures within science had begun to burst the carapace they had outgrown. The issues this posed, and their implications for public well-being, are still with us today.

Notes and References

1. This eassy excludes what would, in some ways, be a separate study of specifically industrial research, experiment, and development, and the role played (or neglected) by British industry in its support. The fact that, within the physical sciences, such distinctions are often difficult to draw, will not escape the reader's notice, and, of course, the effects of fundamental and applied research must be seen in combination in any complete assessment of scientific patronage.

2. This was, of course, a phenomenon common to many European countries. See, for example, Loren Graham, 'The Formation of Soviet Research Institutes: A Combination of Revolutionary Innovation and International Borrowing', *Social Studies of Science*, 5 (1975), 303–30.

3. Government participation in scientific exploration and discovery in aid of commercial and economic interests of a colonial power was evident from at least the seventeenth century. See George Basalla, 'Science and Government in England, 1800–1870', (unpublished Ph.D. thesis, Harvard University, 1963).

4. See, for example, R. M. MacLeod, 'Science and the Civil List, 1830–1914', *Technology and Society*, 6 (1970), 47–55; R. M. MacLeod, 'Of Medals and Men: Reflections on a Reward System in Victorian Science', *Notes and Records of the Royal Society*, 26 (1971), 81–105; R. M. MacLeod, 'The Resources of Science in Victorian England: The Endowment of Science Movement, 1868–1900', in *Science and Society, 1600–1900*, edited by Peter Mathias (Cambridge, 1972), pp. 111–66.

5. Calculated form *Civil Estimates* for 1859/60, 1869/70, and 1879/80; Parliamentary Papers [hereafter P.P.] 1859 (38), XVI. 370; 1868–9 (122) XLII. 1; 1878–9 (23) XLVIII. 1.

6. There is growing evidence to demonstrate that research costs in individual fields of science were increasing as the multiplication of institutions and men had a cumulative impact. Expensive instrumentation included, for example, electrical apparatus (electromagnetos, high voltage storage batteries, and induction coils), photometric, spectrometric and other optical equipment, and eventually, in the 1890s, machinery for producing high vacua and low temperatures. See Paul Forman, J. Heilbron & S. Weart, 'Personnel, Funding and Productivity in Physics circa 1906: a Multinational Statistical Study', *Historical Studies in the Physical Sciences*, forthcoming.

7. This is not to mention the soaring cost of science education through the 'science schools', which grew from £26,000 in 1869, to £188,000 in 1899. Calculated from *Civil Estimates* for 1869/70 and 1899/1900; P.P. 1868–9 (122), XLIII. 1; 1899 (69), LVI. 1.

8. *Royal Commission on Scientific Instruction and the Advancement of Science* [hereafter, Devonshire Commission]: *Eighth Report*, P.P. 1875 [C. 1298], XXVIII. 417, p. 26. The supporting literature is extensive; see George Gore,

Science and the Treasury, 1870–85

'The National Importance of Scientific Research', *Westminster Review*, new series, 43 (1873), 343–66.

9. The Census Returns for 'scientific persons' (which exclude men of science who were university teachers), list 672 in 1861, 909 in 1871, and over 1,200 in 1881, doubling in 20 years; see P.P. 1863 [3221], LIII. Pt. I 1, p. 307; 1873 [C. 872], LXXI. 1, p. 93; 1883 [C. 3722], LXXX. 1, p. x.

10. Devonshire Commission: *Eighth Report*, P.P. 1875 [C. 1298], XXVIII. 417, p. 24.

11. Ibid.

12. 'On National Institutions for Practical Scientific Research', *Quarterly Journal of Science*, 6 (1869), 40.

13. See, for example, A. J. Meadows, *Science and Controversy: A Biography of Norman Lockyer* (London, 1972).

14. Thus, Sir Humphry Davy, 'Government, by the command of our august patrons, has always been found ready to assist us when our enquiries have been connected with the objects of national interest . . .'; 'On the Progress and Prospects of Science', in *The Collected Works of Sir Humphry Davy, Bart*, edited by John Davy, 9 vols (London, 1839–40), VII (1840), p. 6.

15. Joseph Ben-David, *The Scientist's Role in Society: A Comparative Study* (Englewood Cliffs, New York, 1971).

16. See, for example, D. S. L. Cardwell, *The Organisation of Science in England*, second edition, (London, 1972), p. 118 & passim.

17. J. B. & B. L. Hammond, *James Stansfeld* (London, 1932), pp. 91–2.

18. Charles J. Cornish, *Sir William Henry Flower* (London, 1904), pp. 203–4. See Richard Johnson, 'Administrators in Education before 1870: Patronage, social Position and Role', in *Studies in the Growth of Nineteenth-Century Government*, edited by Gillian Sutherland (London, 1972), pp. 110–39.

19. Listed Treasury papers at the Public Record Office [hereafter PRO] concerning science in the period 1850 to 1900, probably number several thousand documents, which relate to scientific activities as different as the Ordnance Survey and the National Physical Laboratory. Of these, however, only several hundred seem to have survived official 'weeding'. These papers include Treasury 'in-letters' (PRO Reference T.1), and Treasury 'Supply' files (PRO Reference T. 165). In addition, there are departmental files, amounting, within flexible definitions of 'science', to several hundreds more.

20. See H. Roseveare, *The Treasury: The Evolution of a British Institution* (London, 1969); M. Wright, *Treasury Control of the Civil Service, 1854–1874* (Oxford, 1969).

21. See, for example, Sutherland, op. cit. note 18. This development is summarized in R. M. MacLeod, 'Statesmen Undisguised', *American Historical Review*, 78 (1973), 1386–405.

22. A full study of government patronage of science would require much more case study material than at present exists. The absence of other work may serve to explain the present author's otherwise excessive self-citation in this essay. The

neglect of such issues even in contemporary work is evident. See, for example, Ian Varcoe, *Organizing for Science in Britain* (Oxford, 1974).

23. This essay considers neither the question of political patronage in staffing, nor, of course, the other important functions of the Treasury, including financial management and budgetary policy. See, for example, Rosevare, op cit. note 20; and Wright, op. cit. note 20.

24. In most cases, the technical 'expert' would have been appointed under Section IV of the Superannuation Act of 1859, consolidated in Clause IV of the Order in Council, 1870. These appointments formed the nucleus of the 'Professional Civil Service', which, by 1912, numbered about 1,200: see *Royal Commission on the Civil Service: Fourth Report*, P.P. 1914 [Cd. 7338], XVI. 1, p. 31.

25. This included expenditure on the geological and ordnance surveys, which in 1870 amounted to £23,067 and £133,500 respectively, and on meteorological research. The latter had begun, in 1855, as a Department under the Board of Trade. In 1867, meteorological research was transferred to a 'Meteorological Committee' under the Royal Society, with an annual budget of £10,000. In 1877, the budget was increased to £14,500 and the Committee transformed into a Council. In 1882, the grant was increased to £15,300, where it remained until 1900. Agricultural research included the work of the Cattle Plague Department formed under the Home Office in 1867, which was transferred with the Veterinary Department to the Privy Council. It was not until 1889 that, with the formation of a Central Board of Agriculture, research into all aspects of agriculture was centralized. Fisheries research had been started, in 1869, by the Scottish Fisheries Board (with a budget of £13,298); in 1882, a Fisheries Board for Scotland was formed. In 1886, a National Fisheries Department was set up by the Board of Trade. 'Science in policy' also related to imperial questions. Special Votes were requested and sanctioned to aid specific enquiries and institutions such as the Imperial Institute (1887), and the London School of Tropical Medicine (1899).

26. *Returns of Commissions of Inquiry appointed since 1830, and expenses of each*, P.P. 1856 (415), XXXVIII. p. 395; *Return of Royal Commissions issued since 1856*, P.P. 1862 (317), XXX. p. 615; *Return of Royal Commissions issued between 1866–84*, P.P. 1888 (426), LXXVIII. p. 491; *Return of Royal Commissions issued in each and every year including 1874*, P.P. 1896, LXXVIII. p. 513.

27. Several contemporary attempts were made to categorize scientific expenditure though never (to my knowledge) by the Treasury; see, for example, R. A. Proctor, 'Money for Science', *Cornhill Magazine*, 32 (1875), 459.

28. R. M. MacLeod, 'The Royal Society and the Government Grant. Notes on the Administration of Scientific Research, 1849–1914', *Historical Journal*, 14 (1971), 323–58.

29. Comparisons with contemporary figures are notoriously difficult. A very crude comparison might be concluded from the fact that in 1974–5, the sum of £352 millions was allocated to government-sponsored services relevant to

Science and the Treasury, 1870–85

agriculture, industry, health, environmental affairs, and the research councils. This represented only 1.5 per cent of the Gross Civil Estimates for that year. However, this figure is to be distinguished from the 'R & D Estimates' (with which it in fact overlaps), which in 1974–5 totalled £517 millions (or 4.7 per cent of Gross Civil Estimates; see *Supply Estimates, 1974–5, Memorandum by the Chief Secretary to the Treasury*, P.P March 1974. Cmnd. 5576.

30. See Royston Lambert, *Sir John Simon, 1816–1904, and English Social Administration* (London, 1963).

31. See, for example, Margaret Deacon, *Scientists and the Sea, 1650–1900: A Study of Marine Science* (London, 1971).

32. *Inaugural Address to the Fifth Annual Meeting of the Devonshire Association For the Advancement of Literature, Science and Art* (Exeter 1866).

33. *Correspondence of Sir Arthur Helps*, edited by E. A. Helps (London, 1871), p. 22.

34. 'Government and "Scientific Investigation",' *The Spectator*, 22 July 1971, p. 882.

35. Charles Wilson, *Chapters from my Official Life* (London, 1916), p. 61.

36. See, for example, Roseveare, op. cit. note 20, p. 186; Wright, op cit. note 20, p. 329; and Basil Chubb, *The Control of Public Expenditure* (Oxford, 1952). For Gladstone's attitude, see his address to the Society of Arts, *Journal of the Society of Arts*, 55 (1862), 504, praising its voluntary endeavours as the supreme 'feature of the English character'. For the weakness in Gladstone's assumptions, see D. G. C. Allen, 'The Society of Arts and Government, 1754–1800', *Eighteenth Century Studies*, 7 (1974), 434–52.

37. See Roseveare, op. cit. note 20, chapter 6; G. Sutherland, *Policy Making in Elementary Education* (Oxford, 1973).

38. *First Report of the Commission appointed by the Treasury on the Method of Selecting Civil Servants*, P.P. 1875 [C. 113], XXIII. 1.

39. According to one observer, the Privy Council had 'been used as a kind of potting shed for new administrative plants'; see K. B. Smellie, *One Hundred Years of English Government* (London, 1937), p. 90.

40. This impression is based on existing Treasury files. The four clerks were: Sir W. H. Clerke, Bt.; G. C. Barrington; G. L. (later Sir George) Ryder; F. A. 'Court Bergne.

41. Roseveare, op. cit. note 20, p. 215.

42. Wright, op. cit. note 20, p. 333.

43. Jeremy Bentham, 'The Rationale of Reward', in *The Works of Jeremy Bentham, published under the Superintendence of his Executor, John Bowring*, 11 vols (Edinburgh, 1838–43), II (1843), p. 256.

44. Ibid.

45. W. E. H. Lecky, *Democracy and Liberty*, 2 vols (London, 1896), I, 275.

46. For example, Joseph Hooker, writing to Darwin in 1876, about the Parliamentary Grant to the Royal Society, complained: 'Government may do much, but it must always be under such vexatious restrictions that it tries a man's temper

and patience, let his patriotism be what it will, to undertake the expenditure of what Government gives, and I fear it must ever be so. Between ourselves, I think there will be a wretched outcome of the Government Fund'; see L. Huxley, *Life and Letters of Sir Joseph Dalton Hooker*, 2 vols (London, 1918), II, 231; Hooker to Darwin, 22 December 1876. Alfred Russel Wallace agreed, on the grounds that 'the State has no moral right to apply funds raised by the taxation of all its members to any purpose which is not directly available for the benefit of all'; see 'Government Aid to Science', *Nature*, 1 (1870), 788–9.

47. Sir George Airy, for example, held a consistently conservative position: 'I think . . . successful researches have in nearly every instance originated with private persons or with persons whose positions were so nearly private that the investigators acted under private influence, without the danger attending connexion with the State. Certainly, I do not consider a Government is justified in endeavouring to force at public expense, investigations of undefined character, and, at best of doubtful validity: and I think it probable that any such attempt will lead to consequences disreputable to science.' See *The English Mechanic*, 831 (1881), 586–7; also *Autobiography of Sir George Biddell Airy*, edited by W. Airy (Cambridge, 1896). The feeling was widespread, though how popular it was is more difficult to say. There is much impressionistic evidence. E.g. Leslie H. Lampitt, in the First Percy Frankland Lecture, recalled to Frankland as one who had no faith in politicians, and who 'fearing the result of the impact of politics on the development of science, was not in favour of research schemes partly supported by Government money'; *Lectures, Monographs and Reports*, 1949, no. 2, Royal Institute of Chemistry (London, 1949), p. 11.

48. See MacLeod, in Mathias, op. cit. note 4, pp. 131–49.

49. Richard Proctor, *Wages and Wants of Science-Workers* (London, 1876), pp. 84–5.

50. As Ralph (later Sir Ralph) Lingen, Permanent Secretary of the Treasury from 1870 to 1875, once said: 'It is well known that there are many Fellows of the Royal Society, whose positions as workers in science need not be too clearly defined, who view with mistrust the liberality of the Government'; see 'Government Grants in Aid of Science', *Nature*, 15 (1877), 369.

51. See Frank Greenaway, *The Science Museum* (London, 1951); and *The Science Museum: The First Hundred Years* (London, 1957).

52. *Hansard* (Commons), 3rd series, 232 (26 February 1877), cols. 1065–6.

53. R. M. MacLeod, 'The X-Club: A Scientific Network in Late-Victorian England', *Notes and Records of the Royal Society*, 24 (1870), 305–22.

54. [George Gore], 'The National Importance of Scientific Research', *Westminster Review*, new series, 63 (1873), 353; A. Strange, 'On the Necessity for State Intervention to secure the Progress of Physics Science', abstract printed in 'Notes and Abstracts of Miscellaneous Communications to the Sections. Mathematics and Physics', *Report of the Thirty-Eighth Meeting of the British Association for the Advancement of Science; held at Norwich in August 1868* (London, 1869), pp. 6–8 (separate pagination from Reports);

Science and the Treasury, 1870–85

Charles Appleton, 'Economic Aspects of the Endowment of Research', *Fortnightly Review*, new series, 16 (1874), 519–36.

55. George Harris, *Civilisation Considered as a Science* (London, 1861), p. 195. Harris (1809–90) was a barrister and amateur anthropologist, a Fellow of the Society of Antiquaries, educated at Rugby and Trinity College, Cambridge.

56. London School of Economics, Welby Collection, R. (S.R.), 1017, 'Civil Service—Miscellaneous', f. 238; Evidence to undated Treasury enquiry (*c.* 1872).

57. David Layton, 'Lord Wrottesley, FRS: Pioneer Statesman of Science', *Notes and Records of the Royal Society*, 23 (1968), 230–46.

58. *Hansard* (Commons), 3rd series, 235 (17 July 1877), col. 1395.

59. F. W. Hirst, *Gladstone as Financier and Economist* (London, 1931), quoted in Roseveare, op. cit. note 20, p. 190.

60. *The Times*, 23 December 1872, quoted in H. Spencer, *The Study of Sociology* (London, 1873), p. 220.

61. Quoted in *Nature*, 6 (1872), 21, 'Mental Darkness in High Places'.

62. Asa Briggs, *Victorian People* (London, 1954), p. 278.

63. Royal Society Scrapbooks (1820–1876), letter from 'F.R.S.' to *The Times* (no date given), citing Disraeli's remark in the Commons that 'when we talk of the learned societies of the nineteenth century [the House must remember] that learned societies no longer consist of learned men'.

64. Royal Society Scrapbook (1820–1876), 'Mr Benjamin Disraeli, F.R.S.', *The Examiner*, 19 February 1876.

65. 'You will remember', Northcote told Edinburgh students during his Rectorial Address in 1884, 'how great is the power which you have acquired and how, in an age when social questions are taking the first place in our attitudes, the scientific man has the means of doing more than even the statesman to remove the causes of sorrow and suffering and to ameliorate the physical condition of the great masses of the people'; *Rectorial Addresses delivered before the University of Edinburgh, 1859–1899*, edited by Archibald Stodart-Walker (London, 1900), p. 248.

66. Robert Cecil, Third Marquess of Salisbury (1830–1903); Prime Minister, 1885–6, 1886–92; 1895–1902; Secretary for India in Disraeli's second government, 1874–8; President of the British Association, 1894. Edward Stanley, fifteenth Earl of Derby (1826–92); Foreign Secretary, 1874–8, under Disraeli; Colonial Secretary under Gladstone, 1882–5.

67. Devonshire Commission: *Fifth Report, with Appendix*, P.P. 1874 [C. 1087], XXII. 51, Question 13,556, 26 November 1872.

68. See 'The Marquis of Salisbury on Scientific Education', *Nature*, 11 (1875), 241; *Hansard* (Commons), 3rd series, 227 (24 January 1876), cols. 791–803.

69. 'Speech on the Medical Profession', in *Speeches and Addresses of Edward Henry Stanley, Fifteenth Earl of Derby*, edited by T. H. Sanderson & E. S. Roscoe, 2 vols (London, 1894), II, 90–1.

70. Stodart-Walker, op. cit. note 65, p. 179.

71. Robert Lowe, (1811–1892), created First Viscount Sherbrooke in 1880. For

his unhappy attempts at raising revenue by imposing a match tax, which earned him the immortal sobriquet of 'Lucifer Lowe', see W. Stanley Jevons *The Match-Tax: A Problem in Finance* (London, 1871). Cf. John Morley, *Life of Gladstone*, 2 vols (London, 1905–6), I (1905), p. 1007. Lowe was forced to withdraw the match tax and to raise income-tax by 2*d.* in the pound instead.

72. Morley, op. cit. note 71, I, 1006.

73. *The Times*, 22 March 1869.

74. *The Telegraph*, 22 June 1869; *Hansard* (Commons), 3rd series, 197 (6 July 1869), col. 1173.

75. Royal Institution Archives, The Journals of Thomas Archer Hirst, f. 1865, 30 March 1870. Lowe supported Hirst for the Assistant Registrarship of London University; see ff. 1942, 1956, 1968.

76. See M. Grant-Duff, *A Victorian Vintage* (London, 1930), p. 26. Darwin was, in Lowe's words, 'the top sawyer of these times'.

77. By twenty-three votes and no blackball; W. White, *The Journals of Walter White* (London, 1899), p. 243.

78. Hirst, op. cit. note 75, 5 August 1872.

79. T. A. Hirst recorded one visit by Lowe to the Lubbock's house at High Elms: 'I was amazed at the respectful familiature our hostess [Lady Lubbock] assumed with the Chancellor. She is evidently a favourite of his. He was very genial and entertaining'; Hirst, op. cit. note 75, f. 1956, 23 November 1872.

80. Ibid., f. 1906.

81. A. Patchett Martin. *Life and Letters of the Rt. Hon. Robert Lowe, Viscount Sherbrooke* (London, 1893), p. 376.

82. Hirst, op. cit. note 75, f. 1968: 'I had a good deal more to do with your position at Greenwich than you can be sure of', Lowe to Hirst, 4 February 1873.

83. Reprinted in E. Ray Lankester, *The Advancement of Science: Occasional Essays and Addresses* (London, 1890), p. 97.

84. Newcastle University Library, MS Letter Books of Sir Charles Trevelyan, vol. 36, ff. 87–8, 6 February 1856.

85. Quoted in Wright, op. cit. note 20, p. 338, from PRO, Hamilton Correspondence, IV, Hamilton to Stansfeld, 21 October 1869.

86. PRO, T1/7253A/18, 718/1872, Minute, Lingen to Lowe, C. 1872.

87. Quoted in Wright, op. cit. note 20, p. 346.

88. Quoted in Wright, op. cit. note 20, p. 346, from PRO, Hamilton Correspondence, IV, Hamilton to Stansfeld, 21 October 1869.

89. By 1877, the economic boom had become a slump; that year proved to be 'a turning point in revenue history'; Roseveare, op. cit. note 20, p. 191. The surplus of £6 million on expenditure of £70 million in 1872–3 had been replaced by liabilities of £10 million on the Estimates of £81 million for 1879.

90. Alpheus Todd, *On Parliamentary Government in England: Its Origin, Development and Practical Operation* (London, 1867), p. 563.

91. PRO, T1/6975B/9208/1870, Lingen, Memorandum, 19 March 1870.

92. Wright argues that Lingen wanted a system of general rules, but did not en-

Science and the Treasury, 1870–85

visage a single unified civil service; Wright, op. cit. note 20, p. 333. Lingen's policy towards science suggests his willingness to have rules for science that were distinct from those applicable to conventional spending.

93. See R. M. MacLeod, *Treasury Control and Social Administration*, Occasional Papers on Social Administration, no. 23 (London, 1968).

94. Cited in Wright, op. cit. note 20, p. 339. Gladstone to Childers, 12 September 1865.

95. Quoted in Roseveare, op. cit. note 20, p. 208.

96. Treasury clerks on committees included, for example, Lord Lingen, Civil Establishments (1886); Lord Welby, Expenditure of India (1894); and Robert Chalmers, Departmental Committee on the National Physical Laboratory (1897).

97. Wright, op. cit. note 20, p. 338.

98. PRO, T1/8708A/18953/1871, Lingen, Minute, 1 June 1871; quoted in Lambert, op. cit. note 30, p. 452.

99. Ibid., p. 314.

100. See R. M. MacLeod, 'The Alkali Acts Administration, 1863–84: The Emergence of the Civil Scientist', *Victorian Studies*, 9 (1965), 85–112; R. M. MacLeod, 'Government and Resource Conservation: The Salmon Acts Administration, 1861–86', *Journal of British Studies*, 7 (1968), 114–50.

101. For the unhappy sequel to Simon's tenure at the Local Government Board, and the gradual suppression of expansionist sentiment, see R. M. MacLeod, 'The Frustration of State Medicine, 1880–1899', *Medical History*, 11 (1967), 15–40. In this case, as elsewhere, departmental Permanent Secretaries were often as anxious as the Treasury to curtail expansion. This factor led to repeated demands from scientific men for authority to answer directly to their political chiefs. Similar rumblings have been heard ever since. See J. B. Poole & K. Andrews, *The Government of Science in Britain* (London, 1972), chapter 6, 'The Scientific Civil Service,' pp. 292–306.

102. Appendix 16, Third Report of the Committee on Public Accounts, 'Memorandum on Grants in Aid', in *Epitome of the Reports of the Committee of Public Accounts, 1857–1937*, P.P. 1937–8 (154), XXII. p. 394.

103. By 1894, this class included votes for the Royal Society, the Meteorological Council, the Royal Geographical Society, the Ben Nevis Observatory, the Royal Academy of Music, the Marine Biological Association, the Royal Society of Edinburgh, the Scottish Meteorological Society, the Royal Irish Academy, and the Royal Zoological Society of Ireland. See PRO, T/165/12, Scientific Investigation, (U.K.), May 1894.

104. *Return of Scientific Societies (Government Grants)*, 1906 (358), LXV. pp. 2–3.

105. Some (like the Royal Society Grant) were awarded without conditions of any kind; some (like the Universities Grant after 1889) specified conditions of administration; some recipients (like the Royal Geographical Society) were required to give reports, while others (for example, the National Galleries) were not always required to do so.

106. The first vote for the Deep Sea Exploring Expedition was taken under Class VII (Special and Temporary), in 1872–3, and remained there until 1876–7, when the Expedition was completed. The vote was then transferred to Class IV (Education, Science and Art) in 1877–8, where it remained, essentially a grant-in-aid, until the *Challenger* Report was finished.

107. 'Our warfare with these Departments is perpetual', Hamilton advised Gladstone, in 1865; PRO, Hamilton Papers, Semi-Official Correspondence, II, 2 August 1865.

108. PRO, T1/7215A/18067/1871, Lingen to Lowe, 21 November 1871.

109. See Simon's efforts to continue vaccination inspection; Lambert, op. cit. note 30, pp. 444–7.

110. Cambridge University Library, Stokes Papers, W. N. Hartley to G. Stokes, 7 March 1892.

111. Robert Lowe's assistance to John Simon is a case in point; see Lambert, op. cit. note 30, p. 362.

112. Helps, op. cit. note 33, p. 331; Helps to Lord Northbrooke, 9 October 1872.

113. In July 1872, Lingen made a last minute attempt to avert parliamentary debate by sending conciliatory letters to both Hooker and the Office of Works urging the reasonableness of Hooker's case; PRO T1/7231A/12009/1872, Lingen Minute, 24 July 1872; *Nature*, 6 (1872), 280–2.

114. *The Times*, 6 July 1872.

115. 'The Treasury and the Privy Council', *The Times*, 18 October 1872.

116. [A. Strange], 'The Tides and the Treasury', *Nature*, 7 (1872), 137–8.

117. PRO T1/6754A/4310/1867, Minute, G. W. Hunt, March 1867.

118. Roseveare engagingly describes Bergne as a 'particularly peppery Principal Clerk who cast his blighting influence over all the vulnerable areas dealt with by the Third Division in the 1880s'; Roseveare, op. cit. note 20, p. 225.

119. PRO, T1/8223B/18995/1885, Bergne to Ridley, November 1885.

120. H. Asquith, *Memories and Reflections* (London, 1927), p. 251.

121. *Dictionary of National Biography* [hereafter *DNB*], Second Supplement (London, 1912), pp. 467–9. There is no definitive biography of Lingen, though one is surely overdue. For his work in the Education Department, see Sutherland, op. cit. note 37, pp. 244–7.

122. The autor of Lingen's obituary described him as 'resolutely determined that the expenditure of public money should be severely checked', and as looking 'with a suspicious and grudging eye upon every claim involving an increase of outlay'; *The Times*, 24 July 1905. His sense of public service at personal cost was Homeric: 'Power is not strutting, not titles ... but work, service, self-denial and self-devotion, quite as often resisting the cry that "something must be done" as in doing. No such preaching should ever appear in minutes, but in example, if it can be set'; Lingen to Arthur Helps, 19 December 1871, quoted in Helps, op. cit. note 33, pp. 316–17.

123. Roseveare, op. cit. note 20, pp. 209–10.

124. PRO, T1/7088B/10480/1870, Lingen, covering minute, *c.* 28 November 1870.

Science and the Treasury, 1870–85

125. See H. Butterworth, 'The Science and Art Department, 1853–1900' (unpublished Ph.D. thesis, University of Sheffield, 1968).
126. PRO, T1/7472/16947/1875, Lingen to W. H. Smith, 11 January 1875.
127. Ibid.
128. Norman (later Sir Norman) Lockyer (1836–1920), astronomer, clerk in the War Office, 1857; Secretary to the Devonshire Commission, 1870; Director of the Solar Physics Observatory and Professor of Astronomical Physics, Royal College of Science, 1890 to 1913; editor of *Nature*, 1869 to 1920; FRS, 1869. See Meadows, op. cit. note 13.
129. PRO, T1/7472/16947/1875, Lingen to W. H. Smith, 11 January 1875.
130. Ibid., Lingen, Minute, *c.* August 1875.
131. PRO, T1/7472/14008/1875, Lingen, Minute, 8 October 1875.
132. PRO, T1/7555B/13366/1876, Lingen, Minute, 12 August 1876.
133. PRO, T1/7164B/1122/1871–2, Lingen, cover note, 25 January 1872.
134. PRO, T1/7652B/9835/1877, Lingen to Richmond, 6 June 1877.
135. PRO, T1/7625B/5238/1877, Lingen, Minute, 28 March 1877; T1/7532B/12922/1876, Lingen, Minute, August 1876.
136. See Basalla, op. cit. note 3.
137. *Hansard* (Commons), 3rd series, 126 (26 April 1853), col. 541.
138. PRO, T1/7652B/9835/1877, Hooker to Lingen, 12 June 1877.
139. PRO, T1/7702B/18125/1878, Lingen to Chairman, Meteorological Council, 9 November 1878.
140. PRO, T1/7662B/19895/1878, Lingen to Ryder, 11 December 1878.
141. Royal Society Council Minutes, p. 273, Lingen to PRS, 23 December 1881.
142. PRO, T1/21690/10260/1881, Lingen to Cavendish, 13 June 1881.
143. PRO, T1/8042B/19497/1882, Lingen to Spottiswoode, 27 December 1872.
144. PRO, T1/8014C/1586/1882, Lingen, Memorandum, 16 February 1883.
145. PRO, T1/8008C/20599/1882, Lingen, Minute, *c.* 3 February 1882.
146. PRO, T1/7522B/6048/1876, Lingen, File cover note, 12 April 1876.
147. PRO, T1/8008C/20599/1882, Lingen, Minute, 3 February 1882.
148. See R. M. MacLeod & Kay Andrews, 'The Origins of the DSIR: Reflections on Ideas and Men', *Public Administration*, 48 (1970), 23–48; and R. M. MacLeod & Kay Andrews, 'The "Pay and Prospects" Problem in British Science, 1880–1918', forthcoming.
149. PRO, T1/8223B/2858/1885, Lingen, Minute, 15 April 1885.
150. PRO, T1/8223B/5351/1885, Spring-Rice, Memorandum, 13 April 1885.
151. See Algernon West, *Recollections, 1832–1886*, 2 vols (London, 1899), II, 243.
152. Roseveare, op. cit. note 20, p. 212.
153. *Second Report on the Civil Service Establishments*, 1888 [C. 5545], XXVII. 1, Question 10, 623.
154. PRO, T1/8267/10849/1886, Welby to Fowler, 7 July 1886.
155. Eleven years after his retirement, Welby applied his experience to the King Edward's Hospital Fund. '. . . if you want limited funds laid out to the best advantage, the experts must not be left uncontrolled. The non-expert common

sense element of management should say we can give you *so much* and not more; we don't interfere in the details, but we fix the limits.' See Lincolnshire Archives Office, Welby Papers, Dep. 24/3/2, vol 6, Welby to Danvers Power, 5 January 1905.

156. There is no definitive life of Mowatt. The *DNB* credits him with raising the reputation of the Treasury for promptness and efficiency.

157. PRO, T1/3872/10439/1899, Mowatt to the Chancellor of the Exchequer, 9 May 1899.

158. D. J. Montgomery, 'The Basis of Scientific Choice: the Criteria for Public Support of Science and Technology', Space Science Laboratory, Berkeley, California, typescript monograph, p. 28. See also the background to the 'criteria debate' in *Criteria for Scientific Development: Public Policy and National Goals: A Selection of Articles from* Minerva, edited by Edward Shils (Cambridge, Massachusetts, 1968).

159. *Nature*, 35 (1887), 481.

160. Calculated from *Civil Estimates* for 1914–15, P.P. 1914 (132), LX. 1.

VIII

THE ROYAL SOCIETY AND THE GOVERNMENT GRANT: NOTES ON THE ADMINISTRATION OF SCIENTIFIC RESEARCH, 1849-1914 [1]

INTRODUCTION

The development of government participation in the support of research is one of the most significant characteristics of nineteenth-century science. As public money became available for science, the social framework of research underwent a profound transformation. This process of transformation is not easy to define, but the response of scientific societies and institutions sometimes provides significant clues.

These clues are likely to be of both academic and topical interest. Given that externalist history, or the history of scientific institutions in the broadest sense, cannot attempt to account for highly individual, subjective, creative flashes of scientific insight,[2] it is still important to enquire into the complex social conditions which affect the rate and direction in which discovery may occur.[3] In so far as the stimulus and recognition of scientific insight and the development of scientific paradigms depend upon such external factors as competition, the search for prestige, the accuracy of instruments and the existence of a *Zeitgeist* responsive to innovation, it is important to understand the characteristics and functions of institutions which reflect their influence. This may prove to be one way of bringing together ' internalist ' and ' externalist ' evidence, which Thomas Kuhn has described as ' perhaps the greatest challenge now faced by [historians of science] '.[4]

Moreover, despite the efforts of political scientists and sociologists, few historians have begun to measure or assess the relative influence of institutions on scientific progress, or to analyze the elusive consequences of decisions taken by

[1] This investigation was supported by a research grant from the Department of Education and Science. For his useful comments on earlier drafts, I am indebted to Professor Christopher Freeman of the Science Policy Unit, University of Sussex. The Tyndall Papers have been cited by permission of the Librarian of the Royal Institution; the Stokes Papers by permission of the Librarian of Cambridge University; and the Palmerston Papers by permission of the Broadlands Trust. I am also grateful for permission to use Council minutes and manuscript material in the possession of the Royal Society.

[2] A. R. Hall, ' Merton Revisited ', *History of Science*, II (1963), pp. 13–14.

[3] D. S. L. Cardwell, ' Science in the Nineteenth Century ', ibid. pp. 140–5.

[4] T. Kuhn, ' The History of Science ', *International Encyclopedia of the Social Sciences* (1968), p. 76.

The Historical Journal, XIV, 2 (1971), pp. 323–358.
Reprinted with permission of Cambridge University Press.

the informal networks and cliques within the ' scientific Establishment '. Such decisions are particularly topical where they involve normative judgments about the merits of supporting different scientists, or different fields of science, by different means for different objects. If pressures of a political, personal, or social nature can be shown to have a probable effect on the pace and reception of discovery, they may bring us closer to understanding factors which have influenced scientific change in different cultures, under different social systems, at different periods of time.

To outline some of these considerations, this paper will concentrate upon a single piece of institutional history—the evolution of the Government Grant to the Royal Society, during the period 1849–1914. The Government Grant is important historically for at least two reasons.[5] In these sixty-four years the Government Grant assisted 938 men of science in 2,316 projects, with sums totalling about £179,000. Among the various reluctant and sporadic public efforts on behalf of science during the nineteenth century, this was a landmark in the extension of state involvement in the life of fundamental research. Indeed, the Grant was the first, and until about 1890, the major continuous source of direct government finance earmarked solely for the support of original scientific investigation; by the outbreak of the First World War, it had become a working model for the first system of professional grants to be launched by the British Government.

The Grant is also important for a second reason. ' Little is yet known ', a D.E.S. report stated in 1967, ' of the manner in which growing points [in science] are recognised and given the far-sighted support that they need '.[6] The study of institutional machinery for the endowment of science affords both a method and a means of examining growth patterns in science over time. A close examination of these patterns, and the published work resulting from government support, may cast fresh light on empirical levels of threshold expenditure thought necessary for research; on the quality and sophistication of work produced under government stimulus; and on the influence of external pressures in ensuring scientific progress in given directions.

The present paper is confined to a description of the Government Grant as an instrument of research policy, and makes no pretence of being an exhaustive study of the many complex factors underlying the formulation of criteria for research support. It does seek, however, to outline questions about such criteria, and to suggest the importance of identifiable but often indirect decisions in the evolution of government policy for science. As events since the First World War have repeatedly shown, the implications of decisions made by small elite groups, using public instruments to develop and even direct research, are fundamental to our understanding of the social history of science.

---

[5] A useful but limited chronology of the Government Grant appears in the *Record of the Royal Society* (London, 1940), pp. 79–80, 185–91.

[6] *Second Report on Science Policy*, Cmnd. 3420 (H.M.S.O., Oct. 1967), para. 18.

I. The Background to Government Patronage

Much myth and mystery surround the origins of the Grant. Traditionally, historians have believed that the Government, in the person of Lord John Russell, Prime Minister and First Lord of the Treasury, approached the Earl of Rosse, President of the Royal Society, in October 1849, with an offer to allocate a given annual sum of money for scientific research.[7] This has been described as an ' unexpected ' act of recognition by the Whig Government of the Society's attempts at internal reform during the late 1840s. It has also been considered an earnest of the Government's intentions towards science, bestowed upon the country's most eminent scientific men.[8]

Events during the 1840s lend some support to both elements of this interpretation. The Government had increasingly come to recognize the use and value of science and to expand its support of scientific enterprise, if only on a moderate scale. Sir Robert Peel, ' whom the science of England ', wrote Sir David Brewster, ' must ever regard as its warmest friend and greatest benefactor ', had undoubtedly contributed greatly to the growing public awareness of science.[9] The Prince Consort had helped bring science and technology to the notice of Court and fashionable society, while the Royal Society of Arts and preparations for the Great Exhibition attracted wide manufacturing interest. Moreover, the British Association, since its inception in 1831, had created a visible movement in favour of public support for science.[10] Between 1833 and 1849, its own scheme of grants had already assisted over fifty men and almost three hundred projects with sums amounting to nearly £15,000.[11]

These factors, however, do not completely explain the Government's motives in approaching the Royal Society in October 1849. Through his friendship with Sir John Herschel and the Marquis of Northampton, Russell had become acquainted with the reform movement in science.[12] But while he may have been personally sympathetic to the Royal Society's need for support, he was not at the

---

[7] *Minutes of the Government Grant Committee* (hereafter abbreviated *Mins.GGC*), 16 Nov. 1849. The date of Russell's letter is given as 24 Oct. and Rosse's reply, 7 Nov. No copy of Russell's letter exists in the Royal Society's files, although an alleged copy was published in a review of the Eighth Report of the Devonshire Commission (see below, note 30) in *Nature*, XII, 19 Aug. 1875, 308.

[8] See Dorothy Stimson, *Scientists and Amateurs : A History of the Royal Society* (New York, 1948), p. 223; Sir Henry Lyons, *The Royal Society, 1660–1940* (Cambridge, 1944), p. 266.

[9] Sir David Brewster, Presidential Address, *Report of the British Association* (1850), pp. xxxviii–xxxix. See Charles S. Parker, *Sir Robert Peel* (London, 1899), I, 162; III, 492 *et passim*.

[10] O. J. R. Howarth, *The British Association for the Advancement of Science : A Retrospect, 1831–1931* (London, 1931), pp. 152–9.

[11] See *Report of the British Association* (1849), p. xvii, with reference to the support of magnetical and meteorological observations.

[12] See *Royal Society Manuscripts*, H.S. 14.4.36, Russell to Herschel, 31 May 1839. No mention of the grant occurs in the published letters and speeches of Russell, or in his official biographies. His most recent biographer admits that ' of science he knew little, and to call his mathematics elementary would be to over-praise him '. A. Wyatt Tilby, *Lord John Russell : A Study in Civil and Religious Liberty* (London, 1930), p. 72.

326

best of times the most likely fount of Government largesse. At the close of 1849, in particular, Russell's faltering ministry had no mandate to promise long-term support for any scientific enterprise. Whether he made such a promise remains unclear, but the Society chose to think he had, and this assumption set the tone for the Grant's future development.

Whatever its precise origins, it seems that the Grant was not, at first, universally welcomed. If the Society were given £1,000 a year, could it use the money to good advantage? Certainly, the British Association was pleased at the prospect of ' this recent and noble act of liberality on the part of the Government '.[13] The Society was less certain. Some Fellows expressed doubts about the viability of a research scheme. In his Presidential Address in November 1850, Lord Rosse admitted his fear that the Grant would be abused, and that the Society's previous unhappy experience in equitably dispensing the small sums at its disposal would simply be repeated on a larger scale. Rosse distrusted the ' continental experience ' which had seen governmental patronage bring personal jobbery and bureaucratic formalism to several European scientific academies. Any steps which might tend in a similar direction were automatically suspect as ' little harmonising with our institutions, or feelings, perhaps prejudices, and [would] only be followed by failure and disappointment '.[14]

Amid this atmosphere of uncertainty, the Council appointed a ' Committee of Recommendations for the Application of the Government Grant ' to consider the Government's offer.[15] The Committee consisted of Professor Richard Owen, Sir Roderick Murchison, Dr William Allen Miller, and the officers of the Society, under the chairmanship of the Lord Chief Baron, Sir Frederick Pollock. Their deliberations were strongly influenced by the example of Henry Victor Regnault, who had received the Rumford Medal in 1848, and that of Peter Andreas Hansen, winner of the Copley Medal in 1850, both of whom had received research assistance paid for by continental governments. Here were two cases ' strikingly brought before us by our own *Proceedings*, illustrating the position that while the man of science supplies the mind, others must often supply the hands '.[16] The Committee also found it instructive that the ' application of very considerable sums in furtherance of scientific objects is not unprecedented in this country, having formed an important feature in the objects of the British Association ever since the institution of that body '.[17] In the end, the scientific results arising from the British Association's research scheme convinced the Committee of the practical value of such an investment.

In March 1850 the Committee issued a report asserting that ' the judicious employment of grants in the way proposed would very materially promote the

---

[13] Presidential Address, *Report of the British Association* (1850), p. xxxviii.

[14] Presidential Address to the Royal Society, 30 Nov. 1850, *Proc.R.Soc.*, v (1850), 1003–4.

[15] *Mins.GGC*, 7 Mar. 1850.

[16] *Proc.R.Soc.*, v (1850), 1003.

[17] *Mins.GGC*, 7 Mar. 1850.

advancement of science'. The best plan, they suggested, would be 'first and chiefly to aid private individual investigations, to assist the reduction of accumulated data, to purchase astronomical and meteorological instruments, and to advance such other scientific objects as may, from time to time, appear to be of sufficient interest '.[18] Following the report of the Committee, the Council created a standing 'Committee of Recommendations', consisting of the entire Council of twenty-one and an equal number of Fellows (see Table I).

There was speculation at first that few people would actually seek aid even when it became available, but these doubts were quickly dispelled. By May 1850, thirteen applications had been received by the Committee, which had now come under the chairmanship of Sir Roderick Murchison. Colonel (later Sir Edward) Sabine was appointed by Rosse to superintend the committee, and remained in the post of secretary for five years. The Committee, which after 1853 became known simply as the 'Government Grant Committee' (GGC), appointed subcommittees of three to review each grant application. In theory anyone could apply for support and no formal account of expenditure was required from grantees. Should a researcher's experiments fail altogether, Sabine later claimed, the responsibility rested with 'those who sanctioned the expenditure, not with the person who proposed it'. Sabine recalled more than one case where the Committee had sanctioned grants 'notwithstanding the impression in the mind of

TABLE I

Original Members of the Government Grant Committee 1850–53

Name	Field
Sir George Airy	Astronomy
Professor William Bowman	Medicine
Mr Robert Brown	Botany
Sir David Brewster	Natural Philosophy
Sir Henry de la Beche	Geology
The Dean of Ely	Geology
Professor James D. Forbes	Geology
Mr Michael Faraday	Natural Philosophy
Professor Thomas Graham	Chemistry
Sir John Herschel	Astronomy
Sir Charles Lyell	Geology
Reverend Dr Humphrey Lloyd	Natural Philosophy
Professor W. H. Miller	Mineralogy
Mr John Phillips	Geology
Professor Baden Powell	Natural Philosophy
Professor John Royle, M.D.	Natural History
Captain William Smythe, R.N.	Geography
Professor William Sharpey	Physiology
Professor Robert Willis	Mechanical Engineering
Reverend Dr William Whewell	Natural Philosophy

[18] Ibid.

TABLE 2

First Grants of the Government Grant Committee (with referee Committees)
27 June 1850 *

Recipient	Project	Amount (£)
1. Armagh Observatory	for publication of the observations made for the re-observation of Bradley's stars. (Rosse, Lloyd, Airy)	350
2. Edward Cooper (aet. 52) (F.R.S. 1853)	for publication of his catalogue of ecliptic stars. (Rosse, Lloyd, Airy)	150
3. Charles Brooke (aet. 46) (F.R.S. 1847)	for construction of an Instrument for the automatic compensation of the effects of temperature on Instruments for measuring magnetic force. (Airy, Christie, Sabine)	100
4. Thomas Wharton Jones (F.R.S. 1840)	for an investigation on inflammation. (Bell, Graham, Sharpey)	100
5. Professor Owen (aet. 46) (F.R.S. 1834)	for drawings of skeleton of the Megatherium. (Darwin, Bell, Sharpey)	100
6. Lt. Col. Sabine (aet. 62) (F.R.S. 1813)	for purchase of new Instruments for Kew Observatory. (Sykes, Royle, Wheatstone)	100
7. J. Stenhouse (aet. 41) (F.R.S. 1848)	to complete researches on chemical relations among the various genera of plants. (Graham, Miller, Royle)	100
Total		£1,000

* Source: *Minutes, GGC*, 27 June 1850.

many of the members that the result disappoints the applicant '.[19] Of the first thirteen applications, seven were accepted (see Table 2). The personal recipients were all Fellows of the Society, and most lived in or near London. The six unsuccessful candidates were not Fellows, and seemed to be working in fields which may have been thought too theoretical or too philosophical to be ' good science '.[20] W. R. Birt, for example, wished £50 to study the ' nature of atmospheric waves ', while H. T. Baxter requested £30 to do research on polar forces in animals and vegetables. Neither was accepted. Baxter applied time and again for assistance, and at last received £30 in 1855. Even then, however, his award was perhaps a nominal gesture. Baxter continued applying till 1865, but never again succeeded in getting assistance. In the period 1850–4, Fellows received 87.6 per cent of the 32 awards made by the GGC. The obvious bias in favour of Fellows, and the

[19] Evidence of Sir Edward Sabine to the Royal Commission on Scientific Instruction and the Advancement of Science (the Devonshire Commission), 10 May 1872. *Mins. Evid.*, Parliamentary Papers (1874), vol. II, xxii, Q. 11,155; Q. 11,160–11,161.
[20] *Mins.GGC*, 27 June 1850.

apparent possibility of discrimination, naturally aroused resentment. The young
T. H. Huxley was among those who denounced the implications of discrimination
for the reputation of the Society. To his sister he wrote in March 1852:

You have no notion of the intrigues that go on in this blessed world of science. Science
is, I fear, no purer than any other region of human activity, though it should be. Merit
alone is very little good; it must be backed by tact and knowledge of the world to do
very much.[21]

II. THE EARLY YEARS OF THE GGC, 1850–5

Amid such vicissitudes, the GGC struggled through its first five years. Some
Fellows looked doubtfully at the first list of grantees, and questioned whether
the money was actually supporting work which would not otherwise have been
done. Rosse himself shared these misgivings, in part because he deplored the
notion of ' outdoor relief ' for science. Privately, he expressed the belief that
science could ' take care of itself in this country '. Publicly, however, he hoped for
the best:

Many . . . have expressed their readiness to undertake new researches on receiving a
certain amount of assistance from the Government Grant; and although none has proposed any very extensive series of experiments, many facts no doubt will be obtained
in various departments of science.[22]

In 1852, Rosse reviewed the Grant's progress, and defined its purpose:

You have all no doubt observed that as science advances, truth has to be sought out
under every variety of circumstances. Sometimes the investigation is easy and inviting,
at other times laborious and perhaps repulsive. When there is an immediate prospect
of striking discoveries, the interest of the subject brings many into the field, and there
is often even a vigorous contest for priority; where, however, the only prize to be obtained is a few dry facts, important in themselves, as opening the way to further progress, but otherwise perhaps of little interest, direct encouragement is necessary.

We cannot overrate the importance of collecting facts: the whole history of the
inductive sciences shows that without facts discovery cannot progress; that we must
in fact, work the rock if we wish to extract the ore.[23]

Thus the Grant was intended to assist collection of facts ' where much labour
and little fame is involved ', on the basis of ' the value of the results expected and
the improbability of their being obtained without pecuniary assistance '. In
practice, Rosse's Baconian philosophy did not wholly govern the Grant's distribution; rather, sums were given *ad hominem*. Thus both empirical and theoretical
projects received support, although a bias towards experimental research was
evident from the first. In 1852, the twelve grants awarded included £505 to

---

21 Quoted in Leonard Huxley, *The Life and Letters of T. H. Huxley* (London, 1900), I, 97, letter
of 5 Mar. 1852. Huxley applied in May 1851 for assistance in publishing his *Rattlesnake* investigations.
The Committee sympathized with his need, but declined his request on the grounds that the Admiralty
should meet his costs.

22 Presidential Address, 1851, *Proc.R.Soc.*, VI, 102–3.

23 Presidential Address to the Royal Society, 1852, *Proc.R.Soc.*, VI, 235.

330

William Thomson for experimental work on the ' evolution of heat and force in different applications of electricity '. Alexander Williamson received £100 for experiments on chemical mass action; James Prescott Joule, £50 for studying the ' electroscope relations of metals '; Richard Owen, £100 for obtaining anatomical drawings of extinct animals; and Miller, Gassiot and Sabine, £150 for the reconstruction and verification of standard meteorological instruments.[24]

During the first five years, the awards remained at a level of ten to twelve per year, and most of these went to established scholars. Some grants, however, did go to young British men of science, who might otherwise have left the country to pursue their career, or left science to earn a living. Thus, Edward Sabine encouraged Tyndall to apply a few months before he was elected to the Society in 1852 for a grant of £50, if that sum would keep him from emigrating. ' If you were to state a definite object ', he wrote Tyndall, ' in your researches and ask for a grant ... I'm sure it will be very favourably received and would very likely be alloted.' [25] The grants to Huxley and Tyndall certainly influenced their decisions to stay in England.

In the years between 1853 and 1855, the whole of the annual grant of £1,000 could not be completely spent. This does not necessarily imply that the scientific community was indifferent to money; on the contrary, it seems to suggest that the Society made little effort to solicit new applications, or to advertise the existence of the Grant outside the Society. Possibly, however, factors other than the ones of scientific merit underlay this cautious policy.

Each year for five years the Grant was renewed. Successive governments under Derby and Aberdeen raised no question about its validity or purpose. But with the succession of Palmerston in 1855, the picture suddenly changed. Rosse's assumption that the Grant would automatically continue was abruptly shattered. In June 1855, James Wilson, Financial Secretary to the Treasury, informed the Society that the Grant would stop at the end of the current year. Its funds had come, he said, from the so-called ' Special Services Fund ' or ' Queen's Bounty ' (Class IV of the Civil Estimates), which was normally applied to charitable purposes. Wilson, a former editor of the *Economist*, and a stern financial reformer, needed little prompting from Palmerston to say that the Treasury ' were not aware of any undertaking for making an annual grant to the Royal Society for scientific purposes ' when ' so many other private bodies were making claims upon the Government's charity '.[26]

The Treasury letter caught the Society and Lord Wrottesley, its new President, completely by surprise. Within a week, however, Wrottesley, former President of the British Association, and veteran of many campaigns to win govern-

[24] See T1/5790B/4075/1853, C. R. Weld, Secretary, Royal Society to Secretary, Treasury, 25 Feb. 1853.

[25] Tyndall Papers (Royal Institution), VIII, fo. 1300, Sabine to Tyndall, 29 Mar. 1852.

[26] T1/5954B/17098/1855, Wilson to Wrottesley, 28 June 1855. See also Royal Society MSS, M.C.5.204, and *Mins.GGC*, 25 Oct. 1855.

ment assistance for science, began to mobilize sentiment. The Duke of Argyll, recently appointed Postmaster-General, and the man of science closest to the Prime Minister, was asked to find the reason for the Treasury's action.

' I am told ', he wrote to Palmerston, ' it [the Grant] has always been most carefully expended by the Council and has often done great good ' . . . ' Every day is proving the dependence of the Arts (sic) upon the pure sciences—and surely it is poor saving to withdraw so small a sum as £1,000 for the encouragement of original science ' from ' the most competent of all our Public Bodies '. The subject, Argyll added, ' was not without its political importance ' : ' The withdrawal was mentioned today at the Crystal Palace by Professor Owen and was heard with much respect and surprise by a crowded company of the Mercantile and Manufacturing classes. I hope you will set this right.' [27]

Palmerston's reply rejected Argyll's assumptions. The history of the Grant, he said, ' proves that the Body to which it was given are masters both of art and science '. According to Palmerston, it was the Society, not the Government, which first raised the question of such a grant, by requesting the sum of £1,000. This sum was to be used for a specific purpose on the understanding that ' the whole might not be wanted and any surplus would be restored '. Far from returning any funds, the Society had continued asking for annual grants of the same amount, as if they were allowances ' to which an established right exists '. In Palmerston's view, the Government could make no such commitment without Parliamentary sanction :

If the public are to contribute £1,000 a year in aid of the resources which in other ways the Scientific Body can dispose of, the case should be stated to Parliament, sufficient reasons should be shown, an Estimate should be presented, and a vote should be prepared.[28]

The Society's position was not clarified when Wrottesley asked Rosse for an explanation. To everyone's surprise, Rosse, then holidaying in Brighton, reported that the original confidential letter from Russell had been mislaid. Neither the Society's secretary nor Rosse's private secretary in Ireland knew its whereabouts. To remove all doubts, Wrottesley asked Rosse to prepare a memorandum for the Council, outlining the sequence of events leading up to October 1849.

In the meantime, attention was drawn to the issue in the House of Lords on 31 July by Lord Brougham. In replying for the Government, Earl Granville repeated that the Grant had come about on the initiative not of the Government, but of Lord Rosse and the Royal Society, who wished temporary assistance ' to enable them to carry out some especial, and as it was understood, temporary object connected with science '.[29]

In his prepared memorandum to the Council, however, Rosse formally repudiated Granville's contention. Lord John, Rosse protested, had written to him first,

[27] Broadlands MSS (Public Record Office), GC/AR/S, Argyll to Palmerston, n.d. (ca. July 1855). [28] Palmerston Letterbooks, B.M. Add. MSS 48579, fo. 70, Palmerston to the Duke of Argyll, 4 July 1855.   [29] Hansard, *Parliamentary Debates*, Third Series, vol. cxxix, col. 1554.

332

asking whether the Royal Society could employ a sum ' effectively for the advancement of science ' and especially for the assistance of ' persons of small means, to enable them to meet the cost of expensive experiments ...' Rosse conceded, however, that the sum was ' not in any one year to exceed £1,000 ' and that Russell was ' unable to give a pledge that his successors would continue the grant '.[30]

It was this last phrase, of course, which worried Wrottesley. On what grounds had the Society proceeded with its annual application? Rosse implicitly admitted that his grounds were singularly weak. Regardless of the impression he had given the Council, the Society and the public at large, he knew Russell had guarded himself against making any lasting pledge:

In speaking with confidence in my address as to the continuance of the Government Grant, I did so on broad principles, and feeling satisfied that we had nothing else to rely upon, I was the more anxious that the information which at best had been entrusted as to the application and rules of the grant should be digested into the shape of a Parliamentary Paper.

I fear that it is now too late; the statement I apprehend would now come with a bad grace ...[31]

Under these circumstances, Wrottesley admitted the force of Palmerston's argument. Nonetheless, he found it regrettable that the Grant had been ' discussed ... in a spirit which was hardly called for or justified by the facts '.[32] In replying to the Treasury, therefore, Wrottesley asked that the Government create a special vote for the ' promotion of science in the United Kingdom ', conceived not as a gratuitous act of charity, but as an endowment for which the Society would act as a trustee ' officially accountable to the Public for its due administration '.[33]

In August 1855, Wrottesley's reply, together with a report of the Grant's operation during the years 1850–4, was presented in a Return to Parliament. Detailed commentaries described the purpose of each award, and the results so far achieved. Altogether about £5,000 had been allocated to about 40 men for 35 different projects. The money had been expended carefully and ' solely in instru-

[30] Royal Society MSS, M.C.5.206. Rosse to Secretary, Royal Society, 25 July 1855. The letter from Russell to Rosse, reproduced in *Nature* in 1876, read as follows: ' As there are from time to time scientific discoveries and researches which cost money and assistance the students of science can often but ill afford, I am induced to consult your lordship, as President of the Royal Society, on the following suggestion :—I propose that at the close of the year the President and Council should point out to the First Lord of the Treasury a limited number of persons to whom the grant of a reward, or of a sum to defray the cost of experiments, might be of essential service. The whole sum which I could recommend the Crown to grant in the present year is £1,000, nor can I be certain that my successor would follow the same course; but I should wish to learn whether, in your lordship's opinion and that of your colleagues, the cause of science would be promoted by such grants.'

[31] Royal Society MSS, M.M.14.13. Rosse memorandum, n.e. (ca. early August 1855).

[32] Presidential Address, 30 Nov. 1855, *Proc.R.Soc.*, VII (1855), 565.

[33] T1/5954/17098/1855, Wrottesley to Wilson, 28 July 1855. See also *Mins.GGC*, 25 Oct. 1855.

ments, materials and other appliances required in performing the experiments and investigations.' With the aid of this sum, Wrottesley argued, the Government had obtained ' for the advancement of science and the national character, the personal and gratuitous services of men of first rate eminence without which this comparatively small assistance would not have been so applied '.[34]

By late October, Wilson had left the Treasury, and his successor, Charles Trevelyan, was given the task of dealing with Wrottesley's proposal. Trevelyan, co-author of the Civil Service Reforms of 1853–4, a patron of the new Victoria and Albert Museum and generally in favour of government support for science and art, was alive to the lessons of the Great Exhibition for British manufacturers. When Granville confessed in the Lords that ' notwithstanding all our skill and industry, in the qualification of the principles of art to our manufacturers we were very much behind other European countries ',[35] there were clear grounds of policy for supporting science. In November, Trevelyan indicated his assent to Wrottesley's request, and provision was made for an annual grant-in-aid to appear for the first time in the Miscellaneous Estimates for 1856–7.[36] Argyll noted the event appreciatively in his Presidential Address to the British Association in 1855, and Palmerston, having upheld the principle of accountability, announced himself pleased to meet the Society's needs.[37] He even allegedly offered Sabine £10,000 of public money, if the Society could use the sum effectively. Sabine reportedly declined,[38] in the belief that a small sum could go a long way in original research.

The Treasury's acceptance of a private ' trust ' of scientists, responsible for public moneys, but neither subject to detailed audits nor accountable to a minister in Parliament, was an important constitutional precedent. The lack of a ministerial voice to defend the ' science vote ' was not an unmixed blessing, as events would prove. But the freedom produced by a grant-in-aid seemed generous at the time. Under the provisions of a grant-in-aid, any money left over at the end of a financial year could be saved by the Society. This permitted the accumulation of a small reserve fund, which, by 1861, amounted to over £1,000. Disappointingly, however, there was not a proportional increase in the number of

[34] *An Account of the Appropriation of Grants . . . placed, by order of the Treasury at the Disposal of the Royal Society, between the Years 1850 and 1854*, Parliamentary Papers, 1854–5 (466), xxx, 605.

[35] Hansard, *Parliamentary Debates*, Third Series, vol. cxxxix, col. 1556.

[36] See T1/5709B/4075/1853 and Royal Society MSS M.C.5.217, Trevelyan to Wrottesley, 2 Nov. 1855. In 1866–7, separate votes for the Royal Society, the Geographical Society, the Academy of Music, the Royal Society of Edinburgh and for Scientific Works and Experiments were combined into a single vote for ' Learned Societies '. In 1873–4, this designation was changed to ' Learned Societies and Scientific Investigations '. See Treasury Blue Notes, T165/5. After 1890–1, the sum was referred to as the vote for ' Scientific Investigations '.

[37] Palmerston Letterbooks, B.M. Add. MSS 48582, fo. 78, Palmerston to Brodie, 25 Jan. 1861.

[38] Evidence of Col. Alexander Strange to the Devonshire Commission, 8 May 1872, *Mins.Evid.*, Parliamentary Papers (1874), II, xxii, Q. 11,042.

applications.[39] In 1857, ten grants were given, totalling less than £875; in 1858, fifteen applications were received and fourteen were accepted, totalling £908. In 1860, the third year of Sir Benjamin Brodie's presidency, the number of applications dropped to twelve.

From time to time, the existence of ' surplus ' funds created certain difficulties for the GGC. The Treasury, for example, were tempted to ask that the annual £1,000 be used to cover all the Royal Society's claims upon public funds.[40] But the Society steadfastly refused to appropriate funds from the Grant for other purposes, such as the publication of the *Philosophical Transactions*.

In the meantime, the GGC had undergone some small modifications. Although the membership of the Committee was supposed to alter from one year to the next, the first major change did not come until 1861, when Gassiot, Murchison, Wheatstone and Wrottesley were put on to the Committee to replace Baden Powell (who had died), Graham, Paget and Horner. In 1862, following the accession of Sir Edward Sabine to the Presidency, the GGC was reconstituted, but the composition of the Committee was not materially altered. At any given time, there was only a limited number of men able and willing to assume, without remuneration, and at some personal inconvenience, such a responsible and time-consuming task. Following this obvious natural law, such men as Airy, Huxley, Faraday, Busk, Tyndall, Lyell, Frankland, Angus Smith and Richard Owen found themselves serving time and again. In consequence, small groups of about thirty Fellows dominated the activities of the GGC for whole scientific ' generations '. It is difficult to assess the significance of this upon the Committee's decisions. It is certain, however, that these small groups were responsible for deciding what kind of science was worthy of encouragement and support.

Whatever may have been the scientific criteria for awards, certain social criteria were obvious. Between 1860–4, Fellows received 94.9 per cent of the 39 grants awarded, while non-Fellows received only 5.1 per cent. Of the 44 grants awarded between 1870 and 1874, 77.3 per cent went to Fellows. This proportion gradually decreased with time (Table 3) but it remained true that Fellows living in London, who played a large role in the affairs of the Society generally, similarly played a large role in the administration of the GGC. We are reminded that it was the Royal Society of *London*. Men of science living in the Midlands—or worse still, in Scotland—naturally had less access to GGC membership. The result was a form of geographical selectivity. For example, an application in 1865 from the young Henry Roscoe of Manchester was rejected even though it promised important information on the chemical action of daylight. Not until 1867 was Roscoe awarded a grant.[41] In 1866, P. G. Tait, afterwards the famous Professor of

[39] When the Vote for 1861–2 was considered, an unspent balance of £1,000 from former years remained in the hands of the GGC. See Royal Society MSS, M.C.6.122. George Hamilton to P.R.S., 24 Jan. 1861.
[40] T1/6174/21247/1858, Brodie to Trevelyan (n.d.): also references to letter from Trevelyan to Wrottesley, 28 Nov. 1857.
[41] *Mins.GGC*, 19 June 1865 and 21 Mar. 1867.

Natural Philosophy at Edinburgh, was refused money to carry out research on the possible dependence of specific heat on gravity; in 1867 another application from him to study the ' dependence of the properties of bodies on the proximity of other masses ' was also declined.[42] Such experience, coupled with the failure of the Society to elect him to its fellowship, could well have contributed to Tait's bitterness, and hostility towards the scientific circle of London.

Throughout the 1860s the level of applications wavered between ten and fourteen, and the number of grants between eight and ten. By the early 1870s, however, the number of applications increased strikingly, and the percentage approved declined. In 1871 alone fourteen applications were received, four were declined and two postponed, but still the Grant was overspent by £200. Increasing applications reduced the number of grants of £100–£200 from 43 to 27, and increased the number under £100 (see Table 4). It quite soon became necessary for the GGC to take a decision about the extent of support which could be given to any single project, or to any single group of applicants.

TABLE 3. *Trends in Awards to Fellows and non-Fellows—1850–1914*

Percentage of total awards

	1850 –54	1855 –59	1860 –64	1865 –69	1870 –74	1875 –79	1880 –84	1885 –89	1890 –94	1895 –99	1900 –04	1905 –09	1910 –14
FRS's	87·5	72·6	94·9	73·3	77·3	75·1	67·2	66·3	59·7	57·9	52·0	52·5	43·5
Non FRS's	12·5	27·4	5·1	26·7	22·7	24·9	32·8	33·7	40·3	42·1	48·0	47·5	56·5

TABLE 4. *Grants to Fellows and Non-Fellows, 1850–1914*

	1850–9	1860–9	1870–9	1880–9	1890–9	1900–14	Totals
less than £50	12	12	37	81	244	830	1,216
£50–99	32	35	69	100	138	227	601
£100–199	43	27	81	97	68	42	358
£200–299	2	7	18	27	12	11	77
£300–399	1	2	23	18	4	3	51
£400–499	—	—	2	1	4	—	7
£500–599	—	—	1	1	—	—	2
£600–699	—	—	—	—	3	1	4
Totals	90	83	231	325	473	1,114	2,316

In the 1870s, the single most expensive science was astronomy, and the single most expensive applicant was Norman Lockyer, discoverer of Helium, editor of *Nature* and secretary to the Royal Commission on Scientific Instruction and the Advancement of Science (the Devonshire Commission) from 1870–5. In 1870,

[42] *Mins.GGC*, 19 June 1866 and 21 Feb. 1867.

Lockyer recommended the purchase of a large reflecting telescope, costing be-tween £600 and £900. The GGC appointed a special Committee to review his application. Their report to the GGC, dated 24 March 1870, set out the ' fairness to all ' principle which had gradually become part of the GGC's ethos. In this case, ' fairness ' involved restricting disproportionate expenditure in expensive fields. Thus, whilst the Committee highly appreciated

the value of Mr. Lockyer's researches and have the fullest confidence in his ability to turn to good account greater optical means than he at present possesses, they do not think, with due consideration of the claims of other branches of science, they would be justified in recommending so large an appropriation for a Government Grant. . .[43]

This principle did not mean that repeated grants would not be made; on the contrary, individuals could and did accumulate large sums in grants. But the Council's decision did mean that by the mid-1870s financial constraints were con-fronting the GGC with the necessity to make certain ' choices ', not only between ' expensive ' and ' inexpensive ' pieces of work within each science, but also, by implication, between different fields of science. The significance of this problem was touched upon in evidence before the Devonshire Commission in 1872, when Colonel Alexander Strange claimed that ' more public money is spent in England in certain branches of natural history than in all other branches of science put to-gether '.[44] The figures suggest this was probably untrue, but the GGC, with a reputation to uphold, could not afford to be the target of such criticism. Certain priorities were therefore established. Assistance towards the publication of catalogues and tables, although an early goal of the Society, was sharply reduced.[45] Expensive observational work was restricted, except in special cases. Moreover, the necessity to limit large expenditures probably encouraged the GGC to steer away from the support of engineering and technology. After Fairbairn's application to conduct riveting experiments was refused in 1865, there is no evidence of other engineers applying for funds, and no hint of any interest in stimulating applications in engineering by the GGC before at least 1900. The GGC, by the exercise of its financial prerogative, helped to separate research in pure science and technology.

The GGC also took new steps to refine its own administrative procedure. In 1872, on the motion of Professor Michael Foster, the Committee agreed to pub-licize its existence by advertising its application deadlines in scientific journals, and began to issue printed application forms. These forms required information about previous work, about the nature and cost of the investigation proposed, and whether means would be found to finance the research after an initial grant from the GGC. The forms placed the assessment of applications on a more uniform footing and probably helped discourage desultory or capricious applications; in

43 *Mins.GGC*, 17 Feb. 1870.
44 Quoted in J. G. Crowther, *Statesman of Science* (London, 1965), pp. 251–2.
45 Howarth, op. cit. pp. 267–8.

content and style, they are remarkably like forms used by government research agencies today.

For the next few years, the sum annually available to the GGC was sufficient to meet most acceptable claims upon its resources. Inevitably, however, wider advertisement brought more applications, and it was not long before its funds were fully stretched. Something of a crisis was reached in 1876 when, faced by eighteen applications for sums totalling £1,025, and with a balance on hand of only £797, the chairman, Sir Joseph Hooker, sponsored a resolution calling for increased government resources.[46] The Committee's resolution happily coincided with the recommendations of the Devonshire Commission, which urged the Treasury to increase the Society's provision for original research. The combined effect of these recommendations brought about a new phase in the history of the Grant.

III. The Government Fund Committee : The 'Direct Encouragement' of Science, 1876–81

The Eighth and last Report of the Devonshire Commission was published in August 1875. After deliberating for five years and taking evidence from scores of scientists, administrators and politicians, the Commission agreed that greater government participation in the financial support of science was a proper national object. The Commission reported that the valuable work being done privately in Britain could not compare with the amount needed to be done to advance science, or the amount being done abroad. Reviewing the unwillingness and inability of learned societies to finance research from their own resources, the Commission admitted that ' the progress of Scientific Research must in a great degree depend upon the aid of Government. As a nation we ought to take our share of the current scientific work of the World.' Without wishing to supersede individual efforts, the Commission recommended that assistance be given to national museums, observatories and institutions, to the scientific departments of civil departments and to the creation of a scientific advisory board for the Government itself. Direct grants, it stated, should be given for deserving projects, and it recommended the extension of government aid, both for out-of-pocket expenses and for personal payments to individual researchers.[47] With this recommendation, the Devonshire Commission added fresh fuel to the growing movement for the ' Endowment of Research ', in which the Government Grant played a central role.[48]

In the spring of 1876, the Conservative Government considered the Commission's recommendations, and the question of increasing aid to scientific research

[46] *Mins.GGC*, 17 Feb. 1876.

[47] *Eighth Report of the Royal Commission on Scientific Instruction and the Advancement of Science* (1875), Parliamentary Papers, 1875 [C.1298], xxviii, pp. 24, 47.

[48] See R. MacLeod, ' The Support of Victorian Science : The Endowment of Research Movement, 1868–1900 ', *Minerva* 1971.

338

was discussed between the Duke of Richmond and Gordon (Lord President), Sir Stafford Northcote (Chancellor of the Exchequer) and W. H. Smith (Financial Secretary to the Treasury). Lord Salisbury and Lord Derby, both of whom had given enthusiastic evidence to the Devonshire Commission, were now in the Cabinet. Together they agreed to sanction a Vote for Research, including provision for personal payment to appear under the Estimates of the Science and Art Department, under the responsibility of the Lord President of the Council.

The decision to give the Science and Art Department control of the Vote was hotly contested by the Treasury. Ralph Lingen, Permanent Secretary, a strong supporter of Gladstonian finance, not only deplored the explosive growth of the Department and the soaring costs associated with scientific education, but also feared that the absence of direct Treasury control of research funds would open the door to unchecked expansion and unproductive spending. In either case, he felt that the role of the Treasury in relation to scientific research was being misconstrued. ' I cannot see ', he wrote, ' what is the obligation of Government while the Royal Commissions are sitting on two Universities with more than £700,000 per annum to dispose of.' [49]

Over Lingen's objections, Richmond went to Sir Joseph Hooker, President of the Royal Society, on 29 April 1876, and proposed a supplementary £4,000 per year for an experimental period of five years, the whole sum of £5,000 being taken under the vote of the Science and Art Department. Richmond also offered a scheme of personal allowances for qualified investigators who were willing ' to devote their whole time to science '. To ensure fairness in administering this ' personal ' fund, he proposed that the GGC be reconstituted to include the Presidents of the fifteen major scientific societies of Scotland and Ireland as ex-officio members. [50]

The Lords of the Committee of Council on Education are fully aware of the difficulties which surround the question of the direct encouragement of research and of the labour and responsibility that must necessarily be entailed on those who undertake to organise the experiment in this country. [51]

' No definite rule ', Richmond conceded, ' can be laid down as to the amount to be awarded in individual cases. These must depend upon various circumstances,

[49] T1/7522B/6048/1876, Minute, R. Lingen to W. H. Smith, 12 Apr. 1876. *Report of the Commissioners appointed to inquire into the property and income of the Universities of Oxford and Cambridge and of other Colleges and Halls therein* (1873), Parliamentary Papers, 1873 (C.856), xxxvii.

[50] These included the Royal Astronomical Society, the Mathematical Society, the Chemical Society, the Zoological Society, the Linnaean Society, the Geological Society, the Physiological Society, the Institution of Civil Engineers, the Institution of Mechanical Engineers, the General Medical Council, the Royal College of Physicians, the Royal College of Surgeons, the British Association, the Royal Society of Edinburgh and the Royal Irish Academy. *Mins.GGC*, 18 May 1876, Richmond and Gordon to P.R.S., 29 Apr. 1876.

[51] *Mins.GGC*, 1 June 1876.

especially on the amount of time which the investigator devotes to the inquiry.'[52]

Hooker agreed to the principle of an increase but insisted that the Society retain a margin of freedom in distributing its own Grant. Although Richmond's proposal might widen the scope of this Grant, it would also place it entirely under departmental control, and make it subject to detailed audit and account. Hooker was wary of being asked to perform a free service for a government department which would, in turn, have complete power of financial control over the Society's decisions.

Thus, Hooker and Lingen, for very different reasons, agreed that the Royal Society and the Treasury should retain their special relationship, regardless of what arrangements might be made with other departments.[53] Following conversations in May 1876, between Hooker and Lord Sandon (Vice-President of the Council and head of the Science and Art Department), a compromise was reached. By this agreement, the Society kept control of its original £1,000 grant-in-aid, in case it wished to approve applications which the Committee of Council on Education wished to reject.[54] At the same time, a new fund would be created and administered by the Science and Art Department, which would follow the advice of a special Committee of the Royal Society.

Lingen accepted the compromise, but there were many details to work out. Lingen opposed the policy of instituting personal salary payments ' where now nothing but assistance towards the cost of experiments . . . is afforded '. In his words, it opened the door ' to a sort of expenditure doubtful both in kind and degree '.[55] In the end, W. H. Smith, the Financial Secretary, backed by the recommendations of the Cabinet, intervened and quashed Lingen's objections.

In the plan for personal payments lay the germ of the modern research fellowship scheme.[56] But doubts about its workability were not confined to the Treasury. The regulation of stipends was not a congenial task, and the idea had itself many opponents in the Royal Society. Hooker's own views were perhaps typical. Two years earlier, he had said that Government should help provide ' appliances and buildings and colleges ' but that private enterprise should ' find the workers and

[52] Ibid.

[53] To Lingen, the advantage of non-ministerial control of scientific research was clear only in a negative, restrictive sense. Only much later were the positive advantages of direct Treasury responsibility exploited by Lloyd George, as Chancellor of the Exchequer, in helping to create the Development Commission and the Medical Research Committee (later the Medical Research Council). In 1915 this spirit was reflected again in the creation of the Advisory Council on Scientific and Industrial Research. See Bernard Schaffer, *A Consideration of the Use of Non-ministerial Organisation in the Administrative and Executive Work of Central Government, with special reference to the period 1832–1919* (University of London, unpublished Ph.D. dissertation, 1956).

[54] *Mins.GGC*, 1 June 1876; Norman Lockyer reprinted and correspondence between the Royal Society and the Government in an enthusiastic leader entitled ' Government Aid to Scientific Research ', in *Nature* (29 June 1876), xiv, 185.

[55] T1/7522B/6048/1876, Lingen to W. H. Smith, 12 Apr. 1876.

[56] See R. MacLeod and E. K. Andrews, ' Scientific Careers of 1851 Exhibition Scholars ', *Nature* 218 (1968), 1011–1016.

340

funds when they require it for their support '.[57] To Darwin he wrote in December 1876:

Government may do much, but it must always be under such vexatious restrictions that it tries a man's temper and patience, let his patriotism be what it will, to undertake the expenditure of what Government gives, and I fear it must ever be so. Between ourselves, I think there will be a wretched outcome of the Government Fund (the £4,000 p.a.). I am sure that if I had uncontrolled selection of persons to grant it to, and was free to use my authority over them, I could have got ten times more done with the money. I shirked the subject in my address.[58]

The subject was heatedly discussed at the famous ' X Club ' later in December, when Tyndall announced that ' a good deal of heart burning is likely to flow from this ... gift. It is not one into the need of which we have fairly and naturally grown, so that it will have to be managed instead of healthily assimilated.' [59] As he predicted, the issue became involved in the broader controversy about whether science flourished best in an ' amateur ' condition, uninfluenced by the state. In 1881, Sir George Airy, Astronomer Royal, advanced a classic defence of the conservative position in a communication to the *English Mechanic*: ' I think ', he said,

successful researches have in nearly every instance originated with private persons, or with persons whose positions were so nearly private that the investigators acted under private influence, without the danger attending connection with the State. Certainly I do not consider a Government is justified in endeavouring to force, at public expense, investigations of undefined character, and, at best, of doubtful validity: and I think it probable that any such attempt will lead to consequences disreputable to science.[60]

Within the Society generally, those on whom the duty of management would fall were probably least happy about the new arrangements. At one stroke the Senior Secretary, who performed most of the administrative work of the new Committee would find his responsibilities vastly increased.[61] Nevertheless, by the end of December 1876, the preliminary work of reorganization was settled, and the new programme was launched. The new ' Committee of £4,000 ' was christened the ' Government Fund Committee ' (GFC), and was furnished with a recommended programme:

(i) To initiate or carry on investigations, and to provide funds for their being carried out, whether by conferring grants on competent persons, or by offering prizes for the solution of problems;

[57] L. Huxley, *Life and Letters of Sir Joseph Dalton Hooker* (London, 1918), II, 231, Hooker to Darwin, 22 Dec. 1876.

[58] Ibid. p. 235.

[59] Tyndall Papers (Royal Institution), vol. XI, fo. 644, Tyndall to Thomas Hirst, 17 Dec. 1876.

[60] *The English Mechanic*, 831 (1881), pp. 586–7.

[61] Spottiswoode told Lord Cavendish that ' as regards personal payments all the Fellows to whom he had spoken desire that the Society may be relieved of them altogether '. Spottiswoode admitted, however, ' the difficulty of administering them otherwise than through the Society ' and agreed to lend his aid. T1/8008C/20599/1881, Spottiswoode to Cavendish, 14 Jan. 1881.

(ii) To consider applications from persons desirous of undertaking investigations; and

(iii) To apply funds for computation and formation of Tables of Constants and other laborious and unremunerative scientific work.[62]

The new GFC included many members of the old GGC, which continued to meet separately once a year. To deal with claims from increasingly more specialized fields of science, the GFC appointed three subcommittees of Recommendations and a General Purposes Committee (see Table 5). The tenure of personal grants was to be limited to twelve months, and project reports were to be received by December of each year. All scientific instruments of permanent value were to become the property of the Royal Society. GGC subcommittees were to meet as often as necessary,[63] whilst the whole GFC would assemble each February to assess the programme and approve the grants recommended to it.

TABLE 5. *First Subcommittees of Recommendations of the Government Fund Committee 1877*

A : Mathematics, Physics and Astronomy

W. G. Adams	Henry Smith
Carey Foster	John Tyndall
Norman Lockyer	William Pole

B : Biology and Geology

Henry W. Acland	
G. J. Allman	George Busk
J. R. Bennett	W. B. Carpenter
P. M. Duncan	W. Carruthers
John Simon	P. L. Sclater

C : Chemistry

F. A. Abel	Lyon Playfair
William de la Rue	Gen. W. Smyth
Edward Frankland	Henry Sorby

D : General Purposes

President and Officers	
Lord Cardwell	G. J. Goschen
John Evans	Lyon Playfair
	Henry Sorby

In January 1878, the membership of each subcommittee was greatly increased. Subcommittee A (mathematics, physics and astronomy) had twenty-two members; subcommittee B (biology and geology) had twenty; and subcommittee C (chemistry) had six. The regulations governing awards were chiefly borrowed from the old GGC, but two new clauses appeared. It was resolved that each grant required the approval of a two-thirds majority from the relevant subcommittee; and that if any application exceeded a ' suitable share ' of the £4,000

---

[62] *Mins.GGC*, 7 Dec. 1876.
[63] Ibid.

342

available each year, the relevant subcommittee would be asked to determine which projects ' they consider the more urgent '. In time, this decision became a landmark in the history of research policy; admitting the necessity of choice on grounds of expense and urgency, it led logically to the criteria of ' timeliness and promise ' used by research councils today.

The GGC's mandate to offer personal stipends had several opponents. In 1880, Sir William Flower, Owen's progressive successor at the Royal College of Surgeons, and future director of the Natural History Museum, declined the chairmanship of subcommittee B, because he deplored the dissipation of government money in the support of ' amateurs ' when so many ' professional ' men were labouring under unsatisfactory conditions in the nation's museums. But he also objected to the support of ' cottage research ' and the demoralization of the scientific entrepreneurs by a programme which would make their lives too easy:

The large increase of this method of subsidising science, accompanied as it is with the (as it appears to me) humiliating necessity of personal application in each case, must do much to lower the dignity of recipients and detract from the independent position which scientific men ought to occupy in this country.[64]

Flower's views were perhaps extreme, but in the same year William Spottiswoode, Treasurer of the Society, admitted the difficulty in taking decisions on personal grants. In principle, it was clearly desirable to permit men of small means to devote time to research which they could not otherwise afford; on the other hand, it was open to question whether the Society should assume responsibility for encouraging individuals ' not yet of independent income ' to interrupt the business of their life merely for the sake of science.[65]

Other questions were equally difficult. Professor George Stokes asked whether the personal grants should go to mature scholars or to ' young men of promise '. If the former, the Society would open itself to criticism for giving money to men who were already reasonably comfortable. If the latter, on what basis would the selection be made? If candidates were required to submit written work, who would referee it? Could the Committee members, who received no fees or travelling expenses, be asked to do so? If testimonials were to be taken up and if interviews were to be held, wouldn't these place a premium on personality and personal acquaintance?[66]

Of course, it was not known whether many would-be men of science were prevented from doing research because they lacked funds. To this question, at least, the Committee received an answer. By March 1877, ninety-eight applications for grants totalling nearly £14,500 had been received. In the end, only

[64] *Mins.GFC*, 19 Feb. 1880; William Flower to Huxley, 27 Jan. 1880.

[65] *Mins.GFC*, 11 Jan. 1877. To help explain the difference between the obvious kinds of grant support, Norman Lockyer devoted the leading article in *Nature* of 1 Mar. 1877 to ' Government Grants in Aid of Science '.

[66] Stokes Papers (University of Cambridge), ' Proposals ', n.d. (ca. 1877).

thirty-three of these projects were approved,[67] but a pool of potential researchers was clearly in existence.

The growing popularity of the grants became alarming when William Thomson (later Lord Kelvin) and William Crookes, both members of the GFC, announced their intention of resigning in order to apply themselves. Their threatened departure could have deprived the GGC of the services of those men of science ' on whose judgement and knowledge the country would place the greatest reliance '.[68] But a compromise solution was found: although no regulation specified a limited term on any subcommittee, those wishing to do research temporarily left the GFC.

The popularity of personal grants also directed fresh complaints against the GGC's bias towards Fellows living near London. In 1877, the Royal Society of Edinburgh and the Royal Irish Academy protested to the Royal Society that the new GFC was insufficiently representative of Scottish and Irish interests. J. H. Balfour of the Royal Society of Edinburgh argued that in twenty-six years' experience of the £1,000 Grant, the whole of the fund, with scarcely one or two exceptions, had gone to F.R.S.s; that less than £1,000 altogether had gone to Scotland and nothing had gone to Ireland at all. John Ingram of the Royal Irish Academy observed that the GFC had twelve representatives from England, but only one from Scotland and one from Ireland.[69]

These complaints were referred to T. H. Huxley, then Senior Secretary of the Society. Huxley agreed that the Scottish and Irish could reasonably be allowed an extra representative, but he rejected their allegation that the GFC consciously restricted its grants to England. Records revealed that between 1850 and 1876, £1,734 had gone to Scotland and £2,054 to Ireland.[70] By far the greater proportion of this assistance, however, had gone to a very few people. In Ireland, for example, only eight men had applied for grants in thirty years, but of those that had applied, and who were also Fellows of the Royal Society, almost all had received grants, some several times over.[71] To Scotland, twenty-four grants had been given, but eighteen of these went to William Thomson and J. P. Joule.[72] Neither Huxley, Balfour nor Ingram seemed to realize this.

If Huxley's intentions were honourable and his reply fair, it remained clear that the Government Grant had been given by the few to the few. It is true that

[67] The records do not reveal the criteria of selection, but Hooker confirmed that no successful application requested more than £300. Presidential Address, 30 Nov. 1877; Proc.R.S., xxvi, 432.

[68] Mins.GFC, 15 Feb. 1877, Norman MacLeod, Science and Art Department, to Secretary, Royal Society, 29 Jan. 1877.

[69] Mins.GFC, 14 June 1877, Memorials from J. H. Balfour, Secretary of the Royal Society of Edinburgh, 27 Feb. 1877 and from John K. Ingram, Secretary of the Royal Irish Academy, 28 Apr. 1877 to the Duke of Richmond and Gordon.

[70] Mins.GFC, 30 Nov. 1877, Huxley to Secretary, Science and Art Department, 5 July 1877.

[71] Thomas Robinson (F.R.S. 1856), the astronomer, received four grants; Edward Cooper (F.R.S. 1853), the astronomer, received four; Maxwell Simpson received seven; and five others received one apiece.

[72] Mins.GFC, 30 Nov. 1877.

344

the percentage of grants going to F.R.S.s did begin to decline from a peak of over 90 per cent in the 1860s. Between 1875–9, 130 grants were given and only 75·1 per cent went to Fellows. But there remained obvious inequalities (see Table 6). There were still grounds for the belief that the Society gave preferential consideration to people living near London and was in fact dominated by London. Lord Wrottesley in his farewell speech in 1858, unconsciously conceded as much when he claimed that there were ' few instances in which meritorious and successful cultivators of the various departments of science, *if resident in the Metropolis* (my italics) have failed in obtaining their share of the government and administration of the Society '.[73] He omitted to mention that only about half of the Fellowship lived in London, that few from the provinces came to the Society regularly, and that in consequence ' many have never heard of the funds we administer . . . in aid of scientific research, nor of the fund for relief of the necessitous, nor of the gratuitous services rendered by the Society to the various Departments of the Government '.[74]

TABLE 6. *Chief Recipients of GGC/GFC Grants for Research Expenses*

Name	Amount	No. of Awards	Years between which awards were given	C'ttee awarding grants
	Over £2,000			
W. K. Parker	2,500	13	1859–88	B
J. N. Lockyer	2,000	14	1867–91	A and B
	£1,000–2,000			
Warren de la Rue	1,950	11	1853–69	A
H. H. Turner	1,820	18	1896–1914	A and B
H. E. Armstrong	1,775	14	1872–1914	C
P. F. Frankland	1,630	17	1863–98	C and B
W. N. Hartley	1,575	13	1873–97	C
Balfour Stewart	1,150	11	1860–87	C
J. Milne	1,200	7	1896–1913	B
Wm. Thomson	1,050	12	1852–87	
	£500–999			
Wm. Crookes	900	6	1863–79	
W. R. Dunstan	900	10	1890–6	C and G
W. H. Perkin	815	13	1901–14	C
George Gore	800	9	1857–85	A
J. Dewar	900	4	1873–??	C and B
S. U. Pickering	735	9	1881–93	C

[73] *Proc.R.Soc.*, IX (1858), 508.   [74] *Proc.R.Soc.*, XXIII (1874), 51.

Thus, although no formal rule had ever been set down, the policy of the Royal Society had apparently become biased towards the promotion of research by the acknowledged leaders of ' English ' science. The Irish and Scottish representatives assumed that the government largesse was to be spread in some equitable fashion over the whole of Britain. Their point of view seems quite reasonable, but it was not the view taken by the GFC. The natural corollary of limited participation was *de facto* concentration of community funds in the hands of a few well-known men with well-established ideas. This could possibly have operated against new men and untried ideas; certainly the men who constantly reappeared on the subcommittees were capable of influencing the direction of research. Scientific networks, with the reciprocal favouritism that they implied, were a natural result of the subcommittee scheme.

During the late 1870s and early 1880s there were visible changes in the Grant's distribution. The dominance of physics, astronomy and chemistry (in that order) during the period 1850–79 had begun to contrast sharply with the increasing percentage of support for the life sciences. In 1870–4, biology accounted for only 17·9 per cent of the budget on average each year, but in 1880–1, its percentage had risen to 28·8 and by 1887–8, it was 54·8. By the turn of the century, grants going to the life sciences commonly equalled or surpassed the number going to physical science.

At the same time, the value of individual grants was decreasing (see Table 4). When surplus funds existed in the old Government Grant, applications were often transferred there. These numbered about eighteen per year, with an acceptance rate of about 84 per cent. But there was already a severe scarcity of funds. Some felt that the grants were becoming ' unprofitable gifts '; more ' rewards ' for merit than actual recompense for time spent or equipment used. George Gore, the Birmingham industrial chemist, wrote that any individual who accepted an award commonly spent £1,000 for every £200 he received. In consequence, ' only scientific men who had other sources of income were able to avail themselves of the grants '.[75] In 1881, however, with such basic questions still unsettled, the five-year experimental period ordained for the Government Fund came to a close. It was time to take stock.

IV. The New Government Grant Committee and 'State Fellowships for Science', 1881–4

In its quinquennial report to the Science and Art Department, the GFC tried to justify its rationale of reward. From a scholarly point of view the experiment had proved successful. Although the Committee admitted that the scientific value of the sponsored work could not easily be measured, the £20,000 expended between 1877 and 1881 had given rise to twenty-one articles in the *Philosophical Transactions* and 150 articles in the proceedings and journals of other scientific

---

[75] George Gore, *The Scientific Basis of National Progress, including that of Morality* (London, 1882), p. 209.

346

societies,[76] and many researches were still in progress. During the five years, 417 applications had been received, of which 181 came in 1878 alone. After 1878, the number declined to 103, 63, then 72, but the GFC insisted that this decline, far from reflecting a reduced interest in the plan, instead represented a decline in the submission of ' useless and unsuitable schemes '. By the end of the period, it was clear that the trend in the number of suitable applications was definitely upward, and that, failing an increase in the total sum of money available, individual amounts to be awarded, ' impartially among all branches of research ',[77] would inevitably decrease. The GFC therefore concluded their report by recommending that the annual budget of £4,000 be increased, and that permission be given to create a Reserve Fund, as the GGC had done, for unremitted expenses.

Earl Spencer, Lord President of the Council in Gladstone's second government accepted the Society's report, and agreed to approach the Treasury. He asked, first, for an annual increase in the Royal Society's grant-in-aid from £1,000 to £3,000 and for authority to confine that sum to non-personal grants; and, second, for authority to grant, through the Science and Art Department, a certain number of ' State Fellowships ' of £200 to £400 per annum, for periods of not more than five years, amounting in aggregate to not more than £2,000 a year.[78] Both would be administered by a single Grant Committee, combining the old GGC and the GFC, which would report on the results of such research considered important enough to justify state assistance.[79]

The Treasury's immediate response was disappointing. Lingen advised the new Financial Secretary, Lord Frederick Cavendish,[80] that ' State Fellowships ' as such were unthinkable; such a policy would ' bring the State into a relation with individual scientific investigations which it is most undesirable that it should occupy '.[81] Lingen's views on personal grants were strongly influenced by his distrust of state sponsorship in general, and by the activities of the Science and Art Department in particular. Between 1871 and 1881 the nation's educational expenditure had soared. The fastest growing sector of the Civil Estimates was Class IV (Education, Science and Art) which doubled four times in forty years, from an average of £296,000 in the decade 1841–50 to an average of £4,480,000 in the five years ending 1886.[82] Much of this was reflected in the Science and Art Department's Vote. As Secretary of the Education Department, Lingen had tried to contain this expense by the payment-by-results system. Now, as Secretary

76 ' Report on the Government Fund ', Mins.GFC, 27 Oct. 1881.

77 Ibid.

78 T165/5, Committee of Council on Education to Secretary, Treasury, 9 Dec. 1881; Cavendish to the Vice-President of the Council, 23 Jan. 1882.

79 T1/8008C/20599/1881, MacLeod to Cavendish, 9 Dec. 1881.

80 Lord Frederick Cavendish (1836–82), second son of the seventh Duke of Devonshire and a distant relative of Henry Cavendish, the chemist. Private secretary to Gladstone, and financial secretary to the Treasury under Gladstone, April 1880–May 1882; succeeded W. E. Forster as chief secretary for Ireland in May 1882, and was assassinated in Phoenix Park, Dublin, the same day.

81 T1/8008C/20599/1881, Lingen to Cavendish, 2 Feb. 1882.

82 See L. Levi, ' Our National Expenditure ', Fortnightly Review, XLII (1887), 876.

of the Treasury, he applied the same test to the science grant. Between 1876 and 1882 Lingen tried to keep the major part of the scientific Vote under his own control through the grant-in-aid device. Only with the greatest reluctance did he let the Science and Art Department become a separate source of research funds. In what was to be a classical statement of government policy towards science, he observed:

The Royal Society is the most eminent and the most generally representative of all the Central Scientific Associations. If the direct prosecution of scientific inquiry is not, as I contend that it is not, the first business of Government, its indirect prosecution . . . cannot be better forwarded than by liberal grants to this Society. Of all the ways to waste money, their scheme of ' State Fellowships ' seem to me one of the least plausible. Real discoveries are not of the sort that South Kensington would either attract or select. Real discovery cannot be ordered like so much clerical or other labour, although plenty of people who can be ordered are all ready to take wages for it. The judicious assistance and encouragement of a body like the Royal Society . . . is probably the least mischievous form of aid, although even that implies the question ' what are you doing ' and ' when may we look for results ', which I believe to be more grievous than poverty with its freedom, to the investigator who is worth anything, and who must far oftener turn back than go forward.[83]

Lingen advised Cavendish to keep science funds under close guard. ' A small grant ', he added, ' has many advantages.'

The real workers whose work is known to be worth much are few; and a small grant obliges selection. It also escapes question. A large grant soon attracts the Parliamentary Philistine. ' Well, what have you got for your money? ' The question is legitimate and fatal. This is why I think the State is better away.[84]

Cavendish, second son of the Duke of Devonshire, and a distant relative of the famous chemist, proposed a compromise. Rather than insisting on the Treasury's right to a close overview of expenditure, he asked the Royal Society to accept the task. The Treasury could have ' no official knowledge of the merits of any particular scientific work or of any individual claimants '. The Society was ' exactly suited to be the intermediary between the State and the individual investigator, especially when supported as would be in the case of the reconstituted GGC, by representatives of other learned bodies '.[85] On the other hand, Cavendish rejected the idea of creating special fellowships under the Science and Art Department. He proposed instead that a single sum be taken on the Estimates, and remitted wholly to the Royal Society, to be spent, as it thought fit, on personal or other expenses associated with scientific research, without the intervention of any government department. The concept of a state fellowship scheme, administered by a Government department—a concept later to bear fruit under the DSIR in 1916—was thus delayed for thirty-five years.

[83] T1/8008C/20599/1881, Lingen to Cavendish, 3 Feb. 1882.
[84] Ibid.
[85] Mins.GFC, 7 Mar. 1882; Cavendish to P.R.S., 20 Feb. 1882.

348

After some discussion with his staff, Cavendish offered to set the new figure at £4,000, instead of the total of £5,000 previously available for research, but to extend the Society's authority for accumulating a ' reserve fund '. This held out the prospect of greater financial flexibility for long-term planning, and the Council agreed. What science may have lost in absolute money terms, the Society believed it gained in financial freedom.[86]

Between 1882 and 1884, the arrangements for this new system were completed. Under the new regulations, the GFC as such was disbanded and its membership was merged with the old GGC. The ' new ' GGC thus consisted of the Council, 21 other Fellows elected by the Council, and the 16 representatives of learned bodies which had previously held *ex-officio* posts on the GFC, together with additional ' weighting' representatives from Ireland and Scotland. Like the GFC, the new GGC had special subcommittees. Subcommittee A (mathematics and physics), under T. A. Hirst, had 21 members; subcommittee B (biology) under Huxley, had 26 and subcommittee C (chemistry) under Frederick Abel, had 11. A new General Purposes subcommittee D was constituted with twelve members under W. W. Smyth to review all novel grants recommended by the other committees.[87] Meetings of the General Committee for final consideration of all recommended grants were to be held twice a year, in May and November, and application deadlines were to be 31 March and 30 September. All grants were to be made for twelve months in the first instance, and were to be renewable only on the basis of a satisfactory research report at the end of the year.

V. Improvement and Elaboration, 1885–1914

Given the reduced total budget, personal grants after 1881 were fewer in number than they had been between 1877–80. Over the period, about 50 men received aid of this kind; individual grants were generally less than £200 per annum (see Table 7a). Altogether, about 114 grants were made, of which 68 went to 26 Fellows, and 45 went to 25 non-Fellows. By far the most heavily subsidized was W. K. Parker, who received £3,150 from Committee B between 1878–87. Other important beneficiaries were Thomas Rupert Jones (Committee B), £625, between 1882–8; Carl Schorlemmer (C) £600 between 1877–80; H. Tomlinson (A), £650 between 1879–86; and C. R. Wright, £600 between 1877–81. Most of the awards were between £100–200, and by far the greater number went to men in the Physical Sciences (see Table 7b).

The altered arrangements of 1883 were accompanied by one major change in spending policy. It was decided in 1884 to transfer many of the small applications to the Donation Fund, and to devote much of the Government Fund to research in the form of large grants, applicable to expensive studies. For example,

[86] See *Mins.GGC*, 7 Mar. 1882 and Spottiswoode's Presidential Address, 30 Nov. 1882, *Proc.R.Soc.*, xxxiv, 307.

[87] *Mins.GGC*, 25 May 1882.

TABLE 7 (a). *Personal Grants by Amount 1877–1914*

	Less than £50	£50–99	£100–199	£200–299	£300 +	Total
1877–80	10	10	23	7	4	54
1881–5	1	15	16	—	4	36
1886–90	4	3	4	—	2	13
1891–1914	5	2	3	1	—	11
	20	30	46	8	10	114

TABLE 7 (b). *Personal Grants by Field*

	A	B	C	D	E	F	Total
1877–80	20	15	19	—	—	—	54
1881–5	14	16	6	—	—	—	36
1886–90	6	6	1	—	—	—	13
1891–1914		5	—	1	3	2	11
	40	42	26	1	3	2	114

£500 was appropriated for the exploration of Kilimanjaro, £300 to assist the exploration of British Guiana, £200 to study the flora of Chile, and £300 for instruments for the Royal Cornwall Polytechnic Observatory.[88] As events later proved, however, the pressure on funds made this desirable policy very difficult to follow in the long term.

The new arrangements did not exhaust the need for further improvements. There was still no satisfactory answer to the question whether individuals should be encouraged to leave careers in medicine, business or the clergy to take up science. In the end, this discussion was overtaken by events, by the growing number of individuals seeking scientific careers and competing for the limited funds. Other questions were merely shifted from one generation to the next. For example, the Regulations still did not specify whether or how often members of sub-committees could be reappointed. In practice, the limited number of eminent men willing and available to serve meant that the same network of individuals continued to control the policies of different subcommittees year after year. Not even the turnover of members in the Council affected the subcommittees, which continued to enjoy a life of their own.[89] Thus, while in subcommittee A, Thomas Hirst was succeeded in 1883 by Warren De la Rue,

---

[88] Presidential Address, 1 Dec. 1884, *Proc.R.Soc.*, xxxvii, 440–1.

[89] In 1880, Spottiswoode told the Society that ten of the ordinary members of the Council retired every year, six were removed according to seniority and four were removed for poor attendance. 'It was', he said, 'rare for any Fellow, except the President, the Secretary or the Treasurer to remain in office for over two years.' *Proc.R.Soc.*, xxxi (1880), 79. But those officers who were among the most active members of the Society were naturally found most frequently on the GGC.

350

subcommittee B was led by Thomas Huxley from 1882–4 and by his friend Joseph Hooker until 1888. Subcommittee C was chaired by Frederick Abel alone from 1881–8. This personal element no doubt helped preserve the continuity of award policy; whether it also inhibited the acceptance of new men or ideas remains unclear.

In the meantime, the degree of confidence enjoyed by the Society fluctuated with the degree of rapport existing between its President and the Permanent Secretary of the Treasury. Between 1881 and 1885, Lingen continued to watch and review every step which involved increased expenditure. In these circumstances, the GGC had to tread carefully. Always suspicious of its ability to manage public funds, Lingen sanctioned sums such as £1,500 for the Eclipse Expedition in 1882 only when the Royal Society contributed significantly from its own grant, and promised ' to keep expenditure within the narrowest limits consistent with the efficient performance of the Service '.[90]

Naturally, Lingen's suspicions were strengthened every time the Society failed to demonstrate a businesslike attitude towards money. When, as in 1881, a small misunderstanding about financial deadlines left the Royal Society with £2,420 unspent at the year's end, Lingen saw it as evidence of fiscal incompetence. Another embarrassing incident occurred in November 1885, when the Council applied for £1,000 to equip a solar eclipse expedition to the West Indies. The proposal was reviewed by the Treasury in the usual way. Minutes were written enquiring why this sum could not be met out of the Society's grant, and the clerk in charge, G. C. Barrington, pontifically concluded that the Royal Society should meet the cost itself. ' However curious the various subjects investigated may be ', he wrote, ' they ... may well be put off for a year in favour of a good eclipse.' [91] The Royal Society rejected this view and submitted a statement showing how its grants had been distributed over the preceding four years. Unfortunately, this information implied that a balance of £1,000 had accumulated from the old annual grant and that residual grant funds amounted to nearly £450.

The scientists had unconsciously made Lingen's point. Faced by the obvious difficulty of asking for more money in these circumstances, the Society hurriedly reduced its request by £400. Of course the very act of reduction was taken as a contrite admission of error. Barrington observed that the £1,000 had been requested ' in a loose sort of way without discussion '. Because a very few pointed questions had reduced the Society's demands by one half, the Treasury reasonably concluded that the scientists ' will find the money required if they are only forced to do so '.[92] In the end, ' looking at past precedents and acknowledging that the Society is not, as a rule, extravagant in their demands ',[93] Sir Matthew Ridley,

[90] Royal Society MSS, MC.12.292, Stokes to Secretary, Royal Society, 23 Dec. 1882, Lingen to P.R.S., 1 Jan. 1883.

[91] T1/8222B/17991/1885, Barrington to M. Ridley, n.d. (ca. Nov. 1885).

[92] Ibid.

[93] T1/8222B/19931/1885, Minutes, Barrington to Ridley and Ridley to Barrington, 28 Dec. 1885.

Chancellor of the Exchequer, merely scolded the Society for ' reckless behaviour ' and granted it £500. But the experience was instructive. If men of science proposed to win government grants, they would have to become more sophisticated in the art of financial management.

Undoubtedly, the question of management was largely a question of personalities. When the gentle classicist, Reginald Welby, succeeded Lingen in 1885, the Treasury found it unnecessary to pursue its earlier passion for keeping the Royal Society under close financial scrutiny.[94] Moreover, the growing prestige of the Society, together with its reputation for economic probity, combined to elevate its requests in the Treasury's esteem. True, the Society still met with occasional rebuffs. F. A'C. Bergne (Principal Clerk of the Treasury's Third Division, responsible for Education and Science) declined funds for the *Catalogue of Scientific Papers* in 1889 on the grounds that ' it has always been a matter of dispute whether assistance from the public purse should be given to specialist undertakings '.[95] Moreover, despite the years of experience in dealing with science, the Treasury clerical staff remained sublimely unaware of the importance of the work it was helping to support. In 1894, Michael Foster pleaded unsuccessfully for an increase in the grant on the grounds that this would produce a corresponding increase of ' valuable and much needed scientific investigation '.[96] But Bergne insisted that ' many of the grants go to researches or reports of very minor importance '. Because the Society had managed to live within its means, the £4,000 was considered ' quite enough for all necessary purposes.' [97] It took the passage of time, the retirement of men like Bergne, and even the cold blast of war to impress the Treasury with the importance of supporting pure research.

The Society's growing prestige and authority did not unite the scientific community. Indeed, the GGC perpetrated certain fundamental discriminations in its distribution of funds. Even the renovated GGC was still suspected of favouring ' known ' men with established reputations or personal connexions who lived in or near London. From 1850, the GGC had claimed to consider ' all scientific inquiries to have an equal claim on the fund whether they belonged to the Royal Society or otherwise '.[98] But, in the continued absence of information about rejected applicants, it was difficult to determine whether the policy had been followed. In any case, the complaints of Scottish, Irish, or even provincial English scientists were never satisfactorily answered.

[94] Thus Welby once minuted, ' My Lords do not desire me to press the Royal Society for more detailed proof of expenditure than will be sufficient to satisfy the ordinary conditions of a grant-in-aid '. Royal Society MSS, M.C.14.39, Welby to P.R.S., 7 May 1885. T1/83771/9135/1888, Welby to Secretary, Royal Society, 5 Oct. 1888. Welby gave the Society greater latitude in handling its funds. As George Hamilton, a senior Treasury official, casually admitted, ' our approval has practically become a formality '. Hamilton to Welby, 10 Aug. 1888.

[95] T1/8377A/7532/1889, Draft, Bergne to P.R.S., 19 Jan. 1889.

[96] *Mins.GGC*, 21 June 1894, Foster to Secretary, Treasury, 26 June 1894.

[97] T1/8834B/10050/1894, Minute, Bergne to Secretary, Treasury, 26 June 1894.

[98] *The Times*, 2 Dec. 1893.

352

In May 1886, Professor Chrystal, President of the Royal Society of Edinburgh, presented yet another petition against what he considered a cabalistic practice, and demanded that the grant of £4,000 should be divided into three separate portions, to be administered by three Committees in London, Edinburgh and Dublin, each answering directly to the Treasury.[99] There is no evidence that the suggestion was even considered. In time, however, the alleged geographical bias was overcome by improvements in communication. In 1913, Sir Archibald Geikie reminded the Society that only a quarter of the grants then went to F.R.S.s,[100] and the rest to deserving scientists throughout the country. With the increasing production of university-trained scientists seeking to continue research, Geikie's contention seems plausible.

By the 1890s, the problem of regionalism was overshadowed by the sheer difficulty of distributing funds among increasingly specialized fields of research. By November 1887, it was already clear to the GGC that the simple tripartite division of science reflected in the subcommittee structure was unsatisfactory, and that large unwieldy subcommittees were often unable to deal with highly specialized applications. The GGC accordingly set up an Administrative Committee consisting of the President, the Council, Professor Flower, Professor Huxley, Sir Joseph Hooker and the Presidents of the Chemical, Linnaean, Geological and Astronomical Societies, to advise on desirable alterations in grant administration. The Committee's report in July 1888 recommended a sweeping revision of the GGC structure and led to the adoption of a new scheme of administration which was destined to last, with slight alterations, to the present day.[101]

These recommendations, cordially approved by Welby, included the long-awaited formal creation of a Reserve Fund and modifications in the grant regulations. 'Ordinary grants' would continue to be awarded for periods of twelve months, and 'personal grants' would be given for periods not exceeding three years, with stipends not exceeding £300 per annum. The number of annual competitions for awards was reduced from two to one. More important, the four old subcommittees were replaced by seven new Grant Boards; each specialist Board would attempt, by covering a much narrower range of scientific discipline, to raise the standards of work in each speciality. The Boards were designated as follows:[102]

Board	Title
A	Mathematics, Mathematical Astronomy, Crystallography and Mathematical Physics
B	Experimental Physics, Observational Astronomy and Meteorology
C	Chemistry and Metallurgy

[99] *Mins.GGC*, 19 May 1886.
[100] Presidential Address, *Proc.R.Soc.*, A, 89, p. 461.
[101] See *The Year Book of the Royal Society of London* (London, 1967).
[102] *Mins.GGC*, 5 July 1888.

Board	Title
D	Geology, Palaeontology, Mineralogy and Geography
E	Botany
F	Zoology and Comparative Anatomy
G	Animal Physiology and Medicine

To ensure efficient administration and to avoid any suspicion of ' nest building ', each Board was to have eight members, each elected for four years. Two were to retire annually, and no one could succeed himself. This was the first time any such regulations about terms had been formally stated. Unlike the old subcommittees, each Board was to be representative, so far as possible, of Scotland and Ireland as well as England and Wales, and each chairman was to be appointed by the Council.

The pressure of claims upon the Society after 1881 reflected the growth of different disciplines in science. The number of grants awarded by Board G (physiology) quadrupled between 1889 and 1914, while grants for Board B (physics) merely doubled (see Table 8). The claims upon Board C (chemistry) grew more slowly than others. Such trends do not necessarily indicate national ' strengths ' or ' weaknesses ' in particular fields, but they suggest the ' tempo ' of new science. Particularly so in biology, where the new interest suggested to some that the life sciences were getting more than their fair share. ' Biology is very well looked after ', wrote *The Times*, ' though admirable biological work is done in other parts of the country without receiving any encouragement.' [103] The relatively rapid growth of biology, medicine and mathematics was in sharp contrast to the comparatively static rate of applications in other fields. Between 1850 and 1900, for example, there was little change in the average number of annual grants in comparative anatomy and palaeontology. There was no clearcut difference between observational and experimental sciences. Geology applications increased very slowly, but applications in botany and zoology remained fairly constant.

TABLE 8. *Distribution of Funds by Sector*, 1890–1914
(% of annual budgets)

Field	1890	1895	1900	1905	1910	1914	Average for 6 years
Physical Sciences (Boards A, B & C)	57·4	46·4	50·6	55·2	46·1	47·5	50·6
Life Sciences (Boards E, F & G)	39·9	46·5	31·2	28·9	44·2	44·9	41·8
Earth Sciences (Board D)	2·7	7·1	18·2	15·9	9·7	7·6	7·6
Totals	100·0	100·0	100·0	100·0	100·0	100·0	100·0

[103] *The Times*, 2 Dec. 1893.

After 1890, the allocation of funds between the major areas of science followed a fairly constant pattern, but it was also clear that experimental sciences were competing with the observational sciences. For example, observational astronomy (B) and geology (D) continued to have the smallest average number of awards and the highest average amount per award, as special assistance was needed for expensive observations and data reductions.

Competing fields were kept at peace by awarding equal sums to projects in each field. No one could complain if physics simply received more applications than zoology, hence received a larger slice of the cake. But in time, the cheaper experimental sciences had a greater chance of winning more, if smaller, grants. Thus, medicine and physics, receiving about equal numbers of grants in 1889–94, thereafter diverged; medical experiments, costing on average about one-half or one-third of the average physics project, increased until, by 1914, twice as many grants were given in medicine as in physics. Nonetheless, over the whole period 1889–1914, the total sums spent on each of these fields were very nearly equal.

In viewing these patterns, several questions remain. This essay has not attempted to consider the quality of science supported by the Society, although this must be a chief factor in any complete historical assessment. Important research was, of course, done outside the auspices of the Royal Society, and it is not clear that the Grant necessarily produced the 'best' work done. Moreover, further research into the age and occupational structure and the distribution of wealth of grant-winners is needed to determine whether young, unknown or poor, independent scientists had a real chance of substantial support. One may discover whether public support was being allocated on the basis of need, prestige, or following some conception of 'timeliness and promise'. The process of rejection is equally important. Unfortunately, lists of rejected applicants were kept only for the period 1870–82, but from these lists it may be possible to make some inferences. We know, at present, only that 216 applicants were deferred or rejected outright in this period, about 75 per cent of whom were not Fellows of the Society. Clearly this group deserves study. Any distribution of funds which could give over £2,000 to two men (W. K. Parker and Norman Lockyer) while limiting most applicants to sums under £100 and rejecting up to 30 per cent of applicants requires close scrutiny. Quite possibly, it will be discovered that the Grant functioned more as a reward system, following a Victorian version of the 'Matthew Rule', than as a scheme for encouraging unorthodox, 'revolutionary' ideas.

The study of such questions will inevitably involve closer study of the Grant Boards and Committees of Recommendations. It is obvious that the grant's administration was dominated by a relatively small number of men, some well known, but many whose names are now forgotten. Although records before 1889 are fragmentary, we have a fairly complete picture for the period 1889–1914. In these twenty-five years, about 270 different scientists sat on the several different boards. The term was four years, but there were no restrictions on the number of terms each could serve, as long as they were not consecutive. Not surprisingly, the same names recur time and again. Eight of the 48 men on Board A appeared more than once. Sir George Stokes served from 1889–90 and again from 1893–6; George Darwin from 1889–91 and from 1895–8; George Chrystal from 1890–3; from 1897–1900 and again from 1904–7. Others, less known, with second and third terms on Board A were J. W. L. Glaisher, P. MacMahon, A. E. H. Love, H. A. Miers and E. J. Whitaker. Of the 46 men on Board B, 11 served more than once, as did 16 of the 39 on Board C; 12 of the 42 on Board D, 14 of the 30 on Board E; 13 of the 43 on Board F, and 15 of the 35 on Board G. Especially on the smallest Boards (C, E and G) it was by no means unusual to find individuals serving 12 years out of 20. After about 1901–2, however, reappointments on most Boards (with the notable exception of C) became much rarer. Whether this reflected an attempt to restrict individual influence or merely the numerical growth of science, is open to conjecture. But beginning in 1905, the term was reduced to three years, and these two factors, in the absence of external pressures for change, suggest that the Society was attempting to distribute its power more widely. Fellows still monopolized the grant,[104] but by 1914, with increasing numbers outside the Society receiving awards (Table 3), the sheer growth of the scientific profession had made some form of redistribution virtually inevitable.

CONCLUSION

The development of the Government Grant during the period 1850–1915 must be seen in both an administrative and scientific context. It would be difficult to associate the Grant with any particular political policy; indeed, the politics of pure science was not a party issue. It began under a Whig ministry and was increased by the Tories; it was later reduced by the Liberals and contained by the Conservatives. It originated in a form of personal patronage at a time in British history when the Cabinet wielded such patronage with reasonable freedom, but it was increased only under the threat of political pressure or repeated representations from the scientific community.[105] The Grant's administration was distinctly influenced by changing relations between the Treasury, the Royal Society and the Science and Art Department, and as such forcibly illustrates the nature of executive action both within the Government and within the scientific community. But the Grant was too small to be affected either by changes in the economic climate or in patterns of government spending and it was probably too small to do more than indicate or describe trends in original

[104] Of the 938 men, overall, 381 (40·6%) were at the time of the award Fellows of the Royal Society; of the 2,316 grants, 1,330 (57·9%) went to Fellows alone. Therefore, about 41% of the successful applicants received 58·9% of the awards. On average, successful Fellows received about 3·5 awards apiece while outsiders received about 1·5 apiece.

[105] In 1919, the Treasury increased the Grant to £5,000; in 1936, to £7,000; £21,000 in 1946 and to £30,000 in 1955. In 1967 it stood at £169,000. *The Yearbook of the Royal Society of London* (London, 1968), p. 125.

research. From the Government's point of view its financial significance dwindled. In 1851 the Grant constituted about 50 per cent of all parliamentary funds in aid of science. By 1880, however, its proportion had already declined to 16 per cent and by 1900, despite an absolute increase in size, it represented only 5 per cent of total government expenditure on scientific activity. Even within the annual vote for ' Learned Societies ', the Grant decreased in proportion from nearly 80 per cent of total expenditure in 1851 to 12 per cent in 1900 and to 9 per cent in 1914. Gradually, as pursuit of original research became identified with the universities, the Royal Society's administrative mantle was assumed by the Privy Council and the Government's ' direct sponsorship ' of undefined original research operating through the learned societies ceased to be significant.

Whatever we may infer about the administrative and financial significance of the Grant, it probably did contribute significantly to the morale of British scientists. Many spoke of it in almost reverential terms. In 1876, for example, Henry Sorby, the geologist, commented that ' many most important discoveries would have been lost to the world if it had not been for the pecuniary assistance afforded by the Government Grant Committee of the Royal Society '.[106] *The Times* in 1883 thought the Grant ' most carefully and skilfully dispensed ' and responsible for raising the whole tenor of scientific research.[107] By it, agreed Michael Foster in 1894, ' many individuals have secured results which, without the grant, would probably have not been obtained at all, or obtained imperfectly after long delay '.[108]

The Grant caught and may have accelerated the wave of advancing specialism in the last quarter of the century. It may have helped certain ' underdeveloped ' areas in science to receive a critical initial thrust. But the Royal Society made little effort to increase its budget or to demonstrate its importance or ' utility '. Some far-sighted Fellows, like Michael Foster, saw the need for greater encouragement which the universities were not yet in a position to offer. Sabine's alleged refusal of £10,000 in 1861 may once have been justified by the belief that the relationship between more money and more good science was not a simple equation.[109] But the Royal Society, in acting out this belief, and in acquiring over the years an impressive reputation for public virtue and economy, neglected the growing needs of British science.[110] As late as 1913, when the need for more

---

106 H. Sorby, ' Unencumbered Research : A Personal Experience ', in *Essays on the Endowment of Research* (London, 1876), p. 174.

107 *The Times*, 1 Dec. 1883.   108 *Mins.GGC.* 21 June 1894.

109 Cf. D. S. L. Cardwell, ' Science in the Nineteenth Century ', *History of Science*, II (1963), 144.

110 By 1900, the income of all its private research funds combined did not exceed £1,400 and most of the other learned societies could spare little from their income for the active encouragement of science. *The Record of the Royal Society* (London, 1940), p. 78. Reviewing the position in 1945, the Royal Society had no doubt ' that if more funds had been available, and if the conditions of grant had been broadened, many more applications would have been received and much other important work could have been accomplished '. *Report on the Needs of Research in Fundamental Science after the War* (London, 1945), p. 17.

money was generally recognized, Sir Archibald Geikie, the ageing President of the Society, had only the mildest criticism of government policy towards the Grant.[111] But with the coming of war, belated appeals for public sympathy were inadequate. The official attitude of the Royal Society was not in this period favourable to increased Government participation in its affairs. This attitude is attributable partly to the Society's traditional distrust of outside interference, and partly to its growing resistance to the ' threat ' of over-professionalization. Usually both factors operated together. The progress of science and the freedom of the Royal Society were conventionally assumed to be identical. Fears that governmental intervention would reduce the Society to a professionalized body in government service clearly worried Sir George Airy in 1881 and appeared as late as 1904 in Sir William Huggins' presidential address.[112] Such fears were reflected in the Society's insistence that it should be considered a ' trustee ' of government funds and not a ' recipient ' of them. The implications of this for science were clear. The duties of a trustee were, in the Society's view, to advance science unselfishly, and not to solicit larger endowments. Only as the mid-Victorian generation of scientists died did resistance to this form of government involvement begin to subside.

The limitations accepted by the Royal Society drew increasing criticism from as early as the 1890s. Some critics feared the Grant would herald the end of the independent scholar. In 1892, a *Times* correspondent published a searing criticism of the Society, in which he deplored what he thought were recent attempts to ' professionalize ' the Society and its facilities. In part, this was a reaction against the ' bread and butter view ' of science and scientific recognition reflected by the growing ' professioriate '. ' The Professor abounds greatly ', he wrote, ' while independent investigators of the type of Joule, Brewster, Spottiswoode, De la Rue, Gassiot, Grove and others who have been the glory of English science, are completely rare [in the Society] '.[113] In fact some of the people most well-supported by the GGC were ' amateurs '. Anti-professionalism could not be suppressed. Lord Rayleigh, speaking in 1908, reminded the Society of its relevance when he deplored the fact that ' the specialization and the increasing cost and complication of experimental appliances ' were having a ' prejudicial effect upon the Society's tradition of non-professional science '.[114] This seemed a curious thing to say on behalf of a Society which had implicitly encouraged specialization by proliferating numbers of grants, fragmenting its Grant Board structure, and providing financial support for specialized research workers.

But the Society had come to fulfil an uncongenial, sometimes invidious bureaucratic task of dispensing a very small sum amongst a relatively large number of able and vocal competitors. ' Even under most favourable conditions ', advised

[111] *Proc.R.Soc.*, A, 89 (1913), p. 464.
[112] Sir William Huggins, *The Royal Society; or Science in the State and in the Schools* (London, 1906), p. 64.
[113] *The Times*, 1 Dec. 1892.
[114] *Proc.R.Soc.*, A, 82 (1908), p. 3.

358

The Times in 1892, ' a single Committee sitting in London is not the most suitable body to determine practically the ultimate distribution of money intended for the encouragement of original work all over the country '.[115] Indeed, by 1914 it was widely felt that the allocation of public funds for science should not be entrusted to a learned society representing only a fraction of the scientific community: it was the responsibility either of a minister, accountable to Parliament, or of the universities, accountable to their patrons and benefactors.

With the outbreak of war and the creation of the DSIR the debate over the support of pure science came to a head. As science and its applications were seen as critical to the nation's security and prosperity, the commitment of the State to the support of fundamental research, whatever form it would take, could not be reversed. During the war and after, however, all schemes could at least look back to the experience of those few hundred men of science who had distributed or received the early blessings of the Parliamentary Grant.

[115] *The Times*, 1 Dec. 1892.

The Support of Victorian Science: The Endowment of Research Movement in Great Britain, 1868–1900

WITHIN the context of broad social changes being wrought by science and technology in Britain during the nineteenth century, four institutional developments were of particular importance to the character of fundamental research. The first following the " Declinist " controversy was the creation of the British Association and the reform of the Royal Society in the 1830s and 1840s. The second was the establishment of research laboratories and scientific museums in the 1840s and 1850s. The third was the reform of science teaching in the schools and universities. The fourth was the inception of the " scientific movement ", with its broad implications for literature, religion and philosophy. One aspect of this movement was the campaign for the " endowment of research ". This campaign produced the first explicit signs of public acceptance of the proposition that research was moving from an occasional pursuit of individuals with private means to an organised activity, undertaken by individuals and groups working full-time in significant numbers within institutions where research occupied a specific and acknowledged place. As such, this campaign exerted a profound influence on the rate and direction of British scientific research and on the social standing of British men of science. The history of this movement illuminates the process by which the claims of research were brought to public attention, and became a part of university life and an object of government policy.

The Background

The movement must be seen as having its origins in the " Declinist " controversy of the 1820s.[1] In the wake of the Napoleonic wars and with French rivalry still in view, a small group of British men of science, led by Sir David Brewster and Charles Babbage, argued that British science had fallen into decline, relative to the Continent, and required government assistance to restore its vitality and identity. Following their campaign, a small shower of honours, pensions and awards descended upon science,[2] the British Association was begun, the Royal Society was

---

[1] Brewster, Sir David. " The Decline of Science ", *Quarterly Revied*, XLIII (1830), pp. 305–42 ; Babbage, Charles, *Reflexions on the Decline of Science and on Some of its Causes* (London, Fellowes, 1830).
[2] See Cardwell, D. S. L., *" The Organisation of Science in England: A Retrospect* (London : Heinemann, 1957). See also MacLeod, R. M., " Science and the Civil List, 1824–1914 ", *Technology and Society*, VI (20 October, 1970), pp. 47–55 ; MacLeod, R. M.,

198

"reformed" and the government began to look with increased favour on new scientific expeditions, explorations and surveys. In 1849, following the exertions of the British Association, an annual parliamentary grant-in-aid of £1,000 was voted to the Royal Society for the promotion of scientific research.

By 1860, however, it was clear that this effort, and the earlier grant scheme of the British Association on which it was modelled, were insufficient.[3] They were insufficient because the nature of research, particularly in the physical sciences, had materially changed. Physics and chemistry in particular had become subjects requiring specialised knowledge, and the few qualified to pursue it could not always afford to pay for it themselves. As William Crookes, reviewing the situation of recent decades, observed in 1876:

The facts and truths that lay near at hand have already been gathered in. We have now to go farther afield, to use costlier, because rarer, materials, to correct the approximate determinations of our predecessors, and in so doing to employ expensive instruments of precision. Little could be done in these days with apparatus such as that used by Dalton or by Davy at the outset of his career. Hence it has become more difficult for a poor man, unaided, to win his way to eminence.[4]

The parliamentary grant helped the amateur scientist by defraying some of his out-of-pocket expenses. But it could not suffice for the "poor man, unaided" who was becoming far more visible in the world of research.

The pursuit of natural science in Britain had long been associated with the amateur activities of the leisured classes. But a rising "middle class" of science, educated not at the ancient universities but at London medical schools, in Germany, or privately, was coming into prominence. In 1850 this group was quite small—of the order of a few hundred. But by 1875 the figure reached into the thousands. This expansion was reflected in the membership of the metropolitan scientific societies which doubled from about 5,000 in 1850 to about 10,000 in 1870.[5] Only a fraction of these persons wished to pursue science teaching vocationally, and even fewer wished to do scientific research full-time, but those who did were discouraged and hampered by the few and dismal prospects open to them. Men such as these sought not personal honours or even "honours for science" in the sense used 30 years before by Babbage and Brewster. Rather, they sought means of livelihood. In the 1850s, stimulated by rapid changes in science itself, and witnessing the triumph of reform in

"Of Medals and Men: A Reward System in Victorian Science", *Notes and Records of the Royal Society* (June, 1971) (in press).

[3] For an analysis of this scheme see MacLeod, R. M., "Scientists, Civil Servants and Fundamental Research: The Parliamentary Grant to the Royal Society", *Historical Journal,* XIII (June, 1971), in press.

[4] Crookes, W., "The Endowment of Scientific Research", *Quarterly Journal of Science,* VI (October, 1876), p. 485.

[5] MacLeod, R. M., and Andrews, K., *Selected Science Statistics relating to Research Endowment and Higher Education, 1850–1914* (Mimeograph, Science Policy Research Unit, University of Sussex, 1967).

social and political affairs generally, " scientific reformers " gathered new strength and fresh purpose. They looked naturally to the state for action and to the universities for reform.

University Reform

Their appeals gained force by association with the movement of reform slowly getting under way within British education generally and at Oxford and Cambridge in particular. As Mark Pattison later observed, it was to the " silent permeative genius of science that the growth of a large and comprehensive view of the function of a University and the desire to discharge it spread among Oxford liberals ".[6] In 1850 Oxford introduced honours schools in modern history and the natural sciences. The same year the Liberal ministry of Lord John Russell responded to a memorial from the Royal Society by appointing royal commissions to inquire into Oxford and Cambridge. Oxford, slumbering under the shrouds of theological studies,[7] had prompted Brewster's sweeping criticisms of university science in 1830, and had caught the fury of Lyell's attacks in 1845.[8] In 1851, reformers' proposals, catalysed by the existence of the commission, led at Cambridge to the creation of the Natural Science Tripos and to regular scientific instruction on an official basis. Following the two commissions, an Oxford University Act in 1854 abolished the Test for matriculation and the B.A. and provided for executive commissioners to reform the expenditures of the colleges and the government of the university. An analogous Act for Cambridge in 1856 freed matriculation from the Test[9] and thus opened the universities to greater numbers of Dissenters. For the first time, too, college fellowships were declared open to merit.

The march of reform was neither smooth nor quick. In 1851, some colleges refused to reveal their incomes to the Royal Commissioners, and refused therewith to share in the endowment of university chairs. At Oxford, especially, there were recurrent protests against the " Germanising " of English universities by the professorial system. One don wrote a tale, in Aristophanic parody, about:

> Professors we, from over the sea,
> From the Land where Professors in plenty be,
> And we thrive and flourish, as well we may,
> In the Land that produced one Kant with a *K*,
> And many Cants with a *C*.[10]

---

[6] Quoted in Campbell, Lewis, *The Nationalisation of the Old English Universities* (London: Chapman, 1901), p. 305.

[7] Until 1871 it was not possible to matriculate at Oxford without a declaration of membership of the Church of England; Cambridge students had to make no declaration till they took their degree. Cambridge, to that extent, was slightly more " open " to Dissenters. Tillyard, A. I., *A History of University Reform from 1800 A.D. to the Present Time* (Cambridge: W. Heffer and Co., 1913).

[8] See Lyell, Charles, *Travels to North America* (London: John Murray, 1845).

[9] M.A.s and Fellowships remained subject to the Test until 1871. See Green, V. H. H., *Religion in Oxford and Cambridge* (London: S.C.M. Press, 1964), pp. 297–305.

[10] Quoted in Campbell, *op. cit.*, p. 81 ff.

Nevertheless, it could not be ignored that comparisons with the Continent invariably cast English scholarship in an unfavourable light. Following the Crimean War, parliamentary interest in university reform revived. In 1864, the Clarendon Commission reported in favour of increasing the proportion of time given to natural science in the great public schools.[11] Meanwhile, movements for technical education, for reform in the Science and Art Department syllabus and for increased numbers of teachers were all gathering strength.[12] By the late 1860s the pace of events quickened. In 1867, following the disappointing performance of British manufacturers in the industrial section of the Paris International Exhibition, Lyon Playfair and the Taunton Commission put the blame on inadequate British secondary education.[13] And in 1868 there appeared two books to awaken fresh controversy about educational reform—Matthew Arnold's *Schools and Universities on the Continent* and a volume of *Suggestions on Academical Organisation* by Mark Pattison, rector of Lincoln College, Oxford. Arnold demonstrated the disadvantages under which Britain laboured in the diffusion of scientific knowledge, while Pattison argued that Oxford by its neglect of research had failed in its highest duty to the country. He thought that the reform of teaching alone would have deleterious consequences. " In the present age ", Mark Pattison wrote, research was vital if the university wished to ensure its future:

In order to make Oxford a seat of education, it must first be made a seat of science and learning. All attempts to stimulate its *teaching* activity without adding to its solid possession of the field of science, will only feed the unwholesome system of examination which is now undermining the educationalist value of the work we do. . . .[14]

The Mid-Victorian Scientific World

Outside the ancient universities, a group of " new men " were rising to prominence in science. Gathering strong support from older " reformers " like Lyon Playfair, they realised that even in the shadow of the Great Exhibition, greater public and private efforts in research would be needed if Britain were to retain her international scientific eminence. This group included at different times such diverse figures as Henry Roscoe in Manchester, Clerk Maxwell in Cambridge, P. G. Tait in Edinburgh, and a

[11] Report of the *Royal Commission on Certain Public Schools* (the Clarendon Commission), 1864, XX, 1. See especially, evidence given by Lyell, Faraday, Hooker and Airy in November 1862.

[12] *Report of the Select Committee on Provision for Instruction in Theoretical and Applied Sciences in the Industrial Classes*, 1867–68 (432), XV, 1. See also the Standing Committee of the Royal Society of Arts on Technical Education, created in January 1867, which reported in July 1868. *Journal of the Society of Arts*, XIV (31 January, 1868), pp. 183–209; XVI (24 July, 1868), pp. 627–42. See also Gore, George, " On Practical Scientific Instruction ", *Quarterly Journal of Science*, VII (1870), pp. 215–229.

[13] *Report Relative to Technical Education of the Schools Inquiry Commission* (the Taunton Commission), 1867, XXVI, p. 267.

[14] Pattison, Mark, *Suggestions on Academical Organisation* (London, 1868), p. 198.

dozen or more who gathered in London around T. H. Huxley, John Tyndall, Thomas Hirst, John Lubbock, Edward Frankland and Norman Lockyer. During the 1850s, these men, mostly under 40 years of age, and mostly " unestablished ", met each other privately or through meetings of the British Association. By the 1860s they were in commanding positions of power and influence in the small world of Victorian science.

In 1864, nine of them came together to create the famous " X-Club ". Most of the members of the X-Club were self-taught in science though a few came from scientific families, and three had German doctorates. Significantly, none had degrees from either Oxford or Cambridge. Through a wide range of public appointments they began to reach into the daily affairs of the civil service, the Royal Society, the British Association, the Science and Art Department and scientific publishing.[15] Of the nine, one gave evidence to the Clarendon Commission in 1862, two were members of the Taunton Commission in 1865, and two were elected to the Society of Arts Committee on Technical Education in 1868. Whatever differences distinguished these nine from each other, they shared at least three characteristics; first, a sound sense of what was important in contemporary physics, chemistry and biology; second, a belief that Britain, however well she had distinguished herself in the Great Exhibition of 1851, lacked a sound foundation of scientific education and research; and third, that increased state and private action was needed to achieve this. Making their case, first in the literary weeklies, then through the *Quarterly Journal of Science* and finally through *Nature,* founded by Lockyer in 1869, their position became known throughout the English-speaking world.

Members of this small London circle differed in many respects from the " cultivators of science " who had rallied round David Brewster's banner at the British Association in 1831. Unlike the " Declinists ", the new scientific elite of the 1860s was much more aware of trends in scientific life and education outside Britain, and much more concerned about the cultivation and diffusion of new knowledge for its own sake and for the good of society.

Like the " Declinists ", however, the members of this new elite were strengthened in their resolve by years of personal financial sacrifice in the pursuit of science and by growing conviction that science was worth continuous public support. Unlike Faraday, who was even then cited as a paragon of indifference to wealth and comfort,[16] they were convinced that the question of a scientific career was often in part a financial one.

[15] MacLeod, R. M., " The X-Club: A Scientific Network in Late-Victorian England ", *Notes and Records of the Royal Society,* XXIV (1970), pp. 305–322.

[16] Faraday's salary at the Royal Institution was £200. After his retirement, he received a pension of £300 from the government, which permitted what was then considered to be a middle-class standard of living. He deliberately avoided contractual arrangements which would have brought him greater wealth, lest they distract him from research. " I cannot afford to become rich ", he allegedly once said. This was widely cited. See Gore, George, " The National Importance of Scientific Research ", *Westminster Review,* XC (1873), p. 358.

From their point of view the ancient universities provided little hope. With few exceptions, such university chairs as there were in science had become unproductive sinecures. Even University College London, with its history of distinguished scientific appointments, offered limited opportunities for research. Outside the universities, conditions were even worse. A. H. Garrod, a physician-turned-physiologist, and later a sub-editor of *Nature*, mocked the prospect of a scientific career as " little more than a phantom. The prospect of a post in any government institution, such as the British Museum, is to say the most, scarcely a pittance, and there are many of the best workers who would undergo many privations rather than have to devote the greater part of their lives to the drudgery of an educational appointment ". [17]

To a scientific man of no private financial means, the alternatives outside the universities were, broadly speaking, three: to teach in secondary schools, to leave the country, or to protest. Britain came near to losing some of its most promising scientific men to the colonies and to the United States. Both Tyndall and Playfair would probably have emigrated to Australia or North America during the 1840s, had not Sir Robert Peel and the Prince Consort contrived new posts in government establishments for them.[18] But such piecemeal attempts did not bring satisfaction. Government had shown itself unwilling to act in a comprehensive fashion; but even the help of government, either through state support or legislative intervention in the universities, was seen as the first step towards the systematic creation of careers in research.

The Devonshire Commission

In its manoeuvres, the London circle tended to act without formal status. Yet its informal influence was decisive when, in August 1868, the British Association heard a call to arms from a little-known ex-Indian Army officer and amateur astronomer, Lieutenant-Colonel Alexander Strange.[19] At the Mathematics and Physics Section of its meeting in Norwich, Strange delivered a paper " On the Necessity for State Intervention to Secure the Progress of Physical Science ". The short paper aroused immediate support. Strange, with Playfair, had recently

[17] *Nature*, IX (29 January, 1874), p. 237.

[18] See Parker, C. S., *Sir Robert Peel* (London: John Murray, Second edn. 1899); Reid, W., *Memoirs and Correspondence of Lyon Playfair* (London: Cassell, 1899).

[19] Alexander Strange (1818–76) was educated at Harrow; he served in the Indian Army as a cavalry officer and later as Inspector of Scientific Instruments for the astronomical and geodetic sections of the trigonometric survey of India. He retired to England in 1861 and held strategic positions on the Council of the Royal Astronomical Society from 1863–67, and was its Foreign Secretary from 1868–73. He was elected to the Royal Society in 1864 (the year the X-Club was formed), and served on its council from 1867–69. His Indian experience made him adamant about the accuracy of measuring instruments, and the part they played in physical research. *The Academy* (25 March, 1876), p. 290; see also Crowther, J. G., *Statesmen of Science* (London: Cresset Press, 1965), pp. 237–269. See " On the Necessity for State Intervention to Secure the Progress of Physical Science ", Address to the Mathematics and Physics Section, *Report of the British Association*, 1868.

been a juror at the Paris Exhibition. When Playfair returned and took up a campaign for technical education, Strange turned to the issue of research in the physical sciences. In his paper, he appealed to one of the British Association's earliest declarations of intention, namely, " to remove any disadvantage of a public kind which impedes (the) progress (of science) ". There was no doubt in Strange's mind that state participation in research was vital. He took it for granted that any abstract question whether scientific investigation should be aided or even carried on by government had already been settled by the irresistible verdict of circumstances.

Following Strange's paper the British Association appointed a committee of 12 in November, 1868, which included Tyndall, Frankland, Thomas Hirst and Huxley—essentially the " X-Club "—plus Lockyer and Playfair. The committee was asked to determine whether there was sufficient provision for the vigorous prosecution of physical science in Britain. In March 1869, the committee issued a circular to several men of science, asking:

(1) Whether any course could be adopted to improve their field, whether by government or by private initiative;

(2) whether there were grounds for asking for such initiative, and

(3) whether the interests of the community were " sufficiently involved in the more vigorous development of scientific knowledge " to warrant the employment of state aid, either

(a) through the creation of new institutes for experimental and observational research;

(b) the extension of old institutions, or

(c) the enlargement of grants to individuals for apparatus and materials.

Several months later, the committee concluded that by any responsible definition there was insufficient national provision for research. Hitherto, research had paid the community " but it had not paid the man ".[20] The advantages conferred on the community by research implied an obligation of the community to support research. This obligation would not be satisfied merely by the establishment of a scientific observatory, by sponsoring physical measurements, the creation of one or two museums and providing out-of-pocket expenses for talented amateurs. It could only be met by diverting substantial sums of money to individuals prepared to pursue a full-time vocation in science.

Many in the British Association shared Strange's view that the surest and most satisfactory source of support would inevitably be governmental. But others feared state interference. *Nature*, for example, published a letter from Alfred Russell Wallace, protesting against what *Nature* has called the " Science Reform movement " because " experience shows that

[20] Crookes, W., " On National Institutions for Practical Scientific Research ", *Quarterly Journal of Science*, VI (January, 1869), p. 48.

public competition ensures a greater supply of the materials and a greater demand for the products of science and art, and is thus a greater stimulus to true and healthy progress than any government patronage ".[21] Moreover, there seemed good grounds for arguing that " where the state has a finger there will be patronage, and the preference of inferior agents who have the support of friendly recommendations, to superior agents who are standing alone ".[22] Already, in any case, the state was spending £140,000 each year on museums, gardens and surveys, while the Science and Art Department estimate for 1869–70 was over £225,000.[23]

There was an important division between those who wanted research supported on its own, and those who wanted research combined with teaching. The X-Club was quietly united on this issue. Tyndall and Frankland, both at the Royal Institution, were conscious of the importance of research support, yet did not directly seek money for research as an end in itself. But outside the X-Club there was disagreement. Lockyer, reflecting the independent tradition of astronomy which he himself cultivated, argued strongly for separate support of independent research, although that research might in practice be linked with university teaching.[24] On the other side, " university men " including A. W. Williamson and Clerk Maxwell argued that research should not at any cost be divorced from instruction. In extreme form, this argument implied that research could be properly supported only through the universities and only with university money. Benjamin Jowett, in sympathetic support of science at Oxford, denied that there was any opposition between original research and a moderate amount of teaching, and added in support of his view: " the greatest discoveries in Physical Science have been made by teachers at the Royal Institution ".[25] Jowett's comment sadly ignored the fact that Royal Institution professors did not " teach " in the traditional Oxford-Cambridge sense of the term. It also implied that no action could be taken unless the universities were willing to take action themselves.

In the end, the belief that teaching and research were interdependent became a valuable weapon in the hands of the British Association, which approached the government for a formal inquiry in late 1869. In February 1870, soon after his election, Gladstone agreed to appoint a royal commission under William Cavendish, seventh Duke of Devonshire, to study the existing national provision for scientific instruction and the advancement of science. Two of the nine members, Huxley and Lubbock, were

---

[21] " Government Aid to Science ", *Nature*, I (13 January, 1870), pp. 279–288.
[22] *Quarterly Journal of Science*, VI (January, 1869), pp. 48–49.
[23] See *Nature*, I (7 April, 1870), pp. 589–90.
[24] Campbell, *op. cit.*, p. 190.
[25] Lockyer, through *Nature*, observed that almost all Continental scientists taught as well as did research, and that even " in this country the greater number of our most distinguished men of science are professors and teachers ". " The Royal Commission on Science ", *Nature*, I (10 February, 1870), p. 375. See also *The Academy*, III (1 December, 1872), p. 460.

members of the X-Club. Another two, William Sharpey and W. A. Miller, had been active in forming research schools at University College London. Another, Samuelson, had served on both the Acland Committee in 1867 and the Society of Arts Committee on Technical Education in 1868.

The Commission sat for six years, met 85 times, interviewed over 150 witnesses and published eight reports and four massive volumes of evidence. Although instructed to look chiefly at scientific instruction in schools, museums and universities, it raised searching questions about the state of British science in general, and about research in particular.[26] Some reports were more conclusive than others; some virtually assumed the wisdom of what they set out to prove. The first report, appearing in March 1871, examined the institutions concentrated in South Kensington, and recomended that, as Huxley and Lockyer had long wished, the government combine the Royal School of Mines and the Royal College of Chemistry into a single science school with a single staff of professors in mathematics, physics, chemistry and biology.[27] The second report, issued in March 1872, dealt with technical education, and endorsed improvements in the policies of the Science and Art Department which had long been approved by the London circle. The third report, on Oxford and Cambridge, appeared in August 1873; the fourth, on national museums, in January 1874; the fifth, on university colleges, in August 1874; and the last three—on schools, the Scottish universities and government provision for science—in June 1875.

The Devonshire Reports provided dramatic evidence of large government spending on " scientific projects " which had been justified on grounds of prospective commercial or military benefit. Indeed, as the support of the famous *Challenger* voyages and the transit of Venus expeditions had amply demonstrated, much could be subsumed under this class of expenditure.[28] But while government had dramatically increased its expenditure on activities related to research since the 1850s, it had excluded explicitly fundamental science, or else had confined support to ends strictly chargeable within the narrow definitions of departmental needs.

During the six years of the Commission's work, reports relayed by Lockyer through *Nature* and the literary quarterlies kept public and scientific interest alive. The distressed state of scientific men became well known, and invidious comparisons with Germany became commonplace. " It is well known to all the world ", lamented *Nature*, that science " is all but dead in England ". By this was meant not the " jury " science of the exhibitions and practical technology, but " that searching

26 *Nature*, IV (17 August, 1871), p. 302.

27 The first brief report was printed in full in *Nature*, III (30 March, 1871), p. 421.

28 *Cf*. " Government and Scientific Investigation ", *Spectator*, 22 July, 1871, pp. 882–884; also Anon., *Correspondence between the Royal Geographical Society and the Government* (London, 1873).

after knowledge which is its own reward ".[29] Whether we confess it or not ", Lockyer wrote, " England, so far as the advancement of knowledge goes, is but a third-rate or fourth-rate power ".[30] Although the logic of his position was not entirely clear, his rhetoric left no room for doubt about his convictions. " It is the question of ' scientific careers ' that is the pressing one, and the one most difficult to settle ", one correspondent wrote.[31]

In 1870, 1871 [32] and again in 1872, Alexander Strange returned to the fray demanding that scientists should be paid salaries like other professionals. " It has hitherto been too much of the custom ", he said, " to treat men of science as exceptions to all the professions, to assume that whilst it is quite proper to enrich and ennoble soldiers who fight for pay, lawyers who evade or apply the law according to circumstances, physicians who kill or cure as seemeth best to them and even divines, whose missions to save souls might be deemed a sufficient privilege . . . the man of science should work for love and die . . . in poverty." In the interpretation of nature, no less than in the interpretation of religion, the labourer should be worthy of his hire.[33]

These appeals were seconded by George Gore, an industrial chemist who had set up his own Institute for Scientific Research in Birmingham. Gore was no university man, and had neither wealth, title, nor professional degree. He earned his living by chemical analyses, a notoriously precarious livelihood, and soon found himself in the " independent " wing of the reform party. " Scientific discovery and research ", he told the Social Science Association at Plymouth in 1872, " is national work and it is the duty of the State to provide and pay for it." The justification was to him obvious:

. . . because the results of it are of immense value and indispensable to the nation; also because nearly the whole benefit of it goes to the nation and scarcely any to the discoverer, and because there exists no other means by which scientific investigators can be paid for their labour.[34]

In Gore's view the only and " most satisfactory way of rewarding scientific discoverers and serving national interests at the same time " would be the creation of salaried state professorships for original research.[35] Gore's suggestion quickly won support. Francis Galton in

[29] " A Voice from Cambridge ", *Nature*, VIII (8 May, 1873), p. 21.

[30] " Our National Industries ", *Nature*, VI (6 June, 1872), p. 97.

[31] *Nature*, II (12 May, 1870), p. 25.

[32] *Cf. Journal of the Society of Arts*, 18 (1870), reported in " The Relation of the State to Science ", *Nature*, I (7 April, 1870), pp. 589–591.

[33] " On the Necessity for a Permanent Commission on State Scientific Questions ", *Journal of the Royal United Service Institution*, XV (1870), pp. 537–566, reprinted in *Nature*, IV (15 June, 1871), p. 133; " On Government Action in Science ", *Report of the Mathematics and Physics Section of the British Association* (1871), p. 56.

[34] Gore, G., " On the Present Position of Science in Relation to the British Government ", *Transactions, Social Science Association* (1873).

[35] Gore, *op. cit.*, p. 360.

English Men of Science, published in 1874, agreed that action was necessary. " Science has hitherto been at a disadvantage . . . in enlisting the attention of the best intellects . . .",[36] Galton warned. Only financial inducements operating, through state-sponsored posts in Government and the universities, would provide the answer.

Gore's views, as a chemist, had particular force, for physical and chemical research seemed particularly in jeopardy. Faraday, Graham, Mattheisen and Miller had died, leaving no obvious heirs. Evidence of Edward Frankland before the Devonshire Commission showed that the number of British articles contributed to the *Journal of the Chemical Society* and *Chemical News* was dwindling. Young men were being turned away from research and lost to the professions. Germany was producing four and a half times as many investigators in chemistry and six times as many scientific papers each year, including half the papers which appeared in British journals.[37] Similar conclusions were drawn for physics, biology and geology.[38] What was true of chemistry was held (without, it must be said, much evidence) to be valid *pari passu* for other fields. Chemists at least had the prospect, however remote, of a commercial career, but there were few opportunities indeed for industrial careers in physics, and none in biology. One professor of biology advised his pupils to give up their study and enter chemistry, as " there was no possibility of a career for them in anything else ".[39]

The Endowment of Research Movement

While advocates of direct state intervention marched past the Devonshire Commission, advocates of less state action and more university action gathered in Oxford. In 1872, just after the second report of the Devonshire Commission, but before it had moved on to Oxford and Cambridge, a new Royal Commission was appointed to inquire into the finances of

[36] Galton, Francis, *English Men of Science* (London: Macmillan, 1874), p. 258.

[37] *Devonshire Commission, 1874, Mins. Evid.*, p. 371. Frankland's estimates, among the first attempts to quantify and compare the British position, were repeatedly accepted without question. See Gore, G., " The Promotion of Scientific Research ", *Fortnightly Review*, XIV (ns) (1873), pp. 510–511; Gore, G., " The National Importance of Scientific Research ", *Westminster Review*, LXIII (ns) (1873), p. 353; Appleton, Charles, " Economic Aspect of the Endowment of Research ", *Fortnightly Review*, XVI (ns) (1874), pp. 522–523 (also reprinted with additions as " The Endowment of Research as a Form of Productive Expenditure " in Pattison, M., *et al., Essays on the Endowment of Research* (London: H. S. King, 1876), pp. 86–124. See also Crookes, W., " The Encouragement of Scientific Research ", *Quarterly Journal of Science*, VI (ns) (1876), p. 468, and Crookes, W., " England's Intellectual Position ", *Journal of Science*, I (3rd Series) (1879), p. 521; and Cardwell, *op. cit.*, p. 96. Even more recent work has not challenged Frankland's calculations.
   Cf. Holt, B. W. G., " Social Aspects in the Emergence of Chemistry as an Exact Science: the British Chemical Profession ", *British Journal of Sociology*, XXI, 2 (June, 1970), p. 182.

[38] See also Brodie, B. C., " Scientific Research and University Endowments ", *Nature*, VII (12 December, 1872), p. 97. On physiological botany see " Obstacles to Scientific Research ", *Nature*, XI (26 November, 1875), p. 62.

[39] Appleton, Charles, " Economic Aspect of the Endowment of Research ", *Fortnightly Review*, XVI (ns), (1874), p. 524, quoted in Proctor, Richard, " The Endowment of Scientific Research ", reprinted in the *Popular Science Monthly*, VII (1875), p. 362.

the colleges at the two ancient universities. In November the same year, a group of about 20 Oxford liberals, reformers and men of science, most of them strongly influenced by continental fashions in historical, theological and scientific research, met at the Freemasons Tavern in London. From this meeting grew the Association for the Study of Academical Organisation, established to consider "the low state of learning and science in the two older universities".[40] Charles Appleton, editor of the *Academy* and fellow of St. John's College, Oxford, believed that the struggle begun by Pattison in 1868 still had far to go.[41] Appleton, a man consumed by enthusiasm for order, preached the German spirit of idealism and *Wissenschaft* to the dry congregation of Oxford dons. He coined, or at least gave new life to, the phrase "endowment of research".[42]

The Oxford reformers' first meeting in London resolved that, whatever the University Commission decided, "The chief end to be kept in view in any redistribution of the revenues of Oxford and Cambridge is the adequate maintenance of mature study and scientific research, as well for their own sakes, as with the view of bringing the higher education within the reach of all who are desirous of profit by it".[43] The resolution was signed by about 70 men and led to discussion on research in different subjects, on the abolition of prize fellowships, the need for more professors, the improvement of teaching and the introduction of new disciplines.

The Association had several meetings and won support in both universities. In May 1873, a memorial urging reform was drafted by Cambridge dons. It asked for the abolition of life fellowships and more efficient provision for teaching and private study. At Lockyer's request, J. S. Cotton wrote for *Nature* a series of leading articles advocating the "endowment of research" and calling attention to the importance of both university reform at Oxford and Cambridge and direct state aid through a national scheme of research fellowships.[44] Soon enemies appeared among dons who controlled college endowments, and among dons disturbed "by being called upon to learn before they taught".[45] There were differences of view among the reformers themselves. Appleton and Pattison preferred not to abolish fellowships or fellowship examina-

---

[40] *Cf.* Roll-Hansen, Diderik, "The Academy, 1869–1879: Victorian Intellectuals in Revolt", *Anglistica*, VIII (1957), p. 77. The Association was given leader space in an article by Brodie in *Nature*, VII (12 December, 1872), pp. 97–98.

[41] Appleton, Charles Edward (1841–1879), classical philologist, man of letters, and vigorous reformer in Oxford University politics and international copyright law. See Appleton, John H., and Sayce, A. H., *Dr. Appleton; His Life and Literary Relics*, (London: Trübner, 1881).

[42] Bruce, H. A., Home Secretary in Gladstone's first administration and formally responsible for the Devonshire Commission, believed the phrase was invented by Mark Pattison (Bruce, H. A., *Life of Lord Aberdare*, II (Oxford, 1902), p. 255). Pattison himself attributed it to Appleton, *The Academy*, 19 February, 1881, p. 127.

[43] *The Academy*, 1 December, 1872, p. 459.

[44] "The Endowment of Research", *Nature*, VIII (26 June, 1873), pp. 157–158; *ibid.* (10 July, 1873), pp. 197–198; *ibid.* (24 July, 1873), pp. 237–238; *ibid.* (31 July, 1873), pp. 257–258; *ibid.* (14 August, 1873), pp. 297–298; *ibid.* (11 September, 1873), pp. 377–378.

[45] *The Athenaeum*, 1 November, 1873, p. 563.

tions, but to convert the fellowship into a body of men whose work ranged from full-time teaching to full-time research. John Stuart Mill also preferred to keep the fellowship system, and to connect teaching closely with research.[46] Such differences among individuals prevented the group from presenting a united front.

Public comment was unsympathetic; while the London circle moved quietly and informally, *Punch* caricatured the Oxford movement as one of " research for endowment ". To make matters worse, Appleton fell out with John Murray, his publisher, over a delicate matter of historical theology, and his name became anathema at Oxford. As one colleague later recalled, the name of " researcher " was invented especially to stigmatise the holders of Appleton's " unpalatable " doctrine. To decry Appleton became a popular pastime: " If you wish to please the dominant party in common rooms, it was only necessary to sneer at research and researchers ".[47] The Association had a second meeting, but in the face of criticism it died late in 1873. Fortunately in August of that year the publication of the Devonshire Commission's third report on Oxford and Cambridge gave Appleton fresh hope. The Commission recommended that the collegiate tutorial system be complemented by new university chairs. In 1870, there were only six science chairs (excluding medicine) at Cambridge, and two of those also were associated closely with medicine. Only one— zoology—was of recent creation (1866). For Oxford, the Commission recommended two new chairs in physics, two in chemistry, one in mathematical physics, one in applied mechanics and engineering and five in medicine and biology.[48] Citing the model of the research laboratory and classes of Sir William Thomson at Glasgow, the Commission said the new professors should be required to advance knowledge as well as to teach. The Commission also recommended reforms in the university museums, and the institution of a doctorate in science.

The creation of new university chairs and degrees at Oxford and Cambridge did not completely satisfy the " researchers ", who were also concerned about the obstacles to the introduction of science in the constituent colleges. At Cambridge in 1869, three quarters of all university prizes and half of all college prizes were awarded in English and classics. The Sedgwick Prize was the only prize available in the natural sciences. After 18 years, the natural science tripos had still not succeeded in arousing wide interest. Between 1861 and 1870, 95 students, 14 of whom ultimately became fellows, took honours degrees in natural science. In

[46] *The Academy*, 19 November, 1881, p. 127.

[47] The conflict between Murray and Appleton is illuminated by correspondence kindly made available to me by John Murray of John Murray, Publishers, London.

[48] In oral evidence Mark Pattison said 20 to 30 science chairs were needed at Oxford and stressed the great need for skilled assistants, demonstrators and university lecturers. See " The Report of the Science Commission on the Old Universities ", *Nature*, VIII (21 August, 1873), pp. 337–341.

1879 there were 73 men placed in the classical tripos, 111 in mathematics, but only 13 in natural science.[49]

Fellowships were the chief endowments which could be used for the promotion of research. In 1871 the net income of Oxford colleges amounted to £300,000, of which £91,545 was paid in fellowships. But for 20 years (1850–70) only 12 of a total of 200 Oxford fellowships had been awarded in science. Cambridge did not give an account of its total income, but reported that college fellowships annually cost £92,820 at £200 to £300 apiece. Among Cambridge colleges, Trinity had one science lecturer, and St. John's had two, both of whom were shared with medicine.[50] But the enumeration of teaching posts tells very little about the amount of research undertaken. "Indeed", Richard Proctor wrote, thinking perhaps of Oxford, "it would seem almost as though election to those well-paid offices had been the sole end and aim of work . . . so thoroughly has original research ceased or become unfruitful when the desired post has been secured".[51] For the most part, salaried teaching posts were associated with heavy teaching duties and offered few opportunities for research. To assist younger men to enter science "free from pecuniary anxiety", the Commission therefore urged the universities to create senior and junior classes within the fellowship and to emphasise scientific subjects in the election of junior fellows.

These far-reaching recommendations were fundamental to the reconstruction of academic life in England over the next half century. More scientific men began to flow to the universities. In 1872 the Board of Studies of the Natural Science School at Oxford attempted to improve the science syllabus, placing emphasis on wide general knowledge of science.[52] In June 1874 the Cavendish Laboratory at Cambridge was formally opened, and *Nature* prophesied that "the genius possessed by Professor Clerk Maxwell and the fact that it is open to all students of the University of Cambridge for researches will, if we mistake not, make this before long a building very noteworthy in English science".[53] But the traditional relationship between college and university could not be quickly transformed. Indeed, not until a change in statutes in 1882 were Cambridge colleges required to make financial contributions to the university.[54]

In the meantime, the "endowment of research" made slow progress.

[49] See *Nature*, CIV (6 November, 1919), p. 256. It must be said that the Natural Science Tripos was not made an independent avenue to an honours degree until 1861. *Cf.* Arthur Gray, *Cambridge University: An Episodical History* (Cambridge, 1926), p. 289.

[50] T. G. Bonney, on "Natural Science at the University of Cambridge", *Nature*, I (3 March, 1870), pp. 451–452.

[51] Proctor, *op. cit.*, p. 358.

[52] But see M. Fosttr's critical review, "The Oxford Scheme of Natural Science", *Nature*, VI (23 May, 1872), pp. 57–58.

[53] "The New Physical Laboratory at the University of Cambridge", *Nature*, X (25 June, 1874), p. 139.

[54] Gray, *op. cit.*, p. 303.

Reviewing the third report of the Devonshire Commission in *Nature*, J. S. Cotton referred to the " absurdity " of the fact that

. . . the lack of pecuniary means can be the main difficulty which has hitherto in the richest country in the world hindered original investigation in the sciences . . . for the permanent Endowment of Research and the continuous support in a worthy position of the researchers, not only the aid of the nation at large, but the wealth and prestige of our ancient universities are required.[55]

The Devonshire Commission's fifth report appeared in August 1874, and announced that only two universities in Britain, Edinburgh and London, actually offered degrees in science.[56] Staff salaries varied widely, and were largely unattractive. Moreover, Owen's College, Manchester, University College, London, and the other university colleges united by the examination system of London University reported that they were unable to expand their science faculties without government help. Industry, with few exceptions, showed little interest. City and merchant guilds could be generous, but were always unpredictable. Private philanthropy in support of scientific research was nowhere to be seen. Government aid, both in capital and maintenance grants, was the only real alternative.

Following the fifth report in August, and the report of the University Commissioners, Appleton renewed his campaign in the *Fortnightly Review*, the *Theological Review* and the *Pall Mall Gazette*. Finally, in the *Spectator* of 24 October, 1874, he published a " Draft Scheme for the Endowment of Research " which remains a noteworthy attempt to define organised research as an appropriate undertaking of a modern university. The chief purpose of endowment was to " prevent the waste of that capacity where it does happen to exist by being diverted into those various practical channels of activity in which men without private means are accustomed to get a living ".[57] According to Appleton's scheme, young graduates would, upon recommendation by their tutors or professors, and perhaps by competitive examination, be chosen for support by a board of electors, to do specific pieces of research for limited and specified periods.

Appleton's scheme was designed to secure for a few " citizen's of the Republic of Science " payment equal to, but not greater than, the average income they would receive in a legal, medical or diplomatic career—a sum, he added reflectively, " enough to live upon . . . perhaps not enough to marry on ". If the candidate showed evidence of succeed-

[55] Cotton, J. S., " The Endowment of Research, V ", *Nature*, VIII (14 August, 1873), p. 297. See also Cotton, J. S., " The Universities Commission Report ", *Nature*, X (15 October, 1874), pp. 475–476 ; (22 October, 1874), pp. 495–496 ; *Nature*, X (14 May, 1874), pp. 21–23.
[56] *Seventh Report of the Royal Commission on Scientific Instruction and the Advancement of Science*, 1875 XXVIII, pp. 3, 6 (hereafter cited as the Devonshire Commission).
[57] *Spectator*, 24 October, 1874, pp. 1329–1330, reviewed in *Nature*, XI (5 November, 1874), p. 2.

ing in his research by the end of his tenure, as indicated by acceptance by the Royal Society or other learned bodies, his " precarious and terminable " grant could be renewed for periods amounting in the end by 10 or 12 years, at a salary rising to the income of a " barrister, or a medical man in fairly good practice, or a clerk who had been a dozen years in a public office, or a junior partner in an average business—say, £800 to £1,000 a year ". If he won fame, he would be eligible for an annuity on an equally liberal scale. To complete his scheme, Appleton suggested that the learned societies should be endowed sufficiently to carry on the business of assessment of scientific achievements, to publish transactions and generally to help men of science set high standards of work. This endowment would also rescue the societies from being forced to admit " from sheer want of funds . . . a multitude of persons who have no pretension to the character of savants ".[58]

Nine months after Appleton's scheme appeared, the eighth Devonshire report was published, and dealt directly with the question of how the state should aid science. From the Civil Estimates of 1869–70, the government spent at most £400,000 on scientific museums, expeditions, learned societies, and the scientific work of central departments. The Commission accepted that the " progress of Scientific Research must in a great degree depend upon the aid of government. As a nation we ought to take our share of the current scientific work of the world ".[59] Accordingly, they followed the recommendations of Strange and *Nature* that the government create a ministry of science and education, with a council of scientific advisers; that the scientific facilities of civil departments be augmented; and that a national technical laboratory and physical observatory be built.[60] The Commission embraced the scientists' recommendations; it would be their own fault, J. S. Cotton observed, if they allowed the issues to " remain any longer in the domain of theory ".[61]

Each of the Commission's recommendations was highly significant to

[58] *Ibid.*, p. 1330. In 1874 Benjamin Jowett prepared a list of " Suggestions for University Reform ". This assessed the slender benefits of previous government action and recommended several fresh steps, including the creation of new chairs at £1,000 apiece and the creation of grants and grades of fellowships and university offices for teaching and research. These innovations at Oxford University which would cost £60,000 p.a. could be met by " taxes " on the colleges. The colleges would also be responsible for aiding new university colleges to be created in large industrial towns. Finally, Jowett's paper recommended the appointment of another royal commission and renewed government intervention to secure the needed changes. Unfortunately Jowett's proposals lay unnoticed until the First World War. *Cf.* Appleton, J. H. and Sayce, A. H., *op. cit.*

[59] *Eighth Report of the Devonshire Commission*, p. 2. Both reports were abstracted at length in *Nature*, XII (12 August, 1875), pp. 285–288; (19 August, 1875), pp. 305–308; (2 September, 1875), pp. 361–363; (9 September, 1875), pp. 389–392; (30 September, 1875), pp. 469–470. The *Seventh Report*, dealing with the Universities of London, Scotland, Trinity College Dublin and Queen's University, Belfast, was reported in *Nature*, XII (11 November, 1875), pp. 21–22.

[60] *Eighth Report*, p. 47. See Strange's letter to *The Times*, 6 February, 1874; see also " A Minister for Science ", *Nature*, IX (12 February, 1874), p. 277. A proposed science council of 30 members was outlined anonymously by Strange in *Nature*, XII (16 September, 1875), p. 431.

[61] *The Academy*, 4 September, 1875, p. 252.

the constitutional development of scientific administration. Over the next 50 years most of them were realised in some form. None however was of more immediate significance to the conduct of basic research than the Commission's recommendation to increase the parliamentary grant of the Royal Society, and to give state stipends to individual men of science.

The Fruits of Protest

Personal Stipends for Research: Between 1875 and 1880 the movement reached its climax. During the life of the Devonshire Commission, Gladstone's government had taken little interest in its proceedings.[62] However, with the accession of Disraeli's second administration in 1875, the reformers' prospects brightened. Derby and Salisbury, both members of Disraeli's new cabinet, had both given evidence before the Commission, strongly urging government participation in the support of research. *Nature* reported its pleased " surprise " that Appleton's scheme had been so well received by the Conservative Government, and remarked that " the general principle of the need of some sort of endowment for science is generally admitted ".[63]

The political question of " patronage " raised by the proposal for individual stipends troubled the Liberals' conscience, but left Derby and Salisbury, themselves amateur scientists of long standing, quite unmoved. In January 1875, Salisbury insisted on the justice of the claims of science to a place in higher education.[64] It followed that scientific men were worth cultivating for the sake of the national interest. " Who knows how many discoveries might be worked out ", Derby asked Edinburgh students in his rectorial address in December 1875,

how many conquests of man over Nature secured if, I do not say a numerous body, but even for some 50 or 100 picked men, such modest provision were made that they might be set apart, free from other cares, for the double duty of advancing and diffusing science. . . . Whatever is done, or whoever does it, I think more liberal assistance in the prosecution of original scientific research is one of the recognised wants of our time.[65]

In a reply to his question in parliament about the Devonshire Commission in February 1876, Lyon Playfair was told that the new

---

[62] Gladstone's aversion to science was well known. W. E. H. Lecky admitted there " were wide tracts of knowledge with which he (Gladstone) had no sympathy. The whole great field of modern scientific discovery was out of his range." See Lecky, *Democracy and Liberty,* Vol. I (London: Longmans, 1896), p. xxxi. Lord Morley recalled that Gladstone watched science " vaguely and with misgiving . . . from any full or serious examination of the scientific movement he stood aside, safe and steadfast within the citadel of Tradition ". Morley, John, *Life of Gladstone* (London: John Murray, 1905), Vol. I. p. 209.

[63] Cotton, J. S., " The Prospects of the Endowment of Research ", *Nature,* XI (5 November, 1874), pp. 1–2.

[64] See Stewart, Balfour (of Owen's College), " The Marquis of Salisbury on Scientific Education ", *Nature,* XI (28 January, 1875), p. 241.

[65] Address to students at Edinburgh, reported in *Nature,* XIII (23 December, 1875), p. 141.

administration was considering what action it should take.[66] In early March, Playfair, with Sir John Hawkshaw, president of the British Association, led two deputations to the government to induce them to act on the Devonshire recommendations. In reply, the deputation was told that the third report (on Oxford and Cambridge) was in the hands of Lord Salisbury, while the government had taken steps to set up a solar physics laboratory for Lockyer in South Kensington. The government, Playfair was assured, was "quite alive to the importance of the subject". That said, the scientific reform issue shifted from the public forum to the council chamber, and became a matter of administrative arrangement. In the spring of 1876, the Treasury agreed to sanction an increased vote of £4,000 for research for a period of five years, to be taken on the estimates of the Science and Art Department, in addition to the £1,000 voted as a grant-in-aid to the Royal Society.[67]

The government's decisions were welcome to Norman Lockyer, who was shortly offered the task of organising the Loan Exhibition of scientific instruments, and then a post at the Royal College of Science.[68] The Science and Art Fund could be used for personal stipends as well as for research expenses.[69] This policy was exactly what Lockyer and *Nature* had sought; to have the sum placed on the vote of the Science and Art Department, in which both Lockyer and Huxley were employed, was perfect. But the apparent success of the London circle and Lockyer's new-found security aroused resentment, particularly among some of the clerks and the senior officials of the Treasury. Although accepted by the government, the new stipends did not meet with administrative approval. Ralph Lingen, Permanent Secretary to the Treasury,[70] opposed on principle the policy of instituting salary payments, "where now nothing but assistance towards the cost of experiments . . . is afforded", because it "opens the door to a sort of expenditure doubtful both in kind and degree".[71] Only the intervention of W. H. Smith, the Finacial Secretary, backed by the Cabinet's recommendations, succeeded in overriding Lingen's objections.

But doubts were not confined to the Treasury. "It is well known",

[66] Hansard, *Parliamentary Debates* (Third Series), 227, c. 551 (21 February, 1876); "Scientific Instruction and the Advancement of Science", *Nature*, XIII (9 March, 1876), p. 371.

[67] For an examination of this arrangement, see MacLeod, R. M., *op. cit.*

[68] See Meadows, A. J., "Lockyer as Astronomer". *Nature*, CCXXV (17 January, 1970), p. 230.

[69] Lockyer loyally reprinted the official correspondence for all to see in "Government Aid to Scientific Research", *Nature*, XIV (29 June, 1876), pp. 185–86.

[70] Ralph (later Baron) Lingen (1819–1905), K.C.B., 1878, raised to peerage on retirement in 1885; educated at Trinity College, Oxford; fellow of Balliol 1841; Secretary to Sir James Kay-Shuttleworth at the Education Department in 1849, and helped introduce system of "payment by results". Strong advocate of aggressive retrenchment as permanent secretary to the Treasury under the Liberal government of 1874–80 and Conservative government of 1880–85. He combined scholarly acumen with a formidable sense of administrative detail.

[71] T1/7522B/6048, Lingen to W. H. Smith, 12 April, 1876.

Lingen said, " that there are many Fellows of the Royal Society, whose positions as workers in science need not be too clearly defined, who view with mistrust the liberality of the government ".[72] Two years earlier, Sir Joseph Hooker, president of the Royal Society, had said that government should help provide " appliances and buildings and colleges ", but that private initiative alone should " find the workers and funds when they require it for their support ".[73] Now, in December 1876, Hooker wrote to Charles Darwin in a similar vein:

Government may do much, but it must always be under such vexatious restrictions that it tries a man's temper and patience, let his patriotism be what it will, to undertake the expenditure of what Government gives, and I fear it must ever be so. Between ourselves, I think there will be a wretched outcome of the Government Fund (the £4,000 p.a.) I am sure that if I had uncontrolled selection of persons to grant it to and was free to use my authority over them I could have got ten times more done with the money.[74]

The subject was heatedly discussed at the X-Club later that month. Tyndall, who had himself endowed research fellowships in physics in America with the $30,000 he had earned from his lecture tour in 1872,[75] ruefully predicted that " a good deal of heart-burning is likely to flow from this . . . gift. It is not one into the need of which we [the Royal Society] have fairly and naturally grown, so that it will have to be managed instead of healthily assimilated ".[76] Professor George Stokes asked whether the personal grants would go to mature scholars or to " young men of promise ". If the former, the Society would open itself to criticism for giving money to men who were already reasonably comfortable. If the latter, on what basis would the selection be made? If candidates were required to submit written work, who would referee it? Could the committee members, who received no fees or travelling expenses, be asked to do so? If testimonials were to be taken up and if interviews were to be held, would these not place a premium on personality and personal acquaintance? [77]

The Royal Society, reluctant executor of the government's benefaction, went ahead as proposed. At the end of December 1876, the new Government Fund Committee was launched on a five-year trial, with the following terms of reference:

(1) To initiate or carry on investigations and to provide private funds for their being carried out, whether by conferring grants on competent persons, or by offering prizes for the solution of problems; (2) to consider applications

---

[72] " Government Grants in Aid of Science ", *Nature*, XV (1 March, 1877), p. 369.
[73] Huxley, Leonard, *Life and Letters of Sir Joseph Dalton Hooker* (London: John Murray, 1918), Vol. II, p. 251, Hooker to Darwin, 22 December, 1875.
[74] *Ibid.*, p. 235.
[75] One was at Harvard, one at Columbia, and one at the University of Pennsylvania. See " Endowment for Scientific Research and Publication ", *Nature*, LI (13 December, 1894), pp. 164–5.
[76] *Tyndall Papers* (Royal Institution), XI, p. 644, Tyndall to Thomas Hirst, 17 December, 1876.
[77] *Stokes Papers* (Cambridge University Library), " Proposals " (1877).

from persons desirous of undertaking investigations; and (3) to apply funds for computation and formation of Tables of Constants and other laborious and unremunerative scientific work.[78]

Claims from different fields of science would be considered by three specialist committees of recommendations and reviewed by a general purposes committee. Individual grants were to be limited to 12 months' tenure and annual reports were required. Three members of the X-Club, two members of the Devonshire Commission and several signatories to Appleton's resolution were among the 26 members of the new committee. *Nature* hailed it as inaugurating " a new era in the scientific activity of our country ".[79]

Almost immediately, however, the award of personal grants to individual research workers and research assistance to university professors intensified the growing separation between scientists in government service and those in academic life. The government's policy generated competition for funds. In 1880, Prof. William Flower, Richard Owen's progressive successor at the Royal College of Surgeons and later director of the Natural History Museum, declined to serve on the Royal Society committee on grounds that government money was being dissipated in the support of amateurs at a time when many professional men in the country's museums were labouring under unsatisfactory conditions. Flower also objected to what he called the encouragement of " cottage research " and the demoralisation of individual scientific men by a programme which made their lives too easy. The programme seemed, in his view, too much like outdoor relief:

The large increase of this method of subsidising science, accompanied as it is with the (as it appears to me) humiliating necessity of personal application in each case, must do much to lower the dignity of recipients and detract from the independent position which scientific men ought to occupy in this country.[80]

The Royal Society stood firm in the belief that it was concerned with the selection of academic rather than government scientists, but neither the Royal Society nor the government had weighed the long-term consequences of the new scheme. William Spottiswoode, Treasurer of the Society, admitted that in principle it was desirable to permit men without sufficient means to do research they could not otherwise afford. But it was questionable whether the Society should assume moral responsibility for encouraging men " not yet of independent income " to interrupt " the business of their life " merely for the sake of science.[81]

[78] *Minutes of the Government Fund Committee* (hereafter abbreviated *Mins. GFC*), 7 December, 1876.

[79] " The Endowment of Research ", *Nature*, XVI (14 June, 1877), p. 117.

[80] *Mins. GFC*, 19 February, 1880.

[81] *Mins. GFC*, 11 January, 1877. To help explain the difference between the existing forms of government support, Norman Lockyer devoted a leading article in *Nature* of March 1, 1877, to " Government Grants in Aid of Science ".

Of course, no one knew exactly how many would-be men of science were not doing research because they could not afford to do so. This question at least was answered three months later in March 1877 when 98 applications for grants totalling nearly £14,500 were received by the Royal Society. In the end only 33 of these projects were approved,[82] but it was clear that a pool of willing research workers did exist. The growing popularity of the grants grew alarming when Sir William Thomson (Lord Kelvin) and William Crookes, both members of the committee, announced their intention of resigning in order to apply for grants themselves. Their threatened departure could have deprived the government of services of those men of science " on whose judgment and knowledge the country would place the greatest reliance ".[83] But fears for the integrity of the scheme soon disappeared. Those wishing research assistance simply left the committee until their grant-aided projects were completed.

In assessing the scheme five years later the Royal Society admitted that the scientific value of work sponsored could not easily be measured. But it was clear that the £20,000 spent between 1877 and 1881 had given rise to 21 articles in the *Philosophical Transactions*, 150 articles in the proceedings and journals of other scientific societies,[84] and many investigations were still in progress. Moreover, the competition weeded out weak candidates. During the first five years 417 applications were received, beginning in 1878 with 181. After 1878 the numbers fell to 103 and later to 72, but the percentage of successful applications increased from 18 per cent. to 58 per cent. The Government Fund Committee assured the Science and Art Department that the declining number of applications reflected a reduction in " useless and unsuitable schemes " rather than a diminished interest in the grant. Applications through the 1880s and 1890s varied between 40 and 80 per year, with a rejection rate varying between 30 per cent. and 50 per cent. The grant continued (and still continues today) to be a means of assisting original studies, regardless of personal status; despite early fears, it found a secure place among British institutions of science.

The " Essays " and the Universities: Action on the Devonshire Commission's recommendations was quickly overtaken by the Conservatives' positive interest in university reform. In the 1850s most Tories had opposed government interference in the universities, largely on the grounds

---

[82] The records do not reveal the criteria of selection, but Hooker confirmed that no successful application requested more than £400. Presidential Address to the Royal Society, 30 November, 1877; *Proceedings of the Royal Society*, XXVI (1877), p. 432.

[83] *Mins. GFC*, 15 February, 1877, Norman MacLeod, Science and Art Department to Secretary, Royal Society, 29 January, 1877.

[84] *Report of the GGC* (1881). *The Academy*, 17 June, 1876, p. 585. *Cf.* the new research fund for the Chemical Society, begun by gifts from T. Hyde Hills and G. D. Longstaff. *Nature*, XIII (13 April, 1876), p. 461.

that university reform was then synonymous with the admission of Dissenters.[85] After 1876, however, this was no longer an issue. With the abolition of Tests at Oxford and Cambridge in 1873, the nonconformist population from which many scientists had traditionally come [86] at last had access to university degrees. In February 1876, to Appleton's great joy, Salisbury, Chancellor of Oxford, introduced the Oxford Reform Bill in the House of Lords. Salisbury's views coincided with Derby's and both were prepared to restore to the university its ancient preeminence over the colleges. University chairs and buildings would be supplied from forfeited " idle fellowships ". " We are of the opinion ", he said,

that the mere duty of communicating knowledge to others does not fulfil all the functions of a University and that the best Universities in former times have been those in which the instructors, in addition to imparting learning, were engaged in adding new stores to the already acquired accumulation of knowledge.[87]

This parliamentary campaign, which *Nature* called the " first fruits " of the Devonshire Commission, was also the climax of Appleton's efforts.[88] In May 1876 Appleton edited a volume *Essays on the Endowment of Research*. Appleton's seven collaborators for the 10 essays included Oxford dons Mark Pattison, Henry Nettleship (Corpus), T. K. Cheyne (Balliol), J. S. Cotton (formerly fellow of Queens') and A. H. Sayce, professor of comparative philology, H. C. Sorby, professor of geology at Sheffield and W. T. Thiselton-Dyer, assistant director of Kew Gardens.[89] The book had a tremendous impact and was reviewed in nearly every major journal in England.[90] *The Spectator* said:

The movement for the Endowment of Research is no longer the impracticable crusade which it appeared to be twelve months ago. The activity of its promoters and the unexpected sympathy which it has inspired in official quarters, has enabled it to make its way into the arena of practical politics.[91]

[85] Campbell, *op. cit.*, p. 80.

[86] *Cf.* Hans, Nicholas, *New Trends in Education in the Eighteenth Century* (London: Routledge and Kegan Paul, 1951).

[87] Hansard Parliamentary Debates (House of Lords), third series (24 February, 1876), 227, cols. 791–803.

[88] Cotton, J. S., " The Government Scheme of University Reform ", *Nature*, XIII (2 March, 1876), p. 342.

[89] The *Essays* included Mark Pattison's " Review of the Situation "; Cotton, J. S., on " The Intentions of the Founders of Fellowships "; Appleton on " The Economic Character of Subsidies to Education ", Appleton again on " The Endowment of Research as a Form of Productive Expenditure "; Sayce on " The Results of the Examination System at Oxford "; Sorby on " Unencumbered Research: A Personal Experience "; Cheyne on " The Maintenance of the Study of the Bible "; Sayce again on " The Needs of the Historical Science "; Thiselton-Dyer on " The Needs of Biology "; and Nettleship on " The Present Relations between Classical Research and Classical Education in England ".

[90] *Cf. The Times* (28 June, 1876); Creighton, H., " The Endowment of Research ", *Macmillan's Magazine*, XXXIV (1876), pp. 186–192; Lankester, E. R., " The Endowment of Research ", *Nature*, XIV (8 June, 1876), pp. 126–129; " Essays on the Endowment of Research ", *Dublin Review*, LXXXVIII (1876), p. 122. See also Crookes, W., " The Encouragement of Scientific Research ", *Quarterly Journal of Science*, VI (ns), (1876), pp. 467–494.

[91] *Spectator*, XLIX (10 July, 1876), pp. 899–900.

The *Essays* illustrated the broad range of opinions held among university men on the question of research. Appleton continued to view research not in terms of natural science, but in terms of *Wissenschaft.* Pattison, for reasons peculiar to Oxford, saw the problem as one of medieval privileges resisting modern scholarship. Sorby spoke for the privately supported amateur who had done well financially on his own and who then wanted to patronise science himself, while Thiselton-Dyer, the biologist, represented the " civil scientists " who valued the application of pure research in nutrition and public health. Practical research in fields such as navigational astronomy and geology was well and good, but it was also necessary, he said, that the state, " without a present utilitarian stimulus should set apart some portion of its income for the systematic attack on problems, the solution of which may be reasonably expected, but which are beyond the scope of teaching establishments ".[92]

The *Essays* were launched in a climate of public opinion already anxious about the threat of foreign scientific competition. With the Devonshire reports, the claims for the endowment of science by the state and by the universities had been put clearly before the public. The Oxford and Cambridge Act of 1877, passed after much debate, continued the direction of reform since 1854, gave the two universities a stronger position *vis-à-vis* their colleges and set up a new body of executive commissioners with powers to revise university and college statutes. At best, however, the commissioners could only use funds which they could extract from the colleges. Moreover, much to *Nature's* annoyance, the commissioners included no one from outside university circles.[93] The " permissive " nature of the Act meant that progress depended upon cooperation between the colleges and the universities. By and large, Oxford colleges, with a few exceptions (including Balliol, Magdalen, Christ Church and Trinity) remained uncommitted to research.[94] At Oxford, " university " money was absorbed by new buildings, and little could be spared for stipends.

The Commissioners were still sitting in 1880 when Gladstone returned to power. Then, just as victory seemed within reach, the reformers began to lose ground.

Obstacles and Reactions

It would be wrong to hold that the arguments of either the London reformers or the Oxford " researchers " were accepted without question, yet they held the stage for nearly 15 years. As time went on, however, delicate questions posed in the 1870s grew in urgency, and the move-

[92] Appleton, *op. cit.*, p. 235.

[93] Jack, William (professor at Manchester) "The Universities Bill", *Nature* XVI (3 May, 1877), pp. 1–2.

[94] Hartley, Sir Harold, " The Contribution of the College Laboratories ", *Chemistry in Oxford* (London: Chemical Society, 1966), pp. 7–10.

ment began to encounter opposition. Even under the Conservatives, "research" was caught up in the flotsam of delayed political promises. The *Essays* and the final Devonshire Report coincided with the great wave of reforming legislation in trade union policy, housing, public health, and food and drugs regulation which fell to the lot of Disraeli's second administration. University reform was a relatively easy matter in some ways, as it did not involve public money and could win political favour in certain quarters. But the government argued, with some justice, that its hands were too full to take on the whole task of reorganising science as the Devonshire Commission recommended, particularly as there was no strong political mandate to do so, and because no one was unequivocally agreed on what should be done.

In any case, to implement all the Devonshire recommendations would have cost a great deal and taken a long time. In terms of political realities, little favour could be won from the electorate for reforms of institutions which affected an exceedingly small group, many of whom were also Liberal in politics. Moreover, some scientists were not pleased by the prospect of government action. Richard Proctor, an old enemy of Norman Lockyer, warned against taxing the people for science. In particular he wrote that a new ministry, as Strange recommended,

having, as an important part of its duty, the control of large sums of money for researches of only philanthropic interest would certainly be objected to by the country at large, and . . . might excite a hostility to science and to scientific men which would most seriously injure the prospects of science in this country.[95]

In the end, only certain recommendations, which were among the least expensive, were accepted by Disraeli's administration. The Conservatives remained in office for too short a time to implement a larger programme, even if such a programme had been feasible, and even if they had wished to carry it out. When Gladstone returned to power in 1880 and again in 1886 and 1892, Liberal "reformers", with their chronic emphasis on retrenchment, brought the "researchers" grave disappointment. Gladstone, never a friend to science in the best of times, set himself against the proposal of a centralised Ministry of Science on constitutional grounds, and against state intervention in science on the principle of "free trade and no favour". Not surprisingly, the reformers lost faith in political action.[96]

Perhaps more significant than the realities of party politics, however,

---

[95] Proctor, R., "Money for Science", *Cornhill Magazine*, XXXII (1875), p. 463.

[96] Crookes, W., "The Encouragement of Scientific Research", *Quarterly Journal of Science*, VI (ns) (1876), p. 486. The Conservatives, said one reviewer, gave forth hostile cries of "confiscation, spoliation, violation, communism, revolution, pious founders and the like", and announced to the reformers: "If you want places for the advance and increase of human knowledge, found them and endow them yourselves." The same writer found liberalism "standing mute, fearing lest its Chinese idol, competitive examinations should be overthrown and his joss house burnt in the struggle".

was the rising tide of opposition to science and the scientific outlook which had emerged during the 1870s and 1880s. By the 1880s, science had severed its connections with theology and the separation had become widely accepted. Gladstone in 1881 declared that the debate had come to an impasse: "let the scientific men stick to their science and leave philosophy and religion to poets, philosophers and theologians".[97] But resentment steadily mounted against the attitudes of the extreme proponents of science, against Tyndall's alleged "materialism" and Huxley's admitted "agnosticism". Science had, by the early 1880s, cut itself off from much popular sympathy and support. Individualists saw science no longer as an instrument of limitless progress, but as one of intellectual and moral subjugation. Coming under attack by moralists and moral reformers like Frances Power Cobbe, scientists were accused of attempting to supplant traditional loyalties by a "priestcraft of science" possessing attitudes and beliefs less and less comprehensible to the average man. For wide sections of the public, the concepts of the unity and uniformity of nature, established first by geology, then by biology and physics, brought what seemed like a threatening prospect of an encompassing, atheistic materialism. This brought the pursuit of science, an activity proclaimed as beneficent, useful and moral by Lord Brougham and the Society for the Diffusion of Useful Knowledge 50 years before,[98] into grave disrepute. Nothing brought this change in attitudes home quite so clearly as the reaction to John Tyndall's address at Belfast in 1874.[99]

Throughout the 1880s literary reviewers repeatedly denounced the "arrogance" of scientists who identified man with the "kingdom of nature" and by so doing reduced his laws and institutions and even his free will to the status of mere animal existence, amenable to the studies of reductionist physiology and psychology.[100] Social and intellectual resistance to physico-chemical reductionism was shortly followed by

[97] Quoted in Brown, Alan, *The Metaphysical Society, Victorian Minds in Crisis,* 1869–1880 (New York, 1947), p. 106.

[98] See, *e.g.,* Hays, J. W., "Science and Brougham's Society", *Annals of Science,* 20 (1964), pp. 227–241.

[99] The intellectual crisis of the 1870s is well illustrated in the history of the Metaphysical Society, which began in 1869 in an attempt to "unite all shades of religious opinion against materialism". See Brown, *op. cit.* The impact of reductionism and atomistic, scientific materialism was darkly illustrated by Tennyson, first in his poem *Lucretius* and later, more optimistically, in the *Higher Pantheism.* For reactions to Tyndall, who more than once had "severely tried the patience not merely of the public but of a large number of his scientific brethren by the rashness with which he had intruded his speculations into regions far beyond those which are properly the province of the Professor of Natural Science", see Wace, Henry, "Scientific Lectures: their Use and Abuse", *Quarterly Review,* CXLV (1878), pp. 35–61, especially pp. 38–39. See also Eve, A. S., and Creasy, C. H., *The Life of John Tyndall* (London: John Murray, 1945), Chap. XV. The Belfast Address was published separately by Longmans, with an explanation by Tyndall, in September 1874, and was reprinted with modifications in Tyndall's *Fragments of Science* (London, 1894). See sixth edition, Vol. II, p. 193. For an intermediate position on the "errors of modern physics", see Tyndall's old enemy, Tait, P. G., *Lectures on Some Recent Advances in Physical Science,* second edition (London: Macmillan, 1876), pp. 1–26.

[100] *Quarterly Journal of Science,* LXIII (1881), p. 204.

references to the "degrading" tendencies of science associated with biological research in France and Germany. The reports of the Royal Commission on Vivisection in 1876, following the Devonshire Commission, and virtually coinciding with the *Essays*, connected the advancement of biological and physiological research with iniquities of animal experimentation.[101] If biology bred brutality, physics and chemistry brought materialism, and all " pure " research, by implication, was suspect. One writer in the *Journal of Science* even argued that " the life that is wholly given over to such pursuits [*i.e.*, research] is a misspent one, and is, as an example, positively injurious to society ".[102] John Ruskin, speaking of Darwin and Tyndall, claimed that science should not be pursued as an end in itself, but should be subordinate to ethics. Where science clashed with ethics, science should give way. Thus, Ruskin opposed the new physical laboratory built in Oxford in 1884.[103] His sentiments were repeated, often out of context, in the growing reaction against vivisection, vaccination and rabies inoculation in the 1880s and 1890s. National leagues for opposition to vaccination and the notification of infectious diseases received wide popular support, particularly among the working classes in London and the north of England, but also among the well-to-do middle classes in the west of England. They were expressive of a broad wave of popular dissatisfaction and disillusionment with the repercussions and implications of science.[104]

Within science there was also division and dissatisfaction. Many held that British science, "noisily accompanied by public begging", was in danger of losing its "dignity".[105] "Hitherto indeed", wrote Grant Allen in 1887, "we Britons have been remarkable as the propounders of the deepest and widest scientific generalisations; it is only of late years that our bookish educators of the new school have conceived the noble

[101] See *Report of the Royal Commission on Vivisection*, 1876, XLI, 277. The ethics of vivisection were debated vigorously in the scientific press and the quarterlies. See *Nature*, XIV (25 May, 1876); Coleridge, Stephen, " The Administration of the Cruelty to Animals Act of 1876 ", *Fortnightly Review*, LXVII (1900), pp. 392–398. Vivisection was also the subject of a second Royal Commission which sat for five years, 1907–12, and issued four voluminous reports. Not until 1912 could the commission report public acceptance of the " experimental method ", and even then inserted a strong reservation against " an exaggerated over-estimation of the usefulness of results obtained from experiments on animals ". *Final Report of the Royal Commission on Vivisection*, 1912 (Cd. 6114), XLVIII, paras. 73–74 and pp. 129–131.

[102] Cited in Fernseed, Frank, " The Future Martyrdom of Science ", *Quarterly Journal of Science* (3rd series) III (1881), p. 202.

[103] Collingwood, W. G., *John Ruskin, His Life and Work* (London: Methuen, 1894), Vol. II, pp. 90, 233.

[104] MacLeod, R. M., " Law, Medicine and Public Opinion: The Reaction to Compulsory Health Legislation, 1870–1907 ", *Public Law* (1967), pp. 107–128 and 189–211. Compare the vast protest literature connected with such women as Catherine Walter (" The Tyranny of Science ", *New Science Review*, II (1895), pp. 341–342) and Frances Power Cobbe (" The Scientific Spirit of the Age ", *Contemporary Review*, 54 (1880), pp. 126–139). See also Anon., *Science in Excelsis* (London, 1875), with its parody of the " Celtic Association for the Promotion of Science ". For analogous commentary in America, see Porter, Noah, *Science and Sentiment: Essays Chiefly Philosophical* (New York: May, 1882).

[105] *Cf.* Proctor, R., " The Dignity of Science ", *Knowledge*, 1 January, 1886, pp. 93, 95.

ambition of turning us all into imitation Germans." [106] The progress of British science in the early nineteenth century had been inexpensive and had been brought about without much state patronage; now it was being alleged that British science was in danger of degraded imprisonment in the fetters of gold.

This opinion was accompanied by the feeling that science should not become the servant of government. An "FRS" deplored in a letter to *The Times*, in September 1876, the current "wretched whining cry for State funds in aid of research". "Hitherto there has generally existed among scientific men in this country a healthy spirit of independence, and it is earnestly to be hoped that it may long continue, and not be found to bow the knee to some official Baal and 'walk after things that do not profit'." [107]

There were also men of science who saw the entire Devonshire Commission as the "mere tools and cats' paws of a needy and designing confederacy" led by Strange and Lockyer.[108] It was charged that Lockyer, having a large family, persuaded the government to give him a "berth" merely for personal reasons.[109] Such assertions could not be proved. But the heat generated by the contest damaged the reputation of the whole endowment of research movement.

In 1876, Proctor published *Wages and Wants of Science Workers*, arguing that the resources for scientific research should be acquired by private efforts.[110] Instead of giving his general approval to the Devonshire Commission's recommendations, Proctor called Lockyer's list of witnesses selective and biased and advised caution in dealing with any wide scheme of endowment that would contribute to "scientific Micawberism".

Finally, the right-wing of the endowment movement—the Oxford group—passed from sight with Appleton's death in 1879. The whole weight of the campaign then fell upon Lockyer and his associates. Although reforms were gradually occurring in the universities, these received less public attention. This meant that criticism was now concentrated, perhaps more than circumstances warranted, on the London group and its provincial supporters. Following *Nature's* guide, a "Birmingham Research Fund" was begun in 1880 by the Birmingham Philosophical Society (itself founded only in 1876). The first decision of the fund's directors was to award a grant of £150 to George Gore. *Nature* reported the news with gratitude:

106 Allen, Grant, "The Progress of Science from 1836–1886", *Fortnightly Review*, XLI (1887), p. 873.
107 *The Times*, 16 September, 1876.
108 *English Mechanic*, 7 January, 1876, p. 415.
109 *Ibid.*
110 Proctor, Richard B., *The Wages and Wants of Science Workers* (London: Smith and Elder, 1876). *Cf.* an enthusiastic review in the *English Mechanic*, 7 January, 1876, p. 415: "Of all the contributions to the literature of the *vexato questo* of the endowment of scientific research which have hitherto appeared, there is scarcely one which seems to us so well calculated to diffuse sound and just views on the subject and to enlighten the general public as to the real end and aim of those who clamour for it. . . ."

"Perhaps nothing would sooner convince our ignorant and one-sided politicians of the reality of science and of the necessity for its national recognition than similar efforts . . . in all our great industrial centres ".[111] Such successes, however, merely stimulated more resentment. Beginning in 1880, Lockyer and his associates became embroiled in lengthy debates, particularly in the pages of the *English Mechanic,* a heady rival of *Nature,* which boasted a circulation "larger than all other English scientific publications put together ".[112] "FRAS ", a regular correspondent of the *Mechanic,* claimed that those "who were the most pushing and clamorous before the Royal Commission were those *who wanted the money themselves* ". They were not really among the "best " scientists anyway, "FRAS " claimed. "It is the pseudo-scientific men, the quacks, advertisers and begging letters of the scientific world who are clamouring to be subsidised." Taking a broad swipe at Lockyer and the South Kensington Science School, he went further.

The "Endowment of Research " has come in these later days to signify the subsidising of such things as Committees on Solar Physics, and not in the very slightest degree the helping of the real student. It means the opening of the National Purse, the shutting of the Nation's eyes, and the seeing what Brompton will send us.[113]

Throughout 1881 allegations against the "endowment intrigue " mounted. Because several of the so-called "Brompton pluralists ", including Huxley and Lockyer, held central posts [114] in connection with South Kensington and government, cries of "jobbery " rose time and again. The *English Mechanic* claimed bitterly that *The Times,* the *Daily News, The Academy* and *Nature* were all united in attempting to suppress its point of view.[115] Soon the debate took on even larger dimensions, when resistance to the "researchers " rose among established scientists holding government posts, who preferred to confine any increased government expenditure in science to their own departments. Some "establishment scientists " lent support to a new Society for Opposing the Endowment of Research which was founded in 1880 with Captain W. Noble, the astronomer, as secretary. In February 1881, Sir George Airy, Astronomer Royal, defined the policy of this group in a letter to Noble, published in the *English Mechanic.* He said:

successful researches have in nearly every instance originated with private persons, or with persons whose positions were so nearly private . . . that the investigators acted under private influence, without the dangers attending conjunction with the State. Certainly I do not consider a Government as justified in endeavouring to force at public expense investigations of undefined

---

[111] *English Mechanic,* 18 February, 1881, p. 539.
[112] *English Mechanic,* 23 September, 1870, Editorial.
[113] *English Mechanic,* 17 December, 1880, p. 349.
[114] *Ibid.,* 11 February, 1881, p. 530.
[115] *Ibid.,* 6 May, 1881, p. 208.

character, and at best of doubtful utility; and I think it probable that any such attempts will lead to consequences disreputable to science.[116]

In 1882 the question was debated at the Social Science Association. The case as put by Rowland Hamilton, secretary of the education section, was simple: " endowment " meant that " those who were engaged in research should, upon due proof that they were engaged, be exempt from carking cares and difficulties ". There was no doubt that " at present any object of research must be investigated by people of independent means ". Such means should exist for men of quality without making them feel " under a personal obligation to anyone ".[117]

The opponents of the endowment of research were encouraged by the early mistakes of the Government Grant Committee. One might, like Airy, contend with some justification that " the world . . . is not unanimous in believing that the (Royal Society's) government grants have been useful ". " It is commonly acknowledged ", he said, even by supporters of research, that they were awarded in a " lax and unbusinesslike way ".[118] *The Times* in 1886 announced that " we hear a good deal from time to time about the endowment of research . . .", but the best scientific efforts were usually supported by private means. Government grants such as they were had " not been so conspicuously successful as to create a very strong desire for their extension ".[119]

The " researchers' " campaign had made its demands in very general terms. No one had carefully worked out who would administer government grants, to whom they would be given, or what criteria would be used in awarding them. These weaknesses were now seized upon by the enemies of the movement within the scientific community itself. Dissension among the scientists reached a climax in 1881, when in that year A. J. Mundella, then vice-president of the Privy Council and well known for his services to education, proposed to endow, under the Science and Art Department, a regular programme of " state fellowships " for science costing £200 to £400 apiece, amounting to at least £2,000 per year. According to his plan, the Royal Society would continue to advise on the merit of individual applications.

To carry out this programme the Treasury and the government looked for guidance to the Royal Society. Unfortunately, the officers of the Royal Society were unable or unwilling to become wholly responsible for awarding national grants from public funds. There was, moreover, a sharp division of opinion on the subject of research within the society itself. Reflecting the views of some fellows, *The Times* remarked in December 1880, that " the election to the vacancies in [the Society's] ranks has of late years

116 *English Mechanic*, 25 February, 1881, pp. 586–587.
117 *Knowledge*, II (29 September, 1882), p. 296; *Transactions of the Social Science Association* (Nottingham, 1883), pp. 319–330.
118 *English Mechanic*, 22 July, 1881, p. 472.
119 *The Times*, 23 December, 1886.

been too manifestly governed by a tendency to set up as an idol something which it is technically fashionable to call ' research ' and to ignore the far higher mental effort which is required for successful ratiocination ".[120]

Under the circumstances the Royal Society stood aloof, and continued to encourage the pursuit of science for its own sake without entering into the practical economic costs of those ideals.[121] Confronted by a raging debate on one side and by a non-committal Royal Society on the other, the Treasury did not know where to turn. It therefore rejected the state fellowship scheme. In the words of Ralph Lingen, Permanent Secretary to the Treasury: " I think it most mischievous to make a parliamentary department the channel of doles ".[122] Such a scheme would, in his view, " bring the State into a relation with individual scientific investigation which it is most undesirable that it should occupy ".[123] The Treasury consented only to aid the Royal Society, as the respected representative of British science.[124] From 1882 to 1914 the government grant remained at £4,000 per year.

Perhaps the last volley in the opposition to endowment was fired in Proctor's own journal—*Knowledge*—shortly before Proctor's death in 1884. He wrote : " Few circumstances have caused true lovers of science in recent times more pain than that outcry for the Endowment of Research. . . ." In epitaph Lewis Carroll wrote a poem " Fame's Penny Trumpet ", which mocked the " researchers' " campaign. But by the early 1890s such opposition (with its chief opponents) had largely died away. What remained was a residue of scepticism among Treasury officials, Lockyer's embittered memories of struggle at South Kensington, and a general optimism in the Royal Society and the universities that the long, slow process of gradual reform would gradually win the day.

Confluence and Consolidation 1890–1900

The endowment of science movement of the 1860s and 1870s, followed by the counter-movement of the 1880s, was followed in turn by a gradual acceptance of the principle of endowment. Institutes for fundamental research, supported both by governmental and private benefactions, gradually emerged. The London School of Tropical Medicine, which concentrated on research, was established in 1899 by the Colonial Office under

[120] *The Times*, 2 December, 1880.
[121] Some of these consequences I have dealt with elsewhere. See MacLeod, R. M., " Scientists, Civil Servants and Fundamental Research: The Parliamentary Grant to the Royal Society, 1850–1914 ", *op. cit.*
[122] T1/8008C/20599, Minute, ca 3 February, 1881.
[123] *Mins. GFC*, 2 March, 1882.
[124] Lingen's logic was fundamental to the Treasury's scientific policy for the next 30 years : " A small grant like the Royal Society equipment grant has many advantages. The real workers whose work is known to be worth much are few and a small grant obliges selection. It also escapes question. A large grant soon attracts the Parliamentary Philistines [asking] ' well—what have you got for your money?'—the question is legitimate and fatal. That is why I think the state is better away." T1/8008C/20599, Lingen to Cavendish, 2 February, 1881.

Joseph Chamberlain. An Imperial Research Fund was launched in 1901 for the study of cancer. Private endowments for bacteriological research were begun at the Jenner (now the Lister) Institute, and the Davy-Faraday Laboratory for physical chemistry at the Royal Institution was opened with a gift from Alfred Mond.[125] The *Daily Telegraph* greeted the Mond bequest with a calm acceptance of the obvious. " Nothing ", it observed, " is better worth buying than scientific fact ". With pardonable licence the *Telegraph* speculated that the Mond grant could possibly do " more for physical science at one stroke than all the Cabinets of Her Majesty have done since the commencement of that reign, one of the greatest glories of which has been the advance of research in England ".[126]

But neither research institutes nor government action could meet the needs of " researchers " for salaries and fellowships. The government grant scheme lagged behind the growing number of young men of science, while the Treasury looked cynically at the alleged " nest-building " of Lockyer and the Science and Art Department at South Kensington.[127] As the Royal Society remained dispassionate and uninvolved, it remained for the universities to provide the base on which " researchers " could build on a significant scale. In 1850 there were about 60 university posts in science and technology (excluding medicine, but including agriculture) in Britain; by 1900, there were over 400. Government assistance, when it came to the universities from 1889 onwards, came principally by way of subsidies in aid of teaching, but this inevitably acted as an indirect endowment of research. The development of " research schools " in the late 1890s, notably at the Cavendish, set the pattern. In 1894, largely through the efforts of Lockyer, Mundella, Huxley and Playfair, money from the Royal Commission for the Exhibition of 1851 was used to begin the first imperial fellowship scheme for scientific research. One of the first " 1851 Exhibitioners " was Ernest Rutherford.[128] The numbers of research fellowships tenable at universities and university colleges also increased. By 1914 there were 170 privately endowed fellowships for science at 24 different institutions (outside Oxford and Cambridge).[129] These had the long-term effect of giving research a firm academic foundation, protected by traditions of freedom in learning and teaching and not subject to Treasury or party politics.

Opponents of endowment still argued that by spending time in research " the prospects of such men would be so injured that it would be difficult

[125] " A Magnificent Endowment ", *The Times*, 3 July, 1894; *The Academy*, 7 July, 1894.
[126] *Daily Telegraph*, 4 July, 1894.
[127] *Cf.* MacLeod, R. M., " The Social Framework of *Nature* in its First Fifty Years ", *Nature*, CCIV, 4 November, 1969, pp. 423–477.
[128] Gray, A., " Fellowships for Research ", *Nature*, LVIII (20 October, 1898), pp. 600–602; MacLeod, R. and Andrews, E. Kay, " Education, Career and Migration Patterns among Commission of 1851 Scholars: A Case Study in the Endowment of Research ", *Nature*, CCXXVIII (1968), pp. 1011–1016.
[129] DSIR 17/1. Total number of Postgraduate and Research Fellowships and Scholarships (1915).

for them after to find congenial employment ". Well into the new century, a scientific man's " prospects " remained very limited. But by 1914 *Who's Who in Science* listed over 1,600 leading men of science in Britain who had in some way found " congenial employments ". In any event, the research community was increasing. In the 42 years between 1858 and 1900 the only doctoral degree in science in England—the London D.Sc.—had only 171 successful candidates, while in the 14 years between 1900 and 1914, 108 more received the degrees. The static assumptions of the Treasury, which had limited the government grant to £4,000 per year while the number of British research workers doubled, and doubled again, had proved baseless. Moreover, as public opinion became persuaded of the needs of fundamental inquiry, the Gladstonian system of " payment by results " could no longer be invoked as a magic phrase to reject all claims for " unfettered research ".

There still remained great difficulties which the scientific reform movement had only partially uncovered. Most British universities gave greater emphasis to education than to research training and " research schools " were not visible in many universities until after the First World War. Moreover, despite the improved " prospects of science ", industry took little interest in research and there were few posts to absorb the growing numbers of research workers. It followed from this industrial indifference that research workers as a class, distinct from the chemists and physicists who led the professional institutions of the 1870s and 1880s, had less and less to do with applied science. Some posts were created at the National Physical Laboratory, which in many ways acted as a " half-way house " between industry and the universities, but it became a commonplace article of British belief " that there is one Science " and the University was its teacher.[130]

By 1900 it was often observed that Britain was falling behind Germany and even further behind America in numbers of science graduates and was employing her graduates outside industrial research. In 1900, there were about 2,000 men of science of graduate standing in Britain, about half of whom were secondary and primary schoolteachers; about 420 (18 per cent.) were university teachers, and about 250 (10 per cent.) were in the civil service. There were only about 225–250 graduate chemists in British industry. Between 1900 and 1914 the momentum generated by the " researchers' " campaign began finally to show results. In these years alone the supply of science graduates reached nearly 6,000, of whom 300 received advanced degrees. By 1914 there were probably well over 7,000 graduate scientists in Britain and more with advanced degrees than there had been scientists altogether in 1850.[131]

[130] *Nature*, CIV (6 November, 1919), p. 257.
[131] Pike, R. M., *The Growth of Scientific Institutions and Employment of Natural Science Graduates in Britain, 1900–1960* (Unpublished M.Sc. dissertation, University of London, 1961).

Unwittingly, the endowment of research movement had helped drive a barrier between science and its industrial applications. By the 1890s the competition for university posts tended to select for early brilliance and grant high social rewards for pure research. Since fellowships were " prizes " and went to the " best ", it was easily concluded that those who did not get them, and who therefore went into industry or teaching, were therefore not the " best ". Provincial universities copied the fellowship pattern previously followed in Oxford, Cambridge and London. The " best "—" the generals of science "—won their prizes, while the " second- " and " third- " class minds, which Huxley called the " rank and file " of science and which was visibly one major source of Germany's technological power, received little benefit from the endowment of research movement, from the Royal Society, or from the universities. Beginning in 1905, under Lockyer's leadership, the British Science Guild tried to draw public attention to the need for more scientists to be better deployed. But despite Lockyer's enthusiasm and the support of Lord Haldane, the British Science Guild failed to win significant industrial or governmental support. Indeed, investment in research was not increased significantly until the national self-examination prompted by the war placed the importance of research training as a national resource firmly among the leading priorities of the state.

Conclusion

The endowment of research movement can be seen in five distinct phases. The first, 1850–1869 saw successive stages of investigation and reform in the universities, the emergence of the London circle, and the manoeuvres of the British Association which culminated in the Devonshire Commission. This phase was followed between 1870 and 1875 by the growth of a working alliance between Oxford-based university reformers and the London circle—men of widely differing social class and scholarly attitude—who proclaimed in *Nature* and the *Academy* their recommendations for endowment and reform. Between 1876–1880 this alliance developed into the endowment of science movement proper, which reached a climax in the eighth report of the Devonshire Commission, the publication of Appleton's *Essays,* the extension of the Government Grant Fund, and the enactment of the university reform Acts. The same period, however, also witnessed growing opposition to research on social, ethical and economic grounds. This resistance became stronger in the fourth phase between 1880 and 1885, reflected in growing hostility towards Lockyer, the collapse of the Oxford reformist wing, and the distraction of government by more pressing issues of domestic and imperial policy. Victory for the " researchers ", however, drew near in the fifth phase from 1885–1900 when university, government and private research establishments and fellowship schemes were begun. Between 1900 and 1915, the efforts of the " researchers " were finally vindicated in the creation of state fellowships for research, including those of the Development Commission and the Department of Scientific and Industrial Research.

In many respects, the endowment of research movement broke new ground. Unlike the "decline of science" debate half a century before, the "researchers'" movement witnessed few calls for public honours or recognition. Instead, it sought a fundamental change in the way in which the government and the universities viewed science. Research claimed to be a national resource, like labour and capital, a productive factor to be cultivated. A new principle was to be invoked. Labourers would be paid not by results, but according to promise, with the anticipation of useful contributions if they were left to follow their own bent. This principle incorporated in the concept of the "research fellowship" represented a great act of faith on the part of the reformers, before which the Treasury not unreasonably paused.

To assure government and the public that science would bring practical and beneficial results, to overcome Treasury scruples, and to negotiate carefully a programme of progress through waves of social disenchantment with the assumptions and image of science, were formidable tasks. The endowment of research movement left an important inheritance. One part of that inheritance was a sense of association, by which a body of scientists, divided sharply in social grounds and personal philosophy, could be bound together by shared convictions and could plead those convictions through press, public meetings and deputations. In this sense the endowment of science movement helped to create the impression that science and research could be identified by certain unifying features and could be considered a collective entity by government.

In the political atmosphere of the 1870s and 1880s—indeed until Balfour and Haldane lifted research out of neglect in the 1890s and 1900s—there was little possibility of achieving in England a sense of political urgency in the support of science. The history of the movement showed that research had not only to justify itself, but had to be seen to justify itself. Specialised research was in many fields elaborating, consolidating, and framing new questions for science, but only a fraction of this activity could be seen to result in ameliorative technology. In the absence of such justification, scientific research would be given a low priority by a political system preoccupied with immediate problems of imperial expansion, economic unrest, inadequate housing, unsystematic education, poverty and unemployment. In a sense, the "researchers'" victory was a paradox. The public acceptance that brought them recognition in universities and research institutes also helped separate them from industry and society at large. The implications of this separation were profound. By its very success the endowment of science movement had helped to sow fundamental questions about the social function of research in modern society.

INDEX

Abel, F.A.: VIII 341, 348, 350
Aberdeen, George Hamilton Gordon,
    4th Earl: V 9–10, 11, 13; VIII 330
Acland, Henry W.: VIII 341
Acland Committee: IX 205
Adams, W.G.: VIII 341
Admiralty: VII 141, 142, 144–5
Advisory Council on Scientific and Industrial
    Research: VIII 339 n.53
agnosticism: IX 221
agricultural research: VII 120, 164 n.25
air aspirators: I 93
Airey, George: IV 68, 76; V 5, 8, 11; VI 89,
    90, 99; VII 151–2, 154, 166 n.47;
    VIII 327, 328, 334, 340, 357; IX 224–5
Aitkin, John: VI 98
Alkali Acts administration (1863–84)
    act of creation (1862–68): I 87–93
    Alkali Act (1863): I 90, 93–4, 98
    Alkali Act (1863) Amendment Act (1874):
        I 96–7, 98–9
    Alkali etc., Works Regulation Act (1881):
        I 107–9
    central control in: I 111–12
    legislative results (1879–84): I 104–10
    local v. central inspection: I 102–4, 105–6,
        107, 108, 111 n.69
    phases of development: I 86–7
    prosecutions: I 89, 102, 104–5
    revision and reappraisal (1868–78):
        I 93–104
    Royal Commission on Noxious Vapours:
        I 86 n.2, 100–104, 112; II 114 n.4
    scientific controls and: I 111, 112
    works not covered: I 100, 104 n.53, 107
alkali inspectors
    appointment: I 87, 90–91
    expenditure on: I 108
    responsibilities, (1864–68): I 91–3; (1868–
        78): I 93–104; (1879–84): I 107–8;
        forces operating to expand: I 111
    salaries: I 90, 94, 97–9, 106, 107–8
    see also Smith, Robert Angus
alkali trade
    statistics relating to: I 87, 100
    see also Alkali Acts administration (1863–
        84)

Allen, Grant: IX 222–3
Allman, G.J.: VIII 341
Althorp (John Charles Spencer, 3rd Earl
    Spencer): V 5, 6, 7
ammonia vapours: I 100, 103–4
animal experimentation: VII 120; IX 222
Appleton, Charles: VII 132, IX 208–9,
    211–12, 213, 216, 218–19, 223
applied scientists, Civil List pensions to:
    V 11
Argyll, George Douglas Campbell, 8th Duke
    of: VIII 331, 333
Armagh observatory: VIII 328
Armstrong, H.E.: VIII 344
Arnold, Matthew: IX 200
Ashby, Eric (Lord Ashby): VI 96
Ashworth, Thomas: II 118 n.21
Associated Sanitary Authorities, Liverpool–
    Merseyside: I 108
association, principle of: IV 68, 87 n.62
Association for Prevention of Noxious
    Vapours (Manchester and
    East Cheshire): I 106
Association for the Study of Academical
    Organisation: IX 208–9
Astronomical Society: see Royal Astronomi-
    cal Society
Ayrton, A.S.: VII 145
Ayrton, William: VI 100

BAAS: see British Association for the
    Advancement of Science (BAAS)
Babbage, Charles: IV 55–6, 60, 62, 63, 64,
    65, 66, 68, 69, 73, 78, 84 n.30; V 11;
    VI 83, 84, 90, 92, 101 n.2; IX 197
Bagehot, W.: IV 57, 59, 75, 78
bailiffs: II 119–20, 123 n.47, 124, 134, 147
Baker, Thomas: II 126, 128
Balfour, A.J.: V 18; IX 23
Ball, Robert: III 30 n.114, 31
Banks, Joseph: IV 58, 59, 60–61, 72; VI 83
Barlow, Peter: IV 65
Barrington, G.C.: VIII 350
Barrow, Isaac: V 5
Barrow, John: IV 68
Baxter, H.T.: VIII 328
Beck, T.S.: IV 72, 73, 75; VI 89–90

A VOW
TO SECURE
HIS LEGACY

A VOW
TO SECURE
HIS LEGACY

BY

ANNIE WEST

First published in Great Britain 2016
By Mills & Boon, an imprint of HarperCollins*Publishers*
1 London Bridge Street, London, SE1 9GF

Large Print edition 2016

© 2016 Annie West

ISBN: 978-0-263-26209-4

C463791324

Printed and bound in Great Britain
by CPI Antony Rowe, Chippenham, Wiltshire

Dedicated to those who work with the
sick and frail: medical staff, technicians,
administrative staff, care workers,
paramedics and volunteers.
Your skills and above all your kindness
make such a difference!

Thanks, too, to the lovely Fabiola Chenet
for your advice. Any errors are all mine!

PROLOGUE

'IMOGEN! WHAT A lovely surprise.' The receptionist looked up from her desk. 'I didn't expect to see
you again.' She paused, her smile fading. 'I was so
sorry to hear about your mother.'

Her voice held a note of sympathy that stirred
grief, even after four months. It was like pressure
applied to a bruise that hadn't faded. The pain was
more intense today because coming here, doing
this, was so difficult. Imogen laced her fingers together to stop them trembling.

'Thanks, Krissy.' The staff here at the specialist's consulting rooms had been terrific with her
mum and her.

Imogen swept her gaze around the familiar space.
The soothing sea-green furnishings, the vase of
bright gerberas on the counter and the waiting room
of people apparently engrossed in their magazines.
She recognised their alert stillness—a desperate
attempt to pretend everything would be all right.
That they'd receive good news from the doctor, de-

spite the fact he had a reputation for dealing with the most difficult cases.

Her stomach swooped in a nauseating loop-the-loop. A chill skated up her spine to clamp her neck.

Swiftly, she turned back to the desk.

'What brings you here?' Krissy leaned in. 'You just can't stay away, is that it? You love our company so much?'

Imogen opened her mouth but her throat constricted. No words came out.

'Krissy! That's enough.' It was Ruby, the older receptionist, bustling in from a back room. She wore an expression of careful serenity. Only the sympathetic look in those piercing eyes gave anything away. 'Ms Holgate is here for an appointment.'

There was a hiss of indrawn breath and a clatter as Krissy dropped the stapler she'd been holding.

'Please take a seat, Ms Holgate. The doctor is running a little late. There was a delay in surgery this morning, but he'll see you shortly.'

'Thanks,' Imogen croaked and turned away with a vague smile in Krissy's direction. She couldn't meet the other woman's eyes. They'd be round with shock. Perhaps even with the horror she'd seen in her own mirror.

For weeks she'd told herself she was imagining things…that the symptoms would pass. Until her GP had looked at her gravely, barely concealing concern, and said he was sending her for tests. Then he'd referred her to the very man who'd tried to save her mother when she'd suffered exactly the same symptoms.

Imogen had had the tests last week and all this week she'd waited for a message from her GP saying there was no need to see the specialist, that everything was clear.

There'd been no message. No reprieve. No good news.

She swallowed hard and made herself cross the room, taking a seat where she could look out at the bright Sydney sunshine rather than at the reception desk.

Pride dictated she play the game, hiding her fear behind a façade of calm. She took a magazine, not looking at the cover. She wouldn't take it in. Her brain was too busy cataloguing all the reasons this couldn't end well.

A year ago she'd have believed everything would be okay.

But too much had happened in her twenty-fifth year for her to be complacent ever again. The world had shifted on its axis, proving once more, as it had in childhood, that nothing was safe, nothing sure.

Nine months ago had come the news that her twin sister—flamboyant, full-of-life Isabelle—was dead. She'd survived paragliding, white-water rafting and backpacking through Africa, only to be knocked over by a driver in Paris as she crossed the street on her way to work.

Imogen swallowed down a knot of grief. Isabelle had accused her of being in a rut, of playing safe when there was a wide world out there to be explored and enjoyed.

Her twin had followed her dream, even knowing the odds of her succeeding were a million to one. Yet she *had* succeeded. She'd moved to France and through talent, perseverance plus sheer luck had snaffled a job with a top fashion designer. She'd had everything to look forward to. Then suddenly her life was snuffed out.

Soon after had come their mother's diagnosis—a brain tumour. Massive, risky to operate on, lethal.

Blindly, Imogen flipped open the magazine on her lap.

When the news had come from Paris she'd protested that there must have been a mistake—Isabelle couldn't possibly be dead. It had taken weeks to accept the truth. Then, as her mother's headaches and blurry vision had worsened and the doctors looked more and more grim, Imogen had been convinced there would be a cure. Fatal brain tumours just didn't happen in her world. The diagnosis was impossible.

Until the impossible had happened and she was left alone, bereft of the only two people in the world who'd loved her.

The past nine months had shown her how possible the impossible actually was.

And now there was her own illness. No mistaking this for anything other than the disease that had struck down her mother. She'd been with her mum as her illness had progressed. She knew every stage, every symptom.

How much longer did she have? Seven months? Nine? Or would the tumour be more aggressive in a younger woman?

Imogen turned a page and lifted her eyes, scanning the room. Was this her destiny? To become a regular here until they admitted there was nothing they could do for her? To become another statistic in the health-care system?

Isabelle's voice sounded in her head.

You need to get out and live, Imogen. Try some-

thing new, take a risk, enjoy yourself. Life is for living!

Imogen snorted. What chance would she have for living now?

She thought of the dreams she'd nurtured, planning and carefully executing every step. Working her way through university. Getting a job. Building professional success. Saving for a flat. Finding a nice, reliable, loving man who'd stick by her as their father hadn't. A man who'd want a lifetime with her. They'd see all the things Isabelle had raved about. The northern lights in Iceland. Venice's Grand Canal. And Paris. Paris with the man she loved.

Imogen blinked and looked down. Open on her lap was a double-page photo of Paris at sunset. Her breath hitched, a frisson of obscure excitement stirring her blood.

The panorama was as spectacular as Isabelle had said.

Imogen's throat burned as she remembered how she'd turned down her sister's invitation, saying she'd visit when she had a deposit saved for a flat and had helped their mum finish that long-overdue kitchen renovation.

Isabelle had ribbed her about planning her life

to the nth degree. But Imogen had always needed security. She couldn't drop everything and gallivant off to Paris.

Fat lot of good that will do you now you're dying. What will you do, spend your money on a great coffin?

Imogen gazed at the Seine, copper-bright in the afternoon light. Her stare shifted to the Eiffel Tower, a glittering invitation. *You'd love it, Ginny—gorgeous and gaudy by night but just so...Paris!*

She'd spent her life playing safe. Avoiding risk, working hard, denying herself the adventures Isabelle revelled in, because she planned to do that later.

There'd be no later. There was only now.

Imogen wasn't aware of getting up, but she found herself striding across the room and out into the sunlight. A voice called but she didn't look back.

She didn't have much time. She refused to spend it in hospitals and waiting rooms until she absolutely had to.

For once she'd forget being sensible. Forget caution. She intended to *live*.

CHAPTER ONE

'TELL ME, *MA CHÉRIE,* will you be at the resort when we visit? It would be so much more convenient having the owner on the premises when we do the promotional photo shoot.' Her voice was intimately pitched, reaching him easily despite the chatter of the crowd in the hotel's grand reception room.

Thierry looked down into the publicist's face, reading the invitation in her eyes.

She was beautiful, sophisticated and, he guessed by the way she licked her bottom lip and pressed her slim frame closer, ready to be very accommodating. Yet he felt no flicker of excitement.

Excitement! He'd left that behind four years ago. Would he even recognise it after all this time?

Bitterness filled his mouth. He'd been living a half-life, hemmed in by conference-room walls and duty, forcing himself to care about minutiae that held no intrinsic interest. *Except those details had meant the difference between salvaging the family's foundering business portfolio and losing it.*

'I haven't decided. There are things I need to sort out here in Paris.'

But soon… A few months and he'd hand over the business to his cousin Henri and, more importantly, the managers Thierry had hand-picked. They'd guide Henri and maintain all Thierry had achieved, securing the Girard family fortune and leaving him free at last.

'Think about it, Thierry.' Her lips formed a glossy pout as she swayed close. 'It would be very…agreeable.'

'Of course I will. The idea is very tempting.'

But not enough, he realised with abrupt clarity, to drag him from Paris. These meetings would bring him closer to divesting himself of his burdens. That held far more allure than the prospect of sex with a svelte blonde.

Hell! He was turning into a cold-blooded corporate type. Since when had his libido taken second place to business?

Except his libido wasn't involved. That was the shocking thing. At thirty-four Thierry was in his prime. He enjoyed sex and his success with women showed he had a talent, even a reputation, for it. Yet he felt nothing when this gorgeous woman invited him into her bed.

Hadn't he known taking on the family business would destroy him? It was sucking the life out of him. It was...

His gaze locked on a figure on the far side of the room, and his thoughts blurred. His pulse accelerated and his chest expanded as he hefted a startled breath.

His companion murmured something and stretched up to kiss his cheek. Automatically, Thierry returned the salutation, responding to her farewell as she joined a group who'd just entered the hotel ballroom.

Instantly, his gaze swung back to the far side of the room. The woman who'd caught his eye stood poised, her weight on one foot, as if about to leave.

He was already pushing his way through the crowd when she straightened and drew back her shoulders. Delectable, creamy shoulders they were, completely bared by that strapless dress. The white material was lustrous in the light of the chandeliers, drawing a man's eyes to the way it fitted her breasts and small waist like a glove before flaring in an ultra-feminine swirl to the floor.

Thierry swallowed, his throat dry despite the champagne he'd drunk. A familiar tightness in his groin assured him that his libido was alive and kicking after all. Yet he barely registered relief. He was too busy drinking her in.

In a room packed with little black dresses and sleek, glittery outfits, this woman stood out like *grand cru* from cheap table wine.

She turned her head, presenting him with an engaging profile, and Thierry realised she was speaking. He halted, surprised that his walk had lengthened to an urgent stride.

Her companion was a gamine-faced woman, pointing out people to the woman in white. The woman in white and scarlet, he amended, taking in the pattern of red flowers cascading around her as she moved. There was white and scarlet on her arms too. She wore long gloves to her elbows, re-minding him of photos he'd seen of his *grand-mère* at balls and parties decades ago.

Thierry's gut clenched as the woman lifted one gloved hand to her throat in a curiously nervous gesture. Who knew gloves could be erotic? But there was no mistaking the weighted feeling in his lower body. He imagined stripping the glove down her arm, centimetre by slow centimetre, kissing his way to her fingers before divesting her of that dress and starting on her body.

Why was she nervous? A shy woman wouldn't wear such a glorious, blatantly sexy concoction.

Heat sparked. His gaze roved her dark, glossy hair swept up from a slim neck. She had full red lips, a retroussé nose and heart-shaped face. Curves that made him ache to touch.

She wasn't just pretty; she was sexy on a level he couldn't resist.

The old Thierry Girard wasn't dead after all.

'You're sure you don't mind?' Saskia sounded doubtful.

Imogen smiled. 'Of course not. I appreciate all you've done these past few days but I'm fine. I'll drink champagne and meet interesting people and enjoy myself.' If she said it enough she might stop being daunted by the glittering crowd long enough to believe it. 'Now go.' She made a shooing gesture, nodding towards the knot of fashion buyers Saskia had pointed out. 'Make the most of this opportunity.'

'Well, for half an hour. I'll look for you then.'

Imogen blinked, overwhelmed anew by the kindness of her sister Isabelle's best friend. Saskia had not only shown her where Izzy had worked and lived, but shared stories about their time together, filling the black well of Imogen's grief with tales that had made Imogen smile for the first time in months.

Saskia had even presented her with the dresses Izzy had made for herself, eye-catching outfits Imogen would never have considered wearing. But here, in Paris, it felt right, a homage to her talented sister. Imogen smoothed her hand down the fabulous satin dress.

'Don't be silly. Go and mingle, Saskia. I don't expect to see you again tonight.' She smiled, making a fair attempt at Izzy's bantering tone, even tilting her head to mimic her sister. 'Since you snaffled me an invitation, I intend to make the most of my only society event. I don't need you cramping my style.'

'Isabelle said you weren't good with lots of new people but obviously you've changed.' Saskia's lips twitched. 'Okay. But join me if you want. I'll be around.'

Imogen kept her smile in place as Saskia left, ignoring the trepidation that rose at being alone, adrift in this sea of beautiful people.

Stupid. This isn't alone. Alone is discovering you're dying and there's no one left in the world who loves you enough to feel more than pity.

Imogen shoved aside the thought. She refused

to retreat into self-pity. She was in Paris. She'd make the most of every moment of the next six weeks—Paris, Venice, London, even Reykjavik. She'd wring every drop of joy from each experience before she returned home to face the inevitable.

She swung around, her full-length skirt swishing around her legs, and refused to feel out of place because other women were in cocktail dresses. Isabelle's dress was too wonderful not to wear.

'Puis-je vous offrir du champagne?' The deep, alluring voice sent heat straight to the pit of her stomach, as if she'd inadvertently taken a gulp of whisky.

French was a delicious language. But surely it had been designed for a voice like this? A voice that sent shivers of sensual pleasure across her skin.

She jerked her head around and then up.

Something she couldn't identify slammed into her. Shock? Awareness? Recognition?

How had she not seen him before? He stood out from the crowd. Not just because of his height but because of his sheer presence. Her skin prickled as if she'd walked into a force field.

She met eyes the colour of rich coffee, dark and inviting, and her pulse pounded high in her throat as if her heart had dislodged and tried to escape.

Deep-set eyes crinkled at the corners, fanning tiny lines in a tanned face. A man more at home out-doors than at a fashionable party?

Except his tall frame was relaxed, as if he wore a perfect dinner jacket every night to mingle with a who's who of French society. His mouth curled up in a tantalising almost-smile that invited her to smile back. Was that why her lips tingled?

Dark hair, long enough to hint at tousled thick-ness. A determined chin. Strong cheekbones that made her think of princes, balls and half-forgotten nonsense.

Imogen swallowed, the muscles in her throat re-sponding jerkily. She cleared her throat.

'*Je suis désolée, je ne parle pas français.*' It was one of her few textbook phrases.

'You don't speak French? Shall we try English?' His voice was just as attractive when he spoke English with that sensuous blurring accent. Plea-sure tickled Imogen's backbone, and her stomach clenched.

'How did you guess? Am I that obvious?'

'Not at all.' His gaze did a quick, comprehen-sive sweep from her head to her hem that ignited a slow burn deep inside. A burn that transferred to her cheeks as his eyes met hers and something passed between them, as tangible as the beat of her heart. 'You are utterly delightful and feminine but not obvious.'

Imogen felt the corners of her mouth lift. Flirting with a Frenchman. There was one to cross off her bucket list. Back home she hadn't been good at flirtation, but here it seemed she didn't have to do anything at all.

'Who are you?' Funny the way dying helped you overcome a lifetime's reserve. Once she'd have been too over-awed to speak to a man who looked so stunningly male. He was one of the most attractive men she'd ever met and despite that aura of latent power he was definitely the most suave. Even that prominent nose looked perfect in his proud face. Just as well his eyes danced or he'd be too daunting.

'My apologies.' He inclined his head in a half-bow that was wholly European and totally charming. 'My name is Thierry Girard.'

'Thierry.' She tried it on her tongue. It didn't sound the same as when he said it. She couldn't quite get the little breath of air after the T, but she liked it.

'And you are?' He stepped closer, his gaze intent. She caught a scent that made her think of mountains—of clear air and pine trees.

'I'm Imogen Holgate.'

'Imogen.' He nodded. 'A pretty name. It suits you.'

Pretty? She hadn't been called that in ages. The last person to do so had been her mum, trying to persuade her into bright colours, saying she hid behind the dark suits she wore for work.

'And now, Imogen, would you like some champagne?' He lifted a glass.

'I can get my own.' She turned to look for a waiter.

'But I brought it especially for you.' She looked down and realised he was holding two glasses, not one. This stranger had singled her out in a room of elegant women and brought her champagne? For a moment she just stared. It was so different from her world, where she paid her way and never had to field compliments from men about anything other than her work.

He raised the other glass, giving her a choice of either. His eyes turned serious. 'Whichever you prefer.'

Her cheeks flushed. He thought she was stalling because she didn't trust him. In case he'd slipped something into one of the glasses.

It was the sort of thing that would have occurred

to her once, for in her real life she was always cautious. But right now she was struggling to absorb the fact she was with the most charming, attractive man she'd ever met. The fact that he offered both reassured her.

She took a glass, meeting his eyes, ignoring the tingly sensation where their fingers brushed. 'Is it champagne from the Champagne region?'

'Of course. That's the only wine that can use the name. You like champagne?'

'I've never tried it.'

He blinked, astonishment on his face. *'Vraiment?'*

'Really.' Imogen smiled at his shock. 'I'm from Australia.'

'No, no.' He shook his head. 'I happen to know the Australians import French wine as well as exporting theirs. Champagne travels the world.'

She shrugged, enjoying his disbelief. 'That doesn't mean I've drunk it.' She eyed the wine with excitement. What better place to taste her first champagne than Paris?

'In that case, the occasion deserves a toast. To new friends.' His smile transformed his face from fascinating to magnetic. Imogen inhaled sharply, her lungs pushing at her ribcage. Her fingers tightened on the glass. That smile, this man, made her feel acutely aware of herself as a woman with desires she'd all but forgotten.

Stop it! You've seen men smile before.

Not like this. This was like standing in a shaft of sunshine. And it was an amazing antidote to the chill weight of despair. How could she dwell on despair when he looked at her that way?

She lifted her glass. 'And to new experiences.'

She sipped, feeling the effervescence on the roof of her mouth. 'I like that it's not too sweet. I can taste…pears, is it?'

He drank too, and she was riveted by the sight of his strong throat and the ripple of movement as he swallowed.

Imogen frowned. There was nothing sexy about a man's throat. Was there? There never had been before and she worked surrounded by men.

But none of them were Thierry Girard.

'You're right. Definitely pears.' He watched her over the rim of the glass. 'To new experiences? You have some planned?'

Imogen shrugged. 'A few.'

'Tell me.' When she hesitated he added, 'Please. I'd like to know.'

'Why?' The word shot out, and she caught her bottom lip between her teeth. Typical of her to sound gauche rather than sophisticated. She just wasn't used to male attention. She was the serious, reserved sister, not the gregarious one with a flock of admirers.

'Because I'm interested in you.'

'Seriously?' As soon as the word escaped heat scalded her throat and face. She squeezed her eyes shut. 'Tell me I didn't say that.'

A rich chuckle snagged at her senses, making her eyes pop open. If his smile was gorgeous, his laugh was... She couldn't think of a word to describe the molten-chocolate swirl enveloping her.

'Why don't you tell me about these new experiences instead?'

Imogen opened her mouth to ask if he was really interested in hearing about them then snapped it shut.

Here was a wonderful new adventure, flirting with a gorgeous French hunk over champagne. She wasn't going to spoil it by being herself. She was going to go with the flow. This trip was about stepping out of her shell, tasting life's excitement.

Chatting with Thierry Girard was the most exciting thing that had happened to her in ages.

'I've got a list. Things I want to do.'

'In Paris?' She loved the way his eyes crinkled at the corner when he smiled.

'Not just here. I'm away from home for a month and a half but I'm only in Paris a fortnight.' She shook her head. 'I'm already realising my plans were too ambitious. I won't fit everything in.'

'That gives you a reason to return. You can do more on your next visit.'

His eyes were almost warm enough to dispel the wintry chill that descended at his words. There'd be no return visit, no second chance.

She had one shot at living to the max. She'd make the most of it, even if it meant stepping out of her comfort zone. She tossed back another mouthful of champagne, relishing the little starbursts on her tongue.

'This is delicious wine.'

He nodded. 'It's not bad. Now, tell me about this list. I'm intrigued.'

She shrugged. 'Tourist things, mainly.' But she refused to feel self-conscious. 'See those Impressionist masterpieces at the Musée d'Orsay, visit Versailles, go for a boat ride on the Seine.'

'You'll have time to fit those in if you have two weeks.'

She shook her head. 'That's only the beginning.

I want to attend a gourmet cooking class. I've always wanted to know how they make those melt-in-the-mouth chocolate truffles.' The ones that were exactly the colour of his eyes.

Her breath gave a curious little hitch and she hurried on. 'I'd hoped to eat at the Eiffel Tower restaurant but I didn't realise I needed to book in advance. Plus I'd love a champagne picnic in the country and to go hot-air ballooning and drive a red convertible around the Arc de Triomphe and... Well, so many things.'

His eyebrows rose. 'Visitors are usually scared of driving there. Traffic is thick and there aren't lane markings.'

Imogen shrugged. She was scared too. But that was good. She'd feel she was really *living*.

'I like a challenge.'

'So I gather.' Was that approval in his expression? 'Have you been hot-air ballooning before?'

'Never.' She took another sip of champagne. 'This is a trip of firsts.'

'Like the champagne?' There was that delicious crinkle around his eyes. It almost lured her into believing Thierry Girard was as harmless as her work colleagues. Yet every feminine fibre screamed she was out of her depth even looking at the ultra-sexy Frenchman. Everything about him, from the breadth of his shoulders to the intriguing dark shadow across his jaw, signalled he was a virile, powerful man. 'Imogen?'

'Sorry, I was distracted.' Her voice was ridiculously husky. The way he said her name turned it into something lilting and special. She lifted her gloved fingers to her throat, as if that could ease her hammering pulse.

The glint in his eyes warned that he understood her distraction. But she refused to be embarrassed. He must be used to women going weak at the knees.

'Tell me about yourself,' she said. 'Do you live in Paris?'

He shook his head. 'Occasionally. I'm here for business meetings over the next week or two.'

'So while I'm out enjoying myself you'll be in meetings? I hope they're not too tedious.'

Nonchalantly, he lifted those impressive shoulders, and a wave of yearning washed through her. She wanted to put her hands on them, feel the strength in his tall body and lean in to see if he tasted as good as he smelled.

Imogen blinked, stunned at the force of her desire. She didn't *do* instant attraction. She didn't fall in a heap in front of any man. But her knees were suspiciously shaky and her instincts urged her to behave in ways that were completely out of character.

Was it champagne or the man? Or maybe the heady excitement of Paris and wearing Isabelle's gorgeous gown. Whatever it was, she approved. She wanted to *feel*, and from the moment her eyes had locked on Thierry's she'd felt vibrantly alive.

'You sound like you have experience of boring meetings.'

Imogen sipped more wine, enjoying the zing on her palate. 'Definitely.' She rolled her eyes. 'Our firm specialises in them. I'd bet my meetings are more boring than yours.'

'I find that hard to believe.'

Thierry took her arm and guided her away from an influx of newcomers. Even through the satin gloves his hands felt hard, capable and incredibly sexy. Trickles of fire coursed from the point of contact then splintered into incendiary darts that trailed through her body to pool down low.

How sad that she could be so turned on by that simple courteous gesture. But that wasn't surprising, given the state of her love life. Or her lack of one.

'Believe it.' She dragged herself back into the

conversation. 'I'm an accountant.' She waited for his eyes to glaze over. 'A tax accountant. I know tedious.'

His lips twitched but he didn't look in the least fazed. If anything there was a spark in his gaze as it swept her from head to toe. Did it linger here and there on the way? Imogen's stomach tightened and her breasts swelled against the satin bodice as she drew a sharp breath. Strange how the lace of her strapless bra suddenly scratched at her nipples when it had been perfectly comfortable before.

'You're not acquainted with French property and commercial law, are you? The phrase "red tape" was invented to describe them. And the meetings…' He shook his head.

'You're a lawyer?' He didn't look like any lawyer she'd seen, except in some high-budget courtroom film with a smoulderingly gorgeous hero.

Thierry laughed, that rich-as-chocolate sound doing strange things to her insides. 'Me, a lawyer? That would be a match made in hell. It's bad enough being a client. My first meeting tomorrow will go all morning. I'd much rather be out of the city.'

'Really? You look like right at home here.' Her gaze skated over his hard body in that made-to-measure dinner jacket. When she lifted her eyes she found him watching her, his quirk of a smile disarming.

'This?' One casual hand gestured to his impeccable tailoring. 'This is camouflage.'

'You're saying you don't belong?' Her pulse raced at the idea of finding another outsider. For, try as she might, she couldn't feel at home in this sophisticated crowd, despite her sister's clothes.

He shrugged, and Imogen watched those wide, straight shoulders with something like hunger. She'd never felt *needy* for a man. Not even Scott. Was it this man or the unfamiliar setting that pulled her off-balance?

'I've been forced to adapt. Business means I need to be in the city. But I prefer being outdoors. There's nothing like pitting yourself against nature. It beats meetings hands-down.'

That explained those eyes. Not just the creases from sun exposure, but his deceptively lazy regard that seemed at the same time sharp and perceptive. As if from surveying distant views?

'Each hour behind a desk is pure torture.'

'You poor thing.' Impulsively, she placed her hand on his arm, then regretted it as she felt the tense and flex of sinew and impressive muscle. There it was

again, that little jolt, like an electric shock. Imogen
jerked her hand back, frowning, and looked at her
glass. Surely she hadn't drunk enough to imagine
it? Just enough to make her do something out of
character, like touch a stranger.

Yet she couldn't regret it. That fierce flick of heat
made her feel more alive than…

'You'd like another?' Thierry gave their glasses
to a waiter and snagged two more.

She took the glass he offered, carefully avoiding
contact with his tanned fingers.

'To red convertibles and champagne picnics and
balloon rides.' His eyes snared hers and her heart
thumped. When he looked at her, the way she imagined men looked at truly beautiful women, she almost forgot what had brought her to Paris. She
could lose herself in the moment.

Imogen raised her glass. 'And to meetings that
end quickly.'

'I'll drink to that.' Thierry touched his glass to
hers, watching her sip her wine. She took time to
taste it. Her lips, a glossy bow, pouted delectably.
Her dark eyelashes quivered, and he knew she was
cataloguing the prickle of bubbles on the roof of
her mouth. She gave a delicate shiver of appreciation, and he found himself leaning closer.

She was so avid. So tactile. Touching her through those long gloves had made his hand tingle! From anticipation and excitement, something he usually experienced while risking his neck outdoors.

Imogen Holgate was an intriguing mix of sensuality and guilelessness.

And he wanted her.

'I can help with the ballooning.'

'Really?' Her eyes widened and he saw flecks of velvety green within the warm sherry-brown of her irises. It must be a trick of the light but her gaze seemed to glow brighter. 'That would be marvellous.'

She took a half step closer, and his breathing hitched. He inhaled the scent of vanilla sugar and warm female flesh. His taste buds tingled and his gaze dropped to her lips, then to the faint, fast pulse at her creamy throat.

He wanted to taste her, right here, now, and discover if she was as delicious as he expected. He wanted to sweep her to some place where he could learn her secrets.

Hazel eyes and vanilla sugar as an aphrodisiac?

His tastes had changed. She was completely different from Sandrine and all the women since her. Yet sexual hunger honed his senses to a keen edge.

He searched out the nearest exit, the part of his brain that was pure hunter planning how to cut her from the crowd when the time was ripe.

'I'd appreciate it if you could.' Her words interrupted his thoughts, or maybe it was that excited smile making her face glow. 'I should have researched it earlier but this trip was on the spur of the moment. Can you recommend a company I could contact?'

It took longer than it should have to remember what they were talking about. 'Better than that. A friend runs a balloon company outside Paris. We used to make balloon treks together.'

'Really?' Her eyes widened and there again was that trick of the light, for they seemed almost pure green now. How would they look when ecstasy took her? The tension in his lower body ratcheted up too many notches for comfort. 'You've been ballooning? Tell me all about it. Please?'

She clutched his arm and that shimmer of sensation rippled up it.

Over the next twenty minutes she peppered him with questions. Not the usual *What's it like up there?* and *Aren't you afraid of falling?* but everything from safety procedures to the amount of fuel required, from measuring height to landing procedure. All the while her expression kept shifting. He didn't know whether he preferred her serious, poutingly curious or dreamy-eyed excited.

She was enchanting. Refreshingly straightforward, yet complex and intriguing. And passionate.

He watched her lips as she spoke and desire exploded.

How long since he'd felt like this?

How long since he'd met a woman fascinated by him and his interest in adventure rather than money, social status or his reputation as a lover?

Plus she was passing through. She'd have no aspirations to tie him down.

Imogen was the perfect short-term diversion.

CHAPTER TWO

THE LIGHTS DIMMED and at the far end of the room a band struck up. The swell of the bass was incongruous in this ornate setting, but no one seemed surprised, even when beams of purple, blue and white light shot across the crowd.

A spotlight caught Imogen's eyes and she flinched, moving closer to Thierry. Instantly, his arm curved protectively around her. She liked that too much, but she had no desire to pull away. Not when every nerve screamed at her to lean into him.

His arm was hard and reassuring as the band's volume rose to a pounding beat. Imogen relished the unfamiliar thrill of being close to all that imposing masculinity. For, despite his perfectly tailored suit, there was no disguising that Thierry was all hard-muscled man.

His hands were a giveaway too. Neat, clean nails, but there were tiny, pale scars across his tanned skin, hinting he did more than wield a pen.

Imogen wondered how they'd feel on her bare flesh.

He said something she didn't hear over a crescendo of music. At the same time the light show became more frenetic, a staccato pulse in time with the drums. Imogen felt it all swirl and coalesce like a living thing. Light stabbed her eyes.

Not now. Please not now!

Just a little more time. Was that too much to ask?

Her stomach cramped and her breathing jammed. She blinked. It wasn't the light from the stage blinding her, it was the white-hot knife jabbing inside her skull. Her vision blurred, pain sawing through her.

'Imogen?' That arm at her back tightened. She caught a drift of something in her nostrils, some essence that reminded her of the outdoors, before the metallic taste of pain obliterated everything. Sheer willpower kept her on her feet, knees desperately locked.

'I...' It came out as a whisper. She tried again. 'I'd like to leave.'

'Of course.' He took the glass from her unresisting hand. 'This way.' He turned her towards the exit but she stumbled, her legs not obeying.

Music shuddered through her, a screaming beat, and in her head the jab, jab, jab of that unseen knife.

Warmth engulfed her and it took a moment to realise it was from Thierry's powerful body as he wrapped his arm around her waist and half carried her from the room.

Imagine what he could do with two arms.

And those hands. You've always had a thing for great hands.

That was her last coherent thought till they were in the peace of an anteroom. She couldn't recall exactly how he'd got her there but the lean strength of his body made her feel anchored and safe, despite the lancing pain.

'Imogen? What is it? Talk to me.' His accent was more pronounced, slurring the words sexily. Even in her dazed state she heard his concern.

'Headache. Sorry.' She tilted her head up, trying to bring him into focus through slitted yes.

'A migraine?' Gently, he pulled her to him, resting her head on his shoulder and palming her hair in a rhythmic touch that amazingly seemed to make the pain recede a little.

She wanted never to move, just sink into his calm strength. The realisation she'd never be held like this again by anyone brought a sob rushing to her throat. She stifled it. Pity wouldn't help.

'Sorry.' She sucked air through clenched teeth as

she straightened. 'Enjoy the rest of the party. It's been—'

'Where are you staying?' His voice was low, soothing.

'Here. Three-hundred and five.' She fumbled in her purse, dragging out her key card. All she had to do was get to her room.

Had he read her befuddled mind? One minute she stood on trembling legs, the next she was swept up in his embrace. She felt bone and muscle, the tickle of his breath on her face. She should have objected. Breathing through excruciating pain, she merely slumped against him, grateful that for once she didn't have to manage alone.

This past year she'd had to be strong, for her mother and more recently for herself. Leaning against Thierry, feeling the steady thud of his heart beneath his jacket, she felt a little of the tightness racking her body ease. Was it her imagination or did the pain pull back a fraction? She shut her eyes, focusing on his iron-hard arms beneath her, the comfort of his embrace.

Another first. Being swept off your feet by a man.

Warm fingers touched hers as he shifted his hold and took the card from her hand.

'Here we are.' His deep voice wrapped around

her. 'Not long now.' A door snicked closed and soon she was lowered onto a mattress. Smoothly, without hesitation, his hands withdrew and Imogen knew a moment's craziness when she had to bite back a plea that he not let her go. There'd been such comfort in being held.

Her eyes shot open and she winced, even in the soft glow from a single bedside lamp. Thierry towered above her, concern lining his brow.

'What do you need? Painkillers? Water?'

Gingerly, she moved, the smallest of nods. 'Water, please.' While he got it she fumbled open her bedside drawer and took out her medication with a shaking hand.

'Let me.' He squatted, popped the tablet and handed it to her. Then he raised her head while she swallowed it and sipped the water, his touch sure but gentle. Stupidly, tears clung to her lashes. Tears for this stranger's tenderness. Tears for the extravagant fantasy she'd dared harbour, of ending the night in Thierry's arms, making love with this sexy, fascinating, gorgeous man.

Fantasy wasn't for her. Her reality was too stark for that. She'd have to make do with scraping whatever small pleasures she could from life before it was too late.

Defeated, she slumped against the pillow, forcing herself to meet his concerned gaze.

'You're very kind. Thank you, Thierry. I can manage from here.'

Kind be damned. He looked into drowning eyes shimmering green and golden-brown and his belly twisted. This woman had hooked him with her vibrancy, humour and enthusiasm, not to mention her flagrant sexiness. Even her slight hesitancy over his name appealed ridiculously. Her vulnerability was a punch to the gut, and not just because he'd aimed to spend the night with her.

'Shut your eyes and relax.'

'I will.'

As soon as you leave. The unspoken words hung between them and who could blame her? He was a virtual stranger. Except he felt curiously like he'd known her half his life or, more correctly, had waited that long to meet her.

A frisson of warning ripped through him but he ignored it. She was no threat. With her tear-spiked lashes and too-pale face, she was the picture of vulnerability. There were shadows beneath her eyes too that he hadn't seen before.

'What are you doing?' Her voice was husky,

doing dangerous things to his body. Thierry had to remind himself it was from pain, not arousal.

He put the house phone to his ear, dialling room service. 'Getting you peppermint tea. My *grand-mère* suffers from migraines and that helps.'

'That's kind but…' Her words petered out as he ordered the tea then replaced the phone.

'Just try it, okay? If it doesn't work you can leave it.' He straightened and stepped back, putting distance between them. 'I'll stay till it's delivered so you don't have to get up.'

She opened her mouth then shut it, surveying him with pain-clouded eyes. Again that stab to his gut. He frowned and turned towards the bathroom, speaking over his shoulder. 'You're safe with me, Imogen. I have no ulterior motives.' *Not now, at any rate.* 'Trust me. I was a Boy Scout, did I tell you?'

When he returned with a damp flannel, he caught the wry twist of her lips.

'I'm to trust you because you were a Boy Scout?' Her voice was pain-roughened but there was that note of almost-laughter he'd found so attractive earlier.

'Of course. Ready to serve and always prepared.' He brushed back a few escaped locks of hair and placed the flannel on her forehead.

She sighed, and he made himself retreat rather than trace that glossy, silk-soft hair again. He pulled up a chair and sat a couple of metres from the bed.

Shimmering, half-lidded eyes met his. 'Are all Frenchmen so take-charge?'

'Are all Australian women so obstinate?'

A tiny smile curved her lips, and she shut her eyes. Ridiculously that smile felt like a victory.

The musical chimes of a mobile phone grew louder, drawing the attention of other café patrons. It was only then that Imogen realised it was her phone chirping away in her bag. In a fit of out-with-the-old-Imogen energy, she'd decided the old, plain ring tone was boring, swapping it for a bright pop tune.

'Hello?'

'Imogen?' His voice was smooth and warm, deep enough to make her shiver.

'Thierry?' The word was a croak of surprise. She'd berated herself all morning for wishing last night hadn't ended the way it had.

The fact Thierry had stayed so long only showed how dreadful she must have looked. And that he was what her mum would have called 'a true gentleman'.

'How are you today? Are you feeling better?'

'Good, thank you. I'm fit as a fiddle.' An exaggeration—those headaches always left her wrung out. But she was perking up by the moment. 'How are you?'

There was a crack of laughter, and Imogen's hand tightened on the phone. Even from a distance his laugh melted something inside. She sank back in her chair, noticing for the first time a blue patch of sky through the grey cloud.

'All the better for hearing your voice.'

She blinked, registering his deep, seductive tone. Her blood pumped faster and she tried to tell herself she imagined it. Nothing, she knew, put men off as much as illness. Even illness by proxy. For a moment Scott's face swam in her vision till she banished it.

'How did you get my number?'

There was a moment's silence. 'Your mobile was on the bedside table last night.'

'You took the number down?'

'You're annoyed?'

Annoyed? 'No. Not at all.' Surprised. Delighted. *Excited!* A little buzz of pleasure zoomed through her.

As she watched, the blue patch of sky grew and a beam of sunlight glanced down on the wet cobblestones, making them gleam. The café door opened behind her and the delicious aroma of fresh coffee drifted out.

'What's on your agenda this evening? Night-time bungee jumping? Motorcycle lessons? Or maybe that ghost tour?'

She smiled, enjoying his teasing. 'I'm still deciding between a couple of options.' Like a long bubble bath, painting her nails scarlet or gathering her courage and finding the dance venue Saskia had mentioned.

'How would you like dinner at the Eiffel Tower? There's an unexpected vacancy.'

'There is?' She sat up. 'But I couldn't get a reservation when I tried.'

'There's one for you now if you want it.'

'Of course I want it!' She squashed a howl of disappointment at the idea of dining in such a romantic setting alone. But she was a pragmatist. She'd learned to face hard truths. Thierry felt sorry for her after last night and had arranged this treat. 'It was kind of you to do that, Thierry. Thank you.'

'Excellent. I'll collect you at eight.'

'Eight?' She blinked, dazed. He was collecting her? He was taking her to dinner?

'Yes. See you then.'

He ended the call, and Imogen stared at the phone. Thierry Girard, the most drool-worthy, fascinating, charming man she'd ever met, was taking her to dinner? She didn't know whether to be stunned or nervous.

She settled for thrilled.

Imogen felt like she floated on air as they drove back to her hotel. The evening had been perfect. The food, the wine, the company, the weight of Thierry's gaze on her like a touch.

When he surveyed the dress of green and bronze her sister Izzy had created, his eyes lingered appreciatively. But when his attention roved again and again to Imogen's bare throat and shoulders, and especially her lips, heat coiled inside, like a clock wound too tight.

It made her laughter at his outrageous stories die, replaced by a hunger that no food could remedy. Was it possible to explode with sheer longing for a man's touch?

Did she have the nerve to follow through? Casual sex wasn't in her repertoire. Yet there was nothing casual about how Thierry made her feel.

The question was, what did he feel? Was tonight a random kindness to a stranger or something else?

Imogen wished she knew. She had absolutely no experience of high-octane, sophisticated men like Thierry Girard.

He stopped the car before her hotel and she turned towards him, only to find he was already out the door, striding around the car. A moment later her door swung open and he was helping her out.

Now. Ask him now before he says goodnight.

But her throat jammed as he hooked her hand over his arm and led her into the grand hotel—her big splurge on this end-of-a-lifetime trip. His heat, his scent, fresh as the outdoors, and the feel of his body against hers, made her light-headed. He led her through the luxurious foyer, past staff who stopped to greet them, to the bank of lifts.

'I—' Her words died as he stepped into the lift with her and hit the button for her floor.

So, he was seeing her to her room. She shot him a sideways look, discovering that in profile his features were taut, as if his earlier good humour had faded.

Abruptly, her anticipation drained away.

Had she misread him? Perhaps he didn't feel that hum of sexual arousal, that edge-of-seat excitement. Maybe he'd used up all his charm entertaining the unsophisticated tourist over dinner. She'd known last night she was out of place at that glamorous party, despite the wonderful dress she wore. Maybe after hours in her company he'd realised it too. Did he regret asking her out?

'You...?' Eyes of ebony locked with hers, and she sagged in Izzy's green stilettos.

Izzy would have known what to say. How to entertain and attract him and, above all, follow through. Imogen's only intimate experience had been with Scott, cautious Scott, who never acted on impulse, never broke rules or took a chance. He'd never made her feel the way Thierry did.

But, cataloguing the tension in her companion's shoulders and the pronounced angle of his strong jaw, she realised her mistake. Thierry's was a casual charm. Of course he didn't want more from her. He was French. He was being polite. And those heavy-lidded looks that stopped her breath? They probably came naturally to him and didn't mean anything.

'It's kind of you to see me to my room.'

The doors slid open, and he ushered her down the hall to her room, her arm clamped to his side.

Probably afraid you'll collapse like you did last night.

'That's the second time you've accused me of

being kind.' His voice sounded tight, but she didn't look at him, delving instead into her purse for her key card.

'You've been wonderful, and I appreciate it. I—' She frowned as he took the card and opened the door.

Did he have to be so eager to say goodnight?

But, instead of saying goodbye, Thierry stepped over the threshold, drawing her in. The door closed behind them and, stunned, Imogen turned. His tanned features looked chiselled, uncompromising, and those liquid, dark eyes…

'I'm not good at "kind".' He stroked a finger down her cheek in a barely there touch that rocketed to the centre of her being. 'In fact, I excel at doing exactly what pleases me most.' His head dipped, and Imogen's breath stalled as his breath caressed her lips. 'And what pleases me most is to be with you, Imogen.'

Imogen swallowed hard. It was what she wanted, what she'd steeled herself to ask. Yet part of her, the cautious, reserved part that had kept her safe for twenty-five years, froze her tongue.

Safe? There was no safe, not any more. Not when she could count the future in months, not decades.

'Or am I wrong?' His hand dropped, and still

she felt his touch like a sense memory. 'Do you not want…?'

'Yes!' Her purse tumbled to the floor as her hand shot out. She clutched his fingers, threading hers through them. The flash of heat from the contact point was like an electric charge. 'I want.'

How badly she wanted. Need was a shimmering wave, engulfing her.

He didn't smile. If anything his features grew harder, flesh pulling taut across those magnificent bones. His fingers tightened around hers.

'I can offer you short-term pleasure, Imogen. That's all.' His eyes narrowed as if he tried to read her thoughts. 'If that's not what you want—'

Her finger on his mouth stopped his words and sent another ripple of sensual awareness through her. Despite his honed, masculine features his lips were surprisingly soft. She felt light-headed just thinking about them on her mouth.

'That sounds perfect.' She drew a breath shaky with grim amusement. 'I'm not in the market for long term.'

The words were barely out when his head swooped and his mouth met hers. Firmly, implacably, no teasing, just the sure, sensual demand of a man who knew what he wanted and, Imogen realised as her lips parted, who knew how to please a woman. The swipe of his tongue, the angle of his mouth, the possessive clasp of his hand around her skull were so *right*; she wondered how she'd gone her whole life without experiencing anything like it.

Whatever she and Scott had shared, it was nothing like this.

Thierry circled an arm around her, pulling her against his hard frame. Everywhere they touched, from her breasts to her thighs, exploded into tingling awareness, as if she'd brushed a live wire. Darts of fire shot to her nipples, her pelvis, even up the back of her neck as he massaged her scalp, and she heard herself moan into his mouth.

He tasted better than chocolate, rich, strong and addictive. She slid her arms around his neck and hung on tight as her knees gave way.

Instantly, the arm at her back tightened. He swung her off the ground, high in his arms, making her feel precious and feminine against his imposing masculinity. His mouth devoured hers, seeking, demanding, yet giving so much pleasure that exultation filled her.

This was a kiss. *This* was desire.

She was greedy for him, hungry for the passion he'd stoked so easily. She pushed her fingers through his hair, its soft thickness enticing.

'More,' she mumbled against his lips.

For answer she felt movement. Then she was on the bed and he over her, his weight pressing her down, his long legs imprisoning hers. She'd never felt anything as erotic as his hard length pinioning her, his breath hot on her neck as he grazed her with his teeth, making her jolt and squirm.

'Thierry!' That scraping little nip at the spot where her neck met her shoulders had her shuddering as great looping waves of delight coursed through her. They swamped her body, arrowing in to concentrate at the sensitive point between her legs.

He shifted his weight, settling low in the cradle of her hips, and she throbbed deep inside.

Urgently, Imogen arched, feeling the strong column of his arousal between her legs, and her brain shorted. She slid her hand down, wrapping around the solid weight of him, needing that contact. Desperate for more.

His breath hissed as he lifted his head. One large hand covered hers, holding her palm against him for a moment then dragging it away.

'Patience, Imogen.' She barely comprehended.

His accent was so thick and her ears so full of her pulse pounding like the thud of a hammer on metal.

'Yes, now.' Was that reedy, desperate voice hers?

His eyes looked smoky, on the edge of focus, as he forced her arm wide, imprisoning her hand. When she shifted and brought her other hand down to touch him he pulled that arm wide too, so she lay spread-eagled.

The action pressed his groin against her pelvis, and her eyelids fluttered. Circling her hips, she moved against him, and to her amazement almost tipped over the edge into ecstasy. How could pleasure be so intense? So instantaneous? With Scott…

Thought died as Thierry murmured something in that lush, deep voice and lowered his head again. His breath feathered the sensitive flesh of her neck and then warm lips pressed just there and… Oh, yes, just there.

Again that powerful pulse through her pelvis, making every muscle clench and every erogenous zone shiver in anticipation.

'No. Don't!' It was a gurgle of sound, a hoarse whisper scraped from the back of her throat, but he heard it. Stilled.

She felt him draw a deep breath, his chest expanding. His hands tightened as if in spasm before loosing their hold. Then he pulled back, lifting his head.

Gone was the urbane sophisticate. Gone was the man in control. The glittering eyes that met hers held an unfamiliar wildness. His lips were a twist of what looked like raw pain.

Imogen watched him open his mouth. He shut his eyes and swallowed. Fascinated, she followed the jerky movement of his throat. Then blazing, dark eyes met hers again. 'You've changed your mind?' Even his voice was unfamiliar.

'Of course not.' How could he even think it? 'But I can't wait. I need you *now*.' Already she was running her hands over him, revelling in the heat of ridged muscle beneath his fine shirt. One hand dipped to his belt buckle and her fingers fumbled in their haste.

Thierry's eyes widened, his body rigid, as if he couldn't trust her words. Hadn't he ever met a woman so eager for him? Impossible!

What was impossible was that she, Imogen Holgate, was so desperate she didn't think she'd survive another minute of his seduction.

He was going to kiss and caress her, taking his time, and she'd self-combust at any moment. She'd never known anything like this spike of arousal.

'Please, Thierry.' Finally, she got his buckle undone and slid the belt free with clumsy hands. 'You can seduce me later. Whatever you like. But I need you inside me now.'

Fire washed from her throat to her hairline. But she didn't care about embarrassment or appearing unsophisticated. *Desire* was too tame a word for this urgent, visceral need. Nothing mattered but being one with this man.

Imogen bit her lip as her fingers slipped on his zip. She tried again and heard his sharp inhale. Hard fingers closed around hers.

He wasn't going to stop her, was he? Not now. She almost sobbed with frustration, her whole body burning like a single, vibrant flame that would at any minute consume her.

'Let me, *ma chérie*.'

Thierry kept his eyes on her face as he shucked his shoes and grabbed one of the condoms he'd brought.

She was glorious, her skin flushed with sexual arousal. Her eyes were bright as stars, veiled by long black lashes. Her reddened lips were plump and inviting, but not as inviting as the rest of her. His movements quickened, sheathing himself as his gaze dropped to proud breasts straining against that tight bodice. A surge of hunger hit and he drew an uneven breath. Despite what she said he needed to rein himself in, not surrender to hunger and take her with no preliminaries. He needed to…

Thierry's thoughts spun away as she reefed up the hem of her dress. Long, pale, toned thighs. Skimpy, emerald-green lace panties. The subtle, enticing scent of vanilla sugar and feminine arousal.

Slender fingers hooked the green lace and she arched her hips up, wriggling, to pull it away.

His hands tangled with hers, stripping the lace off. Then his hands were on her, skimming satin-soft flesh, stroking the dark silk, already damp, at her core.

He didn't register moving closer. But an instant later he was there, pressing against her softness, his hands planted beside her on the bed. Her skirt was up around her waist and her hair had come down on one side, dark tresses curling to her breasts.

A shudder ripped through him. He wanted to feast on her, take his time to build their pleasure, but he couldn't.

It wasn't the tug of her fingers digging into his shoulders that shattered his control, or the tiny, throaty purring sound she made. It was simply that he'd never wanted a woman so urgently.

His hand shook as he lifted her to him. Then in one sure, glorious stroke he surged home, high and hard, till he felt nothing but her, knew nothing but her liquid heat, sweet scent and indescribable pleasure.

Tawny green eyes snared his. Her head pressed back, baring that delectable throat. He heard his name in a throaty, broken gasp. It was the sexiest thing he'd ever heard, and to his amazement was all it took for him to lose the last of his control.

She quivered, jerking and shaking around him, drawing him into the most mind-blowing climax he'd ever experienced.

It was a long, long time before his brain functioned again. Imogen shifted drowsily, and he found himself quickening into arousal again. His immediate thought was to wonder if he'd brought enough condoms.

His second, when her eyes fluttered open and her tentative smile hit him square in the chest, was to congratulate himself on finding her. He'd never known a woman so unstinting in her passion.

Two weeks would barely be enough to enjoy all

she had to offer. Yet that was all they had. She'd be gone in a fortnight.

Thierry felt a flicker of something almost like regret. But it would dissipate. A temporary lover was all he wanted. A couple of months and he'd be free of the shackles that had tied him down for four years. Then he'd leave, ready for adventure and the physical and mental challenges he missed. Which was why Imogen, who could only ever be temporary in his life, was absolutely perfect.

CHAPTER THREE

IMOGEN STARED FROM her hotel window at the London square with its communal garden and neat Georgian buildings. A couple strolled by hand in hand and her stomach did a little somersault. She looked away, lifting her peppermint tea to her lips.

She'd developed a taste for herbal tea since that night in Paris when Thierry had ordered it for her.

Turning, she found her gaze following the couple and felt a pang of regret. They were in their seventies, she'd guess, yet they held hands, heads turned towards each other as if in conversation.

What would it be like to grow old with the man you loved? The question wormed into her brain and she had to slam down a protective portcullis before her thoughts went too far.

Thierry Girard had been a revelation. Any woman would have been in heaven experiencing Paris with him, even if she hadn't spent years buried in a half-life of tedium, hemmed in by caution. Was it any wonder Venice, Reykjavik and London hadn't seemed quite as fabulous as Paris? He'd brought the city alive.

He'd brought *her* alive.

But she couldn't give in to romantic fantasy.

What they'd had had been wonderful and she'd lingered over each memory, loving the hazy sense of wellbeing they brought. But their passion, the romance and sense of connection had been illusory, the product of an affair that could only be short-lived.

She sipped her tea then grimaced as her taste buds did that strange thing again, turning a flavour she enjoyed into a dull, metallic tang. She put the cup down then realised she'd turned too fast, for the nausea rose again. Imogen gripped the table, taking slow breaths.

Her mother hadn't had these symptoms. Did it mean Imogen's condition was different after all? If anything the headaches had eased a little and were less frequent. But the nausea worried her. It was so persistent.

Reluctantly, she turned towards the bathroom. It was silly to consider the possibility of it being anything else. There was no chance a woman in her condition…

She shook her head then regretted it as the movement stirred that sick feeling again.

Clamping her lips, she headed to the bathroom. Of course it was absurd. This must be a new symptom of her deteriorating condition. Though, with the exception of the nausea, she felt better than she had in ages.

What was the point of second-guessing? She needed to see the specialist back in Sydney. He'd explain what was happening. How long she had.

Imogen drew a slow breath, deliberately pushing her shoulders down as tension inched them higher. Whatever the future held, she'd meet it head on.

She crossed the bathroom and reached for the test kit she'd left there. She hadn't had the nerve to look at the result before, telling herself it was nonsense and she'd be better having tea and biscuits to settle her stomach.

Now, reluctantly, she looked down at the indicator.

The world wobbled and she grabbed the counter.

Had her illness affected her eyes? But the indicator was clear. It was only her brain that felt blurry.

Pregnant.

She was expecting Thierry's child.

It was harder, this time, to contact him. He had a new PA who seemed dauntingly efficient and not eager to help.

No, Monsieur Girard wasn't in Paris. No, she couldn't say where he was. Her tone implied Imogen had no right to renew his acquaintance. Had she been placed on some blacklist of importunate ex-lovers? Imogen imagined a throng of women trailing after him, trying to recapture his attention.

Was she to be so easily dismissed? Embarrassment and anger warred, and her grip tightened on the phone.

'When will he be back? It's urgent I speak with him.' She'd taken the first train from London to Paris, checking into a tiny hotel with the last of her travel money.

'Perhaps you'd like to leave a message, *mademoiselle*? He's very busy.' The cool tone implied he'd never find time for her again. Was that an overprotective assistant or a woman acting on orders?

Her crisp efficiency and Imogen's realisation she could only contact him via this dragon brought home the glaring differences between them. Thierry was powerful, mixing in elite social circles and living a privileged life. Employees protected him from unsolicited contact. She was working class and unsophisticated, more at home with a spreadsheet of numbers than at a glittering social event. Only the bright passion between them had made them equals.

Imogen set her chin.

'I need to speak with him in person. It's imperative.'

'As I said, I can take a message...'

But would it be delivered?

Imogen gritted her teeth, staring over the slate-grey roof of the building across the lane. It seemed close enough to touch in this cheap back street. A far cry from the magnificent hotel she'd splurged on during her first stay in Paris.

'Please tell him I need to see him. Five minutes will do.' She bit down grim laughter. How long did it take to break such news? 'I have...important information for him. Something he needs to hear as soon as possible.'

'Very well, *mademoiselle*.' The phone clicked in her ear.

'That's all now.' Thierry looked at his watch. 'Finish those in the morning.'

Mademoiselle Janvier primmed her mouth. 'I find it more efficient to complete my work before leaving and start fresh tomorrow.'

Thierry forbore from comment. His temporary

PA took efficiency to a new level. At least these notes would take no more than half an hour.

He should be grateful. When there'd been that recent glitch in his plans to take over a rival business, her hard work had been invaluable. She'd even tried to match his eighteen-hour work days till he'd put a stop to it. Dedication he appreciated, but sometimes she seemed almost *proprietorial*.

If only she'd smile occasionally.

His lips twitched. That was his unregenerate, unbusinesslike side. The side that preferred being outdoors on a clear evening like this, rather than cooped up with a sour-faced assistant.

That part of him would far rather share a champagne picnic with an intriguing dark-haired beauty whose enthusiasm, sensuality and unexpected flashes of naïveté intrigued.

That couldn't be regret he felt? There'd be excitement enough in his life once he cleared this final hurdle. He'd given up four years of his life and wrought a small miracle, wresting the family business from the brink of disaster. Soon...

He rolled his shoulders. Soon he could take up his real life again. The one that defined him, no matter how irresponsible his *grand-père* branded it. But his *grand-père* had never understood it was the rush of adrenalin, the thrill of pitting himself physically against the toughest challenges, that made him feel *real*. These past years he'd been condemned to a half life.

Adventure beckoned. What would it be first? Heli-skiing or hot-air ballooning? Or white-water rafting? Orsino had mentioned a place in Colorado…

'By the way, there's a woman waiting to see you.'

'A woman?' Thierry checked his diary. He had no appointments.

'A Mademoiselle Holgate.'

'Holgate?' Something inside his chest jerked hard. 'How long has she been waiting?'

His PA's eyes widened as he shot to his feet. 'I warned her she'd have to wait. You had a lot—'

'Invite her in. Immediately!'

Mademoiselle Janvier scurried out, shock on her thin features. It was the first time she'd seen him anything but polite and calm, even when it had looked like his expansion plans, so vital to the solidity of the company, had unravelled.

The door opened and his breathing quickened. He stepped around the desk, elation pulsing.

Elation? He halted, a prickle of warning skating through him.

He and Imogen had enjoyed themselves but Thierry wasn't in the habit of feeling more than casual pleasure at the thought of any woman. Not since Sandrine, a lifetime ago.

He'd learned his lesson then. Women added spice and pleasure, especially now his chance for serious adventure had been curtailed. But none lasted. He made sure of it. Women fitted into the category of rest and recreation.

Thierry frowned as a trim, dark-haired figure stepped into the room and an unfamiliar sensation clamped his belly.

He almost wouldn't have recognised her. Those glorious dark tresses were scraped into a bun that reminded him of Mademoiselle Janvier with her rigid self-control. Imogen wore jeans and a shirt that leached the colour from her face. He'd never seen her in anything but bright colours. And there were shadows under her eyes, hollows beneath her cheekbones.

Again that inexplicable thump to his chest, as if an unseen hand had punched him.

'Imogen!' He started forward but before he reached her she slipped into a visitor's chair.

Thierry pulled up abruptly. It wasn't the reaction he got from women. Ever.

'Thierry.' She nodded, the movement curt, almost dismissive. And her eyes—they didn't glow as he remembered. They looked...haunted as they stared at his tie. Yet there was defiance in the set of her chin. Belligerence in her clamped lips.

What had happened? He'd seen her ecstatic, curious, enthralled. He'd seen her in the throes of passion. His lower body tensed. Those memories had kept him from sleep too many nights since she'd left. He'd even seen her in pain, with tears spiking those ebony lashes. But he'd never seen her look like this.

He grabbed a chair, yanked it around to face her and sank onto it, his knees all but touching her thighs.

She shifted, pulling her legs away, as if he made her nervous. Or as if his touch contaminated.

Something jabbed his gut. Deliberately, he leaned back, gaze bland, his mind buzzing with questions.

'This is an unexpected pleasure.'

'Is it? That's not the impression I got.' Her chin lifted infinitesimally and colour swept her too-pale face. That was better. The woman he knew had sass and vibrancy.

'You've just walked in the door.' He gave her the smile he knew melted female hearts. Despite her tension it was good to see her. He'd missed her more than he'd expected and—

'I suppose I should be grateful you found time out of your busy schedule to see me.'

Imogen bit her lip. This wasn't going right. She'd let fear and anger get the best of her. Anger at how long it had taken to see him, only then to be kept waiting for an hour. And fear. Fear that even with his help, assuming he would help her, the new life growing inside her was likely in danger.

She threaded her fingers together, trying to hide their tremor.

It didn't help that one glance was all she'd needed to fall under Thierry's spell again. He looked wonderful. Strong and fit, so utterly masculine that just sitting beside him was a test of endurance. She wanted to touch him, feel that strong life-force, remind herself there was some hope in this bleak situation.

'I'm sorry you had to wait. I didn't know you were there.'

Imogen waved a dismissive hand, her gaze skating across the huge office with its expansive, and expensive, views over one of Paris's most prestigious neighbourhoods.

'It doesn't matter.' She drew a breath, trying to slow her racing heart, only to discover she'd inhaled his distinctive scent—warm male flesh and clear mountain air. It teased her nostrils and set up a trembling deep inside.

For one self-indulgent instant she let herself remember how glorious it had been between them. How perfect.

But that was over. He'd moved on and she, well, she had more important things to worry about than her attraction to a heartbreaker of a Frenchman.

'I thought you'd be in Australia now. Wasn't it Venice, Reykjavik, London and then home to Sydney?'

He remembered. A tiny curl of delight swirled inside. 'That was the plan.' Her voice emerged husky, not like the firm tone she'd aimed for. 'But things have changed.'

'I'm glad.' His voice caressed. 'I've been thinking of you.'

Surprised, she jerked her head up, their eyes meeting. Instantly, sultry heat unfurled in her belly like coiling tendrils. Her skin drew taut.

She didn't know how Thierry did that. She didn't know whether to be shocked, stoic or despairing that absence hadn't lessened his impact. Even with so much on her mind, that low voice, that slurred ripple of accented sound, made her body hum.

He leaned close, and she sat back, seeing the moment he registered her withdrawal. A frown puckered his brow.

'I came because I had some news.'

He stilled, and she sensed a watchfulness that belied his air of unconcern.

When they'd been together all that powerful energy had been focused on pleasure. Now, in this vast office that screamed authority, with those unblinking eyes trained on her, she saw how formidable Thierry was. Not just as the sexiest, most charismatic man she'd ever met, but because of the power he wielded with such ease.

She swallowed, her throat suddenly parched.

'News?' The word was sharp.

'Yes.' She swiped her top lip with her tongue and a flicker of something crossed his proud features. 'Yes, I...'

Spit it out! How hard is it to say? You've had a week of waiting to get used to it.

'You...?' He leaned forward, and she knew an urge to slide onto his lap and burrow close.

As if Thierry's embrace would make everything right! *Nothing* could make this right.

Again she licked her lips. 'I'm pregnant.'

For what seemed a full minute he said nothing, merely looked at her with a face frozen into harsh lines that emphasised the chiselled hauteur of those superb features.

'You say the baby is mine?'

Mistake number one, Thierry realised when Imogen snapped back in her seat as if yanked by a bungee cord.

Ice formed in her hazel eyes, turning them from warm and a little lost to frozen wasteland. Then there was the taut line of her mouth, the hurt in the way she bit her lip.

He hated it when she did that. He always wanted to reach out and stop her. And she…

Belatedly, he yanked back his thoughts. Pregnant. With his child?

His breath disintegrated and a sense of unreality engulfed him. Like the day, as a kid, when he'd learned his parents had died in a crash outside Lyon. Or four years ago, when his indomitable *grand-père* had had a stroke.

Was it possible?

Of course it was possible. He and Imogen had

spent every night for almost two weeks together, insatiable for each other.

He'd never known any woman to test his control the way Imogen had. He'd plan some outing to tick off her bucket list—a visit to a dance club, or a moonlight picnic—and all the time she was beaming at him, laughing and thrilled at the novelty of new experiences, he was calculating how long before he could get her naked and horizontal. Or just naked enough for sex. As for horizontal... the missionary position was overrated.

Molten heat coiled in his belly.

'There's been no one else. Just you.'

Stupid to feel that punch of pleasure. Thierry forced himself to focus. This was too important.

'Since when?'

'That's not relevant. I—'

'Since when, Imogen?' Stranger things had happened than a woman trying to pin an unexpected pregnancy on some gullible man.

Her chin rose and the expression in her eyes could have scored flesh. 'Seven months.'

So long between lovers? Did that make him special, or a convenient way of ending the drought? Or maybe a target?

'That's very precise.'

'I don't make a habit of sleeping around.'

He'd worked it out. He vividly recalled her charmingly unpractised loving, the shock in her eyes at the ecstasy they'd shared.

'Pregnant.' He paused, frustrated that his brain wouldn't function. Now it had side-tracked into imagining Imogen swollen with his child, her hands splayed over her ripe belly. He'd never lusted after a pregnant woman yet the image in his head filled him with all sorts of inappropriate thoughts.

Diable! He should be concentrating, not mentally undressing her.

He dragged his attention back to her face. 'We used condoms.'

Jerkily she nodded. 'It turns out they're not a hundred percent effective.'

'You're sure about this?' He searched her features. She looked different—drawn and tired. And…was that fear?

'I wouldn't be here if I weren't. I took the test in London. That's why I came to Paris, to find you.'

Thierry stared into those haunted eyes and told himself the sensible thing would be to insist on a paternity test. He had only her word the child was his.

Yet, crazy as it was, he was on the verge of believing her. He'd been with her just two weeks, but he felt he knew her better than any of the women he'd dated.

Even better than Sandrine.

The thought sideswiped him. He'd grown up with Sandrine and had loved her with all his youthful heart.

The memory served its purpose, like being doused in a cold mountain stream. He needed to think critically. He straightened.

'What sort of test was it? One from a pharmacy?'

She nodded. 'That's right.'

Thierry stood, relieved to have a purpose. He strode around the desk and reached for a phone. 'Then the first thing to do is get this confirmed by a doctor.'

The flare of relief in Imogen's eyes intrigued him. She didn't look like a woman trying to catch a man by getting pregnant.

She looked scared rigid.

'Well, that settles that.' Thierry's voice was as delicious as ever, the silky burr a ribbon of warmth threading Imogen's ice-cold body as they left the doctor's rooms.

She'd felt chilled and resentful all through the

consultation. Perhaps because Thierry had insisted he remain, as if he didn't trust her. Perhaps from embarrassment, because she couldn't shake the idea the doctor, for all his professionalism, was quietly judging her and sympathising with Thierry. He'd continually addressed Thierry rather than her. As if she didn't have the wit to comprehend her condition.

Or as if she was an inconvenient problem.

'What does it settle?'

Thierry didn't answer. She darted him a sideways stare and guessed he was brooding over his own thoughts. That wide brow was furrowed, his eyes focused on the glistening cobblestones as they walked.

Yet, distracted as he was, his hand was reassuring in the small of her back. It felt...protective.

Imogen was needy enough right now to appreciate that.

Since the realisation of her fatal condition, she'd felt separated from the world by a wall of glass. Only her brief time with Thierry had seemed *real*. But the news she was pregnant... She'd never felt so frighteningly alone in all her life. Being responsible for another life as she faced the end of her own—how was she going to manage it?

She stumbled, and Thierry's arm slid around her waist, holding her upright and safe. She stopped, her heart hammering high in her throat.

What if she'd fallen? Would such a simple tumble be enough to dislodge that tiny life? Surely not? Yet Imogen's palm crept to her abdomen as fear spiked.

Her baby. She'd never get to see it grow. Never have the opportunity to be a real mother to him or her. But she knew with a sudden fierce certainty that she'd do anything to protect it. Anything to ensure her baby had a good chance at life.

'Here. It's okay. We're at the car.' Thierry clicked open the lock and ushered her into the gleaming sports car that looked like something out of a glossy magazine and which she knew rode like a growling beast eager for the open road.

Suppressing a sigh of relief, she sank into the moulded leather and shut her eyes. The car dipped as he got in then he started it and swung out into the traffic.

Minutes later she opened her eyes and stared glassily at the congested traffic.

'Where are we going?'

'To your hotel. You look like you need rest, and we have to talk.'

Imogen frowned as she recognised a landmark. 'I'm not staying in the centre of the city this time.'

'Then where?'

She told him and his ebony eyebrows slashed down in a frown. 'What on earth are you doing there?'

She shrugged. 'I'd spent all my holiday money. I was due to go home, remember?' She didn't add that she'd been loath to dip into the last of her savings. She'd kept some in the bank in Australia, figuring she'd need something to cover her last months.

'Money didn't seem to be a problem before.'

Was that accusation in his voice? 'Believe it or not, I didn't stay in a five-star hotel to catch myself a rich man—'

'I didn't say that.' The wrinkle on his brow became a scowl and it hit her that Thierry wasn't used to having his intentions questioned.

'I told you before.' She struggled for an even tone, though she felt like shouting or maybe smashing something. It was hard enough to deal with the impossible hand fate had dealt her without coping with his doubt, however reasonable. Imogen dragged in a sharp breath and tried to ignore the twin scents of luxury leather and earthy male that filled her nostrils. 'The trip was a once in a lifetime experience. I splurged on things I'd never normally afford.' She laced her fingers together in her lap. 'Now it's back to reality.'

She pursed her lips to restrain the burst of hollow laughter that threatened. If she gave in to it she feared she'd never stop but hysteria wouldn't help.

They finished the rest of the trip in silence. It continued as he unlocked the door to an apartment in a prestigious old building looking out over the Seine. One glance at the spacious living room with its view of central Paris glittering in the twilight told her she'd stepped into another world. One where wealth was figured in numbers with far more zeroes than she'd ever see.

'Please, take a seat.'

Imogen settled onto a vibrant red lounger that toned with the slash of grey, red and yellow abstract art over the fireplace. A moment later Thierry passed her a tall glass. 'Sparkling water, but I can make tea or coffee if you prefer.'

'This is fine.' Gratefully, she sipped, watching as he strode to the bar in one corner, downed a shot of something then poured himself another before turning towards her.

'Are you all right?' As soon as the words escaped,

she firmed her lips. What a stupid thing to say. Of course he wasn't okay. She was still in shock and she'd had seven days to get used to her pregnancy.

Yet his eyebrows rose in surprise. Because he hadn't expected her to notice he wasn't utterly in control?

Looking at him now, at those broad shoulders that seemed capable of withstanding any weight, at the glinting dark eyes and firm jaw, she realised that, no matter how surprising her news, Thierry Girard was more than capable of handling it.

Exactly the sort of man she needed. For the first time today she felt herself begin to relax, just a little.

'You're absolutely sure it's mine?'

Imogen stiffened, her fingers gripping so hard the water in her glass threatened to slop over the side.

She met searing eyes that probed her very depths. 'For all I know there could have been a man in Venice, one in Reykjavik and one in London too.'

Imogen swallowed hard, tasting indignation. 'You think that was on my must-do list? A lover at every stop?' Despite the harshness she heard in her voice, she couldn't quite keep the wobble from it. Maybe if she was the sort of woman to fall into bed with a stranger so easily she wouldn't have expected so much from Thierry.

She gnawed her lip and dragged her gaze from his. Was she stupid, hoping he'd help? They'd had fun together but she'd been what—a diversion? An easy lay? Certainly something different from the women he was used to in his rarefied world of wealth and privilege.

With careful precision she put her glass on a nearby table and scooted to the edge of her seat, grabbing her bag from where she'd dropped it.

'Where are you going?'

Imogen blinked, sanity returning.

She didn't have the luxury of pride. This wasn't just about her. She had a baby to consider.

'Stop it.' He crossed the space between them in a couple of long strides, making her crane her neck to look up at him.

'What?' Even as she said it his thumb brushed her bottom lip, making her register the salt tang of blood in her mouth. And more, the heady taste of his skin. Imogen had to fight not to dart out her tongue for a better taste.

'Stop torturing that lovely mouth of yours.'

The unexpectedness of that made her blink and sit back. *Lovely mouth?*

'I don't...' She shook her head.

Abruptly he dropped his hand and nodded, and Imogen was horrified at her sense of loss. Surely she was stronger than this?

Her mouth trembled, and she grabbed her glass, taking a long draught of the sparkling water, telling herself the sting of it where her teeth had grazed her skin was a timely reminder that she needed focus.

She straightened her shoulders and looked at a point near his perfectly knotted tie.

'I'm happy to take a paternity test if you like.' She paused, letting that sink in. 'Then, when you believe me, I need your help.'

CHAPTER FOUR

HELP?

In the form of money, he assumed.

Thierry hadn't missed her wide-eyed appraisal of his apartment, the way her hand lingered on the plush fabric of the designer-original lounger and her eyes on the masterpiece of Modernism over the fireplace.

But, if she carried his child, why shouldn't she expect support?

He could afford it. He'd worked like the devil to turn around the family company, not just for his ageing grandparents and cousins, but for himself too. Duty had driven him, but he'd benefited. It had stunned him to discover the wealth he'd always taken for granted was in danger of slipping away while he travelled the world, following his own pursuits. Years of poor management as his grandfather's health deteriorated had taken its toll on the family fortune.

But it was safe now.

Unlike Imogen. The sudden thought disturbed him.

Pregnancy wasn't an illness. It was surely the most natural thing in the world. Yet the sight of her tension, the dark circles beneath her eyes and her pallor drew at something inside him, making him tense and restless.

He turned to stand by the windows. But it wasn't the lights of early evening that he saw. It was her wan reflection. Her shoulders hunched again and she seemed to crumple. Not at all like the vivacious Imogen he'd known.

'What sort of help do you want? To arrange an abortion?' Alone in a foreign country, she could well ask for that sort of assistance. Especially if, as she'd said, her money had run out.

Thierry knocked back a slug of cognac, surprised to discover its taste had unaccountably turned sour.

He scowled at the glass, slamming it down onto a nearby table. He still reeled from the idea of her being pregnant. He hadn't had time to begin imagining an actual child. Yet out of nowhere anger hit him. Anger that she could consider disposing of her baby. *His* baby, if his instincts were correct.

Her equanimity at the thought of a DNA test was convincing, as was his memory of her untutored loving. Imogen wasn't a woman who flitted from man to man, no matter how easily she'd fallen into his arms.

He spun around. 'Is that it? You want to get rid of the baby?'

It would solve his problems, remove any inconvenience. Yet his stomach twisted at the thought. He found himself looming over her, watching the convulsive movement of her pale throat.

'I suppose that would be a solution,' she whispered, looking down at her twisting hands. 'Maybe it's selfish to try...'

'Try what?' He hunkered before her, confused by his desire to take her in his arms even as he wanted to shake her for even considering destroying their baby.

Their baby! Was he really so easily convinced?

Perhaps he was. Adrenalin made his heart pound, just like it used to as he'd waited for the starter's signal at the beginning of a downhill race, his eyes fixed on the treacherous snowy slope before him.

He sensed, with a marrow-deep instinct he didn't even begin to fathom, that the child was his.

Imogen lifted her head and his pulse tripped. Her eyes, more green than brown, glistened over-bright and huge in her taut face.

'I'd hoped…' She shrugged. 'I want to give my baby a chance to *live*. Is that so wrong?'

'Of course not.' Her hands were cool and slight in his. He chafed them gently, telling himself relief was a natural response. 'So you want to keep the child.' He made it a statement.

'Yes. I do.' Her hands gripped his, and he was surprised at her strength. 'I want to keep it.'

'Good. That's one thing sorted.' He made his voice businesslike, as if dealing with unexpected pregnancies was no more difficult than the business challenges he handled daily.

Thierry disengaged his hands and stood. It was hard to think when Imogen clung to him, her eyes devouring him as if he were her last hope. That muddled his brain and he needed his wits.

He sank into a nearby armchair and surveyed her, wondering what it was about this woman that evoked such strong protective instincts in a man who'd spent his life avoiding any form of commitment. He'd perfected the art of being unencumbered until his *grand-père's* illness and the realisation he couldn't avoid the yoke of duty any longer.

'You want my help.'

'Yes. Please.' But instead of meeting his gaze she focused on sipping from the glass of water he'd given her. Suspicion feathered through him, an inkling she was trying to hide something.

'And what form would this assistance take?' Now would come the appeal for money. It was only natural.

She studied the glass in her hand, one finger stroking the condensation on the outside as if it fascinated her. 'I want your help if anything goes wrong.'

Thierry straightened, his hands gripping the plush arms of his chair. 'Wrong? What could go wrong?'

She shrugged, an uneven little movement. 'Things do.'

'Not often. Not with good medical care.' He frowned. Was she scared by pregnancy?

The idea confused him. Where was the woman who'd planned to skydive, climb a glacier and see volcanoes in Iceland? Who'd shown not one hint of fear as he'd taken her hot-air ballooning outside Paris?

Still she stared at the tall glass in her hands.

'Do you need money for health care? Is that it?' He'd assumed she was well-off, given where they'd met and where she'd stayed on her first visit to Paris. Now she seemed skint.

She shook her head. 'No. I should be all right once I'm back in Australia. There's comprehensive health care, plus I have some savings I haven't touched.'

Once she returned to Australia.

So, she didn't intend to stay here through her pregnancy. Thierry ignored the unfamiliar hollow sensation in his gut. It couldn't be disappointment. His lifestyle, and especially the lifestyle he was about to return to—never in one place longer than it took to conquer the next challenge—left no room for a baby. Besides, children were better off with their mothers; everyone said so. If he really wanted he could visit after it was born.

Yet discontent niggled.

And surprise. She didn't want to be with him. She didn't want his money. She only wanted his help if things went wrong.

Common sense told him he was getting out of this lightly. Most men would jump at the chance to divest themselves of such responsibilities.

But Thierry couldn't feel relief. He felt curiously deprived.

'What, exactly, do you want from me, Imogen?' At her name, she looked up, meeting his eyes squarely, and he felt a curious little thump in his chest, as if his heart had thudded too hard against his ribs.

Again that uneven little shrug. Her gaze swerved away, fixing on the view as if it fascinated her. 'I want to know you'll be there wh—if—something happens to me. I want to know you'll take care of him or her.'

She shifted in her seat, skewering him suddenly with a look he could only describe as desperate. Thierry felt the slow crawl of an icy finger up his nape, each individual hair on his neck and arms rising in response.

Not just desperation but fear. What was going on?

'I'm alone, you see. My mother and sister are dead. So if anything were to happen to me...' She swiped her bottom lip with her tongue. 'I know there are some wonderful foster parents out there, but I can't bear the thought of my baby being put into care.'

'It won't come to that. You and the child will be fine.' Thierry leaned towards her, willing her to think logically, despite the panic edging her husky voice.

He hated hearing her so desperate and fearful.

Then the full implication of her words sank in. 'You've got no one back in Australia? No family?'

'No. But I'm used to looking out for myself.' This time her jaw angled higher, as if daring him to feel sorry for her.

Thierry frowned. He might not be accustomed to taking responsibility for others—he might have spent years perfecting what *Grand-père* called his 'damned selfish bachelor lifestyle'—but the idea of Imogen, pregnant and alone, disturbed him. More than disturbed. It sent a shock wave tingling through him as if he'd touched an electric current.

'What about your father?' She'd said her mother and sister were dead but she hadn't mentioned him.

Her lips pulled taut in a grimace. 'I don't know where he is. He used to move around a lot, working in outback mines. And even if I did know how to contact him I wouldn't expect him to raise his grandchild. Not when he walked out on Mum the day he found out she was expecting twins.'

Diable! Thierry's hands closed into fists as he read the careful blankness on Imogen's face. It was the sort of blankness that hid pain, despite her matter-of-fact tone.

What sort of man deserted a woman pregnant with his children?

Then he remembered that moment of relief when he'd entertained the possibility this wasn't his baby.

Or that Imogen might get rid of it and make things easier for them both. A shudder of revulsion ripped through him at the idea he had anything in common with a man like her father, even if only for a split second.

'You needn't worry about that.' His voice sounded harsh and he saw a hint of surprise on her features. 'I won't run scared.'

It was one of the things he'd always prided himself on—his ability to face fear. In his youth he'd stared it down on neck-breaking black ski-runs while the hopes of a nation weighed down his shoulders. Later there'd been adventure sports and his treks into inhospitable territory with his friend Orsino Chatsfield. More recently he'd confronted the ultimate horror: a desk job, hemmed in by solid walls while he came to grips with the ailing Girard business interests.

'You'll take care of our child if I die?'

Thierry surged to his feet. 'You're not going to die.' Years ago he'd been first on the scene in a desert car rally after a crash. The other driver had died in his arms while they'd waited for an airlift and Thierry had never felt so helpless. He refused to countenance such talk from Imogen. 'You're going to have an uneventful pregnancy, a healthy baby and a long, happy life as a mother.'

And, most probably, as someone's wife.

The realisation sent a twang of discontent through his gut.

'You sound so sure.' This time the curve of her lovely mouth, though tiny, was a real smile.

'I am.'

'Thank you, Thierry.' She looked away, but not before he saw her blink back what looked like a glimmer of moisture. Her lashes clumped as if wet, and the sight filled him with unfamiliar feelings.

'Don't.' He leaned down, taking the glass from her hand and putting it aside. Then he tugged her up till she stood before him, shorter than he remembered in her flat shoes. The scent of sweetness and vanilla filled his nostrils as he leaned close. 'There's nothing to cry about.'

Her mouth twisted in a crumpled sort of smile and her palm grazed his cheek. 'You're a good man, Thierry Girard.'

He blinked, transfixed by the mix of emotions flitting across her features. Or perhaps by the strange sensation in the pit of his stomach, as if he'd gone into freefall.

A good man? Focused, yes. Selfish, yes. With a

taste for adventure and good-looking women. And an astute business sense that had surprised everyone, himself included.

Her hand began to slide away and he grabbed it, clamping it against his jaw. He liked its soft warmth against his skin.

'What's going on, Imogen?' She was hiding something. He'd read that in her refusal to hold his gaze. The way she kept looking away, as if scared he'd see too much. But what could it be? He was ready to accept the child was his, even if his lawyers would probably advise a paternity test.

'Nothing.' Her laugh sounded forced. 'Apart from an unexpected pregnancy.'

'Imogen.' He captured the back of her head in his free hand, delving his fingers into the soft luxury of her hair.

Memory hit—of those dark, silky waves slithering over them both as they'd lain naked in bed. Of him tugging gently on her hair so she arched her neck back, exposing her creamy throat to his mouth. Of the taste of her, sweet and addictive.

Fire ignited in his groin and his fingers tightened.

She could break his hold. All she had to do was step back, or tell him to let go.

The voice of reason urged him to do just that. Not to complicate an already fraught situation.

But he didn't.

He stood, looking down, watching a delicate flush steal across her cheeks, turning pallor to peaches-and-cream loveliness. And still she stood, watching him through narrowed eyes, her long dark lashes veiling her expression. She was a contradiction, a conundrum. Vulnerable yet unwavering, alluring and intriguing, a mystery to be solved.

Her lips parted, and he leaned closer, needing to taste. It had been too long.

His lips touched hers, and he realised he'd made a serious error of judgement when sensation exploded, tightening his limbs, his belly, his grip on her. His mouth moved with purpose now. Not for a whisper-soft taste, but with a ravening hunger that hadn't been assuaged since the day Imogen had left Paris.

She tasted so sweet. Lush, feminine and delicious. The scent of her intoxicated him and he bowed her back, thrusting his tongue into her mouth, shocked at how the familiar taste of her blasted at his control. A tremor passed through him, a huge, curling wave of hunger and exultation as she kissed him back, just as ravenous as he.

Her free hand slid up his chest to cup the back of his neck, fingers tight as if defying him to break away. He felt another detonation inside him, her touch, her need, triggering his to even greater heights.

Imogen made a low humming sound in the back of her throat that sent him crazy. From the first he'd lusted after her enthusiasm, her passion. He needed it now. How had he gone so long without it? She was sweet rain after drought, ambrosia after starvation.

Thierry released her hand and wrapped an arm around her, hauling her in to him so she cushioned his burgeoning arousal with her soft belly.

Her belly.

His baby.

Realisation slammed into him. Tension crawled along his limbs to grab his neck and shoulders. A new sort of tension that had nothing to do with sex.

He dragged his mouth free, hauling in air.

Hectic colour scored her cheeks and throat, and her lips were red from his kisses. Her eyelids fluttered as if reluctant to open.

He wanted to grind himself against her, strip her clothes away and lose himself in her welcoming body.

The body that cradled a fragile new life.

The body of a woman who for some reason feared this pregnancy like a physical threat.

What was he thinking?

He wasn't thinking. He was doing what he'd always done—indulging in whatever pleasure beckoned.

Abruptly, he straightened, his hands dropping, engulfed in horror at his lack of control. You'd think that in his thirties he'd have conquered the impulse to act rashly.

But one touch, one taste of Imogen, and thought fled.

He stared into dazed eyes that glowed green and honey-brown and knew he teetered on the edge of control.

Deliberately, he stepped back, his movements stiff and reluctant, forcing his brain to function. There was more he needed to understand. Much more.

'Are you going to tell me the truth now?'

'The truth?' The words sounded like a foreign language. Imogen stared at that firm mouth, the sensuous bottom lip, the taut line it formed when he stopped speaking. 'What do you mean?'

It was all she could do not to sway as she stood,

bereft of his touch, still feeling his body imprinted on hers. She bit her lip, silencing the futile plea that he gather her close again.

She wanted Thierry. Wanted the comfort of him holding her, the taste of him—cognac and that bitter-chocolate tang that was unique to Thierry. She wanted to be naked with him, losing herself to ecstasy.

But he looked distant, even standing so near. His eyes were unreadable, his face taut, prouder, harder than she remembered it. Suspicious.

'What don't you want me to know? You're not telling me the truth.'

Imogen jerked back an unsteady step. Her heart thumped harder. 'I know the pregnancy is a surprise, but it's real. You heard the doctor.' Pride came to her aid, stiffening her backbone. 'Or is it the idea you're the father that you doubt?'

Had she really believed he'd take her word it was his? She pulled her arms across her chest, holding in the welling hurt.

Slowly, he shook his head, his piercing gaze never leaving her face. 'It's not that. There's something more. Something you're hiding. I won't do anything until I know what it is.'

That powerful jaw took on an obstinate cast as

he crossed his arms across his chest, reinforcing that aura of tough, masculine strength despite his suavely tailored jacket. His lips thinned and his nostrils flared.

He looked intimidating. Not like the easy lover she remembered, or the passionate man of seconds ago. There was passion still, but something formidable too.

'You're reneging on what you said? You won't step in if something…happens to me?' Fear clutched. She wasn't even sure if she could carry this child to term but she had to believe she could. And she had to believe there'd be someone to care for it when she was gone.

'Hey.' His voice was soothing, his fleeting touch on her arm gentle. 'Don't get worked up. All I want is the truth. Surely I'm entitled to that?'

'You have the truth. The baby is yours.'

He stood silent, his scrutiny like a weight pushing her down.

She spun away, turning to the windows, vaguely aware of the lights of Paris beyond. Once, a few weeks ago, she'd have revelled in being here, seeing this. Now she felt terrified, scared not so much for herself as for her baby. Despair hovered in the shadows at the corner of her vision, ready to pounce if she let her guard down.

'I can't help unless you tell me what's troubling you.'

She pivoted towards him. 'Help?' She'd wondered if he was looking for an excuse to wriggle out of that.

'I said I would and I'm a man of my word.' He spoke with such authority she couldn't help but believe him.

Imogen hadn't wanted to tell him too soon, scared the knowledge he'd definitely be responsible for their child might frighten him off. Yet surely he deserved to know? The sooner he came to grips with what was to come, the better.

'Whatever it is, I'm sure it'll be okay.'

A laugh ripped from Imogen's throat. The sound scared her—so raw and guttural. It betrayed the fact she clung to calm by the skin of her teeth.

Thierry's dark eyebrows shot up, his gaze interrogative.

'It won't be okay, that's the problem.' Her voice was harsh and raspy. She cleared her throat. 'I'm not going to be a mother and I'm not going to know my child.' Pain settled like a lump of cold metal in her stomach, its chill paralysing. 'I'm dying.'

CHAPTER FIVE

THE NEXT HOUR passed in a haze, for which Imogen was grateful. She'd had enough of pain and grief and though both still threatened like bullies hovering at the edge of a playground, Thierry's presence kept them at bay.

Two things stood out. First, the way he'd gone stark white beneath the bronze of his tanned olive skin when he heard her news. Even the laughter lines at the corners of his eyes had morphed into creases that betrayed shock rather than humour. Second, his gentle solicitude as he'd ushered her back to a chair and pressed a hot drink into her hands.

His touch had been impersonal, as far from his earlier passionate grip as it was possible to be. Dying did that—it distanced you from people, putting up an unseen but unbreakable barrier no one wanted to broach. She'd seen it with her mother—people keeping their distance, as if they feared her brain tumour might be catching.

In Thierry's case, the fire died out of his eyes

as she told him about her condition, and that her mother had died of the same illness just months before. He hadn't protested in disbelief but his face had grown grimmer and grimmer as she'd spelled out what was in store.

'We need to get you to a specialist.' Even his voice had changed, the timbre hollow instead of smooth and rich.

She leaned her head against the back of her chair. 'I have another appointment in Sydney in a couple of weeks.'

'So far away?'

She shrugged. 'I'm not in a hurry, Thierry. I've been through it all with my mother and I know what to expect. Except...' She pressed a hand to her stomach, terror swooping through her as she thought of the danger to her baby.

'Don't.' He hunkered beside her, his hand on hers firm and strong, callused, as if he did more with his time than attend meetings. Heat seeped from his touch. She imagined it as warm tendrils shooting and unfurling, spreading through her chilled body. Was it imagination or did the tightness around her hunched shoulders ease?

Then he said something that threatened to undo her.

'You're not alone now, Imogen.'

He made no ridiculous promises to find a cure when there was none, to snatch her from the jaws of death. That would have meant nothing, just the bluster of someone unwilling to accept the inevitable.

Instead, his words pierced the shaky wall she'd built around her heart. They made her feel less desperate.

She opened her mouth to tell him how precious a gift he'd given her but found she couldn't speak. She gulped down a knot of emotion.

She'd known this man a few short weeks and yet for the first time since she'd lost her mother—in fact since Isabelle had died—she felt something like whole.

'You need to rest. You're exhausted.'

It was true. Sleep had eluded her this week. As if on cue, a mighty yawn rose.

'You're right. I'd better get back to the hotel.'

For answer Thierry slid his arms beneath her and hoisted her up in one smooth movement as he stood. His darkening jaw was just centimetres away and beneath the hand she pressed to his chest came the steady thud of his heartbeat.

Safe, it seemed to say.

For once Imogen let herself ignore the tiny voice

of reality that sneered nothing could keep her safe now. Instead, she let her head sink against his shoulder. Just for a moment it was nice to be cared for. It was a novelty she could get used to.

Except she wouldn't have the chance to get used to it, would she?

He must have heard her hiccup of laughter.

'What is it?'

'Nothing. I'm just tired.'

'Which is why you're going to bed.' He turned and carried her from the room. To her amazement they didn't head towards the foyer but down a wide corridor.

'Thierry? I need to get back to my hotel.'

He stopped. 'Why? Have you got medicine there that you need?'

She shook her head.

'Good. You can sleep here. I'll lend you something to wear and bring you supper once you're in bed.'

Imogen knew she should move, knew she couldn't afford to get used to being cosseted. It would only make things more difficult later. But what woman would willingly give up the pleasure of being in Thierry's powerful arms, even for a short time?

The beautiful bedroom with its high ceilings,

elegant doors and honey-coloured wood flooring spoke of the elegance of another age, even if the *en suite* bathroom she glimpsed was all modern luxury. One quick survey told her this was a guest room. No sign of Thierry's personal belongings. Nor could she imagine him choosing the delicate pale blue and cream bed linens for himself.

He lowered her onto a bed that her weary bones protested was just too comfortable to leave.

Would it be so wrong to stay the night? Independence warred with exhaustion as she sat, swaying.

'Here. You can use this tonight.' She hadn't even noticed Thierry leave but he was entering the room again. He pressed something soft into her hands, and she looked down, seeing a black T-shirt that she knew would look fantastic clinging to his hard chest. Her pulse did the funny little jig that had become familiar during her time in Paris. *He* did that to her.

She looked up into burning dark eyes. Concern etched his face. She wanted to assure him everything would be okay, erase the pain that turned his mouth into a sombre line, but she couldn't find any words to make this right.

Instead, she conjured a half-smile. 'Thank you, Thierry.' She paused, letting herself enjoy the sound of his name on her tongue. Soon she'd have no reason to use it, once she was back home. She shifted, forcing her heavy eyelids up, squaring her shoulders. 'It's thoughtful of you. I'd very much like to stay the night.'

Her hands tightened on the T-shirt. So what if a night of being cared for made the solitude she faced later harder to bear? She'd rather experience these past couple of hours with him, even if only in his apartment, not sharing his bed, than the emptiness of that soulless hotel room.

But it was more than a couple of hours. When the sun rose so did Imogen, staggering a little, groping along the wall as she made her way to the bathroom.

The headache was back. Amazingly, it was the first in weeks, but it clawed at her skull as if some giant bird of prey dug hot talons into her brain.

She was back in bed when the bedroom door opened. Thierry's hair was damp and gleaming black. Tailored charcoal trousers clung to solid thighs and his crisp white shirt revealed a V of tanned flesh where the buttons hadn't all been done up. Despite the miasma of pain, Imogen felt a twinge of pleasure at the sight of him. She regretted now that she had no photo of him. Taking holiday snaps to pore over later hadn't occurred to her. She'd spent her time trying not to think about the future.

'How are you doing?' He sat on the bed and even through the light blanket she felt his warmth. She wanted to snuggle into him and hold him tight, never let go.

She snared a breath. She had to be stronger than that. She couldn't rely on him or anyone else.

Imogen looked up through slitted eyes and read worry on his broad brow.

'Fine,' she lied, loath to make that worry worse. 'Just tired.' That, at least, was true. A week of little sleep had left her on the edge of exhaustion.

A hand brushed the hair from her face, and her eyes fluttered closed. His touch was so soothing, so gentle. Yearning rose in a welling tide.

'Are you sure that's all? Do you need a doctor?'

Her eyes sprang open to find him leaning closer, the spicy fresh scent of his skin making her nostrils flare.

'No doctor. I've had enough of them for now.' Sydney would be soon enough. 'I'm fine, really, just tired.'

'I've brought croissants and juice if you're hungry.' She shook her head, and he frowned. 'I have appointments all morning. I could put them off.'

'Don't be silly.' She tried to sound firm and strong but she suspected her voice was too hoarse. 'I'll get up now and head back to my hotel.'

'You really think I'd let you?'

'Sorry?' Was the ache in her head making her hear things?

'What sort of man do you take me for?' Anger sparked in that gleaming gaze. 'You'll stay here while you're in Paris. I'm just trying to work out whether I can leave you this morning.'

'Of course you can leave me. I'm not your responsibility.' Her brain told her to move, not loll here basking in his concern. But her aching head and tired body didn't want to move. She forced herself to pluck at the blanket, lifting it, ready to get up.

A hard hand clasped her wrist, forcing it and the blanket back down.

'Don't.' His voice caressed rather than ordered, and to her shock, awareness, acute and devastating, jagged through her. 'We'll argue about it later, when you have more energy.' He stroked her hair again and there was magic in his touch. She felt the tension rolling away in little waves. 'For now you need sleep. Promise me you'll stay here till I come back.'

It was pure weakness, she knew, but Imogen was barely surprised to hear the whisper emerge from her lips. 'Just for a while, then.'

When she finally woke, late in a golden afternoon, she was surprised to find herself refreshed, without that horrible hangover feeling after too much pain. Thankful for small mercies, she headed to the bathroom, only to discover her toiletries bag sitting there, and her hair brush. Dazed, she swivelled, looking back through the door to the bedroom. Her suitcase lay, unzipped, on the other side of the room.

He'd gone to her hotel and collected her belongings?

How had he done it? Surely there were rules about not giving strangers access to other people's hotel rooms?

Imogen's brow pleated as she tried to work out how Thierry had done it. And why. It was highhanded, and she should be annoyed, but right now the thought of getting into fresh clothes was just too appealing.

Shaking her head, she stripped off, stepping into the marble-lined shower and a stream of blissfully warm water. She'd work it all out when she was fully awake. But she'd bet Thierry's ability to access her things had something to do with that combination of innate authority and his bone-melting smile. No doubt the hotel employee he'd approached was female.

The thought stirred unwelcome feelings. A jab of what felt like jealousy.

Imogen caught herself up sharply. She had no right to jealousy. Thierry had never been hers in any real sense. Anyway, she wouldn't be with him long enough to worry about other women.

Emerging from the bathroom, she automatically reached for jeans, then paused as she noticed the gorgeous light of late afternoon slanting in the big windows.

She'd been too exhausted yesterday to worry about anything but confronting Thierry and breaking her news. Now she needed to book a flight to Sydney since she had Thierry's word he'd care for their baby.

Which meant this could be her last evening in Paris.

Firming her lips, she put the jeans down and delved into the big suitcase. If this was her last night here…

Fifteen minutes later she stared at herself in the mirror. Izzy's dress in uncrushable scarlet lace clung more than Imogen had anticipated. And it was more suited to evening than late afternoon.

But she didn't care. Red would give her energy and the bravado she needed. Besides, she'd always loved the colour, even though back home she would never consider it. It was so attention-grabbing. So not her.

She loved it. Her last night in Paris; she refused to spend it looking like some quaking little mouse.

Thierry looked up at the sound of footsteps. Not merely footsteps but the tap of high heels, if he was any judge, which he was. His lovers all wore heels. Except Imogen, he realised. She'd been just as likely to turn up wearing flats or tennis shoes, because she was as interested in hot-air ballooning and picnicking as she was in dancing and dining.

No tennis shoes now. His heart revved to a thundering roar as a vision in red appeared in the doorway. Voluptuous, glorious, sexy as hell. The colour was a perfect contrast to the creamy swell of her breasts above the low, square-cut neckline.

She'd left her hair down. It rippled in ebony silk waves around her shoulders.

Thierry's groin tightened. Imogen only wore her hair loose in bed. That had been his secret pleasure, inhaling its indefinable sweet fragrance, rubbing it between his fingers, feeling its caress on his bare skin as they made love.

His gaze dropped to the hemline above her knees and her long, shapely legs. To scarlet stilettos.

His breath rushed out like air from a punctured balloon. Arousal vied with disbelief.

How could she look this way when she was *dying*? The word hung like a dark stain on his consciousness, tearing at his innards, making his gut writhe in denial.

All night and day he'd fought to come to grips with her news. Even now part of him rejected the prognosis as impossible. *Not Imogen.*

'You look stunning.' The words jerked out hoarsely.

She stopped, eyes rounding. 'I do?' Something that might have been pleasure flitted across her face. 'Thank you. I needed something to give me courage for my last night in Paris. I wanted to look…' she shrugged '…well.'

Instantly, guilt rose. Because he was busy lusting after a fatally ill woman. Because he couldn't get up from the seat where he was working on a report for fear she'd see just how well he thought she looked. He scrubbed a hand across his jaw, trying to reorient himself.

'You look more than well. You look blooming.' The red brought colour to her cheeks and the long sleep had lessened the shadows beneath her fine eyes. Savagely he squashed the temptation to stride across and haul her to him, to claim those lips he knew would be soft and inviting, to explore that glorious body.

Because she was dying. The word scourged his brain.

'Sorry? I missed that.' He knew she'd spoken but the rush of blood in his ears had deafened him.

'I asked if you have wi-fi. I need to book my flight home.' She lifted one hand and rubbed her bare arm, as if to counteract a chill. 'I *should* argue about the fact you collected my luggage without permission. And I should move back to the hotel.' She paused, turning towards the window. 'But I don't want to waste time. This will probably be my last night in France and I've got other things to do.'

'Other things?' Dressed like that? He shot to his feet, his papers sliding to the floor. 'Like what?' The way she looked, she'd have men clustered around her the moment she stepped out the door.

A tiny, self-conscious smile lit her face, and Thierry felt as if someone had reached in and grabbed his innards. How much longer would she be able to smile like that?

'I was so busy when I was here last time, I never took one of those dinner cruises on the Seine, even though it was on my list of things to do.'

Was that a hint of a blush? Was she too thinking of all the things they'd done instead of cruising the river?

It was on the tip of Thierry's tongue to say those cruises were crowded with tourists, and the loudspeaker commentary would detract from the ambience of the evening, but he firmed his lips. He wasn't going to spoil it for her.

'So, wi-fi?' She moved farther into the room and Thierry had to force his gaze up to her face instead of on the undulating curves outlined in the tight red dress.

He dragged open his collar as heat rose. She looked so sultry and alluring it was hard to believe she carried a new life inside. Or that she was gravely ill.

Even his lawyer's dire warnings about paternity tests wouldn't stop him doing what he could for her. He'd been told he had no duty to her legally. But legalities weren't the issue.

'I can do better than that.' He cleared his throat, conscious his voice sounded gruff. 'I'll have my PA make the arrangements if you bring me your passport. She can book a dinner cruise too.'

'She's still working?' Imogen glanced at her watch.

'I usually keep much longer business hours than this.' He'd cut them back when she'd been in Paris last time, working like a demon all day so he could have his evenings free for her. He stooped to pick up the reports he'd dropped and put them on the table. 'Mademoiselle Janvier will still be at work, believe me.'

'As long as I can pay you for the air fare.'

Thierry looked at her, standing proud in her high heels. This woman admitted she needed courage to face her last night in Paris and that she was short of cash, yet she refused to take charity when it would be so easy and reasonable.

His heart dipped and skidded to a halt, only to start up again in an uneven rhythm.

She was a wonder. He'd never known a woman like her. Except perhaps his *grand-mère*, whose petite size and exquisite manners hid a spine of steel.

Would he exhibit such courage in Imogen's situation? It was one thing to risk his neck in some dangerous adventure, quite another to be stoic in the face of a steady, fatal decline. The thought of what she faced curdled his blood.

'I'll make sure you get the bill for any air fare.' As if that was going to happen. 'Now, if you'll get me your passport, I'll contact my PA.'

'I don't know which is better, the *tarte tatin* or the scenery.' Imogen sat back, replete, looking from her empty plate to the beautiful, floodlit bridge they were about to pass under. A series of pale, carved stone heads stared sightlessly out from its side, intriguing her. 'I knew the Eiffel Tower looked terrific lit up, and Notre Dame and all the other buildings, but these bridges are amazing.'

Silently she vowed to store the memory of this last night with Thierry to pull out and remember later, when her condition worsened and the shadows closed in.

'So...' Beside her Thierry lifted his glass and sipped. 'It's not the company you're enjoying?'

When he looked at her that way, his eyes gleaming and that hint of a cleft grooving his cheek as he smiled, Imogen's heart leapt. In the subtle light

of the lanterns on deck he looked suavely sophisticated. Yet Imogen knew from experience that his
rangy frame, which showed off a dinner jacket to
perfection, was actually a symphony of lean, hard-
packed muscle and bone. He might look indolent
but the man beneath the sophisticated exterior had
the body of an athlete, and such strength…

Desperately, she dragged her eyes away. Pregnancy, like illness, had no effect on her attraction
to him. If anything her response was sharper, more
urgent. Because she'd developed a craving for his
love-making and, just as importantly, because he
made her feel *special*.

'Are you after a compliment?' Imogen forced herself to smile, hiding her tumble of emotions. Desire,
gratitude, piercing regret and that undercurrent of
fear. Once she left him she'd face her future alone.
She squared her shoulders. 'It's wonderful of you to
make my last night in Paris so memorable. I can't
tell you how much it means.'

'You already have.' A casual gesture dismissed
what he'd done as negligible. But Imogen was no
fool. She'd been about to use the last of her available money to pay for a package tourist-trip. Instead, she'd found herself on a private luxury
cruiser where they were the only guests, waited

on by superb staff and eating one of the best meals of her life. The cost must have been exorbitant.

She leaned forward, reaching for Thierry's arm, till she realised what she was doing and grabbed her water glass instead.

'Don't brush it off as nothing, Thierry. What you've done...' To her horror she felt her throat thicken. 'You should at least let me thank you.'

Over the rim of his glass, Thierry's eyes locked with hers and a tingle of sensation shot through her, spreading to her breasts before arrowing to her womb. Imogen sucked in a stunned breath. Her body's urgent response to him threatened to unravel her totally.

Even the knowledge her condition had apparently killed his desire for her couldn't stop that throb of feminine wanting. She'd read his closed expression and understood he saw her as a victim, a figure of pity, not a desirable woman.

'You want to thank me?' He put his glass down and leaned close. Too close, but she couldn't seem to pull back. 'Good. Because there's something I want you to do.'

'There is?' She couldn't imagine what. Unless, of course, it was the DNA test to prove paternity. She'd heard there were risks involved with those during pregnancy but if it meant giving her child a secure future…

'Yes.' He paused so long tension tightened the bare skin of her shoulders. 'I want you to marry me.'

There was a thud and cold liquid spilled onto her thigh. Vaguely Imogen was aware of Thierry reaching out to grab her water glass before it could roll onto the deck.

She didn't move, just sat, goggling.

'Ah, thank you.' He spoke to the waiter who appeared out of nowhere to mop the tablecloth and clear the plates. All the while Thierry sat there, leaning back now, one arm looped casually over the back of his chair, watching her.

The waiter left.

'What did you say?' Her voice was a croak from constricted muscles.

'I want us to marry. This week.'

He looked so relaxed, as if he'd merely commented on the quality of the meal they'd shared, or on the beautiful old buildings floodlit along the banks of the Seine.

Her pulse fluttered like a mad thing. 'You can't be serious.'

'Never more so.' They approached another bridge

and for a few moments were bathed in light. That was when she saw it, the glint of determination in those espresso-dark eyes. And the arrogant thrust of his chin.

Imogen wasn't aware of moving but she heard a scrape and suddenly she was on her feet, stumbling for the deck's rail. She clutched it with hands that shook.

She didn't know what she felt. This was one shock too many. Her legs wobbled and she had trouble dragging in enough oxygen.

'There's no need for that,' she finally gasped out. 'Is this you trying to be kind?' She didn't need pity, no matter how good his intentions.

Imogen spun around, only to find Thierry standing behind her, just a breath away. His clean scent filled her senses as she fought for air.

'Not kind. Just practical. Planning for the future.' His voice was smoothly persuasive. Dully, she wondered if he used this tone to broker his business deals. Yet, despite his calm demeanour, she sensed he wasn't as relaxed as he appeared.

Good! *Her* heart was racing like a runaway train.

Imogen shook her head. 'I don't see what's practical about it.' She licked dry lips, peering up into

his shadowed features. 'When the time comes…
I'll ensure you're named as the father and—'

'You think it will be that easy? Claiming the child
from the other side of the world? No matter what
the birth certificate says, I'll bet Australian law is
every bit as complex as in France. There'll be one
hurdle after another for me to claim the baby. It
could take months, years.'

The baby. Not *his* baby.

What had she expected? That a mere twenty-four
hours after learning he was going to be a father,
Thierry would have the same powerful connection she felt for the tiny life inside her? Of course
it was too much to ask. All she could do was hope
that with time that would change.

'Do you want to risk the possibility your baby
will be put in care while the legalities are sorted
out?'

Pain scoured her, as if someone took a rusty blade
and scraped it through her womb. Her palm found
her belly, pressing tenderly as if to make sure that
little life was safe inside.

A large hand, warm and callused, covered hers,
splaying gently across her abdomen. She blinked
and looked up into unreadable eyes.

'If we marry there will be no legal hurdles. I'll be

responsible for our child. There will be no waiting, no complications. Only what's best for the baby.' Thierry's voice dropped to a low, crooning note that flowed through her like molten chocolate. Or maybe that was the effect of his touch, so real, so *sure*.

'You know there's a chance the baby might not survive?' She choked back the horror that had haunted her since she'd learned of her pregnancy. The fear that her child might die simply because she wouldn't live long enough for it to survive.

In the gloom away from the lights, she could just make out the fierce jut of Thierry's hard jaw.

When he spoke his voice held an edge she couldn't identify. 'As your husband, I'll be in a position to do everything possible for it. And for you.'

For one enticing moment Imogen let herself imagine leaning on Thierry as she had today, allowing him to take care of her. But ultimately they were strangers.

'I don't belong here, Thierry. My home is in Australia.'

'Yet you admit you've got no one to look after you there.'

'You think I came to Paris to find someone who'd look after me?' She tried to free her hand from his but he simply pressed closer, crowding her against the railing. 'I'm Australian. I belong there.'

'And who will care for you?' His words were like soft blows, hammering at her. 'You have no family. Have you close friends who'll be there whenever you need them? Have you got *anyone*?'

Said like that, he made her sound so pathetic. 'My really good friends have all moved away with jobs or family.' And, while she got on well with her work colleagues, this last year she'd been so wrapped up in grief after Izzy's death, then busy caring for her mother, that she'd got out of the habit of accepting social invitations. She'd effectively cut herself off. 'But I'll be fine. The health service—'

'I'm not talking about people paid to look after you.' His fingers closed around hers and he lifted her hand between them. To her surprise he planted her palm against his mouth and pressed a kiss to it. A kiss that sent heat and wonder coursing through her, reminding her she wasn't dead yet.

'I'm talking about someone who will be there for you. Someone who can deal with the medicos when you're too weary. Someone who'll be on hand to look after our child.'

Imogen's heart swelled. Put that way, the offer was irresistible.

'You know I'm right, Imogen.' His lips moved against her sensitive palm and the low burr of his voice curled around her like an embrace. And something inside, some selfish, needy part of her, urged her to accept.

Silently, she nodded.

An instant later his arms closed about her, pulling her against his hard chest.

Relief filled her. She just hoped she wasn't making a mistake they'd both regret.

CHAPTER SIX

By Saturday they were married.

Thierry steered his car through the congestion of central Paris, hyperaware of the woman beside him, her belongings stored neatly in the back.

He was a married man.

Married and expecting a child.

His hands clamped the wheel. Sweat beaded his hairline and something like panic stirred. Him—responsible for raising a child? The notion was so far out of left field, he still couldn't quite believe it. He could face any number of extreme sports with a thrill of anticipation, yet the idea of being solely responsible for another life filled him with trepidation. He had no experience with kids, no desire for…

He caught the direction of his thoughts and cut it off. Shame pierced him, curdling his belly. So what if he knew nothing about child-rearing? He'd adapt. He'd take it one step at a time, just as he had when forced by injury to give up competitive skiing, and when he'd taken charge of the ailing family company. He had no right to complain, not when Imogen…

No, he refused to go there, at least today. For now it was enough that she was here with him. He was doing what needed to be done, despite his legal advisor's warnings.

He'd never had much time for lawyers. But to be fair the old man had probably been as stunned by his news as Thierry's family would be.

Thierry was the bachelor least likely to tie the knot, much to his grandparents' despair. In his youth he'd vowed never to settle for any other woman since he couldn't have Sandrine. Looking back on that time now, he felt merely curiosity and a twinge of remembered disappointment at the hurt which he'd thought had blighted his life.

How naïve he'd been. Far from being destroyed, his life had been filled to the brim. He'd spent the intervening years doing exactly what he loved— feeding his appetite for pleasure: sport, women, adventure.

'You look happy.'

He turned to see Imogen scrutinising him, as if trying to read him. Why wouldn't she? She'd put her life in his hands, and their child's life.

She'd put on a good show of being indomitable these past few days, but her tiredness betrayed her. He couldn't bear to think of where that would inevitably lead. The knowledge had been like acid eating at him ever since he'd heard. He'd never felt so appallingly *useless*.

'Getting out of the city is cause for celebration, don't you think?' He forced a smile and was rewarded with a slight upward tilt of her lips.

He'd always liked the way she responded to his smile, even when, as now, he guessed she felt out of sorts.

Out of sorts! His smile twisted.

'You don't like the city? I think Paris is fabulous.'

Thierry shrugged, focusing his attention on the road and the van trying to change lanes into a non-existent space between a motorcycle and another car.

'To visit, perhaps, but where we're going there'll be pure air. No fumes or road noise. No crowds either.'

'I thought you enjoyed socialising.'

He shrugged, taking action to avoid a kamikaze motorcyclist. 'I love a good party, but after a while I've had enough of the chatter.'

'So what do you like, then?'

A sideways glance showed her turned towards him, her gaze curious, as if she really wanted to know.

It struck him that most of the women he'd known had had their own agendas—to be seen at the right parties or with the right people, the heir to the Girard fortune being one of the right people. They'd had fun together but how many had tried to know Thierry the man rather than Thierry the CEO or Thierry the scion of one of France's elite families? Or, in the old days, Thierry the famous athlete?

'Surely it's not a hard question?'

Not hard at all. 'Skiing. Downhill and very, very fast.' Once he'd thought that was his destiny. He'd been in the peak of his form training for the Winter Olympics before a busted leg had put an end to those dreams.

'What else?'

Another glance showed she hadn't taken her eyes off him. Of course she wanted to know. He'd be the one raising their child. His hands tightened on the wheel.

'White-water rafting. Rally driving. Rock climbing.'

'You don't like to be still.'

'You could say that. Except for hot-air ballooning. There's nothing quite like that for getting a little perspective in your life.' He didn't add that a lot of his balloon treks took him to inhospitable, often dangerous places where tourists rarely went.

'And when you're not outdoors?'

'These days I'm usually working.' In the past he'd have unwound in the company of some gorgeous woman but lately his interest had waned. Until Imogen. Even today, in jeans and a plain shirt, her lithe curves made his hands itch for physical contact.

Not even telling himself that it was wrong to lust after a dying woman, a woman relying on him, could kill that hot flare of hunger.

'What about you, Imogen? What do you like to do? I don't mean the things on your travel list.' It struck him suddenly that hers really had been a bucket list to be accomplished before she died. The realisation was like an icy hand curling gnarled fingers around his chest, squeezing till his lungs burned.

'You mean, in my ordinary life?'

Thierry nodded, not trusting his voice.

'The list is pretty ordinary, like me. No white-water rafting.'

'*Ordinary* isn't the way I'd describe you, Imogen.' Not with her zest for life, her sense of humour and that entrancing mix of pragmatism and wide-eyed enthusiasm. As for her body… He couldn't go there, not if he wanted to keep his wits on the traffic.

She laughed, but the smoky quality of her voice held a harsh rasp. 'I suppose you think I'm more like a walking disaster zone. Suddenly you've been saddled with—'

'Don't!' Thierry dragged in a breath that grated across his throat. This wasn't the place to rehash their debate about her being a burden. He knew this was the right thing and he refused to resile from that. He forced a smile into his voice. 'You don't get out of answering that easily. Tell me at least three things that make you happy.'

In his peripheral vision, he saw Imogen slump a little in her seat. Then she turned to stare out the window.

'Books. I love reading, anything from romance to history or biography.'

'And? That's only one.'

She hesitated. 'Numbers. I've always liked numbers. There's something…comfortable about working with figures and finding the patterns that create order out of chaos. I suppose that's why I went into accounting.'

Thierry nodded. His cousin, Henri, was the same.

Give him a spreadsheet and he was happy. The trouble was, though Henri was a genius with figures, he showed little aptitude for management. Lately it had become obvious that Thierry's plan of leaving the family company in his charge was fraught with problems.

'And the third?'

'Baking. Well, cooking generally, but baking specifically.'

'What do you bake?' Thierry was intrigued. He didn't know anyone who cooked for pleasure.

He thought of Jeanne, who'd been his grandparents' cook as long as he could remember. She was fiercely protective of her domain, a dumpy little woman with arms as strong as any farm labourer, and fingers that could pinch a boy's ears painfully if he wasn't quick enough stealing fresh-baked pastries. As far as he could tell, she had nothing in common with Imogen.

'Anything. Kneading bread dough is therapeutic but I love making sweet things, like baklava or Danishes. I always get requests at work for my honey-chocolate sponge cake.'

How apt that she tasted like one of her pastries— of vanilla and sugar. Except Imogen was more delectable than any cake he'd ever eaten.

It had been days since he'd tasted her. Yet, despite his determination not to press her when she was unwell, Thierry's craving for her sweet lips had grown, not eased, with abstinence.

'So, I'm pretty boring, really.'

He flicked on the car's indicator and changed lanes, accelerating as they left the city behind.

'You're anything but boring.' Thierry paused, mulling over what she'd told him. 'You like being at home.'

'I suppose so.'

'Tell me about it. What's your home like?'

Imogen shifted in her seat. 'I was saving up for a place of my own when this... When I decided to come to France. I'd been renting, sharing a flat, but I moved back in with my mother while she was ill.'

In other words she'd nursed her mother through her decline. What must it be like, after watching her mother's fatal deterioration, to know in intimate detail what she herself could expect?

Thierry put his foot to the floor and for a short time focused on the satisfying distraction of speed. But it didn't work. His thoughts kept circling back to Imogen.

'Your family home, then. What was it like?'

Again that short laugh, a little ragged around the edges. 'We didn't have one. We moved too often.'

He shot her a questioning look.

'My mother worked hard to qualify as a teacher when Isabelle and I were little, but she had trouble getting a permanent position. She never said so but it might have been because of the demands of raising twins. Anyway, she worked as a casual teacher, filling in where needed, sometimes for a term at a time if we were lucky.'

'In Sydney?'

'All around the state, though in later years she worked in Sydney. By then she'd come to enjoy the challenge of dealing with new pupils and new surroundings all the time. She chose to keep working on short-term placements.'

'Maybe that explains the bond between you all.'

'Sorry?'

'When you speak of your mother or sister I hear affection in your voice. I get the impression you were close.'

She was silent for a few moments. 'I suppose it did draw us closer together in some ways.'

'But not all?' Thierry passed a slow-moving truck then rolled his shoulders. Already he felt a familiar sense of release at leaving Paris.

'Isabelle thrived on new places, making new friends, starting afresh. She was the outgoing one.'

'You're not outgoing?' He thought of her laughter the night they'd met in Paris, the confident way she'd bantered with him. Plus there was the enthusiastic way she embraced every new experience.

Out of the corner of his eye he saw her rub her palm down her jeans. He jerked his attention back to the road, before his mind wandered to places it shouldn't.

'I'm the reserved one, the cautious twin. Izzy would walk into a new classroom and by the end of the day she'd have five new best friends. It would take me weeks or months, and by that stage we'd usually be on the move again. My sister thought it a grand adventure but I...suppose I just wanted more stability and certainty.'

Hence the affinity for creating order out of chaos with numbers. Thierry tried to imagine what it must have been like for such a child, averse to change, being carted around the countryside. It didn't escape him that her other interests—reading and baking—were home-based. It was a wonder she'd crossed the globe in search of adventure.

As if she'd read his thoughts, she spoke. 'My sister followed her dream and took the gamble of coming to France, hoping to work in fashion, though everyone said her chances were slim. I was the one who stayed where I was.'

'I was always looking for adventure,' he said then paused, surprised he'd shared that.

'What sort of adventure?'

'Anything to break the monotony of home.' He sensed her surprise and shot her an amused glance. 'My childhood was the opposite of yours. Everything in my world was so stable it was almost petrified. Things were done the same way they'd always been done.'

If it had been good enough for the Girards to dine in the blue salon a hundred and fifty years ago, the Girards would continue to do so, even if it was a cold room that missed the evening sun in summer. Male Girards entered the diplomatic corps or the military before taking their place managing one of the family enterprises and there was an end to it. Rules covered everything, from his choice of friends to his behaviour in public and in private.

His parents had died when he was a baby so he'd been brought up by his strict grandparents. A psychologist might say he'd rebelled against their outmoded rules and restrictions. But Thierry was pretty sure he'd simply been born with a thirst for adventure.

'We weren't big on family traditions.' Imogen's voice was soft. 'Except spending Christmas Day together, and Easter. Even in the last couple of years the three of us would have an Easter egg hunt in the garden.'

'Your mother too?'

'Of course. She loved chocolate.'

Thierry tried and failed to imagine his *grand-mère* hunting for eggs in their exquisitely kept grounds.

'That sounds like fun. I've never been on an Easter egg hunt.'

'You haven't?' Her face swung towards him again. 'It's not a French tradition?'

'For some. But not in the Girard family.' Easter had meant his best behaviour and, of course, formal clothes. He couldn't recall a time when he hadn't been expected to wear a tie to dinner. No wonder yanking his top button undone was always the first thing he did on leaving the office.

He saw her hand swipe the leg of her jeans again. 'You make your family sound a little daunting.' She paused. 'Are they?' Was that concern in her voice?

Daunting? He supposed his grandparents were, with their formality and strict adherence to old ways, but for all that he loved them.

'They'll welcome you with open arms. They've

all but given up on the idea of me bringing home a bride. But you needn't worry for now. My grandparents spend the summer at their villa on the south coast. And my cousins, aunts and uncles live elsewhere.'

'You share a house with your grandparents?' Surprise tinged her tone. Who could blame her? Until four years ago he'd lived his own life, visiting the Girard estate only occasionally. But it was easier to manage the estate and the family's diverse commercial interests from there since that was where the main offices were located.

'You think it unusual for a thirty-four-year-old?' His smile was tight as he remembered how reluctant that move back home had been. 'My grandfather had a stroke a few years ago and they needed me. But don't worry; we'll be quite private. There's plenty of space.' Even when his grandparents were in residence the place was so big he could go for weeks without seeing them.

Thierry considered explaining to Imogen just what to expect. But she'd been pale today, admitting to a little nausea, which to his astonishment had evoked a visceral pang of possessiveness in him. As if it made the idea of their child suddenly more concrete. She'd been nervous too. Better not to overload her with details. He couldn't guess whether she'd be excited or retreat mentally, as she'd done a few times when unsure of herself.

'Why don't you close your eyes and rest? We'll be travelling for a while.'

The sun still shone brightly when Imogen woke. Her head lolled against the backrest. She hadn't slept well lately but the rhythm of the car had lulled her into relaxation.

She blinked. The rhythm had changed, as if the road surface was different. When she looked through the windscreen she realised they'd left the main *autoroute*. They were in what looked like a park. Great swathes of grass with tall, mature trees dotted the scene. They clustered close to the road.

She frowned. Though paved, it was a narrow road with no lines marked.

'Are we almost there?'

'Almost. You'll see it soon.'

It? Imogen felt befuddled, shreds of sleep still clinging. Presumably he meant the town where he...

She gasped as the car topped a rise and the vista opened up. Her eyes popped.

'You live in a castle?' It couldn't be...but the road

they were on—a private road, she realised belat-edly—headed straight for the next rise where the sun shone off massive walls of darkest honey gold.

She swung around to Thierry but he looked un-moved, as if driving home to a medieval fortifica-tion was an everyday occurrence.

She sat back in her seat, her brain buzzing.

'I don't suppose your place is off to the side some-where? An estate manager's house or something?'

His mouth quirked up in a smile, and he slanted an amused look at her. She felt its impact deep in-side as her internal organs began to liquefy.

He only has to smile and you lose it.

No wonder you let him convince you to go along with this absurd idea.

Even now, hours after the short civil ceremony, she had trouble believing she'd actually married Thierry.

'Are you disappointed? Would you rather live in a cottage?'

Slowly, she shook her head, drinking in his pro-file as he turned back to the road. A castle. Maybe that explained that air of assurance she'd noticed in him from the first. It was more than just the insouciance that came from looking staggeringly handsome in bespoke formal wear, or the comfortable-in-his-skin athleticism of his magnificent body. It was something bred in the bone. And then there were his strongly sculpted features. Were they the result of generations of aristocratic breeding?

'Imogen? You don't like it?'

She turned her head. The walls rose several stories and were punctuated, not with tiny arrow slits, but with large windows that must let in a lot of light. Yet at the corners of the building were sturdy round towers topped with conical roofs, like an illustration of Rapunzel's story.

'I don't know. I can't imagine actually living in a castle.'

'We call it a *château*.'

'Okay, then. I can't imagine living in a *château*.' Imogen half expected to wake up and find she'd dreamt it. A *château*! The word conjured images of royal courts and lavish indulgence. Could anything be more different from the two-bedroom flat she'd shared in suburban Sydney?

'It's like living anywhere else except it costs a lot more to heat and the maintenance bills are a nightmare. But don't worry.' Imogen heard the current of amusement in Thierry's voice. 'It's been modernised through the years. It's even got hot- and cold-running water.'

'I wouldn't expect anything less.' She recalled Thierry's Paris apartment where her bathroom had been expensively modern bordering on sybaritic decadence. He might have restless energy and a hard body sculpted into muscle, but he was a man with a strongly sensuous streak.

Imogen gave a little shiver and clasped her hands together, trying to evict memories of his sensuality and how he'd uncovered a purely hedonistic side to her she'd never known.

'Has your family owned it long?' Her gaze drifted from the fairy-tale towers across the impressive façade.

'A couple of hundred years.'

Tension clamped her shoulders. She'd realised she was marrying into money, but the aristocracy as well? She was going to be totally out of her depth.

Not for long, reminded that persistent inner voice. The reminder dampened her momentary sense of rising panic.

The car slowed and pulled to a halt in front of the imposing building, gravel crunching under the wheels. 'Welcome to your new home, Imogen.'

Her throat clenched. He really was a man in a million. He'd taken her news with something close to equanimity, only the occasional flicker of emotion in his dark eyes betraying his shock. More, he'd not only agreed to take care of their child, he'd taken it upon himself to provide for her too.

'You didn't need to do all this.' She waved futilely. She could have been back in Sydney by now, alone. Instead, he'd brought her to his family home. That meant so much.

'Of course I do. You're carrying my child.'

Of course. His child. She had to keep remembering this was about their baby. She was just along for the ride.

Imogen bit her lip, swallowing a laugh that held no humour.

'Are you okay?' His touch on her arm was light, but she felt the imprint of his fingers in each riotously sensitive nerve ending.

'Perfect.' She turned and gave him her best smile. The one she'd practised so often before heading out to some large social event. She must be slipping, for Thierry didn't look convinced, just sat, watching, as if he read the unease and dismay she tried to hide.

'What's wrong?' Those espresso-dark eyes saw too much.

A litany of worries ran through her head. Her baby's health, her own illness, staying in France for these final months instead of Australia, where at least she spoke the language. Being a burden to Thierry and an unwelcome surprise to his family. If she wasn't careful all those concerns would submerge her just when she needed her strength.

'Neither of us really wants this marriage.' She shook her head. 'It's not what you'd planned for yourself.'

Thierry's scrutiny sharpened and his eyes narrowed. She couldn't read his expression.

'Things don't always work out the way we expect but I'm a firm believer in making the best of any situation.' His hand closed on hers, long fingers threading through hers. 'This is the right thing, Imogen. Trust me.'

CHAPTER SEVEN

IMOGEN PUT THE wicker basket down and sank onto the garden seat. Typically, it wasn't a bare stone seat. Someone had placed cushions on all the outdoor seats, in case she or Thierry or some unexpected visitor chose to stop.

Everything at the *château* was like that—not just elegant and expensive but beautifully cared for. No detail was too small, no comfort overlooked, from the scented bath oils made from herbs grown at the *château*, to crisp white sheets that smelled of sunshine and lavender from the purpose-grown drying hedge. Even the discreetly efficient lift to the top floors was hidden behind ancient panelling so as not to interfere with the ambience.

Imogen closed her eyes, soaking up the late-afternoon sunshine, enjoying the sense of utter peace. There was no sound but the drowse of bees and in the distance a motor. A car maybe, or a tractor. She inhaled, drinking in the heady scent of roses, and felt herself relax.

She'd done the right thing.

Of course she had!

It didn't matter that she felt like she'd forced Thierry into a corner so he'd been obliged to take responsibility for their child. She'd had no other option.

Nor did it matter that she was an outsider here. What mattered was doing right by her baby. If that meant spending her last months in France rather than her own country, so be it.

As if it was hard, living here at the *château*!

For days she'd rested, sleeping more than she could remember ever having done. Jeanne, the Girard's formidable cook-housekeeper, seemed to have made it her mission to tempt Imogen's appetite with one delicious treat after another. And when, with a knowing look, she'd seen Imogen turn pale at the pungent scent of fresh coffee, she'd begun providing herbal teas and delicate, light-as-air crackers that had helped settle Imogen's stomach.

Her thoughts eddied as she drifted towards sleep. It was so easy to relax here. So very peaceful.

The crunch of footsteps woke her. And the murmur of voices. Thierry's voice, a low, liquid blur of sound that flowed through her like luscious caramel pooling deep inside. Imogen kept her eyes closed just a little longer, reluctant to move. Listening to his voice was one of her greatest pleasures. Thierry could read weather forecasts or even tax law aloud and she'd melt into a puddle of pure bliss.

'Imogen?'

She opened her eyes to find him standing before her. He looked every bit as delicious as he sounded. His clothes were plain, tailored trousers and a pale shirt undone at the throat, but there was nothing ordinary about the man wearing them. He looked the epitome of hard athleticism from his solid thighs to his straight shoulders and every hard inch between.

Imogen gave a little quiver of pleasure. Every time she saw him it happened, even now. He made her silly heart stutter.

'I'd like you to meet my grandmother.' He gestured to his side, and her gaze swung to the tiny, grey-haired lady she hadn't even noticed before. A lady with a capital L, Imogen realised in the split second it took to register her immaculate hair and make-up, the sophisticated dark suit that screamed couture and the lustre of elegant pearls at her throat. She wore stockings despite the heat and gorgeous black patent shoes that Imogen wouldn't dare wear on gravel for fear of scuffing them.

Imogen shot to her feet, managing to tip over the basket of roses beside her. Secateurs clattered to the ground.

Eyes as dark as Thierry's, but much sharper, surveyed her from head to toe.

Imogen felt a flush rise to crest in her burning cheeks. She knew her shirt was rumpled, her jeans faded and one canvas shoe had got caked in mud when she'd ventured too near an ornamental pond. Faced with the other woman's elegance, Imogen felt a complete frump. It was one thing to borrow her sister's creations and play at dressing up in Paris. It was quite another to achieve that bone-deep level of stylish sophistication.

'*Bonjour*, Madame Girard.' Imogen paused, searching for the words she'd memorised: *it's very nice to meet you... 'Je suis ravie de vous rencontrer.'* Unexpected nerves made her stumble over even that simple phrase. Quickly, she put out her hand, only to whip it back when she realised she still wore gardening gloves.

'It's a pleasure to meet you at last too.' The other woman's English was crisp if heavily accented. She leaned in and kissed Imogen lightly on the cheeks in a gesture that held no discernible warmth. A light fragrance, perfectly balanced and no doubt worth a fortune, wafted around her. 'We will speak in English, as it's easier for you.'

'Thank you. I'm afraid my French is non-existent.' Under the other woman's assessing scrutiny Imogen almost blurted that she'd learned Japanese and Indonesian at school, but stopped herself before she could babble. Instead, she pulled off the soiled gloves and dropped them on the seat where Thierry had righted the basket of cut flowers.

'It's important that we become better acquainted. You have married my grandson. You are part of the family now.'

Imogen searched her inflection for any hint of welcome. She found none.

'Which is why you left *Grand-père* in Provence and hot-footed it up here,' Thierry murmured. 'It's a delightful surprise to see you.'

Fine eyebrows arched. 'He wasn't up to the journey this time.' She turned to Imogen. 'My husband has been unwell and needs rest. But we felt it important that one of us came to welcome you into the family.'

If the gleam in those shrewd eyes was any indication, it was more a matter of sizing her up. Yet who could blame the older woman?

What had Imogen expected? To be greeted by

Thierry's family with open arms? She suspected she was doomed to disappointment in that case.

It didn't matter what they thought of her, she reminded herself. Unless that affected her child's future. The thought stirred Imogen's protective instincts.

'It's good of you to come all this way, Madame Girard. I'm afraid the news of our marriage must have come as a surprise to Thierry's family.'

'And presumably to your own.' Those keen eyes roved Imogen's face, as if searching for clues.

'I don't have a family.' The bald statement sounded more brutal than she'd intended and she read the shock on the older woman's face. 'I mean—'

'Sadly, Imogen recently lost her mother and her sister.' Warm fingers threaded through hers, and Imogen looked up to find Thierry watching her, his smile reassuring. His hand squeezed hers, and she smiled back gratefully. She wasn't in this alone.

Nevertheless, she felt like an imposter, pretending to be his one true love, the woman he'd spend the rest of his life with.

'I'm very sorry for your loss. That must have been very difficult.'

'Thank you. It was…difficult.' Could she sound

any less sophisticated in front of this stylish matriarch?

'But now you have Thierry.'

Imogen blinked. Did his grandmother think she'd married him because she was lonely? No, more likely trapped him because of his money. 'I'm a very lucky woman.'

To her surprise, she felt Thierry's warm fingers stroke her cheek. 'I'm the lucky one, *chérie*.' His voice dropped to that low, shivery note she hadn't heard in so long. Since they'd shared a bed on her first visit to Paris. Imogen swallowed hard, hit by a surge of longing so strong she found herself swaying towards him. Yet his affectionate display was obviously a show for his grandmother. Thierry didn't want to explain the exact circumstances of their marriage and nor did she.

'You always did have luck on your side, Thierry. Now, if you'll leave us alone, I'd like to get to know your wife a little better.' It wasn't a request but an order.

Thierry ignored it. 'Let's all go inside for coffee. I've no doubt Jeanne has been busy preparing something suitable from the moment you arrived.'

Imogen liked that he wanted to look after her. But

she wasn't totally helpless, even if she *had* turned to him when she hadn't known what else to do.

'We'll come in soon,' she assured him. 'It would be nice if your grandmother could show me the garden. I'm sure she knows the name of those beautiful roses at the end of the walk.' The gardener had mentioned that Madame Girard herself had overseen their planting.

'You're sure?' His eyes searched her face.

She nodded.

'Then I'll see you both inside very soon. There's a call I need to get back to.'

'Go on, Thierry.' His grandmother made a shooing motion. 'I know I interrupted your work. We'll be fine. I don't intend to eat the girl.'

As soon as he was gone Madame Girard turned to her. 'I was surprised to find him in the offices. You didn't want a honeymoon?'

She didn't beat around the bush, did she? But Imogen rather liked that. One of the reasons she felt uncomfortable at big social events was that she'd never excelled at meaningless small talk. Those nights in Paris with Thierry were an exception, when flirting with him had been as easy as breathing.

'He has a lot of work at the moment and he can do

that here.' Imogen had been surprised to discover the rear of the *château* accommodated offices for staff involved in running the Girard family's commercial interests. It was there Thierry spent his days, often working late, though always coming to share meals with her.

'Nevertheless, a bride should expect more of her husband. I'll speak with him.'

Startled, Imogen saw a flash of something like disapproval in the older woman's eyes. On her behalf?

'No! Please, don't. We're content as we are.' The thought of Thierry's grandmother telling him he had to spend more time with her...

'Content? What is that? Have you no passion, girl? No fire?'

Imogen drew herself up. 'It's not a matter of passion. It's a matter of common sense. Anyone can see Thierry has a lot on his mind right now.'

And she'd added to his burdens. It was only since she'd returned to Paris that she'd begun to realise how hard he worked. When he'd been with her before, she'd seen only the carefree side of him, the man who revelled in seeing her pleasure at her first hot-air balloon ride, or tasting her first glass of champagne.

'You're willing to take second place to business while he does so?'

'I have no complaints. Thierry has responsibilities and I knew that when we married.'

'The marriage was very sudden.' Those dark eyes glinted. 'Thierry didn't tell me exactly how long you've known each other but I don't recall him mentioning your name in the past.'

Imogen stared straight back at her interrogator. 'It was a whirlwind romance.'

'I see.' She sounded as if she didn't like what she saw. 'So, perhaps you have mutual friends. Is that how you met? You moved in the same circles?' Her gaze skated over Imogen's rumpled clothes.

Imogen held the basket close, as if that could protect her from the other woman's curiosity. If only she'd been warned of the visit, she'd have dressed up. Which was probably precisely why they'd had no warning. Thierry's grandmother struck her as a very canny woman.

'No, we don't have any mutual friends. We met by chance at a party in Paris and...'

'And he swept you off your feet?'

Imogen shrugged, ignoring the trace of a blush she felt in her cheeks. 'Something like that.' Deliberately, she held the older woman's gaze.

'I see.' Madame Girard tilted her head as if to get a better view of her. 'And your work? Do you have a job?'

Imogen's hands tightened on the basket but she drew a slow breath and released it, reminding herself it was natural Thierry's grandmother wanted to know these things. Did she think Imogen was unemployed, looking for someone to sponge off? One thing was for sure, she wouldn't mistake her for one of the idle rich, not in these clothes.

'I'm an accountant. From Australia. I was visiting Paris on holiday.'

'Where you met my grandson, had a passionate affair and found yourself pregnant.'

Imogen's breath hissed in and for a moment she felt the world wobble around her.

'Come! You need to sit.' A surprisingly firm hand gripped her upper arm, guiding her back down to the seat.

'That's better.' Madame Girard took the seat beside her. 'I don't have any patience with this fainting nonsense.'

'Good.' Imogen lifted her chin. 'Because I don't faint.'

To her amazement the other woman chuckled. The sound was unexpectedly rich and appealing.

'I'm very glad to hear it.' Then she nodded. 'With some coaching, you might even do for him very well.'

'I beg your pardon?' Imogen stared, torn between relief and offence.

'Your clothes, your lack of French… We'll have to work on both if you're to take your place beside Thierry.'

Imogen blinked at the 'we'. His grandmother intended to coach her? Or had pregnancy hormones made Imogen lose the thread of the conversation?

'How did you know I was pregnant?'

'Jeanne, of course. She's been at the *château* for years. As soon as she realised…' Madame Girard gave a fluid shrug. 'Of course she contacted me.'

'Of course.' Imogen paused, caught up in an unexpected tide of relief that she had one less secret to keep from this formidable lady. More than that, sharing the news with another woman made her feel less alone. So often she wished her mother was alive to talk to about the pregnancy. She had so many hopes and fears for this baby.

She chewed her lip. Thinking about that only made everything more difficult. Instead, she should focus on politely declining any make-over attempt. It wasn't as if she'd be here long term, so there was no question of her becoming the perfect wife for Thierry.

The knowledge stabbed, the pain sharper than before. But Imogen kept her expression neutral. She wasn't ready to share *that* with Thierry's grandmother. She already felt like she'd been stripped bare.

Curiosity got the better of her. 'You don't mind that Thierry married so quickly, or that I'm pregnant?'

'I might have, until I saw the way you looked at him.' There was a glimmer of a smile in those eyes so like Thierry's.

'The way I looked at him?'

'Absolutely. The way a woman looks when she's in love.'

Imogen gave up trying to sleep. Instead, she perched on the window seat in her bedroom.

It was twilight and in the distance she saw the haze of indigo mountains. Closer to the *château* were verdant fields and she could smell that sweet scent on the evening air again. Meadow flowers or perhaps something growing in the formal gardens. To the right was a sprinkle of lights from the nearest town.

She lifted her feet, wrapping her arms around her knees, drinking in the view.

But Madame Girard's words stole her peace.

The way a woman looks when she's in love.

Had she really looked at Thierry that way?

Imogen told herself Madame Girard indulged in wishful thinking because she wanted to see her grandson happy.

The bond between the pair had been evident through the evening they'd all spent in *madame*'s apartments—in a wing of the *château* Imogen hadn't visited before. The old lady was shrewd, with a dry sense of humour that had grown on Imogen. But sentimental? Not enough to skew her judgement.

In love.

Imogen had never been truly in love. At the time she'd thought perhaps with Scott... But, though she'd been hurt by the callous way he'd dumped her, her heart hadn't broken.

She admired Thierry. She liked him and was grateful for all he was doing for her and their child. After Scott, who'd resented the increasing time she spent with her mother as she'd faded, Imogen knew how remarkable it was to find a man who didn't run from harsh reality, but helped shoulder her burdens.

How many men would have done as Thierry had?

He wasn't content simply to put his name on the marriage contract. He was meticulous about seeing to her comfort. He never missed a meal with her and his careful attentiveness should have put her at ease.

Instead, it made her restless.

Physically she felt better than she had in weeks. But emotionally? The unwanted truth hammered at her. It wasn't her luxurious surrounds that made her edgy, or meeting Thierry's grandmother. As for her illness—she hadn't precisely become accustomed to it, but she'd learned to live in the moment as much as possible.

It was Thierry who tied her stomach in knots.

She raked her hand through her hair, pulling it back from her face.

She didn't want Thierry's hospitality. Each time he solicitously held her chair at the table or opened a door for her, impatience gnawed. He was caring and charming but there was an indefinable distance between them now.

What she wanted, what she *craved*, was his touch, his passion. Not love, she assured herself, but intimacy.

When she'd had that in Paris she'd felt able to

cope with the future. In some inexplicable way it had given her the strength to face what was to come. Even after all this time she still reached for him in the night, waking to a loneliness even more desolate for his absence.

Had his attraction for her been so short-lived? Or did her illness turn him off? Or her pregnancy?

Or did he hold back from her for some other reason?

A breeze wafted through the window, stirring her nightdress against her breasts and teasing her bare arms. Her eyelids flickered as she thought of Thierry and how sensitive she'd been to his lightest touch. He'd made her body come alive as never before. He'd awakened something in her that refused to go back into hibernation.

A sound drew her attention to the door connecting her room to Thierry's.

Imogen's lips firmed. She wasn't dead yet.

Thierry paused in the act of hauling off his shirt when he heard a tap on his door. Not the door to his private sitting room but the one connecting to Imogen's room. The one he'd tried to ignore since they'd arrived, knowing she slept just metres away.

He'd almost locked it so he couldn't be tempted

to do something reprehensible like forget the state of her health and take what he hungered for.

He let his shirt drop back into place, even doing up some of the buttons again, which was when he noticed the tremor in his hands.

'Thierry?'

He swung around. The door was ajar, and Imogen stood there, her hair tumbling about her shoulders and breasts in shining waves of ebony.

His gut clenched and a hammering started up in his chest. It took a split second to realise it was his heart, throbbing to an urgent new beat.

'Are you okay?' He paced towards her then pulled up short. He needed distance. That pale nightdress revealed too much. Her nipples pressed, proud and erect, against the light fabric and his palms tingled as he remembered how they felt, budding in his hands. How they tasted, sweet as sugar syrup and warm woman on his tongue.

He tried but couldn't stop his gaze skating lower to the hint of the darkness at the apex of her thighs. Thierry swallowed at the memories of her naked in his bed. His lower body turned into cast metal. A film of sweat broke out across his brow and his throat turned desert dry.

'What's wrong?' His voice was hoarse. 'Do you need a doctor?'

She shook her head and, mesmerised, he watched the way those dark locks slid and separated around her pouting breasts. He knew Imogen had a body to please a man. It was only now, worn down by the weight of abstinence, that he realised it could torture just as well.

Never had he been as fervently eager for work as he had been since their wedding. He was actually grateful for the distraction it gave from his wife.

'No, I'm not sick.' Her words had that throaty edge she got when nervous or aroused. Adrenalin shot through him, and he had a battle not to cross the room and haul her close. Of course she wasn't aroused. 'I wanted to talk.'

'Talk?' The last thing he needed was an intimate chat here in his bedroom. 'Can it wait till tomorrow?'

She shook her head and his breathing stalled as he watched her hair caress and frame her beautiful breasts.

Resolutely, he reminded himself that Imogen now fitted under the category of 'duty'. She and their child were his responsibility. He couldn't let himself be distracted by selfish cravings when he had a duty to care for them both. He'd spent years in the pursuit of pleasure. He could be utterly single-minded when it came to doing what he wanted. He couldn't afford to lose focus now and give in to the urge for pleasure. He needed control, purpose, resolve.

Besides, he didn't like the morass of emotions that threatened whenever he thought of Imogen the woman, rather than Imogen his responsibility. He didn't deal in emotion, except for the frustrations and elations of his chosen sports.

'Now's not the time, Imogen. It's late.' He watched her stiffen and silently cursed his harsh tone.

He shoved his hands in his trouser pockets. As if that made it easier to resist the temptation to touch! An ache started in his jaw from clenching his teeth too tight.

'What's bothering you? Is it *Grand-mère*? I know she can be overwhelming at first but she likes you.'

'You can tell that?'

He nodded. 'I think she liked the way you spoke your mind. She isn't one for prevarication.'

'So I gathered.' Imogen gnawed the corner of her bottom lip, and he wanted to reach out and stop her.

'She offended you?'

'No. I rather liked her too, though she made me feel like a fashion disaster.'

'No one expects you to dress up all the time.' Imogen in high heels and that red, clingy dress was branded too clearly on his brain for anything like comfort. It had kept him awake too many nights. Besides, he liked her in jeans; liked the way they shaped her long legs and…

'Just as well.' Something like hurt glowed in her hazel eyes. 'I feel like a fraud going along with her plans to improve me.'

'She means well. And a tutor to help you with French is an excellent idea. I should have thought of it myself.'

'It's not that. I'd like to learn French.' Her gaze slid from his then back. The impact of those eyes on his should have knocked him back on his feet. There was so much *feeling* there. It was like looking into her soul. 'I just don't feel right, pretending I'm your wife for real.'

'You are my wife. Believe me, the ceremony was legally binding, even if it was brief.'

'But I'm not the woman who's going to be with you for the rest of your days. This is a temporary arrangement for my benefit.'

Thierry had never wanted a woman to be with

him for the rest of his days. Not since Sandrine. But he couldn't say that to a woman whose life was measured in months rather than years. The truth was he'd do whatever it took to make her remaining time as easy as possible.

He didn't just lust after Imogen. He didn't just see her as a responsibility. He cared about her.

Which meant he had to keep his focus on her well-being.

'Don't forget the child is mine too. We're in this together, Imogen.'

A little of the tension eased from her features, and he was stunned at how good it felt that he'd been able to do that for her.

'You don't have to worry about anything.' He kept his voice soothing. 'I'll take care of everything.' He paused, wondering whether to tell her his news.

'What is it?' She moved away from the door, her nightgown drifting around her like temptation.

'Sorry?'

'There's something you're not saying.'

Thierry frowned. Since when had she been able to read him? He prided himself on his ability to keep his thoughts to himself.

'Nothing to worry about.' But he saw she didn't

believe him. Perhaps she'd had so much bad news she now expected the worst. 'Just that I've managed to get you an appointment with one of the country's finest specialists. They're sending to Australia for your medical records.'

'I see.' Her mouth twisted, and he wanted to reach out and smooth those plump lips with his thumb, stroke her hair and tell her everything would be all right. But the hell of it was he couldn't.

'That's very good of you. Thanks.' The huskiness had gone from her voice, leaving it flat.

Thierry's muscles bunched as he fought the urge to reach for her. His embrace might soothe her temporarily but at the risk of him taking things too far. And her fragility was for once obvious in her delicate features.

'Was there anything else you wanted to talk about? My *grand-mère*, perhaps?'

'No. I just…' She paused so long he began to wonder what was wrong.

In a flurry of lace and cotton she crossed the floor, planting her hands on his tense shoulders. She was so close he felt her like the earth felt the sun, drawn to her magnetic warmth. Her lashes lifted to reveal eyes of sherry-brown spangled with green that made him think of mountain streams and ecstasy. She cupped the back of his head, narrow fingers sliding through his hair, sending rivers of molten energy straight to his groin.

'I needed to thank you.' She opened her mouth as if to say more then shut it again, her gaze zeroing on his mouth.

An instant later she'd risen on her toes, leaning in so her breasts pushed, soft and enticing, against him. Her lips were hot and sweet on his, seeking, torturing with the promise of delight.

A quake rocked him to the soles of his feet. His hands fisted in his pockets so hard he thought they might never loosen again. He breathed in her scent, tasting her on his lips, and almost lost his resolve. He wanted this so badly. He wanted so much more than he should if he was to look after her as she deserved.

A lifetime's experience in giving in to temptation had him dragging his hands out of his pockets, anchoring them at her sides where he felt the supple shift of toned muscle and the mind-destroying seduction of her in-curving waist.

Something like a growl erupted from the back of his throat and her tiny, answering moan just about undid him. All he had to do was open his mouth and…

With a surge of inexplicable strength he put her from him, stepping back so he held her at arm's length. His arms were shaking and his heart galloped out of control, but he'd done it. By the skin of his teeth he'd actually done what he should have done all along. She didn't have to thank him with the gift of her body. A better man wouldn't have countenanced it even for a second.

'There's no need to thank me, Imogen.' He barely recognised his voice as finally he managed to drag his hands away. 'Not like this.'

Something flashed in her eyes. Something swift and raw that he felt like a smack to the face. But it was gone in a second. Her flushed features set in an expression he couldn't read. Her lips were slightly parted as she dragged in air, and her hazel eyes looked past him as if the far wall fascinated her.

'Truly, Imogen, there's no need for that sort of thanks.'

Slowly, she nodded, then before he realised what she was about she was walking out the door, leaving his hands empty. 'I understand. Goodnight, Thierry.'

CHAPTER EIGHT

IMOGEN SAT STRAIGHT in her seat, braced for bad news. Hope for the best but prepare for the worst, wasn't that the adage? Right now she was hoping the doctor would confirm her child would be safe. The alternative…

A callused hand enclosed hers, long fingers gripping gently.

Startled, she looked around to Thierry beside her. He was watching the doctor pore over her scan results, yet he'd sensed her fear as if attuned to her.

He'd done that before, she remembered, the day his grandmother had arrived. His gentle touch on her cheek then had calmed her, made her feel he was on her side.

Imogen released a shivery breath, trying to find a place of calm amongst her whirling emotions.

Thierry's touch was a two-edged sword. Unashamedly she clung to his hand, grateful for the reminder she wasn't alone. Yet the poignancy of his touch lacerated something fragile inside. He hadn't touched her willingly since that day with his grandmother in the garden. The night she'd gone to him, eager to show how much she needed him, he'd stood aloof.

The memory of his beautiful, big body, so still and unresponsive when she'd offered herself to him, gouged at far more than her self-respect. It felt as if she'd swallowed a razor blade that cut her every time she breathed. The pain of his rejection rivalled even her blinding headaches at their worst.

Had she really invested so much in this man?

Imogen looked away to the framed diplomas on the wall.

Thierry hadn't even bothered to take his hands out of his pockets that night she'd kissed him! So much for rekindling the passion they'd shared. He'd stood there, enduring her touch, till finally he'd grabbed her and put her aside. No words could have made it clearer that for him the physical side of their relationship was dead.

She really had been a temporary fling.

'Imogen?' His low voice curled around her, beckoning, but she refused to turn. She had to hold herself together.

'Madame Girard.' At last the doctor spoke. Imogen squared her shoulders in preparation for the inevitable.

Yet, instead of the grave expression doctors usually reserved for delivering bad news, this man looked animated. Pleased. Her breath caught. Did that mean her baby would be okay? Involuntarily, her fingers clenched around Thierry's.

'You're something of a puzzle, Madame Girard.' The doctor shook his head slowly but there was no mistaking the hint of a smile at the corners of his mouth.

'I am?' Her voice was a husk of sound.

'Your symptoms fit a classic pattern and, combined with your family history...' He spread his hands as if to say there was nothing he could do for her.

Her heart dived and she bit down a gasp of distress.

A chair scraped and Thierry roped a long arm around her shoulders. Warmth enveloped her, the woodsy scent of the outdoors and something more, something beyond mere physical comfort. She leaned into him. No matter that she could do this alone if she had to. She'd never been more grateful for company in her life, even if it came from the man who saw her solely as a form of duty.

'Despite that, I'm pleased to tell you the head-aches and vision problems aren't what you think.'

'Pardon?'

The doctor smiled, his eyes alight. 'Contrary to expectations, you're not suffering the same disease as your mother.'

The air rushed from her lungs as if from a punctured balloon. 'I'm not?'

'Absolutely not. In fact, I can tell you there is no tumour, malignant or otherwise.' His smile became a beam.

Dazed, Imogen shook her head. 'I don't understand.'

'There was never a tumour, though it seems your general practitioner, like you, feared the worst.' He spoke slowly, glancing again at the test results. 'I've consulted with both your family doctor and my specialist colleague in Australia. The one you were supposed to see but didn't.'

She didn't miss the questioning inflection in his voice, or the tightening of Thierry's grip on her shoulder.

'There didn't seem much point. I knew what he was going to say. I just...' She looked up into surprisingly sympathetic grey eyes and found the words tumbling out. 'I couldn't bear facing the diagnosis so soon after losing my mother. I felt trapped.' She hefted a deep breath into too-tight lungs. 'I decided to get away, just for a while, before I had to face all that.' She waved a hand at the reports on his desk. 'But you're saying it's not a tumour? What is it, then?'

'I understand from your family doctor that you also lost your sister recently?'

Imogen could have howled with impatience. Why didn't he just tell her what was wrong with her?

Thierry's warm hand caressed her shoulder in a gesture of support that helped her gather her scattered wits.

'That's right. She died suddenly in an accident.'

'And then your mother became ill?'

Imogen nodded. 'Very soon afterwards. But I don't see how that's relevant.'

Sympathetic grey eyes held hers. 'Stress and grief can do amazing things, Madame Girard.'

'I don't understand.' She leaned forward, dislodging Thierry's grip. 'Please, just tell me what's going on.'

'I'm pleased to say that, on the basis of these very extensive tests, there's nothing physically wrong with you.'

'But that can't be! I'm not imagining those headaches. They're so bad they even affect my vision.'

The doctor nodded. 'I'm sure they are. Tell me, are they still as frequent?'

Imogen hesitated, calculating. 'No, not as often as before.' She spoke slowly. 'I haven't had one since Paris.' She couldn't remember the exact date and darted a sideways glance at Thierry but he wasn't looking at her. His attention was fixed on the doctor.

'So you're saying all this is the result of stress?' Thierry's voice held a note of disbelief that matched her own. 'There's no physical cause?'

'That doesn't make the pain any less real. I have no doubt the symptoms your wife has experienced were every bit as disturbing as ones caused by a tumour.' He looked down at his notes then up at Imogen. 'It seems to me that you've been through a very traumatic time, Madame Girard. The best remedy is rest, and...' a small smile played at his mouth '...something positive in your life. Like a baby to look forward to.'

'You're serious?' Imogen couldn't take it in.

'Absolutely. The symptoms you're experiencing will pass with time.'

A great hiccupping sob rose in her throat, and she crossed her arms around her middle, folding in on herself as shock detonated at her core. Through a blur of emotion she heard the doctor reassure her, telling her he'd be happy to see her again if she had any questions later, and more that she didn't really take in.

All she registered was that she was okay. She and her baby were going to live. Everything would be all right.

And one other detail. The fact that Thierry hadn't touched her again. She missed the warmth of his large, reassuring hand.

'I feel like such a fool,' she said again, watching the streets pass by as Thierry drove them out of the city. 'I just can't believe it. It seems so incredible.'

Thierry didn't say anything. When she turned to look, his profile was set in lines of concentration, his brow furrowed and his mouth firm.

The traffic was heavy, she told herself. Of course he needed to focus on that. Even to her own ears she sounded like a broken record, replaying the same phrases again and again. But she needed to talk about this to make it real. It was so unexpected, so much the miracle she'd never dared hope for, that she couldn't quite believe it.

Her palm covered her belly and gratitude overcame her. Her baby would be all right. She felt the weight of every anxious night ease from her shoulders as tears pricked her eyes. She let her head sink back against the headrest, relief vying with so many other emotions she couldn't get a grip on.

Just as well it was Thierry driving. She wouldn't have trusted herself.

'I still don't believe it,' she murmured. 'The one and only time I act on impulse.' She clasped her hands together. 'All my life I've been cautious, the one who never acted rashly, always considering the pros and cons before making a decision. Yet that one time I acted on the spur of the moment...'

That day in the Sydney waiting room, defeat had pressed down so hard, there'd seemed no room for doubt. She'd *known* she had the same fatal illness as her mother. 'I should have stayed for that appointment instead of haring off to the other side of the globe.'

But if you had, you'd never have met Thierry. You wouldn't be expecting this child.

Shocking as it was to find herself pregnant, Imogen couldn't wish that undone.

She turned and peeked at Thierry through her lashes. His jaw was hard-set, emphasising the strong thrust of his nose and the slashing lines of his cheekbones.

She dragged in a rough breath that didn't fill her lungs. 'All of this…us…' she waved her hand '…is because I acted impulsively. I should have waited and checked my facts.'

Still he said nothing.

'I'm sorry, Thierry. Truly sorry. You must be upset.'

'You think I'd prefer if the doctor had confirmed today that you're dying?' A muscle twitched in his jaw. 'What sort of man do you think I am? You think I'm upset that you're going to live?' Finally, he looked her way, his gaze piercing. 'What have I done to give you such an opinion of me?'

'You know what I mean. If I hadn't jumped to conclusions all this wouldn't have happened. We wouldn't be married. Because of that mistake, we're stuck with each other.'

Unless, of course, they divorced. But for the life of her she couldn't bring herself to mention it. Not yet. Not till she'd had time to absorb everything.

'What's done is done, Imogen. There's nothing to be gained in lashing yourself over it.'

'You think not?' Imogen stared. He seemed far too calm, though now she looked properly, the chiselled stillness of his profile hinted at fierce control. What was he holding back?

'I didn't do it deliberately.' She reached out and placed her palm on his thigh. Instantly, she felt the long muscle beneath her hand bunch tight and solid.

It was the first time she'd reached for him since that night in her room. Imogen looked at her pale hand against the taut, dark fabric of his trousers and wondered with a catch in her chest whether it would be the last time. 'You have to believe me. I wasn't lying or trying to trick you. I truly believed—'

'You think I don't know that?' Again, Thierry's gaze captured hers, shooting fire along veins turned frosty with shock.

'I don't know what you believe.' Thierry had been so good to her, so supportive, but she'd never been able to read him fully except when they shared pleasure. Right now he was giving a good imitation of a graven image. She felt none of the closeness she'd experienced before. She lifted her hand, warm from touching him, and tucked it into her lap.

'Your shock was obvious when the doctor told you the truth. I thought for a moment you might faint.'

Yet he hadn't wrapped his arm around her and hauled her close as he'd done before.

'I believe...' He paused and she could have sworn her heartbeat slowed in expectation. 'That, instead of apologising, you need to celebrate. It's not often a dying woman gets such a reprieve.'

Finally, his mouth curled up at the corner, and Imogen's heart gave a flutter of relief. It took a while to notice the tension in his neck and jaw hadn't eased.

They celebrated with lunch at the sort of restaurant Imogen had read about in guide books but never anticipated visiting. The service was impeccable, the food unlike anything she'd ever tasted and the ambience discreetly elegant. If the wine waiter was surprised they toasted her news with sparkling water, he didn't show it.

Thierry was charming, urbane and witty and, by the time the chef came out to greet them, Imogen felt more relaxed than she had in ages.

It was as she was coming back from the ladies' room that she saw Thierry in conversation with another diner, a fit-looking man with a shock of shaggy blond hair.

'A friend?' she asked as she sat down, watching the stranger walk out the door.

It struck her that she didn't know Thierry's friends. They'd spent all their time together, unless Thierry was working, as he did so many hours in the day.

'Yes, someone from the old days.'

'The old days?' She wished she'd returned to the table sooner.

'The days before I became a respectable businessman.' It should have been a joke but it didn't sound like it.

She tilted her head to one side. 'What did you do before you became respectable?'

'Whatever I pleased.' When he saw her watching, he continued. 'Skiing, parties, trekking, ballooning, more parties.' He swallowed the last of his coffee. 'In fact, I was just invited to a weekend climbing in the Alps.'

'And are you going?'

He shrugged, but she didn't miss the glitter in his eyes. It was the same look she'd seen when he'd told her about some of his far-flung adventures. 'I have too much to do. Too many responsibilities.'

You're one of those responsibilities.

You relied on him when you were desperate and look where that got you both—trapped in a marriage that should never have happened.

'I think you should go.' Imogen wasn't aware

of formulating the words but suddenly they were emerging from her mouth.

'Pardon?'

'Look at the hours you work.' He might be meticulous about joining her for meals but he was usually back at work in the evening. When did he get time off? He'd made time in Paris but now his business seemed to consume most of his waking hours. That and being on hand for her.

'That's because I've got deadlines.'

'Can't they be put back a few days? Long enough for a short break?' She watched his eyes narrow on the coffee cup he twisted with one hand. 'Surely nothing will go wrong if you take a weekend off? What are two days?'

Besides, it would do her good to have a few days alone. She had a lot of thinking to do. After months getting used to the idea of dying, she had to get her head around the notion of living.

Then there was this situation they were in—man and wife in a marriage that now had no built-in end date. Marriage to a man who was protective and caring but no longer desired her.

'You should go,' she urged, her constricting throat making her voice husky.

'Two days,' he mused, frowning. 'I admit, it's tempting.'

* * *

Two days turned into four. In fact, it would be five by the time he returned. Tonight was his fourth night away.

After the freedom of the mountains, the thrill of pitting himself against the elements on some of the region's most treacherous climbs, Thierry had been only too ready to agree when his friends had suggested an extra night at the resort before returning to his normal life.

Yet maybe he was getting too old for this. The hot shower tonight had been bliss on his sorely tried body. He couldn't remember feeling this level of weariness after a few days' climbing. Or maybe he felt out of sorts because he still grappled with the bizarre soap-opera storyline his life had become.

He swirled his cognac, inhaling its rich aroma, then knocked it back in one. The shot of heat to his belly was satisfyingly definite, unlike so much in his life now. He looked up, ignoring the party going on around him, and caught the bartender's eye, gesturing for another.

Thierry rolled his shoulders but couldn't shift the tension that had settled there. The sense of being weighed down. But worse was the roiling morass of *feelings*.

Thierry grimaced. His life had been simple and perfect. Yes, he'd had a little heartbreak in his youth but that had merely left him able to play the field, enjoying freedom in the bedroom as well as in his sports. Even the yoke of the family business hadn't taken that away from him. He'd shouldered massive burdens but he was close to freeing himself of that.

His old life had beckoned. Until Imogen.

He lifted his glass and slugged back another mouthful, ignoring the fact this liquor deserved slow appreciation. He didn't have the patience for that. He needed something to cut through the web of emotions tangling his brain.

He'd never felt such relief in his life as when the doctor had said Imogen was safe. That she and the baby would live. But the news hadn't just brought relief.

Cool logic told him Imogen hadn't deliberately set out to trap him into marriage. He'd been the one to persuade her and there'd been no mistaking her utter shock at the doctor's pronouncement. It wasn't her fault.

Damn it all, he could even sympathise with her walking out of that Sydney waiting room and heading for adventure rather than facing more appointments and treatment. It was the sort of thing he could imagine himself doing.

Yet no amount of logic could shift the sensation that he'd got caught in a net, in a situation far more complex than he'd anticipated. Marrying for the sake of a child was one thing. Acquiring a long-term wife was another. Then there were these feelings that clogged his chest. Half-formed ideas and sensations that were totally unfamiliar.

Thierry wanted his simple life back. Even in the beginning when he'd had to work soul-destroying hours to salvage the business he'd been certain of his purpose, and what little free time he'd had was his own to use as he chose.

Now he felt tethered. Tangled. Worse, he felt... He didn't know what he felt. Just that he didn't like it.

After the wedding he'd put Imogen in that box labelled 'duty'. He'd been able to deal with her as his responsibility when she was off-limits. Now suddenly that label didn't fit and all sorts of insidious ideas were weaving their way through his brain.

The waiter returned, and Thierry gestured for him to leave the bottle. Helping himself, he poured a double. His mouth twisted. He never drank this much. He preferred to keep his wits about him. But that hadn't done much good lately. Maybe he'd find clarity this way. *Something* had to break this untenable bind he found himself in.

He'd lost count of his drinks when he heard a husky whisper beside him. 'Is there enough for me to have a sip?'

He turned and for a second the edges of his vision blurred. But he had no trouble focusing on the woman beside him. Tall, slim, with cornflower-blue eyes and hair the colour of sunlight. Her mouth was wide and her expression aware. Exactly the sort of beautiful woman he'd always preferred. Given her height, he guessed she had long, lissom legs.

Thierry smiled and her pout of enquiry turned into a smile that would have melted the snow off Mont Blanc.

She put a glass on the bar, and he swiped up the cognac bottle, pouring her a measure without spilling a drop. He was congratulating himself on that feat when she leaned in to pick up her drink, pressing against him from breast to knee.

He felt the subtle stretch and arch of her body as she knocked back her drink, her breasts thrusting into his torso. Heat shot through him at that deliberate invitation.

She put her glass down and, holding his eyes,

slowly licked her lips. Her bottom lip shimmered, and Thierry felt a pounding in his head—or was it his chest?—as she slid her arms around his neck.

'How about a private party?' she whispered, her breath tickling his throat.

Then she reached up, pressing her mouth to his, and he found his hands clamping convulsively around her waist.

CHAPTER NINE

THIERRY DROVE ROUND to the offices at the back of the *château*.

He wasn't really in a fit state for work but there'd be crucial matters for his attention after five days away. Two property deals were nearing conclusion and he wanted an update. Plus there'd be the revised schedule for the new ski resort to check.

Besides, he wasn't ready to face his wife.

Wife. That word had become real in ways he'd never imagined when he and Imogen had married in that swift civil ceremony.

A wife was more than a temporary responsibility, a woman to be cared for in her hour of need.

Imogen had ceased being a responsibility and had again become a woman—with all the complications that entailed. Not a woman for a quick liaison but a woman with whom his life was now inextricably entangled.

Because he'd followed his instinct and decided

on marriage. He'd spent his life acting on instinct, even in business, and it rarely let him down.

His mouth set. There was always a first time.

He parked and switched off the ignition. His head beat like a drum, the pounding an insistent, punishing beat reminding him how foolish he'd been last night.

As if alcohol would solve his problems! Not even climbing, one of his favourite sports, had cleared his mind. Instead of enjoying the challenge of the sport, he'd been distracted by thoughts of Imogen and the disturbing emotions she stirred.

As for that debacle in the bar last night!

He leaned back against the headrest, shoving his hand through his hair.

Even drunk, he'd known what the blonde wanted. How could he not? He was the master of the short-term affair.

Too much cognac was a convenient excuse for the fact he'd smiled right back and offered her a drink. As if tangling with one sexy woman would solve the problems he had with another!

He couldn't remember if he'd felt a sizzle of anticipation as she'd sidled up to him, or what, if anything, had gone through his brain. All he knew was, the moment she'd pressed her mouth to his, revulsion had knifed him. Revulsion at her touch and, more, at himself.

His hands hadn't been gentle as he'd shoved her away. He had a suspicion she might even bear bruises from his touch, though last night she'd looked too shocked to register pain.

Thierry scrubbed a hand over his face. It had just been a kiss, a split second of a kiss at that, yet for the first time in his life he'd felt guilty about being with a woman.

Guilt and anger, and that sick swirl in his belly he'd like to believe was the result of too much alcohol. Instead, he suspected it was due to something else entirely.

Shoving the car door open, he swung out, letting it slam, and strode to the offices. He needed an afternoon concentrating on reports, plans and the delicate power play of property negotiations. Anything to take his mind off personal matters.

He made it past most of the offices and had reached the threshold of his own when someone called his name.

Thierry paused, biting down an oath. He wanted privacy, but this was why he was here, to lead the team. He turned and saw one of the legal staff approaching, an envelope in his hand and an expression on his face that had Thierry instantly alert.

'Is there a problem?' Mentally, he flicked through the current investments—commercial property, high-end resorts, the Côte du Rhône vineyard and—

'No problem.' Yet the lawyer's smile looked forced. 'Just tying up loose ends.' He offered the envelope and, to Thierry's surprise, walked quickly away.

Thierry's fingers tingled as he surveyed it. His staff here made a close-knit team, without the formality of the Paris office. They were relaxed and friendly, even in times of high workload. But his senior legal advisor was worried.

Thierry entered his office and shut the door. He strode to the window and slid the contents of the envelope into his hand.

It was just a few pages. Flicking to the back, he saw Imogen's name and signature and a date two days ago, all witnessed. Thierry frowned and flipped to the front.

Minutes later he stood, staring, his hand carving through his hair to clutch his scalp. Dimly, he registered a cramping in his chest that reminded him to suck in air.

This was what his legal staff had done while he'd been away?

The paper crackled as it crumpled in his fist.

Imogen must have asked them to draw this up. No one else would have dared consider it.

He dragged in another breath and searched for calm. It eluded him. Why had she so ostentatiously cut herself off from his wealth, the material support he could provide? It should have felt like a reprieve yet in some obscure way it was a slap in the face, made more insulting because of the shame he felt after last night.

He told himself a single kiss with a stranger didn't taint his honour, yet he felt…stained. It had to be because of this indignity Imogen had engineered. No doubt his employees were gossiping about the fiasco their boss's marriage had become. Thierry had never in his life cared about gossip, but to be made a laughing stock in his own home…

The papers fell as he marched across the room, wrenched open the door and strode out.

She wasn't in her room. A scan revealed nothing except her passport on the dresser beside her purse.

Thierry scowled. Why was her passport out?

The sound of running water penetrated and he

stalked to the bathroom door, pushed it open and walked in.

Behind the clear glass of the shower screen, water sluiced down Imogen's lush body. Her head arched back as she massaged shampoo from her long hair. The pose thrust her breasts out, silhouetting them against the window beyond.

Thierry stilled, his hand on the door knob. Everything inside him collapsed in on itself. Arousal, strong as the tug of the ocean's inexorable current, dragged at his lower body. He didn't notice the pounding in his head any more, just his lungs' short, sharp grabs for oxygen and the thunder of his heartbeat rapping his ribs.

'Thierry?' Her eyes opened wide, and she stood transfixed, glistening and perfect. His gaze traced her raspberry-pink nipples that beaded as he watched, down the plane of her ribcage to her taut belly that showed no sign yet of his child inside.

His child.

His hand tightened on the door as she turned her back to wrench off the taps. The dip and curve of her glistening back was entrancing.

His wife.

The thought curled through him like a beckoning finger, inviting him into the room.

He scooped up a towel and pulled open the shower door. Amazingly, she crossed one arm over her breasts as she turned, her other hand covering her pubic area. As if he didn't recall every slick curve and plane of that gorgeous body!

That was the problem. All this time dealing with Imogen the duty rather than Imogen the sensuous woman had left him sleep-deprived. No wonder he was out of sorts.

'There's no need for modesty, *ma chère*.'

Her chin tilted and something hot jabbed through him. He'd always responded to a challenge.

'I'd prefer you to knock before you come in.'

'It's late for setting ground rules, Imogen. You're my wife and I have a right to be here.' The long walk through the *château* had fuelled his roaring indignation.

His eyes flicked down, taking in her pale skin, blush-pink from the shower, and her sinuous curves.

Reason and patience retreated. He was tired of being patient. More, he was tired of the bitter stew of emotions he couldn't banish. Emotions Imogen had created.

He didn't do emotion. Not with women.

He should have followed through that night she'd kissed him in his bedroom. She wouldn't be tying him in knots if he had. But telling himself his frustration levels were his own fault didn't help. He'd needed that mental and physical distance to keep himself sane and ensure he looked after her as she deserved.

Mouth setting in a crooked line, she snatched the towel from him. He had one last glimpse of tip-tilted breasts jiggling deliciously before she wrapped the massive bath sheet around her, even covering her shoulders, as if knowing how her bare skin inflamed him.

She stared straight back, her look all hauteur, as if he'd crawled out of a Marseilles sewer.

Instead of freezing him, that stare ignited something dangerous. Thierry felt it like a whoosh of flame, razing his carefully nurtured restraint.

No woman looked at him like that. Ever. Especially not the woman for whom he'd done so much!

Thierry's hands were hard and brown against the white towel as he grabbed her shoulders. He felt her fine bones, heard the flurry of her quickened breathing, and that sent fiery heat spilling through his veins.

'What did you think you were doing, drawing up that…that…?' Indignation stole his vocabulary.

'That post-nuptial agreement?' Her chin notched.

'Were you deliberately trying to insult me?'

Her eyes widened. 'Of course not. I don't see the problem.'

'You go to my staff and ask them to draw up a contract specifying you renounce any claim to my assets, weeks *after* we marry. You sign in front of witnesses, and you don't see a problem?' His voice rose and beneath his hold she flinched.

Good! How dared she make him an object of ridicule?

Yet if anything her mouth set tighter. Green fire sparked in her eyes.

'I was doing you a favour. Your lawyers thought so. You should have seen their relief when I explained what I wanted.'

'You think I live my life to please lawyers?' His fingers clamped harder.

'I was doing the right thing.' Her chin jutted and her brilliant eyes met his unerringly. 'You didn't want a permanent wife. If you had, I'm sure you'd have expected a pre-nup. Circumstances have changed and I wanted you to know I'm not hanging around, aiming for a share of your wealth.'

Not hanging around? Was that why her passport was out? Warning jangled, and Thierry yanked her body full against his, soft to his rigid frame. He let go of her shoulders and wrapped his arms around her, pinioning her.

Memory assaulted him. Of that woman last night, her body pressed to his, her lips against his mouth. And all he felt was disgust. Because she hadn't been Imogen.

It was his wife he wanted. No one else.

That truth had hammered at him all day. There'd been no evading it, no matter how he'd tried.

Imogen had burrowed under his skin, destroying his interest in other women. That was bad enough. Worse was the fact she now acted as if she didn't want him! She deliberately provoked.

'What did I ever do to suggest I believed you were after my money?' His words were sharp as a lash, and he felt her tense. He breathed deep, nostrils flaring as he dragged in the scent of damp, sweet woman. 'When have I *ever* insulted you as you've insulted me? You make me look like a mercenary, gullible fool, scared you're going to fleece me. A man who needs saving from his own decisions!'

'That wasn't my intention.' Her eyes widened. This close, he caught the shock in those sherry-brown depths.

'You think I'm so incompetent I need protecting from my actions?'

'I think you're overreacting.' Her finger jabbed his chest. 'I saw your expression after the doctor said I wasn't ill. I saw your doubts.' She tried to stare him down. 'You were wondering if I'd deliberately misled you, weren't you? You suspected I was some gold-digger who'd set up an elaborate scam.'

Fury spiked in Thierry's gut, because for a split second the question *had* surfaced. That was what his lawyer had warned. But Thierry had dismissed the idea. Instead, he'd trusted her, ignoring any such doubt as unworthy.

How many men would have done that?

Besides, Imogen's reaction at the doctor's news had been absolutely genuine.

'What you saw was shock,' he ground out between clenched teeth. 'You'll pardon me for that, given everything that went before. Or are you the only one allowed to be taken by surprise?'

'It was more than surprise. You were quiet. You weren't...' For a split second he'd have sworn he read vulnerability in her expression but then she shoved her finger into his chest again, as if *he* were at fault.

He, who'd done nothing but look after her from the start!

'Weren't what?' he growled.

She shook her head and a slick ribbon of dark hair slid over her shoulder. 'You're saying you weren't regretting this marriage? You weren't regretting *me*?'

'You think I'd rather the doctor had confirmed you were dying? *That's* what you think of me?'

Deliberately, he lashed his anger higher, ignoring the fact there was a grain of truth in her words—he'd never expected to have a real marriage, only a short-term solution to the problem of caring for Imogen and her child.

Her eyes held his. 'Why are you so angry, Thierry?' Her breath came in short bursts that pushed her breasts against his torso and sent need quaking through him. Being close to her spun him out till he teetered on the brink of control. 'I don't understand. I was trying to do the right thing, making it clear I didn't expect more from you.'

He stared down at the mutinous line of her mouth. The mix of anger and hurt in her eyes.

Why *was* he angry?

What she said made sense. Yet he didn't want that

sort of favour. At some deep, primitive level her action carved at his honour, his masculine pride.

Was it the careless way she spurned the fortune he'd worked like a slave to secure that needled? Or that he couldn't conquer the unfamiliar mix of emotions she'd stirred?

Or was it that the gesture felt like a rejection of *him*?

He hadn't known rejection since he was twenty and Sandrine had chosen another man. Since then he'd ensured his liaisons were short and easy, ones he could walk away from without a backward glance. Always he was in control—the hunter, the seducer, the one to leave.

The thought of Imogen spurning him made him wild. The fire spread from his belly, coursing out in molten waves.

'Why have you got your passport out?'

She blinked. 'I wondered if I should book a flight to Australia. Clearly, you're not going to want me here long term.'

'Clearly?'

Her eyes skated away from his, and he felt something loosen inside.

'I don't belong here, Thierry. That's obvious.'

He ignored the strange, queasy sensation her words provoked. 'You were going to run away?'

Her gaze met his again in a clash that should have struck sparks. 'Of course not. I was waiting till you came home to talk about it.' For the first time he read hesitation in her expression. 'Now you're here we can discuss it. Just give me time to get dressed.' She gripped the towel tighter and made to take a step back. But he didn't let her go. Instead, his arms closed hard around her.

Imogen's head jerked up, consternation battling something he couldn't identify in her expression.

Why was she worried? She wasn't afraid of him. She'd made that clear. She was ready to walk out on him.

'No.' The word emerged from his tight throat. 'You're not going anywhere.'

She scowled and shoved her hands against his chest as if to push him away. The movement shifted the towel, revealing a tempting sliver of peachy, pale skin. 'What's wrong with you, Thierry? I don't understand.'

Nor did he. That made his anger burn brighter. The fact that it was instinctive, uncontrollable, totally inexplicable.

He just knew that none of this was right.

He'd be damned if he'd let her leave before he worked it out.

'Then understand this.' Hauling her to him, he took her mouth in a swooping kiss that started as punishing but morphed in a heartbeat to urgent, hungry, demanding. Desperate.

A moment's hesitation, a stillness that made something like fear rise in him, then her lips opened beneath his like a fragile blossom responding to sunlight.

This was what he wanted. What he'd craved. Imogen's fragrance, her taste, invaded his senses, a sweet, addictive flavour that blasted the back off his head as she tentatively moved her mouth against his.

One arm lashed about her waist and his other roved up to cup the back of her neck, supporting her as he bowed her back. She clung to his shirt and he knew a surge of triumph.

A shudder racked her, and he felt it from his mouth, down all the places where their bodies melded, right to the soles of his feet, braced wide to support them both. His brain told him to pull back; he was being too rough. Then he heard her little throaty moan, tasted it in his mouth.

He knew that sound. Imogen losing control. Imogen turning to flame and rapture in his arms. Imogen abandoned and eager.

Thierry's anger drained and with it the fear he'd refused to acknowledge. Fear that he'd lost her. Energy coursed through him; arousal weighted his groin and turned his body from flesh and bone to forged metal.

In a single, unhesitating movement, he swept an arm beneath her legs and scooped her up against his chest. Still they kissed, their lips fused with a passion that obliterated all else.

Her arms crept higher till he felt her fingers against his neck, holding tight. He wanted to whoop in exultation. Except that would mean lifting his mouth from hers. And the way she was kissing him, as if she'd been starved of him, just as he'd been without her... He refused to give that up.

Thierry spun round, lifting his eyes just enough to navigate into Imogen's bedroom.

Six strides and he was beside the bed. An instant later and she fell onto the coverlet, and he with her, arms around her, his body pressing her down. She hitched her arms tighter around his neck and pressed her mouth urgently against his.

With one hand he wrenched back the towel from her damp body, his fingers brushing soft flesh and dissolving his brain. Urgently, he fumbled at his belt buckle. He couldn't recall ever being this desperate, this uncoordinated.

He breathed hard through his nostrils, trying to find focus. He would have lifted his mouth but Imogen gripped his skull so hard he succumbed to mutual hunger and contented himself with fumbling one-handed.

One slim, bare leg slid alongside his, then folded over the back of his thigh, as if trapping him against her.

Did she really fear he'd withdraw now?

Not with the taste of her on his tongue, vanilla sugar and feminine spice. Not with her mouth demanding, playing, teasing his. And her body moving sinuously beneath him. Those tiny, circling movements drove him insane. He had to get naked, quickly, before he lost it.

He'd lost count of the weeks since he'd had Imogen. It felt like half a lifetime. The need for her rose, eclipsing all else. Finally, he wrenched his belt undone, then the button on his trousers. But in the process the back of his hand brushed the soft, warm skin of her belly.

A shaft of awareness struck him. Not sexual awareness but something new. Something powerful and tender. Bracing himself better on his other elbow, he turned his hand and spread his palm over her stomach.

There was a roaring in his ears, a pounding like a hundred horses behind his ribcage, and a strange new sense filling it. It was wonder, possessiveness and a fierce tug of protectiveness all rolled into one.

Imogen's head fell back and suddenly he could breathe again, though in rasping breaths so harsh they tore at his lungs. Or maybe that was because of the look in her eyes. It was something like wonderment and it erased his searing temper in an instant.

Thierry slid his hand lower, entranced by the incredible silky texture of her flesh and the fact that his child lay nestled there.

He wanted to pound himself against her, fill her hard and fast till they lost their minds in ecstasy. But thought of the child gave him pause. Exultation warred with caution—the primitive against the civilised.

'Our baby,' he murmured, stunned by the reality of it.

Imogen's hand covered his, gently pressing. Her eyes glowed as if he'd just given her the best compliment in the world.

'I thought you didn't really want it.'

He shook his head. In truth he hadn't thought too much about it as a living, breathing child. He'd focused on getting through the pregnancy, seeing Imogen cared for. Intellectually, he'd understood there was a baby, but touching her belly, knowing that new life lay just centimetres below his palm... It was a humbling experience.

He shook his head. 'I would never reject it.' That, at least, was the truth.

Imogen lay panting, watching expressions flicker across Thierry's strong features. He'd taken her from zero to two hundred in a heartbeat with that glorious, savage kiss that had melted her bones. Now his tenderness threatened to melt her heart.

Our baby. Finally, he'd said it. More than said it. He felt how special this was—it was there in his touch, his stillness, his expression.

Suddenly, he was moving and Imogen bit back a cry as he levered himself away. She had to clench her hands to stop herself reaching for him.

But he didn't go far, just pulling back far enough to strip the towel wide, leaving her completely exposed. He bent, his mouth grazing her belly softly in a caress that drew her skin tight with wanting and wonder.

Imogen looked down at his glossy dark hair against her skin, that proud face, his large, capable hand clamping her hip while his lips skated across the place where their baby lay.

Her heart turned over at Thierry's tenderness, and stupidly, tears pricked the back of her eyes. Rapidly, she blinked them back.

'You really do care about the baby.' The revelation tightened her throat.

His eyes met hers and connection throbbed between them, strong as the beat of her heart. 'Of course I care.'

Imogen shook her head, confused by what she thought she saw in his eyes. 'There's no need for this…us.' She stumbled over the words, hating the idea that, for the sake of their baby, he might pretend to want her too.

'No need?' His dark brows scrunched together.

She tried to hitch herself higher in the bed but his weight imprisoned her.

'You don't want me. There's no need to pretend.'

'Not *want* you?' His eyes rounded.

Imogen looked away, too aware suddenly of her nakedness. 'When I went to your room, when I wanted you, you rejected me.' Sheer pride kept her voice steady when it felt like she was crumbling into a thousand humiliated pieces.

'Listen to me, Imogen.' His hand was warm and compelling as he cupped her chin, turning it so she was forced to meet his gaze. 'I never, not even for a moment, stopped wanting you.'

'But—'

'But I tried to ignore that because I needed to look after you. I thought you were too sick, too fragile—'

'Fragile!' Her eyes bulged.

Thierry nodded. 'I was trying to protect you from me.' Slowly the grim line of his mouth eased into a rakish smile that made her heart dance. 'But you're not ill now, are you?' His voice grazed her nerves like suede on silk.

Imogen opened her mouth to argue, to probe, but abruptly he was gone, sliding down her body. 'Thierry?'

He positioned himself low, his strong hands urging her thighs up and out, leaving her wide open to him. Imogen's breath stalled, her protest disintegrating as those midnight-dark eyes snared hers. His mouth dipped to touch her in that most sensitive spot and a shiver of powerful excitement shot through her. She'd waited so long for his loving.

Wonder filled her at the idea he, like she, had suffered from the careful distance they'd maintained.

Imogen swallowed hard, but before she could formulate words his mouth caressed her again. This time the bolt of pleasure rocked her to the core.

Seconds later, her heart quivering from the smoky expression in his eyes, the flames erupted and her whole body lit up from the inside. The climax was more powerful than any Imogen remembered. She found herself sobbing his name, her hands biting his shoulders as waves of pleasure rolled through her.

Afterwards he didn't smile. There was no satisfaction like he'd shown in the past when she hadn't been able to contain her response to him. His expression was serious, completely intent as he gently lowered her legs, stroking her thighs till the racking shudders of ecstasy abated.

Through half-closed eyes she watched him undress, revealing the lean, powerful body that was so superbly masculine and honed to perfection. His movements were methodical and slow, as if he didn't understand how much she needed him, even after that climax. No, because of it. She needed Thierry, his body joined with hers.

Finally, he covered her with his hard frame, careful to take his weight on his arms. Heavy thighs pressed against hers, the rough silk dusting of his chest hair tickled her nipples and she sighed, relishing his heavy erection nudging her.

Imogen clutched his shoulders, trying to draw him closer, but he resisted, his jaw locked in an expression of determination that flummoxed her. But soon she understood.

It wasn't enough that he'd already reduced her to white-hot ash with that blast of sexual release. He was determined to do it again, with his superb body and his hand between her legs.

'I want you. Now,' she gasped, letting go of his shoulder and reaching for him. But she'd barely brushed her fingers across that hot erection when he captured both her wrists and shackled them above her head with one hand.

'Thierry!' But his mouth met hers, stopping her complaints, and all the while he made love to her with a slow, sure eroticism that made her tremble all over again. Heat sparked anew and she jerked hard beneath his touch as rapture took her.

How long he pleasured her she didn't know but she saw stars over and over again. Her breathing fractured and her body was limp and boneless from an overload of delight.

All the while those dark eyes held hers, his touch sure and fatally sensual, dragging response after response from her. Imogen told herself she should have stopped him, demanded what she wanted. But how could she when it seemed he knew her better than she did? He played her body like a maestro conducting a symphony. A symphony that left her euphoric and sated.

She felt as if those caresses had indelibly imprinted him on her body, marking her as his, so that in future she'd respond to no man but him. She was lost in the heady delight of his touch, his slow, seductive kisses and the magic he wove.

Finally, he came to her, joining them with one slow surge that brought him right to the heart of her. For an instant he held steady there and she wondered if she'd ever know again such a sensation of being one with another being. It was wonderful and scary and, despite her exhaustion, arousing.

Wrapping her arms around his slick torso, she held him close. He was determined to take things slowly, his movements measured, despite the way his heart pounded. Looking up, she saw the sheen of sweat on his forehead and the grit of a jaw locked, as if in pain. His heat was like a furnace, branding her.

A flash of suspicion hit. Was he afraid he'd injure the baby? Was that what kept his powerful body so tight?

As soon as the notion surfaced she knew it was true. He'd been mightily aroused from the moment he'd confronted her in the bathroom and still he held himself in check.

Her hands slid down the sleek curve of his back and around the impressive, taut curve of his buttocks. They flexed at her touch, and she tightened her grip, hearing Thierry's breath hiss. She turned her head, stretching higher to touch her lips to his ear. Then she whispered to him, confiding exactly what she wanted him to do to her.

She'd barely begun when he lost his slow rhythm and a burst of hoarse French filled her ears. A large hand clamped her breast, kneading, as Thierry's hips jerked powerfully, rocking into her, filling her faster and faster.

Imogen held tight, revelling in his urgency. She nipped at his earlobe and suddenly there was a roar of sound, a fierce, undulating wave of delight as he powered into her, no longer in control, as vulnerable to ecstasy as she'd been.

Heat pumped into her, an unfettered liquid throb that she'd never before experienced.

Dazedly, Imogen realised it was the first time they hadn't used protection. Maybe that was why this felt so momentous. So starkly real as she held Thierry's shuddering body protectively close. Not just satisfying, but as if together they'd discovered some primeval secret that would bind them for ever.

Finally, he slumped in her arms, his mouth at her neck, his weight pressing her down as exhaustion and satiation claimed them.

Imogen's last thought was a hope that, whatever they'd just experienced, it would change everything between them.

CHAPTER TEN

'ARE YOU HUNGRY?' The warm rumble of Thierry's voice made Imogen stir and stretch. She'd been lying in a haze of wellbeing, her mind drifting.

She opened her eyes and discovered soft lamplight filled the room. 'How long did I sleep?' She rolled over to find him propped against the headboard beside her. He looked scrumptious with his rumpled hair, the dark shadow on his jaw, and a casual shirt and jeans.

'You got dressed!'

His chuckle was like honey, rich and enticing, and her insides curled. Delight feathered her spine and between her thighs she felt a pulse flutter into life.

Responding again to the sensual promise in Thierry's voice should have been impossible after all they'd just shared. Yet when her eyes met his the impact of that connection jolted through her. She watched his smile fade.

'I had to get dressed or shock the staff when I

went to get us a snack. You might prefer me naked but they wouldn't.'

Imogen wouldn't bet on it. No woman in her right mind would object to seeing a man like Thierry in all his glory—beautifully proportioned, every muscle honed and full of lean power. Watching him walk naked across a room was one of the treats she'd most missed when they'd said their goodbyes in Paris. He was built like an athlete in his prime, moving with effortless masculine grace.

'What time is it?' Surely it had been early afternoon when he'd confronted her in the bathroom? After her long walk in the sun, grappling with her options for the future, she'd felt weary and hot, ready for a cool shower.

He shrugged. 'Late. I cancelled dinner while you slept but Jeanne insisted I bring a tray to you.'

Imogen rose on her elbows. 'You should have woken me.'

Thierry didn't answer. His gaze was on her breasts, uncovered now by the sheet that someone had pulled over her. Heat suffused Imogen. Because she was so exhausted by their love-making she didn't even remember covering herself? Or because of the jangle of excitement when he looked at her that way—as if she were some delicacy for his enjoyment? She was so weak where he was concerned. Look how she'd gone up in flames in his arms!

Imogen grabbed the sheet and pulled it higher.

'Don't.' His arm shot out, fingers circling her wrist. 'Please.' His deep voice grated.

She swallowed, a delicate shiver rippling through her as he let go her wrist to touch her breast with gentle fingers. Was it his touch or the pleading tone that made her hesitate?

A gasp caught in her throat as pleasure cascaded through her. Her nipple beaded to an aching pout as he circled her breast.

'Thierry.' It was half groan, half plea, and she didn't have time to feel self-conscious about it because in another second he was there, his breath warm on her flesh, his eyes glittering greedily.

One arm pulled her close while the other cupped her breast as he lowered his mouth. Her skin tingled as he blew over her nipple, creating delicious quivers of reaction that spread across her back, down her belly and straight to her womb. Then his mouth was on her, drawing her in, offering bone-melting delight.

Imogen cradled his dark head in her hands, holding him to her while her hips turned towards him, pressing close through the bedclothes. She loved the softness of his hair in her hands, such a contrast to the hard muscle and bone of his powerful body.

When finally he dragged his head up her breathing was ragged and needy and she had trouble focusing on his expression.

'I came here to talk,' he murmured. 'But that can wait.' Already, he was peeling the sheet lower, his big, warm hand smoothing down her ribs.

She covered his fingers with hers, stopping his progress.

'You want to talk?'

'Later will do.' A hungry smile curled the corner of Thierry's mouth, and Imogen knew a compelling temptation simply to lie back and enjoy his attentions. Nothing in all her life made her feel so good as when he made love to her.

Except ever since the doctor's news, she'd wanted to talk with Thierry. Not the casual chatter that he'd used to fill her 'celebration' lunch, but to sort out things between them.

Lustrous dark eyes surveyed her. Oh, the promise in that heated look! 'It can wait.'

How she'd craved that from him all this time when he'd been punctiliously polite, like a courteous stranger.

Nerves stabbed her. He'd said he still desired her, had already proved it, yet maybe she wouldn't like what he'd say. They needed to clear the air and decide where they went from here. It took all her courage to do what she knew she must.

'No, it can't.' She put her hand on his shoulder, stopping him when he would have bent again to her breast. She felt the bunch and flex of muscle beneath her hand and knew she didn't have the power to hold him off. Instead, he chose to respect her wishes.

Finally, she felt some of his urgency abate a fraction as he eased back, resignation on his face. 'You choose the damnedest times to chat.'

A bubble of laughter rose to her lips but she smothered it, realising it was generated by nerves, not amusement. 'You were the one who suggested we talk.'

'That was before.' He moved his hand to tweak her nipple. She gasped as a chord of erotic energy drew tight and alive to the core of her being. Slowly, Thierry smiled. 'Are you sure you don't want to talk later?'

Of course she wasn't sure. She was only human.

Too human when it came to Thierry. For a woman who had no trouble resisting men, she found herself totally unstuck with this gorgeous hunk of a Frenchman. Even the lazy satisfaction of her well-used body didn't prevent a quiver of anticipation at the look in his eyes.

'We need to talk now.' Her voice, throaty and full, gave her away but finally, after close scrutiny, he nodded and rolled away from her to sit up.

Imogen gnawed at her lip rather than howl her frustration at the distance between them.

This is what you wanted, remember!

Physically, she was besotted with the man. She yanked up the sheet, determined to cover herself, and almost groaned out loud at the sensual torture of crisp cotton against her aroused nipples.

Out of the corner of her eye she saw him watching. Was that a smirk?

Did he know how turned on she was after the way he'd fondled her? Of course he knew! He was enjoying her reaction.

Setting her mouth, Imogen let go of the sheet and wriggled up into a sitting position, propping a second pillow behind her. Warm air caressed her breasts but it was the heat of Thierry's gaze that she felt like a touch.

He wasn't smiling now. He was focused on every sway and jiggle of her bare breasts with an intensity that almost stopped her breath.

Good! Served him right.

Casually, she reached for the sheet, drawing it slowly over her chest and tucking it tight under her arms.

She turned to him. 'You're ready to talk?'

'Witch.' But there was amusement in his eyes despite the tension in his features.

If she was, then it was because of him. Thierry Girard had turned a cautious mouse of a woman into one more than happy to flaunt herself before her lover. One with more confidence in her body than she'd had before. One ready to take on the challenge of living instead of dying.

Imogen felt an answering smile tug her mouth. She loved it when he was like this—charming, fun and oh-so-sexy. Far better than when he'd been politely distant. Or when he'd looked grim and implacable.

'Thierry? We've got things to discuss.'

Slowly, he raised his gaze to hers and once more she felt that sensation of melding, of connection. It warmed her in places that had been too long cold.

'Let's eat first.' He swung away and lifted a tray from the bedside table, busying himself ensuring it was stable.

In any other man those quick, restless movements would have made her wonder if he was nervous.

But this was Thierry, über-confident and competent, literally the lord of all he surveyed from his ancient *château*. What reason could he have to be nervous?

She was the outsider, the unwanted complication in his world.

Thick, dark hair fell across his brow, giving him a casual, boyish look that tugged at her heart.

Imogen's breath caught as she remembered his grandmother's words. Did she really look at him with love in her eyes? Was that why she was so desperate for more than his polite goodwill? Why she craved his smiles and this precious sense of them sharing not just their bodies, but some other intimate connection?

The idea made her simultaneously ecstatic and horrified. Trepidation and tentative hope danced along her nerves. But she couldn't bring herself to believe it was true. It was far too dangerous a thought.

'Fruit, quiche or trout?'

Imogen made herself focus on the lavish spread between them. Jeanne had done them proud. She could barely see the tray for the luscious food piled upon it.

Suddenly she realised she was ravenous. 'Everything.' She plucked a gleaming strawberry from a bowl. Her eyes closed as she bit into it. It tasted of sunlight and sweetness. She'd never known food to taste as good as here at Thierry's *château*. Because it was locally grown and fresh, or because her new lease of life made her appreciate small delights even more?

When she opened her eyes it was to find Thierry staring at her mouth, his expression taut and hungry. She gulped down the rest of the fruit, her throat constricting.

They had so much to sort out, but at least on a purely physical level the connection was as strong as ever. The intensity of Thierry's love-making earlier had given her hope and relief after these lonely days when he'd been away. Ever since her doctor's appointment she'd felt strangely alone, even when he was with her. He'd withdrawn mentally.

Not even the fact her headaches were fading had made her feel better. The last one, the first night Thierry had been away climbing, had been a mere shadow of the previous piercing agony.

'You're sure you want to talk?' His voice was pure temptation and the look in his eyes told her she'd enjoy every moment of *not* talking. But they needed to clear the air.

'Why were you so angry earlier?' Imogen had never seen him in a temper and riding that lashing storm had been shocking. Yet on some level she'd thrilled to the vibrancy in him, excited by it.

Because he cared enough to be angry?

That sounded masochistic and she wasn't fool enough to want a man who took out his frustrations on her. Yet she sensed Thierry's anger was rare. After all, he'd taken in his stride all the complications she'd presented him with, never once blaming her or losing his cool. It was more that his flash of temper had broken down the wall between them, the wall she hadn't seen him build till it was too late.

'I apologise for that.' A pulse ticked in his jaw as he helped himself to cheese and home-made crackers. 'I overreacted. I see now you were trying to make a point.' Suddenly, he looked up, his eyes, dark as bitter coffee, snaring hers. 'But there was no need to prove yourself.'

Imogen spread her hands. 'It was important to make it clear I didn't want any more from you. You've done so much, acted so…honourably.' That old-fashioned word seemed apt. For surely that was what Thierry's grave concern, his gentleness and the efforts he'd gone to on her behalf, amounted to?

'It's done now. I suggest we forget it.' Yet he hadn't. There was an edge to his voice.

'But there's something bothering you.'

He dropped his gaze to her breasts, and her nipples peaked against the crisp cotton. 'From here everything looks perfect.'

Heat crept from her breasts to her throat and face. She still hadn't grown used to such blatantly carnal looks. They threatened to turn her brain as well as her bones to mush. After all, she'd spent twenty-five years avoiding risk, playing safe.

Thierry and her—this connection between them—had been easier to cope with when she'd been able to write it off as a flare of passing attraction, a desperate fling of a dying woman. But she had a full life before her now. She had to come to grips with what was happening.

Her whole being lit up when he looked at her that way. Focusing was almost impossible.

'Why do I get the feeling you're changing the subject?'

Thierry blinked and for an instant she read tension in that powerful frame.

'Things have changed,' he said finally. 'You were right about that.'

Imogen's frustration levels rose when he didn't

continue. If he wouldn't confront the elephant in the room, she would.

'I'm not dying. Which means we've saddled ourselves with marriage when we needn't have.' The words tasted bitter.

'Saddled?' His nostrils flared as if in distaste.

'Come on, Thierry. Don't tell me you wanted a permanent wife. Marriage made sense when I thought I was dying and it meant you could claim our baby. But now—'

'Now you want to back out of it?'

'It's not a matter of backing out. It's a matter of being sensible.' The thought of leaving him tore at something vital inside her. But she owed him. That knowledge threatened to shatter every certainty she'd once harboured.

All her life she'd been risk-averse, carefully building security for herself, keeping herself independent of any man, she realised. No wonder Scott had found it so easy to walk away from her, using the time she'd devoted to her mother as an excuse. Now it seemed her happiness was bound up with a man she'd met just months ago.

Yet she couldn't hold Thierry to this marriage, not unless they were both committed to it. 'You were kind to me when I most needed it. I don't want to repay you with a complication you never wanted.'

No matter how she yearned for him.

Sexual attraction alone was not a sound basis for a relationship. As far as she knew, that was all he felt for her, plus responsibility for their baby.

'You think of our child as a complication?'

She struggled to read his inflection.

'It was unexpected, but I can't regret it. I was referring to me being a complication in your life.' Why was he so obtuse? His quick understanding was one of the things she loved about him.

Loved.

Something clenched in the deepest recesses of her soul.

It was true. It was really true.

Here she was, trying to convince him he didn't need a spouse, when all the time...

Imogen sucked in a deep breath, dizzy with the implications of the one crucial fact she'd been avoiding for weeks.

'Imogen?' Thierry's frown grew, lines ploughing his forehead and carving around his mouth.

Helplessly, she stared at him. She was in far too deep when the sight of his concern threatened to undo her resolve. She tried to tell herself that it was natural she'd grown fond of him when he'd been so wonderful.

But *fond* didn't go anywhere near describing her visceral need for Thierry. A need that was far more than physical.

Imogen crossed her arms as if to hide the tumultuous throb of her heart hurling itself against her ribs.

'I could be on a flight in a day or two.' She dragged the words out. 'There's no need for…' She waved her hand across the bed as words dissolved.

'You *want* to leave?' He leaned close, his finger stroking her cheek, pushing her hair back over her shoulder. It was all she could do not to turn into his touch and nestle her cheek against his palm.

She wanted so much. Thierry. This closeness. His passion—definitely his passion—but far more. She swallowed hard over a knot of pain.

Against the odds she'd shared a wonderful affair with a man who in every way the world counted was far out of her league. Now, when it should be over and they should be saying their goodbyes, it tore her apart.

Because it was true.

She'd fallen in love with Thierry Girard.

She wanted to be with him, not just now, sharing

pleasure, but always, growing old together. Being a part of him just as he'd become a vital part of her.

'I'm trying to do what's right.' And it had never been so hard. To her horror her mouth crumpled with the effort of holding in so much welling emotion.

'I don't want you to go.' The words circled the still air and eddied deep inside her. Her head shot up, eyes locking with his.

'You don't?'

His smile was crooked and devastatingly sexy. 'I want you here, *chérie*.'

Imogen's heart locked in her throat. Could it be?

'Is it so bad being here with me?' he murmured, his hand trailing down her throat to her bare collarbone.

'Of course not. I…' She swallowed hard, trying to find her voice. 'I like it here.'

She'd like anywhere so long as Thierry was with her. The enormity of her feelings blindsided her. How had she gone from casual attraction to full-blown love in such a short space of time? Maybe because she wasn't made for casual affairs. That was why she'd been so cautious with her heart and her body before this.

'I'm glad. I'd wondered if it might be too quiet for you here.'

Imogen shook her head. She loved the peace of the estate. Besides, it was only minutes to the nearest town and a short drive to the nearest city. But what made it perfect was Thierry's presence.

'You really want me to stay?' Did he hear the longing in her voice? Hurriedly, she went on briskly. 'I'd rather you were totally honest.'

Thierry hesitated and there was something in his eyes that made her uneasy. As if he hid something.

Yet what could he hide? He had been trustworthy, honest and generous from the night they'd met. He'd even pulled back from her physically when he'd believed her ill, putting her wellbeing before his own sexual needs.

He wouldn't lie to her.

'I want you to stay, Imogen.' His gaze bored into hers, and she felt the impact right to her core. Slowly, he smiled and it was as if he'd flicked a switch, releasing the tension straining between them.

'Think about what we've got.' His hand dropped to the sheet covering her, his long fingers brushing her breasts in deliberate provocation. 'We like each other. We're sexually more than compatible.'

He lifted his hand away and it was only then Imogen discovered how far she'd leaned forward into his touch. 'And we're having a child. Why not stay together?'

Dazed as much by his touch as his words, Imogen sank back against the pillows, her body heavy and lax.

'You want to stay married?' She needed to hear him spell it out.

'I do.' That smile devastated her brain, making logic almost impossible. 'It makes sense, Imogen.'

Part of her wanted to exult. He wanted her here, and not just as a temporary girlfriend. Imogen knew that a future with Thierry would be everything she'd never dared to hope for. Because when she was with him she felt...

'What we have is good, isn't it?'

Good?

Imogen's thoughts screeched to a halt.

Good. That insipid word couldn't describe how she felt when she was with Thierry.

She opened her mouth then closed it. Her neck prickled, the hairs standing to attention as finally her sluggish brain moved into gear.

She'd been on tenterhooks, wondering if he

wanted her gone, but it was only now she realised what was missing.

Imogen met those gleaming eyes that she'd seen kindle with desire, crinkle with laughter or warm with concern. She took in those straight shoulders that she'd leaned on in moments of weakness and those capable hands that had helped her when she'd needed it. Thierry was caring, passionate and considerate.

But he doesn't love you.

There was no urgency in him, no desperation. Just calm logic and, yes, liking.

Imogen's heart skated to a bruising halt then lurched into a discordant rhythm so powerful she felt queasy.

Now she understood!

'This is you making the best of the situation, isn't it? Making do.' She recalled him talking in those terms in Paris, about not pining for the impossible, but adapting to whatever situation he found himself in.

'Why not?' That insouciant Gallic shrug made a mockery of her secret hopes and dreams. 'I'm expected to marry some time and here we are with a baby on the way.'

He must have noticed her breathless rigidity because he went on with a smile guaranteed to turn any woman to a puddle of pure longing. 'We like each other.' His hand settled on one of hers, lightly stroking an intricate scroll of desire from her wrist to her thumb. 'Sex between us is fantastic and we respect each other.'

'You said that before.' Her voice sounded scratchy. Were those the only reasons he could come up with for them to stay together?

'They're important.' The skin between his eyebrows pinched, as if he was surprised or annoyed she wasn't gushing with delight. 'I couldn't marry a woman I didn't respect.' His mouth curved in a way that devastated her resolve. 'As for the sex...' He shook his head. 'I can't remember it ever being so good.'

Imogen sat utterly still, scared that if she moved something, like her stupid heart, might shatter.

He wants to stay married to you because the sex is good. And because you're conveniently providing him with a child.

No doubt he wants one to inherit the estate and the villa on the south coast, and all the other things the Girard family have amassed. He wants an heir.

She'd been dreaming of love but Thierry laid out their relationship as if it was a business merger.

Her lips flattened. That was how he saw this—a neat solution to a difficult problem. A way of keeping his child while getting companionship and sex into the bargain.

She had no illusions she was the sort of woman he'd marry in normal circumstances, but Thierry had proved himself a realist through and through. Why yearn for caviar when you have fish and chips already on the table?

Imogen felt her hair slide around her face and neck as she shook her head. 'I don't think that's a good basis for marriage.'

His hand tightened, long fingers shackling her wrist. Did he feel her pulse hammering? He leaned in, crowding her against the pillows. For the first time since this conversation began she felt disadvantaged, naked beneath the sheet while he was dressed.

'Of course it's a good basis for marriage.' His eyes narrowed. Fervently she hoped he couldn't read her thoughts. 'Unless you're after some fantasy of romance. Is that it?'

Self-preservation made her shake her head, even as her soul cried out that that was exactly what she wanted.

'I didn't think so.' His lips quirked up in the hint

of a smile. 'You're like me, *chérie*—too practical to want hearts and flowers and sentimental protestations of undying love.'

Dry-eyed, Imogen gritted her teeth. Thierry couldn't know how she felt about him. He'd never deliberately trample over her feelings. Yet that didn't stop the pain from each dismissive word.

'You don't believe in love?'

His lips quirked. 'Once. I fell in love with a girl from a neighbouring estate. But she married someone else. At the time I thought my heart was broken but I'm old enough now to realise that's just a fiction. I've been happy with my life. It wasn't blighted by rejection after all.'

His expression was reflective as he stroked her palm, making her shiver. 'What we have is precious, Imogen, even if it doesn't go by the name of love. Respect, liking and a baby—those make a good starting point.'

'Don't forget the sex,' she said, hiding pain behind a twisted smile.

'Oh, I don't. Not for a moment.' He pressed his mouth to the spot below her ear where she was most sensitive. Instantly, tremors of heat racked her, and she shivered. Yet her heart ached.

'Let me warm you properly, Imogen.' He reached

for the tray between them, made to lift it away, but she put a shaky hand on his arm.

'No. Don't. I'm hungry.' The food would be sawdust in her mouth but she couldn't have sex with him, not now. Not knowing she'd given her heart to him and he only saw her as a convenient solution to a problematic situation.

She didn't care about his wealth or his power. But she wanted to *matter* to someone, to be the most important thing in their life. And that someone was Thierry. Because that was how she felt about him. Once she'd have settled but now she didn't want to *make do*. She wanted *everything*.

But he didn't believe in love. Would he ever? If he did, would it be for her or some woman from his own set, privileged and sophisticated?

Bile rose, and she almost choked.

'Are you all right?' The concern in his eyes was real.

Thierry did care. Just not enough.

'Fine,' she croaked, reaching for the sparkling water on the tray. She had to hold the glass in both hands so as not to spill it, but at least that gave her something to concentrate on other than Thierry's piercing gaze.

She felt his scrutiny like a touch. He wanted an answer.

What was she going to do? Flounce home and give up any chance he might, over time, begin to care for her as she did him? Or stay here like some charity case, making do with what he handed out, maybe breaking her heart little by little each day?

The mineral water tasted unbearably metallic, and she put it down with a grimace.

'Maybe I won't have anything to eat after all.'

'You're unwell? Morning sickness?' Thierry whipped away the tray, getting off the bed to put it on a nearby table. Imogen's breath eased out in a sigh of relief. She needed space to think.

'I'm a little out of sorts.' After one swift glance at his frown she looked away, watching her hands smooth the rumpled sheet. How had she gone from ecstasy to misery in such a short space of time?

It wasn't as if he'd led her on. He'd been marvellous. It was all her own doing, because she'd made the mistake of believing the fantasy. Because she loved him.

'I'll get you some herbal tea.'

'No. Nothing, thanks.' She doubted she'd keep anything down.

'Lie down then and I'll stay here till you sleep.'

'No!' Her head shot around to find him staring at her curiously. 'No, there's no need.'

See? He was caring. The sort of man any woman

would want, even if he didn't love her. Was she crazy to wish for more?

She must be. Why would a man born to his world of privilege and power fall for someone as ordinary as her?

A warm hand closed around hers. He stood beside the bed, so close she had to crick her neck to meet his eyes. They were unfathomable, deep and steady, yet she felt the intensity of his stare through every part of her being.

'So you'll stay, Imogen? You agree?'

She imagined tension in his voice. Clearly, she was projecting her own emotions.

'I...'

'You won't regret it. We're good together; you know it.'

Good. There was that word again.

She didn't want good. She wanted spectacular, amazing, special. She wanted love.

She gnawed at her lip, torn between fighting for what she wanted and the craven impulse to take whatever Thierry offered. She wasn't sure she'd like the woman she'd become if she did that.

'Stay, Imogen.' His voice was compelling, his hold tight.

She swallowed hard. 'I'll stay. For now. Let's see how it goes.'

CHAPTER ELEVEN

SEE HOW IT GOES.

She was going to see how it went.

As if he were on probation!

Thierry frowned, flipping another page of the contract before realising he hadn't taken in a word.

Disgusted, he shoved his chair back from the desk.

His ability to concentrate, even in a crisis, had always been one of his strengths. It had saved his hide more than once on long-distance motor rallies and while climbing. It had been one of the few assets he'd had in the early days when he took on this business.

Until today concentrating on what needed to be done hadn't been a problem. Even when he'd yearned for the wind in his hair and a far more physical challenge than that presented by corporate negotiations. He'd always given his all to the job at hand, knowing the sooner he solved a problem and moved on, the sooner he'd be free.

Nowadays he even found satisfaction in developing and expanding the business, finding new opportunities.

Not today.

A month today since Imogen had agreed to stay and *see how it goes.*

A month and no resolution.

He felt like he was on trial.

He surged to his feet and stalked to the window, staring at the blue sky that mocked his mood. He felt dark, stormy and miserable.

Thierry folded his arms over his chest. Made miserable by a woman. It didn't seem possible. Never had it happened in all the years since Sandrine had rejected him and his volatile young heart had counted itself broken.

Since then he'd enjoyed women but never wanted or expected anything serious.

Naturally, that had changed with Imogen. She was his wife so they needed a secure, meaningful relationship. One based on respect.

That was what he'd offered her and still she refused to commit to staying.

What more could she want?

He spun around, his gaze driving unerringly through the office's glass wall to his cousin

Henri's desk. There he was, his head bent towards Imogen's.

Heat blasted Thierry's gut as he watched the pair, so at ease, totally absorbed in the accounts Thierry personally found incredibly dull. But Imogen and Henri spoke the same language. The language of numbers.

When Imogen had complained she didn't have enough to keep her busy—as if she needed to work when he could provide for her!—Thierry had suggested she assist with the accounts. It had been a masterstroke and a disaster. Imogen was happy with the opportunity to work as an accountant again, her smiles becoming more genuine and frequent, at least in the office. More than that, she'd proved a valuable asset, her skills obviously top notch.

But her happiness at work only made him realise how rarely she smiled with him. He missed those lit-from-within smiles, so incandescent they were contagious.

His eyes narrowed as he heard a laugh and watched Imogen and Henri share some joke.

Thierry wanted to stride out and yank her away. Insist she share the joke with him as once she would have.

Except it didn't work like that. With him she

was polite, friendly, as she was with Jeanne or his grandparents when they visited. But never was he treated to those delicious gurgles of pure joy that had entranced him when they'd met. Or those cheeky, teasing grins.

He missed that. Missed Imogen. It was as if the most vital part of her was locked somewhere he couldn't reach.

Sometimes when they made love he felt he'd almost breached that gap, reached the woman locked behind her reserve. For, despite initial protests, Imogen hadn't been able to deny the passion between them. They shared a bed and his one solace was that in his arms she went up in flames as surely as the propane that fuelled his balloon flights. She was mesmerising, her passion all he could ask for.

Yet afterwards a curious blankness replaced the smoky flare of rapture. She'd withdraw mentally. For the first time ever Thierry found himself wanting to dig deeper, even discuss her *feelings*!

She drove him crazy.

He wrapped a palm around the back of his neck. He was too close to the edge.

Thierry glared through the glass. *Diable.* He wasn't jealous of his cousin, was he?

Impossible. Yet he found himself striding across the office, only to slam to a halt, his hand on the door.

Think, man! What are you going to do? Go out and drag her off to your bedroom?

The idea appealed, especially when he saw her smile at Henri as the younger man touched her hand then pointed to something on the screen. Waves of heat battered at Thierry, turning his belly into a churning morass.

Okay, he admitted it. He was jealous. He knew there was nothing between them except liking and professional admiration but that didn't lessen his envy.

Thierry dropped the door handle as if it burned with an electric current. He took a step back.

What was happening to him?

He wasn't interested in examining his feelings. He wanted action. But abducting his wife and ravishing her till she cried his name in rapture, while perfect in its own way, would leave him disgruntled when she withdrew again.

Sex wasn't the answer. Not alone. He had to find another way to connect with Imogen.

'Imogen.' She stilled, her heart pattering as that deep voice turned her name into a caress.

Would she ever *not* respond to it?

Slowly, she turned, willing her breathing to steady as espresso-dark eyes snared hers and she tingled all over. It was hard, sometimes, to remember Thierry saw her as a convenient wife, not the love of his life. That heavy-lidded stare sizzled with a promise she'd almost swear held more than physical desire.

Except she was done with fantasy. She was back into self-protection mode, carefully weighing her options for the future. She owed her baby that.

'Thierry.' She stumbled a little over his name. Last time she'd said it had been just hours ago, in that big, luxurious bed of his, and she hadn't said it: she'd screamed it in pleasure. 'Did you need this report? We're almost done.' Casually, she glanced at Henri, hoping he'd take up the conversation.

'It's not about the report,' Thierry said. 'I need you.'

Imogen's head snapped around. But the banked embers in his eyes had disappeared, or maybe she'd imagined that. Thierry looked all business.

'Of course. Excuse me, Henri?'

'Yes, fine.' He turned back to the spreadsheet. 'We've almost sorted this. You'll have it in ten minutes, Thierry.'

'No rush. So long as I get it by this evening.'

Imogen frowned. An hour ago the report had been urgent. But her thoughts frayed when Thierry put a hand under her elbow as she stood.

Once she'd loved those little courtesies. Now they were exquisite torture.

'You want me for something?' Her voice was only a little husky.

'I do.' To her surprise, he escorted her out to the car park where the sun shone warm on her face. 'I suppose I'll need to get another car,' he murmured as they approached his.

'You will?' The words flummoxed her. He adored his low-slung sports car.

'There's no room for a baby seat in this.'

The idea of Thierry replacing his streamlined beast with a family sedan stunned her. He really was serious about being an involved father.

If she stayed.

'Why are we here?' She stood back when he opened the passenger door. 'I've got work to do.'

'You've done your share today.'

Imogen shook her head. 'It's early—'

'You married the boss, so there are perks. Besides...' his expression turned serious '...you need to look after yourself. You're still getting morning sickness.'

'Only a little.' She found it better if she kept herself busy. Between the accountancy work, intensive French lessons and the hours she spent with Jeanne learning the secrets of French baking, every waking hour was filled. Soon she'd have to decide whether to leave, but having time on her hands hadn't helped her reach a decision. All it had done was depress her.

'Well, today we have somewhere else to be.' He held open the door. Imogen wavered, for suddenly it hit her—she'd deliberately arranged her days to spend as little time as possible with her husband.

Because she was afraid he'd convince her to stay?

'Please, Imogen. It's important.' His mouth flattened. Curiously, she read strain in his proud features and restlessness in the way his hand slid along the open door.

'What's wrong?' Anxiety leapt into her chest. She'd learned no one was immune to bad news and she'd never seen Thierry look this way, as if suppressing agitation.

'Nothing's wrong. Can't you just trust me?'

Imogen looked into the face of the man she loved and knew that was the one thing she'd always done.

He'd never deliberately hurt her. He'd gone to re-markable lengths to protect her.

She laid her hand on his where it shifted along the door. Instantly, he stilled, and she felt the familiar thrill of connection. 'Of course I trust you.' What-ever Thierry wanted, she'd help him if she could. She owed him that.

Yet she was careful not to meet that gleaming gaze as she slid into the passenger seat.

'I can't believe it. This is amazing!' The wind caught her words as hair streamed across her face. Imogen laughed, lifting her free hand to pull her hair back.

The air rushed around her, skimming her body just as the small sailing boat skimmed the lake's sparkling waters. The sensation of speed, the huff and ripple of the wind against canvas and the joy-ous sense of adventure were like champagne in her blood. Her skin tingled, and her heart felt lighter than it had in months.

Thierry beamed, his face creasing into grooves that accentuated his devastating appeal. He looked totally at ease, his long frame swaying, adjusting easily each time the small boat shifted. Yet she'd seen how quickly he could move, coming to her aid whenever an unexpected change in conditions threatened her fragile confidence. She was a complete novice.

But he'd made sailing so easy.

Her hand clenched on the tiller. That was what he'd always done, wasn't it? Make things easy for her. Their affair. Their baby. Even dying. No matter what she'd faced, he'd been at her side.

Her heart lurched against her ribs. She loved him so much. How was she supposed to walk away? Was she mad, even considering it?

'I knew you'd take to it.' He linked his arms behind his head, stretching those long legs towards her till they almost touched.

'You couldn't possibly know that.'

'Of course I did. Face it, Imogen, we're the same. Both with a taste for adventure.'

Automatically, she shook her head. She wasn't like Thierry. Those extreme sports he enjoyed made her hair curl. 'You've got me wrong, Thierry. I'm ordinary and cautious. I'm an accountant, remember? Until recently I'd never done anything exciting. Only the threat of dying got me out of Australia.'

'But it did, didn't it? You didn't stay, waiting for the end, but went out and found your true self.' He sounded satisfied, almost smug, as if today's surprise sailing treat was a major win in some way she couldn't fathom.

'I'm afraid not.' How could he have got her so wrong? 'My true self belongs at home or in an office. This is just…' She shrugged. 'My sister was the courageous one, not me.'

The wind shifted and the little boat shivered as Imogen struggled to guide it. Instantly, Thierry was beside her, his shoulder against hers, his hand over hers on the tiller. Seconds later they were gliding easily over the water again. He lifted his hand but didn't move away.

A sense of wellbeing filled her, and for once Imogen didn't fight it, just accepted this glorious moment, with the rush of wind, the thrill of sailing and Thierry beside her.

'You don't think it took courage to look after your dying mother? Even though it cost you your lover? You don't think you were courageous when you faced what you thought was your own death? Or when you planned to face pregnancy alone?'

'I didn't have any choice. That wasn't courage. That was necessity.'

Thierry lifted her free hand to his lips and her heart sang. 'You're wrong, Imogen. You're exciting

and marvellous and brave. We're well matched—
because we both have a taste for *life*.'

She opened her mouth to disagree but his finger
on her lips stopped her. 'We *are*, Imogen. Don't
you feel it whenever we're together?'

The trouble was she did. But she told herself it
was because she'd fallen for him, hook, line and
sinker. Whereas he— Well, Thierry wouldn't fall
for someone like her.

'You're talking to a woman who has just spent
days learning how to make the perfect choux pas-
try. I'm no daredevil.'

Thierry shook his head. 'You think it's so black
and white? That we aren't all complex? I might love
motor rallies and alpine climbing but I never spent
all my time doing that. Do you know how many
hours I spent beneath the engine of my rally car,
getting it tuned to perfection? Or planning the op-
timal route for a trek?' He slipped his arm around
her, his embrace warming her in places she couldn't
name.

'You don't understand. I'm not the woman you
think I am. That woman in Paris wasn't the real
Imogen.'

'Wasn't she?' His voice was a deep burr that did
wicked things to her heart and her self-control.

'You've spent so long putting yourself in a pigeon-hole you can't see that you're more complex than you ever imagined.' He paused. 'I think that's why you're afraid to take a chance on me.'

Before she could say anything he rose and took up a position just far enough away that she couldn't touch him. But his eyes held hers, bright and challenging.

'We have so much going for us, Imogen. Why won't you give us a chance? Us and our child?'

Because I'm scared. I'm terrified to love you when you don't love me back.

'Trust your instincts, Imogen. Think of the good times we could have together.' His was the voice of temptation, coursing through her like liquid chocolate.

Of course she wanted to stay. That was the trouble. It was too easy to imagine being with him, spending time together, not just at the *château* or in his arms, but *living*, sharing adventures like this.

'All you have to do is let go of your fear and trust in us.'

Let go of her fear! After living with fear so long that was easier said than done. Yet the temptation to trust in him was almost overwhelming. Only a lifetime's caution held her back.

But what was she holding back from? Fear of not being loved? If she walked away from Thierry she'd sever whatever bond they already had. Plus she'd destroy any chance that he'd ever love her.

Did she ask too much, expecting him to love after such a short time, just because she loved him? Imogen frowned. Looked at that way, she seemed impatient and greedy.

Imogen stared at his sprawled body, apparently relaxed, yet with eyes so watchful. He'd deliberately distanced himself when it would be easy to persuade her with his arm around her. Her mind always went to mush when he touched her.

He was being noble, damn him, and to her chagrin that only made it harder to deny him. But he wouldn't be the man she adored if he wasn't decent and caring. Look at today—giving her this first exhilarating taste of sailing.

Her thoughts stuck and circled. Thierry had shared his love of the outdoors with her, his delight in speed and adventure.

He wasn't blocking her out of his life, or taking her for granted like the convenient bride she'd imagined herself.

He was letting her in.

Imogen stared hard at the man before her, the

tautness of his shoulders and hands revealing he was anything but relaxed. He wasn't cold-blooded. He might see marriage as a pragmatic solution to their situation but Thierry was passionate and caring. He didn't love her but surely there was a chance he might one day?

If she stayed.

Her heart pounded like stampeding wild animals and she blinked, blinded by the sudden brightness of sunshine on glittering water.

'Watch out!' A moment later he was with her again, his firm body hot beside her, his strong hand guiding hers.

The boat shifted, poised for a moment, then turned and caught the wind, flying across the water.

But it wasn't the speed that caught the breath in Imogen's throat.

She sank against him, her head against his chest, his tantalising scent stimulating her senses. She closed her eyes and felt the tension leave her.

Really, she had only one choice.

'You win, Thierry. I'll stay.'

It might be the biggest gamble of her life, the only gamble, but she'd play it to the end.

CHAPTER TWELVE

THIERRY'S HANDS CAME around her waist, pulling her back against him. In the mirror she read that familiar smile, and her stomach tumbled over itself as it had that first night in Paris.

'You look good enough to eat.' He pressed a kiss to her neck, and she shivered as desire spiked.

'Seriously, this dress is right for tonight?' It was her first formal event as Thierry's hostess and nerves had struck. When he'd mentioned it a month ago she'd told herself wearing one of Izzy's creations would be perfect. The full-length white satin with crimson flowers would give her confidence. It was the dress she'd worn the night she'd met Thierry and it felt like a lucky talisman.

Should she have taken his offer to buy something new?

'This dress is perfect.' He spread his palm over her belly, now rounded just enough that she'd had to find a dressmaker to let out the dress a little.

'Even if I'm making it strain at the seams?' Surely

she'd put on weight in the past week? Soon she'd need new bras too.

Thierry's hand slid up to her breasts straining against the satin. His light touch made her knees quiver. 'The only problem will be the disgruntled women when all men watch you, *ma chérie.*'

Imogen's lips twitched. 'Sweet talker.'

'Siren.' His hand stroked her budding nipple, and she gasped in exquisite arousal. Pregnancy made her even more sensitive to his touch. And he knew it. In the mirror his smile was pure erotic invitation as she sank back against him.

It had been so easy to give in and agree to live as Thierry's wife. He made her feel desired, appreciated, supported. Even if he didn't love her, surely that was enough to begin a marriage? And their sex life just got better and better. She read familiar heat in his expression.

'Thierry! We don't have time. And I've got my make-up on.'

Firmly, she stifled a wish that he felt more than sexual attraction. She needed patience. One day surely…?

He pressed an open-mouthed kiss to her neck that made her shiver, then stepped back. Instantly, she felt bereft. She was as needy as ever and now she'd opened her heart to him too.

'I'll be good. Besides, I have something for you.'

'You do?' She made to turn but he stopped her.

'Stand there.' She watched, dumbfounded, as he lowered a magnificent necklace over her head. The dressing-room light flashed on brilliant gems and old gold that glowed with the patina of age. Imogen was dazzled as the weight of the necklace settled on her.

'I've heard of rubies the size of pigeons' eggs...' she said shakily.

'You think it too old-fashioned?'

'It's gorgeous,' she murmured. 'I just hope it's not as precious as it looks. Tell me it's costume jewellery.'

He shook his head. 'It's real. You're my wife, my hostess. You need to look the part. This has been in the family for generations. Besides, it matches your dress.'

He was right. The crimson glow of the central stone matched the flowers on her dress and the ornate necklace paired well with the simplicity of the strapless bodice.

Her fingers fluttered over it, her eyes wide. She looked different—not like the woman she knew.

Disquiet shivered through her, but she forced it aside. Naturally Thierry wanted her to do him proud tonight. The session he'd organised for her with a beautician had been a thoughtful gift. Thierry's grandmother had spent hours coaching her on the who's who of French society that would be at tonight's party. Plus, with her language tutor's help, Imogen felt reasonably competent with introductions and very basic conversation.

She smoothed her gloved hands down her dress, telling herself she'd be fine. It wasn't that she was scared of crowds, just that they weren't her thing. But with Thierry at her side she'd be fine. More than fine. She'd shine.

Only Thierry didn't stay at her side.

For an hour he was with her, his arm around her waist, greeting their guests, turning these sophisticated strangers into people she could relax and laugh with. Most of them, if curious about her, were friendly.

But after a while they got separated. Occasionally he'd turn his head to check on her, his eyebrows raised in question, and she'd nod, silently letting him know she was okay.

She was a professional woman, used to meeting

strangers. She didn't need her hand held, even if some of the glitterati were rather daunting.

There was one woman in particular—Sandrine. A tall, slender blonde who looked like she'd stepped from a glossy magazine. She was the most beautiful woman Imogen had ever seen, with a long sweep of platinum hair, perfect features and an assurance that allowed her to wear backless silver lamé and a fortune in diamonds with casual insouciance.

But it wasn't the other woman's beauty that made Imogen stare, it was the realisation that this was the woman who'd broken Thierry's heart. Sandrine made it clear they'd known each other since the cradle. Several times in their short conversation she'd subtly reinforced the fact that Imogen was an outsider in this milieu.

When Thierry was beside Imogen that didn't matter. But as the evening wore on it was harder not to make comparisons between herself and the glamorous blonde so at home in these superb surroundings.

Imogen dragged her attention back to the couple talking with her about Australia, reminiscing about a trip to an exclusive resort she'd heard of but never visited.

'I was disappointed,' the husband said, 'not to

see those dangerous snakes we hear about.' The twinkle in his eyes belied the complaint.

Imogen smiled. 'I can recommend some nature reserves for your next visit.' She glanced down and noticed their glasses were empty. Looking around, she couldn't see any of the waiters brought in for tonight's party.

'If you'll excuse me, I'll send someone over with drinks.'

'No, no, it's fine. It's no trouble.'

Nice as it was to chat, it felt good to do something practical, attending to guests' needs. It made her feel less of an imposter in this well-heeled crowd. To be fair, though, not all the invitees were rich. There were locals and friends of Thierry who shared an interest in extreme sports.

Imogen was moving to the end of the room where the bar was set up when a woman's voice slowed her steps.

'Of course she's pregnant, what other reason could there be? He's married her to make the child legitimate. She's not Thierry's type. When has any-one ever seen him with a brunette? And as for the rest… Thierry deserves someone with panache, someone who fits in.'

Pale blonde hair swung across the speaker's elegant bare back.

Sandrine. Thierry's old friend. His first love.

Imogen's chest tightened and she faltered to a stop. Was that why Thierry was adamant he'd never want a love match? Because he'd given his heart to this woman and no one else would fill her place?

It was one thing to know her husband had once been disappointed in love. It was quite another to discover the object of his affection was the most stunningly beautiful woman she'd ever seen.

Did she seriously expect him to love her when his taste ran to svelte goddesses?

'Oh, come on, Sandrine.' An American accent this time. 'You can't know that. I say it was love at first sight. You just have to look at her to know she's head over heels in love with him. I think it's sweet.'

Imogen pressed a hand to her suddenly queasy stomach. She needed to keep moving. She didn't want to hear the speculation about her marriage.

Before she could move, Sandrine shrugged. 'I couldn't agree more. I feel sorry for the poor little thing.' Her voice dropped and the woman with her leaned closer.

Despite her resolve to move on, Imogen found herself waiting with bated breath.

'Didn't you see the photo in that scandal rag a month or so ago? Thierry kissing some blonde in a hotel bar when he was supposed to be on a climbing trip? The way he held her, it was obvious they'd just got out of bed.'

'Imogen. There you are. I was hoping to find you.' Startled, Imogen swung round to see Poppy Chatsfield beside her. The tall, red-headed model was another of the sophisticated set but her smile was warm.

Imogen blinked, trying to focus. Her stomach heaved and she almost stumbled as the floor rippled beneath her. A chill clamped her spine, freezing each vertebra in turn.

Thierry kissing another woman.

Thierry holding another woman...

'Imogen?' A hand gripped her elbow and she found herself ushered to the side of the room. 'You need to sit. In your condition you shouldn't be standing so long.'

A ragged laugh escaped Imogen's lips as Poppy led her to an antique sofa. 'Does *everyone* here know I'm pregnant?'

'Of course not.' Poppy sat beside her. 'But

Thierry and Orsino are old friends; he just told us the news. I came to congratulate you.' She paused, her concerned gaze roving Imogen's face. 'Can I get you something? Water? I found sipping it slowly sometimes helped the morning sickness.'

'No. I'm okay.' Imogen felt her mouth stretch in a grimace. Okay? How could she be okay? If what Sandrine had said was true… She wrapped her arms around her midriff, holding in the searing hurt.

'If you'll take my advice, you won't pay any attention to Sandrine.'

Imogen's gaze met Poppy's and heat washed her face. How many people had heard?

Poppy went on, her voice soft. 'I don't know what she said but I have a good idea it's what made you feel sick.'

Despite the haze of hurt and disappointment, Imogen found herself liking this woman.

'That's better. You look less like you're going to faint.'

'That's not going to happen.' Imogen straightened, drawing breath and putting a hand to her hair. 'But thank you. I appreciate your concern.'

Poppy nodded. 'You should know, Sandrine is—'

'I know. Years ago she and Thierry were an item.'

'Actually, I was going to say Sandrine isn't a complete witch, even if she's not at her best tonight. She's piqued because you married Thierry.'

'Why should she be piqued? She rejected him. She's been married to someone else for years.'

'Yes, and in all that time she's had the satisfaction of seeing Thierry go from one woman to another, never settling. As if he couldn't get over her.' Poppy nodded. 'Imagine how she feels after years thinking his heart was hers. Now you come along, stealing him. It's obvious he's fallen for you.'

Imogen pressed her hands together, wishing she could take comfort in Poppy's words.

Thierry hadn't fallen for her. He'd told her they were well-matched because neither expected hearts and flowers and declarations of love.

Did that explain the other woman? Imogen swallowed convulsively at the thought of them together.

That must have been the weekend after they'd learned there'd been no need for them to marry because she was going to live. Imogen had known Thierry was rocked by the news, as she was, but he'd denied it.

A blonde. Sandrine had said brunettes weren't his type. Imogen's stomach churned so hard she thought she'd be ill. His taste ran to blondes like Sandrine and the woman in that bar.

Imogen stared blankly at the chattering crowd. How many had seen that photo? How many knew he'd betrayed her with another woman?

Clearly, Thierry didn't think it a betrayal—because he didn't love her, or because such things were accepted here? Did he expect her to put up with his affairs? Was that how he saw their marriage working?

This time the pain was a piercing white-hot blade to the heart.

'Imogen? You're worrying me. Shall I find Thierry?'

She jerked her head around to meet Poppy's stare. 'No,' she croaked. She couldn't face that yet. She needed time to digest this.

'I'm just…' Dazed, she searched for words to reassure Poppy. 'It's so crowded and close. I just can't get my breath.' It was true as far as it went.

Poppy squeezed her hand. 'You poor thing. I was the same when I was pregnant with Sofia.'

'If you'll excuse me, I'll head outside for some fresh air.' Imogen stood, locking her knees when they wobbled. She wasn't going to collapse in a pathetic heap, especially amongst Thierry's friends.

'I'll come with you.' Imogen was about to protest when Poppy whispered in her ear. 'You won't get far alone. Everyone wants to talk with you. If you're with me, you've got an excuse not to stop and chat.'

Minutes later Imogen rested her palms on the stone balustrade of the terrace. The buzz of the crowd was a muted hum and the high-riding moon washed the scene silver.

Imogen made herself turn to Poppy. 'That's better. Thank you. I'm okay now, so you can go back to Orsino. He's probably wondering where you are.' She was desperate to be alone.

Poppy waved a careless hand. 'No, he won't. He and Thierry are busy planning their grand trip.'

'Grand trip?' Imogen hadn't heard anything about a trip. But then she was probably the only person here who hadn't known about his other woman. Her fingers clenched on stone as revulsion welled.

'Oh, just the usual. For years they've been planning their next big adventure—the one they'll take as soon as Thierry's free.'

'Free?' The word tore from Imogen's choked throat. Free of her? She frowned. But then why insist they stay married?

'Free of the business.' Poppy bent her head, tsking as she disentangled her bracelet from a sequin on her dress.

'What do you mean, free of the business?'

Poppy looked up, astonishment on her features. 'You don't know?' She paused. 'Maybe I got it wrong,' she said quickly. 'I—'

'Please, Poppy. I need to know.'

Did Poppy hear the strain in her voice? Finally, she shrugged but she didn't look comfortable. 'Only close friends know. Thierry wouldn't talk about it in public.'

Clearly whatever *it* was, he hadn't thought to share it with his wife.

Disappointment hammered at Imogen's heart. She'd been fooling herself that if she was patient one day things would change between them!

How many secrets did Thierry hide?

'Thierry was dragged kicking and screaming into the family business when his grandfather became ill.'

Imogen nodded. 'He had a stroke.' She knew that, at least.

'Thierry hates being cooped up behind four walls—says it will send him crazy one day, being tied down. He vowed to set the company on its feet then step aside, find some good managers and take up his old life. He and Orsino used to do a lot of balloon treks together, rally driving too, and climbing.'

She paused, her glance darting to Imogen as if for confirmation she already knew this. Imogen said nothing, just turned to look at the cold, moonlit garden.

'For ages they've talked about a big trek to celebrate his freedom when it comes. Last I heard, it would be white-water rafting somewhere inhospitable. Somewhere you wouldn't catch me, ever. I'll stay where there are some creature comforts, thank you very much.'

Imogen recalled seeing Thierry across the crowd with Orsino Chatsfield. The two handsome, dark-haired men were easy to spot, given their height. But it was the animation on Thierry's face and the intensity of their conversation that she'd noticed.

Poppy turned towards her. 'Perhaps we could spend some time together when they're away? Get to know each other better?'

'That's a lovely idea.' Imogen forced the words out before her throat closed on a ball of wretched emotion. She liked Poppy. In other circumstances she could imagine them as friends. But it wasn't going to happen.

The pain morphed from a piercing stab to a heavy, slow-grinding ache pressing down, robbing her of air.

What more did she need to convince her this marriage was all wrong? He wasn't interested in settling down any more than he believed in love. He begrudged the time he spent in one place saving the family firm. How much more would he come to resent the woman and child who tied him down even further?

He'd put a good face on a bad situation. No doubt about it, her husband didn't shirk from what he believed to be his duty. Having met his grandparents, she realised he'd had responsibility drummed into him from an early age.

Something in her chest tore in an excruciating, slow-motion rip of anguish. Her heart?

'I'm afraid things are a little up in the air at the moment. A little…complicated.' She tried for a casual smile but knew it didn't convince, by the sombre way Poppy surveyed her.

'Of course. I don't mean to pressure you. A new marriage can be challenging as well as exciting.' Her laugh held a jarring note. 'Orsino and I went through hell before we worked out we loved and trusted each other.' She touched Imogen briefly on the arm. 'Just remember, if ever you need to talk, I'm available. I know how hard it can be, married to one of these take-charge men.'

'Thanks, Poppy. That's kind of you.' Imogen gulped, overcome by her empathy and kindness. She struggled for a lighter tone. 'I suppose we'd better get back inside before we're missed.' She couldn't think of anything worse. But she had her pride. She'd see the evening out then decide what to do.

Except she knew she'd run out of options.

She'd given her heart and soul to a man who didn't love her. Who could never love her. Who couldn't even give her his loyalty. He liked her, and he shared himself as much as he could with her, but ultimately she and their child were encumbrances, like the business he'd stepped in to save and couldn't wait to be rid of.

Her fond dream of him returning her feelings was just that—a dream.

There was only one thing any self-respecting woman could do. It was just a pity she hadn't done it months ago.

CHAPTER THIRTEEN

'IMOGEN?' THIERRY FLICKED on the light switch only to find his bedroom empty.

Where was she? She'd come upstairs when the last of the guests had left. There'd been fine lines of tiredness on her face yet that stubborn streak had seen her determined to play hostess to the end, despite his suggestion she retire early.

Thierry smiled. She'd been magnificent. He'd wondered if such a big function would be too much but she'd sailed through it with ease. Every time he'd looked over she'd been the centre of some eager group.

Afterwards he'd remained chatting with Orsino, who was staying with Poppy in one of the guest suites. It had been too long since they'd caught up. It was only now as work turned from manic to manageable that he realised how little he'd seen of his friends, as opposed to business contacts.

He marched across the room and opened the

bathroom door. Empty. Where was she? His belly tightened in a premonition of trouble.

A few strides took him to the dressing room, but it too was empty. He scowled, thinking of her pale features as she'd headed upstairs and cursed himself for not seeing her to their room, despite her protests.

Thierry whipped around and back into the bedroom. Flicking off the light, he stepped towards the sitting room. That was when he noticed the strip of light under the adjoining bedroom door.

His heart slammed his ribs as he stopped midstride. What was she doing in her old bedroom? Incoherent thoughts jostled his brain. Was she ill? Was it the baby?

He wrenched open the door. The room looked peaceful in the glow of a bedside lamp and he heard water running in the bathroom.

He was almost at the bathroom door when he noticed the laptop open on the bed. One glance sent a sucker punch to the gut.

Thierry staggered, stared, and felt the world tilt.

Diable! Imogen had seen this? He went hot then cold as wave after wave of prickling remorse hit him.

He didn't want to, but Thierry took a step closer,

then another. The photo was even worse close up. The blonde leaned into him, every line of her body taut and hungry as they kissed. From this angle, and with his hands at her waist, it looked like he'd been utterly lost to passion.

What had Imogen thought when she'd seen it? Flicking down the screen, scanning the snide little magazine commentary, he saw it was dated too. She'd have been in no doubt when this was taken.

His belly turned to lead. It was no good telling himself there'd been nothing in it. That didn't stop the guilt.

The door opened behind him, and his head flicked around.

'Hello, Thierry.' Imogen looked composed but pale.

'Are you all right?' He started towards her but stopped at the look on her face. Closed. Shuttered. Distant. He'd never seen her like that and it made something catch hard under his ribs.

'Why wouldn't I be?' She took off her watch and put it on the dressing table.

Thierry frowned. 'I was worried when you weren't in our room. What are you doing here?'

She shrugged as she moved things on the dressing table. Avoiding him? He stepped closer.

'I'm very tired and a bit queasy. I thought it better to sleep here.'

If she was tired, why wasn't she in bed?

The answer was easy: she'd been checking on him, trawling the media to find that incriminating photo. He tried to whip up indignation but found only regret.

'About that photo…' Her head swung round, her gaze meshing with his, and for a split second pure energy blasted through him, like he'd tapped into an electric current. 'It wasn't the way it looks.'

She walked past him and turned off the laptop, taking it to the dressing table.

'Imogen? I said it wasn't like it seems.'

'If you say so.'

'I do say so.' His fingers closed around her bare arm. The swish of her silky nightdress against his knuckles reminded him of the hours of pleasure they'd shared in his bed. It made her curious composure all the more disturbing. 'Why don't you say anything?'

Her eyes met his, more brown than green now and strangely flat.

'I'm tired. Can't we talk in the morning?'

'You've got to be kidding.' She'd seen that photo and withdrawn as if he were a stranger. Anger stirred. It was more palatable than the guilt lining his belly. 'We need to talk now.'

Her mouth flattened. 'I've had enough for one night.'

But instinct told him he couldn't delay. Keeping his hold on her arm, he led her to the bed. Her chin jutted mutinously but she said nothing as he sat beside her.

'Aren't you curious about the woman in the photo?' If he'd seen a picture of her in the arms of another man he'd have been more than curious. He'd want to rip the guy's arms off.

'Not particularly.' Her blank tone didn't match the fire in her eyes.

'She kissed me.' Thierry felt a shudder pass through her. 'I was drinking in the bar the last night of the climbing trip—'

'You don't have to justify yourself.'

But he did. He couldn't bear for her to believe he'd been with someone else. 'She asked for a drink then she kissed me.'

'I'm sure it happens to you all the time.' The hint of a snarl in her tone stirred tentative hope. Anger he could deal with. It was this...*nothing* that scared him.

'Nothing happened, Imogen. Just a kiss. What you saw was me pushing her away.'

Hazel eyes held with his, searching, then Imogen looked away. He felt her sag. 'If you say so.'

'I *do* say so.' How could he convince her? Her listlessness scared him. Where was his vibrant Imogen? Why wasn't she reacting? Even to hear her yell would be a relief.

'Right. Now that's cleared up, I'm going to sleep.'

Thierry stared. 'What's going on, *chérie*?'

'Don't!' She stiffened. 'Don't call me that.' She yanked her arm free and shuffled along the bed, putting distance between them. Her hand came up to cradle the spot where he'd held her, as if he'd hurt her, though his touch had been careful.

'I'm not your *chérie* and I never will be.'

'What are you talking about?' His pulse hammered a tattoo of fear. 'Of course you are. You're my wife.' He didn't like where this was going. He'd never seen her act so.

'A convenient wife—not your dear or your sweetheart, or whatever the translation is.' She waved her hand dismissively, and Thierry felt a plummeting sensation in his belly. 'I know it's just a word, a little nothing that slips out easily, but...' She turned her profile to him. 'But I don't want your casual endearments.'

'Imogen—'

'And since you insist on talking now...' she turned to him '...you should know I've decided to leave. This isn't working.'

Thierry shot to his feet, stalking across the thick carpet. 'Because of one stupid photo? I explained that. Nothing happened! I give you my word.' He squared his shoulders. A Girard's word was rock-solid, unquestionable.

She didn't look impressed. She hugged her arms around her, and he had to work not to let his gaze linger on her breasts, straining against her night-gown. 'It's not because of the photo.'

He strode across to loom over her so she had to arch her neck to look at him. 'Don't lie, Imogen.' Pain settled like a weighted blanket. 'We've always had the truth between us.' It was one of the things he'd most appreciated about her. She was direct and open, someone he could believe in.

'You want the truth?' Abruptly, the blankness was gone and heat shimmered in her eyes. 'The truth is marrying you was the biggest mistake of my life. I've had enough and I'm going home. I've booked a flight to Australia. Once I'm there I'll see about a divorce.'

The light dimmed and for a second Thierry's vision blurred, like the time he'd almost knocked himself out on a ski run in Austria. He braced himself, bending his knees slightly to counteract the sensation that he was swaying.

Yet nothing counteracted the horrible clogging in his chest, or the fierce pain slicing through his gullet.

'You're not going anywhere.' He didn't consciously form the words. They simply shot from his stiff lips.

'You're going to stop me by force?' Her eyebrows rose, giving her a haughty look that reminded him of his grandmother at her most disapproving. But his grandmother had never struck fear into him as Imogen did.

He stumbled back then steadied himself. 'I won't let you go.'

In a slither of fabric, she rose, standing toe to toe with him. 'You can't stop me.'

He shook his head, trying to fathom what had happened. Only hours ago everything had been fine.

'You know I can.' His voice was low and urgent

and when he touched her cheek he felt as well as heard her sudden intake of breath. 'We're good together, Imogen. You can't seriously want to give that up.'

Her head reared back and his hand fell. 'Sex?' She sneered. 'Yes, that's good. But why would I uproot myself just for that? It was a mad idea to think of staying in France.'

Thierry's eyes widened at her determination, and fear engulfed him. More than that. Fear was what he'd felt in the accident that had ended his Olympic skiing career. And the time his parachute had jammed before finally releasing.

This was more. This was on a level he'd never experienced. It was slow, grinding terror. Instead of creating a surge of defiant adrenalin that gave him courage to face danger, this weakened his very bones.

It made him feel…helpless.

'You think this is just about *sex*?' He saw her flinch and realised his voice had risen to a roar.

Thierry backed up, astonished at his loss of control. He never shouted. He never lost control. But he'd never felt anything like this visceral dread.

Before he could apologise she spoke, so softly and steadily the contrast with his own exclamation shamed him. 'If this relationship isn't about sex, tell me what it *is* about, Thierry.'

Her gaze held his gravely, and he swallowed. He flexed his hands.

'Our child...'

She dropped her eyes, her shoulders sagging before that bright hazel gaze met his again. 'Our child will do very well without this. It doesn't need us to live together in a farce of a marriage to be happy and healthy. I'd never try to cut you out of its life.'

So, he was to be a long-distance parent? Outrage flared.

'A farce? There's nothing farcical about this marriage, Imogen.' Fury leavened the horror. After all he'd done, all he offered, that was what she thought of them together? 'It's real. As real as French law can make it.' As real as *he* could make it.

'I don't care about the law, Thierry.' She folded her arms. 'I care about the fact I've married a man who doesn't love me. Who can never love me.' Her eyebrows rose as if in challenge. 'I want more. It was a mistake thinking I could settle for less.'

'I told you I didn't sleep with that woman.' This time, instead of anger, he felt desperation. Why wouldn't she believe him?

She shook her head. 'This isn't about her. This is

about the fact you'll never really want *me*. Not for myself, just for the heir I'm providing, and because physically we're compatible.'

Imogen paced to the window, and Thierry tracked her with his eyes, willing down the need to haul her close and seduce her into forgetting this nonsense. Seduction wouldn't work this time.

His gut clenched in panic.

'We talked about this.' He kept his voice low and persuasive. 'We've got the basis of a great marriage.'

'No!' This time the shake of her head splayed dark tresses around her shoulders. 'I've changed, Thierry. Once upon a time I'd have been willing to put up with second best, with not quite achieving the dream. Once I didn't dare to dream because I was too busy being cautious. But thinking I was dying gave me courage.' She paused, a wistful smile curving her lips.

'So did you, Thierry. You helped me to be brave. You encouraged me to follow my dreams.' She hefted a breath that lifted her lovely breasts. 'My dream is to love and be loved. As simple and as huge as that.'

She rubbed her hands up her arms as if cold. Did she too feel the draught of icy air coursing around him?

'I understand you'll never love me, Thierry. You explained you don't believe in romance. Plus, I'm not the woman for you. I'm not blonde or sophisticated.' She shrugged. 'The woman you met in Paris wore borrowed plumage, just like tonight, and pretended to fit in, though she knew she was an outsider. I don't belong in your world, so it's better I go.'

'To find a man to love?' The words grated from his throat, leaving it raw.

Her face twisted with what looked like anguish. Except *he* was the one being torn apart.

'If I can.'

He stalked forward, grabbing her hands. They were cold. He looked down at her small, capable fingers in his and knew he couldn't bear to release her. It was asking too much.

'No.' His voice was a scrape of sound.

'Sorry?'

'You can't do that.'

Thierry watched his thumbs trace a possessive path across her knuckles. He imagined their hands together in twenty years, forty years, veined and wrinkled. The image made him feel…right inside. The idea of Imogen giving herself to another man, growing old with *him* instead, turned Thierry's stomach.

'You can't do it to me.'

'To *you*?'

Thierry met her questioning eyes. Instantly heat, recognition and emotion slammed into him. All those feelings that had been growing since the night he'd looked across a crowd in Paris and seen Imogen.

At first he'd thought it simple attraction, sexual desire with a dollop of curiosity and vicarious pleasure in watching her wide-eyed excitement at so many new experiences. But his feelings went way beyond that. They had almost from the first.

She tugged to free herself and his grip tightened.

'Let me go, Thierry.' Desperation laced her words. It gave him hope when moments ago there'd been none. There must be a reason she sounded as desperate as he felt.

'I can't.' It was the simple truth. How had she put it? *Simple and huge.* The truth was so huge it felt like he'd swallowed the sun.

Thierry met his wife's eyes, willing her to believe, to understand, to share what he felt. 'I can't, Imogen, because I love you.'

Thierry's hands on hers kept her standing as the room whirled. His arm came around her, strong and sure. Yet it was the look in his eyes that held her immobile. A look she'd never seen.

How was that for wishful thinking?

'Don't lie, Thierry.' She choked on the words.

He held her gaze, and she could almost believe she read desperation there. Enough to feign love now he realised it was what she wanted?

'I don't lie, Imogen.' He spoke gravely.

How badly she wanted this to be true! Enough to half-believe him, though it defied logic. 'I can't take any more, Thierry. Not tonight.'

'This can't wait.' Before she knew it she was high in his arms, cradled against his chest. She tried to be strong, but found her cheek nestling against him. His unique scent filled her. If this was the last time he held her she was determined to commit every detail to memory.

He moved, and her heart hammered, but he wasn't carrying her to bed. She was grateful. He'd be hard to resist if he tried to seduce her. Surely it was relief, not disappointment, she felt when he settled on the window seat, cradling her?

'I love you, Imogen.' The words vibrated through his body into hers. They wafted warm air in her hair.

'Thierry. Please.' She swallowed pain. 'Don't pretend. I won't stop you seeing our baby. You'll still have access.'

'This isn't about the baby. It's about us.'

Imogen turned her face into his chest, absurdly seeking comfort from the very man she shouldn't. 'It's not about us. This is pride speaking. You just don't want to let go.' Not after he'd shown his bride to his friends and all those society people.

'Of course I won't let you go. Not without a fight. It's taken a lifetime to find you.'

Shock caught her throat. Sincerity throbbed in every word. But it couldn't be.

Tilting her head, she leaned back enough to see him. Tension accentuated the planes and angles of that remarkable face. His mouth was grim, but his eyes looked lost. Surely not!

'Don't play games, Thierry.' Her voice scraped. 'It's cruel. That's not you.'

His arms tightened. 'What would be cruel is losing you. I love you, Imogen. Nothing matters but that.'

Her heart thudded in her throat and there was a rushing in her ears. 'You don't believe in love. You told me.'

'I was an arrogant, ignorant fool.' He brushed

her cheek with a touch so tender it made her eyes well. 'Don't cry, Imogen. I want you to be happy.'

She opened her mouth to tell him she'd be happy if he released her. But it wasn't true.

'I'm not your type. I'm not tall and glamorous or—'

'You're so much my type I don't think I could live without you.' Her heart squeezed. 'As for me chasing blondes…' He shook his head. 'My tastes have matured. I never loved any of them.'

'Not even Sandrine?'

His mouth twisted. 'Does it make me sound old if I admit that was youthful folly? I was besotted but I'm glad she married someone else. We'd have made each other unhappy. We're too alike, too self-centred.'

'You're not.' His care for her had been anything but.

'I am. Now I've found you, I'll do anything to keep you.'

'Like pretend to love me.'

He cupped her cheek, holding her so she couldn't look away.

'There's no pretence. From the first you were different. I didn't know how or why but I felt it. Didn't you?' He barely paused. 'I told myself you were a breath of fresh air, a diversion, but you were much more. I was on the point of trying to find your address in Australia when you appeared at my office.'

'Really?' Her breath stilled.

'Really. I didn't know I was in love. Obviously I'm a slow learner. But it's true. I've been falling for you since that night in Paris.'

Hope vied with disbelief, stealing her words, jumbling her thoughts.

'But the woman you met in Paris wasn't the real me. I'm boring and—'

A crack of laughter stopped her. 'Boring? Anything but. You're more exciting than anyone I know.'

Imogen shook her head. 'You don't understand.'

'I understand. You're cautious, you like to weigh your options. You love numbers and order. But there's more. That woman in Paris is just another side to your personality, even though you suppressed her for years. You weren't pretending, just letting her loose.' His smile was so tender her heart turned over. 'Your zest for life is contagious and you help me be the man I want to be. The thought of losing you…' To her amazement, his voice cracked.

'Thierry?'

'Don't ever say you're not glamorous.' The authoritative confidence was back in his voice. 'You're the most gorgeous woman on the planet, whether you're in a ballgown, or old jeans or nothing.' His voice dipped. 'Preferably nothing.'

'Now you're lying,' she gasped.

He smiled. 'You're the most extraordinary woman in the world. I love you, Imogen. Stay with me and in time maybe you'll love me back.'

Her heartbeat snagged. He truly didn't know?

'But you don't want a wife to tie you down. You want freedom. A life of adventures like the one you're planning with Orsino.'

He shook his head. 'Before you I pined for what I'd lost—the freedom to take off at a moment's notice. I told myself I hated the job I'd been forced to do and it was true in the beginning. But I've come to realise I enjoy commerce. I like the cut and thrust of it, sizing up opportunities and making the most of them.' His smile was self-deprecating.

'I've had to do a lot of growing up recently. From self-absorbed playboy to responsible adult. It was hard but I'm happy with the outcome.' Thierry's thumb stroked her cheek.

'I'd already decided I need balance in my life. Now the business is on track, I can step back a little and have a life outside the office. But I don't want to step back totally. I want to run the business and find time for a little climbing or ballooning. But what I want most of all…' His voice dipped to that low, earthy note that always thrilled her. 'Is to be with you and our baby.'

Thierry paused, his gaze meshing with hers. Imogen felt hope and excitement pound through her. 'That's going to be the most exciting adventure of my life. I wouldn't miss it for anything.' His thumb brushed her cheek.

'I'll give it all up, the treks, the business, whatever, if it means you'll stay with me. I'll move to Aus—'

Imogen put her hand to his lips. They were warm and soft, at odds with his harsh expression. 'You'd do that? Give up all this?'

'I love you, Imogen.' His lips moved against her hand, his words balm to her aching heart. 'All I want is to be with you. The rest is nothing.'

The *château*, the place in society, the birthright, were less precious than her?

'Ah, *mon coeur*, don't cry. Please, it breaks my heart.'

He leaned in to kiss the hot tears sliding down her cheeks, and she bit back a sob. Her heart felt too full, as if it were going to burst.

She clutched his shoulders, trying to reassure herself this was real. 'You mean it?'

'I've never been more serious about anything in my life.' His expression was so solemn, so earnest. 'Stay with me and I'll prove it to you. No man could ever love you more than I do and one day, I hope, you'll feel the same way about me.'

Fire caught Imogen's throat as she smiled through her tears.

'Not *one day. Now.*'

He stared blankly as if he couldn't make sense of her words.

She slid her hands up to cup the back of his head, a quiver of excitement filling her at the knowledge dreams really did come true.

'I'm in love with you, Thierry. I have been since Paris. Since that first night.' She waited for his satisfied smile. Instead, she read shock then wonder on his proud features. 'You swept me off my feet, my darling.'

He closed his eyes, murmuring something in French under his breath that sounded heartfelt and urgent. When he opened them again she caught the dark gleam of excitement she'd loved from the beginning.

'You truly love me?'

She nodded. 'That's why I was so miserable, so ready to leave. I thought I could love you and live with you even though you didn't return my feelings. But then—'

'Then you thought I was a selfish, ungrateful brute who didn't understand what a treasure I had in you.'

Suddenly he swooped her up in the air then deposited her on the window seat. Before she could catch her breath he knelt before her, drawing her hands into his.

'Thierry? What are you doing?'

Midnight eyes held hers, and she couldn't look away, for they were filled with love. The same love welling inside her.

'Imogen, will you make me the happiest man in the world? Will you marry me and live with me for the rest of our lives?'

'But we're already married.'

'I want to marry you again—properly this time. With us both giving our hearts. A marriage of love, not convenience.'

'Oh, Thierry!' She blinked back fresh tears.

'You don't like the idea?' He frowned.

'I love the idea! I can't think of anything I'd like more.'

MILLS & BOON®
Large Print – July 2016

The Italian's Ruthless Seduction
Miranda Lee

Awakened by Her Desert Captor
Abby Green

A Forbidden Temptation
Anne Mather

A Vow to Secure His Legacy
Annie West

Carrying the King's Pride
Jennifer Hayward

Bound to the Tuscan Billionaire
Susan Stephens

Required to Wear the Tycoon's Ring
Maggie Cox

The Greek's Ready-Made Wife
Jennifer Faye

Crown Prince's Chosen Bride
Kandy Shepherd

Billionaire, Boss...Bridegroom?
Kate Hardy

Married for Their Miracle Baby
Soraya Lane

His loving smile, his tender kiss on her palm, told her he felt the same, but there was a mischievous glint in his eyes. 'Women love shopping for wedding dresses and the trimmings for a big wedding.'

'A big wedding?' She pretended to pout. 'What if I want to get married in a hot-air balloon or—'

His kiss stopped her words. When he pulled back he was grinning. 'Whatever you want, *mon coeur.* Perhaps we could go somewhere more comfortable to discuss the options.'

Imogen felt that smile to the soles of her feet. 'You have the best ideas, Thierry.' She put her hand in his and let him draw her to her feet, knowing he was right. The future together would be the adventure of their lifetimes.

* * * * *

Also available in the
ONE NIGHT WITH CONSEQUENCES
series this month
BOUND TO THE TUSCAN BILLIONAIRE
by Susan Stephens

And look out for THE SHOCK CASSANO BABY
by Andie Brock in September 2016.

A TYCOON TO BE RECKONED WITH

A TYCOON TO BE RECKONED WITH

BY

JULIA JAMES

MILLS & BOON

First published in Great Britain 2016
By Mills & Boon, an imprint of HarperCollins*Publishers*
1 London Bridge Street, London, SE1 9GF

Large Print edition 2016

© 2016 Julia James

ISBN: 978-0-263-26229-2

C463472599

Our policy is to use papers that are natural, renewable and recyclable products and made from wood grown in sustainable forests. The logging and manufacturing processes conform to the legal environmental regulations of the country of origin.

Printed and bound in Great Britain
by CPI Antony Rowe, Chippenham, Wiltshire

For IHV, who gave me my love of opera.

CHAPTER ONE

'YOU KNOW, IT'S you I blame.'

Bastiaan's aunt tried to laugh as she spoke, but it was shaky, Bastiaan could tell.

'It was you who suggested Philip go and stay in your villa at Cap Pierre!'

Bastiaan took the criticism on board. 'I thought it might help—moving him out of target range to finish his university vacation assignments in peace and quiet.'

His aunt sighed. 'Alas, it seems he has jumped out of the frying pan into the fire. He may have escaped Elena Constantis, but this female in France sounds infinitely worse.'

Bastiaan's dark eyes took on a mordant expression. 'Unfortunately, wherever in the world Philip is he will be a target.'

'If only he were less sweet-natured. If he had your...*toughness*,' Bastiaan's aunt replied, her gaze falling on her nephew.

'I'll take that as a compliment,' Bastiaan replied dryly. 'But Philip will toughen up, don't worry.' *He'll need to*, he thought caustically. Just as he himself had had to.

'He's so impressionable!' his aunt cried. 'And so handsome. No wonder these wretched girls make a beeline for him.'

And, of course, so rich, Bastiaan added cynically—but silently. No point worrying his already anxious aunt further. It was Philip's wealth—the wealth he would be inheriting from his late father's estate once he turned twenty-one in a couple of months—that would attract females far more dangerous than the merely irksome spoilt teenage princess Elena Constantis. The real danger would come from a very different type of female.

Call them what one liked—and Bastiaan had several names not suitable for his aunt's ears— the most universal name was a familiar one: gold-diggers. Females who took one look at his young, good-looking, impressionable and soon to be very rich cousin and licked their lips in anticipation.

That was the problem right now. A woman who appeared to be licking her lips over Philip. And the danger was, Bastiaan knew, very real. For Philip, so Paulette, his housekeeper at Cap Pierre, had informed him, far from diligently writing his essays, had taken to haunting the nearby town of Pierre-les-Pins and a venue there that was most undesirable for a twenty-year-old. Apparently attracted by an even more undesirable female working there.

'A singer in a nightclub!' his aunt wailed now. 'I cannot believe Philip would fall for a woman like that!'

'It *is* something of a cliché...' Bastiaan allowed.

His aunt bridled. 'A cliché? Bastiaan, is that all you have to say about it?'

He shook his head. 'No. I could say a great deal more—but to what purpose?' Bastiaan got to his feet. He was of an imposing height, standing well over six feet, and powerfully built. 'Don't worry...' he made his voice reassuring now '...I'll deal with it. Philip will *not* be sacrificed to a greedy woman's ambitions.'

His aunt stood up, clutching at his sleeve. *'Thank you,'* she said. 'I knew I could count on you.' Her eyes misted a little. 'Take care of my darling boy, Bastiaan. He has no father now to look out for him.'

Bastiaan pressed his aunt's hand sympathetically. His maternal uncle had succumbed to heart disease when Philip had just started at university, and he knew how hard her husband's death had hit his aunt. Knew, too, with a shadowing of his eyes, how losing a father too young—as he himself had when not much older than Philip—left a void.

'I'll keep Philip safe, I promise you,' he assured his aunt now, as she took her leave.

He saw her to her car, watched it head down the driveway of his property in the affluent outskirts of Athens. Then he went back indoors, his mouth tightening.

His aunt's fears were not groundless. Until Philip turned twenty-one Bastiaan was his trustee—overseeing all his finances, managing his investments—while Philip enjoyed a more than generous allowance to cover his personal spending. Usually Bastiaan did nothing more than cast a casual eye over the bank and credit card statements, but an unusually large amount—twenty thousand euros—had gone out in a single payment a week ago. The cheque had been paid into an unknown personal account at the Nice branch of a French bank. There was no reason— no *good* reason—that Bastiaan could come up with for such a transfer. There was, however, one very bad reason for it—and that he *could* come up with.

The gold-digger had already started taking gold from the mine....

Bastiaan's features darkened. The sooner he disposed of this nightclub singer who was making eyes at his cousin—and his cousin's fortune—the better. He headed purposefully to his study. If he was to leave for France in the morning, he had work to do tonight. Enterprises with portfolios the size of Karavalas did not run themselves. His cousin's fortune might be predominantly in the form of blue chip stocks, but Bastiaan preferred to diversify across a broad range of investment opportunities, from industry and property to en-trepreneurial start-ups. But, for all their variety, they all shared one aspect in common—they all made him money. A *lot* of money.

The cynical curve was back at Bastiaan's mouth as he sat himself down behind his desk and flicked on his PC. He'd told his aunt that her son would toughen up in time—and he knew from his own experience that that was true. Memory glinted in his dark eyes.

When his own father had died, he'd assuaged his grief by partying hard and extravagantly, with no paternal guardian to moderate his excesses. The spree had ended abruptly. He'd been in a casino, putting away the champagne and generally flashing his cash lavishly, and it had promptly lured across a female—Leana—who had been all over him. At just twenty-three he'd been happy to enjoy all she'd offered him—the company of her luscious body in bed included. So much so that when she'd fed him some story of how she'd stupidly got herself into debt with the casino and was worried sick about it, he'd grandly handed her a more than handsome cheque, feeling munificent and generous towards the beautiful, sexy woman who'd seemed so keen on him...

She'd disappeared the day the cheque had cleared—heading off, so he'd heard, on a yacht belonging to a seventy-year-old Mexican millionaire, never to be seen again by Bastiaan. He'd been royally fleeced and proved to be a complete mug. It had stung, no doubt about it, but he'd learnt his lesson, all right—an expensive one. It wasn't one he wanted Philip to learn the same way. Apart from taking a large wedge of his money, Leana had damaged his self-esteem—an uncomfortably sobering experience for his younger self. Although it had made him wise up decisively.

But, unlike Bastiaan, Philip was of a romantic disposition, and a gold-digging seductress might wound him more deeply than just in his wallet and his self-esteem. That was not something Bastiaan would permit. After his experience with Leana he'd become wise to the wiles women threw out to him, and sceptical of their apparent devotion. Now, into his thirties, he knew they considered him a tough nut—ruthless, even...

His eyes hardened beneath dark brows. That was something this ambitious nightclub singer would soon discover for herself.

Sarah stood motionless on the low stage, the spotlight on her, while her audience beyond, sitting at their tables, mostly continued their conversations as they ate and drank.

I'm just a divertimento, she thought to herself, acidly. *Background music.* She nodded at Max on the piano, throat muscles ready, and he played the opening to her number. It was easy and low-pitched, making no demands on her upper register. It was just as well—the last thing she wanted to do was risk her voice singing in this smoky atmosphere.

As she sang the first bars her breasts lifted, making her all too aware of just how low-cut the bodice of her champagne satin gown was. Her long hair was swept over one bare shoulder. It was, she knew, a stereotypical 'vamp' image— the sultry nightclub singer with her slinky dress, low-pitched voice, over-made-up eyes and long blonde locks.

She tensed instinctively. Well, that was the idea, wasn't it? To stand in for the club's missing resident *chanteuse,* Sabine Sablon, who had abruptly vacated the role when she'd run off with a rich customer without warning.

It hadn't been Sarah's idea to take over as Sabine, but Max had been blunt about it. If she didn't agree to sing here in the evenings, then Raymond, the nightclub owner, lacking a *chanteuse,* would refuse to let Max have the run of the place during the day. And without that they couldn't rehearse…and without rehearsals they couldn't appear at the Provence en Voix music festival.

And if they didn't appear there her last chance would be gone.

My last chance—my last chance to achieve my dream!

Her dream of breaking through from being just one more of the scores upon scores of hopeful, aspiring sopranos who crowded the operatic world, all desperate to make their mark. If she could not succeed now, she would have to abandon the dream that had possessed her since her teenage years, and all the way through music college and the tough, ultra-competitive world beyond as she'd struggled to make herself heard by those who could lift her from the crowd and launch her career.

She'd tried so hard, for so long, and now she was on the wrong side of twenty-five, racing towards thirty, with time against her and younger singers coming up behind her. Everything rested on this final attempt—and if it failed… Well, then, she would accept defeat. Resign herself to teaching instead. It was the way she was currently earning her living, part-time at a school in her native Yorkshire, though she found it unfulfilling, craving the excitement and elation of performing live.

So not yet—*oh, not yet*—would she give up on her dreams. Not until she'd put everything into this music festival, singing the soprano lead in what she knew could only be a high-risk gamble: a newly written opera by an unknown composer, performed by unknown singers, all on a shoestring. A shoestring that Max, their fanatically driven director and conductor, was already stretching to the utmost. Everything, but *everything*, was being done on a tiny budget, with savings being made wherever they could. Including rehearsal space.

So every night bar Sundays, she had to become Sabine Sablon, husking away into the microphone, drawing male eyes all around. It was not a comfortable feeling—and it was a million miles away from her true self. Max could tell her all he liked that it would give her valuable insight into roles such as *La Traviata*'s courtesan Violetta, or the coquettish Manon, but on an operatic stage everyone would know she was simply playing a part. Here, everyone looking at her really thought she *was* Sabine Sablon.

A silent shudder went through her. Dear God, if anyone in the opera world found out she was singing here, like this, her credibility would be shot to pieces. No one would take her seriously for a moment.

And neither Violetta nor Manon was anything like her role in Anton's opera *War Bride*. Her character was a romantic young girl, falling in love with a dashing soldier. A whirlwind courtship, a return to the front—and then the dreaded news of her husband's fate. The heartbreak of loss and bereavement. And then a child born to take his father's place in yet another war...

The simple, brutal tale was told as a timeless fable of the sacrifice and futility of war, repeated down the ages, its score haunting and poignant. It had captivated Sarah the first moment she'd heard Max play it.

What must it be like to love so swiftly, to hurt so badly? she'd wondered as she'd started to explore her role. For herself, she had no knowledge—had never experienced the heady whirlwind of love nor the desolation of heartbreak. Her only serious relationship had ended last year when Andrew, a cellist she had known since college, had been offered a place in a prestigious orchestra in Germany. It had been his breakthrough moment, and she had been so glad for him—had waved him off without a thought of holding him back.

Both of them had always known that their careers must come first in their lives, which meant that neither could afford to invest in a deeply emotional relationship which might jeopardise their diverging career paths. So neither had grieved when they'd parted, only wished each other well. Theirs had been a relationship based primarily on a shared passion for music, rather than for each other—friendship and affection had bound them, nothing more than that.

But this meant she knew that in order to portray her character now—the War Bride—as convincingly as she could, she would need to call on all her imagination. Just as she would need all her operatic abilities to do credit to the challenging vocal demands of the hauntingly beautiful but technically difficult music.

She reached the end of her song to a smattering

of applause. Dipping her head in acknowledge-
ment, she shifted her weight from one high-heeled
foot to the other. As she straightened again, sending her gaze back out over the dining area, she
felt a sudden flickering awareness go through
her. She could hear Max start the introduction to
her next number but ignored it, her senses suddenly on alert. She heard him repeat the phrase,
caught him glancing at her with a frown, but her
attention was not on him—not on the song she
was supposed to have started four bars earlier.
Her attention was on the audience beyond.

Someone was looking at her. Someone standing at the back of the room.

He had not been there a moment ago and must
have just come in. She shook her head, trying
to dismiss that involuntary sense of heightened
awareness, of sudden exposure. Male eyes gazed
at her all the time—and there was always movement beyond the stage…diners and waiters. They
did not make her pause the way this had—as if
there were something different about him. She
wanted to see him more clearly, but the light was
wrong and he was too far away for her to discern

anything more than a tall, tuxedo-clad figure at the back of the room.

For the third time she heard Max repeat the intro—insistently this time. And she knew she had to start to sing. Not just because of Max's impatient prompt but because she suddenly, urgently, needed to do something other than simply stand there, pooled in the light that emphasised every slender curve of her tightly sheathed body. Exposed her to that invisible yet almost tangible scrutiny that was palpable in its impact on her.

As she started the number her voice was more husky than ever. Her long, artificial lashes swept down over her deeply kohled eyes, and the sweep of her hair dipped halfway across her jawline and cheekbone. She forced herself to keep singing, to try and suppress the frisson of disturbed awareness that was tensing through her—the sense of being the object of attention that was like a beam targeted at her.

Somehow she got through to the end of the number, pulling herself together to start the next one on time and not fluff it. It seemed easier now, and she realised that at some point that sense of being under scrutiny had faded and dissipated.

As if a kind of pressure had been lifted off her. She reached the end of the last number, the end of her set, with a sense of relief. She made her way offstage, hearing canned music starting up and Max closing down the piano.

One of the waiters intercepted her. 'There's a guy who wants to buy you a drink,' he said.

Sarah made a face. It wasn't unusual that this happened, but she never accepted.

The waiter held up a hundred-euro note. 'Looks like he's keen,' he informed her with a lift of his brow.

'Well, he's the only one who is,' she said. 'Better take it back to him,' she added. 'I don't want him thinking I pocketed it and then didn't show.'

Her refusal got Max's approval. 'No time for picking up men,' he said, flippantly but pointedly.

'As if I would…' She rolled her eyes.

For a moment, it crossed her mind that the invitation to buy her a drink might be connected to that shadowy figure at the back of the room and his disturbing perusal of her, but then she dismissed the thought. All she wanted to do now was get out of her costume and head for bed. Max started opera rehearsals promptly every morning, and she needed to sleep.

She'd just reached her dressing room, kicking off her high heels and flexing her feet in relief, when there was a brief knock at the door. She only had time to say, 'Who is it?' before the door opened.

She glanced up, assuming it would be Max, wanting to tell her something that couldn't wait. But instead it was a man she'd never seen before in her life.

And he stilled the breath in her lungs.

CHAPTER TWO

BASTIAAN'S EYES ZEROED in on the figure seated at the brightly lit vanity unit with its trademark light-bulb-surrounded mirror. Backlit as she was by the high-wattage bulbs, her face was in shadow.

But the shadows did nothing to dim her impact. If anything it emphasised it, casting her features into relief. On stage, she'd been illuminated in a pool of light, her features softened by the distance at which he'd sat. He'd deliberately taken a table at the rear of the room, wanting at that point only to observe without being noticed in return.

It hadn't taken him more than two moments to realise that the female poised on the stage possessed a quality that signalled danger to his young, impressionable cousin.

Allure—it was an old-fashioned word, but that was the one that had come to his mind as his eyes had rested on the slender figure sensu-

ously draped in low-cut clinging satin, standing in a pool of soft, smoky light, her fingers
lightly curved around her microphone, the lustrous fall of her long blonde hair curled over her
bare shoulder like a vamp from the forties.

Her mouth was painted a rich, luscious red, her
eye make-up was pronounced, with long, artificial lashes framing luminous eyes. Seeing her
now, close up, she was even more alluring.

No wonder Philip is smitten!

His eyes completed his swift scrutiny and he
was interested to see a line of colour running
along her cheekbones. *Curious...*he thought.
Then the tightening of her mouth told him what
had accounted for that reaction. It was not a
blush—a woman like her probably hadn't blushed
since puberty—it was annoyance.

Why? he found himself wondering. Women
were not usually annoyed when he paid them
attention. Quite the reverse. But this *chanteuse*
was. It was doubly unusual because surely a
woman in her profession was well used to male
admirers courting her in her dressing room.

An unwelcome thought crossed his mind—was

it his cousin's wont to hang out here? Did she invite him to her changing room?

Just how far has she got with him?

Well, however far it was, it was going to stop from now on. Whatever story she'd trotted out to Philip in order to get him to give her money, the gold mine was closing down...

She was looking at him still, that scarlet mouth of hers pressed tightly, and something sparking now in her eyes.

'*Oui?*' she said pointedly.

His eyelids dipped over his eyes briefly. 'Did the waiter not pass on my invitation?' he asked, speaking in French, which he spoke as well as English and a couple of other languages as well.

Her arched eyebrows rose. 'It was you?' she said. Then, without bothering to wait for a reply, she simply went on, 'I'm afraid I don't accept invitations to share a drink with any of the club's guests.'

Her tone was dismissive, and Bastiaan felt a flicker of annoyance at it. Dismissive was not the kind of voice he was used to hearing in women he was speaking to. Or indeed from anyone he was speaking to. And in someone whose career relied on the attention and appreciation of others, it was out of place.

Perhaps she thinks she does not need to court her audience any longer? Perhaps she thinks she already has a very comfortable exit from her profession lined up?

The flicker of annoyance sparked to something sharper. But he did not let it show. Not now—not yet. At the moment, his aim was to disarm her. Defeating her would come afterwards.

'Then allow me to invite you to dinner instead,' he responded. Deliberately, he infused a subtly caressing note into his voice that he'd found successful at any other time he'd chosen to adopt it.

That line of colour ran out over her cheekbones again. But this time there was no accompanying tightening of her red mouth. Instead she gave a brief smile. It was civil only—nothing more than that, Bastiaan could see.

'Thank you, but no. And now...' the smile came again, and he could see that her intention was to terminate the exchange '...if you will excuse me, I must get changed.' She paused expectantly, waiting for him to withdraw.

He ignored the prompt. Instead one eyebrow

tilted interrogatively. 'You have another dinner engagement?' he asked.

Something snapped in her eyes, changing their colour, he noticed. He'd assumed they were a shade of grey, but suddenly there was a flash of green in them.

'No,' she said precisely. 'And if I did, *m'sieu*—' the pointedness was back in her voice now '—I don't believe it would be any of your concern.' She smiled tightly, with less civility now.

If it were with my cousin, mademoiselle, it would indeed be my concern... That flicker of more than annoyance came again, but again Bastiaan concealed it.

'In which case, what can be your objection to dining with me?' Again, there was the same note in his voice that worked so well with women in general. Invitations to dine with him had never, in his living memory, been met with rejection.

She was staring at him with those eyes that had gone back to grey now, the flash of green quite absent. Eyes that were outlined in black kohl, their sockets dramatised outrageously with make-up, their lashes doubled in length by artificial means and copious mascara.

Staring at him in a way he'd never been stared at before.

As though she didn't quite believe what she was seeing. Or hearing.

For just a second their eyes met, and then, as if in recoil, her fake lashes dropped down over her eyes, veiling them.

She took a breath. *'M'sieu,* I am desolated to inform you that I also do not accept invitations to dine with the club's guests,' she said. She didn't make her tone dismissive now, but absolute.

He ignored it. 'I wasn't thinking of dining here,' he said. 'I would prefer to take you to Le Tombleur,' he murmured.

Her eyes widened just a fraction. Le Tombleur was currently the most fashionable restaurant on the Côte D'Azur, and Bastiaan was sure that the chance to dine at such a fabulous locale would surely stop her prevaricating in this fashion. It would also, he knew, set her mind instantly at rest as to whether he was someone possessed of sufficient financial means to be of interest to her. She would not wish to waste her time on someone who was not in the same league as his young cousin. Had she but known, Bastiaan thought cynically, his own fortune was considerably greater than Philip's.

But of course Philip's fortune was far more accessible to her. Or might be. If she were truly setting Philip in her sightline, she would be cautious about switching her attentions elsewhere—it would lose her Philip if he discovered it.

A thought flickered across Bastiaan's mind. She was alluring enough—even for himself... Should *that* be his method of detaching her? Then he dismissed it. Of course he would not be involving himself in any kind of liaison with a woman such as this one. However worthy the intention.

Dommage... He heard the French word in his head. *What a pity...*

'*M'sieu...*' She was speaking again, with razored precision. 'As I say, I must decline your very...*generous*...invitation'.

Had there been a twist in her phrasing of the word 'generous'? An ironic inflection indicating that she had formed an opinion of him that was not the one he'd intended her to form?

He felt a new emotion flicker within him like a low-voltage electric current.

Could there possibly be more to this woman sitting there, looking up at him through those absurdly fake eyelashes, with a strange expression in her grey-green eyes—more green now than grey, he realised. His awareness of that colour-change was of itself distracting, and it made his own eyes narrow assessingly.

For just a fraction of a second their eyes seemed to meet, and Bastiaan felt the voltage of the electric current surging within him.

'Are you ready to go yet?'

A different voice interjected, coming from the door, which had been pushed wider by a man—a youngish one—clad in a dinner jacket, half leaning his slightly built body against the doorjamb. The man had clearly addressed Sabine, but now, registering that there was someone else in her dressing room, his eyes went to Bastiaan.

He frowned, about to say something, but Sabine Sablon interjected. 'The gentleman is just leaving,' she announced.

Her voice was cool, but Bastiaan was too experienced with women not to know that she was not, in fact, as composed as she wanted to appear. And he knew what was causing it…

Satisfaction soared through him. Oh, this sultry, sophisticated *chanteuse*, with her vampish allure, her skin-tight dress and over-made-up face, might be appearing as cool as the proverbial cucumber—but that flash in her eyes had told him that however resistant she appeared to be to his overtures, an appearance was all it was...

I can reach her. She is vulnerable to me.

That was the truth she'd so unguardedly—so unwisely—just revealed to him.

He changed his stance. Glanced at the man hovering in the doorway. A slight sense of familiarity assailed him, and a moment later he knew why. He was the accompanist for the *chanteuse*.

For a fleeting moment he found himself speculating on whether the casual familiarity he could sense between the two of them betokened a more intimate relationship. Then he rejected it. Every male instinct told him that whatever lover the accompanist took would not be female.

Bastiaan's sense of satisfaction increased, and his annoyance with the intruder decreased proportionately. He turned his attention back to his quarry.

'I shall take my leave, then, *mademoiselle*,' he

said, and he did not trouble to hide his ironic inflection or his amusement. Dark, dangerous amusement. As though her rejection of him was clearly nothing more than a feminine ploy—one he was seeing through...but currently choosing to indulge. He gave the slightest nod of his head, the slightest sardonic smile.

'*A bientôt.*'

Then, paying not the slightest attention to the accompanist, who had to straighten to let him pass, he walked out.

As he left he heard the *chanteuse* exclaim, 'Thank goodness you rescued me!'

Bastiaan could hear the relief in her tone. His satisfaction went up yet another level. A tremor—a discernible tremor—had been audible in her voice. That was good.

Yes, she is vulnerable to me.

He walked on down the corridor, casually letting himself out through the rear entrance into the narrow roadway beyond, before walking around to the front of the club, where his car was parked on the forecourt. Lowering himself into its low-slung frame, he started the engine, its low, throaty growl echoing the silent growl inside his head.

'*Thank goodness you rescued me!*' she had said, this harpy who was trying to extract his cousin's fortune from him.

Bastiaan's mouth thinned to a tight, narrow line, his eyes hardening as he headed out on to the road, setting his route back towards Monaco, where he was staying tonight in the duplex apartment he kept there.

Well, in that she was mistaken—most decidedly.

No one will rescue you from me.

Of that he was certain.

He drove on into the night.

'Give me two minutes and I'll be ready to go,' Sarah said.

She strove for composure, but felt as if she'd just been released from a seizure of her senses that had crushed the breath from her lungs. How she'd managed to keep her cool she had no idea—she had only know that keeping her cool was absolutely essential.

What the hell had just happened to her? Out of nowhere…the way it had?

That had been the man whose assessing gaze she'd picked up during her final number. She'd been able to feel it from right across the club— and when he'd walked into her dressing room it had been like…

Like nothing I've ever known. Nothing I've ever felt—

Never before had a man had such a raw, physical impact on her. Hitting her senses like a sledgehammer. She tried to analyse it now—needing to do so. His height, towering over her in the tiny dressing room, had dominated the encounter. The broad shoulders had been sleekly clad in a bespoke dinner jacket, and there had been an impression of power that she had derived not just from the clearly muscular physique he possessed but by an aura about him that had told her this man was used to getting his own way.

Especially with women.

Because it hadn't just been the clear impression that here was a wealthy man who could buy female favours—his mention of Le Tombleur had been adequate demonstration of *that*—it had been far, far more…

She felt herself swallow. *He doesn't need money to impress women.*

No, she acknowledged shakily, all it took was those piercing dark eyes, winged with darker brows, the strong blade of his nose, the wide, sensual curve of his mouth and the tough line of his jaw.

He was a man who knew perfectly well that his appeal to women was powerful—who knew perfectly well that women responded to him on that account.

She felt her hackles rise automatically.

He thought I'd jump at the chance!

A rush of weakness swept through her. Thank God she'd had the presence of mind—pulled urgently out of her reeling senses—to react the way she'd managed to do.

What was it about him that he should have had such an effect on me?

Just what had it been about that particular combination of physique, looks and sheer, raw personal impact that had made her react as if she were a sliver of steel in the sudden presence of a magnetic field so strong it had made the breath still in her body?

She had seen better-looking men in her time, but not a single one had ever had the raw, visceral, overpowering impact on her senses that this man had. Even in the space of a few charged minutes…

She shook her head again, trying to clear the image from her mind. Whoever he was, he'd gone.

As she got on with the task of turning herself back into Sarah, shedding the false eyelashes, heavy make-up and tight satin gown, she strove to dismiss him from her thoughts. *Put him out of your head*, she told herself brusquely. *It was Sabine Sablon he wanted to invite to dinner, not Sarah Fareham.*

That was the truth of it, she knew. Sabine was the kind of woman a man like that would be interested in—sophisticated, seductive, a woman of the world, a *femme fatale*. And she wasn't Sabine—she most definitely was not. So it was completely irrelevant that she'd reacted to the man the way she had.

I haven't got time to be bowled over by some

*arrogantly smouldering alpha male who thinks
he's picking up a sultry woman like Sabine. However much he knocked me sideways.*

She had one focus in her life right now—only
one. And it was *not* a man with night-dark eyes
and devastating looks who sucked the breath
from her body.

She headed out to where Max was waiting to
walk her back to her *pension*, some blocks away
in this harbourside *ville* of Pierre-les-Pins, before carrying on to the apartment he shared with
Anton, the opera's composer.

As they set off he launched into speech without preamble. 'I've been thinking,' he said, 'in
your first duet with Alain—'

And he was off, instructing her in some troublesome vocal technicalities he wanted to address
at the next day's rehearsal. Sarah was glad, for it
helped to distance her mind from that brief but
disturbing encounter in her dressing room with
that devastating, dangerous man.

Dangerous? The word echoed in her head, taking her aback. *Had* he been dangerous? Truly?

She gave herself a mental shake. She was being

absurd. How could a complete stranger be dangerous to her? Of course he couldn't.

It was absurd to think so.

CHAPTER THREE

'BASTIAAN! FANTASTIC! I'd no idea you were here in France!' Philip's voice was warm and enthusiastic as he answered his mobile.

'Monaco, to be precise,' Bastiaan answered, strolling with his phone to the huge plate-glass window of his high-rise apartment in Monte Carlo, which afforded a panoramic view over the harbour, chock-full of luxury yachts glittering in the morning sunshine.

'But you'll come over to the villa, won't you?' his cousin asked eagerly.

'Seeking distraction from your essays...?' Bastiaan trailed off deliberately, knowing the boy had distraction already—a dangerous one.

As it had done ever since he'd left the nightclub last night, the seductive image of Sabine Sablon slid into his inner vision. Enough to distract anyone. Even himself...

He pulled his mind away. Time to discover just

how deep Philip was with the alluring *chanteuse*. 'Well,' he continued, 'I can be with you within the hour if you like?'

He did not get an immediate reply. Then Philip was saying, 'Could you make it a bit later than that?'

'Studying so hard?' Bastiaan asked lightly.

'Well, not precisely. I mean, I *am*—I've got one essay nearly finished—but actually, I'm a bit tied up till lunchtime...'

Philip's voice trailed off, and Bastiaan could hear the constraint in his cousin's voice. He was hiding something.

Deliberately, Bastiaan backed off. 'No problem,' he said. 'See you for lunch, then—around one... Is that OK?' He paused. 'Do you want me to tell Paulette to expect me, or will you?'

'Would *you*?' said Philip, from which Bastiaan drew his own conclusion. Philip wasn't at the villa right now.

'No problem,' he said again, making his voice easy still. Easier than his mind...

So, if Philip wasn't struggling with his history essays at the villa, where was he?

Is he with her now?

He could feel his hackles rising down his spine. Was that why she had turned down dining with him at Le Tombleur? Because she'd been about to rendezvous with his cousin? Had Philip spent the night with her?

A growl started in his throat. Philip might be legally free to have a relationship with anyone he wanted, but even if the *chanteuse* had been as pure as the driven snow, with the financial probity of a nun, she was utterly unsuitable for a first romance for a boy his age. She was nearer thirty than twenty...

'Great!' Philip was saying now. 'See you then, Bast—gotta go.'

The call was disconnected and Bastiaan dropped his phone back in his pocket slowly, staring out of the window. Multi-million-pound yachts crowded the marina, and the fairy tale royal palace looked increasingly besieged by the high-rise buildings that maximised the tiny footprint of the principality.

He turned away. His apartment here had been an excellent investment, and the rental income was exceptional during the Monaco Grand Prix, but Monte Carlo was not his favourite place. He far preferred his villa on Cap Pierre, where Philip was staying. Better still, his own private island off the Greek west coast. That was where he went when he truly wanted to be himself. One day he'd take the woman who would be his wife there—the woman he would spend the rest of his life with.

Although just who she would be he had no idea. His experience with women was wide, indeed, but so far not one of his many female acquaintances had come anywhere close to tempting him to make a relationship with her permanent. One thing he was sure of—when he met her, he'd know she was the one.

There'd be no mistaking that.

Meantime he'd settle himself down at the dining table, open his laptop and get some work done before heading off to meet Philip—and finding out just how bad his infatuation was…

'I could murder a coffee.' Sarah, dismissed by Max for now, while he focussed his attentions on the small chorus, plonked herself down at the table near the front of the stage where Philip was sitting.

He'd become a fixture at their rehearsals, and Sarah hadn't the heart to discourage him. He was a sweet guy, Philip Markiotis, and he had somehow attached himself to the little opera company in the role of unofficial runner—fetching coffee, refilling water jugs, copying scores, helping tidy up after rehearsals.

And all the time, Sarah thought with a softening of her expression, he was carrying a youthful torch for her that glowed in every yearning glance that came her way. He was only a few years older than her own sixth-formers, and his admiration for her must remain hopeless, but she would never dream of hurting his feelings. She knew how very real they seemed to him.

Memory sifted through Sarah's head. She knew what Philip was experiencing. OK, she could laugh at herself now, but as a music student she'd had *the* most lovestruck crush on the tenor who'd taken a summer master class she'd attended. She'd been totally smitten, unable to conceal it—but, looking back now, what struck her most was how tolerant the famous tenor had been of her openly besotted devotion. Oh, she probably hadn't been the only smitten female student, but she'd always remembered that he'd been kind, and tactful, and had never made her feel juvenile or idiotic.

She would do likewise now, with Philip. His crush, she knew perfectly well, would not outlast the summer. It was only the result of his isolation here, with nothing to do but write his vacation essays…and yearn after her hopelessly, gazing at her ardently with his dark eyes.

Out of nowhere a different image sprang into her head. The man who had walked into her dressing room, invaded her space, had rested his eyes on her—but not with youthful ardour in them. With something far more powerful, more primitive. Long-lashed, heavy-lidded, they had held her in their beam as if she were being targeted by a searchlight. She felt a sudden shimmer go through her—a shiver of sensual awareness—as if she could not escape that focussed regard. Did not want to…

She hauled her mind away.

I don't want to think about it. I don't want to think about him. He asked me out, I said no—that's it. Over and done with.

And it hadn't even been *her* he'd asked out,

she reminded herself. The man had taken her for Sabine, sultry and seductive, sophisticated and sexy. She would have to be terminally stupid not to know how a man like that, who thought nothing of approaching a woman he didn't know and asking her to dinner, would have wanted the evening to end had 'Sabine' accepted his invitation. It had been in his eyes, in his gaze—in the way it had washed over her. Blatant in its message.

Would I have wanted it to end that way? If I were Sabine...?

The question was there before she could stop it. Forcibly she pushed it aside, refusing to answer. She was *not* Sabine—she was Sarah Fareham. And whatever the disturbing impact that man had had on her she had no time to dwell on it. She was only weeks away from the most critical performance of her life, and all her energies, all her focus and strength, had to go into that. Nothing else mattered—*nothing*.

'So,' she said, making her voice cheerful, accepting the coffee Philip had poured for her, 'you're our one-man audience, Philip—how's it going, do you think?'

His face lit. 'You were *wonderful*!' he said, his eyes warm upon her.

Damn, thought Sarah wryly, she'd walked into that one. 'Thank you, kind sir,' she said playfully, 'but what about everyone else?'

'I'm sure they're excellent,' said Philip, his lack of interest in the other performers a distinct contrast with his enthusiasm for the object of his devotion. Then he frowned. 'Max treats you very badly,' he said, 'criticising you the way he does.'

Sarah smiled, amused. 'Oh, Philip—that's his job. And it's not just me—he's got to make sure we all get it right and then pull it together. He hears *all* the voices—each of us is focussing only on our own.'

'But yours is *wonderful*,' Philip said, as though that clinched the argument.

She gave a laugh, not answering, and drank her coffee, chasing it down with a large glass of water to freshen her vocal cords.

She was determined to banish the last remnants from the previous night's unwanted encounter with a male who was the very antithesis of the one sitting gazing at her now. Philip's company eased some of the inevitable tension that came from the intensity of rehearsals, the pressure on them all and Max's exacting musical direction. Apart from making sure she did not inadvertently encourage Philip in his crush on her, sitting with him was very undemanding.

With his good-natured, sunny personality, as well as his eagerness and enthusiasm for what was, to him, the novelty of a bohemian, artistic enterprise, it wasn't surprising that she and the other cast members liked him. What had been more surprising to her was that Max had not objected to his presence. His explanation had not found favour with her.

'*Cherie*, anyone staying at their family villa on the *Cap* is loaded. The boy might not throw money around but, believe me, I've checked out the name—he's one rich kid!' Max's eyes had gone to Sarah. 'Cultivate him, *cherie*—we could do with a wealthy sponsor.'

Sarah's reply had been instant—and sharp. 'Don't even *think* of trying to get a donation from him, Max!' she'd warned.

It would be absolutely out of the question for her to take advantage of her young admirer's boyish infatuation, however much family money there might be in the background. She'd pondered whether to warn Philip that Max might be angling for some financial help for the cash-strapped en-semble, but then decided not to. Knowing Philip, it would probably only inspire him to offer it.

She gave a silent sigh. What with treading around Philip's sensibilities, putting her heart and soul into perfecting her performance under the scathing scrutiny of Max, and enduring her nightly ordeal as Sabine, there was a lot on her plate right now. The last thing she needed to be added to it was having her mind straining back with unwelcome insistence to that unnerving vis-itation to her dressing room the night before.

At her side, Philip was glancing at his watch. He made a face.

'Need to go back to your essays?' she asked sympathetically.

'No,' he answered, 'it's my cousin—the one who owns the villa on the *Cap*—he's turned up on the Riviera and is coming over for lunch.'

'Checking you aren't throwing wild all-night parties, is he?' Sarah teased gently, although Philip was the last type to do any such thing. 'Or holding one himself?'

Philip shook his head. 'Bastiaan's loads too old for that stuff—he's gone thirty,' he said ingenuously. 'He spends most of his time working. Oh, and having hordes of females trailing around after him.'

Well, thought Sarah privately, if Cousin Bastiaan was from the same uber-affluent background as Philip, that wouldn't be too surprising. Rich men, she supposed, never ran short of female attention.

Before she could stop it, her mind homed back to that incident in her dressing room the night before. Her eyes darkened. Now, *there* was a man who was not shy of flaunting his wealth. Dropping invitations to flash restaurants and assuming they'd be snapped up.

But immediately she refuted her own accusation.

He didn't need money to have the impact he had on me. All he had to do was stand there and look at me...

She dragged her mind away. She had to stop this—she *had* to. How many times did she have to tell herself that?

'Sarah!' Max's imperious call rescued her from her troubling thoughts.

She got to her feet, and Philip did too. 'Back to the grindstone,' she said. 'And you scoot, Philip. Have fun with your cousin.' She smiled, lifting a brief hand in farewell as she made her way back to the stage.

Within minutes she was utterly absorbed, her whole being focussed only on her work, and the rest of the world disappeared from sight.

'So,' said Bastiaan, keeping his voice studiedly casual, 'you want to start drawing on your fund, is that it?'

The two of them were sitting outside on the shaded terrace outside the villa's dining room. They'd eaten lunch out there and now Bastiaan was drinking coffee, relaxed back in his chair.

Or rather he appeared to be relaxed. Internally, however, he was on high alert. His young cousin had just raised the subject of his approaching birthday, and asked whether Bastiaan would start to relax the reins now. Warning bells were sounding.

Across the table from him, Philip shifted position. 'It's not going to be a problem, is it?' he said.

He spoke with insouciance, but Bastiaan wasn't fooled. His level of alertness increased. Philip was being evasive.

'It depends.' He kept his voice casual. 'What is it you want to spend the money on?'

Philip glanced away, out over the gardens towards the swimming pool. He fiddled with his coffee spoon some more, then looked back at Bastiaan. 'Is it such a big deal, knowing what I want the money for? I mean, it's *my* money...'

'Yes,' allowed Bastiaan. 'But until your birthday I...I *guard* it for you.'

Philip frowned. 'For me or *from* me?' he said.

There was a tightness in his voice that was new to Bastiaan. Almost a challenge. His level of alertness went up yet another notch.

'It might be the same thing,' he said. His voice was even drier now. Deliberately he took a mouthful of black coffee, replaced the cup with a click on its saucer and looked straight at Philip. 'A fool and his money...' He trailed off deliberately.

He saw his cousin's colour heighten. 'I'm not a fool!' he riposted.

'No,' agreed Bastiaan, 'you're not. But—' he held up his hand '—you could, all the same, be made a fool *of.*'

His dark eyes rested on his cousin. Into his head sprang the image of that *chanteuse* in the nightclub again—pooled in light, her dress clinging, outlining her body like a second skin, her tones low and husky...*alluring*...

He snapped his mind away, using more effort than he was happy about. Got his focus back on Philip—not on the siren who was endangering him. As for his tentative attempt to start accessing his trust fund—well, he'd made his point, and now it was time to lighten up.

'So just remember...' he let humour into his voice now '...when you turn twenty-one you're going to find yourself very, *very* popular—cash registers will start ringing all around you.'

He saw Philip swallow.

'I do know that...' he said.

He didn't say it defiantly, and Bastiaan was glad.

'I really won't be a total idiot, Bast—and...and

I'm not ungrateful for your warning. I know—'
Bastiaan could hear there was a crack in his
voice. 'I know you're keeping an eye on me because…well, because…'

'Because it's what your father would have expected—and what your mother wants,' Bastiaan
put in. The humour was gone now. He spoke with
only sober sympathy for his grieving cousin and
his aunt. He paused. 'She worries about you—
you're her only son.'

Philip gave a sad smile. 'Yes, I know,' he said.
'But Bast, please—do reassure her that she truly
doesn't need to worry so much.'

'I'll do that if I can,' Bastiaan said. Then, wanting to change the subject completely, he said, 'So,
where do you fancy for dinner tonight?'

As he spoke he thought of Le Tombleur.
Thought of the rejection he'd had the night be-
fore. Unconsciously, his face tightened. Then, as
Philip answered, it tightened even more.

'Oh, Bast—I'm sorry—I can't. Not tonight.'

Bastiaan allowed himself a glance. Then, 'Hot
date?' he enquired casually.

Colour ran along his cousin's cheekbones. 'Sort
of…' he said.

'Sort of hot? Or sort of a date?' Bastiaan kept his probing light. But his mood was not light at all. He'd wondered last night at the club, when he'd checked out the *chanteuse* himself, whether he might see Philip there as well. But there'd been no sign of him and he'd been relieved. Maybe things weren't as bad as he feared. But now—

'A sort of date,' Philip confessed.

Bastiaan backed off. He was walking through landmines for the time being, and he did not want to set one off. He would have to tread carefully, he knew, or risk putting the boy's back up and alienating him.

In a burst, Philip spoke again. 'Bast—could I…? Could you…? Well, there's someone I want you to meet.'

Bastiaan stilled. 'The hot date?' he ventured.

Again the colour flared across his cousin's cheeks. 'Will you?' he asked.

'Of course,' Bastiaan replied easily. 'How would you like us to meet up? Would you like to invite her to dinner at the villa?'

It was a deliberate trail, and it got the answer he knew Philip had to give. 'Er…no. Um, there's

a place in Les Pins—the food's not bad—though
it's not up to your standards of course, but—'

'No problem,' said Bastiaan, wanting only to
be accommodating. Philip, little did he realise
it, was playing right into his hands. Seeing his
cousin with his *inamorata* would give him a
pretty good indication of just how deep he was
sunk into the quicksand that she represented.

'Great!'

Philip beamed, and the happiness and relief in
his voice showed Bastiaan that his impressionable, vulnerable cousin was already in way, way
too deep...

CHAPTER FOUR

BEYOND THE SPOTLIGHT trained on her, Sarah could see Philip, sitting at the table closest to the stage, gazing up at her while she warbled through her uninspiring medley. At the end of her first set Max went backstage to phone Anton, as he always did, and Sarah stepped carefully down to the dining area, taking the seat Philip was holding out for her.

She smiled across at him. 'I thought you'd be out with your cousin tonight, painting the Côte d'Azur red!' she exclaimed lightly.

'Oh, no,' said Philip dismissively. 'But speaking of my cousin...' He paused, then went on in a rush, 'Sarah, I hope you don't mind...I've asked him here to meet you! You *don't* mind, do you?' he asked entreatingly.

Dismay filled her. She didn't want to crush him, but at the same time the fewer people who knew she appeared here nightly as Sabine the better. Unless, of course, they didn't know her as Sarah the opera singer in the first place.

Philip was a nice lad—a student—but Cousin Bastiaan, for all Sarah knew, moved in the elite, elevated social circles of the very wealthy, and might well be acquainted with any number of people influential in all sorts of areas...including opera. She just could not afford to jeopardise what nascent reputation the festival might build for her—not with her entire future resting on it.

She thought rapidly. 'Look, Philip, I know this might sound confusing, but can we stick to me being Sabine, rather than mentioning my opera singing?' she ventured. 'Otherwise it gets...complicated.'

Complicated was one word for it—*risky* was another.

Philip was looking disconcerted. 'Must I?' he protested. 'I'd love Bastiaan to know how wonderful and talented you really are.' Admiration and ardent devotion shone in his eyes.

Sarah gave a wry laugh. 'Oh, Philip, that's very sweet of you, but—'

She got no further. Philip's gaze had suddenly

flicked past her. 'That's him,' he announced. 'Just coming over now—'

Sarah craned her neck slightly—and froze.

The tall figure threading its way towards their table was familiar. Unmistakably so.

She just had time to ask a mental, *What on earth*? when he was upon them.

Philip had jumped to his feet.

'Bast! You made it! Great!' he cried happily, sticking to the French he spoke with Sarah. He hugged his cousin exuberantly, and went on in Greek, 'You've timed it perfectly—'

'Have I?' answered Bastiaan. He kept his voice studiedly neutral, but his eyes had gone to the woman seated at his cousin's table. Multiple thoughts crowded in his head, struggling for pre-dominance. But the one that won out was the last one he wanted.

A jolt of insistent, unmistakable male response to the image she presented.

The twenty-four hours since he'd accosted her in her dressing room had done nothing at all to lessen the impact she made on him. The same lush blond hair, deep eyes, rich mouth, and another gown that skimmed her shoulders and breasts, moulding the latter to perfection…

He felt his body growl with raw, masculine satisfaction. The next moment he'd crushed it down. So here she was, the sultry *chanteuse*, making herself at home with Philip, and Philip's eyes on her were like an adoring puppy's.

'Bastiaan, I want to introduce you to someone very special,' Philip was saying. A slight flush mounted in the young man's cheeks and his glance went from his cousin to Sarah and back again. 'This…' there was the slightest hesitation in his voice '…this is Sabine.' He paused more discernibly this time. 'Sabine,' he said self-consciously, 'this is my cousin Bastiaan—Bastiaan Karavalas.'

Through the mesh of consternation in Sarah's head one realisation was clear. It was time to call it, she knew. Make it clear to Philip—and to his cousin Bastiaan—that, actually, they were already 'acquainted.' She gave the word a deliberately biting sardonic inflection in her head.

Her long fake lashes dipped down over her eyes and she found herself surreptitiously glancing at the dark-eyed, powerfully built man who had just sat down, dominating the space.

Dominating her senses…

Just as he had the night before, when he'd appeared in her dressing room.

But it wasn't this that concerned her. It was the way he seemed to be suddenly the only person in the entire universe, drawing her eyes to him as irretrievably as if he were the iron to her magnetic compass. She couldn't look away—could only let her veiled glance fasten on him, feel again, as powerfully as she first had, the raw impact he had on her, that sense of power and attraction that she could not explain—did not want to explain.

Call it. She heard the imperative in her head. *Call it—say that you know him—that he has already sought you out…*

But she couldn't do anything other than sit there and try to conjure up some explanation for why she couldn't open her mouth.

Into her head tumbled the overriding question—*What the hell is going on here?*

Because something was—that was for sure. A man she'd never seen before in her life had turned up at the club, bribed a waiter to invite her to his table, then confronted her in her dressing room to ask her out… And then he reappeared as Philip's cousin, unexpectedly arrived in France…

But there was no time to think—no time for anything other than to realise that she had to cope with the situation as it was now and come up with answers later.

'*Mademoiselle…*'

The deep voice was as dark as she remembered it—accented in Greek, similar to Philip's. But that was the only similarity. Philip's voice was light, youthful, his tone usually admiring, often hesitant. But his cousin, in a single word, conveyed to Sarah a whole lot more.

Assessing—guarded—sardonic. Not quite mocking but…

She felt a shiver go down her spine. A shiver she should not be feeling. Should have no need of feeling. Was he *daring* her to admit they'd already encountered one another?

'*M'sieu…*' She kept her voice cool. Totally neutral.

A waiter glided up, seeing a new guest had arrived. The business of Bastiaan Karavalas ordering a drink—a dry martini, Sarah noted absently—gave her precious time to try and grab some composure back.

She was in urgent need of it—whatever Bastiaan Karavalas was playing at, it was his physical presence that was dominating her senses, overwhelming her with his raw, physical impact just the way it had last night in her dressing room. Dragging her gaze to him set her heart quickening, her pulse surging. What *was* it about him? That sense of presence, of power—of dark, magnetic attraction? The veiled eyes, the sensual mouth…?

Never had she been so aware of a man. Never had her body reacted like this.

'For you, *mademoiselle*?' the deep, accented voice was addressing her, clearly enquiring what she would like to drink.

She gave a quick shake of her head. 'Thank you—no. I stick to water between sets.'

He dismissed the waiter with an absent lift of his hand and the man scurried off to do his bidding.

'Sets?' Bastiaan enquired.

His thoughts were busy. He'd wanted to see whether she would disclose his approach to her the previous evening, and now he was assessing the implications of her not doing so.

He was, he knew, assessing a great deal about her... Predominantly her physical impact on him. Even though that was the thing least relevant to the situation.

Or was it?

The thought was in his head before he could stop it. So, too, was the one that followed hard upon its heels.

Her reaction to him blazed from her like a beacon. Satisfaction—stabbing through him—seared in his veins. That, oh, *that*, indeed, was something he could use...

He quelled the thought—this was not the time. She had taken the first trick at that first encounter, turning down the invitation he'd so expected her to take. *But the game, Mademoiselle Sabine, is only just begun...*

And he would be holding the winning hand!

'Sa...Sabine's a singer,' Philip was saying, his eyes alight and sweeping admiringly over the *chanteuse* who had him in her coils.

Bastiaan sat back, his eyes flickering over the

slinkily dressed and highly made-up figure next to his cousin. 'Indeed?'

It was his turn to use the French language to his advantage—allowing the ironic inflection to work to her discomfiture…as though he doubted the veracity of his cousin's claim.

'Indeed, *m'sieu*,' echoed Sarah. The ironic inflection had not been lost on her and she repaid it herself, in a light, indifferent tone.

He didn't like that, she could see. There was something about the way his dark brows drew a fraction closer to each other, the way the sensual mouth tightened minutely.

'And what do you…sing?' he retaliated, and one dark brow lifted with slight interrogation.

'Chansons d'amour,' Sarah murmured. 'What else?' She gave a smile—just a little one. Light and mocking.

Philip spoke again. 'You've just missed Sabine's first set,' he told Bastiaan.

His glance went to her, as if for reassurance— or perhaps, thought Bastiaan, it was simply because the boy couldn't take his eyes from the woman.

And nor can I—

'But you'll catch her second set!' Philip exclaimed enthusiastically.

'I wouldn't miss it for the world,' he said dryly. Again, his gaze slid to the *chanteuse*.

A new reaction was visible, and it caught his attention. Was he mistaken, or was there, somewhere beneath the make-up, colour suffusing her cheekbones?

Had she taken what he'd said as sarcasm?

If she had, she repaid him in the same coin.

'You are too kind, *m'sieu,*' she said.

And Bastiaan could see, even in the dim light, how her deep-set eyes, so ludicrously enhanced by false eyelashes and heavy kohled lids, flashed fleetingly to green.

A little jolt of sexual electricity fired in him. He wanted to see more of that green flash...

It would come if I kissed her—

'Sa...Sabine's voice is wonderful.'

Philip cut across his heated thoughts. Absently, Bastiaan found himself wondering why his cousin seemed to stammer over the singer's name.

'Even when she's only singing *chan*—'

Sarah's voice cut across Philip's. 'So, M'sieu

Karavalas, you have come to visit Philip? I believe the villa is yours, is it not?'

She couldn't care less what he was doing here, or whether he owned a villa on Cap Pierre or anywhere else. She'd only spoken to stop Philip saying something she could see he was dying to say, despite her earlier plea to him—

Even when she's only singing chansons *in a place like this.*

I don't want him to mention anything about what I really sing—that I'm not really Sabine!

Urgency filled her. And now it had nothing to do with not wanting Bastiaan Karavalas to know that Sarah Fareham moonlighted as Sabine Sablon. No, it was for a quite different reason—one that right now seemed far more crucial.

I can't handle him as Sarah. I need to be Sabine. Sabine can cope with this—Sabine can cope with a man like him. Sabine is the kind of sophisticated, worldly-wise female who can deal with such a man.

With the kind of man who coolly hit on a woman who'd taken his eye and aroused his sexual interest, arrogantly assuming she would comply without demur. The kind of man who rested assessing, heavy-lidded eyes on her, drawing no veil over what he saw in her, knowing exactly what impact his assessment of her was having.

That kind of man…

Philip's enthusiastic voice was a relief to her.

'You ought to spend some time at the villa, Bast! It really is a beautiful place. Paulette says you're hardly ever there.'

Bastiaan flicked his eyes to his cousin. 'Well, maybe I should move across from Monaco and stay awhile with you. Keep you on the straight and narrow.'

He smiled at Philip, and as he did so Sarah suddenly saw a revelation. Utterly unexpected. Gone—totally vanished—was the Bastiaan Karavalas she'd been exposed to, with his coolly assessing regard and his blatant appraisal, and the sense of leashed power that emanated from him. Now, as he looked across at Philip, his smile carved deep lines around his mouth and lightened his expression, made him suddenly seem… different.

She felt something change inside her—uncoil as if a knot had been loosened…

If he ever smiled at me like that I would be putty in his hands.

But she sheered her mind away. Bastiaan Karavalas was unsettling enough, without throwing such a smile her way.

'Make me write all my wretched essays, you mean—don't you, Bast?' Philip answered, making a face.

But Sarah could see the communication running between them, the easy affection. It seemed to make Bastiaan far less formidable. But that, she knew with a clenching of her muscles, had a power of its own. A power she must not acknowledge. Not even as Sabine.

'It's what you came here for,' Bastiaan reminded him. 'And to escape, of course.'

His dark eyes flickered back to Sarah and the warmth she'd seen so fleetingly as he'd smiled at his young cousin drained out of them. It was replaced by something new. Something that made her eyes narrow minutely as she tried to work out what it was.

'I offered the villa to Philip as a refuge,' he informed Sarah in a casual voice. 'He was being plagued by a particularly persistent female. She made a real nuisance of herself, didn't she?' His glance went back to his cousin.

Philip made another face. 'Elena Constantis *was* a pain,' he said feelingly. 'Honestly, she's got boys buzzing all over her, but she still wanted to add *me* to her stupid collection. She's so immature,' he finished loftily.

A tiny smile hovered at Sarah's lips, dispelling her momentary unease. Immaturity was a relative term, after all. For a second—the briefest second—she caught a similar smile just tugging at Bastiaan Karavalas's well-shaped mouth, lifting it the way his smile at Philip had done a moment ago.

Almost, *almost* she felt herself starting to meet his eyes, ready to exchange glances with him—two people so much more mature than sweet, young Philip...

Then the intention was wiped from her consciousness. Its tempting potency gone. Philip's gaze had gone to her. 'She couldn't be more different from *you*,' he said. The warmth in his voice could have lit a fire.

Sarah's long, fake eyelashes dipped again. Bastiaan Karavalas's dark gaze had switched to her, and she was conscious of it—burningly conscious of it. Conscious, too, of what must have accounted for the studiedly casual remark he'd made that had got them on to this subject.

Surely he can't think I don't realise that Philip is smitten with me?

Bastiaan was speaking again. 'Sabine is certainly much *older*,' he observed.

The dark eyes had flicked back to her face—watching, she could tell, for her reaction to his blunt remark. Had he intended to warn her? To show her how real his cousin's infatuation with her was?

How best to respond...? 'Oh, I'm ancient, indeed!' she riposted lightly. 'Positively creaking.'

'You're not old!' Philip objected immediately, aghast at the very idea. Adoration shone in his eyes. Then his gaze shifted to the dance floor in front of the stage, where couples had started to congregate. His face lit. 'Oh! Sabine—will you dance with me? Please say yes!'

Indecision filled her. She never danced with Philip or did anything to encourage him. But right now it would get her away from the disturbing, overpowering impact of Bastiaan Karavalas.

'If you like,' she replied, and got to her feet as he leapt eagerly to his and walked her happily out on to the dance floor.

Thankfully, the music was neither very fast—fast dancing would have been impossible in her tight gown—nor so slow that it would require any kind of smoochy embrace. But since most of the couples were in a traditional ballroom-style hold with each other, that was the hold she glided into.

Philip, bless him, clearly wasn't too *au fait* with so formal a dancing style, but he manfully did his best. 'I've got two left feet!' he exclaimed ruefully.

'You're doing fine,' she answered encouragingly, making sure she was holding him literally at arm's length.

It seemed an age until the number finally ended.

'Well done,' she said lightly.

'I won't be so clumsy next time,' he promised her.

She let her hand fall from his shoulder and indicated that he should let go of her too—which he did, with clear reluctance. But Philip's crush on her was not uppermost in her mind right now.

She was just about to murmur something about her next set, and this time make sure she headed off, when a deep voice sounded close by.

'Mademoiselle Sabine? I trust you will give me equal pleasure?'

She started, her head twisting. Bastiaan Karavalas was bearing down on them as the music moved on to another number. A distinctly slower number.

He gave her no chance to refuse. An amused nod of dismissal at his cousin and then, before she could take the slightest evasive action, Sarah's hand had been taken, her body was drawn towards his by the placing of his large, strong hand at her waist, and she was forced to lift her other hand and let it rest as lightly as she could on his shoulder. Then he was moving her into the dance—his thigh pressing blatantly against hers to impel her to move.

Instinctively Sarah tried to preserve her composure, though her heart was pounding in her ribcage. Her body was as stiff as a board, her muscles straining away from him as if she could increase the narrow gap between their bodies. His answer was to curve his fingers into her waist, and with effortless strength secure his hold on her again.

He smiled down at her.

It was a smile of pure possession.

Sarah could feel her blood surging in her body, quickening in every vein, heating her from within as she moved against his possessive clasp.

'So, *mademoiselle*, on what shall we converse?'

His smile had given way to a question in which both irony and amusement were mingled. And something else too—something she could not give a name to, but which seemed to send yet another quiver of excruciating physical awareness of his closeness to her.

Yet again she found herself clinging to the persona of Sabine. Sabine could cope with this—Sabine could let the potently powerful Bastiaan Karavalas sweep her off and yet keep her cool about it. Keep her composure. So what would Sabine do...say...?

'The choice is yours, *m'sieu*,' she answered, managing to keep her tone somewhere between insouciant and indifferent. Social...civil...just this side of courteous. She made herself meet his gaze, the way Sabine undoubtedly would—for what would Sabine be overset by in those dark, sensual eyes? And Sabine's ridiculously long fake lashes helped, Sarah thought with gratitude, because their length made it easier for her to look at him with a veiled expression—helped her feel protected from the impact those deep, dark eyes were having on her...

Abruptly, he spoke, yanking her back to full focus. 'Why did you not mention that you had already made my acquaintance?' he said.

Sarah felt her eyes widening. There was only one answer to give. 'Why didn't *you*?' she said. She sought to copy the dismissive inflection that Sabine would surely give.

Her answer was a sudden opacity in his gaze. 'You must know why—' he said.

From his dark, deep-set eyes a message blazed that was as clear as day...as old as time.

Sarah could feel her breath catch in her throat, her pulse leap—and suddenly Sabine, with all her worldly defences, felt a long, long way away.

'Why did you refuse to come to dinner with

me?' Again, the question was blunt—challeng-ing. Taking her by surprise.

'You were a complete stranger.' She sought for the only explanation that was relevant—whether or not it was one that Sabine would have made.

Thoughts flickered across her mind like ran-dom electric currents. Would Sabine have found that objectionable? Or would she have made her decision about whether to let a man take her to dinner—and what might follow—on quite dif-ferent grounds?

Such as if the man were the most devastating male she'd ever set eyes on—who'd had the most powerful impact on her she'd ever experienced— who'd stilled the breath in her lungs and sent her pulse into overdrive...

But she was given no opportunity to think co-herently about that, or about anything at all, be-cause now his eyes had a glint in them that was setting her pulse racing even faster.

'Well, I am not a stranger now.'

Not when I hold you in the intimacy of this em-brace...your soft, satiny body in my arms, the warmth of your palm against mine, the brush of your thighs as we move to the music together...

He felt the flush of heat beating in his veins. Telling him how susceptible he was to what she possessed.

The power to make him desire her...

His senses were overpowering him. There was a lingering perfume about her—not cloying, as he might have expected, but faintly floral. Her hair, curved around her shoulder as it was, was not sticky with spray but fine and silky. He wanted to feel it running through his fingers. Wanted to drink in the fine-boned beauty of her face, see again that flash of emeralds in her eyes...

A sudden impulse possessed him. To wipe her complexion free of the mask of make-up covering it and see her true beauty revealed.

'Why do you wear so much make-up?' His question came from nowhere—he hadn't meant to ask it.

She looked momentarily startled. 'It's stage make-up,' she answered. She spoke as if she found it hard to believe he'd asked.

He frowned. 'It does not flatter you,' he stated.

Now, *why* had he said that? he grilled himself. Why tell this woman such a thing?

Because it is the truth—she masks her true beauty, her true self, behind such excess.

Her expression changed. 'It's not designed to flatter—only to withstand the stage lighting. You don't imagine that I wear these spiders on my eyes for any other reason, do you?' Her voice was dry.

'Good,' he said, giving a brief nod.

Even as he did so he realised he was way off agenda. What on earth was he *doing*, talking about her stage make-up? Let alone expressing approval—relief?—that it *was* only make-up. He sought to resume the line of enquiry he'd started. That was the reason he was dancing with her— so that he could continue his assessment of her. Purely for the purposes for which he'd arrived in France, of course…

To free his cousin from her.

Free her from Philip—

The thought was there—indelible, inadmissible. He wiped it instantly. There was no question of freeing *her* from his cousin. It was Philip— only Philip—he was concerned about. That was what he had to remember.

Not the way her body was moving with his to

the soft, seductive cadences of the music, drawing them closer and closer to each other...

Not the way her fragrance was coiling into his senses. Not the way his eyes were lingering on her face...her parted lips... The way he was feeling the soft breath coming from her...intoxicating him...

The melody ended. He stopped abruptly. Even more abruptly she disengaged herself from his grasp. But she did not move—simply stood there for a moment, continuing to gaze at him. As if she could not stop...

Her breasts, Bastiaan could see, were rising and falling as if her breathing were rapid—her pulse was more rapid still. Colour was in her cheeks, beneath the thick layer of foundation. He could just see it...sense it...

Her gaze was dragged from him, back across to where Philip was sitting, his expression a mixture of impatience at her absence, discontent that she had been dancing with his cousin, and his usual fixed regard of uncritical admiration.

She walked across to him—her dress felt tighter suddenly, and she was all too conscious of the swaying movement of her hips. She could almost *feel* Bastiaan Karavalas watching her...

She reached the table. Philip stood up immediately, his chair scraping.

'Phew!' she said, pointedly not resuming her seat. 'I'm worn out by dancing. Two dances and two partners—quite an evening for me!' She spoke with deliberate lightness, obvious humour. Reaching for her glass of water, she took a quick gulp, finding she needed it, then set it down. 'I must go backstage,' she said. 'Prep for my next set.'

Conscious that Philip's cousin was standing behind her, she could say very little else to Philip. She took a step away, encompassing Bastiaan Karavalas in her movement.

'I'll bid you goodnight,' she said, making her voice sound nothing more than effortlessly casual.

She had to get control back—the way Sabine would. Sabine would have been utterly unfazed by that slow, seductive dance with Bastiaan Karavalas. Sabine wouldn't have felt as if her whole body were trembling, her senses overwhelmed. No, Sabine would stay composed, unruffled—

would be well used to men like Bastiaan Karavalas desiring her.

Philip was speaking and she made herself pay attention, drag her thoughts away from his cousin.

'I'll see you tomorrow at the...here...?' he asked.

Sarah was relieved that he'd just avoided saying *at the rehearsal.*

She smiled. A warm smile. Because she didn't want to hurt him, and his feelings were so transparent. 'Why not?' she said lightly. 'Unless...' And now her eyes found Bastiaan again. 'Unless you and your cousin have plans...? You must make the most of him while he's here.'

Dark lashes flickered over even darker eyes. She saw it—caught it. 'I may well be here some time,' Bastiaan Karavalas said. 'It all depends...'

She made no answer—could only give a vague, brief smile and bestow a little wave on Philip, because she wanted to be nice to him, and he was so young, and felt so much...

And then she was gone, whisking away through a little door inset into the wall beside the low stage.

Slowly, Bastiaan sat down. Philip did too, but Bastiaan said nothing—his head was full. Far too full. Only one thought was predominant— he wanted to hear her sing...he wanted to feast his eyes on her again.

Feast so much more than his eyes...

CHAPTER FIVE

As SARAH TOOK her place on the stage she was burningly aware of those dark, heavy eyes upon her. It was the same sensation she'd had the previous night, when she hadn't known who was watching her—had only been able to feel it. As she felt it now, again, that same sense of exposure. But now there was so much more—now there was a frisson running through her body, her veins, that came from his heavy-lidded perusal.

Why? The question kept circling in her head. Why was she reacting like this? Why was this man—this dark, disturbing cousin of Philip— able to arouse such a response in her? Never, *never* before had she been so affected by a man.

By a man's desire for her.

Because it is a desire that echoes in me too...

That was the truth of it. Out of nowhere, like a bolt of lightning crashing into tinder-dry trees, he'd set her alight....

A sense almost of panic swept over her.

I can't handle it. I'm not used to it. No man has ever made me feel this way—like I'm on fire, burning from the inside. I don't know what to do—how to react...

Nothing with Andrew had prepared her for this. Nothing!

I didn't know it was possible to feel this way. To feel this overwhelmed—this helpless.

This aroused...

Standing there in the spotlight, knowing that the dark, heavy eyes of Bastiaan Karavalas were resting on her, that she was exposed to his view, her body had reacted as if her flesh were aflame.

She wanted to run, bolt from the stage, but that was impossible. Impossible to do anything but continue to stand there, the microphone between her fingers, her voice intimate.

While Bastiaan Karavalas looked his fill of her.

No! The cry came from within. *It isn't me he's gazing at—it's Sabine. Sabine is standing here, feeling like this.*

And Sabine—Sabine could handle it. Of course she could. Sabine was not helpless or overwhelmed by the blatant desire in those dark, heavy eyes.

Or by her own desire…

Sabine was who she must be to cope with what was happening to her, with the fire that was running in her veins, burning her senses. That was what she clung to as she worked her way through her numbers.

Never had her set seemed longer, and how she got through it she wasn't sure, but in the end she was heading off stage, filled with relief.

As she gained her dressing room she saw Philip waiting. He launched in as soon as he could.

'Sarah—this Sunday—will you…will you come over to the villa for lunch?' He got the words out in a rush, his eyes filled with eager hope. 'I've been wanting to ask you, but it was Bast who suggested it.'

She felt a quiver inside her, even though she strove to stanch it. *Why? Why had Bastiaan Karavalas suggested inviting her to his villa?*

And the only answer she could think of sent that quiver vibrating through her again, quickening her pulse.

I don't have time for this. I don't have time to

have Bastiaan Karavalas looking at me the way he does, have the impact on me he does. I just don't have time—not now. And I can't cope with it anyway—can't cope with him. I don't know how to respond or react. And, anyway, it isn't me he's inviting—it's Sabine! Sabine's the one he's drawn to—not me. He wants what Sabine would offer him...

The hectic thoughts tumbled through her mind, incoherent and confused. She had to answer somehow—but what? And how?

'So, will you come? Please say yes,' Philip's eager voice pressed.

She pulled herself together forcibly. 'I'm...I'm not sure...' she got out.

'What's this you're plotting?'

Max's voice sounded behind her. It sounded amused, but with a pointedness in it that Sarah was not deaf to.

Philip turned. 'I was asking Sarah if she would come over to the villa for lunch on Sunday with my cousin and me,' he relayed.

'Cousin?' Max raised his eyebrows.

'My cousin—Bastiaan Karavalas,' supplied

Philip. 'It's his villa I'm staying at. He's visiting me from Greece.'

'Karavalas…' murmured Max.

Sarah knew he was storing the information away and would check it out later—just as he'd checked out Philip's name. Any cousin of Philip's would be rich as well, and for that reason she knew she might be disheartened by what Max said next, but she could not be surprised.

Max smiled at Philip. 'Why wait till Sunday?' he said blandly. 'Make it tomorrow—I'll rejig the schedule so Sarah can get away at noon. How would that be?'

Philip's face lit. 'Fantastic! I'll go and tell Bast now. Brilliant!'

He beamed at Sarah and Max, and then rushed off to front of house.

Sarah turned to Max. 'Max—' she began, about to remonstrate.

Max held up a hand. 'Say nothing. I know your opinion about asking Philip for money. But…' his voice changed 'But this Bastiaan Karavalas, the cousin—well, that's a different matter, isn't it? A grown man who owns a villa on Cap Pierre—and presumably a whole lot else—doesn't require kid-glove-handling, does he? So, *cherie*, off you go to lunch with these lovely rich people and make yourself agreeable to them.'

Sarah's expression hardened. 'Max, if you think—'

'*Cherie*, it's just lunch—nothing more than that. What did you *think* I was suggesting?'

He sounded amused, and it irritated Sarah. 'I don't know and I don't care,' she shot back, shutting her dressing room door in his face.

Consternation was flooding through her. She did not *want* to go over to Bastiaan Karvalas's villa and spend the afternoon there. She didn't want to spend a single moment more in his company. Didn't want another opportunity for him to work his dark, potent magic on her senses…

I don't need this distraction. I have to focus on the festival—it's all that's important to me. Nothing else. I want Bastiaan Karavalas gone—out of my life!

She stilled suddenly as she started to change out of her costume. Her mind raced.

Maybe going to the villa wasn't so bad an idea after all. Maybe she could turn the invitation to her advantage. Find an opportunity to get Bastiaan Karavalas on his own and suggest that it would be a really good idea for him to whisk Philip away. Distance would soon cause his youthful crush to atrophy.

And it would take Bastiaan Karavalas away as well... Stop him disturbing her the way he did so that she could get back to the only important thing in her life now: preparing for the festival. Not being swept away by what was in his dark, desiring eyes.

Yes. She took a steadying breath. That, surely, would make it worth enduring an afternoon of his company. Because there was no other reason for wanting to spend an afternoon with Bastiaan Karavalas.

Liar, said a voice inside her head. A voice that whispered to her in Sabine's soft, seductive tones...

'She'll come over tomorrow!' Philip exclaimed happily as he re-joined Bastiaan.

'How surprising...' murmured Bastiaan.

Of course Mademoiselle Sabine had jumped at the invitation to get a foot...literally...in the door.

His cousin completely missed the sardonic note

in his voice. 'Isn't it?' he answered. 'Considering how—' he stopped short.

Bastiaan cocked an eyebrow. 'Considering...?' he prompted.

'Oh, nothing,' Philip answered hastily, but looked as if he were hiding something.

Yet again the question fired in Bastiaan's head. *How far has this infatuation gone? What is Philip hiding?*

But surely his instincts were correct? Philip was not radiating the aura of a young man who had achieved possession of the object of his desire and devotion. He was still worshipping at the altar.

A silent growl of raw, male satisfaction rasped through him. Its occurrence did not please him. Just the opposite. Damnation—the very thought that he could be *glad* that Philip was still merely mooning over the delectable blonde singer for any other reason than that it meant that it would be easier separating him from Sabine, extricating him from her toils, was unacceptable.

He changed the subject deliberately. 'So—tonight... Do you want to come over to Monte? We can eat out and you can stay at my apartment.'

Again, it was a deliberate trail, to discover whether Philip would otherwise have been heading towards La Belle Sabine for a midnight tryst...

To his satisfaction Philip was perfectly amenable to this suggestion, helping Bastiaan to confirm his judgement that, however besotted Philip was with the woman, it had not yet progressed to anything more...tangible.

Then another, more unwelcome thought struck him. *Is she holding out on bestowing herself upon him until he has control over his own funds?*

Was that her game plan? His expression hardened as they left the club. He was looking forward to lunch tomorrow—it would give him more time to study her. Assess her.

All for the sake of rescuing his cousin, of course. Not for any other reason...

None that he would permit.

'Stop!' Max threw his hand up impatiently. 'I said *sostunuto*, not *diminuendo*! If you can't tell the difference, Sarah, believe me—I can! Take it again.'

Sarah drew her breath in sharply but said nothing, though her jaw was set. Max was being particularly tyrannical this morning, and Alain, her tenor, playing The Soldier, was fractious. So was she, she admitted to herself. She was hitting vocal difficulties all over the place, and it was frustrating the hell out of her. The rehearsal session was not going smoothly and Max was finding fault with all of them. Nerves were getting jittery all round.

She shut her eyes to center herself.

'In your own time, Sarah,' came Max's sarcastic prompt.

Somehow her next attempt managed to assuage him, and he turned his exacting attention to Alain and his apparently many flaws, before resuming his attack on Sarah for the next passage that displeased him.

By the time he dismissed her Sarah felt ragged. She definitely needed fresh air and a change of environment. For the first time she actually felt grateful that she was to have the afternoon off, courtesy of Philip's invitation. As she scooped up her bag she heard Max start in on the alto and the baritone, and hurried to make her escape from the fraught atmosphere.

Philip had texted to say he'd pick her up from her *pension*, where she headed now to change into something suitable for having lunch at a millionaire's villa on the exclusive Cap Pierre.

Just what constituted 'suitable'? she pondered.

In the end there was only one outfit that was possible. It was one she'd bought when she'd first arrived in France to join the opera company, after the school term had ended. It wasn't her usual floaty, floral style, but a chic sixties-style shift in a shade of green that suited her fair colouring.

She pushed her hair back with a white band, and completed the retro look with pastel lipstick, frosted eyeshadow and a lot of eyeliner.

She studied her reflection—yes, definitely more Sabine than Sarah. Just what she needed.

'Oh, my goodness!' she exclaimed as she stepped outdoors and immediately saw the low, lean, bright red Ferrari parked there.

'Isn't it a beauty?' Philip said lovingly. 'It's Bast's. He keeps it in Monte Carlo—he has an apartment there as well—and he's letting me drive it today.'

He sounded awestruck at the prospect.

'Bast's already at the villa,' Philip explained,

helping her into the low, luxurious passenger seat. 'So...' He looked at her expectantly, his eyes alight, as he started the engine with a throaty growl. 'What do you think?'

She gave a laugh. 'Terrifying!' she said feelingly.

He laughed, as though he could not possibly believe her, and moved off. He was obviously thrilled by driving such a powerful, fabulous car, and Sarah wisely let him concentrate. The road leading out on to the *Cap* was a residential one, with a modest speed limit.

It was only five minutes to the villa, and she could see Philip's reluctance to abandon the vehicle when he arrived. It seemed, she thought dryly, and not with regret, that she finally had a rival.

Well, any rival was to be welcomed, even one with wheels. What she really wanted to conjure up, though, was a flesh and blood rival to take his mind off *her*—someone suitable for his age and circumstances. She frowned slightly. What had Bastiaan Karavalas been saying the previous evening? About dispatching Philip to his villa in the first place because he'd been pursued by some spoilt teen in Greece? That was a *good* sign, because it could only mean that Philip's cousin would be amenable to her suggesting that another rescue was needed.

Except that I'm going to have to speak to him alone.

That was *not* something she wanted to have to do. Not even behind the protection of being Sabine. But right now she would grab any protection she could.

Walking into the white-plastered, low-rise villa, set in spacious grounds out on the promontory of the *Cap,* she felt the need of Philip's familiar innocuous presence as they crossed the cool, stone-floored hall into a wide reception room and she saw the tall, sable-haired figure of Bastiaan Karavalas strolling in from the vine-shaded terrace beyond to greet them.

As she had the night before, and the first time she'd laid eyes on him, Sarah felt an instinctive, automatic reaction to him. It was like a switch being thrown inside her—a buzz of electric current in her veins, a kick in her heartbeat. She saw his dark eyes narrow as they lit on her, and the electric current ran again—and then Philip was greeting him and ushering her forward.

'Here we are, Bast,' he said cheerfully. 'Is lunch ready? I'm starving. Are we eating out on the terrace?'

'We've time for a drink first,' Bastiaan replied, and Sarah saw that he was carrying a champagne bottle in one hand and three glasses loosely by their stems in the other. 'But let's head out anyway. *Mademoiselle...?'*

He stepped aside from the door to let her go through first. It meant passing close to him, and she felt his eyes on her as she walked out on to the terrace. Then all thoughts of the disturbing Bastiaan Karavalas left her.

'Oh, this is *beautiful*!' she heard herself exclaim.

The wide, shady terrace, roofed by vines and vivid bougainvillaea, opened to verdant lawns beyond, which were edged with richly foliated bushes and sloped down to a glittering azure pool, behind which stretched the even more glitteringly azure reaches of the Mediterranean Sea.

'Welcome to my villa, Sabine,' said Bastiaan.

She turned at the accented voice. His eyes were sweeping over her and she could feel their impact. Feel the electricity course through her again.

Not in a tuxedo, as she had previously seen him, but in a pair of long, pale grey chinos and a short-sleeved, dark burgundy open-necked polo shirt, which moulded his powerful torso. He looked lean, lithe and devastatingly attractive. She felt her stomach give a little clench of appreciation.

'Sab—come and sit down,' Philip was saying, indicating the ironwork table set for lunch.

He'd taken to calling her 'Sab' on the way there, and Sarah was glad. It might make him less likely to call her Sarah. She was also glad about her choice of outfit. OK, so she was probably slightly too smartly dressed for what was clearly going to be an al fresco meal, with Bastiaan in casual clothes and Philip in his customary designer-labelled T-shirt and jeans, but her retro-chic dress felt almost like a costume—and that *had* to help her be Sabine and not Sarah, who was perilously out of her depth in such deep waters as swirled about this powerfully, devastatingly sensual male...

As she carefully seated herself where Philip was holding a chair out for her, in a position that afforded her a view right out over the gardens, she could feel those heavy-lidded eyes on her while Bastiaan settled himself at the head of the table.

'May I tempt you to champagne, Sabine?' The deep-voiced question required an answer.

'Thank you,' she said politely. Inside, the inner voice that whispered to her so seductively in Sabine's husky tones was teasing her... *You tempt me to so much more...*

She silenced it sharply, making herself look not at the man who drew her eyes, but instead out over the beautiful gardens to the sea beyond. Her expression softened. It really was absolutely beautiful, she thought with genuine pleasure. Private, verdant, full of flowers, with the azure sea sparkling beyond—a true Mediterranean idyll.

'What a beautiful spot this is!' she could not help exclaiming warmly. 'If it were mine I'd never leave!'

'Oh, Bast has an entire island to himself at home,' Philip answered. 'This place is tiny in comparison.'

Sarah's eyes widened. Bastiaan saw it as he busied himself opening the champagne. *Thank you, Philip*, he thought, *that was helpful*. His appreciation was sincere—he wanted to see how Sabine reacted to his wealth. Whether it would cause her to turn her attentions to him instead of his cousin.

And would that be helpful too? Again he found himself contemplating using that method to detach her from Philip. It might be so much... *swifter.*

Enjoyable...

His eyes rested on her as he filled their glasses. He was still trying to get past his first reaction to her when he'd walked out on to the terrace. It had been—*surprise.*

Oh, he'd known, obviously, that she wouldn't turn up for lunch in a skin-tight evening gown and a face full of stage make-up. But he'd expected her to wear some kind of flashy strapless brief sundress, exposing a lot of thigh and with a slashed décolletage, and to be adorned with jangly gold jewellery, her hair in a tousled mane. But her stylishly retro look had a chicness to it that drew his eye without condemnation.

Interesting, he found himself thinking. She had changed her image decisively. At the nightclub she had been all sultry vamp. Today she had moved on a couple of decades to the swinging sixties—almost as though she'd made a costume change between acts...

But then, he thought caustically, putting on an act was what a woman like Sabine was all about, wasn't it? From standing on a stage singing throaty, amorous numbers for strangers, to manipulating the emotions of a smitten, impressionable youth.

His eyes hardened minutely as they rested on her. *You will find it harder to manipulate me, mademoiselle...*

If there was any manipulating to be done, then it would be coming from *him*—not her. He would be the one to steer her in the precise direction he wished her to go—away from Philip. *And to me instead?* Again the thought played in his mind provocatively. Temptingly.

'I imagine a private island is just about *de rigueur* for a Greek tycoon, isn't it?' she was saying now, lightly, with a clear infusion of amusement in her voice.

Bastiaan sat back in his chair, lifting his glass. 'Do you take me for a tycoon, *mademoiselle*?' he riposted.

But there was a deep timbre in his voice all the same. She felt it like a low vibration in her body.

'Oh, surely you could be nothing less, *m'sieu*?' she answered in kind. 'With your private island in the Aegean!'

She had matched the slight tinge of ironic inflection that had been in his voice and suddenly there seemed to be a flicker in his dark eyes, a slight curve of his mouth, as if for her alone... Something she didn't want to be there.

Something she did...

No, no I don't. And, anyway, isn't it bad enough that I've got to deal with Philip's bad attack of calf love? The last thing I need is to develop a crush of my own on his cousin.

She paused. Crush? Was *that* what she was calling this strange, disturbing electricity between them? This ridiculous, absurd awareness of his overpowering physical impact on her? A *crush*?

Negation leapt in her. No, this was no crush. There was only one cause for what she was feeling about this man who had walked into her dressing room that night, who had taken her in his powerful, controlling clasp on the dance floor, who was now watching her, his heavy eyes half lidded, waiting for her to reply in similar vein...

Desire. Raw, insistent desire. Desire bred of her burning awareness of his presence, of his physical existence—the way the tough line of his jaw squared his face, the way the strong column of his throat rose from the open neck of his polo, the way the sable darkness of his hair feathered the broad brow, the way his shirt moulded across the strength of his shoulders, his torso...

Desire—that was the only word for it. The only name to give what she was feeling now as her body flushed with heat, with awareness...

Desperation spiked in her. It was like a sideways sweeping wave, knocking her askew, derailing her. And she could not allow it to happen. Not with her whole life's ambition consuming her right now. That was all she must think of—that was all she must focus on.

Not on this man who can make my pulse catch just by letting his dark, dark eyes rest on me, setting my senses afire...

It was a fire she had to quench—and fast.

She reached for her champagne, needing its potency to regain control of herself.

'Bast's island's in the Ionian Sea, not the Aegean,' Philip was saying. 'Off the west coast of Greece. Not far from Zakynthos.'

Sarah turned her head towards him, half reluctant, half grateful to drag her gaze away from his darkly disturbing cousin. 'I don't know Greece at all,' she said. 'I've never been.'

'I'd love to show you. You'd love Athens!' Philip replied immediately, his voice full of enthusiasm.

A low laugh came from the other end of the table. 'A city full of ancient ruins? I doubt it. I'm sure Sabine would prefer sophisticated cities, like Milan or Paris.'

She didn't correct him. The real Sabine, wherever she was right now, probably *would* prefer such cities, and at the moment that persona was hers. She'd better let the issue lie.

She gave a very Gallic shrug, as she had so often seen her French mother give.

'I like warm climates,' she answered, which seemed an unrevealing comment to make, and was true as well. The Yorkshire winters she'd grown up with had never been her favourite, nor her mother's either. She had preferred the soft

JULIA JAMES

winters of her native Normandy. She looked at Philip again. 'I couldn't stand the frozen East Coast USA winters you have at uni.'

Philip shivered extravagantly. 'Neither can I!' He laughed. 'But we get snow in Greece sometimes—don't we, Bast?'

'There is even skiing in the mountains,' his cousin agreed.

'Bast skis like a champion!' Philip exclaimed, with open admiration for his older cousin.

'I was at school in Switzerland,' Bastiaan said laconically, by way of explanation.

Sarah's glance went back to Bastiaan. 'Is that why your French is so good?' she asked.

'Oh, Bast's fluent in German as well—aren't you, Bast? And English, of course. *My* English is probably better than my French, actually, so really we should be speaking—'

'Tell me more about your private island.' Sarah's voice cut across Philip, preventing him from finishing his sentence. She was starting to think that this was ridiculous—all this stuff about her being Sabine. She should just come right out with it—trust Philip's cousin with her real identity and be done with it.

But she was conscious of a deep reluctance to do so. Partly, she knew, for the reason she'd given Philip—but that was not the overwhelming reason. Being Sabine gave her...*protection*. Protection from the onslaught on her senses that Bastiaan Karavalas was making on her.

'My private island?' Bastiaan echoed her. 'What can I tell you? Acreage? Location? Value?'

There was a quizzical expression in his voice, and he spoke lightly, yet Sarah could see a twist at the corner of his mouth. She found herself wondering at it, but her focus had to be on continuing the conversation. She didn't really care that much about Bastiaan Karavalas's island, but it had been the first thing she'd been able to think of asking about in order to interrupt Philip.

'What do you do on it?'

The quizzical expression came again, but this time she had the feeling it was genuine—as if her question had been unexpected. She watched him lift his champagne flute to his mouth.

'Do?' he said. 'Very little.' He gave a sudden smile, taking a mouthful of champagne. 'I take a dinghy out sometimes...swim, chill...not much else. Oh, I read sometimes too—or just watch the sun set with a glass of beer at my side. Nothing exciting. You, *mademoiselle*, would find it very dull.'

Even as he spoke Bastiaan found himself wondering. Why hadn't she followed up on his deliberate mentions of its size and value? Gone on to draw him out about the other properties he owned? Like his villa in the Caribbean, his condo in Manhattan, his apartment in London, his mansion in Athens... It was inconsistent of her. She'd been keen to get him to talk about owning the island in the first place, getting him to reveal to her just how wealthy he actually was.

'Au contraire,' she riposted, and Bastiaan became aware of the greenness of her eyes. 'It sounds very relaxing.'

She held his gaze a moment, and into his head sprang the image of just how he might 'relax' with such a woman on his private island... He felt a kick go through him—one that told him her impact on him was as powerful as ever.

Should I respond to it? Respond to the allure she has for me? Use it for my own purpose?

The questions came—but not the answers... And the very fact that the questions were forming in his mind indicated the temptation they presented. Showed him the answers he wanted to give...

His thoughts were interrupted by Paulette, emerging with the lunch tray. Philip got to his feet to take it from her and was rewarded by a beaming smile—clearly his young cousin had become a favourite of the housekeeper. As he and Philip started to unload it, he noticed Sabine was helping as well, passing plates of *charcuterie* and *fromage*, salads and crusty baguette slices.

'Would you like wine, or are you happy to stick to champagne?' Bastiaan enquired of his guest courteously.

Sarah smiled. 'What girl wouldn't be happy to stick to champagne?' she replied humorously.

She was working hard to keep her tone light, inconsequential. After lunch she must find an opportunity to get Bastiaan on his own, to broach to him her recommendation that it might be best to remove his young cousin to another place that offered less distraction. But even as she determined to do it she found herself dreading it. Dreading being on her own with Bastiaan Karavalas for any time at all.

Roughly, she shook such thoughts from herself. Sought to find something innocuous to say… 'Though if I drink too much at lunchtime I may well fall fast asleep in the afternoon.'

Bastiaan laughed, and yet again Sarah felt her pulse quicken. 'You would be quite welcome,' he said, and indicated the sun loungers that were set out on the lawn beneath the shade of a parasol.

'Don't tempt me,' she riposted, reaching for a piece of bread.

But you do *tempt me, Mademoiselle Sabine— you tempt me greatly…*

Again, the words took shape in his head before he could unsay them. Unthink them…

As he started to help himself to lunch Bastiaan could feel thoughts swirling. Would it *really* be so bad to let his interest in Sabine take the direction in which he could feel it drawing him? Had since his first moment of setting eyes on her.

She tempts me—and without a doubt she feels desire for me, answering my desire for her…

He could hear the arguments in his head already—as tempting as this beautiful woman was.

It would achieve the end I seek…the purpose of my journey—it would take her away from Philip, set him free from his infatuation. And give me what I want...

There was so much in its favour. Why should he reject such a solution to the problem?

Through half-veiled eyes he watched as Philip fussed over her, offering her dishes from the table.

'Chicken, brie and grapes would be lovely,' she said.

Her smile on his cousin was warm, and Bastiaan could see Philip drinking it in. Out of nowhere, a needle pricked Bastiaan beneath the skin.

I want her to smile like that at me.

Jerkily, he reached for the champagne bottle, refilled their glasses.

'So...' said Sarah, glancing between the two of them, casting about for something else to say that would be innocuous. 'Philip seems very smitten with that scarlet monster of yours that he picked me up in.'

'Monster?' said Philip immediately. 'She's a beauty!'

'Her growl is terrifying!' Sarah countered, with a little laugh.

'Wait till I drive you fast in it!' Philip exclaimed. 'Then you'll hear her *roar*!'

She shuddered extravagantly, but Bastiaan addressed Philip directly. 'No,' he said firmly. 'I know you love the idea of racing around in a car that powerful, but I'm not having you smash yourself up. Or, worse, my *car*,' he added, to lighten the rejection.

A mutinous look flashed briefly across Philip's face. Sarah could see it.

'Sab would be perfectly safe with me.'

Bastiaan shook his head. Inside, his thoughts were not just on the safety of Philip driving the powerful performance car. No way was Sabine going to use *his* car to further her aims with his cousin. It was not Sabine who needed to be kept safe—it was Philip.

'Come out with me instead,' he said. 'I'll show you its paces. We'll do the Grande Corniche. How about tomorrow?' he suggested.

Philip's face lit. 'Great!' he enthused. His expression changed. 'But…er…in the afternoon, OK?'

Bastiaan nodded. 'Yes. Do your studies in the morning, then I'll reward you with a spin after lunch.' He turned to Sabine. 'As you know,' he said deliberately, 'my cousin is here first and foremost to complete his university vacation assignments. Not to jaunt around on holiday, entertaining *you.*'

Sarah's face tightened. 'Yes, I am aware of that,' she said coolly. Did he think *she* was inciting Philip to neglect his studies? Well, all the more reason to confront him this afternoon— warn him that he needed to remove Philip yet again.

And I need Bastiaan gone too. I haven't got time for distractions—least of all by a man like this.

His gaze held hers, and for a moment, timeless and impossible, she felt as if her heart had stopped beating.

What power does he have? The question coiled in her mind like smoke. And the answer twisted in the same sinuous shape… *Too much.*

'Good,' replied Bastiaan. Her eyes had darkened in colour again. He wondered at it. Then a more potent thought overrode that. *Emeralds*, he found himself thinking—that was the jewel for her. *Emeralds with the slightest hint of aqua—at her throat, her ears...*

The vision of her draped in such jewels was instant, vivid. They would enhance her blonde beauty, catching the fire of her emerald eyes, displaying that beauty for him and him alone. He felt desire, raw and insistent, growl within him whenever he succumbed to the temptation of thinking about this beautiful, alluring woman— so unsuitable for his naive, infatuated cousin...

But for me it would be different.

Of course it would—to him she presented no danger. Sophisticated, worldly-wise, closer to his age than to Philip's... Whatever his opinion of women who sought to part impressionable young men from their money, *he* was not susceptible to such wiles. *He* was not vulnerable to a woman like her.

But she... Ah, *she* would be vulnerable to *him*. Vulnerable to the desire for him that he could read in her like a book—a desire he shared and made no attempt to conceal. Why should he? For him there was no risk in succumbing to the flame that ran between them.

He took another fortifying mouthful of champagne, making his decision. Resolution streamed within him. *Yes, he would do it!*

Long lashes dipped over his dark eyes. He reached forward across the table, moving a bowl of ripe, succulent peaches towards Sabine. 'May I entice you?' he asked. And in his eyes was an expression that in no way indicated that it was to the fruit he was referring...

Her eyes flickered. He could see it. See the hint of green fire that signalled just as much as her dilating pupils that her sexual awareness of him was radiating out on all frequencies. He smiled, drawing an answering smile from her—an instinctive response. She took a peach and he was minutely aware of the delicate length of her fingers, the pale gloss of her nails.

'Thank you,' she murmured, and dragged her gaze away from him, as though she found it difficult to do so.

He saw the heightened colour on her cheeks as she placed the peach on her plate and started to slice it diligently, head bowed a little, as if she needed to focus on her task. Her chest was rising and falling a little faster than it had been before.

Bastiaan sat back, lifting his champagne glass, satisfaction in his eyes.

Philip was helping himself from the fruit bowl as well, but unlike Sarah he bit enthusiastically into the peach from his hand, spurting juice. 'These are *really* good,' he said enthusiastically.

Sarah flicked her eyes to him. 'Aren't they?' she agreed. 'Just ripe and perfect.'

She was glad to talk about the ripeness of the fruit. Glad to turn her head to Philip and talk about something else. Glad to do *anything* to drag her consciousness away from the man at the opposite end of the table. Glad, too, a few minutes later, when Paulette arrived with a tray of coffee.

Sarah started to gather up the used plates, but the housekeeper snatched them from her, muttering darkly and casting meaningful glances between her and Philip.

Surely she doesn't think I'm encouraging Philip? Sarah thought.

Another thought struck her, even more unwelcome. Did *Bastiaan* think that as well?

No, he couldn't. Of course not! She was doing her utmost to be nothing more than casually friendly—easy-going and relaxed, spending most of her time deflecting his compliments to her. A man as worldly-wise as Bastiaan Karavalas would surely be able to read her reaction to Philip's youthful ardency as easily as if she had written it large.

As easily as he must be able to read my reaction to him...

She felt her stomach clench. The knowledge that Bastiaan Karavalas could see into her feelings towards him was both dismaying and arousing. Fiercely she tried to suppress the arousal, but even as she tried she felt her eyes going to him, almost meeting his as they did so, before she continued handing plates to the unappreciative Paulette. And she felt, in that fleeting mingling before she dipped her lashes to veil her eyes, the tremor of attraction flare and catch.

He knows how he affects me—knows how he makes me feel. It's impossible to hide it from him.

A thought speared into her troubled consciousness. Coming without volition. What if *Philip* knew how attracted she was to his cousin? What if she responded openly to Bastiaan Karavalas's desire for her—hers for him? Would that destroy Philip's crush for her in an instant? Surely it would. It might be harsh, but it would be effective.

And it would give me a reason to succumb to what is happening to me.

As if standing on the edge of a precipice, she hauled herself back from the brink. Was she *insane* to think such a thing? She must be. Whether she was being Sabine or herself, whether Philip did or did not have a hopeless infatuation with her, Bastiaan Karavalas had no place in her life— *none.* Whatever the power of his sensual impact on her, she must ignore it. Suppress it. Walk away from it.

Speak to Bastiaan this afternoon—explain how he should take Philip away—and then get back to what is important. The only thing that is important to you at this time.

Making her final attempt to launch her professional career. Nothing else. *No one* else.

'Sab, did you bring your swimming costume?'

Philip's question cut across her thoughts. She looked startled. 'No—no, I didn't.'

His face fell, then brightened as Bastiaan spoke.

'No problem. There's a wide collection of assorted swimwear in the guest suites. I'm sure there'll be something to fit you.' Bastiaan's eyes glanced over her, as if assessing her figure's size, and her eyes automatically went to his as he spoke.

'Great!' exclaimed Philip. 'When we've had coffee I'll show you where to change.'

She gave him a flickering uncertain smile. She ought to make her excuses and leave—try and have that word she needed with Bastiaan before she did so. But as she sat sipping her coffee, replete with lunch, champagne coursing gently in her veins, she had no energy to make such a move.

Her gaze slipped out over the beautiful gardens beyond the terrace. Out of nowhere she felt a different mood take hold as she committed herself to staying longer. It really was *so* beautiful here, with the gardens and the dazzlingly blue sea beyond. All she ever saw of the Côte d'Azur was the walk back to her *pension* and the local shops around the harbour. By day she was focussed only on rehearsals, by night she posed as Sabine. A relentless schedule of work. Why not relax a little now?

Why don't I make the most of being here? Who

could ask for anything more lovely and enjoy-
able? And surely the longer I spend in Bastiaan's
company the more used I'll get to him—the more
immune I'll feel. The less I'll react to him.

Yes, that was the way to look at it. Extended
exposure to him would surely help to dissipate
this ridiculous flaring of her senses every time
he glanced at her...

It was a confidence that was comprehensively
annihilated as she emerged from the villa in the
swimsuit Philip had found for her. Even though
it was a one-piece, and she had a matching tur-
quoise sarong wrapped around her, she burned
with self-consciousness as she felt Bastiaan's
eyes go straight to her from where he and Philip
waited by the pool loungers.

But it was not just her own body that she was
so conscious of. Nor was it the sight of Philip,
his slenderly youthful physique clad in colour-
ful board shorts with a fashionable logo, sport-
ing snazzy wrap-around sunglasses that was
causing her breath to catch. No, it was the way
her eyes had gone immediately to the powerful
torso of Bastiaan...to the sculpted pecs and abs,
the strong biceps and wide shoulders. His hip-

hugging dark blue trunks were sober compared with Philip's. His eyes were not shaded by dark glasses, and she could feel the impact of his gaze full on, even through her own sunglasses.

She made a play of making herself comfortable on a sun lounger, and then—again self-consciously—she unknotted the sarong and let it fall to either side of her, exposing her swimsuit-clad body and bare thighs.

'The bikinis didn't tempt you?'

Bastiaan's deep voice threw the question at her and Sarah gave an inner shudder at the thought of exposing even more flesh to Bastiaan Karavalas.

'They're hopeless for swimming in,' she said lightly. She relaxed her shoulders into the cushioned lounger and lifted her face to the sun. 'Oh, this is *gorgeous*,' she said feelingly, as the heat of the sun started to penetrate her skin after the cool of the interior of the house.

'Are you a sun-worshipper?' Bastiaan asked, amusement in his voice.

'When I can be,' she answered, still lightly.

'I'm surprised you're not more tanned, given that you only work nights,' he said.

She glanced towards him uncertainly. The reason she was pale was because she'd spent the first part of the summer in the north of England, teaching, and her days here were spent in rehearsal. But all she could say—again in that same deliberately light voice—was, 'I'm working on it!' Then, in order to avoid any more awkward questions, she gave a little yawn. 'Do you know, I really *do* think I might have a little siesta? Champagne at lunchtime has made me sleepy.' She slid her dark glasses off her face—no point getting white circles around her eyes—and gave a swift smile to her hosts. 'Wake me up if I start snoring,' she warned them humorously.

'You could *never* snore!' Philip said immediately, clearly aghast at the idea of his goddess doing anything so un-goddess-like.

His cousin gave a low laugh. He found that her throwaway comment, so insouciantly self-mocking, appealed to him. But then, of course, almost everything about Mademoiselle Sabine was appealing. Everything physical, at least.

Bastiaan's eyes clouded meditatively as he let his gaze rest on her slim, lissom body. Her eyes were closed, and that allowed him to study her face at leisure, while his cousin busied himself fiddling with his iPod's playlist and fishing out earphones now that the object of his admiration was so annoyingly determined to doze off.

She really is incredibly lovely to look at.

That was the thought uppermost in Bastiaan's consciousness. She had taken off her make-up, he realised, presumably to replace it with sun cream, but it had not dimmed her beauty in the least. He found himself studying her face as she lay there with her eyes studiedly closed. Curious thoughts flitted across his mind. Now she was neither *film noir* vamp nor sixties siren.

So who is she?

The question was in his mind...but he was finding no answer.

He frowned. What did it matter what image Sabine Sablon chose to present to him? What did it matter that she appeared to have an engaging sense of humour about herself? What did it matter that as she lay there, her face bare of make-up, being blessed by the sun's rays, all he could see in her was beauty...?

All he could feel was desire...?

He settled himself on his lounger and started to make his plans. The first step, he knew, must be to remove Philip from the vicinity—and for that he had an idea forming already.

Then it would be time to turn his attentions to the woman—the beautiful, alluring woman who was lying so close to him—and bring her right up close and very, *very* personal…

CHAPTER SIX

SARAH SAT, MERMAID-LIKE, on the sun-warmed rock at the sea's edge, watching Bastiaan approach her through the water with swift, powerful strokes. He and Philip were racing each other from the shore to the pontoon moored a little way off. Philip was on the pontoon now, timing Bastiaan.

She watched Bastiaan getting closer to her and tensed. She really must grab this moment to try and speak to him. She'd been looking for an opportunity since she'd woken from her siesta and they'd all headed down to the sea. So far Philip had stuck to her like glue, delighted to introduce her to the delights of the villa's private stretch of rocky shoreline and encouraging her to swim out with him to the pontoon.

As Bastiaan's long arm touched the rock and he twisted in the water, his muscles bunched to start on his return, she leant forward.

'Bastiaan…?'

It was the first time she'd addressed him by his name directly, and it sounded odd to her. Almost…*intimate.*

Dark eyes lifted to her immediately, a question in them. 'Yes?' There was impatience in his voice, and more, too.

'Can I…can I speak with you privately…before I go?'

Dark brows tugged together, then relaxed. 'Of course,' Bastiaan said smoothly. 'I am at your service, Sabine. But not right now.'

Was he being sarcastic, ironic, or was he just in a hurry to complete his race? Maybe the latter, for he twisted his powerful torso and plunged back into his strokes, face-down in the water, threshing with fast, vigorous movement towards the pontoon.

Sarah breathed out, feeling her tension ease a tad. Well, she'd done it, but she didn't look forward to it—didn't want *any* private conversation with Bastiaan Karavalas on any subject whatsoever.

In her head, silent but piercing, came a single word. *Liar.*

An hour or so later, after a refreshing dip in the villa's pool, she announced that she needed to be going. She glanced at Bastiaan, hoping he would remember her request to speak to him.

Smoothly, he took her cue. 'Let me show you back to where you got changed,' he said.

He gestured with his arm towards the villa's interior and Sarah walked ahead of him, glad that the sarong around her was veiling her somewhat.

As they gained the marble-floored hall she heard him speak.

'So, what is it you want to say to me?'

His tone was neutral, yet Sarah felt that she could hear in its timbre a kind of subtext. She paused at the foot of the stairs and turned. Now that the moment had come she felt excruciatingly awkward. Should she *really* tell this forbidding man who had such dangerous power over her senses that his young cousin was hopelessly enamoured of her? Did he need telling in the first place? Wasn't it obvious that Philip was smitten? Maybe she didn't have to broach the subject at all—

But her cowardly hopes were dashed by the

pointedly enquiring look in his dark eyes and the mordant expression in them.

She lifted her chin. 'It's about Philip—' she blurted out.

One eyebrow rose quizzically. She became crushingly conscious of his bared torso, tanned and muscular, and his still damp hip-hugging swim shorts. Of the way his wet hair was slicked back, accentuating the sculpted line of his cheekbones and jaw.

'I…I think it might be a good idea if he went… went somewhere else to complete his essays.' The words came out in a rush.

Something changed in Bastiaan's eyes. 'Why?' he asked bluntly.

She felt colour run into her cheeks, which were already hot from exposure to the sun. 'Isn't it obvious?' she returned. Her voice was husky, her words reluctant to come, resonating with the awkwardness she felt.

Long lashes dipped over deep-set eyes, and suddenly his expression was veiled.

'Ah, yes,' he said slowly. He inclined his head minutely towards her. 'Well, I shall see what I can do to accomplish what I can in that respect.'

His eyes met hers. 'It may take a day or two, but I think I can see a way.'

His eyes were still holding hers, and his expression was still veiled. For a moment—just a fraction of a moment—she wondered whether she'd made her predicament plain to him.

Then he was speaking again. His tone of voice had changed. 'The bedroom you changed in is the third along the landing,' he informed her. 'Please make use of the en suite bathroom to shower and wash your hair if you wish.' Then he'd turned away and was heading back outside.

Sarah mounted the staircase with a sense of relief. It was done—she'd given Bastiaan Karavalas the warning about Philip that she'd needed to, and now she could leave him to it. Whatever plan he came up with to remove Philip from his villa and her vicinity, he would, she was pretty sure, do it effectively. Everything about him told her that he was a man who achieved everything he set himself to do. Of that she had no doubt whatsoever.

Bastiaan stood in the night-dark garden of his villa, contemplating the dim vista of the sea beyond. It was way gone midnight, but he was not tired. After Philip had driven Sabine back to the *ville*, openly thrilled to be let loose with his cousin's Ferrari again, even on the tame roads of the *Cap*, they'd both headed out to dine in Villefranche. It had been a relaxed meal, and their conversation mostly about cars, with Philip grilling him on competing makes and models and which was the absolute best amongst them all.

Bastiaan had been glad to indulge him, even though he knew that his aunt lived in terror of her son's eager enthusiasm for such powerful and potentially deadly machines—but anything that took Philip's mind off the siren charms of Sabine Sablon was to be welcomed.

Well, Philip would not be available for very much longer. Bastiaan was setting his plans in place.

He was refining them now as he stood in the cool night, with stars pricking out in the heavens and catching the swell of the sea with their trickles of light. Across the bay he could hear faint music, coming from one of the restaurants along the harbour. On his island in the Ionian there was no sound from any source other than nature.

A slight frown drew his brows together. Sabine had said how relaxing his remote island sounded—had she meant it? It was unlikely—nothing about Sabine Sablon indicated that her natural habitat was anything that resembled a small, unpopulated island where the nearest night-life was a fast speedboat away.

And yet today at the villa she had seemed happy to while away the afternoon swimming and sunbathing, openly enjoying the easy-going, lazy relaxation of it all. She had been admiring of the gardens and the sea views, appreciative of the peace and quiet, content to do nothing but let the time pass.

Confounding his expectations of her.

His expression changed. Until, of course, the very end of the afternoon. When she'd made her move on him…changing her allegiance from Philip to himself.

Bastiaan's mouth twisted. That request of hers to speak to him privately had been transparent in its objective. As transparent as her suggestion, made in an intimate husky voice, that their path would be smoother without young Philip to get in their way. Well, in that he would oblige her—and be glad to do so. For she was, of course, playing right into his hands with her suggestion.

The twist at his mouth turned into a smile. A smile of satisfaction.

Of anticipation.

Soon—very soon now—his cousin would be safe from her charms, and *he* would be enjoying them to the hilt.

Sarah's voice was low, throaty, as she finished the last number of her final set of the evening. It had been days since she'd spent the afternoon at Bastiaan Karavalas's villa, and Philip had been noticeable by his absence. He hadn't shown up at the next morning's rehearsal, and she'd picked up an apologetic text from him mid-morning, saying that he was working on his essays, then heading off with Bastiaan in the Ferrari. Nor had he turned up at the club in the evening—another apologetic text had said he was staying at Bastiaan's Monte Carlo apartment. Since then there'd been silence.

Sarah knew why—Bastiaan was doing his best to keep Philip preoccupied and away from her. She could only be grateful: it was, after all, what she'd asked him to do, and what she knew was best for Philip. For herself too.

And not just because it was keeping the disturbing impact of Bastiaan himself away from her—essential though that was for her fractured peace of mind. More than ever she needed to focus on her work. She could afford no distraction at all—not now. Least of all now.

Anxiety bit at her. She was hitting a wall—a wall that was holding her back, holding them all back, and making Max tear into her mercilessly.

They had reached the scene where the War Bride received news of her husband's death. Her aria in it was central to the drama—the fulcrum on which it turned. Although technically it was hard to sing, it was not that that was confounding her.

Max had been brutal in his criticism.

'Sarah—your husband is *dead*! A brief while ago you were rapturously in love—now all that has been ripped from you—*destroyed*! We *have* to hear that! We have to hear your despair, your disbelief. But I don't hear it! I don't hear it at *all*!'

However hard she'd tried, she hadn't been able

to please him. Had not been able to get through that wall.

He'd made her sing an earlier aria, declaring her love, dazzled by the discovery of her head-long tumbling into its lightning-swift ecstasy, so that she could use it to contrast with her plunge into the depths of grief at its loss. But she still hadn't been able to please him.

'You've gone from love to grief in *days*—from bride to widow. We need to hear that unbearable journey in your voice. We need to hear it and believe it!'

She'd thrown up her hands in frustration. 'But *that's* what I can't do! I can't *believe* in it! People don't fall in love just like that only for it to end a few days later. It doesn't happen.'

In her head she remembered how she had wondered, on first hearing the tragic tale, what it must be like to love so swiftly, to hurt so badly. Unreal…quite unreal…

Her mind skittered onto pathways she should not go down.

Desire—yes. *Desire* at first sight—that was real. *That* she could not deny. Across her vision strolled Bastiaan Karavalas, with his night-dark eyes and his hooded, sensual regard that quickened her blood, heated her body. Desire had flamed in her the moment she had seen him, acknowledged his power over her...

But desire isn't love! It's not the same thing at all. Of course it isn't.

She recalled Max's exasperated rasp. 'Sarah, it's a *fable*! These characters are archetypes—timeless. They're not people you see in the street. Anton—talk to her—*make* her understand!' He'd called across to where the composer had been sitting at the piano.

But it didn't matter how much Anton went through the text with her, elucidated the way his music informed and reinforced the words she sang, she was still stuck. Still could not break through.

Max's tension cast a shadow over them all as he stepped up the intensity of their rehearsals, becoming ever more exacting. Time, as he constantly reminded them all, was running increasingly short, and their performance was not yet up to the standard it had to be. Time and again he halted them in mid-song, demanding they repeat, improve, perfect their performance. Nerves were jittery, tempers fraying, and emotions were running high amongst them all.

Now, standing on the stage, finally lowering the microphone as she took a smattering of applause for Sabine's tedious repertoire, Sarah felt resentment fill her. Max was working them all hard, but he was working her harder than everyone else. She knew it was for her own good, for the good of her performance, the good of them all, but she was giving everything she had and it was still not enough. From somewhere, somehow, she had to find more.

Tiredness lapped at her now, and the lazy, sunlit afternoon she'd spent at the villa seemed a long time ago—far longer than a handful of days.

Memory played back the verdant flower-filled gardens, the graceful loggia and the vine-shaded terrace, the sparkling water of the pristine pool and the deep azure of the glorious Mediterranean beyond. The complete change of scene—to such a beautiful scene—had been a tonic in itself, a respite both from the rigours of rehearsal and the banal tiresomeness of performing her nightly cabaret. It had been relaxingly enjoyable despite the disturbing presence of Bastiaan Karavalas.

Because of it...

The realisation was disquieting—and yet it sent a little thrill through her at the same time. She tried to quell it. She felt it, she told herself sternly, only because she was standing here with the hot spotlight on her, in her skin-tight gown, just as she had been that first night when she'd felt his unknown eyes upon her.

More memories stirred. Her eyes moved briefly to the dance floor between the tables and the stage, and warmth flushed through her, as if she could still feel the firm, warm clasp of Bastiaan Karavalas's hands on her as they'd danced. Still feel the shimmering awareness of his physical closeness, the burning consciousness of her over-powering attraction to him.

An attraction she could not explain, could not cope with and certainly could not indulge .

She must not think about him—there was no point. He and Philip were both gone, and her only focus must be the festival performance ahead of her. So what was the point of the strange little pang that seemed to dart into her, twisting as it found its mark somewhere deep within? None.

Bastiaan Karavalas was gone from her life and she must be glad of it.

I must!

She straightened from her slight bow, glancing out over the dining tables beyond before making ready to leave the stage.

And looked straight at Bastiaan Karavalas.

As her eyes lighted on the dark, familiar form, she felt a kick inside her that came from the same place as had that pang, only moments earlier. She hurried off the stage, aware that her heart was beating faster. *Why was he here?* Just to tell her how he'd removed Philip? Or was there another reason—a reason she would not give name to?

But Max did. 'You've lost your young, rich admirer, I see, *cherie*, and replaced him with a new one. Cultivate him—I've looked him up and he's worth a fortune!'

Sarah's jaw tightened, and she would have said something harsh, but there were tight lines of ingrained stress around Max's mouth and she could see tiredness in his face. He was working as hard as any of them—*harder.* And if she was working late nights, then so was he.

'I don't know what he's doing here,' she replied with a shrug.

Max gave his familiar waspish smile. 'Oh, come now—do you need it spelled out?'

She gave another shrug, not bothering to respond. Bastiaan thought she was Sabine—not Sarah. For a moment a thought struck her. Should she introduce Max to Bastiaan—see if he couldn't persuade him to sponsor their production? But that would mean explaining that she was Sarah, not Sabine—and all her objections to that disclosure still held. She just could not afford to let her role as Sabine contaminate her identity as an opera singer, compromise her future reputation.

'Well?' Max prompted. 'Off you go to him—it's you he's here to see, that's obvious. Like I say, be nice to him.' His eyes were veiled for a moment. 'Just don't be late for rehearsal tomorrow, OK?'

'Oh, for God's sake!' she snapped at his implication.

Whether he was joking or not, she didn't care. She was too tired to care. But if Bastiaan had taken the trouble to turn up here, she had better return the courtesy.

Max was now on his phone to Anton and she left him to it, making her way through to the front of house. Her emotions were mixed. She felt strange—both a sense of reluctance and a stirring of her blood. They warred within her.

As she approached Bastiaan's table he got to his feet. He seemed taller than ever—and suddenly more forbidding, it seemed to her, his lean body sheathed in a custom-made tuxedo. Was it because of the momentary tightening of his features? The veiling of his dark eyes? Whatever it was, she felt a shimmer go through her. Not just of an awareness that was quickening her pulse, but of its opposite as well—a kind of instinctual reserve.

She would keep this as brief as possible—it was the only sensible thing to do.

'M'sieu Karavalas,' she greeted him, with only the slightest smile at her mouth, a nod of her head.

An eyebrow lifted as he held a chair for her. 'Bastiaan, surely?' he murmured. 'Have we not advanced that far, *mademoiselle*?'

There was light mockery in his invitation to use his given name while reserving more formality for his own addressing of her. A mockery that played upon what he knew—*must* know—about her receptiveness to his masculine potency, his own appreciation of her charms...

She made no reply, merely gave a flickering social smile as she sat down while he resumed his seat.

'So, what have you done with Philip?' she asked. She kept her tone light, but this was, after all, the only reason that his cousin was here.

She saw a dark flickering cross his eyes. 'I've just returned from driving him to Paris,' he answered.

Sarah's eyes widened in surprise. *'Paris?'*

Bastiaan lifted his cognac glass. 'Yes,' he said smoothly. 'He's meeting his mother there, and visiting family friends.'

'So, how long will he be away?' she asked. She sought to keep her tone light, still, but it was hard—every nerve-ending was quivering with the overpowering impact this man had on her.

'Long enough.'

There was a hint of a drawl in his voice and it made her stare at him. She tried to quash the sudden flare in her veins as his veiled, unreadable gaze rested on her. A gaze that suddenly seared its message into her.

'And now, having disposed of the problem of my young cousin,' Bastiaan was saying, his voice dragging across her nerve-endings and making them flare with a kind of internal shiver that she felt in every cell of her body, 'we can move on to a far more interesting subject.'

Something in his face changed and he shifted slightly, relaxing back, it seemed to her, and lifting his cognac glass, his long, strong fingers curved around the bowl. His eyes rested on her with an open expression in them that was pinioning her where she sat.

She could not answer him. Could only sit, lips slightly parted, feeling her heart start to race. The rest of the room had disappeared. The rest of the *world* had disappeared. There was only her, sitting there, her body shimmering with a sensual awareness of what this man could do to her...

And then a smile flashed suddenly across his features. 'Which is, Mademoiselle Sabine, the subject of where we should dine tonight.' He paused, a light in his eyes. 'Last time you disdained my suggestion of Le Tombleur. But, tell me, does it meet with your approval tonight?'

'Tonight?' Her echo of his question was hollow, hiding the shock beneath. Hiding the sudden, overwhelming spike of adrenaline that had shot into her veins as she'd realised what he intended.

Amusement played about his well-shaped mouth. 'Do we need to wait any longer, Sabine?'

All pretence at formality was gone now. All pretence at denial of what had flared between them from the very first. There was only one reality now—coursing through her veins, pounding in her heart, sheering across her skin, quickening in her core.

This man—this man alone—who had walked into her life when she'd least expected it, least wanted it, could least afford to acknowledge it. This man who could set her pulse racing… in whose dark, disturbing presence her body seemed to come alive.

Temptation overwhelmed her. The temptation to say *Yes! Yes!* to everything he was offering. Simply to let his hand reach across the table to hers, to let him raise her to her feet, lead her from here and take her where he wanted…

To a physical intimacy, a sensual intensity, an embarkation into realms of sensuous possibility that she had never encountered before.

And why not? *Why not?* She was free, an adult and independent woman. Her emotional ties to Andrew, such as they'd been, were long gone. She was no ingénue—she knew what was being offered to her…knew it was something that would never come again in her life. For there could never be another man who would affect her the way this man could.

She could go with him as Sabine—the woman he took her to be—as assured as he in the world that this dark, powerful man moved in. A world of physical affairs that sated the body but left the heart untouched. As Sabine she could indulge in such an affair, could drink it to the full, like a glass of heady champagne that would intoxicate the blood but leave her clear-headed the following day.

The temptation was like an overpowering lure, dominating her senses, her consciousness. Then, like cold water douching down upon her, she surfaced from it.

She was not Sabine.

She was Sarah. Sarah Fareham. Who had striven all her life towards the moment that was so close now—the moment when she would walk out on stage and give the performance upon which her future life would depend.

I can't go with him—I can't.

She felt her head give a slow, heavy shake.

'C'est impossible.'

The words fell from her lips and her eyes were veiled beneath the ludicrously over-long false eyelashes.

His face stilled. 'Why?'

A single word. But she did not answer. Could not. Dared not. She was on a knife's edge—if she did not go now, right now, she would sever her resolve. Give in to the temptation that was lapping at her like water on a rising tide.

She shook her head again, drained her coffee cup with a hand that was almost shaking. She got to her feet. Cast one more look at him. One last look.

The man is right—the time is wrong.

'Goodnight, *m'sieu*,' she said, and dipped her head and walked away. Heading to the door beside the low stage, moving back towards her dressing room.

Behind her, Bastiaan watched her go. Then, slowly, he reached for his cognac. Emotion swelled within him but he did not know what it was. Anger? Was that it? Anger that she had defied his will for her?

Or anger that she had denied what burned between them like a hot, fierce flame?

I want her—and she denies me my desire...

Or was it incomprehension?

He did not know, could not tell—knew only that as his fingers clenched around the bowl of his cognac glass he needed the shot of brandy more than he needed air to breathe. In one mouthful he had drained it, and then, his expression changing, he pushed to his feet and left the club. Purpose was in every stride.

CHAPTER SEVEN

SARAH'S FINGERS FUMBLED with the false eye-lashes as she peeled them off her eyelids, then with shaky hands wiped the caking foundation off her face, not bothering to tackle her dark eye make-up. She felt as if she was shaking on the inside, her mind shot to pieces. She'd made her-self walk away from him, but it hadn't seemed to help.

All she could see in her vision was Bastiaan Karavalas, saying in his low, deep voice, 'Do we need to wait any longer?'

Emotion speared in her—a mix of panic and longing, confusion and torment. An overwhelm-ing urge to get away as swiftly as possible, to reach the safe haven of her room in the *pension*, surged through her. She wouldn't wait to change. She simply grabbed her day clothes, stuffing them into a plastic bag and seizing up her purse, then headed for the rear exit of the club. Max was long gone and she was glad.

She stepped out into the cool night air of the little road that ran behind the club—and stopped dead.

Bastiaan's Ferrari blocked the roadway and he was propped against it, arms folded. Wordlessly he opened the passenger door.

'Give me one reason,' he said to her, 'why you will not dine with me.'

His voice was low, intense. His eyes held hers in the dim light and would not release them. She felt her mouth open to speak—but no words came out. In her head was a tumult, a jumble of thoughts and emotions and confusion.

He spoke for her. 'You can't, can you? Because this has been waiting to happen since I first set eyes on you.'

The intensity was still in his voice, in his gaze that would not let her go.

She was still trying to find the words she had to find, marshal the thoughts she had to think, but it was impossible. Impossible to do anything but succumb. Succumb to the emotions that were coursing through her. Impelling her forward.

She felt one last frail, hopeless thought fleeting through her tumbling mind.

I tried—I tried to stop this happening. Tried to deny it, tried to prevent it. But I can't—I can't deny this any longer. I can't.

It was all she could manage. Then, as she sank into the low, plush seat of the powerful, sleek car, she felt herself give in entirely, completely, to what was happening. Succumbing to the temptation that was the darkly devastating man closing the door on her, lowering himself in beside her, reaching to the ignition to fire the powerful engine and moving off into the night with her at his side.

Taking her where he wanted to take her.

Where she wanted to go.

She stole a sideways look at him. Their gazes clashed. She looked away again, out over the pavements and the buildings along the roadway. She knew what she was doing—and why. Knew with every pulse of blood in her veins and in the jittering of her nerves, which were humming as if electricity were pouring through her—a charge that was coming out of the very atmosphere itself.

Enclosed as she was, only a few inches away from the long, lean body of the man next to her, she felt the low, throaty vibration of the ultra-powerful engine of the car—was aware of the sleek, luxurious interior, of the whole seductive ambience of sitting beside him.

She knew that her body was outlined by her stage dress, that her image was that of a woman in the full glamour of her beauty. And that the man beside her, clad in his hand-made tuxedo, with the glint of gold of his watch, the cufflinks in his pristine cuffs, the heady, spiced scent of his aromatic aftershave, had contrived to make the situation headily seductive.

She gave herself to it. It was too late now for anything else. Far too late.

'Where are we going?' she asked. Her voice was low-pitched and she could not quite look at him. Could not quite believe that she was doing what she was doing.

He glanced at her, with half a smile curving his sensual lips. 'I attempted once before to take you to Le Tombleur—perhaps this time you will acquiesce?'

Had there been a huskiness discernible in his

voice as he'd said the word 'acquiesce'? She couldn't be sure—could only be sure that there was some kind of voltage charging her body right now, one she had never experienced before. Somewhere inside her, disappearing fast, there was a voice of protest—but it was getting feebler with every moment she was here with Bastiaan, burningly conscious of his powerful masculine presence, of the effect he had on her that she could not subdue.

Beyond the confines of the car the world was passing by. But it was far, far away from her now. Everything was far, far away.

It did not take long to get to the restaurant, set in the foothills of the Alpes-Maritimes above the crowded coastline of the Riviera. She was helped from the car, ushered inside by the tall, commanding man at her side. The *maître d'* was hurrying forward, all attention, to show them to a table out on the terrace, looking down on where the lights of the Riviera glittered like a necklace of jewels.

She eased into her seat, ultra-aware of the tightness of her gown, the voluptuousness of her figure. Her eyes went yet again to the man sitting

opposite her, studying his menu. What was it
about him that he could affect her the way he did?
Why was she so overwhelmed by him? Why had
she been so fatally tempted to succumb to what
she knew she should not be doing? To dine here
with him *à deux*...

And what would happen afterwards...?

Her mind skittered away. She did not think—
did not dare think. Dared only to go on sitting
there, occupying herself by opening the menu,
glancing blindly down at the complex listings.
Was she hungry? She could not tell. Could tell
only that her heart rate was raised, that her skin
was flushed with heat...that her eyes wanted only
to go on resting on the man opposite her.

'So, what would you like to eat?'

Bastiaan's voice interrupted her hopeless
thoughts and she was glad. She made herself give
a slight smile. 'Something light,' she said. 'In this
dress anything else is impossible!'

It had been a mistake to make such a remark,
however lightly it had been said. It drew a wash
of scrutiny from the dark, long-lashed eyes. She
felt her colour heighten and had to fight it down
by studying the menu again. She found a dish

that seemed to fit the bill—scallops in a saffron sauce—and relayed it to Bastiaan. He too chose fish, but a more robust grilled monkfish, and then there followed the business of selecting wine to go with it.

Choices made, he sat back, his eyes resting on her at his leisure. Satisfaction soared through him. Her yielding had not surprised him in the least, but it had gratified him. Now, at last, he had her to himself.

His sensation of satisfaction, of the rightness of it all, increased. Yes, seducing her would, as he had always planned, achieve his goal of quashing any ambitions she might have had concerning his cousin, but as they sat there on the secluded terrace, with the night all around them, somehow his young cousin seemed very...irrelevant.

'So,' he began, 'tell me about yourself, Sabine?' It was an innocuous question—and a predictable one—but he could see a veil flicker over her eyes.

'Myself?' she echoed. 'What is there to tell that is not evident? I am a singer—what else?' She sounded flippant, unconcerned. Studiedly so.

'What part of France do you come from?' Another innocuous polite enquiry—nothing more than that. Yet once again he saw that flicker.

'Normandy,' she answered. 'A little place not far from Rouen.' Her mother's birthplace, it was the part of France she knew best, and therefore it seemed the safest answer to give.

'And have you always wanted to be a singer?'

The lift of a shoulder came again. 'One uses the talents one is given,' she replied. It was as un-revealing an answer as she could think to give.

Bastiaan's eyes narrowed minutely.

Sarah saw the narrowing. Could he tell she was being as evasive as she could? She was glad that the sommelier arrived at that moment, diverting Bastiaan. But as the man departed, and Bastiaan lifted his wine glass, she felt his dark eyes upon her again.

'To our time together,' he said, and smiled.

She made herself lift her own glass and meet his eyes. It was like drowning in dark velvet. She felt her blood quicken, her breath catch. A sense of unreality overwhelmed her—and yet this was real…vividly, pulsingly real. She was sitting here, so close to the man who could set her senses on fire with a single glance.

Oh, this was ridiculous. To be so…so overcome by this man. She *had* to claw back her composure. If she were going to take refuge in being Sabine then she must be as poised and cool as that protection provided. With an inner breath she set down her glass and then let her glance sweep out across the glittering vista far below.

'If the food is as exceptional as the location, I can understand why this place has such a reputation,' she murmured. It seemed a safe thing to say—and safe things were what she was clutching at.

'I hope both please you,' he replied.

His lashes dipped over his eyes. It was clear to him that she did not wish to talk about herself, but her very evasiveness told him what he wanted to know—that she was, indeed, a woman who presented to the world what she chose to present. For himself, he did not care. Sabine Sablon would not, after all, be staying long in his life.

'Does this have a Michelin star yet?' Sarah asked, bringing her gaze back to him. Another safe thing to ask.

'One. But a second is being targeted,' he answered.

'What makes the difference, I wonder?' Sarah asked. Safe again...

He lifted his wine glass. Talking about Michelin stars was perfectly acceptable as a topic. It lasted them until their food arrived, and then they moved on to the subject of the Côte d'Azur itself—how it had changed and developed, what its charms and attractions were.

It was Bastiaan who talked most, and he soon became aware that Sabine was adept at asking questions of him, keeping the conversation flowing.

And all the time, like a deep, powerful current in a river on whose surface aimless ripples were circling, another conversation was taking place. One that was wordless, silent, yet gaining strength with every politely interested smile, every nod, every lift of a fork, of a glass, every glance, every low laugh, every gesture of the hand, every shift in body position...every breath taken.

It was a conversation that could lead to only one end...take them to only one destination.

The place he had determined she should go. The place she could no longer resist him taking her to.

* * *

Sarah climbed back into the car and Bastiaan lowered his tall frame into the driving seat beside her. Immediately the space confining them shrank. Her mind was in a daze. Wine hummed in her veins—softening her body so that it seemed to mould to the contours of the leather seat. She heard the throaty growl of the engine and the powerful car moved forward, pressing her further into her seat. She could feel the low throb of her beating heart, the flush of heat in her skin.

But it was in *Sabine's* breast that her heart was beating. It was Sabine whose senses were dominated by the presence of this magnetic, compelling man beside her. Sabine who was free to do what she was doing now—ignoring everything in the world except this man, this night...

Sabine, alluring, sensual and sophisticated, could yield to the overpowering temptation that was Bastiaan Karavalas and all that he promised. Sabine had led her to this place, this time, this moment—a moment that Sabine would wish to come...would choose to be in...

This is going to happen. It is going to happen and I am not going to stop it. I want it to happen.

She did. It might be rash, it might be foolish, it might be the thing she had least expected would happen during this summer, but she *was* going to go with Bastiaan Karavalas.

This night.

And as for tomorrow...

She would deal with that then. Not now.

Now there was only her, and him, and being taken to where he was taking her. Wordless. Voiceless. Irreversible.

He took her to his apartment in Monte Carlo.

It was as unlike the villa on Cap Pierre as she could imagine. In a modern high-rise block, its decor sleek and contemporary. She stood by the huge-paned glass windows, gazing out over the marina far below, seeing the glittering lights of the city scintillating like diamonds, feeling the rich sensuality of her body, the tremor in her limbs.

Waiting...

Waiting for the man standing behind her, his presence, his scent overpowering her. Waiting for him to make his move...to take her into his arms...his embrace...his bed.

She heard him murmur something, felt the

warmth of his breath on the nape of her neck, the drift of his hands around her shoulders, so light, feather-light, and yet with a silken power that made her breath catch, her lips part as the tremor in her limbs intensified. She felt the powerful touch of his palms glide down her bare arms, fasten on her wrists, and with a movement as subtle as it was irresistible, she felt him turn her towards him.

She lifted her face to him, lips parted, eyes deep and lustrous. She was so close she could feel the strength and heat of his body, feel the dark intensity of his gaze, of those eyes holding hers, conveying to her all that she knew was in her own eyes as well.

He smiled. A slow pull of his mouth. As if he knew what she was feeling, as if he were colluding with the strange, strong, heavy pulse of the blood in her veins. His eyes worked over her face leisurely, taking in every contour, every curve of her features.

'You are so beautiful...' It was a husky statement. 'So very beautiful...'

For one long, timeless moment his eyes poured into hers as they stood there, face to face, and then his hands closed around her slender, pliant waist and drew her to him slowly, very slowly, as if each increase in the pressure of his hands drawing her to him was almost against his will and yet as impossible for him to resist as it was for her to resist.

Nor did she want to—she wanted only to feel his mouth making its slow descent to hers, wanted him to fuse his lips to hers, to take her mouth, possess it, mould it to his, open it to his...

And when he did her eyes could only close, her throat could only sigh with a low sound of absolute pleasure, as with skill and sensual slowness his mouth found hers to take it and taste it. Somewhere inside her, very dimly, she could feel heat pooling. Her heart seemed to cease its beating as she felt the rich, sensual glide of his lips on hers, his mouth opening hers to him, his kiss deepening.

His hold on her waist tightened, strengthened, as the shift of his stance changed so that she was being cradled against him, and with a little shimmer of shocked response she felt how aroused he was.

His arousal fired hers so that her blood surged,

her breath caught, the melding of her mouth to his quickened and deepened. Her hands lifted, closing around the strong breadth of his back, splaying against the smooth fabric of his dinner jacket. She felt her breasts crush against the wall of his chest. She heard his low growl, felt his palms pull her tighter against him.

Excitement flared through her. Every cell in her body was alive, sensitive, eager for more of what she was already experiencing. And then, as if on a jerking impulse, he swept her body into his arms, as if she were nothing more than a feather. He was striding away with her, his mouth still fastened upon hers, and the world beyond whirled as he deposited her heavily upon the cold satin surface of a wide, soft bed and came down beside her.

His mouth continued devouring hers, and one thigh was thrown over her as a kind of glory filled her. Desire, open and searing, flooded her. She felt her breasts tighten and tingle and threw back her head to lift them more. Another low growl broke from him, and then her arms were being lifted over her head and pinioned with one hand while his palm closed possessively over the sweet, straining mound of her breast. She gasped with pleasure, groaning, her head moving restlessly from side to side, her mouth, freed from his, abandoned and questing.

Was this her? Could it be her? Lying like this, flaming with a desire that was consuming her, possessing her, shameless and wanton?

His heavy thigh lay between hers and she felt her hips writhe against it, wanting more and yet more of the sensations that were being loosened within her. Did she speak? And if she did, what did she say? She did not know—knew only that she must implore him to bestow upon her what she was craving, yearning for, more and more and more...

Never had she felt like this, so deeply, wildly aroused. As if she were burning with a flame that she had never known.

He smiled down at her. 'I think it is time, *cherie*, that we discarded these unnecessary clothes...'

He jack-knifed to his feet, making good on his words. She could not move—could only gaze at him in the dim light as he swiftly, carelessly, disposed of what he was wearing. And then his hard, lean body was lowering down beside her, his weight indenting the mattress. She felt his nakedness like a brand, and suddenly, out of nowhere, her cheeks were flaring, her eyelids veiling him from her sight.

He gave a low, amused laugh. 'Shy?' he murmured. 'At *this* point?'

She couldn't answer him—could only let her eyes flutter open. And for an instant—just an instant—she thought she saw in the dim light a question suddenly forming in his...

But then it was gone. In its place a look of deep, sensual appreciation.

'You are beautiful indeed, *cherie*, as you are... but I want to see your beauty *au naturel.*'

A hand lifted to her shoulders, easing the straps away first on one side, then the other. With a kind of sensual delicacy he peeled her gown down her body to her waist, letting his gaze wander over her in that lazy, leisurely fashion that made the heat pool in her body. Then he tugged it further still, over her hips, taking with it her panties, easing the material down her thighs to free her legs. Now only her stockings remained, and with a sense of shock she realised what it was he was seeing of her...

'Shall I make love to you like this?' he asked, and there was still that lazy, sensual amusement in his voice.

She answered him. No, she would *not* be arrayed like that for him.

With swift decision she sat up, peeling her stockings from her body, tossing them aside with the belt that fastened them. Her hair was tumbling now, free and lush over her breasts, as she sat looking at him where he lay back on the coverlet, blatant in his own nakedness. She gazed down at him, pushing back her hair with one hand. He was waiting—assured, aroused, confident—conspiring with her to make the next move, and she was glad to do so.

Draping her long hair around one shoulder, she leant forward. Her breasts almost grazed his bared chest as she planted her hands either side of him.

'Where shall I start?' she heard herself murmur, with the same warm, aroused amusement in her voice as his had held.

An answering amusement glittered in his dark eyes. 'Take me,' he said, and the amusement was there in his deep voice too. 'I am yours.'

She gave a low, brief laugh, and then her mouth was gliding, skimming over the steel-hard contours of his chest. Lightly...arousingly.

For interminable moments he endured it, his arousal mounting unbearably, as she deliberately teased and tempted him. And then, with an explosive edge, he knew he could take it no longer. He hauled her down on him—fully on him—and the satisfaction he knew as he heard her gasp was all he needed to hear. He rolled her over beneath him, and with a thrust of his thigh parted her.

His mouth found hers—claiming and clinging, feasting and tasting. Urgency filled him. He wanted her *now*.

Almost he succumbed to the overwhelming urge to possess her as she was. But that would be madness—insanity. With a groan of self-control he freed himself, flung out an arm sideways and reached into the bedside drawer.

She was seeking to draw him back, folding her hands around him, murmuring, and he could hear the breathless moans in her throat as she sought him.

'Wait—a moment only...'

It was almost impossible for him to speak. His

arousal was absolute…his body was in meltdown. He *had* to have her—he *had* to possess her. Had to complete what he had wanted to do from the very first moment of laying eyes upon her lush, alluring body, since he had first felt the response in those emerald eyes…

Oh, she might be as mercenary as he feared, as manipulative as he suspected, but none of that mattered. Only this moment mattered—this urgency, this absolute overriding desire for her that was possessing him.

A moment later he was ready, and triumph surged through him. At last he could take what he wanted—possess *her*, this woman who would belong to no one else but him…

She was drawing him down on her, her thighs enclosing his as her body opened to him, and with a relief that flooded through him he fused his body deep, deep within her own…

Immediately, like a firestorm, sensation exploded within him and he was swept away on burning flames that consumed him in a furnace of pleasure. For an instant so brief he was scarcely conscious of it, he felt dismay that he had not waited for her. But then, with a reeling sense of amazed wonder, he realised that she had come with him into the burning flames…that she was clinging to him and crying out even as he was, and that their bodies were wreathed in a mutual consummation that was going on and on and on…

Never before had he experienced such a consummation. Never in all his wide and varied experience had the intensity been like this. It was as if his whole mind and body and being had ignited into one incredible, endless sensation—as if their bodies were melding together, fusing like molten metal into each other.

When did it change? When it did it start to ebb, to take him back down to the plane of reality, of consciousness? He didn't know—couldn't say. Could only feel his body shaking as it returned slowly, throbbingly, to earth. His lungs were seizing and he could feel his heart still pounding, hear his voice shaking as he lifted himself slightly from her, aware that his full weight was crushing her.

He said something, but he did not know what.

She was looking at him—gazing up with an expression in her eyes that mirrored what he knew was in his own. A kind of shock. She was stunned by what had happened.

For one long moment they seemed just to stare at each other disbelievingly. Then, with a ragged intake of breath, Bastiaan managed to smile. Nothing more than that. And he saw her eyes flutter closed, as if he had released her. A huge lassitude swept over him, and with a kind of sigh he lowered himself again, settling her sideways against him, pulling her into his warm, exhausted body.

Holding her so close against him was wonderful, reassuring, and all that he wanted. His hands spread across her silken flanks, securing her against him, and he heard her give a little sigh of relaxation, felt one of her hands close over his, winding her fingers into his, and then, with a final settling of her body, she was still, her breathing quietening as she slipped into sleep.

In his final moment of remaining consciousness Bastiaan reached back to haul the coverlet over them both and then, when they were cocooned beneath, he wrapped his arm around her once more and gave himself to sleep, exhausted, replete, and in that moment possessing all that he wanted to possess on earth.

Something woke her—she wasn't sure what. Whatever it was, it had roused her from the deep slumber into which she'd fallen…a slumber deeper and sweeter than she had ever known.

'Good morning.'

Bastiaan, clad in a towelling robe, was looking down at her. His dark eyes were drinking her in. She did not answer. Could not. Could only hear in her head the words that had forced their way in.

What have I done? Oh, God, what have I done?

But she didn't need to ask—the evidence was in her naked body, in her lying in the bed of Bastiaan Karavalas.

Memory burned like a meteor, scorching through the sky. Awareness made her jack-knife. 'Oh, God—what time is it?' She stared at him, horror-struck.

His face pulled into a frown. 'Of what significance is that?' he demanded.

But she did not answer him—did not do anything except leap from the bed, not caring that she was naked. Not caring about anything except snatching, from wherever she could see them, her clothes from the previous night.

Dismay and horror convulsed her. She pushed into the bathroom, caught sight of herself in the huge mirror, and gave a gasping groan. Three minutes later she stumbled out—looking ludicrous, she knew, with her tangled hair tumbling over her shoulders, her evening dress from the night before crumpled and idiotic on her. But she didn't care—couldn't care. Couldn't afford to care.

She might be wearing Sabine's clothes, left over from the night before, but Sabine herself was gone. Sarah was back—and she was panicking as she had never panicked before.

'What the *hell*…?' Bastiaan was staring at her.

'I have to go.'

'*What?* Don't be absurd.'

She ignored him. Pushed right past him out into the reception room and stared desperately around, looking for her bag. Dimly she remembered that her day clothes were in a plastic bag that must, she thought urgently, still be in the footwell of Bastiaan's car. But there was no time for that now. No time for anything except to get out of here and find a bus stop...

Oh, God, it will take for ever to get back. I'll be late—so late. Max will be furious!

She felt her arm caught, her body swung round. 'Sabine—what is going on? Why are you running away?'

She stared, eyes blank with incomprehension. 'I have to go,' she said again.

For a second there was rejection in his eyes, and then, as if making a decision, he let her go.

'I'll call a cab—' he said.

'No!'

He ignored her, crossed to a phone set by the front door, spoke swiftly to someone she assumed was the concierge. Then he hung up, turned to look at her.

'I don't know what is going on, or why. But if you insist on leaving I cannot stop you. So—go.' His voice was harsh, uncomprehending. His expression blank.

For one timeless moment she was paralysed. Could only stare at him. Could only feel as if an explosion was taking place inside her, detonating down every nerve, along every vein.

'Bastiaan, I—'

But she could not speak. There was nothing to say. She was not Sabine. She was Sarah. And she had no place here…no place at all…

He opened the front door for her and she stumbled through.

As she ran for the elevator she heard the door slam behind her. Reverberating through every stricken cell in her body.

CHAPTER EIGHT

BASTIAAN WAS DRIVING. Driving as though he were being chased by the hounds of hell. The road snaked up, high into the Alpes-Maritimes, way beyond the last outpost of the Riviera and out into the hills, where bare rock warred with the azure skies. Further on and further up he drove, with the engine of the car roaring into the silence all around him.

At the top of the pass he skidded to the side, sending a scree of stones tumbling down into the crevasse below. He cut the engine but the silence brought no peace. His hands clenched over the steering wheel.

Why had she run from him? *Why?* What had put that look of absolute panic on her face?

Memory seared across his synapses. What had flamed between them had been as overwhelming for her as it had been for him—he knew that. Knew it with every male instinct he possessed.

That conflagration of passion had set them both alight—*both* of them.

It has never been like that for me before. Never.

And she had gazed at him with shock in her eyes, with disbelief.

Had she fled because of what had happened between them? Had it shocked her as it had shocked him? So that she could not handle it, could not cope with it?

Something is happening, Sabine, between us—something that is not in your game plan. Nor in mine.

He stared out over the wide ravine, an empty space into which a single turn of the wheel would send his car—himself—hurtling. He tried to make himself think about Philip, about why he had come here to rescue him from Sabine Sablon, but he could not. It seemed…irrelevant. Unimportant.

There was only one imperative now.

He reached for the ignition, fired the engine. Nosed the car around and headed back down to the coast with only one thought in his head, driving him on.

* * *

Max lifted his hand to halt her. 'Take it again,' he said. His voice was controlled, but barely masking his exasperation.

Sarah felt her fingers clench. Her throat was tight, and her shoulders and her lungs. In fact every muscle in her body felt rigid. It was hopeless—totally, absolutely hopeless. All around her there was a tension that was palpable. Everyone present was generating it, feeling it. She most of all.

When she'd arrived at rehearsal, horrendously late, Max had turned his head to her and levelled her with a look that might have killed her, like a basilisk's. And then it had gone from bad to worse...to impossible.

Her voice had gone. It was as simple and as brutal as that. It didn't matter that Max wasn't even attempting to get her to sing the aria—she could sing nothing. Nothing at all.

But it was not the mortification of arriving so late to rehearsal, her breathless arrival and hectic heartbeat that were making it impossible for her to sing. It was because inside her head an explosion had taken place, wiping out everything that had once been in it.

Replacing it only with searing white-hot memory.

Her night with Bastiaan.

It filled her head, overwhelming her, consuming her consciousness, searing in her bloodstream—every touch, every caress, every kiss. Impossible to banish. Impossible for anything else to exist for her.

'Sarah!' Max's voice was sharp, edged with anger now.

She felt another explosion within her. 'I *can't.*' The cry broke from her. 'I just can't! It isn't there—I'm sorry... I'm *sorry*!'

'What the hell use is sorry?' he yelled, his control clearly snapping.

And suddenly it was all too much. Just too much. Her late arrival and the collapse of her voice were simply the final straw.

Alain, her tenor, stepped forward, put a protective arm around her shoulder. 'Lay off her, Max!' he snapped.

'And lay off the rest of us too!' called someone else.

'Max, we're exhausted. We *have* to have a break.'

The protests were mounting, the grumbling turning into revolt. For a dangerous moment Max looked as if he wanted to yell at them all, then abruptly he dropped his head.

'OK,' he said. 'Break, everyone. Half an hour. Get outside. Fresh air.'

The easing of the fractured tension was palpable and the company started to disperse, talking in low, relieved voices.

Alain's hand dropped from Sarah's shoulder. 'Deep breaths,' he said kindly, and wandered off to join the general exodus outdoors.

But Sarah couldn't move. She felt nailed to the floor. She shut her eyes in dumb, agonised misery.

Dear God, hadn't she said she must have no distractions. *None.* And then last night—!

What have I done? Oh, what have I done!

It was the same helpless, useless cry she'd given as she'd stood in Bastiaan's apartment naked, fresh from his bed.

Anguish filled her—and misery.

Then, suddenly, she felt her hands being taken.

'Sarah, look at me,' said Max.

His voice had changed—his whole demeanour had changed. Slowly, warily, she opened her eyes. His expression was sympathetic. Tired lines were etched around his eyes.

'I'm sorry,' he said. 'We're all burning out and I'm taking it out on you—and you don't deserve it.'

'I'm so sorry for arriving late,' she replied. 'And for being so useless today.'

But Max squeezed her hands. 'You need a break,' he said. 'And more than just half an hour.'

He seemed to pause, searching her strained expression, then he nodded and went on.

'Should I blame myself?' he asked. There was faint wry humour in his dry voice. 'Wasn't I the one who told you not to be late this morning? Knowing who'd turned up to see you? No, no, *cherie*—say nothing. Whatever has happened, it's still going on in your head. So…'

He took a breath, looking at her intently.

'What I want you to do is…go. Go. Whatever it takes—do it. I don't want to see you again this week. Take a complete break—whether that's to sob into your pillow or… Well, whatever! If this rich cousin of Philip is good for you, or bad, the point is that *he's* in your head and your work is not.' His voice changed. 'Even without last night you've hit the wall, and I can't force you through it. So you must rest, and then—well, we shall see what we shall see.'

He pressed her hands again, his gaze intent.

'Have faith, Sarah—have faith in yourself, in what you can accomplish. You are so nearly there! I would not waste my genius on you otherwise,' he finished, with his familiar waspish humour.

He stepped back, patting her hands before relinquishing them.

'So—go. Take off. Do anything but sing. Not even Sabine's dire ditties. I'll sort it with Raymond—somehow.'

He dropped a light kiss on her forehead.

'*Go!*' he said.

And Sarah went.

Bastiaan nosed the car carefully down the narrowing street towards the harbour. She was here somewhere—she had to be. He didn't know where her *pension* was, but there were a limited number, and if necessary he would check them all out. Then there was the nightclub as well—someone there at this time of day would know where she might be.

I have to find her.

That was the imperative driving him. Conscious thought was not operating strongly in him right now, but he didn't care. Didn't care that a voice inside his head was telling him that there was no reason to seek her out like this. One night with her had been enough to achieve his ends—so why was he searching for her?

He did not answer—refused to answer. Only continued driving, turning into the area that fronted the harbour, face set, eyes scanning around as if he might suddenly spot her.

And she was there.

He felt his blood leap, his breath catch.

She was by the water's edge, seated on a mooring bollard, staring out to sea. He felt emotions surge through him—triumph shot through with relief. He stopped the car, not caring whether it was in a parking zone or not. Got out. Strode up to her. Placed a hand on her shoulder.

'Sabine...' His voice was rich with satisfaction. With possession.

Beneath his hand he felt her whole body jump. Her head snaked around, eyes widening in shock.

'Oh, God...' she said faintly.

He smiled. 'You did not truly believe I would let you go, did you?' he said. He looked down at her. Frowned suddenly. 'You have been crying,' he said.

There was disbelief in his voice. Sabine? Weeping? He felt the thoughts in his head rearrange themselves. Felt a new one intrude.

'What has made you cry?' he demanded. It was not *him*—impossible that it should be him.

She shook her head. 'It's just...complicated,' she said.

Bastiaan found himself hunkering down beside her, hands resting loosely between his bunched thighs, face on a level with hers. His expression was strange. His emotions stranger. The Sabine who sat here, her face tear-stained, was someone new—someone he had never seen before.

The surge of possessiveness that had triumphed inside him a moment ago on finding her was changing into something he did not recognise.

But it was moving within him. Slowly but powerfully. Making him face this new emotion evolving within him.

'No,' he contradicted, and there was something
in his voice that had not been there before. 'It is
very simple.' He looked at her, his eyes holding
hers. 'After last night, how could it be anything
else?'

His gaze became a caress and his hand reached
out softly to brush away a tendril of tangled hair
that had escaped from its rough confines in a
bunched pleat at the back of her head. He wanted
to undo the clasp, see her glorious blond mane
tumble around her shoulders. Although what she
was wearing displeased him, for it seemed to be
a shapeless tee shirt and a pair of equally shapeless cotton trousers. And her face was blotchy,
her eyes strained.

Yet as he spoke, as his hand gently brushed
the tendril from her face, he saw her expression
change. Saw the strain ebb from her eyes, her
blotched skin re-colour.

'I don't know why you ran from me,' he heard
himself say, 'and I will not ask. But...' His hand

now cupped her chin, feeling the warmth of her skin beneath his fingertips. 'This I *will* ask.'

His eyes rested on hers—his eyes that had burned their way into hers in the throes of exquisite passion. But now they were simply filled with a single question. The only one that filled his head, his consciousness.

'Will you come with me now? And whatever complications there are will you leave them aside?'

Something shifted in her eyes, in the very depths of them. They were green—as green as emeralds. Memory came to him. He remembered how he'd wanted to drape her in emeralds. It seemed odd to him just then. Irrelevant. Unimportant. Only one thing was important now.

The answer she was giving him with her beautiful, emerald-green eyes, which were softening even as he held them. Softening and lightening and filling with an expression that told him all he needed to know.

He smiled again. Not in triumph this time, nor in possession. Just smiled warmly upon her.

'Good,' he said. Then he drew her to her feet. His smile deepened. 'Let's go.'

He led her to his car and helped her in.

* * *

The rest of this week, thought Sarah.

The wealth of time seemed like largesse of immense proportions. The panic that had been in her breast and the tension that had bound her lungs with iron, her throat with barbed wire, were gone. Just...*gone*. They had fallen from her as she had risen to her feet, had her hand taken by Bastiaan. Her feet felt like cushions of air.

I've been set free!

That was what it felt like. As if she had been set free from all the complications that had been tearing into her like claws and teeth ever since she'd surfaced that morning, realizing what she'd done. What *she*—Sarah, not Sabine—had done. And now... Oh, now, it didn't matter—didn't matter who she was.

Max understood—understood the entire impossibility of what had been tying her in knots for days now, ever since Bastiaan Karavalas had walked into her life.

Right man—wrong time.

But no more—not for a precious handful of glorious, wonderful, liberating days.

I can do what I've been longing to do—what I

succumbed to doing last night. This man alone is different from any I've ever known. What happened last night was a revelation, a transformation.

She quivered with the memory of their passion as he started the car, gunning the engine. She turned to look at him, her eyes as bright as stars.

'Where are we going?' she asked.

She had asked that last night and he had taken her to a new, glittering realm of enchantment and desire, passion and fulfilment.

'My villa,' he answered, his eyes warm upon her before he glanced back to steer the car out of the little town, along the road that curved towards the *Cap.*

Gladness filled her. The apartment in Monte Carlo was glitzy and glamorous, but it did nothing for her. It was his villa that charmed her.

'Wonderful…' she breathed. She felt as light as air, floating way, way up into the sky—the carefree, bright blue sky, where there were no complications to tether her down.

I'm free from everything except seizing with both hands this time now! Right man—right time. Right now!

Her spirits soared, and it seemed they were at the villa in minutes. For a brief interlude Sarah felt self-conscious about encountering Paulette again. If the woman had considered her a threat to Philip, what might she think of her cavorting with her employer? But Paulette, she discovered, had a day off.

'So we'll have to make our own lunch,' Bastiaan told her.

He didn't want to make lunch—he wanted to make love. But his stomach was growling. He was hungry. Hungry for food, hungry for her. He would sate both appetites and life would be good. *Very* good.

He had Sabine back with him, and right now that was all he wanted.

As he headed towards the kitchen he glanced out of the French windows to the terrace beyond. Only a few days ago they had lunched there, all three of them—he and Sabine and Philip.

It seemed a long time ago.

'So...' Bastiaan set down his empty coffee cup on the ironwork table on the villa's shady terrace and leant back in his chair, his eyes resting on Sabine. 'What shall we do now?'

The expression in his eyes made it totally clear what he would like to do—he'd sated his hunger for food, and now he wanted to sate a quite different hunger.

Across from him, Sarah felt her pulse give a kick—when Bastiaan looked at her like that it was hard to respond in any other way. Lunch had been idyllic. Simple *charcuterie* and *fromage*, with huge scarlet tomatoes and more of the luscious peaches they'd had the other day. It had felt a little odd to be here again, receiving such intimacy from Bastiaan.

Has it really happened? Am I really here with Bastiaan, and are we lovers?

But it was true—it really was—and for the rest of this glorious week it could go on being true.

A rich, sensuous languor swept through her as his gaze twined with hers. A wicked sparkle glinted in her own.

'The pool looks irresistible…' she murmured provocatively.

She almost heard him growl with frustration, but gallantly he nodded. 'It does indeed—especially with you in it.' His eyes glinted too. 'Do you want me to guide you back to the room you changed in last time? Or—' and now there was even more of a wickedly intimate glint in his eyes '—shall we dispense with swimsuits altogether?'

She laughed in answer, and disappeared off to change. Maybe they could go skinny-dipping at night, under the stars...?

The water was wonderfully refreshing, and so was Bastiaan's company. There was a lot of playful frolicking, and from her more covert—and not so covert—appreciation of his strong, muscled physique. A thrill went through her. For now—for this brief, precious time—he was hers. How wonderful was that?

Very wonderful—and more than wonderful: incredible.

It was incredible when, on retiring to the bedroom in the villa to shower in the en-suite bathroom, she discovered Bastiaan could wait no longer.

He stepped inside the shower, hands slicking down her wet, tingling body. She gasped in shock and then in arousal as skilfully, urgently and devastatingly he took possession of her. As her legs wrapped around him and he lifted her up her head fell back in ecstasy, and it seemed to her that she had been transformed into a different person. A person who was neither the sultry Sabine nor the soprano Sarah, but someone whose only existence was to meld herself with this incredible, sensual male, to fuse her body with his, to burn with him in an explosion of physical pleasure and delight.

Afterwards, as they stood exhausted, with the cooling water streaming over them, her breath coming in hectic pants, he cut the shower, reached for huge fleecy towels and wrapped her up as if she were a precious parcel.

He let his hands rest over her damp shoulders, his eyes pouring down into hers. 'What do you do to me?' he asked. There was a strange quality in his voice, a strange expression in his dark eyes.

She let her forehead rest on his chest, the huge lassitude of the aftermath of passion consuming her now. She could not answer him for it was a question that was in her own being too.

He swung her up into his arms, carried her through into the bedroom, lowering her down upon the cool cotton coverlet, coming down beside her. He drew her into his sheltering embrace, kissed her nape with soft, velvet kisses. And then exhausted, sated, complete, they slept.

When they awoke they made love again, slowly and softly, taking their time—all the time in the world—in the shuttered late-afternoon light of the cool room. And this time Bastiaan brought her to a different kind of ecstasy—a slow, blissful release that flowed through her body like sweet water after drought.

Afterwards they lay a little while in each other's loose embrace, and then Bastiaan lifted his head from the pillow.

'I know,' he told her, 'a great way to watch the sunset.'

It was indeed, Sarah discovered, a wonderful way to watch the sunset.

He took her out to sea in a fast, sleek motor launch that they boarded from the little quay at the rocky shore below the villa. Exhilaration filled her as Bastiaan carved a foaming wake in the darkening cobalt water, the sun low on the surface, turning the Mediterranean to gold as it kissed the swell.

He cut the engine, letting the silence settle around them, and she sat next to him, his arm casually around her shoulder, his body warm against hers. She could feel the gentle bob of the waves beneath the hull, feel the warmth of the sun on her face as she lifted it to its lingering rays. It was as if they were the only people in the world. Here out on the water, with Bastiaan's arm around her, she felt as if all that lay beyond had ceased to be.

Here there were no complications.

Here there was only Bastiaan.

What is happening to me?

The question wound in her mind between the circuits of her thoughts, seeking an answer she was not ready to find. It was far easier simply to go on sitting there, with the warm air like an embrace, the hugeness of the sea all around them, the rich gold of the setting sun illuminating them. This—now—was good. This was all she wanted. This was her contentment.

They headed back to shore in the gathering dusk.

'Would you like to eat out or at the villa?' Bastiaan asked.

'Oh, don't go out,' she said immediately. Then frowned. 'But I'm not very good at cooking, and I don't want you to have to...' she said uncertainly. Could a man like Bastiaan Karavalas really cook a meal?

He gave a laugh. 'We'll have something delivered,' he told her. 'What would you like?'

'Pizza?' she suggested.

He laughed again. 'Oh, I think we can do better than that,' he said.

And indeed they could.

On the Côte d'Azur, when money was no object, it seemed that gourmet meals could be conjured out of thin air.

As she took her place at the table on the terrace, in the warm evening air, it was to discover that a team of servers had arrived from a nearby Michelin-starred restaurant and were setting out their exquisite wares.

She and Bastiaan had already shared a glass of champagne before the meal arrived, and she felt its effervescence in her veins. Now, as the team from the restaurant departed, Bastiaan lifted a glass of rich, ruby Burgundy.

'To our time together,' he said. It was the same toast he'd given the night before, at Le Tombleur.

Sarah raised her own glass.

Our time together...these few precious days... She felt emotion pluck at her.

From his seat, Bastiaan rested his eyes on her. She looked nothing like she had the night before when they had dined. And he was glad of it. She was wearing a pale blue kimono that he had found in a closet. In sheerest silk, it was knotted at the waist and had wide sleeves, a plunging neckline that gave the merest hint of the sweet swell of her breasts. Her glorious hair was loose, cascading down her back. She wore no make-up. Needed not a scrap of it.

How beautiful she is. How much I desire her!

He tried to remember why it was he had seduced her. Tried to remember his fears for Philip. Tried to remember how he had determined to foil her machinations. But his memory seemed dim. Flawed.

As he gazed on her they seemed unreal, those fears. Absurd...

Did I misjudge her?

That was the question that uncoiled itself in his

mind. The question that pressed itself against his consciousness. The question which, with every passing moment he spent with her, seemed more and more...*unnecessary.*

Thoughts flitted through his mind. What evidence, after all, *was* there against her? Oh, Philip was lovestruck—that was undeniable. His every yearning gaze told Bastiaan that. But what of her? What of her behaviour towards Philip?

I thought her nothing more than a blatant gold-digger—trying to exploit Philip's youth and vulnerability. But is she—was she?

I thought that she had blatantly switched her attentions to me—had manoeuvred me to get rid of Philip from the scene.

But why, then, had she been so reluctant to go with him when he'd sought her out on his return from Paris? And why had she fled from him in his apartment that first morning? If she'd been no better than he'd thought her, wanting him for his wealth, she should have clung to him like glue. Not wept by the quayside while he'd searched so urgently for her.

Was that the behaviour of the woman he'd thought her to be? It couldn't be—it just *couldn't.*

There is no evidence against her. From the very start she has confounded my suspicions of her— time after time. All I have to go on, other than my fears for Philip, is that payment that he made.

That was the truth of it. Had he been conjecturing everything else about her? Feeding his suspicions simply because he'd wanted to protect his young cousin? He took a breath, fixed his eyes on her as she lifted her wine glass to answer his toast, looked across at him and smiled—her eyes like incandescent jewels, rich and glowing.

Emotion leapt in him, and in his head he heard his own voice, searing across his thoughts.

There could be an explanation for why Philip paid out that money. All I have to do is ask him. There is no reason—none—to fear that it was to Sabine. She could be completely innocent of the suspicions I've had of her.

As innocent as he wanted her to be. Wanted so much for her to be…

'To us,' he said, and let his eyes mingle and meld with hers—the eyes of this woman who could be everything he wanted her to be. And nothing he did not.

From this moment on he would not let his

fears, his suspicions, poison him. Would not let anything spoil his enjoyment of this moment, this time with her.

And nothing did—that was the bliss of it. Cocooned with her at the villa, he made love to her by day and by night—and *every* time it took him by storm. A storm not only of the senses but of something more.

What is it you do to me?

That was the question that came every time she lay cradled in his arms, her head on his chest, her arm like a silken bond around his waist, her body warm and flushed with passion spent.

The question had no answer—and soon he did not seek an answer. Soon he was content simply to let the hours pass with her. Time came and went, the sun rose and set, the stars wheeled in the clear sky each night as they lay out on the pool loungers, gazing upwards, hand in hand, the cool midnight breeze whispering over their bodies, the moon rising to cast its silver light upon them.

Who *was* this woman? Bastiaan asked of himself, thinking of all that he knew of her. It no longer seemed to matter. Not any more.

Sometimes he caught fragments of her life—a passing mention of the garden at a house in Normandy where, so he surmised, she must have grown up. The climate and the terrain so different from this sun-baked southern shore. Once he tried to draw her out about her singing, but she only shook her head and changed the subject with a smile, a kiss.

Nor did she talk to him about *his* life—only asked him about Greece. How it was to live there, with so much history, the history of millennia, pressing all around him. Of how he made his money, his wealth, she never spoke. She seemed quite oblivious to it. She did not ask to leave the villa—was content to spend each day within its confining beauty.

Meals were delivered, or concocted by them both—simple, hearty food, from salads and *charcuterie* to pasta and barbecues, prepared with much laughter and consumed with appetite. An appetite that afterwards turned to passion for each other.

I didn't know it would be like this—having Sabine with me. I didn't think it would be this... this good.

He tried to think back to a time when it had not been like this—when Sabine had not been with him, when all he'd had were his fears for Philip, his suspicions of her. But it seemed very far away—blurring in his head. Fading more and more with each hour. All that mattered to him now was being as they were now, lying side by side beneath the stars, hand in hand.

He felt her thumb move sensuously, lightly over his as their clasped hands hung loosely between them. He turned his head towards her, away from the moon above. She was gazing across at him, her face dim in the moonlight, her eyes resting on him. There was a softness in her face, in her eyes…

'Bastiaan…' Her voice was low, a sweet caress.

His eyes found hers. Desire reached into his veins. He drew her to her feet and wound his fingers into hers. Speared his hand into her hair, let his mouth find hers.

Passion, strong and sweet and true, flared at his touch. Drove them indoors to find each other, again, and yet again, in this perfect, blissful time they had together.

CHAPTER NINE

'MY *PENSION* IS just there,' Sarah said, pointing to the corner of the street. 'I won't be five minutes.'

Bastiaan pulled the car over to the kerb and she dashed inside. She wanted to change into something pretty for the day. They were finally emerging from the villa, and Bastiaan was set on taking her to a place he was amazed she hadn't seen yet.

The picturesque little town of St Paul de Vence, up in the hills behind the coastline, was famous as a place frequented by artists. She was happy enough to go there—happy enough to be any-where in the world right now, providing Bastiaan was with her and she with him.

Bastiaan. Oh, the name soared in her head, echoed deep inside her. She was seizing all that he was holding out to her so that there was noth-ing else except being with him, day after precious day, night after searing night.

It's as if I were asleep and he has woken me. Woken my senses, set them alight.

In her head, in her heart, emotion hovered like a fragile bubble, iridescent and glistening with light and colour. A bubble she longed to seize but dared not—not now, not yet. But it filled her being, made her breathless with delight, with joy. Joy that brought a smile to her face now, as she ran into the *pension*, eager to be as quick as possible so she could re-join Bastiaan without delay.

Five minutes later she was running down the stairs again, pausing only to snatch at the mail in her room's pigeonhole, dropping the envelopes into her handbag before emerging out onto the roadway. She jumped into the car and off they set.

Bastiaan's gaze was warm upon her before he focussed on the way ahead.

She's changed her image yet again, he found himself thinking. This one he liked particularly, he decided. Her hair was in a long plait, her make-up no more than a touch of mascara and lip gloss, and her skin had been warmed by the sun of the past few days to a golden honey. Her outfit was a pretty floral calf-length sundress in

pale blue and yellow. She looked fresh and sum-
mery and beautiful.

And *his*. Oh, most definitely, definitely his!

Emotion surged within him. What it was, he
didn't know—and didn't care. Knew only that it
felt good—*so* good...

The route out of the *ville* took them past the
nightclub where she sang. As they drove by he
saw her throw it a sideways glance, almost looking at it askance, before turning swiftly away. He
was glad to have passed it too—did not want to
think about it. It jarred with everything that was
filling him now.

He shook his head, as if to clear it of unwelcome thoughts. At the villa, safe in its cocoon,
the outside world had seemed far, far away. All
that belonged in it far, far away.

Well, he would not think of it. He would think
only of the day ahead of them. A day to be spent
in togetherness, on an excursion, with lunch in a
beautiful place, a scenic drive through the hin-
terland behind the coast.

The traffic lights ahead turned red and he
slowed down to a halt, using the opportunity to
glance at Sabine beside him. She was busying

herself looking at the contents of an envelope she'd taken out of the bag on her lap. It was, he could see, a bill from the *pension*. She gave it a cursory check, replaced it in her bag, then took out another envelope. Bastiaan could see it had a French stamp on it, but she was turning it over to open it, so he could not see the writing on the front.

As she ripped it open and glanced inside she gave a little crow of pleasure. 'Oh, how sweet of him!'

Then, with a sudden biting of her lip, she hurriedly stuffed the envelope back inside her handbag, shutting it with a snap.

Abruptly the traffic lights changed, the car behind him sounded its horn impatiently, and Bastiaan had to move off. But in the few seconds that it took a chill had gone down inside him.

Had he really seen what he'd thought he'd seen?

Had that been a cheque inside that envelope?

He threw a covert sideways glance at her, but she was placing her bag in the footwell, then getting out her phone and texting someone, a happy smile playing around her mouth.

Bastiaan found he was revving the engine, his

hands clenching momentarily around the steering wheel. Then, forcibly, he put the sudden burst of cold anger out of his head. Why should Sabine *not* receive mail? And if that mail were from a man what business was it of his? She might know any number of men. Very likely did…

Another emotion stabbed at him. One he had not experienced before. One he never had cause to experience. Rigorously, he pushed it aside. Refused to allow his mind to dwell on the question that was trying to make itself heard. He would *not* speculate on just who might be sending her correspondence that she regarded as 'sweet.' He would not.

He risked another sideways glance at her as he steered through the traffic. She was still on her phone, scrolling through messages. As his gaze went back to the road he heard her give a soft chuckle, start to tap a reply immediately.

Bastiaan flicked his eyes towards her phone screen, hard though it was to see it from this angle and in the brightness of the sun. In the seconds his glance took a face on the screen impinged—or did it? It was gone as she touched the screen to send her message, but he could feel his hands clenching on the wheel again.

Had that been Philip?

The thought was in his head before he could stop it. He forced it out. It had been impossible to recognise the fleeting photo. It could have been anyone. *Anyone.* He would not let his imagination run riot. His fears run riot...

Instead he would focus only on the day ahead. A leisurely drive to St Paul de Vence...strolling hand in hand through its narrow pretty streets, thronged with tourists but charming all the same. Focus only on the easy companionable rightness of having Sabine at his side, looking so lovely as she was today, turning men's heads all around and making a glow of happy possession fill him.

It would be a simple, uncomplicated day together, just like the days they'd spent together at his villa. Nothing would intrude on his happiness.

Into his head flickered the image of her glancing at the contents of that envelope in her lap. He heard again her little crow of pleasure. Saw in his mind the telltale printing on the small piece of paper she'd been looking at...

No!

He would not think about that—*he would not.*
Leave it be. It has nothing to do with you. Let
your suspicions of her go—let go completely.

Resolutely he pushed it from his mind, lifting
his free hand to point towards the entrance to
the famous hotel where they were going to have
lunch. She was delighted by it—delighted by everything. Her face alight with pleasure and happiness.

Across the table from him Sarah gazed glow-
ingly at him. She knew every contour of his face,
every expression in his eyes, every touch of his
mouth upon her…

Her gaze flickered. Shadowed. There was a
catch in her throat. Emerging from the villa had
been like waking from a dream. Seeing the outside world all around her. Being reminded of its
existence. Even just driving past the nightclub
had plucked at her.

The days—the nights—she'd spent with Bastiaan had blotted out everything completely. But
now—even here, sitting with people all around

them—the world was pressing in upon her again. Calling time on them.

Tomorrow she must leave him. Go back to Max. Go back to being Sarah again. Emotion twisted inside her. This time with Bastiaan had been beyond amazing—it had been like nothing she had ever known. *He* was like no man she had ever known.

But what am I to him?

That was the question that shaped itself as they set off after lunch, his powerful, expensive car snaking its way back towards Cap Pierre. The question that pierced her like an arrow. She thought of how she'd assumed that a man like him would be interested only in a sophisticated seductive affair—a passionately sensual encounter with a woman like Sabine.

Was that still what she thought?

The answer blazed in her head.

I don't want it to be just that. I don't want to be just Sabine to him. I want to be the person I really am—I want to be Sarah.

But did she dare? That was what it came down to. As Sabine she had the protection of her persona—that of a woman who could deal with transient affairs…the kind a man like Bastiaan would want.

Would he still want me if I were Sarah?

Or was this burning passion, this intensity of desire, the only thing he wanted? He had said nothing of anything other than enjoying each hour with her—had not spoken of how long he wanted this to last or what it meant to him, nor anything at all of that nature.

Is this time all he wants of me?

There seemed to be a heaviness inside her, weighing her down. She stole a sideways look at Bastiaan. He was focussed on the road, which was building up with traffic now as they neared Nice. She felt her insides give a little skip as her gaze eagerly drank in his strong, incisive profile—and then there was a tearing feeling in its place.

I don't want to leave him. I don't want this to end. It's been way, way too short!

But what could she do? Nothing—that was all. Her future was mapped out for her and it did not include any more time with Bastiaan.

Who might not want to spend it with her anyway. Who might only want what they were having now. And if that were so—if all he'd wanted all along was a kind of fleeting affair with Sabine—then she must accept it.

Sabine would be able to handle a brief affair like this—so I must be Sabine still.

As Sarah she was far too vulnerable...

She took a breath, steeling herself. Her time with Bastiaan was not yet up—not quite. There was still tonight—still one more precious night together....

And perhaps she was fearing the worst—perhaps he wanted more than this brief time.

Her thoughts raced ahead, borne on a tide of emotion that swelled out of her on wings of hope. Perhaps he would rejoice to find out she was Sarah. Would stand by her all through her final preparations for the festival—share her rejoicing if they were successful or comfort her if she failed and had to accept that she would never become the professional singer she had set her sights on being.

Like an underground fire running through the root systems of a forest, she felt emotions flare within her. What they were she dared not say. Must not give name to.

Right man—wrong time...for now...

But after the festival Bastiaan might just become someone to her who would be so much more than this incandescent brief encounter.

'Shall we stop here in Nice for a while?'

Bastiaan's voice interrupted her troubled thoughts, bringing her back to the moment.

'They have some good shops,' he said invitingly.

The dress she was wearing was pretty, but it was not a designer number by any means. Nor were any of the clothes she wore—including that over-revealing evening gown she wore to sing in. He found himself wanting to know just how a dress suitable for her beauty would enhance her. Splashing out on a wardrobe for her would be a pleasure he would enjoy. And shopping with her would keep at bay any unnecessary temptation to worry about the cheque she had exclaimed over. He would not think about it—would not harbour any suspicions.

I'm done with such suspicions. I will banish them—not let them poison me again.

But she shook her head at his suggestion. 'No, there's nothing I need,' she answered. She did not want to waste time shopping—she wanted to get back to the villa. To be with Bastiaan alone in the last few dwindling hours before she had to go.

He smiled at her indulgently. 'But much, surely, that you *want*?'

She gave a laugh. She would not spoil this last day with him by being unhappy, by letting in the world she didn't want to think about. 'What woman doesn't?' was her rejoinder.

Then, suddenly, her tone changed. Something in that world she didn't want to let in yet demanded her attention. Attention she must give it—right now.

'Oh, actually…could we stop for five minutes? Just along here? There's something I've remembered.'

Bastiaan glanced at her. She was indicating a side street off the main thoroughfare. Maybe she needed toiletries. But as he turned the car towards where she indicated, a slight frown creased his forehead. There was something familiar about the street name. He wondered why—where he had seen it recently.

Then she was pointing again. 'Just there!' she cried.

He pulled across to the pavement, looked where

she was pointing, and with an icy rush cold snaked down his spine.

'I won't be a moment,' she said as she got out of the car. Her expression was smiling, untroubled. Then, with a brief wave to him, she hurried into the building.

It was a bank. And Bastiaan knew, with ice congealing in his veins, exactly which bank it was—a branch of the bank that Philip's cheque for twenty thousand euros had been paid into...

And in his head, imprinted like a laser image, he saw again the telltale shape of the contents of that envelope she'd opened in the car that morning, which had caused her to give a crow of pleasure. Another cheque that he knew with deadly certainty she was now paying into the very same account...

A single word seared across his consciousness with all the force of a dagger striking into his very guts.

Fool!

He shut his eyes, feeling cold in every cell of his body.

'All done!' Sarah's voice was bright as she got back into the low-slung car. She was glad to have completed her task—glad she'd remembered in time. But what did *not* gladden her was having had to remember to do it at all. Letting reality impose itself upon her. The reality she would be facing tomorrow...

Conflict filled her. How could she want to stay here as Sabine—with Bastiaan—when Sarah awaited her in the morning? Yet how could she bear to leave Bastiaan—walk away from him and from the bliss she had found with him? Even though all the hopes and dreams of her life were waiting for her to fulfil them...

I want them both!

The cry came from within. Making her eyes anguished. Her heart clench.

She felt the car move off and turned to gaze at Bastiaan as he drove. He'd put on dark glasses while she'd been in the bank, and for a moment—just a moment—she felt that he was someone else. He seemed preoccupied, but the traffic in the middle of Nice was bad, so she did not speak until they were well clear and heading east towards Cap Pierre.

'I can't wait to take a dip in the pool,' she said lightly. She stole a glance at him. 'Fancy a skinny-dip this time?' She spoke teasingly. She wanted to see him smile, wanted the set expression on his face to ease. Wanted her own mood, which had become drawn and aching, to lighten.

He didn't answer—only gave a brief acknowledging smile, as fleeting as it was absent, and turned off the main coastal route to take the road heading towards Pierre-les-Pins.

She let him focus on the road, her own mood strained still, and getting more so with every passing moment. Going through Pierre-les-Pins was harder still, knowing that she must be there tomorrow—her time with Bastiaan over.

Her gaze went to him as he drove. She wanted, needed, to drink him in while she could. Desire filled her, quickening in her veins as she gazed at his face in profile, wanting to reach out and touch, even though he was driving and she must not. His expression was still set and there was no casual conversation, only this strained atmosphere. As if he were feeling what she was feeling...

But how could he be? He knew nothing of what she must do tomorrow—nothing of why she must leave him, the reality she must return to.

Urgency filled her suddenly. *I have to tell him—tell him I am Sarah, not Sabine. Have to explain why...*

And she must do it tonight—of course she must. When else? Tomorrow morning she would be heading back to the *ville*, ready to resume rehearsals. How could she hide that from him? Even if he still wanted her as Sarah she could spend no more time with him now—not with the festival so close. Not with so much work for her yet to do.

A darker thought assailed her. Did he even *want* more time with her—whether as Sarah or Sabine? Was this, for him, the last day he wanted with her? Had he done with her? Was he even now planning on telling her that their time together was over—that he was leaving France, returning to his own life in Greece?

Her eyes flickered. His features were drawn, with deep lines around his mouth, his jaw tense.

Is he getting ready to end this now?

The ache inside her intensified.

As they walked back inside the villa he caught her hand, stayed her progress. She halted, turning to him. He tossed his sunglasses aside, dropping them on a console table in the hallway. His eyes blazed at her.

Her breath caught—the intensity in his gaze stopped the air in her lungs—and then, hauling her to him, he lowered his mouth to hers with hungry, devouring passion.

She went up like dry tinder. It was a conflagration to answer his, like petrol thrown on a bonfire. Desperation was in her desire. Exultation at his desire for her.

In moments they were in the bedroom, shedding clothes, entwining limbs, passions roused, stroked and heightened in an urgency of desire to be fulfilled, slaked.

In a storm of sensation she reached the pinnacle of her arousal, hips straining to maximise his possession of her. His body was slicked with the sheen of physical ardour as her nails dug into his muscled shoulders and time after time he brought her to yet more exquisite pleasure. She cried out, as if the sensation was veering on the unbearable, so intense was her body's climax. His own was as dramatic—a great shuddering of his straining body, the cords of his neck exposed as he lifted his head, eyes blind with passion. One last eruption of their bodies and then it was over, as though a thunderstorm had passed over a mountain peak.

She lay beneath him, panting, exhausted, her conscious mind dazed and incoherent. She gazed up at him, her eyes wide with a kind of wonder that she could not comprehend. The wildness of their union, the urgency of his possession, of the response he'd summoned from her, had been almost shocking to her. Physical bliss that she had never yet experienced.

And yet she needed now, in the aftermath, to have him hold her close, to cradle her in his arms, to transform their wildness to comfort and tenderness. But as she gazed upwards she saw that there was still that blindness in his eyes.

Was he still caught there, on that mountain peak they'd reached together, stranded in the physical storm of their union? She searched his features, trying to understand, trying to still the tumult in her own breast, where her heart was only slowly climbing down from its hectic beating.

Confusion filled her—more than confusion. That same darkening, disquieting unease that had started as they'd driven back from Nice. She wanted him to say something—anything. Wanted him to wrap his arms about her, hold her as he always did after the throes of passion.

But he did no such thing. Abruptly he was pulling away from her, rising up off the bed and heading into the en-suite bathroom.

As the door closed behind him an aching, anxious feeling of bereavement filled her. Unease mixed with her confusion, with her mounting disquiet. She got out of bed, swaying a moment, her body still feeling the aftermath of what it had experienced. Her hair was still in its plait, but it was dishevelled from their passion. Absently she smoothed it with her hands. She found that they were trembling. With the same shaky motion she groped for her clothes, scattered on the floor, tangled up with his.

From the bathroom came the sound of the shower, but nothing else.

Dressed, she made her way into the kitchen. Took a drink of water from the fridge. Tried to recover her calm.

But she could not. Whatever had happened between them it was not good. How could it be?

He's ending it.

Those were the words that tolled in her brain. The only words that could make sense of how he was being. He was ending it and looking to find a way of doing so. He would not wish to wound her, hurt her. He would find an...*acceptable* way to tell her. He would probably say something about having to go back to Athens. Maybe he had other commitments she knew nothing about. Maybe...

Her thoughts were jumping all over the place, as if on a hot plate. She tried to gather them to-gether, to come to terms with them. Then a sound impinged—her phone, ringing from inside her bag, abandoned in the hallway when Bastiaan had swept her to him.

Absently she fished it out. Saw that it was Max. Saw it go to voicemail.

She stared blindly at the phone as she listened to his message. He sounded fraught, under pres-sure.

'Sarah—I'm really sorry. I need you to be Sa-bine tonight. I can't placate Raymond any longer. Can you make it? I'm really sorry—' He rang off.

She didn't phone back. Couldn't. All she could

do was start to press the keys with nerveless fingers, texting her reply. Brief, but sufficient.

OK.

But it wasn't OK. It wasn't at all.

She glanced around the kitchen, spotted a pad
of paper by the phone on the wall. She crossed
to it, tore off a piece and numbly wrote on it,
then tucked it by the coffee machine that was
spluttering coffee into the jug. She picked up her
bag and went out into the hallway, looked into
the bedroom. The tangled bedclothes, Bastiaan's
garments on the floor, were blatant testimony to
what had happened there so short a while ago.

An eternity ago.

There was no sign of Bastiaan. The shower was
still running.

She had to go. Right now. Because she could
not bear to stay there and have Bastiaan tell her
it was over.

Slowly, with a kind of pain netting around her,
her mind numb, she turned and left the villa.

Bastiaan cut the shower, seizing a towel to wrap
himself in. He had to go back into the bedroom.

He could delay it no longer. He didn't want to. He didn't want to see her again.

Wanted to wipe her from existence.

How could I have believed her to be innocent? How could I?

He knew the answer—knew it with shuddering emotion.

Because I wanted her to be innocent—I didn't want her to have taken Philip's money, didn't want it to be true!

That was what was tearing through him, ripping at him with sharpest talons. Ripping his illusions from him.

Fool! Fool that he had been!

He closed his eyes in blind rage. In front of his very eyes she'd waltzed into that bank in Nice, paid in whatever it was she'd taken from Philip—or another man. It didn't matter which. The same branch of that bank—the very same. A coincidence? How could it be?

A snarl sounded in his throat.

Had that cheque she'd paid in this afternoon been from Philip too? Had that postmark been from Paris? Had it been his writing on the envelope? His expression changed. The envelope would still be in her bag, even if the cheque were not. That would be all the proof he needed.

Is she hoping to take me for even more?

The thought was in his head like a dagger before he could stop it. Was that what was behind her ardency, her passion?

The passion that burns between us even now, even right to the bitter end...

Self-hatred lashed at him. How could he have done what he'd just done? Swept her to bed as he had, knowing what she truly was? But he'd been driven by an urge so strong he hadn't been able to stop himself—an urge to possess her one final time...

One final time to recapture all that they'd had—all he'd thought they'd had.

It had never been there at all.

The dagger thrust again, into the core of his being.

He wrenched open the door.

She was not there. The rumpled bed was empty. Her clothes gone.

Emotion rushed into the sudden void in his head like air into a vacuum. But quite what the emotion was he didn't know. All he knew was that he was striding out of the room, with nothing more than a towel snaked around his hips, wondering where the hell she'd got to.

For a numb, timeless moment he just stood in the hallway, registering that her handbag was gone too, so he would not be able to check the writing on the envelope. Then, from the kitchen, he heard the sound of the coffee machine spluttering.

He walked towards it, seeing that the room was empty. Seeing the note by the coffee jug. Reading it with preternatural calm.

Bastiaan—we've had the most unforgettable time. Thank you for every moment.

It was simply signed 'S.'

That was all.

He dropped it numbly. Turned around, headed back to the bedroom. So she was walking out on him. Had the sum of money she'd extracted this time been sufficient for her to afford to be able to do so? That was what Leana had done. Cashed his cheque and headed off with her next mark, her geriatric protector, laughing at the idiot she'd fooled and left behind.

His mouth tightened. Well, things were different now. *Very* different. Sabine did not know that he was Philip's trustee, that he knew what she had taken and could learn if she'd taken yet more today. She had no reason not to think herself safe.

Is she still hoping to take more from Philip?

Memory played in his head—how Philip had asked him to loosen the purse strings of his main fund before his birthday—how evasive he'd been about what he wanted the money for. All the suspicions he'd so blindly set aside leapt again.

Grim-faced, he went to fetch his laptop.

And there it was—right in his email inbox. A communication today, direct from one of Philip's investment managers, requesting Bastiaan's approval—or not—for Philip's instruction to liquidate a particular fund. The liquidation would release over two hundred thousand euros…

Two hundred thousand euros. Enough to free Sabine for ever from warbling in a second-rate nightclub.

He slammed the laptop lid down. Fury was leaping in his throat.

Was that what Philip had texted her about? Bastiaan hadn't been mistaken in recognizing him as the sender—he could not have been. Was that why she'd given that soft, revealing chuckle? Was that why she'd bolted now, switching her allegiance back to Philip?

Rage boiled in Bastiaan's breast. Well, that would never happen—*never*! She would *never* go back to Philip.

She can burn in hell before she gets that money from him!

His lips stretched into a travesty of a smile. She thought herself safe—but Sabine Sablon was *not* safe. She was not safe at all…

And she would discover that very, very shortly.

CHAPTER TEN

SARAH REACHED FOR the second false eyelash. Glued it, like the first, with shaky hands. She was going through the motions—nothing more. Hammers seemed to be in her brain, hammering her flat. Mashing everything inside her. Misery assailed her. She shouldn't be feeling it—but she was. Oh, she was.

It was over. Her time with Bastiaan was over. A few precious days—and now this.

Reality had awaited her. Max had greeted her with relief—and apology. And with some news that had pierced the misery in her.

'This is your last night here. Raymond insisted you show up just for tonight—because it's Friday and he can't be without a singer—but from tomorrow you're officially replaced. Not with the real Sabine—someone else he's finally found. And then, thank God, we can all decamp. We've been given an earlier rehearsal spot at the festival so we can head there straight away.'

He'd said nothing else, had asked no questions. Had only cast an assessing look at her, seeing the withdrawal in her face. She was glad of it, and of the news he'd given her. Relief, as much as she could feel anything through the fog of misery encompassing her, resonated in her. Now there was only tonight to get through. How she would do it, she didn't know—but it would have to happen.

As she finished putting on her lipstick with shaky hands she could feel hope lighting inside her. Refusing to be quenched. *Was* it over? Perhaps it wasn't. Oh, perhaps Bastiaan *hadn't* been intending to end it all. Perhaps she'd feared it quite unnecessarily. Perhaps, even now, he was missing her, coming after her...

No! She couldn't afford to agonise over whether Bastiaan had finished with her. Couldn't afford to hope and dream that he hadn't. Couldn't afford even to let her mind go where it so wanted to go—to relive, hour by hour, each moment she'd spent with him.

I can't afford to want him—or miss him.

She stared at her reflection. Sabine was more alien than ever now. And as she did so, the door of her dressing room was thrust open. Her head flew round, and as her gaze fell upon the tall, dark figure standing there, her face lit, joy and relief flaring in her eyes. Bastiaan! He had come after her—he was not ending it with her! He still wanted her! Her heart soared.

But as she looked up at him she froze. There was something wrong—something wrong with his face. His eyes. The way he was standing there, dominating the small space. His face was dark, his eyes like granite. He was like nothing she had seen before. This was not the Bastiaan she knew…not Bastiaan at all…

'I have something to say to you.'

Bastiaan's voice was harsh. Hostile. His eyes were dark and veiled, as if a screen had dropped down over them.

Her heart started to hammer. That dark, veiled gaze pressed down on her. Hostility radiated from him like a force field. It felt like a physical blow. What was happening? Why was he looking at her like this? She didn't know—didn't understand.

A moment later the answer came—an answer that was incomprehensible.

'From now on stay away from Philip. It's over. Do you understand me? *Over!*' His voice was harsh, accusing. Condemning.

She didn't understand. Could only go on sitting there, staring at him, emotion surging through her chaotically. Then, as his words sank in, a frown convulsed her face.

'Philip?' she said blankly.

A rasp of a laugh—without humour, soon cut short—broke from him. 'Forgotten him already, have you? Well, then…' and now his voice took on a different note—one that seemed to chill her deep inside '…it seems my efforts were not in vain. I have succeeded, it seems, in…*distracting* you, *mademoiselle.*' He paused heavily and his eyes were stabbing at her now. 'As I intended.'

His chest rose and fell, and then he was speaking again.

'But do not flatter yourself that my…*attentions* were for any purpose other than to convince you that my cousin is no longer yours to manipulate.'

She was staring at him as if he were insane. But he would not be halted. Not now, when fury was coursing through his veins—as it had done since the veils had been ripped from his eyes—since he'd understood just how much a fool she'd made of him. Not Philip—*him!*

I so nearly fell for it—was so nearly convinced by her.

Anger burned in him. Anger at her—for taking him for a fool, for exploiting his trusting, sensitive cousin and for not being the woman he'd come to believe, to hope, that she was.

The woman I wanted her to be.

The irony of it was exquisite. He'd seduced her because he'd believed her guilty—then had no longer been able to believe that she was. Then all that had been ripped and up-ended again—back to guilt.

A guilt he no longer wanted her to have, but from which there could be no escape now. *None.*

He cut across his own perilous thoughts with a snarl. 'Don't play the innocent. If you think you can still exploit his emotional vulnerability to you…well, think again.'

His voice became harsh and ugly, his mouth curling, eyes filled with venom.

'You see, I have only to tell him how you have

warmed *my* bed these last days for his infatuation to be over in an instant. Your power over him extinguished.'

The air in her lungs was like lead. His words were like blows. Her features contorted.

'Are you saying…?' She could hardly force the words from her through the pain, through the shock that had exploded inside her, 'Are you saying that you seduced me in order to…to separate me from Philip?' There was disbelief in her voice. Disbelief on so many levels.

'You have it precisely,' he said heavily, with sardonic emphasis. 'Oh, surely you did not believe I would not take action to protect my cousin from women of your kind?'

She swallowed. It was like a razor in her throat. 'My kind…?'

'Look at yourself, Sabine. A woman of the world—isn't that the phrase? Using her *talents*—' deliberately he mocked the word she'd used herself when she'd first learnt who he was '—to make her way in the world. And if those *talents*—' the mockery intensified '—include catching men with your charms, then good luck to you.' His voice hardened like the blade of a

knife. 'Unless you set your sights on a vulnerable stripling like my cousin—then I will wish
you only to perdition! And ensure you go there.'

His voice changed again.

'So, do you understand the situation now? From
now on content yourself with the life you have—
singing cheap, tawdry songs in a cheap, tawdry
club.'

His eyes blazed like coals from the pit as he
gave his final vicious condemnation of her.

'A two-cent *chanteuse* with more body than
voice. That is all that you are good for. Nothing
else!'

One last skewering of his contemptuous gaze,
one last twist of his deriding mouth, and he
was turning on his heel, walking out. She could
hear his footsteps—heavy, damning—falling
away.

Her mouth fell open, the rush of air into her
lungs choking her. Emotion convulsed her. And
then, as if fuse had been lit, she jerked to her feet.
She charged out of the dressing room, but he was
already stepping through the door that separated
the front of house from backstage. She whirled
about, driven forward on the emotion boiling up

inside her. A moment later she was in the wings at the side of the stage, seizing Max by the arm, propelling him forward.

Anger such as she had never felt before in her life, erupted in her. She thrust Max towards the piano beside the centre spot where her microphone was. She hurled it into the wings, then turned back to Max.

'Play "Der Hölle Rache".'

Max stared at her as if she were mad. *'What?'*

'Play it! Or I am on the next plane to London!'

She could see Bastiaan, threading his way across the dining room, moving towards the exit. The room was busy, but there was only one person she was going to sing for. Only one—and he could burn in hell!

Max's gaze followed hers and his expression changed. She saw his hands shape themselves over the opening chord, and with a last snatch of sanity took the breath she needed for herself. And then, as Max's hands crashed down on the keyboard, she stepped forward into the pool of light. Centre stage.

And launched into furious, excoriating, maximum *tessitura*, her full-powered *coloratura*

soprano voice exploding into the space in front
of her to find its target.

Bastiaan could see the exit—a dozen tables or so
away. He had to get out of here, get into his car
and drive...drive far and fast. *Very* fast.

He'd done it. He'd done what he'd had to do—
what he'd set out to do from that afternoon in
Athens when his aunt had come to see him, to
beg him to save her precious young son from
the toils of a dangerous *femme fatale*. And save
him he had.

Saved more than just his cousin.

I have saved myself.

No!

He would not think that—would not accept it.
Would only make for the exit.

He reached the door. Made to push it open angrily with the flat of his hand.

And then, from behind him, came a crash of
chords that stopped him.

He froze.

'Der Hölle Rache.' The most fiendishly difficult soprano aria by Mozart. Fiendish for its crip-
plingly punishing high notes, for the merciless

fury of its delivery. An aria whose music and lyrics boiled with coruscating rage as *Die Zauberflöte*'s 'Queen of the Night' poured out seething venom against her bitter enemy.

'Hell's vengeance boils in my heart!'

Like a remotely operated robot, turning against his will, Bastiaan felt his body twist.

It was impossible. Impossible that this stabbing, biting, fury of a voice should be emanating from the figure on the stage. Absolutely, totally impossible.

Because the figure on the stage was *Sabine*. Sabine—with her tight sheath of a gown, her *femme fatale* blonde allure, her low-pitched voice singing huskily through sultry cabaret numbers.

It could not be Sabine singing this most punishing, demanding pinnacle of the operatic repertoire.

But it was.

Still like a robot he walked towards the stage, dimly aware that the diners present were staring open-mouthed at this extraordinary departure from their normal cabaret fare. Dimly aware that he was sinking down at an unoccupied table in front of the stage, his eyes pinned, incredulous, on the woman singing a few metres away from him.

The full force of her raging voice stormed over him. There was no microphone to amplify her voice, but she was drowning out everything except the crashing chords of the piano accompanying her. This close, he would see the incandescent fury in her face, her flashing eyes emerald and hard. He stared—transfixed. Incredulous. Disbelieving.

Then, as the aria *furioso* reached its climax, he saw her stride to the edge of the stage, step down off it and sweep towards him. Saw her snatch up a steak knife from a place setting and, with a final, killing flourish, as her scathing, scything denunciation of her enemy was hurled from her lips, she lifted the knife up and brought it down in a deadly, vicious stab into the tabletop in front of him.

The final chords sounded and she was whirling around, striding away, slamming through the door that led backstage. And in the tabletop in front of him the knife she'd stabbed into it stood quivering.

All around him was stunned silence.

Slowly, very slowly, he reached a hand forward and withdrew the knife from the table. It took a degree of effort to do so—it had been stabbed in with driving force.

The entire audience came out of their stupor and erupted into a tremendous round of applause.

He realised he was getting to his feet, intent on following her wherever she had disappeared to, and then was aware that the pianist was lightly sprinting off the stage towards him, blocking his route.

'I wouldn't, you know,' said the pianist, whom he dimly recognised as Sabine's accompanist.

Bastiaan stared at him. 'What the *hell* just happened?' he demanded. His ears were still ringing with the power of her voice, her incredible, unbelievable voice.

Sabine's accompanist made a face. 'Whatever you said to her, she didn't like it—' he answered.

'She's a *nightclub* singer!' Bastiaan exclaimed, not hearing what the other man had said.

The accompanist shook his head. 'Ah, no…actually, she's not. She's only standing in for one right now. Sarah's real musical forte is, as you have just heard, opera.'

Bastiaan stared blankly. 'Sarah?'

'Sarah Fareham. That's her name. She's British. Her mother is French. The real Sabine did a runner, so I cut a deal with the club owner to get free rehearsal space in exchange for Sarah filling in. But he's hired a new singer now—which is very convenient as we're off tomorrow to the festival venue.'

Bastiaan's blank stare turned blanker. 'Festival…?' He seemed to be able to do nothing but echo the other man's words, and Bastiaan had the suspicion, deep down, that the man was finding all this highly amusing.

'Yes, the Provence en Voix Festival. We—as in our company—are appearing there with a newly composed opera that I am directing. Sarah,' he informed Bastiaan, 'is our lead soprano. It's a very demanding role.' Now the amusement was not in his voice any more. 'I only hope she hasn't gone and wrecked her voice with that ridiculous "Queen of the Night" tirade she insisted on.' His mouth twisted and the humour was back in his voice, waspish though it was. 'I can't think why—can you?'

Bastiaan's eyes narrowed. It was a jibe, and he

didn't like it. But that was the absolute, utter least of his emotions right now.

'I have to speak to her—'

'Uh-uh.' The pianist shook his head again. 'I really wouldn't, you know.' He made a face again. 'I have *never* seen her that angry.'

Bastiaan hardly heard him. His mind was in meltdown. And then another question reared, hitting him in the face.

'Philip—my cousin—does *he* know?'

'About Sarah? Yes, of course he does. Your cousin's been haunting this place during rehearsals. Nice kid,' said Max kindly.

Bastiaan's brows snapped together uncomprehendingly. Philip *knew* that 'Sabine' was this girl Sarah? That she was in some kind of opera company? Why the hell hadn't he told him, then? He spoke that last question aloud.

'Not surprisingly, Sarah's being a bit cagey about having to appear as Sabine,' came the answer. 'It wouldn't do her operatic reputation any good at all if it got out. This festival is make-or-break for her. For *all* of us,' he finished tightly.

Bastiaan didn't answer. Couldn't.

She trusted Philip with the truth about herself—but she never trusted me with it!

The realisation was like a stab wound.

'I have to see her.'

He thrust his way bodily past the pianist, storming down the narrow corridor, his head reeling, trying to make sense of it all. Memory slashed through him of how he'd sought her out that first evening he'd set eyes on her. His face tightened. Lies—all damn lies.

Her dressing room door was shut, but he pushed it open. At his entrance she turned, whipping round from where she was wrenching tissues from a box on her dressing table.

'Get out!' she yelled at him.

Bastiaan stopped short. Everything he had thought he'd known about her was gone. Totally gone.

She yelled at him again. 'You heard me! Get out! Take your foul accusations and *get out*!'

Her voice was strident, her eyes blazing with the same vitriolic fury that had turned them emerald as she'd hurled her rage at him in her performance.

'Why didn't you *tell* me you weren't Sabine?' Bastiaan cut across her.

'Why didn't *you* tell *me* that you thought me some sleazy slut who was trying it on with your precious cousin?' she countered, still yelling at him.

His expression darkened. 'Of course I wasn't going to tell you that, was I? Since I was trying to separate you from him.' A ragged breath scissored his lungs. 'Look, Sabine…'

'I am *not* Sabine!'

Sarah snatched up a hairbrush from her dressing table and hurled it at him. It bounced harmlessly off his broad chest. The chest she'd clung to in ecstasy—the chest she now wanted to hammer with her fists in pure, boiling rage for what he'd said to her, what he'd thought of her…

What he'd done to her…

He took me to bed and made love to me, took me to paradise, and all along it was just a ghastly, horrible plot to blacken me in Philip's eyes.

Misery and rage boiled together in the maelstrom of her mind.

'I didn't know you weren't Sabine. Do *not* blame me for that,' Bastiaan retaliated, slashing a

hand through empty air. He tried again, attempting to use her real name now. 'Look… Sarah…'

'Don't you *dare* speak my name. You know
nothing about me!'

His expression changed. Oh, but there *was*
something he knew about her. From the shred-
ded remnants of his mind, the brainstorm consuming him, he dragged it forth. Forced it across
his synapses.

She might be Sabine, she might be Sarah—it
didn't matter—

'Except, of course,' he said freezingly, each
word ice as he spoke it, 'about the money. Philip's money.'

She stilled. 'Money?' She echoed the word as
if it were in an alien tongue.

He gave a rough laugh. Opera singer or nightclub singer—why should it be different? His
mouth twisted. Why should 'Sarah' be any more
scrupulous than 'Sabine'?

'You took,' he said, letting each word cut like
a knife, 'twenty thousand euros from my cousin's personal account. I know you did because
this afternoon you paid another cheque into the

very same bank account that the twenty thousand euros disappeared into.'

Her expression was changing even as he spoke, but he wouldn't let her say anything—anything at all.

'And this very evening, after you'd oh-so-conveniently cut and run from my villa, I got a request to release *two hundred thousand* euros from my cousin's investment funds.' His eyes glittered with accusation. 'Did you not realise that as Philip's trustee I see *everything* of his finances—that he needs my approval to cash that kind of money? Running back to him with whatever sob story you're concocting will be in vain. Is *that* why you left my bed this afternoon?'

'I left,' she said, and it was as if wire were garrotting her throat, 'because I had to appear as Sabine tonight.'

She was staring at him as if from very far away. *Because I thought you'd had all you wanted from Sabine.*

And he had, hadn't he? That was the kill. blow that struck her now. He'd had exactly wh he'd wanted from Sabine because all he'd wante was to separate her from Philip and to keep his money safe.

Behind the stone mask that was her face she was fracturing into a thousand pieces...

Her impassivity made him angry—the anger like ice water in his veins. 'I'll tell you how it will be,' he said. 'Philip will go back to Athens, safely out of your reach. And you—Sabine, Sarah, whoever the hell you are—will repay the twenty thousand euros that he paid into your bank account.'

Her eyes were still on him. They were as green and as hard as emeralds.

'It wasn't my bank account,' she said.

Her voice was expressionless, but something had changed in her face.

A voice came from the doorway. 'No,' it said, 'it was mine.'

CHAPTER ELEVEN

SARAH'S EYES WENT to Max, standing in the doorway.

'What the *hell* have you done?' she breathed.

He got no chance to answer. Bastiaan's eyes lasered him. 'Are you claiming the account is yours? *She* went into that bank this afternoon.'

'To pay in a cheque for three thousand euros my father had just sent me to help with the expenses of mounting the opera. I paid it directly into Max's account.'

She was looking at Bastiaan, but there was no expression in her face, none in her voice. Her gaze went back to Max.

'You took Philip for *twenty thousand euros*?' There was emotion in her voice now—disbelief and outrage.

Max lifted his hands. 'I did not ask for it, *cherie*. He offered.'

Bastiaan's eyes narrowed. Emotion was coursing through him, but right now he had only one focus. 'My cousin *offered* you twenty thousand euros?'

Max looked straight at him. 'He could see for himself how we're stretched for funding—he wanted to help.' There was no apology in his voice.

Bastiaan's eyes slashed back to Sarah. 'Did you know?'

The question bit at her like the jaws of a wolf. But it was Max who answered.

'Of course she didn't know. She'd already warned me not to approach him.'

'And yet,' said Bastiaan, with a dangerous silkiness in his voice, 'you still did.'

Max's eyes hardened. 'I told you—he offered it without prompting. Why should I have refused?' Something in his voice altered, became both defiant and accusing. 'Are we supposed to starve in the gutter to bring the world our art?'

He got no answer. The world, with or without opera in it, had just changed for Bastiaan.

His eyes went back to Sarah. Her face was like stone. Something moved within him—something that was like a lance piercing him inside—but he ignored it. He flicked his eyes back to Max, then to Sarah again.

'And the two hundred thousand euros my cousin now wishes to lavish on a fortunate recipient?' Silk over steel was in his voice.

'If he offered I would take it,' said Max bluntly. 'It would be well spent. Better than on the pointless toys that rich men squander their wealth on,' he said, and there was a dry bitterness in his words as he spoke.

'Except—' Sarah's voice cut in '—that is exactly what Philip is planning to do.'

She opened a drawer in the vanity unit, drew out her phone, called up a text, pointed the screen towards Bastiaan.

'This is the text he sent me today, while we were driving to St Paul de Vence.' Her voice was hollow.

His eyes went to it. Went to a photo of the latest supercar to have been launched—one of those he and Philip had discussed over dinner in Villeneuve.

The accompanying text was simple.

Wouldn't this make a great twenty-first birthday present to myself? I can't wait!

Underneath, he could read what she had replied.

Very impressive! What does Bastiaan think? Check with him first!

Sarah was speaking. 'I was as tactful as I could be—I always have been. I don't want him hurt, whatever he thinks he feels about me, but I never wanted to encourage him. And not about this, either,' she replied, in the same distant, hollow voice. 'I know you're not keen on him having such a powerful car so young.'

Harsh realisation washed through Bastiaan like a chilling douche. Philip had been so evasive about why he wanted money released from his funds...

But it wasn't for her—none of the money was for her...

And she was not, and never had been, the person he'd thought her...not in any respect whatsoever. Neither nightclub singer, nor gold-digger, nor any threat at all, in any way, to Philip.

My every accusation has been false. And because of that...

His mind stopped. It was as if he were standing at the edge of a high cliff. One more step forward and he would be over the edge. Falling to his doom.

Sarah was getting to her feet. It was hard, because she seemed to be made of marble. Nothing seemed to be working inside her at all. Not in her body, not in her head. She looked at Bastiaan, at the man she'd thought he was. But he wasn't. He was someone quite different.

'You'd better go,' she said. 'My set starts soon.' She paused. Then, 'Stay away from me,' she said. 'Stay away—and go to hell.'

From the doorway, Max tried to speak. 'Sarah...'

There was uncertainty in his voice, but she just looked at him. He gave a slight shrug, then walked away. Her eyes went back to Bastiaan, but now there was hatred in them. Raw hatred.

'Go to hell,' she said again.

But there was no need to tell him that. He was there already.

He turned and went.

Sarah stood for one long motionless, agonising, endless moment, her whole body pulled by wires of agony and rage. Then tears started to choke her. Tears of fury. Tears of misery.

Aching, ravening misery.

* * *

His aunt was staring at him from across her drawing room in Athens. Bastiaan had just had lunch with her and Philip, and now, with Philip back at his studies, his aunt was cornering him about his mission to the Riviera.

'Bastiaan, are you telling me that this girl in France is actually some sort of opera singer and *isn't* trying to entrap Philip?'

He nodded tautly.

His aunt's expression cleared. 'But that's wonderful.' Then she looked worried. 'Do you think he's still…*enamoured*, though? Even if she isn't encouraging him?'

He shook his head. 'I don't think so. He's full of this invitation to go to the Caribbean with Jean-Paul and his family.' He cast his aunt a significant look. 'Plus, he seems to be very taken with Jean-Paul's sister, whose birthday party it is.'

Philip's mother's face lit. 'Oh, Christine is a sweet girl. They'd be so well-suited.' She cast a grateful look at her nephew. 'Bastiaan—*thank you*. I cannot tell you how grateful I am for setting my mind at rest about that singer and my boy!'

His eyes were veiled for a moment, and there was a fleeting look that he hid swiftly. His expression changed. 'I made one mistake, though,' he said.

More than one...

His throat closed, but he forced himself to continue. 'I let Philip drive my car while we were there—now he's determined to get one of his own.'

His aunt's face was spiked with anxiety. 'Oh, Bastiaan—please, stop him. He'll kill himself!'

He heard the fear in her voice, but this time he shook his head. 'I can't stop him—and nor can you. He's growing up. He has to learn responsibility. But—' he held up a hand '—I *can* teach him to drive a car like that safely. That's the deal I've struck with him.'

'Well...' her acquiescence was uneasy, but resigned '...if you do your best to keep him safe...'

'I will,' he said.

He got to his feet. He needed to be out of there. Needed it badly. He was heading off to his island, craving solitude. Craving anything that might stop him thinking. Stop him feeling...

No—don't go there. Just...don't.

As he walked towards the front door Philip

hailed him from his room. 'Bast! You will come, won't you? To Sarah's premiere? It would be so great if you do. You only ever saw her as Sabine—she'd love you to see what she can really do. I know she would.'

His eyes veiled. What Sarah would love was to see his head on a plate.

'I'll see,' he temporised.

'It's at the end of next week,' Philip reminded him.

It could be tomorrow or at the end of eternity for all the difference it would make, Bastiaan knew. Knew from her brutal, persistent refusal to acknowledge any of his texts, his emails, his letters. All of them asking…*begging* one thing and one thing only…

His mind sheered away—the way he was training it to. Day by gruelling day. But it kept coming back—like a falcon circling for prey. He could sail, he could swim, he could walk, he could get very, very drunk—but it would not stay out of his head.

Three simple words. Three words that were like knife-thrusts to his guts.

I've lost her.

* * *

'Sarah?'

Max's voice was cautious. It wasn't just because of the thorny issue of Philip's generosity and Max's ready acceptance. He was treating her with kid gloves. She wished he wouldn't. She wished he would go back to being the waspish, slave-driving Max she knew. Wished that everyone would stop tiptoeing around her.

It was as if she had a visible knife wound in her. But nothing was visible. Her bleeding was internal...

It was their first rehearsal day at the festival site, a small but beautiful theatre built in the grounds of a château in northern Provence. She was grateful—abjectly grateful—to be away from the Riviera...away from the nightclub. Away from anything, everything, that might remind her of what had happened there...

But it was with her day and night, asleep and awake, alone and with others, singing or not.

Pain. A simple word. Agonizing to endure. Impossible to stop.

'Are you sure you want to start with that aria?'

Max's enquiry was still cautious. 'Wouldn't you rather build up to it?'

'No,' she said.

Her tone was flat, inexpressive. She wanted to do this. Needed to do it. The aria that she had found impossible to sing was now the only one she wanted to sing.

She took her position, readied herself—her stance, her throat, her muscles, her breathing. Anton started to play. As she stood motionless, until her entry came, thoughts flowed through her head...ribbons of pain...

How could I not understand this aria? How could I think it impossible to believe in it—believe in what she feels, what she endures?

Her bar came. Max lifted his hand to guide her in as the music swelled on its pitiless tide. She gazed blindly outward, not seeing Max, not seeing the auditorium or the world. Seeing only her pain.

And out of her pain came the pain of the War Bride, her anguished voice reaching out over the world with the pain of hopes destroyed, happiness extinguished, the future gone. The futility, the loss, the courage, the sacrifice, the pity of war...all in a single voice. *Her* voice.

As her voice died away into silence...utter silence... Anton lifted his hands from the keyboard. Then he got to his feet, crossed to her. Took her hands. Kissed each of them.

'You have sung what I have written,' he told her, his voice full. It was all he said—all he needed to say.

She shut her eyes. Inside her head, words came. Fierce. Searing.

This is all I have. And it will be enough. It will be enough!

But in the deepest recesses of her consciousness she could hear a single word mocking her.

Liar.

Bastiaan took his seat. He was up in the gods. He'd never in his life sat so high above the stage, in so cheap a seat. But he needed to be somewhere where Philip, down in the stalls, could not see him.

Bastiaan had told him that, regrettably, he could not make it to the opening night of *War Bride*.

He had lied.

What he did not want—could not afford—was for Philip to let Sarah know he would be there.

But he could no more have stayed away than remained in a burning building.

Emotion roiled within him as he gazed down. Somewhere behind those heavy curtains she was there. Urgency burned in him. She had blocked him at every turn, denied him all access.

Even Max, when he'd asked for his intervention, had simply replied, 'Sarah needs to work now. Don't make any more difficulties for her.'

So he'd stayed away. Till now.

Tonight—tonight I have to speak to her. I have to.

As the house lights went down and the audience started to settle, conversation dimming, he felt his vision blur. Saw images shape themselves—tantalizing, tormenting.

Sabine, her eyes glowing with passion, gazing up at him as they made love.

Sabine, smiling, laughing, holding his hand.

Sabine—just being with her, hour by hour, day by day, as they ate, as they swam, as they sunbathed and stargazed.

Sabine—so beautiful, so wonderful.

Until I threw her away.

He had let fear and suspicion poison what they'd had. Ruin it.

I did not know what I had—until I lost it.

Could he win it back? Could he win *her* back?

He had to try—at least he had to try.

'OK, Sarah, this is it.' Max was pressing his hands on her shoulders, his eyes holding hers. 'You can do it—you know you can.'

She couldn't respond, could only wait while he spoke to the others, reassuring them, encouraging them. He looked impeccable in white tie and tails, but she could see the tension in him in every line of his slight body. She could hear the audience starting to applaud and the tuning up of the players in the orchestra die away as Max, their conductor for the evening, took the podium.

She tried to breathe, but couldn't. She wanted to die. Anything—anything at all to avoid having to do what she was going to have to do. What she had been preparing for all her life. What she had worked for in every waking second, allowing nothing else to lay claim to an instant of her time, a moment of her concentration.

Least of all the man who had done what he had to her. Least of all him. The man who was despicable beyond all men, thinking what he had of her, judging and condemning her as he had, while all the while…all the while…

He made love to me and thought me nothing better than a cheap little gold-digger. Right from the start—from the very moment he laid eyes on me. Everything was a lie—everything! Every moment I spent with him was a lie. And he knew it the whole time!

No, she had not allowed such vicious, agonizing thoughts into her head. Not one. She'd kept them all at bay—along with all those unbearable texts and voicemails that she'd deleted without reading or listening to. Deleted and destroyed, telling him to go to hell and stay there. Never, ever to get in touch again.

Because all there was in her life now was her voice—her voice and her work. She had worked like a demon, like one possessed, and blocked out everything else in the universe. And now this moment, right now, had come. And she wanted to die.

Dear God, please let me do OK. Please let me get it right—for me, for all of us. Please.

Then the small chorus was filing out on to the stage, and a moment later she heard Max start the brief overture. She felt faint with nerves. As they took their places the familiar music, every note of which she knew in every cell of her body, started to wind its way through the synapses of her stricken brain. The curtain rose, revealing the cavern of the auditorium beyond, and now the chorus was starting their low, haunting chant—their invocation to vanishing peace as the storm clouds of war gathered.

She felt her legs tremble, turning to jelly. Her voice had gone. Completely gone. Vanished into the ether. There was nothing—nothing in her but silence…

She saw the glare of the stage lights, the dimness of the auditorium beyond, and on his podium Max, lifting his baton for her entrance cue. She fixed her eyes on him, took a breath.

And her voice came.

High and pure and true. And nothing else in the universe existed any more except her voice.

* * *

Unseen, high above in the gods, Bastiaan sat motionless and heard her sing.

The knife in his guts twisted with every note she sang.

For the whole duration of the opera, as it wound to its sombre conclusion, Bastiaan could not move a muscle, his whole being riveted on the slender figure on the stage. Only once did he stir, his expression changing. During the heartrending aria of grief for her young husband's death, with the agony of loss in every note. His eyes shadowed. The poignancy of the music, of her high, keening voice, struck deep within him.

Then the drama moved on to its final scene, to her song to the unborn child she carried, destined to be another soldier, in yet another war. And she, the War Bride, would become in her turn the Soldier's Mother, destined to bury her son, comfort his widow—the next War Bride, carrying the next unborn soldier...

As her voice faded the light on the stage faded too, until there was only a single narrow spot upon her. And then that, too, faded, leaving only the unseen chorus to close the timeless tragedy with a chorale of mourning for lives yet to be lost in future conflicts. Until silence and darkness fell completely.

For a palpable moment there was complete stillness in the house—and then the applause started. And it did not stop. Did not stop as the stage lights came up and the cast were there, Sarah, and the other soloists stepping forward. The applause intensified and the audience were rising to their feet as Max walked out on to the stage with Anton at his side, and then both of them were taking Sarah by the hand, leading her forward to a crescendo of applause.

Bastiaan's palms were stinging, but still the applause continued, and still his eyes were only for her—for Sarah—now dropping hands with Max, calling her tenor forward, and the other soloists too, to take their share of the ovation, breaking the line to let the chorus take theirs, and then all the cast joined in with applause for the orchestra taking their bows.

He could see her expression—beatific, transfigured.

He could stay still no longer. He rose from his seat, jolted down the staircase to the ground floor, out into the fresh night air. His heart was pounding, but not from exertion. Walking swiftly, purposefully, he pushed open the stage door, walked up to the concierge's booth.

'This is for Max Defarge. See that he gets it this evening.' He placed the long white envelope he'd taken from his inside jacket pocket into his hand, along with a hundred-euro note to ensure his instruction was fulfilled. Then he walked away.

He couldn't do this. What the hell had he been thinking? That he could just swan into her dressing room the way he had that first night he'd seen her sing?

Seen Sabine sing—not Sarah!

But the woman he'd heard tonight had not been Sabine—had been as distant from Sabine as he was from the stars in the sky. That knife twisted in his guts again, the irony like acid in his veins. That he should now crave only the woman he had thrown away....distrusted and destroyed.

His mobile phone vibrated. Absently he took it out—it was a text from Philip.

Bast, you missed a sensation! Sarah was brilliant and the audience is going wild! Gutted you aren't here. Am staying for the after-party soon as the audience clears. Can't wait to hug her!

He didn't answer, just slid the phone away. His heart as heavy as lead.

CHAPTER TWELVE

SARAH WAS FLOATING at least six inches off the ground. The champagne that Max had splashed out on was contributing, she knew, but mostly it was just on wings of elation—the buoyancy of abject relief and gratitude that she had given the performance of her life.

Elation filled them all—hugs and kisses, tears and laughter and joy lifting them all above the exhaustion that their efforts had exacted from them. But no one cared about exhaustion now—only about triumph.

She could scarcely believe it, and yet it was true. All true. Finally all true.

'Am I dreaming this?' she cried to her parents as they swept her into their arms. Her mother's face was openly wet with tears, her father's glowing with pride.

Her mother's hand pressed hers. 'Whoever he is, my darling—the man you sang about—he's not worthy of you.' Her voice was rich with sympathy and concern.

Sarah would not meet her mother's eyes.

Her mother smiled sadly. 'I heard it in your voice. You were not singing of the loss of your soldier. It was real for you, my darling—*real*.'

Sarah tried to shake her head, but failed. Tried to stop the knife sliding into her heart, but failed. She could only be grateful that Max was now embracing her—for the millionth time—and drawing her off to one side. He found a quiet spot in the foyer area where the after-party was taking place and spoke.

'This has just been given to me,' he said.

His voice was neutral. Very neutral. Out of his pocket he took a folded piece of paper and opened it, handing it to Sarah. She took it with a slight frown of puzzlement. Then her expression changed.

'I'm glad for you,' she said tightly. It was all she could manage. She thrust the paper back at Max.

'And for yourself?' The question came with a lift of the brow, speculation in his eyes, concern in his voice.

She gave her head a sharp, negative shake.

Turned away bleakly. Heading back into the throng, she seized up another glass of champagne, more hugs, more kisses. And suddenly, a huge bear hug enveloping her.

'Oh, Sarah…Sarah—you were brilliant. Just *brilliant*! You were *all* brilliant!'

It was Philip—sweet, lovely Philip—his face alight with pleasure for her. She hugged him back, glad to see him. But automatically, fearfully, she found her gaze going past him. And there was another emotion in her eyes—one she did not want to be there but which leapt all the same.

It died away as he spoke again. 'I just *wish* Bast could've been here. I told him I really, *really* wanted him to hear you do your real stuff—not all that inane Sabine garbage.' He released her from his hug.

She smiled fondly. 'Thank you for all your loyalty and support. It means a great deal to me,' she said sincerely, because his youthful faith in her had, she knew, been a balm to her. 'And Philip?' She pressed his hands, her voice serious now. 'Listen—don't *ever* let types like Max take money off you again. He was out of order.'

He coloured again. 'I wanted to help,' he said.

For a second, just a second, her eyes shadowed with pain. Philip's 'help' had exacted a price from her and she had paid heavily. Was still paying.

Would pay all her life...

'You did,' she said firmly. 'And we're all grateful—you helped make all this possible!' She gestured widely at the happy scene around them.

'Great!' He grinned, relieved and reassured.

She, too, was relieved and reassured. Philip's crush on her was clearly over, there was no light of longing in his eyes any more. Just open friendliness. 'We all liked you hanging around—with or without that hefty donation to us. Oh, and Philip?' Her face was expressive. 'That monster car you want to get for yourself—please, just do *not* smash yourself up in it!'

He grinned again. 'I won't. Bast's teaching me to drive it safely.' He blew her a kiss as he headed off. 'One day I'll deliver you to the artists' entrance at the Royal Opera House Covent Garden in it—see if I don't.'

'I'll hold you to that,' she said fondly.

She turned away. Covent Garden... Would she

make it there? Was what had happened tonight the first step on her journey there?

Fierce emotion fired through her.

I have to make it. I have to!

Work and work alone must consume her now. No more distractions.

The words echoed in her head, mocking her. How often had she said them?

Even right from the start, when her eyes had set on the man who had invaded her dressing room that night, invaded her life…

Invaded my heart…

She felt a choke rising in her throat, constricting her breathing. She forced it back. She would not give in to it. Would not give in to the bleakness that was like a vacuum inside her, trying to suck all the joy out of this moment for her.

My work will be enough—it will be!

That was all she had to remember. All she had to believe.

Lie though it was…

An hour later she had had enough of celebration. The exhaustion she'd blanked out was seeping through her again.

Her parents had gone, yawning, back to their hotel in the nearby spa town. Philip was getting stuck into the champagne with the chorus, with a lot of laughter and bonhomie.

Helping herself to a large glass of water, Sarah found her feet going towards the French windows. Cool fresh air beckoned her, and she stepped out onto a paved area. There was an ornate stone-rimmed pond at the end of a pathway leading across the lawn, with soft underwater lights and a little fountain playing. She felt herself wandering towards it.

Her elation had gone. Subsumed not just by exhaustion but by another mood. Seeing Philip had not helped her. Nor had what Max had disclosed to her. Both had been painful reminders of the man she wanted now only to forget.

But could not.

She reached the pond, trailed her fingers in the cool water, her gaze inward. Back into memory.

Sun sparkling off the swimming pool as Bastiaan dived into it, his torso glistening with diamond drops of water. His arm tight around her as he steered the motorboat towards the gold of the setting sun. His eyes burning down at her with passion and desire. His mouth, lowering to hers...

She gave a little cry of pain. It had meant nothing—nothing to him at all. False—all false!

Bitter irony twisted inside her.

I thought he wanted me to be Sabine—a woman of the world, alluring and sensual, willing and eager for an instant romance. But all along Sabine was the woman he wanted to destroy.

And destroy her he had.

Too late she had discovered, after a few brief, fleeting days of passion and desire, how much more she wanted. Wanted as Sarah—not Sabine.

Pain shot through her again. And too late she had discovered what she was to Bastiaan…what she had been all along, through every kiss, every caress, every moment she'd spent with him.

Discovered that she had lost what she had never had at all.

The choke rose in her throat again, but she forced it back. She would not weep, would not shed tears. She snatched her hand from the water, twisted around, away from the stone pond.

And looked straight at Bastiaan.

* * *

He walked towards her. There was a numbness in him, but he kept on walking. She stood poised, motionless, looking so achingly beautiful, with her gold hair coiled at her nape, her slender body wreathed in an evening gown of pale green chiffon.

As he drew closer, memory flashed. The two of them sitting behind the wheel of his boat, moving gently on the low swell of the sea, her leaning into him, his arm around her waist, as he turned its nose into the path of the setting sun, whose golden rays had burnished them as if in blessing.

Another memory, like a strobe light, of them lying together, all passion spent, during the hours of the night, her slender body cradled in his. Another flash, and a memory of the fragrance of fresh coffee, warm croissants, the morning sun reaching its fingers into the vine-shaded terrace as they took their breakfast.

Each memory became more precious with every passing hour.

Each one was lost because of him. Because of what he'd done to her.

He could not take his eyes from her. Within him emotion swelled, wanting to overtake him, to impel him to do what he longed to do—sweep her into his arms. He could not—dared not. Everything rested on this moment—he had one chance...one only.

A chance he must take. Must not run from as he had thought to do, unable to confront her in the throng inside, at the moment of her triumph in her art. But now as she stood there, alone, he must brave the moment. Reclaim what he had thrown from him—what he had not known he had possessed.

But I did know. I knew it with every kiss, every embrace, every smile. I knew it in my blood, my body—my heart.

As he came up to her, her chin lifted. Her face was a mask. 'What are you doing here? Philip said you weren't here. Why did you come?'

Her words were staccato. Cold. Her eyes hard in the dim light.

'You must know why I am here,' he said. His voice was low. Intense.

'No. I don't.' Still staccato, still that mask on

her face. 'Is it to see if I'm impressed by what you've done for Max? All that lavish sponsorship! Is it by way of apology for your foul accusations at me?'

He gave a brief, negating shake of his head and would have spoken, but she forged on, not letting him speak.

'Good. Because if you want to sponsor him—well, you've got enough money and to spare, haven't you? I want none of it—just like I never wanted Philip's.' She took a heaving breath, 'And just like I want nothing more to do with you either.'

He shut his eyes, receiving her words like a blow. Then his eyes flared open again. 'I ask only five minutes of your time, Sab—Sarah.'

He cursed himself. He had so nearly called her by the name she did not bear. Memory stabbed at him—how he had wondered why Philip stammered over her name.

If I had known then the truth about her—if I had known it was not she who had taken money from Philip...

But he hadn't known.

He dragged his focus back. What use were regrets about the past? None. Only the future counted now—the future he was staking this moment on.

She wasn't moving—not a muscle—and he must take that for consent.

'Please…please understand the reasons for my behaviour.'

He took a ragged breath, as if to get his thoughts in order. It was vital, crucial that he get this right. He had one chance…one chance only…

'When Philip's father died I promised his mother I would always look out for him. I knew only too well that he could be taken advantage of. How much he would become a target for unscrupulous people.'

He saw her face tighten, knew she was thinking of what Max had done, however noble a cause he'd considered it.

He ploughed on. 'Especially,' he said, looking at her without flinching, 'women.'

'Gold-diggers,' she said. There was no expression in her voice.

'Yes. A cliché, but true all the same.'

A frown creased between Bastiaan's eyes. He

had to make her understand what the danger had been—how real it could have been.

If she had truly been the woman I feared she was.

'I know,' he said, and his mouth gave a caustic curl of self-derision, 'because when I was little older than Philip, and like him had no father to teach me better, a woman took me to the cleaners and made a complete fool of me.'

Did he see something change in her eyes? He didn't know—could only keep going.

'So when I saw that twenty thousand euros had gone from Philip's account to an unknown account in Nice…when I heard from Paulette that Philip had taken to hanging around a nightclub endlessly and was clearly besotted with someone, alarm bells rang. I *knew* the danger to him.'

'And so you did what you did. I know—I was on the receiving end.'

There was bitterness in her voice, and accusation. She'd had enough of this—*enough.* What was the point of him going on at her like this? There wasn't one. And it was hell—just hell on earth—to stand here with him so close, so incredibly close.

So unutterably distant… Because how could he be anything else?

She made herself say the words that proved it. 'I get the picture, Bastiaan. You seduced me to safeguard Philip. That was the only reason.' There was a vice around her throat, but she forced the words through.

She started to turn away. That vice around her throat was squeezing the air from her. She had to get out of here. Hadn't Bastiaan Karavalas done enough to her without jeopardizing everything she had worked to achieve?

'*No.*'

The single word, cutting through the air, silenced her.

'No,' he said again. He took a step towards her. 'It was not the only reason.'

There was a vehemence in the way he spoke that stilled her. His eyes were no longer veiled… they were burning—burning with an intensity she had never seen before.

'From the moment I first saw you I desired you. Could not resist you even though I thought you were Sabine, out to exploit my cousin. *Because* I thought that it gave me…' he took a breath '…a justification for doing what I wanted to do all along. Indulge my desire for you. A desire that you returned—I could see that in every glance you gave me. I knew you wanted me.'

'And you used that for your own ends.' The bitterness was back in her voice.

He seemed to flinch, but then he was reaching for her wrist to stay her, desperate for her to hear what he must say—*must* say.

'I regret everything I did, Sarah.' He said her name with difficulty, for it was hard—so hard—not to call her by the name he'd called her when she was in his arms. 'Everything. But not—not the time we had together.'

She strained away from him. 'It was fake, Bastiaan. Totally fake.' There was harshness in her voice.

'Fake?' Something changed in his voice. His eyes. His fingers around her wrist softened. 'Fake...?' he said again.

And now there was a timbre to his voice that she had heard before—heard a hundred times before...a thousand. She felt a susurration go through her as subtle as a breath of wind in her hair. As caressing as a summer breeze.

'Was *this* fake?' he said,

And now he was drawing her towards him and she could not hold back. The pulse in her veins was whispering, quickening. She felt her breath catch, dissolve.

'Was *this* fake?' he said again.

And now she was so close to him, so close that her head was dropping back. She could catch the scent of his body, the warmth of it. She felt her eyes flutter shut and then he was kissing her, the softness of his lips a homage, an invocation.

He held her close, and closer still, cupping her nape to deepen his kiss.

Bliss eased through her, melting and dissolving. Dissolving the hard, bitter knot of pain and anger deep inside her. He let her lips go, but his eyes were pouring into hers.

'Forgive me—I beg you to forgive me.' His voice was husky, imploring. 'I wronged you—treated you hideously. But when I made those accusations at you—oh, they were tearing me to pieces. To have spent those days with you, transforming everything in my life, and then that final day…' He shut his eyes, as if to shut out the memory, before forcing himself to open them again, to speak to her of what had haunted him. 'To think myself duped—because how could you be that woman I'd feared you were when what we had was so…so wonderful.'

His voice dropped.

'I believed all my fears—and I believed the worst fear of all. That you were not the woman I had so wanted you to be…'

He gazed down at her now, his hand around her nape, cradling her head, his eyes eloquent with meaning. And from his lips came the words he had come here to say.

'The woman I love—Sabine or Sarah—*you* are the woman I love. Only you.'

She heard the words, heard them close, as close as her heart—the heart that was swelling in her breast as if it must surely become her very being, encompassing all that she was, all that she could be.

She pressed her hand against the strong wall of his chest, glorying in feeling her fingers splay out over the hard muscle beneath his shirt. Feeling the heat of his body, the beat of his heart beneath her palm.

Wonder filled her, and a whitening of the soul

that bleached from her all that she had felt till now—all the anger and the hurt, the fury and the pain. Leaving nothing but whitest, purest bliss.

She gazed up at him, her face transformed. He felt his heart turn over in his breast, exultation in it.

'I thought it impossible...' she breathed. 'Impossible that in a few brief days I could fall in love. How could it be so swift? But it was true—and oh, Bastiaan, it hurt so *much* that you thought so ill of me after what we'd had together.'

To love so swiftly—to hurt so badly...

She saw him flinch, as if her words had made a wound, but he answered her.

'The moment I knew—that hellish moment when I knew everything I'd feared about you, all I'd accused you of was false...nothing but false... I knew that I had destroyed everything between us. You threw me out and I could do nothing but go. Accept that you wanted nothing to do with me. Let you get on with your preparations for tonight without my plaguing you.'

His voice changed. 'But tonight I could keep silent no longer. I determined to find you—face you.' A rueful look entered his dark eyes. 'I bottled it. I was too…too scared to face you.' His gaze changed again, becoming searching. 'What you've achieved tonight—what it will bring you now—will there be room for me? *Can* there be?'

She gave a little cry. 'Oh, Bastiaan, don't you see? It's *because* of what I feel—because now I know what love is—that I can achieve what I have tonight…what will be in me from now for ever.'

She drew back a little.

'That aria I sang, where the War Bride mourns her husband's death…' She swallowed, gazing up at him with all her heart in her eyes. 'She sings of love that is lost, love that burns so briefly and then was gone. I couldn't sing it. I didn't understand it until—'

He pulled her into his arms, wrapping them tight around her. 'Oh, my beloved, you will *never* feel that way again. Whatever lessons in love you learn from me will be happy ones from now. Only happy ones.'

She felt tears come then, prickling in her eyes, dusting her lashes with diamonds in the starlight. Bastiaan—*hers*. Her Bastiaan! After such torment, such bliss! After such fears, such trust. After such anger, such love...

She lifted her head to his, sought his mouth and found it, and into her kiss she poured all that was in her heart, all that she was, all that she would be.

An eternal duet of love that they would sing together all their lives.

EPILOGUE

SARAH LAY ON the little sandy beach, gazing up at the stars which shone like a glittering celestial tiara overhead. There was no sound but the lapping of water, the night song of the cicadas from the vegetation in the gardens behind. But her heart was singing—singing with a joy, a happiness so true, so profound, that she could still scarcely credit it.

'Do you remember,' the low, deep voice beside her asked, 'how we gazed up at the stars by the pool in my villa at Cap Pierre?'

She squeezed the hand that was holding hers as she and Bastiaan lay side by side, their eyes fixed on eternity, ablaze overnight in the Greek sky.

'Was it then?' she breathed. 'Then that I started to fall in love with you?'

'And I with you?'

Her fingers tightened on his. Love had come

so swiftly she had not imagined it possible. And hurt had followed.

But the pain I felt was proof of love—it showed me my own heart.

Now all that pain was gone—vanished and banished, never to return! Now, here with Bastiaan, as they lay side by side on the first night of their married life together, they were sealing their love for ever. He had asked her where she wanted to spend her honeymoon but she had seen in his eyes that he already knew where he wanted them to be.

'I always said,' he told her, 'that I would bring my bride to my island—that she alone would be the one woman I would ever want here with me.'

She lifted his hand to her mouth, grazing his knuckles with a kiss.

'I also always said—' and his voice was different now, rueful and wry '—that I would know who that woman would be the moment I set eyes on her.'

She laughed. She could do that now—now that all the pain from the way he had mistrusted and misused her was gone.

'How blind I was! Blind to everything that you

truly were! Except...' And now he hefted himself on to one elbow, rolled on to his hip to gaze down at her—his beloved Sarah, his beloved bride, his beloved wife for all the years to come. 'Except to my desire for you.'

His eyes blazed with ardour and she felt her blood quicken in its veins as it always did when he looked at her like that, felt her bones melting into the sand beneath her.

'That alone was true and real! I desired you then and I desire you now—it will never end, my beautiful, beloved Sarah!'

For an instant longer his gaze poured into hers, and then his mouth was tasting hers and she was drawing him down to her. Passion flared and burned.

Then, abruptly, Sarah held him off. 'Bastiaan Karavalas—if you think I am going to spend my wedding night and consummate my marriage on a beach, with pebbles digging into me and sand getting into places I don't even want to think about, then you are—'

'Entirely right?' he finished hopefully, humour curving his mouth.

'Don't tempt me,' she said huskily, feeling her resolve weaken even as she started to melt again.

But you do tempt me...

The words were in Bastiaan's head, echoing hers, taking him back—back to the time when he had been so, so wrong about her. And so, so right about how much he wanted her. He felt his breath catch with the wonder of it all. The happiness and joy that blazed in him now.

He got to his feet, crouched beside her, and with an effortless sweep scooped her up into his arms. She gave a little gasp and her arms went around his neck, clinging to him.

'No,' he said firmly, 'you're right. We need a bed. A large, comfortable bed. And, as it happens, I happen to have one nearby.'

He carried her across the garden into the house behind. It was much simpler than the villa in Cap Pierre, but its privacy was absolute.

The grand wedding in Athens a few hours ago, thronged with family and friends, with Sarah's parents, his aunt and his young cousin— Philip having been delighted at the news of their union—and even his own mother, flown in from LA, seemed a world away.

Max had delivered Sarah fresh from rehearsals for a production of *Cavalleria Rusticana*—with himself directing and Sarah singing 'Santuzza' at a prestigious provincial opera house in Germany—making it very clear to her that the only reason he was tolerating her absence was because she happened to be marrying an extremely wealthy and extremely generous patron of the opera, whose continued financial sponsorship he fully intended to retain.

'Keep the honeymoon short and sweet!' Max had ordered her. 'With your career taking off, it has to come first!'

She'd nodded, but had secretly disagreed. Her art and her love would always be co-equal. Her life now would be hectic, no doubt about that, and future engagements were already being booked up beyond her dreams, but they would never—*could* never—displace the one person who for all her life would stand centre stage to her existence.

She gazed up at him now, love blazing in her eyes, as he carried her into the bedroom and lowered her gently upon the bed, himself with her.

'How much...' he said huskily, this man she loved. 'How much I love you...'

She lifted her mouth to his and slowly, sweetly, passionately and possessively, they started together on their journey to the future.

* * * * *

If you enjoyed this story,
check out these other great reads from
Julia James.

CAPTIVATED BY THE GREEK
THE FORBIDDEN TOUCH OF SANGUARDO
SECURING THE GREEK'S LEGACY
PAINTED THE OTHER WOMAN
THE DARK SIDE OF DESIRE

Available now!

MILLS & BOON®
Large Print – September 2016

Morelli's Mistress
Anne Mather

A Tycoon to Be Reckoned With
Julia James

Billionaire Without a Past
Carol Marinelli

The Shock Cassano Baby
Andie Brock

The Most Scandalous Ravensdale
Melanie Milburne

The Sheikh's Last Mistress
Rachael Thomas

Claiming the Royal Innocent
Jennifer Hayward

The Billionaire Who Saw Her Beauty
Rebecca Winters

In the Boss's Castle
Jessica Gilmore

One Week with the French Tycoon
Christy McKellen

Rafael's Contract Bride
Nina Milne

816 Rom LP

MILLS & BOON®
Large Print – October 2016

Wallflower, Widow...Wife!
Ann Lethbridge

Bought for the Greek's Revenge
Lynne Graham

An Heir to Make a Marriage
Abby Green

The Greek's Nine-Month Redemption
Maisey Yates

Expecting a Royal Scandal
Caitlin Crews

Return of the Untamed Billionaire
Carol Marinelli

Signed Over to Santino
Maya Blake

Wedded, Bedded, Betrayed
Michelle Smart

The Greek's Nine-Month Surprise
Jennifer Faye

A Baby to Save Their Marriage
Scarlet Wilson

Stranded with Her Rescuer
Nikki Logan

Expecting the Fellani Heir
Lucy Gordon

MILLS & BOON®

Why shop at millsandboon.co.uk?

Each year, thousands of romance readers find their perfect read at millsandboon.co.uk. That's because we're passionate about bringing you the very best romantic fiction. Here are some of the advantages of shopping at www.millsandboon.co.uk:

* **Get new books first**—you'll be able to buy your favourite books one month before they hit the shops

* **Get exclusive discounts**—you'll also be able to buy our specially created monthly collections, with up to 50% off the RRP

* **Find your favourite authors**—latest news, interviews and new releases for all your favourite authors and series on our website, plus ideas for what to try next

* **Join in**—once you've bought your favourite books, don't forget to register with us to rate, review and join in the discussions

Visit **www.millsandboon.co.uk**
for all this and more today!